LEARNING Microsoft® Office FrontPage® 2003

Catherine Skintik

Vice President and Publisher: Natalie E. Anderson
Executive Acquisitions Editor: Jodi McPherson
Executive Editor: Jennifer Frew
Manufacturing Buyer: Natacha St. Hill Moore
Production Manager: Gail Steier de Acevedo
Technical Editor: Kathy Berkemeyer
Cover Designer: Amy Capuano
Composition: Shu Chen and Catherine Skintik
Associate Director, Multimedia Production: Karen Goldsmith
Manager, Print Production: Christy Mahon
Printer/Binder: Quebecor World Book Services/Dubuque
Cover Printer: Phoenix Color Corporation

10 9 8 7 6 5 4
ISBN 0-13-146452-3

Contents

LESSON 9: ADVANCED INTERACTIVE WEB SITE FEATURES: DISCUSSION GROUPS AND DATABASES

LESSON 10: WEB-SITE MANAGEMENT

Introduction

How We've Organized the Book

Each lesson in **Learning Microsoft® Office FrontPage® 2003** is made up of several exercises. Lessons are comprised of exercises designed for using FrontPage 2003 in real-life business settings. Every application exercise (except for the Critical Thinking exercises) is made up of seven key elements:

- **On the Job**. Each exercise starts with a brief description of how you would use the features of that exercise in the workplace.
- **Exercise Scenario**. The FrontPage tools are then put into context by setting a scenario.
- **Terms**. Key terms are included and defined at the start of each exercise, so you can quickly refer back to them. The terms are boldfaced in the text.
- **Notes**. Concise notes describe and outline the computer concepts.
- **Procedures**. Hands-on mouse and keyboard procedures teach all necessary skills.
- **Application Exercise**. Step-by-step instructions put your skills to work.
- **On Your Own**. Each exercise concludes with a critical thinking activity that you can work through on your own. You may or may not be supplied with data for the exercise, and you are challenged to use the data to create or modify a Web site. The *On Your Own* sections can be used as additional reinforcement, for practice, or to test skill proficiency.
- In addition, each lesson ends with **Critical Thinking Exercises**. As with the *On Your Owns*, you need to rely on your own skills to complete the task. The Critical Thinking Exercise also includes a Challenge Exercise that you must complete on your own or with the cooperation of teammates.

Working with Data and Solution Files

As you work through the exercises in this book, you'll be creating, opening, and saving files. You should keep the following instructions in mind:

- Many exercises instruct you to open a file from the CD-ROM that comes with this book. The data files are used so that you can focus on the skills being introduced—not on creating complex Web sites. The files are located in the **Datafiles** folder on the CD-ROM.
- It is recommended that you create a folder with a name such as My Webs and copy the data files to this folder as instructed on the next page. Use this folder also when you create new Web sites. Keeping all your Web site files in this solution folder will make it easier for you to locate Web sites and files that are used in more than one exercise.
- The Directory of Data Files on CD-ROM lists the data files you can use to complete each exercise.
- Unless the book instructs otherwise, use the default settings when working with FrontPage. If someone has changed the default software settings for the computer you're using, your exercise files may not look the same as those shown in this book. In addition, the appearance of your files may look different if the system is set to a screen resolution other than 800 x 600.

To Access the Files Included with This Book

1. Insert the *Learning Microsoft Office FrontPage 2003* CD in the CD-ROM drive.
2. Navigate to your CD-ROM drive; right-click **start** and choose Explore from the shortcut menu.
3. Navigate to your CD-ROM drive.
4. Right-click the **datafiles** folder.
5. Navigate to the location where you wish to place the folder.
6. Right-click and choose Paste from the Shortcut menu.

Support Material

A complete instructor support package is available with all the tools teachers need:

Annotated Teacher's Guide includes entire student book with teacher notes, course curriculum guide, and lesson plans. Solution files included on CD-ROM. (ISBN: 0-13-116916-5)

Test Booklet with TestGen CD-ROM includes application pretests, posttests, and final exam. Includes customizable test bank on CD-ROM. (ISBN: 0-13-127055-9)

Solutions Manual includes printouts of exercise solutions with solution file CD-ROM. (ISBN: 0-13-147209-3)

Solution Files on CD-ROM. (ISBN: 0-13-127054-0)

Visual Aids, 25-slide PowerPoint presentation correlated to the book. (ISBN: 0-13-147440-5)

Directory of Data Files on CD-ROM

Exercise #	File Name	Page #
1	Boxes	10
2	No data files	16
3	No data files	25
4	Cooking, roast.doc OYO: Swap, merchandise,doc	33, 34
5	methods.doc, food.doc OYO: logistics.doc	41
6	Drive	49, 50
7	information.doc	51
8	Vinyl	62
9	Conservatory, PC030015.jpg, spring.jpg, cactus.jpg OYO: Refuge, eagle.jpg	71
10	desert.jpg, holiday.jpg	78
11	Ross, rossfinal.jpg, rossvideo.avi, heading.gif OYO: soaring.mpeg	85
12	rossanimation.swf, ross1.gif, ross2.gif, ross3.gif, ross4.gif, ross5.gif OYO: refugeanimation.swf	92
13	Deepcreek, lake1.jpg, deepanimation.swf, P8160.jpg, lake2.jpg, butterfly.jpg, cliff.jpg, flower.jpg, pool.jpg, trail.jpg, waterfall.jpg	96, 97
14	Reunion, trace.jpg, bette.jpg	105
15	No data files	113
16	Fastfinish OYO: Management	121
17	No data files	126
18	No data files	131
19	Eastfork, riding.doc	134
20	Coach	142
21	responses.htm	147
22	Parrot, finches.wav OYO: Winter	153
23	No data files	158
24	Coffee, shadowlayer.jpg	164, 165
25	No data files	172, 173
26	Bank	174, 175

Exercise #	File Name	Page #
27	Richmond	183
28	Gardens OYO: Cats, alley.gif	190
29	specials.htm OYO: FAQs.htm	195
30	links.htm	200
31	Daycare, ballbullet.gif	202, 203
32	Salon OYO: Club	210
33	certificates.htm	215
34	Tutor	221
35	No data files	227
36	Summer	229, 230
37	Tour	239
38	No data files	245
39	No data files	251
40	Alumni	253
41	Levy	261
42	No data files	269
43	Sharks OYO: Striders	276
44	sharkfaqs.htm, results.htm OYO: dailylogs.xls, mileage.htm	284
45	Pledge, playlist.htm, mailform.doc, summerpledge.htm	287, 288
46	Books	298
47	No data files	304
48	No data files	311
49	Ariel, Arielbooks.mdb OYO: Wedding, wedding.mdb	317
50	No data files	323, 324
51	Exchange, cyber.mdb	326, 327
52	Wildlife OYO: Reinhardt	335
53	No data files	340
54	Clifton	347
55	Plantscapes OYO: deer3.jpg	356
56	No data files	362
57	Harbor	364, 365

LESSON 1

Introduction to Microsoft® Office FrontPage® 2003

Exercise 1

◆ **About Microsoft Office FrontPage** ◆ **Start FrontPage 2003** ◆ **FrontPage Window** ◆ **Open FrontPage Web Site** ◆ **Open Web Page** ◆ **FrontPage Views** ◆ **Close FrontPage Web Site** ◆ **Exit FrontPage 2003** ◆ **Web Design Guidelines**

On the Job

Microsoft Office FrontPage 2003 is an application that enables its users to create Web pages and Web sites easily, even with very little Web design experience. FrontPage's views allow Web designers to enter text, organize files and folders, create a Web-site structure, check hyperlinks on a Web's pages, keep track of tasks relating to Web-site development, and run reports to identify potential problems.

In this exercise, you will examine a FrontPage Web site that is under construction for More Than Boxes. You will start FrontPage 2003 and open the Web site and its individual Web pages. You will explore FrontPage's views and learn how each one helps you work on a specific Web element. You will close the Web site and exit FrontPage 2003. Finally, you will learn some basic design guidelines.

Terms

Code view
In FrontPage Page view, a view that shows the author the Web page's HTML coding and text.

Design view
The view in which a Web author inserts text and graphics.

Folder List
A list of the files and folders contained in the current FrontPage *Web site*. The Folder List can be displayed in all views but Reports and Tasks view.

home page
The first page of a *Web site*. The home page usually outlines what the site has to offer, somewhat like a book's table of contents. All pages in the site are usually linked (via *hyperlinks*) to the home page.

hyperlink
Text or a graphic that, when clicked, connects to one of the following: another place on the same *Web page*, another Web page on the same *Web site*, another Web page on a different Web site, an e-mail address, or any other file or document on the same computer, network, or the Internet.

Navigation pane
This pane, which can be displayed instead of the *Folder List* in Page view, displays a graphical representation of how the pages of a Web are connected.

Preview view
The view that shows the Web designer approximately what the Web page will look like in a *Web browser*.

Split view
A view that shows both Design view and Code view in a single view.

task pane
A pane that opens at the right side of the FrontPage window to give Web authors a list of options for the current activity.

Web browser
A software program that allows a person to display Web text containing hyperlinks and use those links to open new Web pages.

Web page

A document created using HTML that can be posted on the World Wide Web by a *Web server*.

Web server

A network or computer connected to the Internet that contains information for a Web site that can be accessed by a browser.

Web site

A group of related *Web pages* served up by a Web server on the World Wide Web. A typical Web site has a *home page* and includes *hyperlinks* to other Web pages on the site.

Web Site pane

A new interface in FrontPage 2003 that gives authors access to site information and views.

Notes

About Microsoft Office FrontPage

- Microsoft Office FrontPage is one of the most popular Web-design products in use today, with millions of users worldwide.
- FrontPage's tools and Web-design options make it easy for anyone to create a Web page, even without extensive computer or design experience.
- FrontPage users don't need to know HTML coding to produce sophisticated Web pages.
- FrontPage 2003 offers new features that improve editing and publishing, enhance Web page graphics, and enable users to create sophisticated dynamic effects in Web sites.
- **Web pages** are separate documents that are stored in a **Web site** on a **Web server**.

Start FrontPage 2003

- Start FrontPage 2003 using the Start>All Programs>Microsoft Office>Microsoft Office FrontPage 2003 menu command (see illustration below).

Start FrontPage from All Programs menu

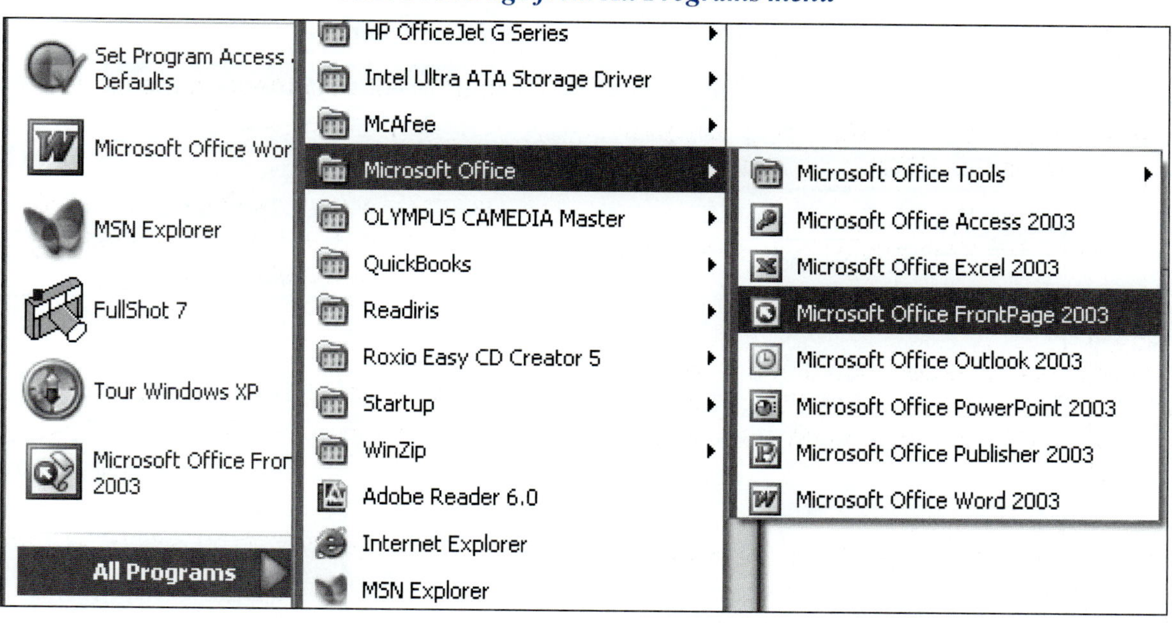

FrontPage Window

- The FrontPage window contains several features that all Microsoft Office programs have in common: a title bar, a menu bar, toolbars, and a status bar.
- When FrontPage starts, it may display either a blank Web page (*new_page_1.htm*) or a list of files for the Web site that was in use the last time the program was exited.
- To open a different Web site or create a new Web site or page, the author can display the task pane (see illustration below).
- The **task pane**, which displays at the right side of the FrontPage window, contains links to recently opened Web pages as well as links that allow Web authors to create new Web pages and sites.
  - ✓ *Authors can close the task pane to see more of the current Web page by clicking the Close button in the upper-right corner of the task pane.*
  - ✓ *If a Web site was open the last time FrontPage was exited, FrontPage displays that site's files, as shown in the illustration at the top of the next page.*
- FrontPage displays the site's files (pages) and folders in the Folder List at the left side of the window.
- The Web Site pane to the right of the Folder List gives more information about the site's contents and also supplies buttons at the bottom of the tab for accessing FrontPage's other views.
- The Web Site pane displays information related to the current view. For example, if an author selects the Navigation button at the bottom of the Web Site pane, the pane displays the navigation structure of the Web.
- The Web Site pane replaces the Views bar used in earlier versions of FrontPage. Placing the views buttons on this pane rather than on a bar allows for more room in the window to work on Web pages.

A new, blank Web page and the task pane

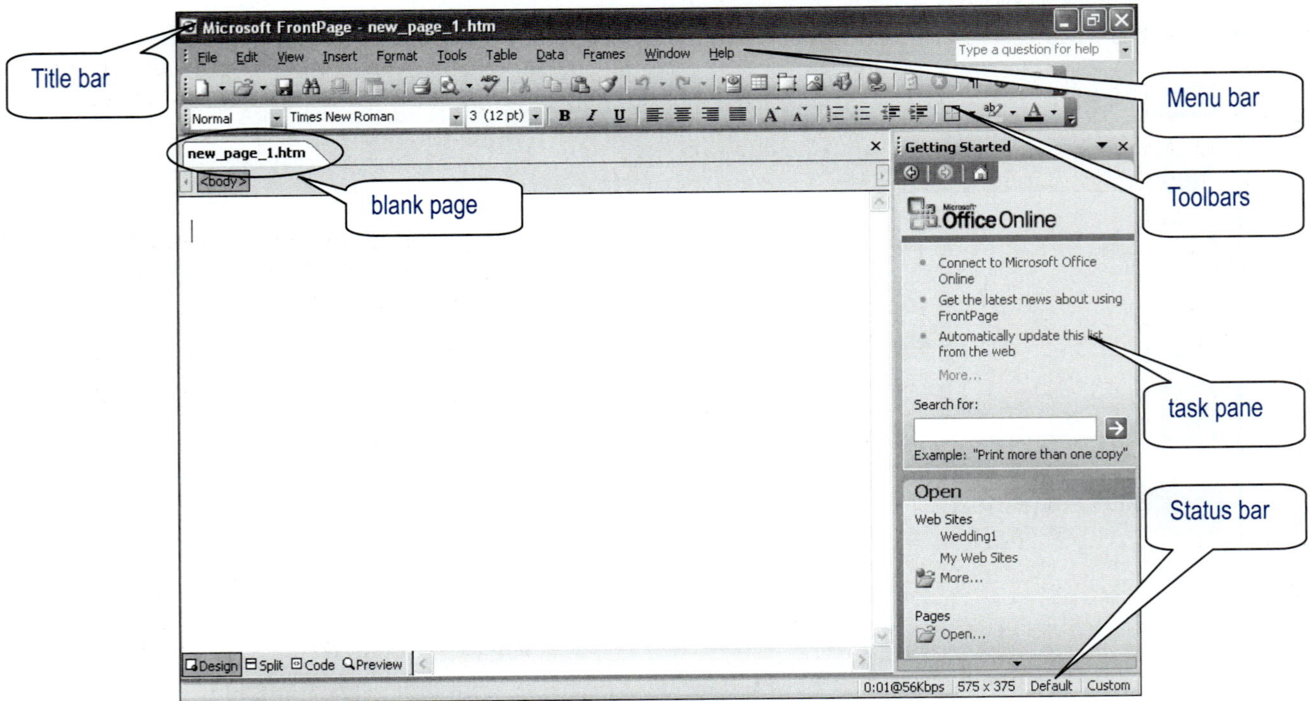

Previously used Web site opens in FrontPage

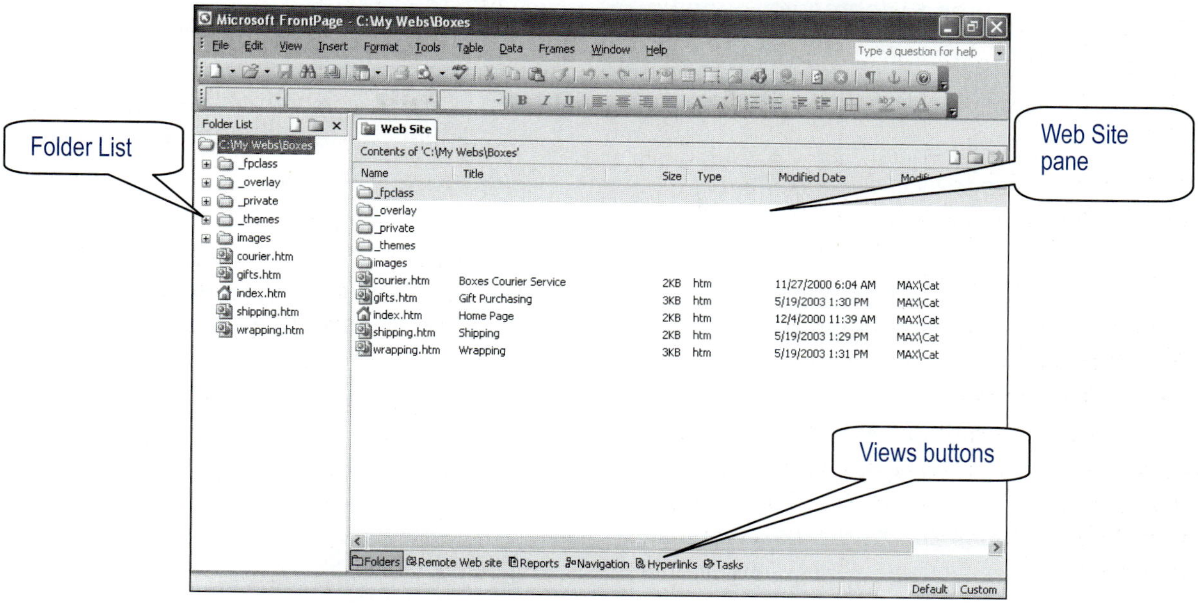

Open FrontPage Web Site

- If an existing Web site opens when FrontPage starts, the Web author can choose to continue working on that site or close it. He or she can then open another existing Web site or begin work on a new one.
- To open an existing Web site, use:
  - The File>Open Site command on the menu bar.
  - The Open Site button on the Standard toolbar (or click the drop-down arrow of the Open button to display the Open Site command).
  - A link in the task pane.
- Using the menu or toolbar method to open an existing Web site prompts FrontPage to display the Open Site dialog box, from which the Web author can navigate to the site where the existing Web site is stored.

Open Web Page

- All FrontPage Web sites display the site's files and folders in the Folder List at the left side of the window.
- To work on a Web page, the Web author must first open it. To open a Web page (or the Open File dialog box):
  - Double-click the Web-page name in the Folder List.
  - Use the File>Open command on the menu bar.
  - Click the Open button on the Standard toolbar.
- The chosen Web page appears in its own pane in the FrontPage window, on top of the Web Site pane. Each open page has a tab at the top of the page containing its name.
- The **home page** of the current Web site is named *index.htm* in the Folder List (see illustration above).

FrontPage Views

- FrontPage has seven views that allow the Web author to complete different tasks relating to the current site. These views are:
  - Page
  - Folders
  - Remote Web site
  - Reports
  - Navigation
  - Hyperlinks
  - Tasks
- To switch views, display the Web Site pane and click the appropriate button at the bottom of the pane, or choose a view from the View menu.

  ✓ *You can choose Page view only on the View menu. There is no Page button at the bottom of the Web Site pane.*

Page View

- Page view is active after a Webmaster opens a page from the Folder List. Page view allows an author to enter and edit the text and graphics that make up each Web page.
  - ✓ *Authors can close the Folder List to see more of the current Web page by clicking the Toggle Pane button on the Standard toolbar or by deselecting Folder List on the View menu.*
- After a navigation structure has been created for the site, clicking the Navigation button at the bottom of the Folder List opens the Navigation pane. The **Navigation pane** illustrates how the pages in the site are linked together.
  - ✓ *A navigation structure specifies the way pages in the site relate to one another. You will learn how to create a navigation structure in Lesson 6, Exercise 32.*
- Each open Web page has a tab at the top of the display on the screen, similar to the tabs on file folders. Web authors can easily move from one page to another by clicking the page's tab.
- Four view buttons at the bottom of the Web page (see illustration below) give Web designers additional control over the contents displayed in the page.
- **Design view** allows Web authors to enter and modify text and graphics on the Web page. This is the default view for Page view.
- **Split view** shows both Design view and Code view, so Webmasters can see how the page will look in a browser as well as the code used to create the page.
- **Code view** shows the HTML code that controls the display of objects and text on the Web page.
  - ✓ *You will work with Code view in Exercise 2 and Exercise 4.*
- **Preview view** lets Web designers see roughly what the Web page will look like when opened in a user's **Web browser**. Web authors can also use Preview view to verify the page's hyperlinks.

Folders View

- To work in a view other than Page view, first click the Web Site tab to display the Web Site pane. Buttons for different views display across the bottom of the pane.
- Click the Folders button at the bottom of the Web Site pane to display Folders view. The files and folders that make up the current site then display in the Web Site pane.
- In Folders view, the Web Site pane provides information about each Web page in the site, such as the site title, size, type, and the date last modified.
- Use Folders view to rename or move Web pages.

FrontPage Page view (Design view)

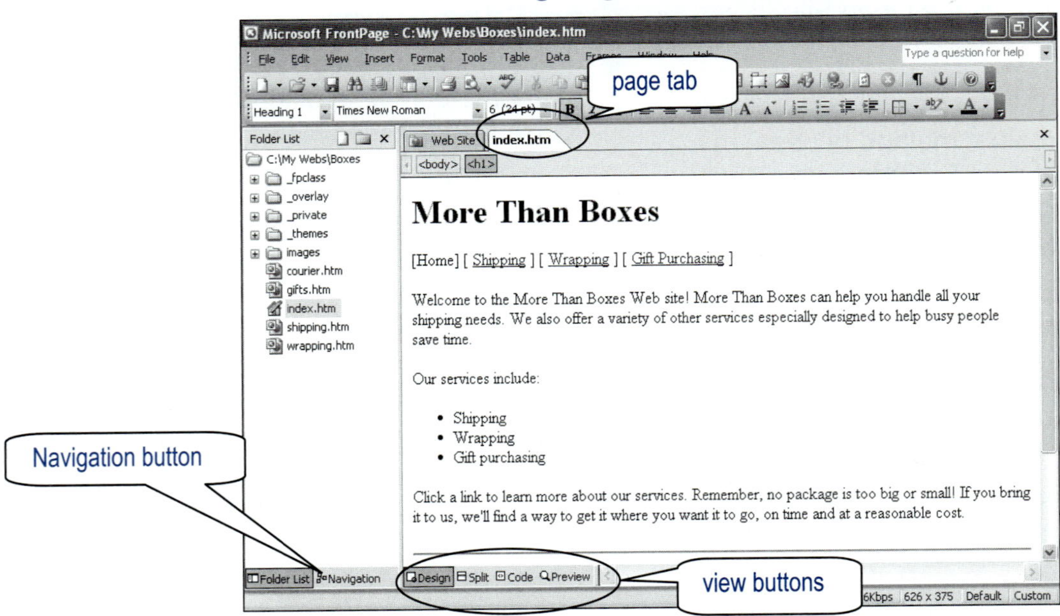

Remote Web Site View

- Click the Remote Web site button at the bottom of the Web Site pane to display this view. The Remote Web site view allows a Webmaster to specify the site to which a FrontPage Web site will be published.
- After establishing the remote site, the Webmaster can control the publishing process from this view: select pages to publish, republish or hide pages, and so on.
- A Webmaster can also choose to view the published Web site or the publishing log in this view, as well as open the remote site in FrontPage for further editing.

  ✓ *You will work with Remote Web site view in Lesson 7, Exercise 37.*

Reports View

- Reports view summarizes information about the current site and lets the Webmaster check for problems in the site. Click the Reports button at the bottom of the Web Site pane to display this view.
- Reports can identify broken hyperlinks, graphics that will load slowly, and Web pages that are not yet linked.
- Use Reports view to check Web pages for problems *before* publishing the site—or at any time during the site-creation process.

  ✓ *You will work with Reports view in Lesson 10, Exercise 55.*

Navigation View

- Navigation view displays a graphical representation of a site's linked pages (see illustration below).
- The site's home page is shown at the top of the navigation structure. Pages that are subordinate to the home page appear below the home page, as in an organization chart.
- The Folder List also displays in Navigation view. The author can easily add Web pages to the navigation structure simply by dragging them from the Folder List to the navigation structure.

  ✓ *You will learn how to add a Web page to the navigation structure in Lesson 6, Exercise 32.*

FrontPage Navigation view

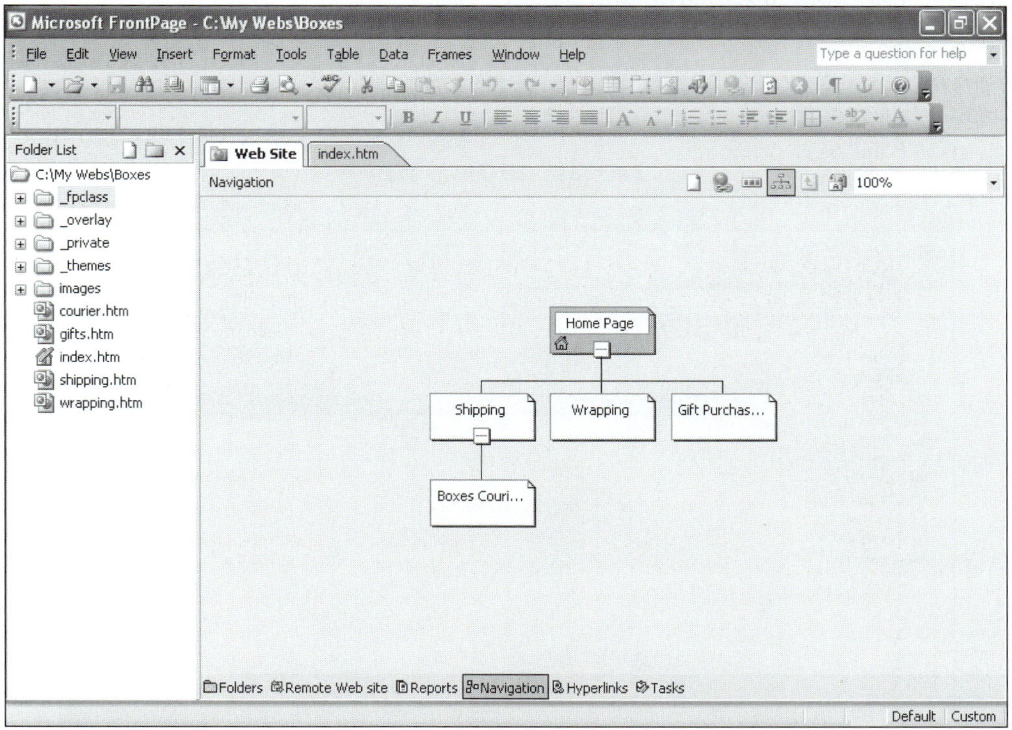

Hyperlinks View

- Hyperlinks view shows how the pages in a Web site are connected to each other and to pages outside the Web by **hyperlinks** (also called simply *links*).
- Use Hyperlinks view to make sure that all pages in a site are correctly linked.
- Hyperlinks view also shows pictures and other objects (such as sounds) that appear on a Web page.

  ✓ *You will work further with Hyperlinks view in Exercise 6.*

Tasks View

- FrontPage includes Tasks view to help organize and keep track of the tasks involved in creating a Web site (see illustration below).
- A Web author might create tasks to finalize content, locate appropriate graphics, check accessibility, and test links, for example.
- Use Tasks view to create a new task, set a priority for it, and assign the task to a particular person.
- After tasks have been entered, monitor the status of each task and mark it as complete when finished.

  ✓ *You will have a chance to create and modify tasks in Lesson 6, Exercise 35.*

Close FrontPage Web Site

- After completing work on a Web site, close the site. Closing the site ensures that it will not display the next time someone starts FrontPage on the computer.
- After a Web site has been closed, FrontPage remains open so the author can work on another site if desired.
- Close a Web site using the File>Close Site command on the menu bar.

Exit FrontPage 2003

- As for any application, exit Microsoft FrontPage after working with it.
- The common Microsoft Office command for exiting also works in FrontPage; choose File>Exit from the menu bar or click the Close button in the top-right corner of the program window.
- If a Web site is open when the Web author issues the Exit command, FrontPage will close the site *and* exit the program.

Two tasks in Tasks view

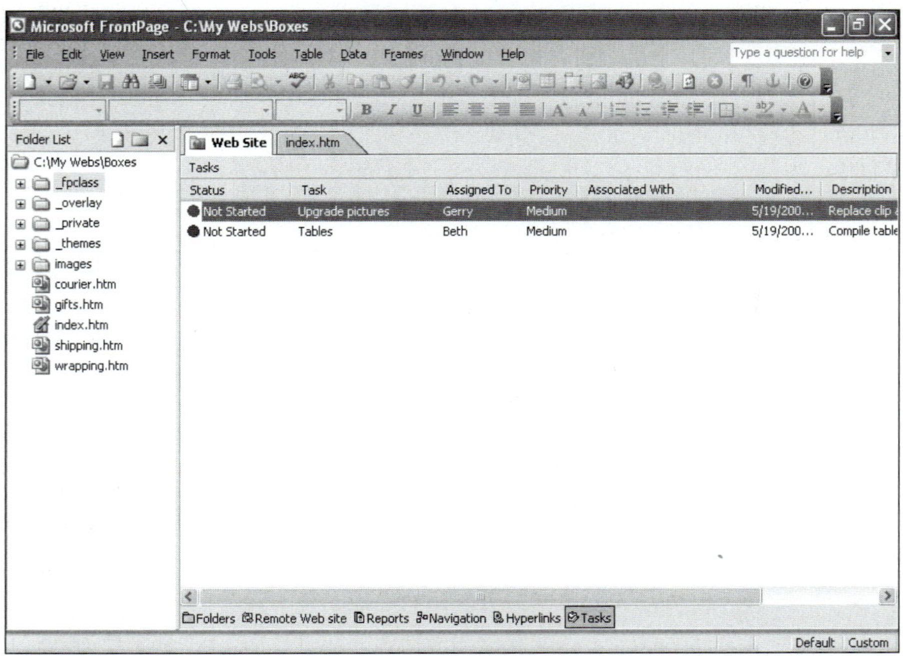

Web Design Guidelines

- As with any document you design, the Web pages you create should be easy to comprehend and pleasing to the eye. You should also make it easy for your viewers to navigate your site and find the information.
- Don't use too many fonts on a single page. Doing so can make a page appear busy and cluttered.
- Be consistent in your designs. Consistency in design helps the people reading your document find their way around. Applying the same formats (such as font size, style, and color) to your headings, using the same colors throughout the site, and placing certain elements in the same place on each page of your site makes your site easier to view and navigate.
- Repetition also provides a comfort level for the viewer. For example, if you use a certain graphic (such as a company logo) on the main page of a Web site, you could use that graphic on each page of the site.
- Group related elements together to create order and balance in your designs. Make sure it is clear which block of text a heading belongs to, or what heading a graphic relates to. Create a relationship among elements by placing them in proximity to each other. Sometimes you will want to reinforce proximity by placing a border around related headings and text, or applying similar colors to like objects.
- Create a balance between your text, graphics, and white space on each page. White space is any area on a page (even if the background of the page is a color other than white) that is not filled with elements such as text or graphics. White space provides places of rest for the reader's eyes and sets off elements to provide emphasis.
- Be careful to choose complementary colors and to use colors that don't interfere with comprehension of text. For example, make sure there is contrast between the color of your text and the color of the page background.

Procedures

Start Microsoft FrontPage 2003

1. Click **start** .... Ctrl+Esc on Windows taskbar.
2. Click **All Programs**.............. P
3. Click **Microsoft Office**.
4. Click **Microsoft Office FrontPage 2003**.

Open FrontPage Web Site

1. Click **Open Site** button on the Standard toolbar.
   ✓ *If the Open Site button does not display on the Standard toolbar, click the Open button's drop-down arrow and click Open Site.*

   OR

   a. Click **File**................. Alt+F

   b. Click **Open Site** I
2. Click **Look in** arrow ..... Alt+I
3. Select drive or folder.
   ✓ *If necessary, double-click folder name.*

   OR

   Click folder to open in Places bar.
4. Click Web to open.
5. Click Open ..... Alt+O

Open Web Page *(Ctrl + O)*

- Double-click Web page to open in Folder List.

OR

1. Click **Open** button

   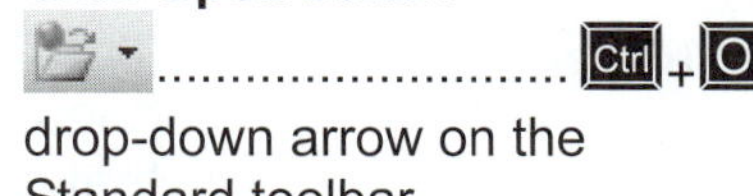

   drop-down arrow on the Standard toolbar.

   OR

   a. Click **File** .... Alt+F

   b. Click **Open** .... O
2. Double-click Web page to open.

   OR

   a. Click Web page to open.

   b. Click Open Alt+O

Change FrontPage View

- Click desired button at bottom of Web Site pane.

OR

1. Click **View** .... Alt+V
2. Click one of the following seven views:
   - **Page** .... P
   - **Folders** .... F
   - **Remote Web Site**.......... W
   - **Reports** .... R
   - **Navigation** .... N
   - **Hyperlinks** .... H
   - **Tasks**............................ A

Close FrontPage Web Site

1. Click **File** .... Alt+F
2. Click **Close Site** .... E
3. Press **Enter** .... Enter

Exit Microsoft FrontPage 2003

- Click **Close** button ⊠ .... Alt+F, X in program window.

Exercise Directions

1. Start Microsoft FrontPage 2003.
2. Close any open Web sites, if necessary.
3. Open **Boxes**.
4. Open **index.htm**.
   ✓ *If your page opens in Code view, click the Design button at the bottom of the page.*
5. Open **shipping.htm**.
   ✓ *Double-click the file name in the Folder List to open the Web page quickly. If the Folder List is not showing, click View>Folder List.*
6. Click the **index.htm** page tab to activate it.
   - Click the Navigation button at the bottom of the Folder List to see the Navigation pane.
   - Click the Folder List button at the bottom of the pane to redisplay the Folder List.
7. Click the Preview button at the bottom of the Web page. Notice that the blinking insertion point disappears, because you cannot edit the text in this view.
8. Click the Design button to return to Page view.
9. Switch to Folders view to see information about the files and folders in the current Web site.
10. Switch to Reports view and view the Site Summary report.
11. Switch to Navigation view to see the navigation structure of the Web site.
12. Switch to Hyperlinks view. Click **index.htm** in the Folder List if necessary to display the hyperlinks to and from the home page.
13. Switch to Tasks view and review the two tasks outstanding for this Web site.
14. Close the Web site.
15. Exit Microsoft FrontPage 2003.

On Your Own

1. Start your Web browser.
2. From your browser's home page, navigate to Web sites that interest you.
3. Pay attention to the design of Web pages you visit. When you find a page with a design you like, print it out or create a sketch of the way text and graphics appear on the Web page.
4. Exit your Web browser and log off, if necessary, when you have finished gathering five Web-site designs.
5. Using the designs you have printed or sketched, identify several "rules" of good Web-site design. For example:
   - Good balance between text and graphics.
   - Text is readable; background not distracting.
   - Web page loads fairly quickly.
   - Interesting use of color; good graphics, and/or multimedia objects.
6. In groups of three or four, compare your list of rules. Together, compile a checklist of rules that cover both appearance and functionality. Keep a copy of this list for use throughout the course to evaluate designs.
7. Submit your five Web-site designs (make sure to include the URL where you located the site) and list of rules to your instructor.

Exercise 2

◆ **About HTML** ◆ **HTML Tags**
◆ **View HTML Code in FrontPage**
◆ **Display HTML Tags in Design View**

On the Job

Hypertext Markup Language (HTML) is the scripting language used to create Web pages. HTML tags provide formatting instructions that browsers use to display text and graphics on a Web page. While Microsoft Office FrontPage 2003 allows Web authors to create Web sites without knowing HTML, it also provides a number of ways to work directly with HTML tags, if desired, using Code and Split views and the Quick Tag selector. HTML tags can also be displayed in Design view.

In this exercise, you will examine the HTML code of the Boxes Web site you viewed in Exercise 1. You will identify specific HTML tags that format the Web page and its text. Finally, you will display HTML tags in Design view.

Terms

attribute
A property of an HTML tag that specifies formatting or a file name.

closing tag
An *HTML tag* that directs browsers to stop displaying a format or feature. See also *opening tag*. Tags that require opening and closing tags are also called non-empty tags and containers.

closing tag switch
The forward slash (/) that indicates a closing tag.

HTML (Hypertext Markup Language)
The scripting language used to create Web pages so that they can be viewed, read, and accessed by any computer running on any type of operating system.

HTML tag
Contains the HTML codes that define specific format options on an HTML document (Web page).

nested tag
An HTML tag that is enclosed within another HTML tag.

one-sided tag
An *HTML tag* that does not need a closing tag. Browsers stop displaying the format or feature at the next new line. Also called *standalone tag* and *empty tag*.

opening tag
An *HTML tag* that directs browsers to display a format or feature. See also *closing tag*.

value
A property of an HTML tag that specifies directions, measurements, or other information for an attribute.

wicket
The technical term for the brackets that enclose *HTML tags*. Most people are more familiar with these characters as less-than (*left wicket*, <) and greater-than symbols (*right wicket*, >).

Notes

About HTML

- **HTML (Hypertext Markup Language)** is the scripting language used to create Web pages.
- HTML was developed to format Web pages specifically for the World Wide Web (WWW). This language does not belong to any single person or company.
- The value of using HTML is that Web pages formatted with HTML coding will look more or less the same in any browser on any computer.
- Every item on a Web page is controlled by HTML codes. HTML coding describes not only the appearance of text but also the page's layout.
- A Web author can write HTML code in a Web-design program such as Microsoft Office FrontPage 2003, in a word-processing program, or even in a simple text program, such as Windows Notepad.

HTML Tags

- HTML codes within a Web page are called **HTML tags**.
- All opening HTML tags have the following structure:
  - A left **wicket** (<).
  - The tag element (or name), such as *body*.

    ✓ *The tag element should be all capital letters or all lowercase letters for ease of comprehension. FrontPage uses all lowercase letters by default.*
  - Any **attributes** necessary to display specific formatting, a graphic, or another file. Attribute **values** give precise directions, measurements, or other information.

    ✓ *Attributes values are usually enclosed in quotation marks within the wickets.*
  - A right wicket (>).
- Most HTML coding requires an **opening tag** and a **closing tag**. The opening tag directs the browser to begin displaying a particular format or feature; the closing tag instructs the browser to stop displaying the format or feature.
- A closing tag contains the same tag element as the opening tag. However, the closing tag contains only the element without any accompanying attributes, and it appears with a **closing tag switch**, a forward slash (/). For example:

```
<title>More Than Boxes</title>
```

- Any text that appears *between* the opening and closing tags is affected by that tag's specific formatting. For example, in the following script, the words *special sale* will appear in bold on the Web page:

```
<p>Welcome to the <b>special
sale</b> page.</p>
```

- HTML tags can be **nested** as shown above, with several sets of opening and closing tags appearing between other opening and closing tags.
- A few HTML tags are **one-sided tags**, which are also called **standalone tags** and **empty tags**. These tags do *not* require a closing tag. The browser turns off the format or feature specified by a one-sided tag when it reads the next new line.

Common HTML Tags

- HTML includes dozens of tags. Some of the most common are listed in the table below.

TAG(S)	DESCRIPTION
<html> </html>	Begins and ends an HTML document.
<head> </head>	Begins and ends the head section of an HTML document. The head section contains the document title and other information about the document. It does not display in the browser.
<title> </title>	Encloses the Web-page title, the words that appear in a browser's title bar when the page is opened in the browser.
<body> </body>	Begins and ends the portion of the Web page that contains the text and other elements.

TAG(S)	DESCRIPTION
<h1> </h1>	Specifies the first heading level on a Web page; pages can contain up to six heading levels.
<p> </p>	Begins and ends a paragraph on the Web page.
<b> </b>	Turns on and off bold formatting.
<i> </i>	Turns on and off italic formatting.
<font> </font>	Changes the font of text between the tags; the font tag requires an attribute to identify the new font.
<align> </align>	Changes the alignment of text between the tags; the align tag requires an attribute such as *center* to specify the alignment.
<ol> </ol>	Begins and ends an ordered (numbered) list.
<ul> </ul>	Begins and ends an unordered (bulleted) list.
<li> </li>	Identifies each item in a list.
 	One-sided tag that inserts a line break (but not a new paragraph).
<a> </a>	Identifies a hyperlink.
<img> </img>	Indicates where a picture appears on a Web page.

View HTML Code in FrontPage

- FrontPage automatically applies HTML tags to text, pictures, and other components as Web authors add them. FrontPage users do not have to know HTML coding to create sophisticated effects on their Web pages.
- However, many Webmasters prefer to work directly with HTML. FrontPage offers several features that make it easy to view and use HTML coding.
- FrontPage users can click the Code tab at the bottom of a Web page to view the HTML tags applied to text and other elements on that page (see illustration below).
- To make it easy for FrontPage users to identify HTML tags, FrontPage displays the tags in purple type. Attributes display in red, and attribute values display in blue. The Web page's text displays in black type.
- Lines of code are numbered to make it easy to locate tags and text.
- FrontPage users can modify text and HTML tags or even create an entire Web page in Code view.
  ✓ *You will enter text in Code view in Exercise 4.*

Web page in Code view

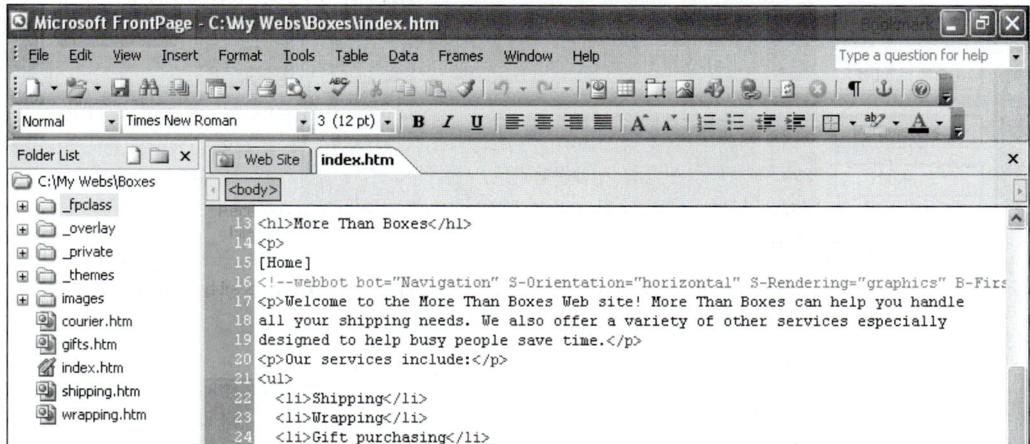

- In FrontPage 2003, Webmasters have the option of working in Split view. Split view, shown below, displays both HTML code and the design view of a Web page.
- Split view provides a "best of both worlds" approach to creating Web pages.
- The Design view portion of the pane lets authors see formatted text and graphics and other Web page elements in place.
- The Code view portion of the pane allows a Webmaster to view the code FrontPage has applied and modify it as desired. After making changes in the Code pane, an author must press F5 to see the changes in the Design view pane.
  - ✓ *Authors can adjust the amount of content shown in each pane by dragging the split bar between the two panes.*

Web page in Split view

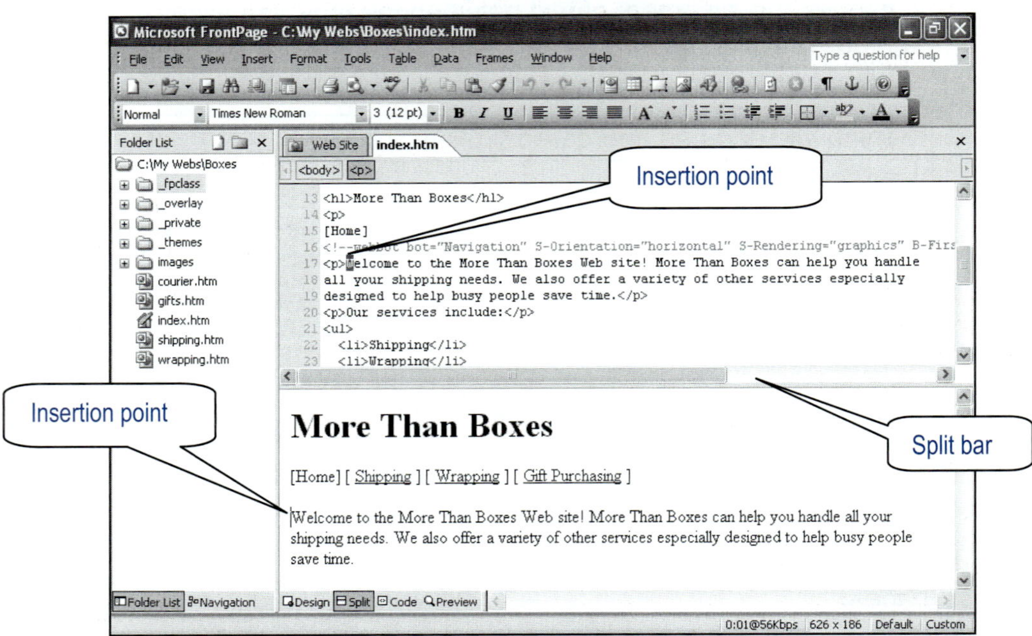

Display HTML Tags in Design View

- FrontPage 2003 allows a Webmaster to work with HTML tags in Design view as well as Code and Split view.
- In Page view, FrontPage displays the Quick Tag Selector above the page's content (see illustration below).

Quick Tag Selector

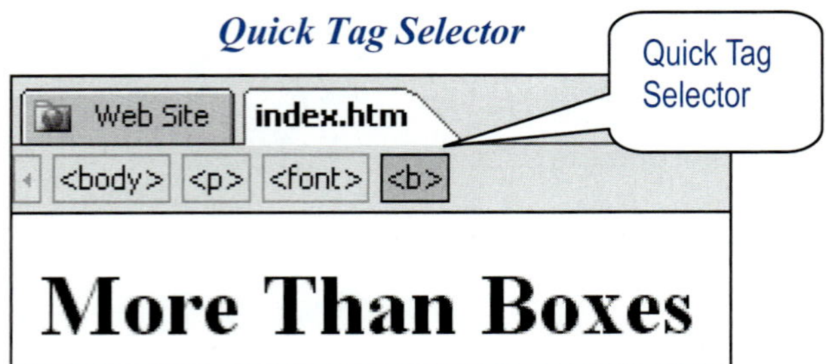

- The Quick Tag Selector lists tags that apply to the page at the insertion point. A Webmaster can easily select the page content controlled by the tag by simply clicking the tag in the Quick Tag Selector.
  - ✓ *Or, rest the mouse pointer on the tag in the Quick Tag Selector to display an outline around the content controlled by the tag.*
- It is then an easy process to modify the selected page content as desired.
- Placing the mouse pointer on a tag in the Quick Tag Selector displays a down arrow to the right of the tag name. Clicking this arrow displays a menu of further options.
- Clicking the Edit Tag option, for example, displays the Quick Tag Editor, as shown in the illustration at the top of the next page.
- The Quick Tag Editor displays the selected tag with its attributes and values. The Webmaster can edit the tag in the Quick Tag Editor, making it unnecessary to switch to Code or Split view.
  - ✓ *Click the Enter checkmark on the Quick Tag Editor to confirm the edit and close the Editor.*

Use Quick Tag Editor to edit HTML in Design view

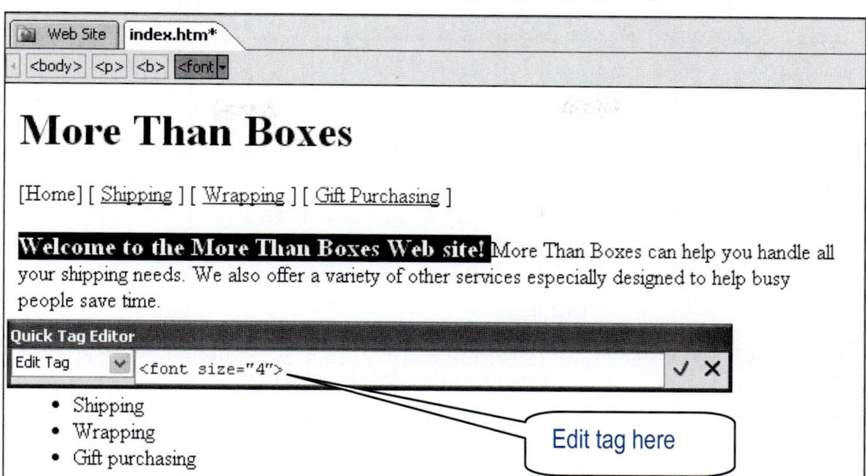

- FrontPage supplies another way to view HTML tags in Design view.
- In Design view, choose View>Reveal Tags from the menu bar. FrontPage displays the HTML tags on top of the Design view (see illustration below), and also displays the usually hidden paragraph symbols.
- HTML tags remain displayed until they are turned off again by deselecting the Reveal Tags command on the View menu.

Design view with Reveal Tags active

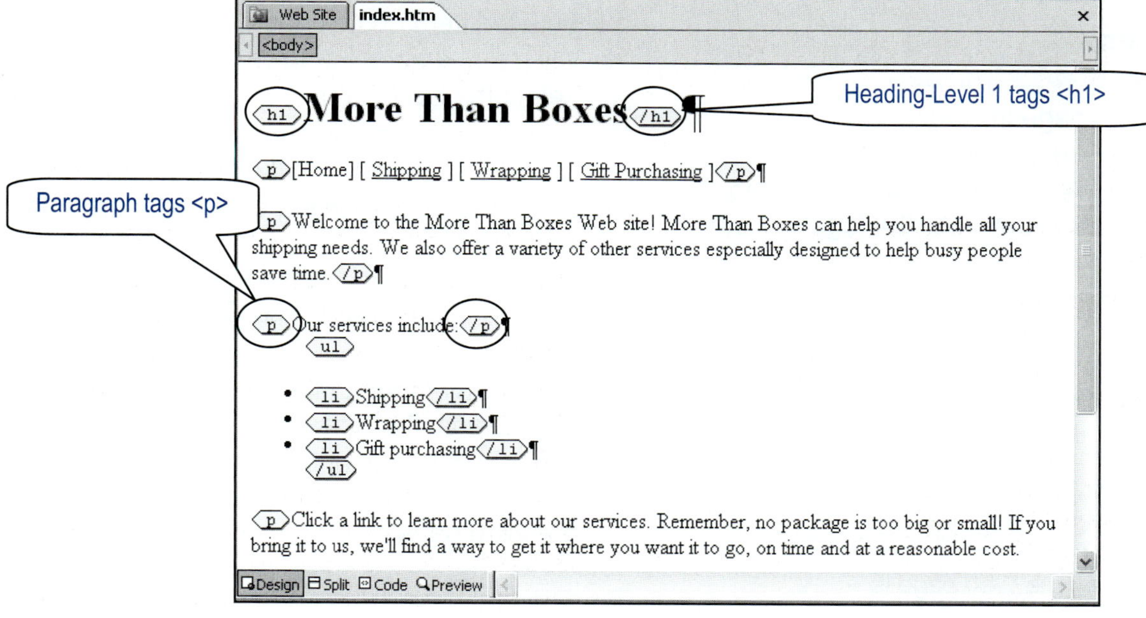

Procedures

View HTML Code in FrontPage

In FrontPage Page view:

- Click **Code** button Code at the bottom of the page.

OR

- Click **Split** button Split at the bottom of the page.

To return to Design view:

- Click **Normal** button Design at the bottom of the page.

Use the Quick Tag Selector

1. Click on the page to position the insertion point in the desired line.
2. Click the tag in the Quick Tag Selector to select the desired tag and all text controlled by the tag.
3. To modify the tag:
   a. Position the mouse pointer over the tag in the Quick Tag Selector to display a down arrow.
   b. Click the down arrow to display shortcut menu.
   c. Click **Edit Tag**................ E
   d. Edit the tag as desired.
   e. Click **Enter** button ✓.

Display/Hide HTML Tags

(Ctrl+/)

1. Click **View** .... Alt+V
2. Click **Reveal Tags**.............. G

Exercise Directions

1. Start FrontPage 2003.
2. Close any open Web sites, if necessary.
3. Open **Boxes**.
4. Open **index.htm**.
5. Display the Web page in Code view.
6. In the blanks provided below, write the HTML code (from the opening tag to the closing tag and including all text between the tags) for the following items:
   - The current Web page's title is

     ____
   - The first-level heading on the Web page is

     ____
   - The first item of the bulleted list is

     ____
   - The hyperlink on the Web page is

     ____

   ✓ *The HTML code for the hyperlink includes an attribute enclosed in quotation marks.*
7. Display the Web page in Design view.
8. Click to the left of the word *Shipping*, the first bulleted item on this page.
9. Click the <li> tag in the Quick Tag Selector to select the bullet item.
10. With the mouse pointer over the <ul> tag in the Quick Tag Selector, click the tag's down arrow.
11. In the Quick Tag Editor, change the <ul> tag to **<ol>**.
12. Display the Web page in Split view, and note how the numbered list is selected in both panes.
13. Display the page in Design view and show HTML tags, if necessary.
14. What HTML tags appear at the beginning and end of the series of hyperlinks near the top of the Web page?

    ____
15. Hide the HTML tags.
16. Leave the Web site open for the On Your Own exercise.

On Your Own

1. In the **Boxes** Web site, open **shipping.htm**.
2. Display the Web page in Code view.
3. Locate the HTML code for the Web's picture.
4. What is the file name of the picture?

   ____

   ✓ *Hint: The picture's file name includes a .gif file name extension.*
5. What word is used as a hyperlink near the bottom of the page?

   ____
6. What is the name of the file that the hyperlink will open?

   ____
7. Open **wrapping.htm**.
8. Display HTML tags in Design view.
9. There is extra space above the first paragraph of text to allow room for the picture. What HTML tags provide the extra space?

   ____
10. Hide the HTML tags.
11. Display the Web page in Split view.
12. Position the insertion point just to the left of the first word in the first paragraph (*If*). Note in the code pane that this word has a font size of 4 applied to it.
13. Select the word using the <font> tag in the Quick Tag Selector and click the tag's drop-down arrow. Choose to remove the tag.
14. Confirm the tag has been removed in the Code pane.
15. Close the Web site and save the page if prompted.
16. Exit FrontPage 2003.

Exercise 3

◆ **Create Web Site Using Template** ◆ **Enter Text**
◆ **Spell Check Web-Page Text** ◆ **Add Meta Tag**
◆ **Create New Web Page** ◆ **Save Web Page**
◆ **Save All** ◆ **Preview Web Page**

On the Job

FrontPage 2003 makes it easy to create a new Web site by offering a number of templates. After the Web site has been created, Web authors can enter text and add Web pages as necessary to complete the site. FrontPage supplies a spelling checker to help authors find typographical errors. To ensure that Web search tools will include the site in search results, Web authors can add meta tags that contain keywords. FrontPage's Preview options allow the author to see Web pages as they will display in a browser.

In this exercise, you will begin working on a Web site for the Glass Works Art Glass Studio. You will create a new one-page Web site using a template, enter text on the home page, and check the page's spelling. You will add a meta tag for the site, add a new Web page to the site, and save your changes. Finally, you will preview the site's pages to check their appearance.

Terms

code snippets
Chunks of code that can be stored by name and inserted in any Web page.

insertion point
The blinking vertical line that marks the location where text will appear when typed.

meta tag
An HTML tag that includes keywords that can be used to identify the contents of the Web page or site to *search engines*.

search engine
A program that searches Web pages for information you want to find (e.g., AltaVista, Yahoo!, Lycos, Google).

template
A predesigned page or Web site that contains settings, formatting, and layout elements. Templates can be used by Web authors to create Web sites without making many design decisions.

Web page title
Title of a Web page that appears in a browser's title bar when the page opens in the browser.

Notes

Create Web Site Using Template

- The easiest way to create a new FrontPage Web site is to use one of FrontPage's Web site **templates**.
- FrontPage Web site templates include simple one-page Web sites as well as other more complex sites such as those for discussion groups or customer support Web sites.
- Using a template ensures that pages and folders are properly created for the site.

To choose a new Web site template, use:

- The File>New command on the menu bar to display the New task pane and then click the More Web site templates link.
- The drop-down arrow of the Create a new normal page button on the Standard toolbar and then click Web Site.

■ The Web Site Templates dialog box (see illustration below) displays available Web site templates.

Web Site Templates dialog box

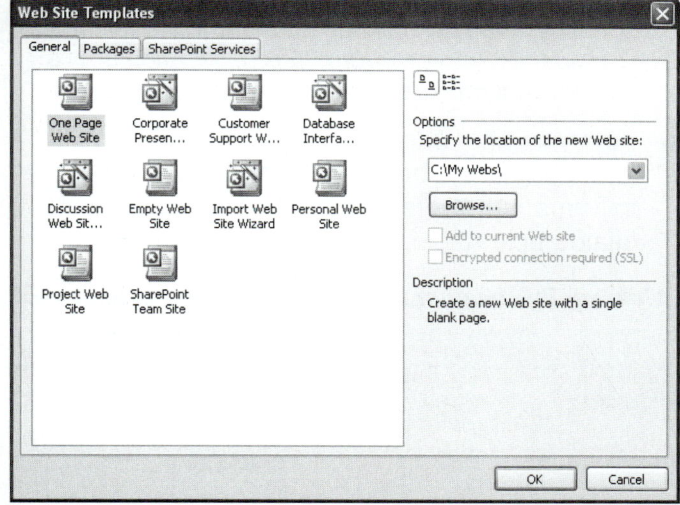

■ To specify a location for the new Web site, click the Browse button to navigate to the folder in which to store the site. After the user opens the folder, it displays as the path in the *Specify the location of the new Web site* text box.

■ The user must also type the name of the site itself in this text box. Click following the folder path and type the name of the site to create the site's folder. All files created for the site will be stored in this folder.

✓ *When creating Web sites, it is essential that all necessary files remain in the same folder.*

■ The One Page Web Site template is useful for starting a simple site. It supplies two empty folders for storing files and the default home page, index.htm.

Enter Text

■ After creating a new Web site, the Web author can then open the index.htm home page to enter text.

✓ *Some templates, such as the Empty Web Site template, do not supply a home page. The Web author can create a home page if desired. You will use the Empty Web Site template in Exercise 7.*

■ In a new Web page, a blinking **insertion point** indicates where text will appear when the Web author begins typing.

■ As in a word-processing document, FrontPage Web authors do not have to press Enter at the end of a line of text. Authors should continue typing until reaching the end of the paragraph.

■ Pressing the Enter key at the end of a paragraph moves the insertion point to the beginning of a new paragraph.

■ FrontPage automatically inserts space between paragraphs, so it is unnecessary to press the Enter key twice between paragraphs—as is often done in word-processing documents.

✓ *You can also enter text directly in Code view. You will work with Code view in the following exercise.*

Spell Check Web-Page Text

■ Like all documents aimed at the public, Web pages should be free of spelling and grammar errors.

■ FrontPage's spell checking options help Web authors locate and correct obvious spelling errors. Authors can:

- Check spelling automatically as they type.
- Run the Spelling program to check an entire page or site.

■ As the Web designer types, words that do not appear in FrontPage's spelling dictionary are marked with a wavy, red underline.

■ Right-click an underlined word to display a shortcut menu that offers choices for correcting the unrecognized word (see illustration below).

"Unrecognized" words display a wavy underline

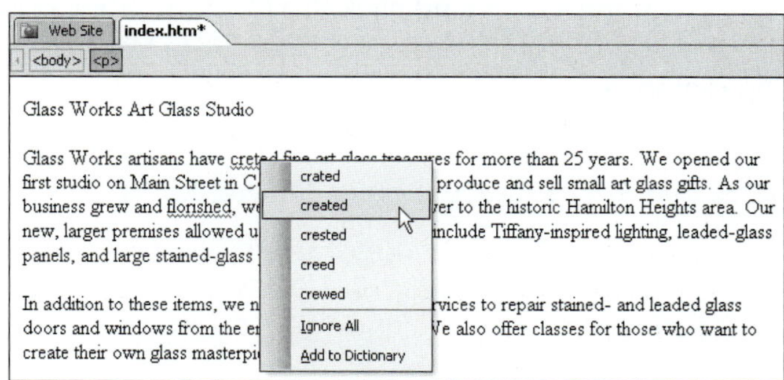

✓ *FrontPage's spelling checker might underline proper names or specialized terms that are spelled correctly. Authors can choose to ignore these words to prevent the spelling checker from identifying them again.*

- To run the Spelling program, use:
  - The Tools>Spelling command on the menu bar.
  - The Spelling button on the Standard toolbar.
- The Spelling program locates each word on a Web page that does not appear in FrontPage's dictionary and allows the author to change the word or ignore it and continue with the check.
- In Page view, the Spelling program will check only one Web page at a time. To check the spelling of an entire Web site, switch to Folders view before running the Spelling program.

Add Meta Tag

- Because the World Wide Web includes millions of Web sites, users frequently employ **search engines** to find Web pages they want to view.
- Search engines gather information about Web sites and pages not only from the text on pages but also from information contained within a Web document's **meta tag**.
- Web-site designers add user-defined meta tags to Web sites to identify important topics in those sites.

✓ *All FrontPage Web pages also include default meta tags containing information on how to display the page, such as its language and character set information.*

- Add a user-defined meta tag to a page using the Page Properties dialog box or FrontPage's new Code Snippets feature.

Insert Meta Tag Using Page Properties Dialog Box

- To use the Page Properties dialog box to enter a meta tag, use the File>Properties command on the menu bar and click the Custom tab. Click the Add button to open the User Meta Variable dialog box.
- A meta tag requires an attribute name and values such as those shown at the top of the next column.

Adding meta tag name and value attributes

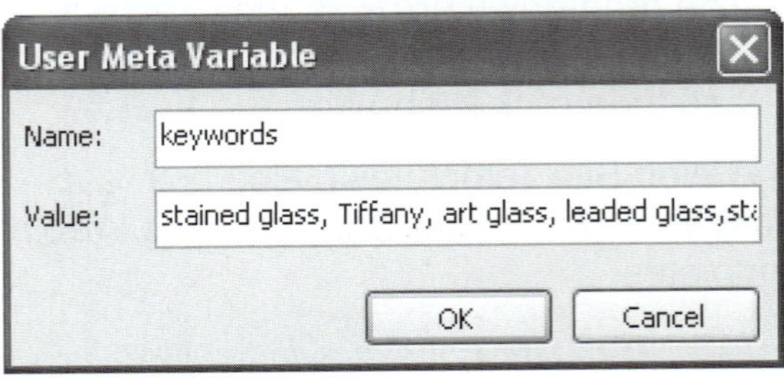

✓ *The value can contain more than one word and spaces between words (see illustration above). Value items are separated by commas.*

- After the user supplies the name and values and clicks OK, the user-defined meta tag information displays in the Page Properties dialog box, as shown below.

Meta tag information in the Page Properties dialog box

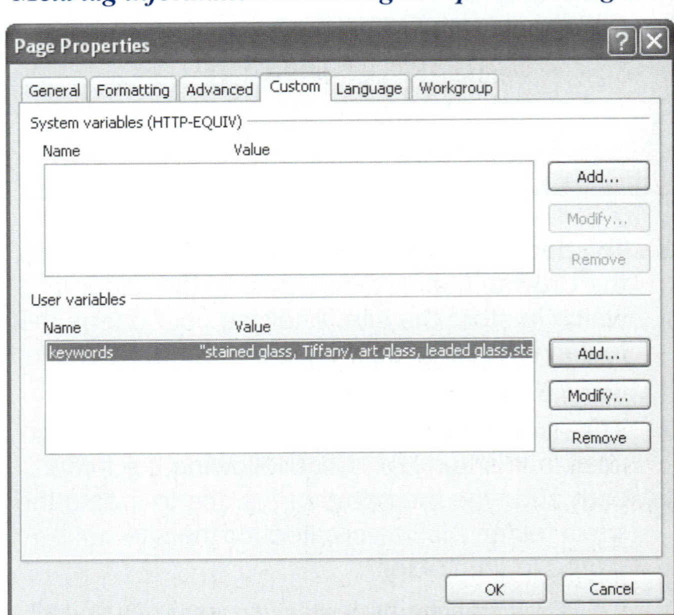

- Meta tags appear in the head section of the Web page, as shown in the illustration at the top of the next page. Information in this section is not visible when the page is viewed in a browser.

Meta tags display in the head section of the page

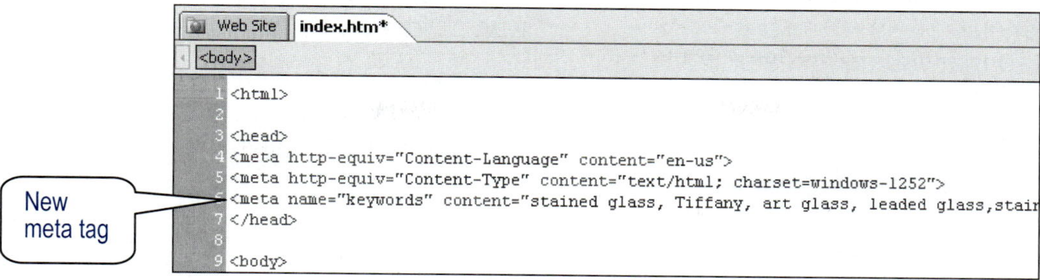

Insert Meta Tag Using Code Snippets

- In FrontPage 2003, a Webmaster can also enter meta tags using the **code snippets** feature. Code snippets are chunks of HTML code that are named and stored for use in any Web page.
- Use the Edit>IntelliSense>List Code Snippets command on the menu bar to open a window containing code snippets (see illustration below).

Code snippets window

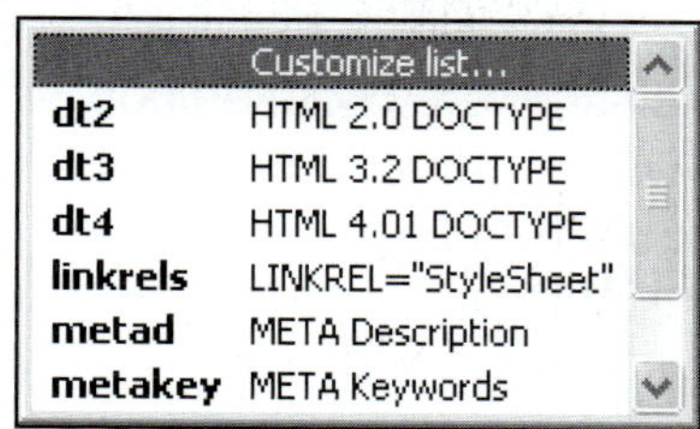

- To insert a code snippet, position the insertion point in Code view where the snippet should appear, and then double-click the desired snippet to insert it. It may then be necessary to enter values or text to complete the code.
- In the illustration below, for example, the metakey (keywords) code snippet has been inserted in the code pane. The insertion point is blinking at the point the Webmaster will need to type the values for the meta tag.

Meta tag inserted as a code snippet

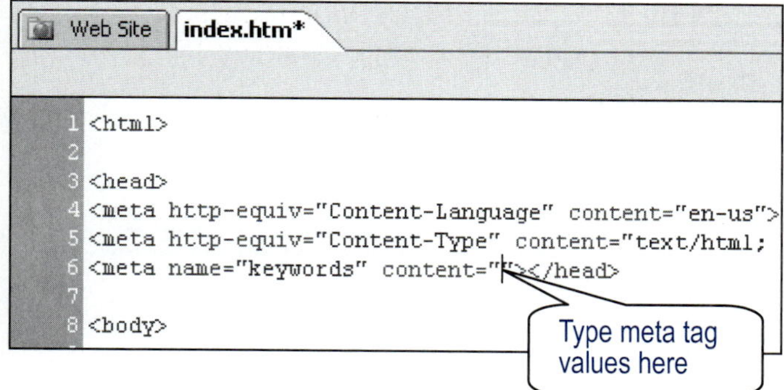

- FrontPage 2003 includes eight default snippets that can be used to perform common tasks such as inserting meta tags. Webmasters can also create their own code snippets to add to the list using the Page Options dialog box.
  - ✓ *You will create and use a code snippet in Exercise 5.*

Create New Web Page

- Most Web sites consist of more than one page. New pages can be added to a Web site at any time, even before text is added to any page.
  - ✓ *FrontPage supplies a number of page templates to create specific types of Web pages. You will work with some of these templates, such as frames pages, in later exercises.*
- To add a new normal Web page (a page not based on a template), use:
  - The File>New command on the menu bar to display the task pane and then click the Blank page link.
  - The Create a new normal page button on the Standard toolbar.
- The new Web page opens into the workspace. The page is named new_page_x.htm by default.
  - ✓ *The x in the default file name above stands for a number that will change depending on how many new Web pages have been created in the current FrontPage session.*
- New Web pages can be added in Page view, Folders view, and Navigation view.
  - ✓ *You will add a Web page in Navigation view in Lesson 6, Exercise 32.*

Save Web Page

- New Web pages should be saved with a descriptive name so that you do not later have to guess at the page's subject.
- To save a Web page, use:
  - The File>Save command on the menu bar.
  - The Save button on the Standard toolbar.
- When saving a Web page, the Web author can also change the **Web page title** (see illustration below).

Set new title for Web page

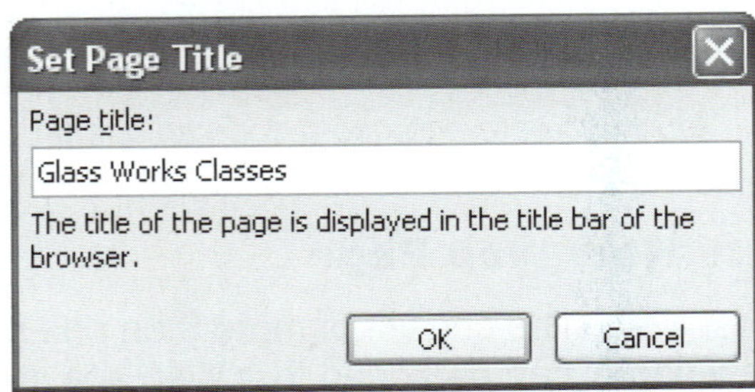

- The Web-page title appears in a user's browser title bar when he/she opens the page in a browser.
- After a Web page has been saved, named, and titled, it can be resaved at any time to update the file to reflect any recent changes. Simply click the Save button on the Standard toolbar.

  ✓ *A Web page that has been changed since the last save shows an asterisk (*) in the tab at the top of the page.*

Save All

- In a Web site of more than one page, authors commonly make changes to several pages in a single editing session.
- To save time, FrontPage offers the File>Save All menu command. Save All saves changes to all open Web pages at the same time.
- After Web pages have been modified and saved, they can be closed by clicking the Close button at the far right of the shaded area above the page.

Preview Web Page

- FrontPage's preview options allow the author to see approximately what a Web page will look like in a user's browser.
- Previewing can help authors judge the effectiveness of the page's text and graphics as well as identify layout problems.
- To preview a Web page, use:
  - The Preview button at the bottom of the page in Page view.
  - The Preview in Browser button on the Standard toolbar.
- Preview view displays in FrontPage. Use this view to quickly check hyperlinks or other Web-page elements.
- The Preview in Browser option gives a more accurate view of how the Web page will look when opened into a user's browser.

  ✓ *You must save a Web page before previewing it if you have made changes since the last save.*

- FrontPage 2003 allows a Web author to specify the desired browser and window size for the preview. Specifying window sizes allows a designer to see how the page will appear for different monitor sizes.
- Clicking the Preview in Browser's down arrow displays a list of browser settings, such as Microsoft Internet Explorer 6.0 (640 × 480) or Microsoft Internet Explorer 6.0 (800 × 600). Select any item on the list to see the preview in the designated browser and window size.
- Click the Edit Browser List button on the list to open the Edit Browser List dialog box (see illustration below).

Edit Browser List dialog box

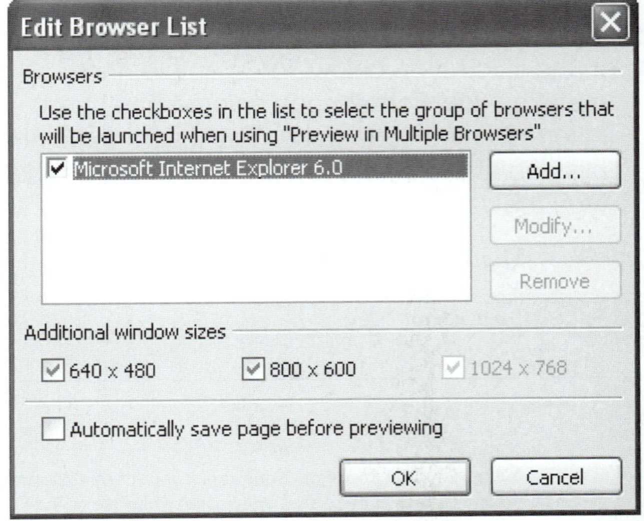

- Click the Add button to add a new browser to the list, and select window sizes for the new browser using the check boxes. The new browser and window sizes then display on the Preview in Browser button's drop-down list.
- The previewed page displays in the selected browser, as shown in the illustration below. (This illustration shows the Microsoft Internet Explorer 640 × 480 view option.)
- Note that it is not necessary to close and open the browser numerous times while working on a Web site. Often, the Webmaster can save changes in FrontPage and simply click the Refresh button in the browser to see the latest version of the Web page under construction.

Web page previewed in Microsoft Internet Explorer

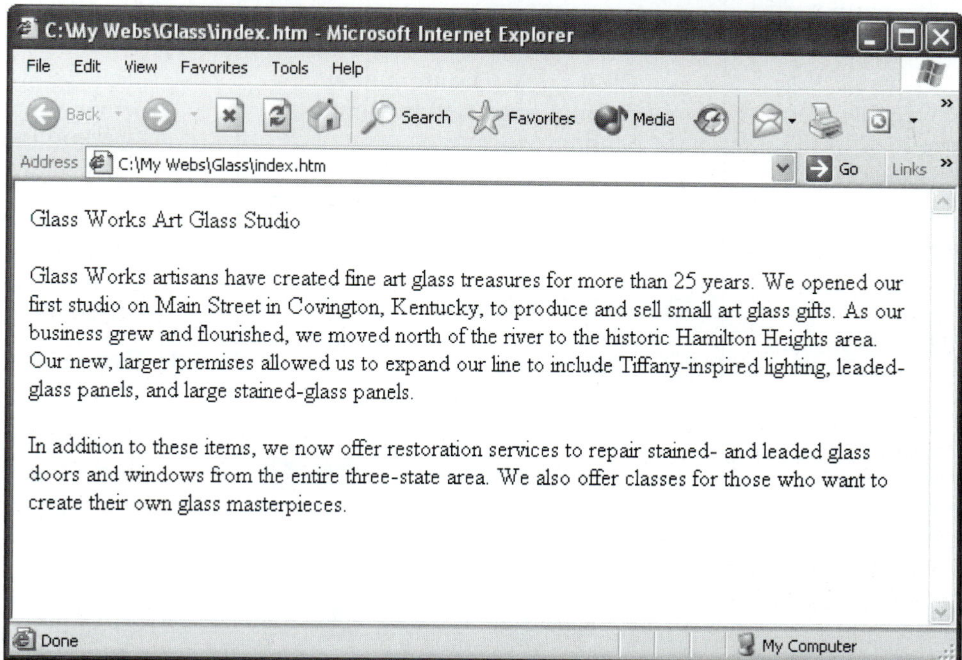

Procedures

Create Web Site Using Template

1. Click (**Create a new normal page** button) drop-down arrow on the Standard toolbar.
2. Click **Web Site** .... W
3. Complete steps 4–10, below.

OR

1. Click **File** .... Alt+F
2. Click **New** .... N
3. Click **More Web site templates** link.

In Web Site Templates dialog box

4. Choose the desired template.
5. Click Browse... .
6. Select drive and folder to store Web in.
7. Click **Open** .... Alt+O
8. Click after the text in the **Specify the location of the new Web site** text box and type new Web name.
9. Click OK .... Enter

Enter Text

1. Click to position insertion point, if necessary.
2. Begin typing.
3. Do not press the **Enter** key twice between paragraphs or to end a line.
4. Press **Spacebar** only once after periods and other punctuation marks.

Spell Check Web-Page Text (*F7*)

✓ *You cannot spell check a page in Preview view.*

1. Click .... F7 (**Spelling** button) on the Standard toolbar.

   OR

   a. Click **Tools** .... Alt+T
   b. Click **Spelling** .... S
2. Choose one of the following options:
   - **Change** word (or all instances of word)
   - **Ignore** word (or all instances of word)
   - **Add** word to spelling dictionary

OR

1. Right-click a word with a wavy, red underline to display a shortcut menu of possible corrections.
2. Click the desired correction on the shortcut menu.

Add Meta Tag

1. Click **File** .... Alt+F
2. Click **Properties** .... R, R, Enter
3. Click **Custom** tab in Page Properties dialog box.
4. Click Add... in **User variables** section.
5. Type name attribute in **Name** text box.
6. Type keywords or descriptive text for value attribute in **Value** text box.

   ✓ *Separate value items with commas (,).*
7. Click OK twice .... Enter

OR

In Code view

1. Click **Edit** .... Alt+E
2. Click **IntelliSense** .... N
3. Click **List Code Snippets** ... L
4. Position insertion point in code where new snippet should appear.
5. Double-click snippet in code snippet window to insert.
6. Type contents values.

Create New Web Page

- Click (**Create a new normal page** button) on the Standard toolbar.

OR

1. Click **File** .... Alt+F
2. Click **New** .... N
3. Click **Blank page** in New task pane.

Save Web Page (*Ctrl+S*)

To save Web page for first time

1. Click (**Save** .... Ctrl+S button) on the Standard toolbar.

   OR

   a. Click **File** .... Alt+F
   b. Click **Save** .... S
2. Type new name for Web page in **File name** text box.
3. Click Change title... button......................... Alt+C
4. Type new **Page title** in text box.
5. Click OK .... Enter
6. Click Save ..... Alt+S

   ✓ *After saving the Web page initially, use File>Save or the Save button on the Standard toolbar to save changes.*

Save All

1. Click **File** .... Alt+F
2. Click **Save All**..................... L

Close Web Page

- Click ☒ (**Close** button) at far right of shaded area above Web page.

Preview Web Page

- Click Preview (**Preview** button) in Page view.

OR

- Click (**Preview in Browser** button) on the Standard toolbar.

OR

- Click down arrow on (**Preview in Browser** button) and select browser or browser window option.

Add Browser to Preview

1. Click down arrow on (**Preview in Browser** button) on the Standard toolbar.
2. Click **Edit Browser List**...... E
3. Click Add... (**Add** button) in Edit Browser List dialog box.
4. Type browser name.
5. Type command to open browser.
6. Click OK.
7. Select window sizes for new browser.
8. Click OK.

Exercise Directions

1. Start FrontPage 2003.
2. Close any open Web sites, if necessary.
3. Create a new Web site using the One Page Web Site template. Name the Web site **Glass**.
   - ✓ *In the Web Site Templates dialog box, click the One Page Web Site template. Click the Browse button to navigate to the folder where you will store your sites for this course and click the Open button to open that folder. In the Web Site Templates dialog box again, click at the end of the folder path in the Specify the location of the new Web site text box and type* ***Glass*** *as the Web site name.*
4. Open **index.htm**.
   - ✓ *If the page opens in Code view, click the Design button at the bottom of the page.*
5. On the blank Web page, type the paragraphs shown in Illustration A, including the two misspellings (circled below).
6. Use the Spelling program to correct the spelling errors on **index.htm**.
7. Create a new meta tag with the name **keywords**. Insert the following values: **stained glass, Tiffany, art glass, leaded glass, stained glass repairs, stained glass supplies**.
   - ✓ *You can use the Page Properties dialog box to insert the meta tag or use the metakey code snippet in Code or Split view.*
8. Switch to Code view if necessary to see the new meta tag keywords in the head section of the Web page.
9. Add a new page to the Web.
10. Save the page as **classes.htm** and change the Web-page title to **Glass Works Classes**.
11. On the new page, type the paragraphs shown in Illustration B.
12. Check spelling on the **classes.htm** page.
13. Use the Save All command to save changes to both Web pages.
14. Preview **classes.htm** in Preview view. If you have several browser window sizes available on the Preview in Browser drop-down list, try all sizes to see the difference in the preview.
15. Switch to **index.htm**.
16. Preview **index.htm** in the browser.
17. Close the browser.
18. Close the Web site.
19. Exit FrontPage 2003.

Illustration A

Glass Works Art Glass Studio

Glass Works artisans have creted fine art glass treasures for more than 25 years. We opened our first studio on Main Street in Covington, Kentucky, to produce and sell small art glass gifts. As our business grew and florished, we moved north of the river to the historic Hamilton Heights area. Our new, larger premises allowed us to expand our line to include Tiffany-inspired lighting, leaded-glass panels, and large stained-glass panels.

In addition to these items, we now offer restoration services to repair stained- and leaded-glass doors and windows from the entire three-state area. We also offer classes for those who want to create their own glass masterpieces.

Illustration B

Glass Works Classes

Even if your only contact with glass pieces has been that vase you dropped last week, you can learn to create beautiful boxes, panels, and even lamp shades. Many patterns are available to take the anxiety out of designing your project.

For the Beginner

If you have never worked with glass before, try our Beginners' Class. This class meets every Wednesday for six weeks. You choose your project and we teach you the skills you need to create it.

On Your Own

1. Start FrontPage 2003.
2. Create a new Web site for a company, organization, or club. Name the Web site **OYO3**.
3. Enter general introductory text on the **index.htm** page.
4. Specify suitable meta keywords for the site.
5. Add at least one new Web page and save it with an appropriate name and title.
6. Enter text on the new Web page(s).
7. Check spelling on both Web pages and save all changes.
8. Preview the Web site in your browser.
9. Close the browser.
10. Close the Web site.
11. Exit FrontPage 2003.

Exercise 4

◆ Web Fonts ◆ Text Alignment
◆ Copy Format (Format Painter) ◆ Insert File
◆ Rename Page ◆ Create Page Content in Code View

On the Job

Using FrontPage's formatting options, the Web author can change text font, size, style, and color to add visual interest to a Web site. Changing paragraph alignment is another way to emphasize text. Files created in other Microsoft Office 2003 applications, such as Word, can be inserted into FrontPage, eliminating the need to retype information. After editing Web-page content, the Web designer can change the page's name and title in Folders view. Text can be entered in Code view to make sure formats are correctly applied.

In this exercise, you will work on a Web site created by a local food and cookware shop called Home Cooking. You will apply text and paragraph formats to add visual interest to the Web pages, insert a file to add text to a page, and rename a page to reflect its new content. Finally, you will enter text in Code view.

Terms

alignment
The horizontal placement of paragraphs or lines of text on a document or in a browser content area. One can align text to the left, center, or right, or justify text. Also called *justification*.

font
A complete set of characters designed in a specific style, such as Arial or Times New Roman.

font style
Font characteristics, such as bold, italics, and underline, that are used for text emphasis.

point (pt)
The standard measurement for fonts. There are 72 points to an inch.

sans serif font
A font design that has no cross-strokes (or "serifs") at the top and bottom of the characters; it is straight-edged. For example: T

serif font
A font design that has small cross-strokes (or "serifs") at the top and bottom of the characters. For example: T

Notes

Web Fonts

- A **font** is a complete set of letters, numbers, and symbols in a particular design.
- FrontPage's default font is Times New Roman, a **serif font** that is easy to read both on the screen and in printed publications.
- Serif fonts such as Times New Roman are most often used for the main body of text on a Web page. These fonts have a "formal" or "conservative" feel.
- **Sans serif fonts** are considered less formal and are often used for headings or for body text on personal Web pages.

- Font choices are capable of conveying a wide variety of moods and attitudes. Keep in mind, though, that some browsers may be unable to display unusual fonts correctly.
- To change the font on a Web page, use:
  - The Format>Font command on the menu bar.
  - The Font list box on the Formatting toolbar (see illustration below).

Font list on Formatting toolbar

- Fonts can be changed before typing text or they can be applied to existing text. Select any existing text before choosing a new font.
- A font can be further modified by changing its font style, size, and/or color. These changes can all be made in the Font dialog box (see illustration below), via toolbar buttons, or by using keyboard shortcuts.

Change multiple formats in the Font dialog box

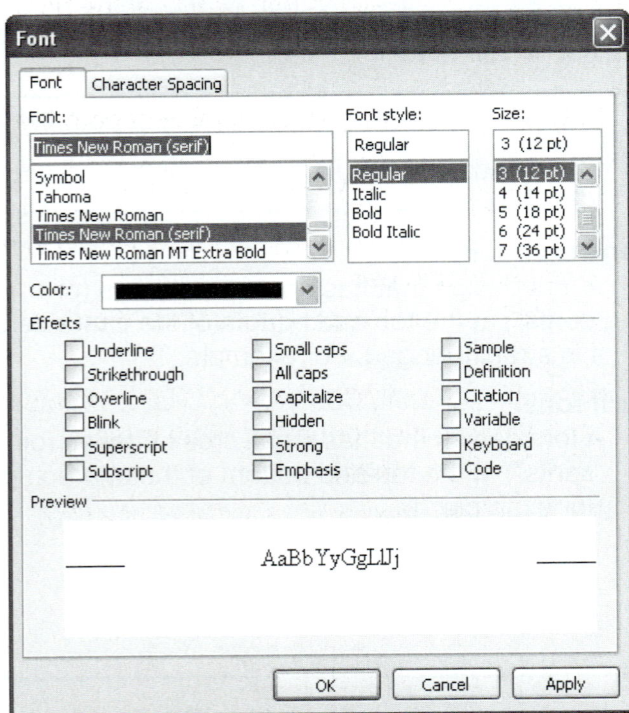

- After applying a formatting change, users can reverse the change by clicking the Undo button on the Standard toolbar. To remove several different format changes, use the Format>Remove Formatting command on the menu bar.

Font Size

- Fonts are measured in **points**. The default size for Web page text is 12 points.
- However, HTML coding requires that font sizes be specified as a single number from 1 to 7. For this reason, the Font Size list box on the Formatting toolbar displays both the HTML number-increment font size and the more familiar point size (see illustration below).

Font Size list (Formatting toolbar)

3 (12 pt)

- To apply a new font size, use:
  - The Format>Font command on the menu bar.

    ✓ *To apply a new size to existing text, select the text first.*
  - The Font Size list box on the Formatting toolbar (see illustration above).
  - The Increase Font Size or Decrease Font Size button on the Formatting toolbar.

    ✓ *These buttons increase or decrease text by one HTML font increment each time they are clicked.*

Font Style

- Web page text can be emphasized by changing its **font style**.
- The font styles most often applied to Web-page text are bold and italics. In Web pages, the underline font style is generally avoided because a user could easily (and understandably) confuse an underlined word with a hyperlink.

  ✓ *Multiple font styles may be applied to the same text to provide additional formatting possibilities. For example, both bold and italic font styles can be applied.*
- To apply a font style, use:
  - The Format>Font command on the menu bar.
  - The Bold, Italic, or Underline button on the Formatting toolbar (see illustration below).
  - Keyboard shortcuts: Bold, Ctrl+B; Italics, Ctrl+I; Underline, Ctrl+U.

Font Style buttons (Formatting toolbar)

B I U

✓ *To apply a new font style to existing text, select the text first.*

Font Color

- By default, all Web-page text is black because black is the color that is easiest to read on most backgrounds.
- To add visual interest to a Web page, text color can also be changed.
- Formatting headings in color emphasizes them so they stand out from surrounding body text.
- The color of body text may be changed to improve readability on a dark background.
- To apply a new color to text, use:
  - The Format>Font command on the menu bar.

    ✓ *To apply a new font color to existing text, select the text first.*
  - The drop-down arrow to the right of the Font Color button on the Formatting toolbar, and then choose a color from the color palette (see illustration below).

    ✓ *Rest the pointer on a color swatch in the palette to display a ScreenTip that provides the color's name.*

Font Color button and color palette (Formatting toolbar)

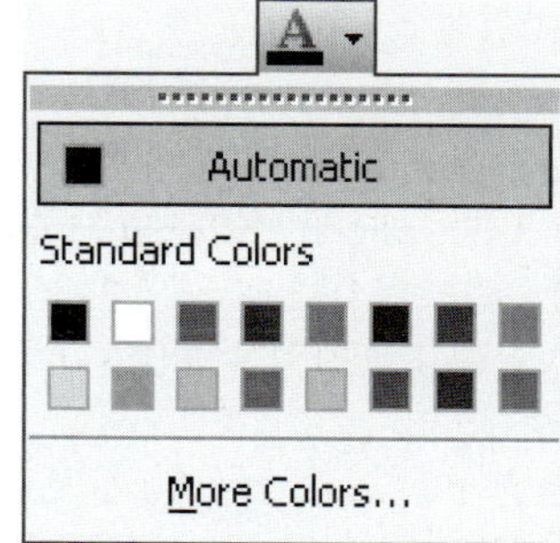

- Note that the color palette includes both standard colors and custom colors that the Web designer has added to the Web.

  ✓ *You learn more about creating custom colors in Lesson 2, Exercise 8, page 00.*
- Clicking More Colors opens the More Colors dialog box, where a Web designer can select from many more colors in a large palette. If the designer applies a color this way, it is added to the color palette in a section called Document Colors.

Code Cues

Web page colors are assigned *hexadecimal* values in HTML code. For example, the hexadecimal code for navy blue is #000080. Find the hexadecimal value for any color by selecting it in the More Colors dialog box and looking at the numbers in the Value box.

Text Alignment

- By default, Web-page text is left aligned. This means that text lines up evenly at the left edge of the browser content area and breaks unevenly at the right edge.
- **Alignment** can be changed to emphasize portions of text on a Web page. Users can choose from the following alignments:

ALIGNMENT	DESCRIPTION
Left (default)	Aligns text evenly at the left edge of the browser content area.
Center	Aligns text in the middle of the browser content area.
Right	Aligns text evenly at the right edge of the browser content area.
Justify	Aligns text evenly at both the left and right edges of the browser content area.

- To apply a new alignment, click anywhere in the paragraph and use:
  - The Format>Paragraph command on the menu bar.
  - The Align Left, Center, Align Right, or Justify button on the Formatting toolbar (see illustration below).
  - Keyboard shortcuts: Left, Ctrl+L; Center, Ctrl+E; Right, Ctrl+R.

Alignment buttons (Formatting toolbar)

Code Cues

Use the align attribute in the paragraph tag to set alignment in HTML code. Alignment options are values for the align attribute.
For example: <p align="center">

Copy Format (Format Painter)

- Achieving just the right look for headings and text on a Web page may mean applying a number of different formats, such as a new font, font style, color, and alignment.
- To avoid having to make the same series of formatting changes to similar kinds of text (for example, headings), the user can quickly apply the same formats to other portions of text with the Format Painter tool located on the Standard toolbar.
- When clicked in formatted text, the Format Painter tool "copies" all formats (including character and paragraph formats) at that location.
- To "paste" the formats elsewhere, click the paintbrush-shaped pointer on the text to format.
- To "paste" a format to multiple locations in the document, double-click the Format Painter tool. Click the Format Painter button to deselect it when you are through.
- Using the Format Painter tool saves a considerable amount of formatting time and ensures that similar kinds of text are formatted the same way.

Insert File

- In the process of constructing a Web site, some materials may be created in other applications, such as a word processor.
- FrontPage's Insert>File menu command makes it easy to insert the entire contents of a file at the location of the insertion point.
- Using this command eliminates the need to retype information that has already been created in another application.
- Text inserted using this command automatically takes on the formatting of the Web page's paragraph style.

  ✓ *You will work with Web page styles in the next exercise.*

Rename Page

- As Web-site construction proceeds, it might become necessary to change the name of an existing Web page to reflect its contents more accurately.
- Both the Web-page name and title can be changed in Folders view simply by clicking the name or title until the item is highlighted. The new name or title can then be entered over the existing one (see illustration below).

  ✓ *A Web-page name can also be changed in the Folder List at any time.*

- When changing a Web-page's name, authors must take care to type the .htm file name extension at the end of the new name. FrontPage supplies a warning dialog box if this extension is not included.

Change Web-page name and title in Folders view

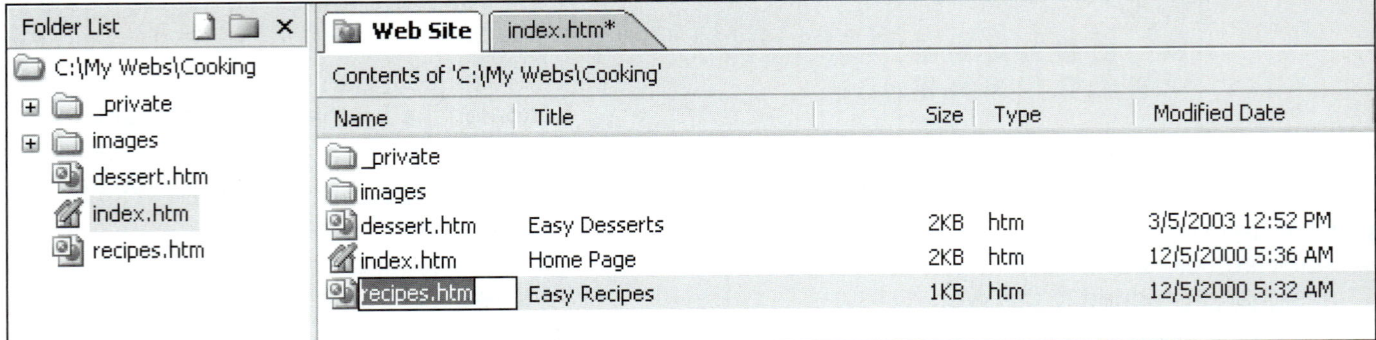

Create Page Content in Code View

- In FrontPage 2003, creating page content using HTML codes is easier than ever. The Webmaster can work directly with HTML codes in either Code view or the Code pane of Split view.
- FrontPage 2003 includes a number of useful features that can help both experienced and novice HTML coders insert HTML tags and format the code for easier comprehension.

  ✓ *To review common HTML tags, see Exercise 2.*

Code IntelliSense

- Microsoft IntelliSense technology has been built into FrontPage 2003 to make it easy to insert HTML tags.
- Typing the opening wicket displays a window containing HTML tags. Type the first letter of the tag to go to the correct section of the window (see illustration below).

Code IntelliSense offers list of HTML tags

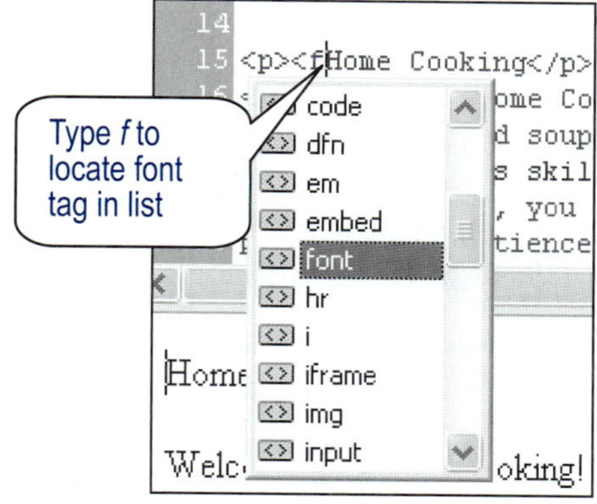

- Select the tag and press Enter to insert it. Typing the closing wicket automatically inserts the closing tag as well.
- If the HTML tag requires an attribute, pressing the spacebar after entering the tag displays another window containing attributes that can be used with that tag.
- The illustration below, for example, shows the attributes that can be used with the <font> tag. After inserting the attribute by pressing Enter, the Webmaster can type any necessary values to complete the tag.

Attributes available for the current tag

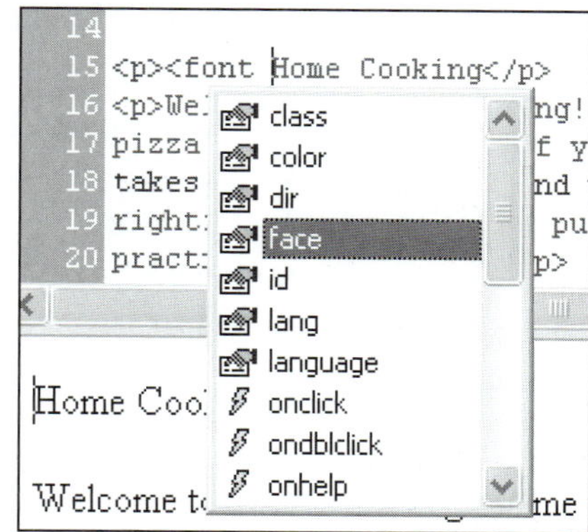

- Code IntelliSense helps to eliminate errors that can creep into code from mistyping tags, failing to provide a closing tag, or other syntax errors.

Code Manipulation Aids

- For experienced HTML coders, FrontPage 2003 includes a number of shortcuts and other features to speed code entry.
- The Edit>Code View command on the menu bar provides an extensive list of shortcuts and features for inserting, aligning, and marking code (see illustration below).

Code view options

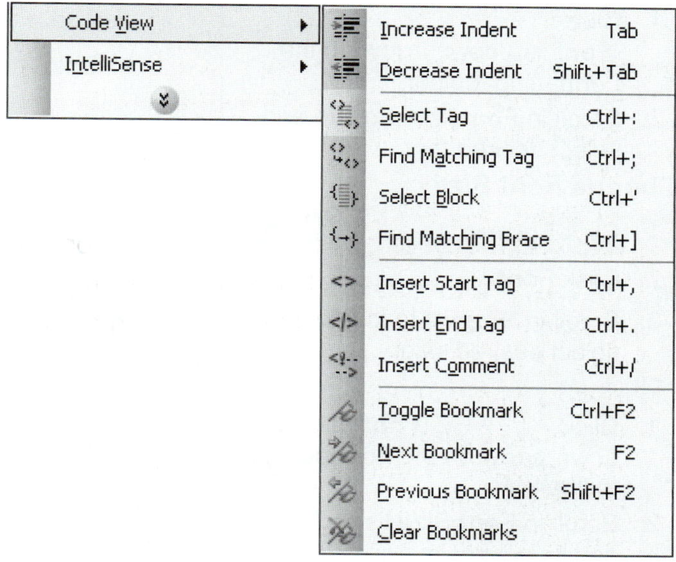

- Use the Increase Indent and Decrease Indent commands to apply or remove indention to lines of code to make them easier to read.

  ✓ *Or, select a block of code and press Tab or Shift + Tab to modify indention.*

- Use Select Tag or Select Block to select a portion of code.
- Use Find Matching Tag or Find Matching Brace to locate the closing tag or brace for a section of code. These options help an author ensure that the code is complete.
- Use the Insert commands, or their shortcut keys, to quickly insert an opening tag, end tag, or comment.
- Use bookmarks to identify specific locations in the code.

- These options, and especially their shortcut keys, can help an author who wants to do the majority of page creation in Code or Split view to insert code both quickly and correctly.

Procedures

Change Font

1. Click **Format** .... Alt+O
2. Click **Font** .... F
3. Scroll in **Font** list to locate and select desired font.

OR

1. Click Times New Roman (**Font** list) down arrow on the Formatting toolbar.
2. Scroll in **Font** list to locate and select desired font.

Change Font Size

1. Click **Format** .... Alt+O
2. Click **Font** .... F
3. Scroll in **Size** list to locate and select desired size.

OR

1. Click 3 (12 pt) (**Font Size** list) down arrow on the Formatting toolbar.
2. Scroll in **Font Size** list to locate and select desired size.

OR

- Use toolbar buttons to change font size by HTML number–increment font size:
  - Increase Font Size
  - Decrease Font Size

Change Font Color

1. Select text to change.
2. Click **Format** .... Alt+O
3. Click **Font** .... F
4. Click **Color** drop-down arrow and select color, or click **More Colors**.

OR

1. Click (**Font Color** button) down arrow on the Formatting toolbar.

   ✓ *If the color you want is currently displayed on the button, simply click the button.*
2. Click desired color on the font color palette.

Change Font Style

1. Click **Format** .... Alt+O
2. Click **Font** .... F
3. Click new style in **Font style** list.

OR

- Use desired toolbar button:
  - Bold .... Ctrl+B
  - Italic .... Ctrl+I
  - Underline .... Ctrl+U

Change Text Alignment

1. Click **Format** .... Alt+O
2. Click **Paragraph** .... P
3. Click **Alignment** drop-down arrow and select desired alignment.

OR

- Use desired toolbar button:
  - Align Left .... Ctrl+L
  - Center .... Ctrl+E
  - Align Right .... Ctrl+R
  - Justify

Copy Format (Format Painter)

1. Click text with format(s) to copy.
   - Click (**Format Painter** button) on the Standard toolbar once to apply formats to one location only.
   - Double-click (**Format Painter** button) to apply formats to more than one location.
2. Click (or select) text to copy format(s) to.
3. Click (**Format Painter** button) again to deselect it, if necessary, after pasting formats as desired.

Insert File

1. Click **Insert** .... Alt+I
2. Click **File** .... F
3. Click **Look in** arrow.
4. Select desired drive or folder.

   ✓ *If necessary, double-click folder name.*
5. Change file type in **Files of type** list box, if necessary.
6. Click desired file name.
7. Click Open ..... Alt+O

Rename Page

Rename page in Folders view

1. Switch to Folders view.
2. Click once on Web-page name to select all page information.
3. Click again on Web-page name.

   ✓ *Do not double-click the Web-page name.*

   Web-page name is highlighted and surrounded by a border.
4. Type a new Web-page name to replace the original one.

   ✓ *Type the .htm file name extension at the end of the new Web-page name.*
5. Click away from the Web-page name to complete the change.

   OR
   - Press **Tab** .... Tab

     to select and change Web-page title.

Rename page in Folder List

1. Click Web-page name in Folder List *twice*.
2. Type new Web-page name.
3. Press Enter.

Use Code IntelliSense

In Code or the Code pane of Split view

1. Position the insertion point where the new tag should appear.
2. Type **<** (the opening wicket) to display the tag list.
3. Type the first letter of the desired tag, if necessary, to go to the correct area of the tag list.
4. Select the desired tag.
5. Press Enter to insert the tag.
6. To insert an attribute for the tag, press the spacebar, and then select the appropriate attribute from the attribute list.
7. Type **>** (the closing wicket) to complete the tag and insert the end tag as well.

Use Code Manipulation Aids

In Code or the code pane of Split view

1. Position the insertion point if necessary where code should be manipulated.
2. Click **Edit** .... Alt+E
3. Click **Code View** V
4. Choose desired command from pop-out menu.
   - **Increase Indent** .... Tab
   - **Decrease Indent** . Shift+Tab
   - **Select Tag** ..... Ctrl+Shift+;
   - **Find Matching Tag** .... Ctrl+;
   - **Select Block** .... Ctrl+'
   - **Find Matching Brace** .... Ctrl+]
   - **Insert Start Tag** ...... Ctrl+,
   - **Insert End Tag** .... Ctrl+.
   - **Insert Comment** ..... Ctrl+/
   - **Toggle Bookmark** .... Ctrl+F2
   - **Next Bookmark** F2
   - **Previous Bookmark** .... Shift+F2
   - **Clear Bookmarks**

Exercise Directions

1. Start FrontPage 2003.
2. Open **Cooking**.
3. Open **recipes.htm**.
   ✓ *This Web site is still under construction and needs more text. As you build this page, refer to Illustration A for guidance on how the page should look.*
4. Position the insertion point below the first paragraph and insert the file **roast.doc**.
   ✓ *You will have to change the* Files of type *setting to* All Files (*.*) *to locate this file in the Data folder.*
5. Scroll to the top of the recipe and notice that each recipe ingredient appears in a separate paragraph. Also, one ingredient is missing. Fix the ingredients list:
   - Switch to Split view.
   - Locate the closing Paragraph tag </p> that follows the first ingredient (*2 cans of mushroom soup)* and delete the closing tag.
   - Use Code IntelliSense to insert a Break tag <br>.
     ✓ The Break tag <br> starts a new line but not a new paragraph. In Page view, you can create the same effect by pressing Shift+Enter.
   - Delete the Paragraph tag <p> at the beginning of the next line and type the following text:
     **1 envelope dried onion soup mix
**
   - Press the **Enter** key.
6. Press F5 to update Design view and check the ingredients list.
7. In the Code pane of Split view, select the three lines that contain ingredients and indent them so they will be easy to find in the code.
8. The content of the Web is now focused on main dishes. Change the Web-page name to **main.htm** and the title to **Easy Main Dishes**.
   ✓ *To change the title in Folders view, click twice on the title and then type a new Web-page title.*
9. Make the following formatting changes on the page. As you change formats, notice the codes applied in the code pane of the Split view.
   - Center the recipe title (*Easy Pot Roast*) and the paragraph below it.
   - Right-align the *Use: Oven* paragraph.
   - Center the following line: *Be careful when opening the foil!*
   - Boldface the *Use: Oven* text.
   - Italicize the following phrases in the first and last paragraphs, below the ingredients list: *You'll also need:* and *Serve with:*.
   - Apply bold and italic formatting to the *Be careful when opening the foil!* line.
10. Open **index.htm** and **dessert.htm**.

11. On **dessert.htm**, in the code pane of Split view, locate the <p> </p> tags in line 13. Click between the opening tag and the closing tag and enter the following content using IntelliSense:
    <font face="Impact" size="6">Easy Desserts</font></p>
    ✓ *If you don't have Impact, use another sans serif font.*
12. Update the Design view to see the new, formatted text.
13. Select the text in the Design pane and change the color of the heading to Maroon.
14. Click anywhere in the heading and copy the formats with the Format Painter.
    ✓ *Double-click the Format Painter button to copy formats to more than one location.*
15. Click the **main.htm** page tab to activate that page and paste the heading formats to the *Easy Main Dishes* heading.
16. Click the **index.htm** page tab to activate that page and paste the heading formats to the *Home Cooking* heading.
17. Save changes to all pages.
18. Preview the **main.htm** page in the browser. It should look similar to Illustration A on the following page.
19. Close the browser and the Web site.
20. Exit FrontPage 2003.

Illustration A

Easy Main Dishes

These recipes will give you a start on a home-cooked meal. Don't forget to add vegetables and fruit to maintain a balanced diet.

Easy Pot Roast

This easy meal gives you pot roast and gravy without a fuss or a mess.

Use: Oven

2 cans mushroom soup
1 envelope dried onion soup mix
1 3 – 4 lb. chuck roast or arm roast

You'll also need: a baking dish (approx. 9x13) and aluminum foil (preferably heavy duty)

Line the baking dish with foil. Tear off another long piece of foil (long enough to wrap around the pot roast and fold over). Lay the long piece of foil in the baking dish. In the center of the foil, dollop most of the first can of mushroom soup and then sprinkle half of the envelope of dried onion soup over it. Carefully place the chuck roast on top of the onion-soup/mushroom-soup mixture. Spoon remaining mushroom soup from first can and about half the soup from the second can over the roast. Sprinkle on the remaining dry onion soup mixture. Fold foil over the roast and seal edges securely. Place the pan in the oven and cook for 3 to 4 hours.

Be careful when opening the foil!

Serve with: hot noodles or mashed potatoes, steamed carrots, and a green salad

On Your Own

1. Start FrontPage 2003.
2. Open **Swap**.
3. Open **index.htm**.
4. Change the font, size, and color of the first heading on the Web and apply the same formats to the first headings on the **items.htm** and **books.htm** pages.
5. On the **items.htm** page, insert the file **merchandise.doc** below the last paragraph.
6. In HTML view, change Paragraph tags <p> to Break tags <br> as necessary to make the items listed under the *Home Furnishings, Kitchenware,* and *Crafts* headings match the items listed below the *Collectibles* and *Toys* headings.
7. While you are still in HTML view, add a new item after *Pots and pans*: **Silver, glassware, and dishes**.
8. Format the merchandise category headings as desired.
9. Change the **items.htm** page name to **merchandise.htm** and the page title to **Swap Merchandise**.
10. Preview the **merchandise.htm** page in the browser.
11. Close the browser.
12. Close the Web site.
13. Exit FrontPage 2003.

Exercise 5

◆ About Styles ◆ Bulleted and Numbered Lists
◆ Create Definition Lists ◆ Insert Special Characters (Symbols)
◆ Copy Text from Other Application
◆ Create and Use a Code Snippet

On the Job

FrontPage 2003 provides a number of styles to format text with a single click of the mouse. Styles such as those for bulleted, numbered, and definition lists are used to organize Web-page text. FrontPage 2003 includes many special characters such as punctuation marks, mathematical symbols, and foreign-language characters for use in text. When text to be included in a Web page has already been prepared in another Microsoft Office 2003 application, it can be copied and pasted into a FrontPage Web page. Use code snippets to quickly insert HTML code in any Web page.

In this exercise, you will continue working on the Home Cooking Web site. You will use styles to format headings and create bulleted and numbered lists. You will copy text from a Microsoft Office Word document and use that text to create a definition list. You will insert special characters in several of the Web pages. Finally, you will create a code snippet to format text on a Web page.

Terms

bullet
A small symbol or character that begins each item in a *bulleted list*.

bulleted list
An unordered list in which each item is preceded by a special character called a *bullet*.

definition list
A list that consists of terms and their definitions. Each term appears on a separate line with its definition in an indented paragraph below the term.

numbered list
An ordered list in which each item is preceded by a number and items appear sequentially.

special characters
Characters such as punctuation symbols, foreign-language characters, mathematical signs, and other symbols used in text.

style
A set of formats (such as font, size, and alignment) with a specific name that can be applied to text.

Notes

About Styles

- A **style** is a named set of formats that is applied to a specific document element to ensure consistency within the document.
- For example, in FrontPage 2003, the Heading 1 style supplies formats suitable for the first heading on a Web page.

- In FrontPage, applying a "style" means applying the specific set of formats via HTML tags for proper display in a Web browser.
- For example, when the Web designer applies the Heading 1 style to text, FrontPage automatically applies the Heading-Level 1 tag <h1>.
- Applying styles in FrontPage eliminates the need to insert HTML tags manually to achieve specific text effects. Using styles also ensures that text elements, such as headings, are formatted the same way throughout the Web site.
- FrontPage's Style list offers the Web designer six heading styles and an additional ten styles for body text.
- To apply a style to text, use the Style list on the Formatting toolbar (see illustration below).

FrontPage Style list (Formatting toolbar)

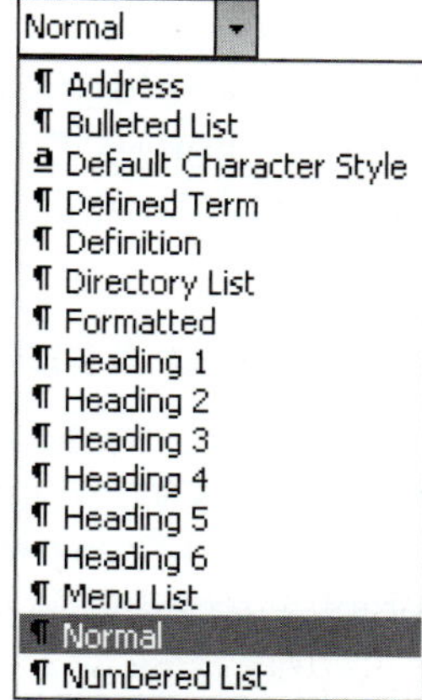

- Designers can modify FrontPage's styles if desired. After a style has been modified, all text formatted with that style is automatically updated to display the new format.

  ✓ *You will modify and create new styles in Lesson 5, Exercise 29.*

- If text has already been formatted with fonts, styles, or colors, applying a FrontPage style will *not* replace existing formatting with the style's formatting.

  ✓ *To remove existing formatting, do one of the following: use the Format>Remove Formatting menu command, delete format attributes in Code view, or use Format Painter to paste the desired formats.*

Bulleted and Numbered Lists

- Lists are used to organize information on Web pages.
- The two most frequently used types of lists are bulleted lists and numbered lists:
  - Use a **bulleted list** to organize text items that do not have to be in a specific order (see illustration below).

    ✓ *Bulleted lists are so called because the small character at the beginning of each list item is called a* ***bullet****.*

  - Use a **numbered list** to organize text items that must appear in a specific order (see illustration below).

Bulleted and numbered lists on a Web page

Payment Options

You can use:

- Cash
- Personal check with one additional form of identification (state ID, driver's license, or school ID)
- Credit card

Selling Options

To reserve a stall at the Swap:

1. Fill out the Swap Information form to provide a general description of your merchandise.
2. Mail or bring the form to Sycamore Town Hall by the close of business on September 12, along with the $15 application fee.
3. You will receive your stall number and receipt by mail or in person.

- The HTML tags for these lists reflect their use. The Unordered List tag <ul> is for a bulleted list; the Ordered List tag <ol> is for a numbered list.
- To apply bulleted or numbered list formatting to a text item, use:
  - The Numbering or Bullets button on the Formatting toolbar.
  - The Numbered List or Bulleted List style from the Style list on the Formatting toolbar.
- Applying one of these styles to text automatically indents the text and displays a bullet or number before each list item.
- After the Bulleted List or Numbered List style has been applied to a paragraph, all subsequent paragraphs will have the same format. To turn off the style, press Enter twice or click the Numbering or Bullets button again to deselect the style.

Create Definition Lists

- A **definition list** is a special type of list that includes terms and their definitions. This type of list is useful for glossaries or to create headings above indented paragraphs (see illustration below).
- Definition lists are created using the Defined Term and Definition styles (see illustration below). These styles may be applied as text is entered or applied to existing text.
  - When the Defined Term style is applied to a term as it is typed, the Definition style is automatically applied to the next paragraph.
  - When existing text is formatted as a definition list, the Defined Term and Definition styles must be applied to each term and definition.

> **Code Cues**
>
> Use the <dl> tag to begin a definition list. Format the defined term with the <dt> tag and the definition with the <dd> tag, as shown below.

Definition list with defined terms and definitions

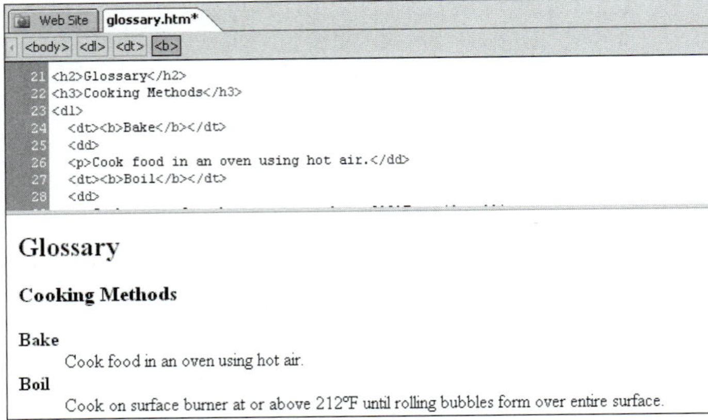

Insert Special Characters (Symbols)

- It is sometimes necessary to insert **special characters** on a Web page, such as copyright symbols (©), foreign-language characters (á), fractions (¼), or punctuation characters (—).
- FrontPage's Insert>Symbol menu command gives the author access to most popular special characters (see illustration below).

Symbol dialog box

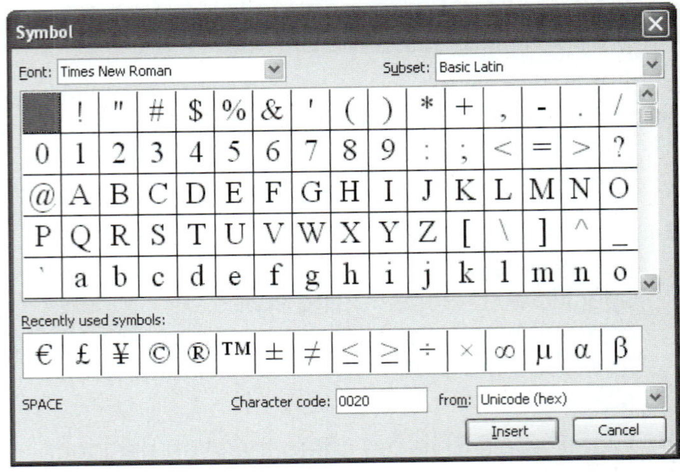

✓ *The Recently used symbols area of the Symbol dialog box allows the Web author to find symbols that have been used recently.*

- Locate the current font in the Font list to make sure symbol characters match the text around them.
- The Symbol dialog box remains open after a character has been inserted. This makes it easy to insert several symbols without reopening the dialog box.

Copy Text from Other Application

- Exercise 4 discussed the Insert>File menu command, which allows Web authors to insert the entire contents of a Microsoft Office file at the insertion point.
- FrontPage users also have the option of inserting any part of a file created in another application using the Copy and Paste commands.
- To copy and paste information, use:
  - The Edit>Copy and Edit>Paste commands on the menu bar.
  - The Copy and Paste buttons on the Standard toolbar.
  - Keyboard shortcuts: Copy, Ctrl+C; Paste, Ctrl+V.
- If the information to be copied has been created with a Microsoft Office application such as Word or Excel, the author can employ the Office Clipboard to handle the copying and pasting process.
- The Office Clipboard allows the author to store up to 24 different copied items and then paste them in another Office application.

✓ *The Clipboard also stores items that have been removed using the Cut command, Cut button on the Standard toolbar, or the Cut keyboard shortcut, Ctrl+X.*

- Web authors control the Office Clipboard contents using the Clipboard task pane. Click the down arrow in the task pane's title bar and select Clipboard to display the Clipboard task pane.
- When the Clipboard task pane is open, copying or cutting text places an application icon and the first few lines of text (or a description) on the Clipboard (see illustration below).
- To paste an item from the Clipboard into another application, simply click the item in the Clipboard task pane.
- To quickly insert all items from the Clipboard, use the Paste All button.
- To clear the Clipboard's contents, click the Clear All button.

Clipboard task pane stores two Word items

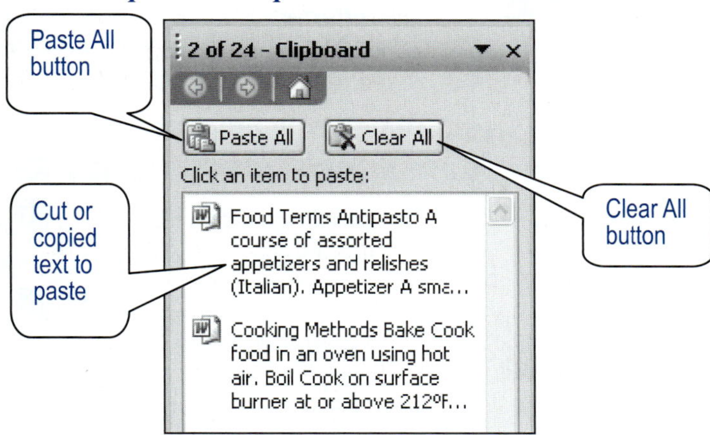

Create and Use a Code Snippet

- Code snippets are chunks of HTML code that a Web author uses frequently. A code snippet can be any code or content that can be entered in the Code pane of a page.
- Code snippets can be used, for example, to apply specific formats to Web-page text. When creating the snippet, the Web author can insert a vertical bar (or pipe) character (|) that indicates where to insert text that will be formatted with the snippet's code.
- To create a code snippet, use the Tools>Page Options command on the menu bar to open the Page Options dialog box, and then click the Code Snippets tab.
- Click the Add button to create a new snippet. In the Add Code Snippet dialog box, shown at the top of the next page, insert a name for the snippet, a description of its purpose, and the HTML tags that make up the snippet.
- After the code snippet has been created, it displays in the code snippet list that the Web author can display using the Edit>IntelliSense>List Code Snippets command on the menu bar.

Create a new snippet

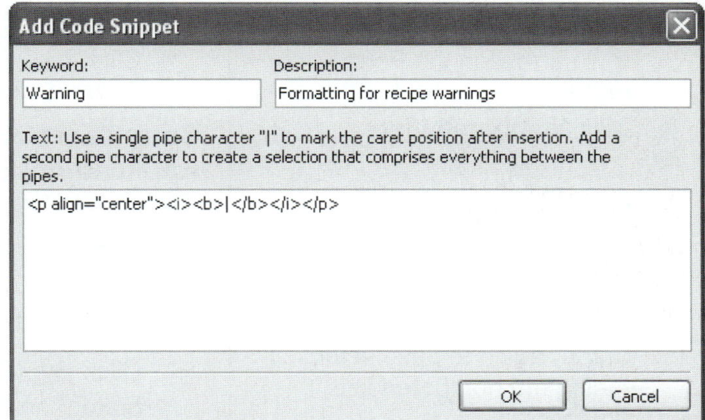

- Code snippets can be edited by displaying the Code Snippets tab in the Page Options dialog box, selecting the snippet to be edited, and clicking the Modify button. Make any necessary adjustments in the Modify Code Snippet dialog box.
- Code snippets can also be deleted from the code snippets list. Display the Code Snippets tab in the Page Options dialog box, select the snippet to delete, and click the Remove button.

Procedures

Apply Style

1. Click Normal (**Style** list) down arrow on the Formatting toolbar.
2. Click desired style.

Create Bulleted List

1. Click Normal (**Style** list) down arrow on the Formatting toolbar.
2. Click **Bulleted List**.

OR

1. Click (**Bullets** button) on the Formatting toolbar.
2. Click (**Bullets** button) again to deselect it, ending the bulleted list.

Create Numbered List

1. Click Normal (**Style** list) down arrow on the Formatting toolbar.
2. Click **Numbered List**.

OR

1. Click (**Numbering** button) on the Formatting toolbar.
2. Click (**Numbering** button) again to deselect it, ending the numbered list.

Create Definition List for New Term

1. Type term.
2. Click Normal (**Style** list) down arrow on the Formatting toolbar.
3. Click **Defined Term**.
4. Press **Enter**...................... Enter
5. Type definition.

Create Definition List for Existing Term

1. Click term.
2. Click Normal (**Style** list) down arrow on the Formatting toolbar.
3. Click **Defined Term**.
4. Click definition.
5. Click Normal (**Style** list) down arrow
6. Click **Definition**.

Insert Special Characters (Symbols)

1. Click **Insert**.................. Alt+I
2. Click **Symbol**...................... S
3. Click desired symbol.
4. Click Insert .... Alt+I
5. Click Close when finished inserting symbol(s).

Copy Text from Other Application Using Commands

Ctrl+C, Ctrl+V

In another Microsoft Office 2003 application

1. Select text or item to copy.
2. Click (**Copy**........... Ctrl+C button) on the Standard toolbar.

   OR

   a. Click **Edit**................ Alt+E
   b. Click **Copy**..................... C

In Microsoft Office FrontPage 2003

1. Position insertion point where you want to paste copied data.
2. Click (**Paste** .... Ctrl+V button) on the Standard toolbar.

   OR

   a. Click **Edit**................ Alt+E
   b. Click **Paste** .... P

Copy Text from Other Application Using Clipboard

In another Microsoft Office 2003 application

1. Click **Edit**..................... Alt+V
2. Click Office Clipboard......... B
3. Select text or item to copy.
4. Click (**Copy** .... Ctrl+C button) on the Standard toolbar.

   OR

   a. Click **Edit** .... Alt+E
   b. Click **Copy** C

In Microsoft Office FrontPage 2003

1. Display task pane and open **Clipboard**.
2. Click item in Clipboard task pane to paste.

Create Code Snippet

1. Click **Tools**................. Alt+T
2. Click Page Options............. A
3. Click Code Snippets tab.
4. Click Add... .... Alt+A to open Add Code Snippet dialog box.
5. Type keyword and description for snippet.
6. Type HTML tags that make up snippet, inserting | where the insertion point should appear after the code is inserted.
7. Click OK twice.
8. Insert code snippet as directed in Exercise 3.

Exercise Directions

1. Start FrontPage 2003.
2. Open the **Cooking** Web site you used in Exercise 4.
3. Open **index.htm**.
4. In Design view, apply the Heading 2 style to the *Our Mission* and *What You'll Find Here* headings.
5. Apply the Heading 1 style to the *Home Cooking* heading at the top of the Web page.
   ✓ *The only format applied is bold style because the formats you applied in Exercise 4, take precedence over the default Heading 1 HTML tags. You can verify this in Code view.*
6. Create a bulleted list from the second, third, and fourth paragraphs below the *What You'll Find Here* heading (*recipes, cooking techniques*, and *cooking supplies*).
7. Open **main.htm**.
8. Apply the Heading 3 style to the recipe title *Easy Pot Roast*.
9. Position the insertion point following the right-aligned phrase *Use: Oven,* type a comma and a space, and insert **325**.
10. Insert a degree symbol (°) following *325*. (Click the down scroll arrow once in the Symbol dialog box to display this symbol.)
11. Click in the paragraph of directions that begins *Line the baking dish*. Apply the Numbered List style.
12. Press **Enter** at the beginning of each new sentence to create new numbered items.
    ✓ *If any of your new numbered items has an extra space before the first word, delete the space.*
13. Open **dessert.htm**.
14. Apply the Heading 3 style to the heading *No Bake Cookies*.
15. Insert the ½ symbol and a space in front of *cup milk* and *cup peanut butter* in the ingredients list.
16. Create a new code snippet with the keyword **Warning**, and the description **Formatting for recipe warnings**.
17. Type the following code for the snippet:
    <p align="center"><i><b>|</b></i></p>
    ✓ *You can find the vertical bar, or pipe, character above the Enter key on the keyboard.*
18. On the **dessert.htm** page in Split view, locate line 49 and select and delete any code in this line. With the insertion point in line 49, insert the Warning code snippet. At the location of the insertion point in the snippet, type the following sentence:

    Be careful not to burn yourself while scooping out the cookies!
19. Press F5 to see the new content in the Design pane.
20. Create a new blank page with the name **glossary.htm** and the page title **Glossary**.
21. Insert the heading **Glossary** and apply the Heading 2 style.
22. In Microsoft Word, open **methods.doc** and **food.doc**.
23. In each document, copy the title and first five terms and definitions to the Office Clipboard.
24. In FrontPage, with the **glossary.htm** page open, paste the Cooking Methods item and then the Food Terms item.
25. Apply the Heading 3 style to the headings *Cooking Methods* and *Food Terms*.
26. Create a definition list from the terms.
    ✓ *For best results, position the insertion point just to the left of each item and then apply the appropriate style. Use Split view to help you position the insertion point correctly.*
    ✓ *Because this text is copied from another Office application, FrontPage displays the style MsoNormal for the definitions. The definitions will display correctly, however.*
27. Boldface each term.
28. Save all changes and preview the **glossary.htm** page in the browser. Your Web page should look similar to the one shown in Illustration A.
29. Close the browser.
30. Close the Web site.
31. Exit FrontPage 2003.

Illustration A

Glossary

Cooking Methods

Bake

Cook food in an oven using hot air.

Boil

Cook on surface burner at or above 212ºF until rolling bubbles form over entire surface.

Broil

Similar to roasting; food is cooked on one side at a time over intense heat.

Brown

Cook meat in skillet or oven at medium to high temperature for a brief time to seal in juices.

Roast

Similar to baking, but at a higher temperature and always uncovered.

Food Terms

Antipasto

A course of assorted appetizers and relishes (Italian).

Appetizer

A small portion of food served before the main course.

Bisque

Thick soup of pureed shellfish or poultry combined with cream.

Canapé

A thin piece of bread or toast spread or topped with cheese, caviar, or other foods.

Drippings

Fats and juices resulting when meat cooks.

On Your Own

1. Start FrontPage 2003.
2. Open **Swap**.
3. Open **index.htm**.
4. Apply a heading style to the two subordinate headings on this Web page. You may want to create a code snippet to apply the formatting.
5. Create a bulleted list from the three information paragraphs below the *Harvesting the Bargains* heading, beginning with the *Days* paragraph.
6. Insert em dashes (—) following the words *Days, Time,* and *Location* in the bulleted list.
   ✓ *Delete the spaces after the words Days, Time, and Location before inserting the em dashes.*
7. Open **merchandise.htm**.
8. Insert the registered symbol (®) following *Beanie Babies*.
9. Create a new blank page and name it **sales.htm**, with the page title **Buying and Selling**.
10. Open **logistics.doc** in Microsoft Word.
11. Copy the text above the *Advertising* paragraph and paste it on the new Web page.
12. Insert an appropriate heading for the Web page with a heading style of your choice.
13. Apply heading styles to the two headings on the Web page, *Payment options* and *Selling options*.
14. Apply bullets and numbers to organize the two lists on the Web page.
15. Open **books.htm**.
16. Below the introductory paragraph, create a definition list that describes several categories of books, such as Classics, Mysteries, General Fiction, Nonfiction, etc. Create definitions for each category to describe or give examples of types of books for that category.
17. Save all changes and close the Web site.
18. Exit FrontPage 2003.

Exercise 6

◆ **About Hyperlinks** ◆ **Insert Hyperlinks** ◆ **Hyperlink Tips**
◆ **Insert Bookmarks** ◆ **Hyperlink to Bookmark**
◆ **Test Hyperlinks (Hyperlinks View)**

On the Job

Text and graphics can be turned into hyperlinks. Hyperlinks can access a location on the same Web page, a Web page within the same site, a different Web site, an e-mail address, or other documents or files. To simplify the process of setting up hyperlinks to and from specific locations on Web pages, the Web designer can use bookmarked locations as hyperlink targets. New hyperlinks can be checked in FrontPage's Hyperlinks view.

You have volunteered to help the Madison Community Center create a Web site for its yearly blood drive. In this exercise, you will insert text and graphic hyperlinks in the Web site, add a hyperlink to an e-mail address, and create a navigation bar. To make it easier for readers to navigate within the site, you will insert bookmarks and hyperlinks to them. Finally, you will check all hyperlinks in Hyperlinks view.

Terms

bookmark
A location in a Web page that has been given a name. This named location can become the *target* of a *hyperlink*.

broken hyperlink
A hyperlink whose target is not available. Also called *broken link*.

hyperlink
Text or a graphic that, when clicked, connects to one of the following: another place on the same Web page, another Web page on the same Web site, another Web page on a different Web site, an e-mail address, or any other file or document on the same computer, network, or the Internet. Also called a *link*.

mailto link
When clicked, automatically creates and addresses a new e-mail message (to the address specified) in the user's default e-mail application.

navigation bar
A group of hyperlinks to other pages in a Web site. Each Web page's navigation bar should have the same hyperlinks in the same order. Also called *nav bar*.

target
The page or program that opens when a hyperlink is clicked. Also called the *destination*.

Notes

About Hyperlinks

- **Hyperlinks** are the means by which users navigate Web pages and Web sites. Hyperlinks can be classified as internal or external. An *internal hyperlink* takes the reader to a different location on the same Web page or in the same Web site. An *external hyperlink* takes the reader to another, independent Web site.
- Hyperlinks are created using a word or phrase, a graphic, or even a part of a graphic.

  ✓ *A hyperlink created from part of a graphic is called a hotspot or image map. You will work with hotspots in Lesson 2, Exercise 10.*
- By default, text hyperlinks are formatted in a different color and with the underline font style so they stand out in the browser content area.
- To find out if text or a graphic is a hyperlink, place the mouse pointer over it. The mouse pointer takes the shape of an upward-pointing hand when positioned over a hyperlink.

  ✓ *When the pointer is on a hyperlink, the hyperlink address displays at the far left of the status bar.*

Insert Hyperlinks

- The process of inserting a hyperlink is the same when using either text or a graphic for the hyperlink object.
- To create a hyperlink, select the text (or graphic) that will become the hyperlink and use:
  - The Insert>Hyperlink command on the menu bar.
  - The Insert Hyperlink button on the Standard toolbar.
  - The Insert Hyperlink keyboard shortcut: Ctrl+K.

  ✓ *To select a graphic, click it once.*
- The Insert Hyperlink dialog box (see illustration below) allows the Web author to identify the hyperlink target. A **target** is the page, program, or location in the current (or an external) Web site that will display when the hyperlink is clicked.
- The Insert Hyperlink dialog box contains a number of options to help the author set up and display the hyperlink. He or she can:
  - Select an option in the Link to bar to specify the location of the target or create a new target.
  - Type new text for the hyperlink in the Text to display text box, if desired.

  ✓ *The Text to display text box becomes inactive when a graphic is selected as the hyperlink.*

Insert Hyperlink dialog box

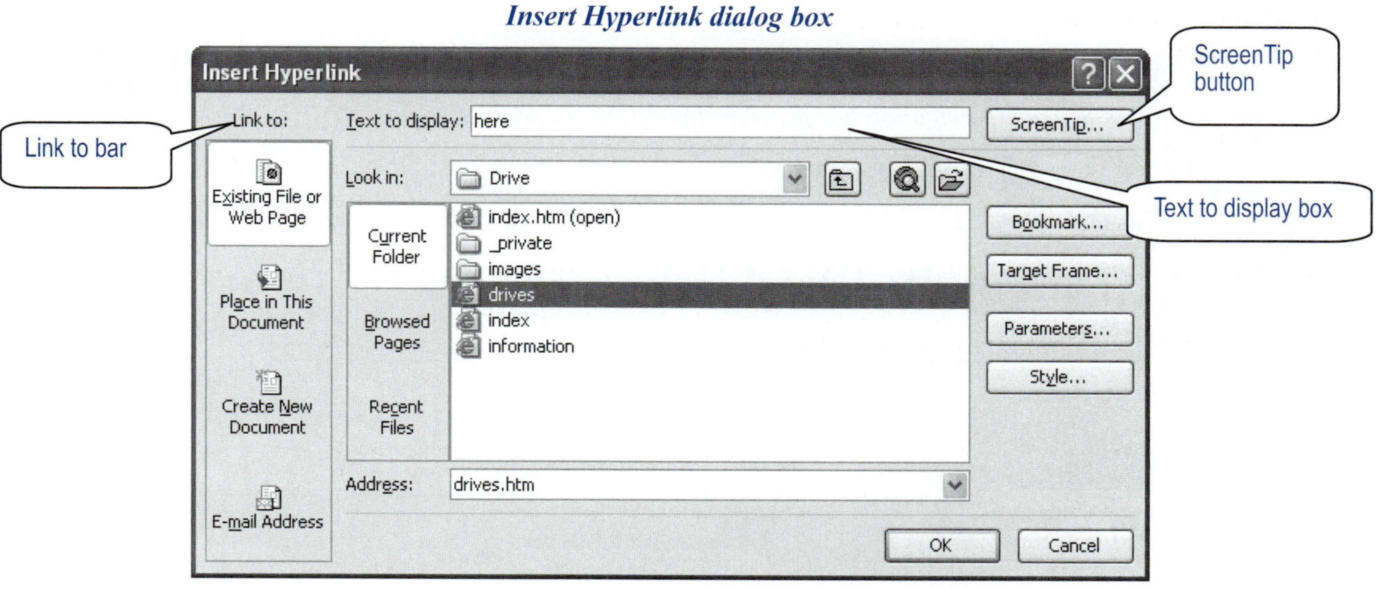

- Click the ScreenTip button in the upper-right corner of the Insert Hyperlink dialog box to create a ScreenTip (see illustration below) that displays when the pointer rests on the hyperlink.

ScreenTip displayed on a graphic hyperlink

- Use the Look in area to display a Web or Internet address; locate a page in the current folder, recently browsed Web pages list, or recently opened files list; and select the target page.
- Insert or display the target's address in the Address text box.
- Click the Bookmark button to create a hyperlink to a bookmark.
- Use the Target Frame button to specify which frame the target will open in.

✓ *You will learn more about frames and linking to frames in Lesson 4, Exercise 21.*

- Select the Parameters button to display specific results from a database region in a Web page.
- Change the format of the displayed hyperlink with the Style button.

Hyperlink to E-Mail Address (mailto: link)

- A hyperlink to an e-mail address is called a **mailto: link**. Such links are frequently included on Web pages as ways for viewers to contact the Web author for more information.
- When a *mailto: link* is clicked, the user's default mail program starts and automatically addresses a new message to the e-mail address specified by the hyperlink.
- Although a Web author can create a link to an e-mail address using the Insert Hyperlink dialog box, there is an easier way: FrontPage automatically recognizes the format of any e-mail address typed in a Web page and creates a link for that address.

  ✓ *When typing an e-mail address, press the Spacebar once after the address to enable the AutoFormat As You Type feature that formats the hyperlink automatically.*

Navigation Bars

- A group of hyperlinks to other Web pages in a site (internal hyperlinks) is called a **navigation bar**. A navigation bar created by an author is a *user-defined navigation bar*.

  ✓ *You will learn how to let FrontPage create a navigation bar for you in Lesson 6, Exercise 33.*

- Navigation bars are usually inserted near the top or along the left side of the browser content area to give users easy access to other pages in a Web site.
- Page names in a navigation bar can be enclosed in brackets (e.g., [Home Page]) or other special symbols (see illustration below).

Navigation bar provides hyperlinks to other Web pages

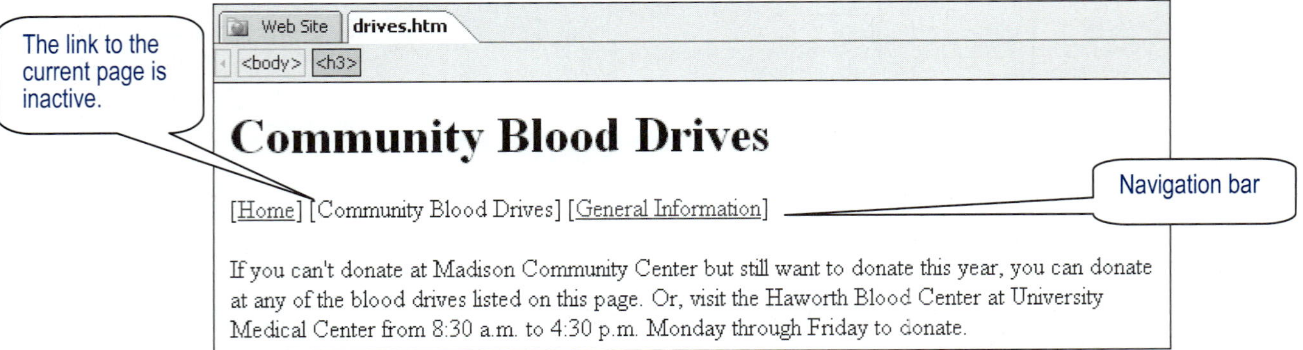

- Navigation bars generally include links to all Web pages in the site, in the same order on each page's navigation bar. No hyperlink is created to the current page, as shown in the illustration on the previous page.

Hyperlink Tips

- In FrontPage 2003, Web authors can modify the appearance of a hyperlink in Page view.
- To remove the underline formatting from a hyperlink, for example, simply click on the link and deselect the Underline button on the Formatting toolbar.
- Hyperlinks can be checked in Page view in several ways:
  - In Design view, point to the hyperlink. The address of the target displays at the far-left end of the status bar.
  - In Design view, press Ctrl and click on the link.

  ✓ *Web authors can also check hyperlinks by previewing Web pages in the browser.*

Code Cues

In HTML code, a hyperlink is designated by the <a> tag, which takes the href attribute and page name value. For example: <a href="index.htm"> If a hyperlink isn't working properly, check Code or Split view to make sure the correct page is entered as the attribute value.

- Hyperlinks can be copied from page to page using the Copy button on the Standard toolbar, the Edit>Copy menu command, or a keyboard shortcut.

  ✓ *Copying hyperlinks saves times when creating navigation bars. Create the navigation bar and its hyperlinks on one Web page, then copy the entire navigation bar and paste it on other pages in the Web.*

- Hyperlinks can also be removed if desired. To remove a hyperlink, right-click the hyperlink, click Hyperlink Properties on the shortcut menu, and then click the Remove Link button in the Edit Hyperlink dialog box.

  ✓ *If you copy a navigation bar from page to page, you will need to remove the hyperlink to the current page and insert a hyperlink to the page you copied the navigation bar from.*

- When a Web page containing hyperlinks is renamed, FrontPage warns the author that other pages are linked to it and asks if the author wants to update links to the current page. Answering *Yes* automatically updates all hyperlinks to the displayed Web page.

Insert Bookmarks

- A **bookmark**, which is a named location in a document, can be used in a Web page as the target of a hyperlink.
- Bookmarks can consist of text or merely a location on a Web page.
- Bookmarks are most often used to help readers move easily in a long Web page.
- For example, a bookmark can be inserted at the top of the Web page, and several hyperlinks to that bookmark can appear at regular intervals down the page to allow users to return to the top of the page quickly.
- To create a bookmark, select text (or position the insertion point as desired) and click the Insert>Bookmark command on the menu bar.
- In the Bookmark dialog box, the Web author can accept the suggested bookmark name or create a new one (see illustration at the top of the next page).

Create a new bookmark

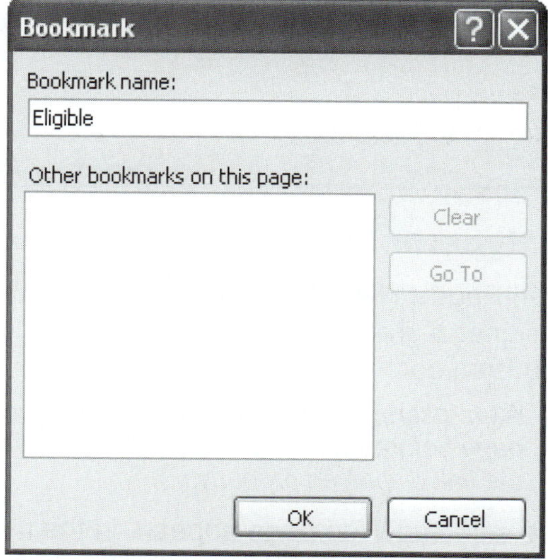

- Text designated as a bookmark displays a dashed underline on the Web page in Page view. If no text has been selected for the bookmark, a small underlined flag marks the location of the bookmark.

Hyperlink to Bookmark

- After bookmarks have been defined on a Web page, hyperlinks can be created to those bookmarks.
  - ✓ *Save a Web page after defining bookmarks to make bookmarks available for hyperlinks.*
- To create a hyperlink to a bookmarked location, use the Bookmark button in the Insert Hyperlink dialog box and then select the bookmark from the list displayed in the Select Place in Document dialog box (see illustration below).
  - ✓ *The address of a bookmark is displayed as the bookmark name preceded by a pound sign (#): #Eligible.*

Select a bookmark as the target of a hyperlink

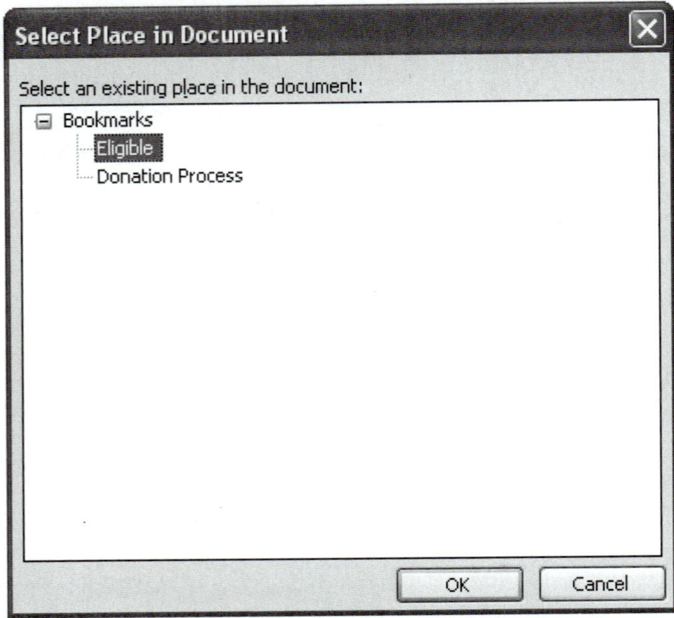

Test Hyperlinks (Hyperlinks View)

- FrontPage's Hyperlinks view gives the Web designer a graphical picture of the hyperlinks to and from each page in a Web site.
  - ✓ *After inserting a link on a Web page, save the page before switching to Hyperlinks view to see the link displayed properly.*
- The selected Web page appears in the middle of the view (see illustration below), with links *from* other pages to the left and links *to* other pages to the right.
- In Hyperlinks view, lines that end with an arrow are hyperlinks to other Web pages. Lines that end in bullets (such as the line to the images/Community.jpg image in the illustration below) lead to multimedia files such as pictures or sounds.
- A line that is not solid (such as the line to info.htm in the illustration above) is a **broken hyperlink**. In this case, a link has been created to a page that does not yet exist in the Web site.
  - ✓ *Another way to identify broken links is to run a report on a Web site. You will learn how to use reports to identify problems such as broken links in Lesson 10, Exercise 55.*
  - ✓ *The Recalculate Hyperlinks command also identifies and fixes hyperlink problems. You will use this command in Lesson 10, Exercise 53.*
- Linked Web pages display a small **plus sign (+)** on the page icon in Hyperlinks view. This plus sign indicates that the current page has links to other pages.
- Clicking a plus sign for a Web page expands the view to show the other pages linked to that page.
  - ✓ *After a Web page's hyperlinks have been expanded, the plus sign becomes a* ***minus sign*** *(–). Click the minus sign to collapse the hyperlinks.*
- To change the central Web page in Hyperlinks view, simply click the desired page in the Folder List.

Check hyperlinks in Hyperlinks view

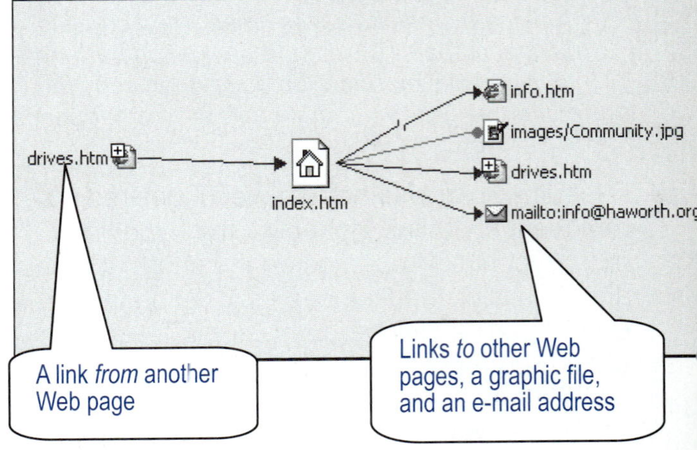

Procedures

Insert Hyperlink (*Ctrl+K*)

1. Select text or object to become hyperlink
2. Click (**Insert Hyperlink** button) on the Standard toolbar. .... Ctrl+K

   OR

   a. Click **Insert** .... Alt+I

   b. Click **Hyperlink** I
3. Click location in **Link to** bar, if necessary.
4. Type link text in **Text to display** text box, if necessary.
5. Click **ScreenTip** .... Alt+P and type ScreenTip as desired for the link.
6. Click target Web page in **Look in** list or type **Address**.
7. Click OK .... Enter

Hyperlink to E-Mail Address (mailto: link)

1. Click Web page at location of e-mail address.
2. Type e-mail address.
3. Press **Spacebar** .... Space

Remove Hyperlink

1. Right-click hyperlink in Normal Page view.
2. Click **Hyperlink Properties** on shortcut menu. .... K
3. Click Remove Link ... Alt+R

Insert Bookmarks (*Ctrl+G*)

1. Select text to bookmark.

   OR

   Position the insertion point in area of Web page to bookmark.
2. Click **Insert** .... Alt I
3. Click **Bookmark** .... K
4. Type **Bookmark name**, if necessary.
5. Click OK .... Enter

Hyperlink to Bookmark

In Insert Hyperlink dialog box

1. Click **Bookmark** .... Alt+O
2. Click desired bookmark in Bookmarks list.
3. Click OK twice.

Test Hyperlinks (Hyperlinks View)

1. Save all pages in the Web site.
2. Display the Web Site pane and click the **Hyperlinks** button at the bottom of the pane.
3. Click Web page to check in Folders List.
4. Click **plus sign (+)** to expand hyperlinks for a Web page.

   OR

   Click **minus sign (-)** to collapse hyperlinks for a Web page.

Exercise Directions

1. Start FrontPage 2003.
2. Open **Drive**.
3. Open **index.htm**.
4. Use the picture at the top of the Web page to create a hyperlink to **information.htm**. Create the following ScreenTip for this hyperlink: **Click here for General Information**.
5. Switch to Preview view to test the ScreenTip.
6. Return to Design view and locate the word *here*, toward the end of the second body paragraph.
7. Select the word *here* and create a hyperlink to **drives.htm**.
8. Insert bookmarks as follows:
   - Click just to the right of the picture at the top of the Web page and insert a bookmark named **Top**.
   - Select the word *Eligible* in the third heading on the Web page and create a bookmark using the selected word as the bookmark name.

     ✓ *Remember to save the page before going on to the next step, or the bookmarks may not be available in the Insert Hyperlink dialog box.*
9. Create hyperlinks to the bookmarks:
   - In the second paragraph of body text on the Web page, select the word *eligible* and create a hyperlink to the Eligible bookmark.
   - At the bottom of the page, select the words *Back to Top* and create a hyperlink to the Top bookmark.

10. In the last paragraph of text on the Web page, position the insertion point at the end of the paragraph and type the following *mailto: link*: **info@haworth.org.**
    - ✓ *Press the Spacebar after typing the e-mail address to apply hyperlink AutoFormat. Then delete the extra space and type a period.*
11. Open **drives.htm**. Click at the beginning of the first full paragraph of text, press **Enter**, and then move the insertion point up into the new paragraph.
12. Type the following navigation bar: **[Home] [Community Blood Drives] [General Information]**
13. Create a hyperlink from *Home* to **index.htm**.
14. Copy the navigation bar you just created.
15. Open **information.htm**, click at the end of the first heading, and press **Enter** to create a new paragraph.
16. Paste the copied navigation bar in the new paragraph.
17. On **drives.htm**, create a hyperlink from *General Information* in the navigation bar to **information.htm**.
18. On **information.htm**, create a hyperlink from *Community Blood Drives* in the navigation bar to the **drives.htm** page.
    - ✓ *You do not have to create a link from* Home *because the link was copied with the navigation bar.*
19. Save all pages. Switch to Hyperlinks view and check hyperlinks to and from **index.htm**.
20. On the right side of the **index.htm** icon, expand the hyperlinks for the **information.htm** page.
21. Save all changes and preview **index.htm** in the browser.
22. Check hyperlinks to and from each Web page in the browser. Test the *mailto: link* but do *not* send a message.
23. Close the browser and the Web site.
24. Exit FrontPage 2003.

On Your Own

1. Start FrontPage 2003.
2. Open **Swap**.
3. Open **index.htm**.
4. Create a navigation bar above the first paragraph of text on the Web page. Insert hyperlinks to appropriate pages.
5. Copy the navigation bar and paste it on the other pages in the Web. Remove links as necessary so that no page will be linked to itself.
6. Open **merchandise.htm**.
7. Create a bookmark at the top of the Web page with an appropriate name.
8. Add text at the bottom of the Web page to direct readers back to the top of the Web document and link this text to the bookmark.
9. Under the Books category heading, create a hyperlink from the word *Books* in the description to the Books page.
10. View the hyperlinks in Hyperlinks view to check that all Web pages are linked properly.
11. Preview the Web in the browser.
12. Close the browser and the Web site.
13. Exit FrontPage 2003.

Exercise 7

◆ **Critical Thinking** ◆ **Challenge**

You are an enthusiastic runner and a member of the Monroe Milers, a local running group. You and your fellow Milers have decided to create a Web site with information about your group and training information for upcoming marathons. In this exercise, you will create the Web site, add pages, enter text, and format that text. You will also add meta tags so browsers will be able to locate your site, and add hyperlinks for easy navigation.

Exercise Directions

1. Start FrontPage 2003.
2. Create a new Web site using the Empty Web Site template. Name the Web site **Milers**.
3. Create a new blank page for the Web and save it as **index.htm**. Change the Web-page title to **Home Page**.

   ✓ *FrontPage will assign the index.htm name by default to the first page created in an empty Web.*
4. On **index.htm**, enter the text shown in Illustration A on the following page.

   ✓ *Use a long dash symbol in the second paragraph of text.*
5. Spell check the text.
6. Insert a meta tag named **keywords** containing values appropriate for the Web site (e.g., running, marathon, etc.).
7. At the end of the last paragraph of text, insert the following *mailto: link:* **Milers@stargate.net**
8. Add a new page and save it as **info.htm** with the Web-page title **Information**.
9. Insert the Word file **information.doc** from the Data disk in the new Web page.
10. Make the following changes to this Web page (see Illustration B for a portion of the completed page):
    - Format the list of three items below the first paragraph (*Beginner, Intermediate, Advanced*) as a numbered list.
    - Below the *Week 1* heading are three paragraphs: *Goal, Details,* and *Notes*. Change the closing Paragraph tag </p> at the end of the *Goal* and *Details* paragraphs to Break tags <br>. Delete the opening Paragraph tag <p> at the beginning of the *Details* and *Notes* paragraphs.
    - Make the same changes to HTML code in the paragraphs below the *Week 2* and *Week 3* headings.
    - In Design view, display HTML tags to verify your changes.
    - Hide HTML tags.
    - Format the three terms and their definitions below the *Definitions* heading as a definition list.
11. On both open Web pages, apply styles and formats to display the text clearly and attractively. Change alignments, fonts, font styles, sizes, and colors as desired.

    ✓ *Copy formats to save time, or create code snippets to apply formats.*
12. Rename the **info.htm** page as **training.htm** with the Web-page title **Training**.
13. On **index.htm**, locate the word *here* in the last paragraph of text and create a hyperlink to **training.htm**.
14. On **training.htm**, create bookmarks for each term in the definition list. Create another bookmark to the left of the heading *Week 1* named *Up*.
15. In the training information for each week, create hyperlinks from the terms *SR*, *RW*, and *MR* to the bookmarked definitions.
16. Insert the following word below the definition list: **Up**. Link this word to the Up bookmark.
17. Test your bookmark links in Preview Page view.
18. Locate the words *Runner's World* in the paragraph below the *Training Plans* heading. Create a hyperlink to the Runner's World Web site (www.runnersworld.com).

    ✓ *In the Insert Hyperlink dialog box, type this address in the Address text box.*

19. Create navigation bars for both Web pages.
20. Save all changes.
21. Check the hyperlinks in Hyperlinks view. Be sure to view the **training.htm** page to check your link to the Runner's World site. Make any necessary changes and save.
22. Preview the entire site in the browser. Check your hyperlinks on both Web pages.
    - ✓ *If you jump to the Runner's World Web site, use the browser's Back button to return to your Web.*
23. Close the browser and make any necessary changes to hyperlinks.
24. Close the Web site.
25. Exit FrontPage 2003.

Illustration A

Monroe Milers

Welcome to the home page of the Monroe Milers, a group of runners from the greater Monroe area in Ohio. Our most important goal is to have fun as we train for and run in local races.

We have another goal, however—to raise money for local charities. Before every race we run, we line up sponsors willing to make a donation for each mile we run. In the last few years, we've raised over $5,000 for local charities, including the Juvenile Diabetes Foundation, Leukemia and Lymphoma Society, and American Heart Association.

This year we are setting our sights on a new challenge: running a marathon. Most of the Monroe Milers are "middle-distance" runners whose longest races are half marathons. Our home base, which is situated between two highly regarded marathons (Cincinnati's Flying Pig Marathon and the Columbus Marathon), has finally prompted us to undertake one of these marathons together.

We have a couple of options to consider when running in our marathon:

- We can run individually.
- We can create one or more relay team(s), which would be good for those of us who might not be able to run the whole distance.

If you're already a member of the Monroe Milers, click here for more information on training. If you'd like to join the Milers, contact us at

Illustration B

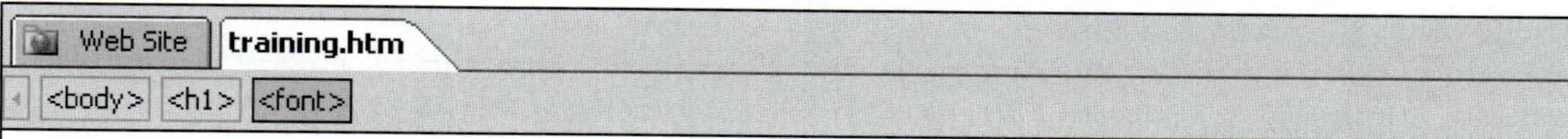

Training

[Home Page] [Training]

Runners need 5 to 6 months of training before the actual race. Most training schedules identify three levels of running fitness:

1. Beginner
2. Intermediate
3. Advanced

Many training plans are available on the Internet (see the excellent plans at Runner's World). Here is a sample training plan for the first few weeks of training from a local source:

Week 1

Goal: Run 3 or 4 days
Details: SR of 15:00, 15:00, 15:00, and 20:00
Notes: Try running every other day using the same route or a different route. Use RW if necessary.

Week 2

Goal: Run 3 or 4 days
Details: SR of 15:00, 15:00, 15:00, and 20:00
Notes: Keep your pace steady; you're building endurance in these early weeks.

Challenge Exercise

1. Using online and offline resources (magazines, books, the Internet, etc.), interviews with family and teachers, and your own personal observations, write a short report that analyzes the impact the World Wide Web has had on society.
2. Write the report in a word processing program or Notepad. Remember to cite sources for the information you found.
3. Go online and search the Internet for sites that give advice and guidelines on Web design. (See Appendix C for help on searching, if necessary.)
4. Note the URLs of helpful sites that give you good design ideas.
5. Create a new Web site using the One Page Web Site template. Name the Web site **Resources**.
   - On the index.htm page, enter text that introduces yourself and your interest in Web design.
   - What do you intend to use the course for?
   - What Web sites would you like to create for your family, school activities, or community?
   - What information might you include on those Web sites?
6. Add a new page to the Web site called **DesignResources**. On this new page, list the sites related to Web design that you found in your search and create links to them.
7. Add another page to the Web site titled **Report**. On this page, insert the file containing the report you wrote in step 1.
8. Add headings and subheadings throughout your Web site as appropriate.
9. Apply formatting to the heading text and paragraph text throughout your Web site. Change font type, size, and color, and text alignment as desired.
10. Make sure you can navigate from one page on your site to all other pages in the Web site.
11. Check your Web design against the guidelines given on page 9 and against the checklist you and your peers created on page 10. Revise your site as necessary.

LESSON 2

Add Graphic Web Elements

Exercise 8

◆ Change Page Background (Color) ◆ Create Custom Color
◆ Insert Horizontal Line (Web Divider)
◆ Create Drawing Using Office Drawing Tools
◆ Wrap Text ◆ Create WordArt Graphic

On the Job

FrontPage supplies a rich collection of features that can be used to add graphic elements to a Web site. A background color for pages adds immediate visual interest. For more subtle colors, create a custom color. Graphic horizontal lines are not only decorative but also useful in establishing regions on the page. Web authors can create drawings right on a page using the Office drawing tools and can create graphic objects from words using the WordArt feature.

In this exercise, you will add graphic elements to Classic Vinyl's new Web site. You will select and then customize a background page color, insert horizontal lines to group information on a page, and create a simple drawing using the Office drawing tools. You will create a graphic using WordArt. Finally, you will explore options for wrapping text around graphics.

Terms

drawing canvas
A feature that provides a "container" for drawing objects, allowing objects within it to be resized and moved as a group on a page (or to another Office application).

handles
Small circles or squares surrounding an object that indicate the object is currently selected. Handles can be used to resize an object.

properties
Characteristics of an object; for example, the color scheme on the desktop is one of the desktop's properties. Changing the properties of an object lets you customize that object.

text wrap
Option that allows text to flow around a graphic object on the left or right.

Web-safe colors
Colors that display the same way in any browser.

Notes

Change Page Background (Color)

- One of the quickest ways to add visual interest to a Web is to change the color of the page's background.
- By default, the background is white, the color that provides the most contrast to black text.
- To change the background color, use the Format>Background command on the menu bar and then click the Background down arrow to display a palette of colors.

- Clicking the More Colors option on this palette displays the More Colors dialog box (see illustration below), where the Web author can choose from many more colors for the background.
  - ✓ *Take care when choosing a background color to select a color that does not obscure the text or make it difficult to read.*

Hexadecimal value

More Colors dialog box

> **Code Cues**
>
> In HTML code, background color is controlled by the bgcolor attribute in the <body> tag. Use a hexadecimal value to specify the actual color. For example, <body bgcolor="FFFFCC"> supplies a light yellow page background.

Create Custom Color

- The More Colors dialog box shows a palette of **Web-safe colors**. These colors display with the same color values in any browser.
- Web-safe colors are designated using six pairs of numbers or letters: 00, 33, 66, 99, CC, and FF. The combination for each color is called its *hexadecimal* value, because it is made up of six numbers or letters.
- Note in the illustration above, for example, that the color white has a hexadecimal value of FFFFFF. Black has the value 000000.
- Web-safe colors, while safe to use for any browser, often don't offer the subtlety of color a Web designer might desire. A designer may therefore wish to create a custom color for Web page elements such as text, background, and other objects.
- To create a custom color:
  - If known, type the hexadecimal values of the color in the Value box in the More Colors dialog box.
  - Click the Custom button to open the Color dialog box, shown below.

Color dialog box

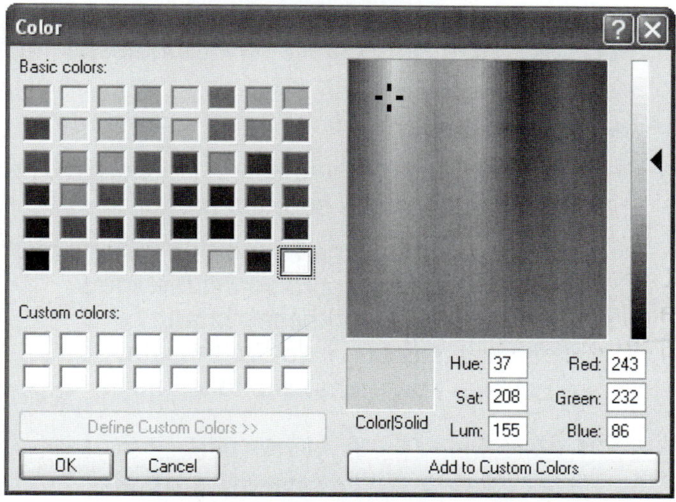

- This dialog box allows a Web designed to specify a color using either of two color models: HSL (Hue, Saturation, Luminosity), or RGB (Red, Green, Blue).
- Type the desired values in the supplied boxes, or drag the pointer in the color gradient to create a new color. Dragging the slider at the right side of the dialog box adds white or black to the chosen color for more subtle effects.
- To save the new color, click the Add to Custom Colors button. The color is then stored in the Custom colors grid and is available to use on the Web page.
  - ✓ *If a browser is unable to display a custom color, it will approximate the color through a process called* dithering.

Insert Horizontal Line (Web Divider)

- Web pages can be divided into sections to group information.
- Insert a horizontal line to create a graphic border between sections on a page.
- To insert a horizontal line, use the Insert>Horizontal Line command on the menu bar. A default horizontal line appears below the insertion point.

✓ *To position the horizontal line correctly, make sure the insertion point is at the end of a paragraph.*

✓ *The HTML tag for a horizontal line is <hr>. This is a one-sided tag.*

- The default horizontal line is a gray, three-dimensional line that extends the entire width of the page.
- Change the horizontal line's **properties**, or formats, in the Horizontal Line Properties dialog box. To change line formats:
  - Double-click the line.
  - Right-click the line and select Horizontal Line Properties from the shortcut menu.
  - In the Horizontal Line Properties dialog box (see illustration below), adjust the line's width or height (thickness), change alignment, select a color for the line, or remove its three-dimensional shading.

Horizontal Line Properties dialog box

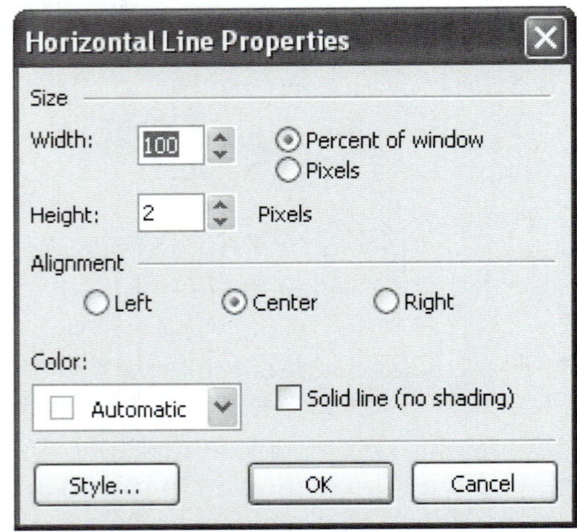

Create Drawing Using Office Drawing Tools

- FrontPage 2003 includes the Office drawing tools that are standard in other Office applications such as Word and Excel.
- The Drawing tools are displayed on the Drawing toolbar (see illustration below). To display the Drawing toolbar:
  - Click the View>Toolbars command on the menu bar and select the Drawing toolbar.
  - Click the Drawing button on the Standard toolbar.
  - Right-click the Standard or Formatting toolbar and select the Drawing toolbar.

✓ *To determine the function of each tool, rest the pointer over it to see a ScreenTip with the tool's name.*

Insert New Drawing

- The Web author can draw shapes and lines directly on a FrontPage Web page. However, if a drawing consists of more than one shape, the author should consider creating the drawing within a drawing canvas.
- The **drawing canvas** is a "container" for drawing objects. The drawing canvas makes it easy to move or resize a number of drawing objects as one unit.

✓ *The drawing canvas can be copied and pasted anywhere on a Web page or within a Web site, or even to another Office application.*

- Display a new drawing canvas using the Insert>Picture>New Drawing command on the menu bar.
- The drawing canvas displays with a hatched border and the Drawing Canvas floating toolbar (see illustration at top of next page).

Drawing tools on the Drawing toolbar

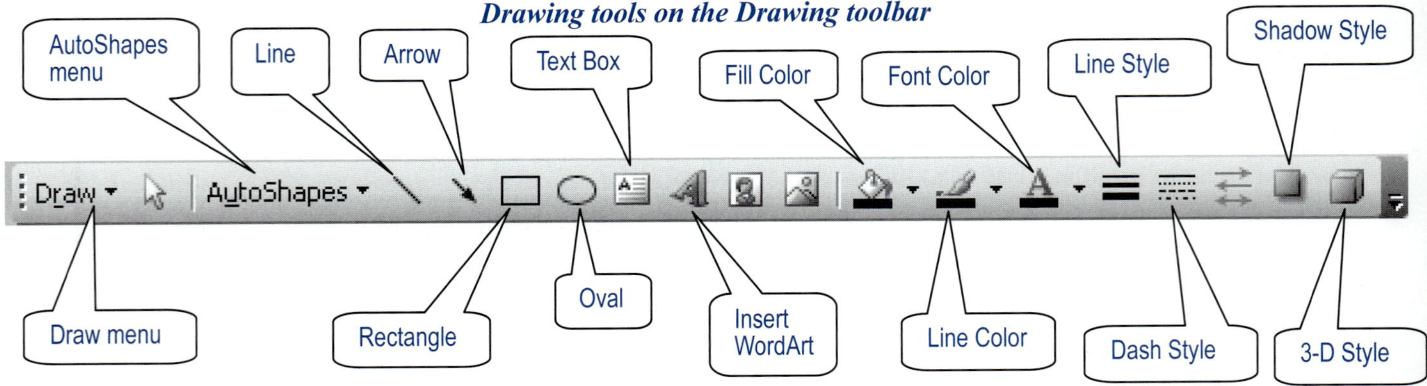

New drawing canvas on a page

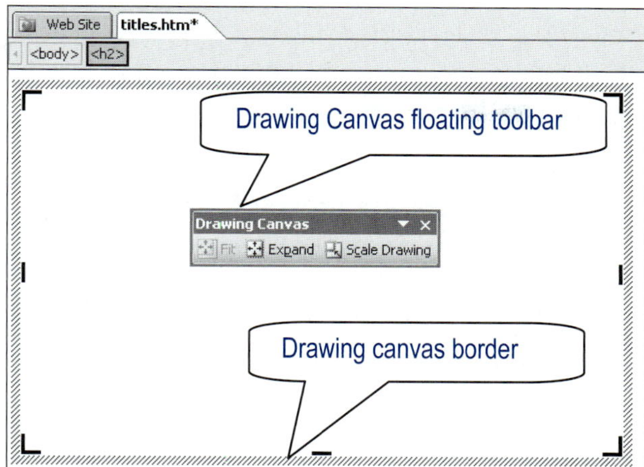

- After completing a drawing within a canvas, click the Fit button on the Drawing Canvas toolbar (or drag a corner or side mark) to reduce the canvas size to fit the drawing.

Use Drawing Tools

- The Drawing toolbar contains buttons to create lines and shapes, buttons to format objects, and menus (Draw and AutoShapes) that contain additional formatting and shape options.

  ✓ *You will use AutoShapes in Exercise 12.*

- The toolbar also contains tools for creating other kinds of graphic objects such as text boxes and WordArt graphics and for inserting clip art pictures and pictures from files.

  ✓ *You will insert clip art and pictures from files in Exercise 9.*

- To draw an object, select the appropriate tool and, with the crosshair pointer, drag on the Web page until the shape is the right size.

  ✓ *Hold down Shift while drawing a rectangle to create a perfect square or while drawing an oval to create a perfect circle.*

- A new object is surrounded by **handles**, small circles or squares that indicate the object is currently selected (see illustration below).

Rectangle drawn using the Rectangle tool

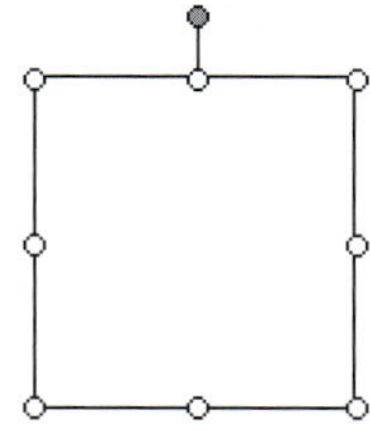

- A new drawing object also displays the green rotate handle that allows the user to rotate the object around a central axis.
- To add color to an object, select it and use the Fill Color button (to add color inside the shape) or the Line Color button (to change the outline color).

  ✓ *Select More Fill Colors on the Fill Color palette to display more colors or Fill Effects to choose a gradient, patterned, or textured fill.*

- Use the Line Style button to change the weight (thickness) of the line or object outline or the Dash Style button to add dashed effects to lines.
- Use the Shadow Style button to add a shadow effect to an object or the 3-D Style button to apply three-dimensional effects to an object.
- Insert a text box in a drawing to hold text. A text box is drawn like any other shape and displays an insertion point for typing text (see illustration below).

Text box inserted in an object

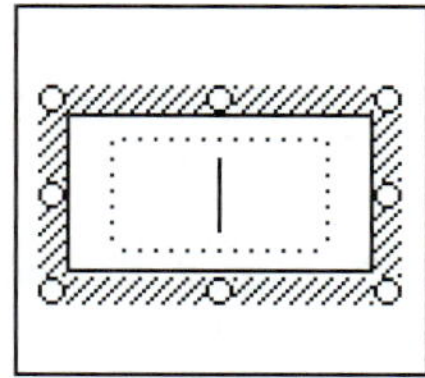

- FrontPage 2003 creates a text box using table formatting. The dotted outline shown in the illustration above marks the border of the table cell.

  ✓ *You will learn more about tables in Lesson 3.*

- The Web author can format text within a text box with fonts, styles, sizes, colors, and alignments.
- To change the outline or fill for a text box, double-click the text box selection outline to display the Format Text Box dialog box.

Work with Objects

- Commands on the Draw menu help the user to manipulate objects.
  - Use the Group command to bind objects together so they can be moved as a single unit.

  ✓ *Grouped objects can be ungrouped using the Ungroup command.*

- Click the Order command to send an object behind another object or to the back or to bring an object forward or to the front of the drawing.
- The Nudge command moves the currently selected object by small increments.

■ Resize an object by dragging a handle in the direction to resize. Dragging a corner handle adjusts width and height at the same time.

■ Objects can be moved anywhere within a drawing canvas by selecting them and dragging them to the new location using the four-headed arrow pointer.

■ Objects can be copied and pasted just like text. Copy objects to ensure similar parts of a drawing are identical or to place an identical drawing on the same or another Web page.

Wrap Text

■ Inserting a graphic object such as a drawing canvas or a picture pushes existing text down to the lower-right corner of the object.

■ To avoid leaving a large empty space to the right of the object, Web designers can apply a **text wrap** option to allow text to flow around the object (see illustration below).

Text wrapped around a drawing canvas

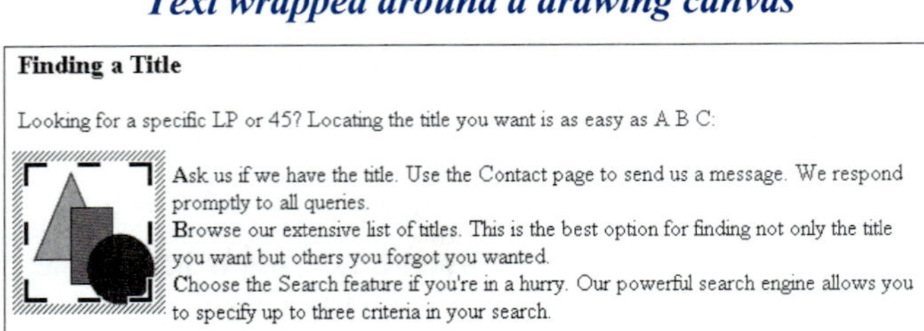

■ To wrap text around a graphic, double-click the graphic to open a properties dialog box and click the Layout tab. Text can be wrapped at the left or right side of an object.

✓ *A table can also be used to control layout of text and graphics on a page. You will learn how to control layout with a table in Lesson 3, Exercise 14.*

Create WordArt Graphic

■ Office's WordArt feature allows the user to create a graphic from text using one of 30 different decorative formats.

■ To create a WordArt graphic, use:

- The Insert>Picture>WordArt command on the menu bar.
- The Insert WordArt button on the Drawing toolbar.

■ Create the graphic from existing text or type the text to transform into a graphic.

■ After the Web author selects a WordArt style and format options (such as font, size, and font style), WordArt displays the graphic along with the WordArt floating toolbar (see illustration below).

WordArt graphic on a Web page

■ Use options on the WordArt toolbar (see illustration below) to modify the WordArt graphic.

✓ *To select a WordArt graphic and display the WordArt toolbar, click on any part of the WordArt text.*

WordArt toolbar

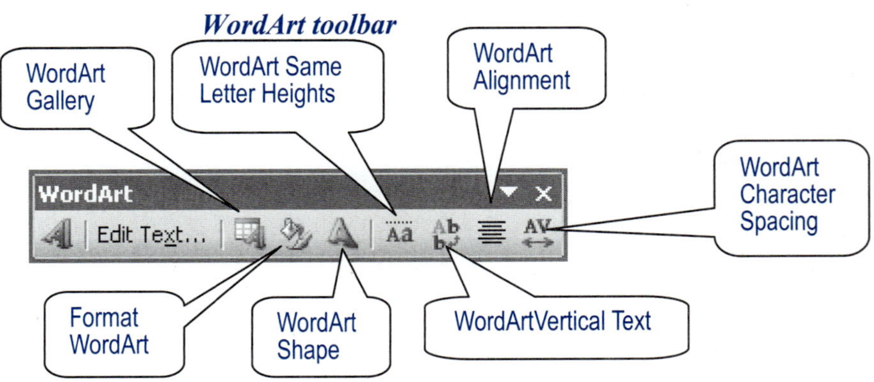

- Click the WordArt Gallery button to select a new WordArt style.
- The Format WordArt button opens the Format WordArt dialog box, where Web authors can select new line color, fill color, size, and layout options.
- Use the WordArt Shape button to select a new shape for the graphic.
- Clicking the WordArt Same Letter Heights button makes lowercase letters and capital letters the same height.
- The WordArt Vertical Text button transforms the graphic from horizontal orientation to vertical orientation.
- The WordArt Alignment button offers alignment options such as centering and right alignment.
- Use the WordArt Character Spacing button to change the amount of space between characters in the WordArt graphic.

■ A WordArt graphic can be resized or moved like any other graphic. Use the yellow diamond handle to adjust the shape of the graphic.

■ A WordArt graphic might not display in a browser exactly as it displays in FrontPage's Page view. Visitors to a Web site will still see a visually interesting graphic object, however.

Procedures

Change Page Background (Color)

1. Click **Format** .... Alt+O
2. Click **Background** .... K
3. Click **Background** down arrow.
4. Select color from palette or click **More Colors**.

Create Custom Color

In More Colors dialog box

- Type new hexadecimal value if known.

OR

1. Click [Custom...] button.
2. Drag pointers to create new color, or type values in supplied boxes for Hue, Saturation, Luminosity or Red, Green, Blue.

Insert Horizontal Line (Web Divider)

1. Position insertion point at location below which horizontal line should appear.
2. Click **Insert** .... Alt+I
3. Click **Horizontal Line** L
4. To change line properties: Double-click horizontal line.

   OR

   - Right-click horizontal line and click **Horizontal Line Properties** .... Z
5. In Horizontal Line Properties dialog box, change line width, size, alignment, or color.

Insert New Drawing Canvas

1. Click **Insert** .... Alt+I
2. Click **Picture** .... P
3. Click New Drawing .... N
4. Create drawing objects.
5. Reduce size of drawing canvas by clicking [Fit] (**Fit** button) on Drawing Canvas toolbar.

Display Drawing Toolbar

1. Click **View** .... Alt+V
2. Click **Toolbars** .... T
3. Click **Drawing**.

OR

- Right-click any toolbar and select **Drawing**.

OR

- Click (**Drawing** button) on Standard toolbar.

Use Drawing Tools

1. Select tool on Drawing toolbar.
2. Drag crosshair pointer in Web page to create object.

   ✓ *Hold down Shift to create perfect square or circle.*
3. Add color to object using:
   - (**Fill Color** button) on Drawing toolbar.

     ✓ *Click down arrow to choose from palette or select More Fill Colors or Fill Effects.*
   - (**Line Color** button) on Drawing toolbar.

     ✓ *Click down arrow to choose from palette or select More Line Colors or Patterned Lines.*
4. Change line format using:
   - (**Line Style** button) on Drawing toolbar.
   - (**Dash Style** button) on Drawing toolbar.
5. Insert text box by clicking (**Text Box** button) on Drawing toolbar.
6. Format text box by double-clicking text box selection outline.

Work with Objects

1. Group objects:

   a. Click first object, hold Shift, click additional objects.

   b. Click **Draw** menu on Drawing toolbar.

   c. Click **Group** .... G

2. Order objects:
   a. Select object and click **Draw**.
   b. Click **Order** .... R
   c. Click **Bring to Front**, **Send to Back**, **Bring Forward**, or **Send Backward**.
3. Adjust position of object:
   a. Select object and click **Draw**.
   b. Click **Nudge** .... N
   c. Click **Up**, **Down**, **Left**, or **Right**.
4. Move object by selecting it, placing pointer on selection border until it becomes a four-headed arrow, and dragging object to new position.
5. Copy object:
   a. Select object.
   b. Click (**Copy** button) on Standard toolbar.
   c. Deselect object.
   d. Click (**Paste** button) on Standard toolbar.

Wrap Text

1. Double-click graphic.
2. In properties dialog box, click Layout tab.
3. Select wrap option.

Create WordArt Graphic

1. Click **Insert** .... Alt+I
2. Click **Picture** .... P
3. Click **WordArt** .... W

   OR

   Click (**Insert WordArt** button) on Drawing toolbar.
4. Select WordArt style.
5. Type text for graphic if necessary and select font, size, and style.
6. To change WordArt formats, use WordArt toolbar options.

Exercise Directions

1. Start FrontPage 2003.
2. Close any open Webs, if necessary.
3. Open **Vinyl**.
4. Open **index.htm**.
5. Apply a background color to the Web page:
   - In the Background color palette, click More Colors.
   - Choose the lightest yellow color in the More Colors dialog box palette.
6. Customize the background color by changing the Red, Green, and Blue values to **254**, **245**, and **218**, respectively.
7. Apply the same background color to the other pages in the Web.

   ✓ *Hint: If you added the custom color correctly, it will appear in the Custom Colors section of the Background color palette.*
8. Activate **titles.htm** and insert horizontal lines:
   - Insert a horizontal line below the introductory paragraph.
   - Insert a horizontal line above the 1970s heading.
   - Change the height of each horizontal line to 4 pixels and change the color to Navy.
9. Delete the 1960s and 1970s headings and remove the remaining paragraph space.
10. Position the insertion point to the left of the first 1960s title and insert a new drawing canvas.
11. Draw the graphic shown in the next column as follows:
    - Draw a perfect square about 1.5 inches wide (or 108 px). Select the square and fill it with the color Red.

      ✓ *If the entire drawing canvas fills with Red, click Undo, select the square again, and click the Fill Color button.*
    - Draw a perfect circle of a size that will easily fit inside the square, as shown in the illustration. Fill the circle with the Gray color.
    - With the circle still selected, click Fill Effects on the Fill Color palette. On the Gradient tab, click the Horizontal shading style.
    - Draw a smaller circle for the record label, fill it with Yellow, and position it in the center of the larger circle.
    - Group the two circles and position them as shown in the illustration.

      Use the Nudge command for fine positioning.
    - Change the order to bring the rectangle to the front.
    - Insert a text box in the square, change text alignment to Center, and type **1960s**.

Record album graphic

12. Remove the text box's border and fill. Boldface the text and change its font if desired.
    ✓ *Hint: select No Fill and No Line in the respective dialog boxes.*
    ✓ *Don't worry if you see a dashed border around the text. It won't show in the browser.*
13. Reduce the size of the drawing canvas to fit the drawing.
    ✓ *Click Fit on the Drawing Canvas toolbar.*
14. Apply the Left wrapping style to the drawing canvas.
    ✓ *You might need to apply text wrap twice to achieve the correct effect.*
15. Copy the drawing canvas and paste it to the left of the first 1970s title.
16. Adjust the text wrap if necessary. Change the text in the text box to **1970s**. If desired, change the color of the square and the text. Your page should look similar to Illustration A.
17. Activate **index.htm**.
18. Create a WordArt graphic using the *Classic Vinyl* heading at the top of the page:
    - Choose the second style from the left in the second row of WordArt styles.
    - Change the color of the graphic to Dark Blue.
      Click Format WordArt on the WordArt toolbar, select the Fill Color down arrow, and choose Dark Blue.
19. Preview the Web in the browser.
20. Close the browser and the Web site.
21. Exit FrontPage 2003.

Illustration A

Popular Titles

[Home] [Popular Titles] [Shipping]

If you're looking for mainstream hit albums from the 60s and 70s, you might find what you're looking for in the following list. Contact us at classicvinyl@earthstar.net for more details or to check for a title not listed here.

The Beatles, Abbey Road. Apple. VG+. $10.00
The Beatles, Revolver. Capitol. VG. $10.00
The Beatles, Rubber Soul. Capitol. VG. $10.00
The Beatles, Sgt. Pepper. Capitol. VG+ $11.00
Blind Faith. Atco. VG+. $10.00
Cream, Disraeli Gears. Reaction. G. $7.00
Crosby, Stills, and Nash. Atlantic. VG. $10.00
Crosby, Stills, Nash, and Young, Deja Vu. Atlantic. VG+. $10.00
The Doors. Elektra. G. $8.00
It's a Beautiful Day. Columbia. G. $8.00
Led Zeppelin. Atlantic. VG. $8.00
The Moody Blues, Days of Future Passed. Deram. VG. $10.00
Simon & Garfunkel, Sounds of Silence. Columbia. VG. $11.00

Dire Straits. Warner. VG++. $12.00
Elton John. MCA. VG. $10.00
Elton John, Tumbleweed Connection. MCA. VG. $10.00
Fleetwood Mac, Rumours. Warner. VG+. $10.00
Genesis, And Then There Were None. Atlantic. VG. $8.00
Led Zeppelin. Atlantic. VG. $10.00
Mott the Hoople, All the Young Dudes. CBS. G. $7.00
Pink Floyd, Dark Side of the Moon. Capitol. VG+. $11.00
Pink Floyd, Meddle. Capitol. VG. $10.00
Pink Floyd, The Wall. Columbia. VG+. $12.00
Rolling Stones, Hot Rocks. Abkco. VG+. $15.00
Rolling Stones, Sticky Fingers. Abkco. VG+ $10.00
Steely Dan, The Royal Scam. ABC. VG. $10.00
Traffic, The Low Spark of High Heeled Boys. Island. VG+. $10.00

On Your Own

1. Start FrontPage 2003.
2. Create a Web site for a collection of items you own or know about. Name the Web site **Collect**.
   ✓ *For example, CDs, books, video games, stuffed animals, dolls, antique toys, etc.*
3. Create a home page to introduce your collection. If necessary, research on the Internet to find out historical facts or interesting information about the items in the collection.
4. Create a Web page to display the collection information. Apply the same background color to both Web pages.
5. Divide the collection into logical parts using horizontal lines.
6. Create a drawing to illustrate an item in the collection or the collection as a whole.
7. Use shapes, fills, and text in your drawing.
8. Create WordArt headings for the Web pages.
9. Add hyperlinks to link pages.
10. Preview your Web site in the browser and then make any modifications necessary.
11. Close the browser and the Web site.
12. Close FrontPage 2003.

Exercise 9

◆ **Insert Picture** ◆ **Save Picture in Web**
◆ **Insert Background Image**
◆ **Import, Rename, and Move Picture File** ◆ **Picture Ethics**

On the Job

Most Web pages include pictures to add visual interest or illustrate the page's subject matter. Pictures include clip art drawings, photos, or other line drawings and may be inserted from FrontPage, from a file on the computer, or from a network or the Internet. The Web author can move pictures to or save pictures in the Web site's images folder and change formats as necessary to modify the picture. Authors can also use pictures as background images to give Web pages visual interest and texture.

In this exercise, you will add pictures to the Summers Conservatory's new Web site. You will insert a FrontPage clip art picture and a photo file and save them in the images folder. You will import a picture, rename it, move it into the images folder, and use it as a background. Finally, you will modify the background picture and apply it to another page.

Terms

clip art
Predrawn graphics that can be inserted into a document or Web page.

embedded picture
A picture inserted into a Web page that thus becomes part of the page's code.

GIF (Graphics Interchange Format)
A standard format for image files on the Web. The file name extension for GIF images is *.gif*, pronounced "giff" or "jiff."

import
Bring a file into a document or Web site from another file location on the computer, a network, or the Internet.

inline
A graphic or other object positioned directly in the text of a Web page at the insertion point. Inline pictures can be moved or aligned like any other text character.

JPEG (Joint Photographic Experts Group)
A standard format for image files on the Web used for high-quality pictures. The file name extension for JPG images is *.jpg*, pronounced "jay-peg."

PNG (Portable Network Graphics)
A standard format for image files on the Web similar to GIF but without licensing restrictions.

Notes

Insert Picture

■ Pictures add visual interest to a Web page or provide illustrations of the Web page's subject. Pictures can also be used on a Web page as hyperlinks to open other pages.

✓ *Pictures can also be inserted in tables designed to control page layout. See Lesson 3, Exercise 14.*

- To display correctly and load quickly, pictures used on Web pages are usually created with one of the following formats:
  - **GIF**. GIF format allows up to 256 colors that can be easily manipulated.

  ✓ *For example, a color in a GIF picture can be made transparent.*

  - **JPG**. JPG graphics allow the Web designer to change the quality of the image to reduce file size.
  - **PNG**. This format is similar to GIF in that it supports transparency, and it also allows a designer to control the degree of transparency. PNG files can be compressed more than GIF files to reduce image file size.

  ✓ *Some browsers will not support PNG format without use of special settings.*

- If a picture created in another graphics file format is used on a Web page, FrontPage will automatically convert the picture to either a GIF or JPG format.
- Authors have a number of options for inserting pictures in a Web site. FrontPage offers an extensive collection of clip art from Office, and authors can also insert a picture file stored on the computer, a network, or the Internet.

  ✓ *FrontPage's Photo Gallery feature creates a collection of pictures on a Web page. You will work with the Photo Gallery feature in Exercise 12.*

Insert Clip Art

- **Clip art** pictures are predrawn graphics supplied by a program for use in that program. Office includes hundreds of clip art pictures organized by category for easy access.

  ✓ *Clip art is also available free on the Internet or from purchased CD collections.*

- To locate clip art pictures, use the Clip Art task pane. Position the insertion point where the picture should appear and then:
  - Click the Insert>Picture>Clip Art command on the menu bar.
  - Click the Insert Clip Art button on the Drawing toolbar.

  ✓ *If the task pane is already open, you can click the Other Task Panes down arrow at the top of the task pane and click Clip Art.*

- In the Clip Art task pane, type a keyword in the Search for box to identify a picture subject.
- Authors can specify the type of results to show—Clip Art, Photographs, Movies, or Sounds—by clicking the *Results should be* down arrow and selecting or clearing check boxes.
- Click Go to begin a search for pictures that match the topic.

  ✓ *For best success, the computer must have an active connection to the Internet at the time of the search.*

  ✓ *To organize clip art, sounds, and other media clips on the current computer, click Organize Clips near the bottom of the task pane. To access additional media clips from Microsoft, click the Clip art on Office Online.*

- FrontPage displays a palette of pictures that match the search topic (see illustration below). To see more pictures at once, click the Expand button above the palette. To change the search topic, type a new keyword in the Search for box.

Search results for "alphabets"

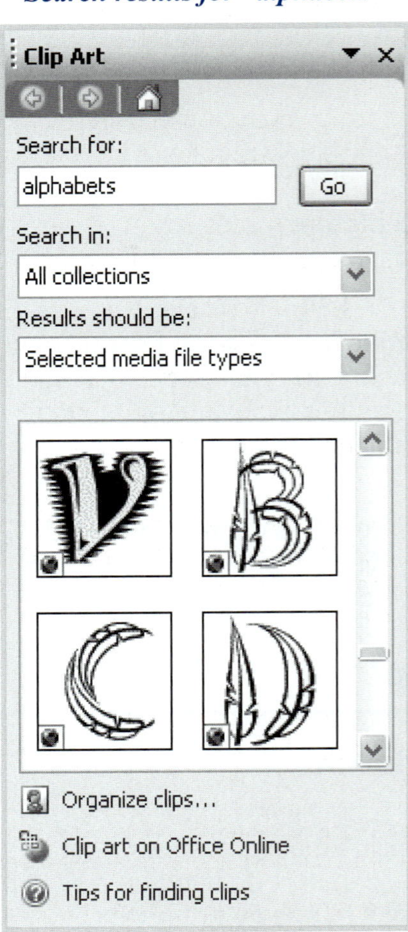

Pictures toolbar

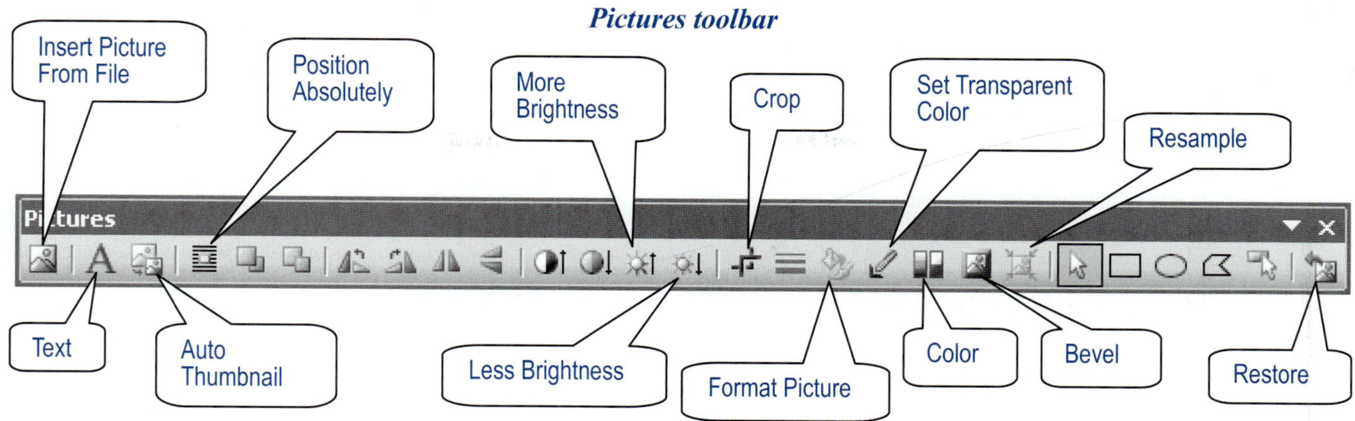

- Click an image to insert it on the page, or click the image's down arrow to see a shortcut menu of other options.
- FrontPage may insert the clip art picture at an extremely large size. Resize the picture quickly using the Specify size Width and Height spin boxes in the Picture Properties dialog box.
  - ✓ *Once the graphic is a manageable size, its size can be further adjusted by dragging a corner selection handle.*
- Pictures are inserted **inline**. That is, they appear on the text baseline like any other text character.
- An inline picture can be moved the same way as a text word or character. Align a picture using the alignment buttons on the Formatting toolbar.
- Text can be wrapped around clip art just as around a drawing canvas using options in the Picture Properties dialog box.
- When a picture is inserted or selected, FrontPage also displays the Pictures toolbar (see illustration above), which contains a number of tools for formatting and modifying the picture.
  - ✓ *To display the toolbar if it does not display automatically, click View>Toolbars>Pictures. You will work with tools on the Pictures toolbar later in this exercise and in Exercise 10.*

Insert Image from File

- Any picture can be stored as a file on a computer's hard drive, on a network, or on the Internet.
  - ✓ *In Exercise 11, you will learn how to insert pictures from a scanner or digital camera.*
- To insert a picture stored as a file, use:
  - The Insert>Picture>From File command on the menu bar.
  - The Insert Picture From File button on the Drawing toolbar.
- By default, FrontPage looks in the current Web site first for picture files. Use the Picture dialog box to navigate to the location where the picture file is stored.
- Pictures inserted from files can be resized and moved in the same way as clip art graphics.

Resizing and Resampling

- When a picture is resized, the display size changes but the file size of the picture does not change.
- To achieve best picture quality, a Webmaster usually should *resample* the picture.
- Resampling a picture adjusts pixel size to match display size and results in a clearer picture after a resizing operation.
- FrontPage 2003 prompts an author to resample after resizing by displaying the Picture Actions box at the bottom right of the picture. Clicking the box displays options for changing only size or resampling the picture (see illustration below).

Choose to resize only or resize and resample

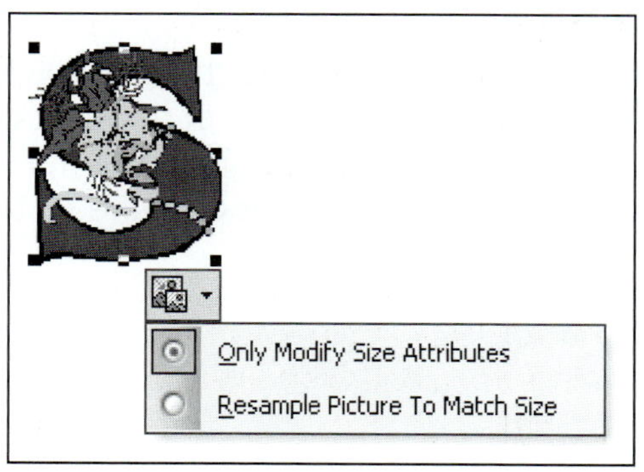

Save Picture in Web

- A picture inserted in a Web page is also referred to as an **embedded** picture.
- When a page is saved after a picture has been inserted, FrontPage prompts the Web designer to save the embedded file.
- Embedded files are saved in the Web site's images folder. Authors can rename the file if desired and specify the folder in the Save Embedded Files dialog box (see illustration below).

Saving an embedded picture

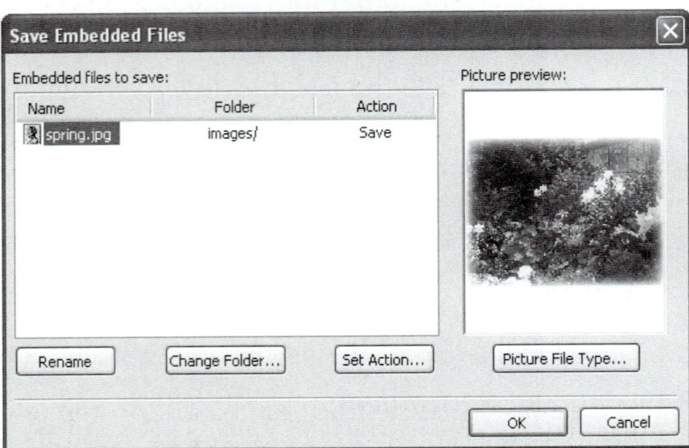

- The Picture File Type button in the Save Embedded Files dialog box also allows the author to change the file format or adjust JPG picture settings.

  ✓ *You will learn more about changing picture formats in Exercise 10.*

- Once a picture has been stored in a Web site's images folder, it is available for use on any page in the Web (just drag it from the folder to the desired position).
- If the picture may need further manipulation, a Webmaster can specify what program to open the picture in, such as an illustration program or photo editing program.
- FrontPage 2003 allows an author to specify the desired picture editor using the Open With command, shown at the top of the next column. To display the shortcut menu that contains the Open With command, right-click the picture.

Specify a picture editor

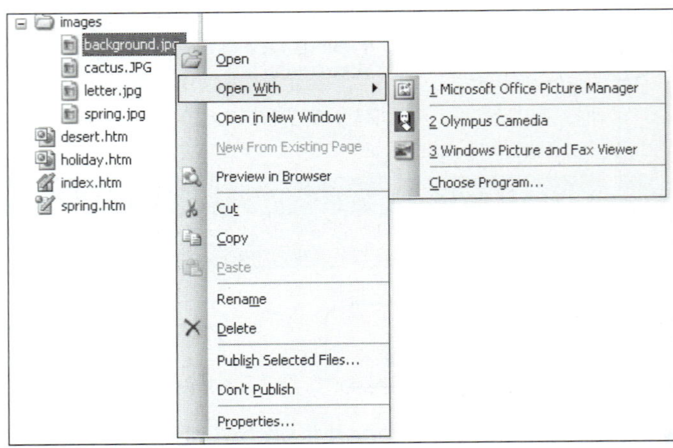

Insert Background Image

- Pictures can be used to supply a graphic background for a Web page. Background pictures provide visual interest and texture to a page.
- Web designers insert background pictures using the Format>Background command on the menu bar to open the Page Properties dialog box (see illustration below).

Specify a background picture for a page

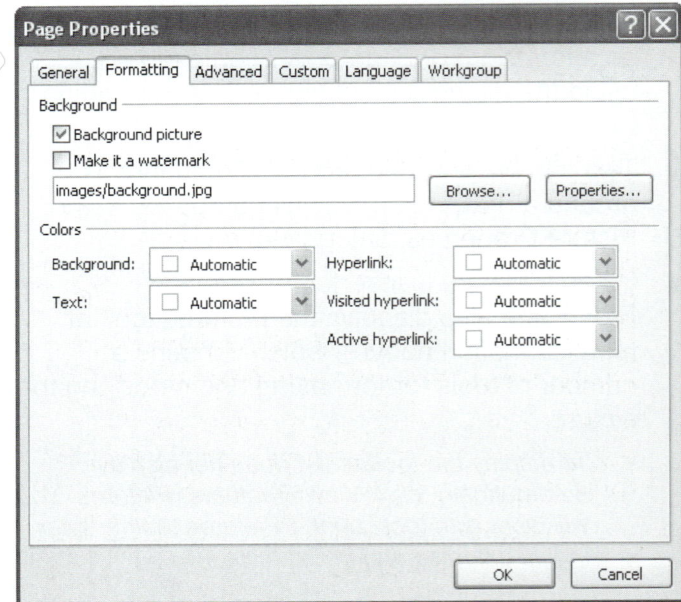

- A background picture does not have to be an illustrative photograph or drawing. Some versions of Microsoft Windows offer desktop textures that can readily be used as Web backgrounds. Office's Stationery files also make good backgrounds.

  ✓ *To locate Stationery backgrounds, browse to Program Files>Common Files>Microsoft Shared>Stationery. Look for the files with Bkgrd in their names.*

Modify Background Image

- Background pictures can easily overwhelm the text on a Web page.
- "Tone down" a background picture using tools on the Pictures toolbar:
  - Use the More Brightness button to lighten colors.
  - Use options on the Color button's drop-down menu to change the picture to grayscale or to "wash out" the picture to make it much less bright.
- A Web author may also use an outside program such as a photo editor or illustration program to apply effects or filters to modify pictures. (Modify pictures before importing them into the Web site.)

Import, Rename, and Move Picture File

- Another way to add a picture to a Web is to **import** it.
- To import a picture (or any other HTML file or other file), use the File>Import command on the menu bar.
- Locate files to import using the Import dialog box (see illustration at top of next column).
- Imported pictures can be renamed easily in Folders view using the same procedure as for renaming any file.

  ✓ *To review renaming a file in Folders view, see Lesson 1, Exercise 4.*

- Imported pictures should be stored in the images folder along with other pictures. Use Folders view or the Folder List to drag the imported picture into the images folder.

Import a picture or other file

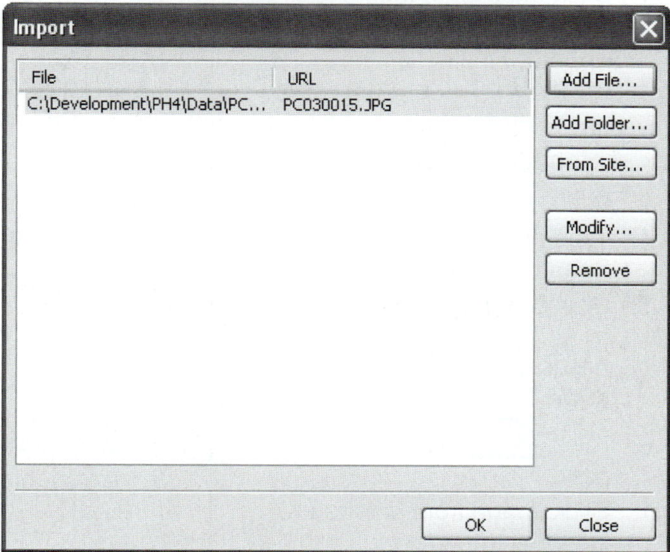

Picture Ethics

- The Internet stores millions of pictures—clip art, photographs, line drawings, maps, and so on—that can easily be copied for use in other Web sites.
- Most Web sites that offer collections of clip art or other pictures allow copying for personal use but forbid use on a commercial site.
- Using a copyrighted picture without permission is considered to be a violation of copyright laws and may result in legal action.
- Web authors should check a site carefully for copyright or fair use information and secure permission if required before copying a picture.
- The same care should extend to pictures of family or friends. Authors should secure permission from anyone whose picture will be published on the Internet for the entire world to see.

Procedures

Insert Clip Art

1. Click **Insert** .... Alt+I
2. Click **Picture** .... P
3. Click **Clip Art** C

   OR

   Click (**Insert Clip Art** button) on Drawing toolbar.
4. Type picture keyword in Search for text box.
5. Choose type of results to show by selecting or clearing check boxes on *Results should be* down list.
6. Click Go (**Go** button) in task pane.
7. Click image from palette to insert picture in page.

Insert Image from File

1. Click **Insert** .... Alt+I
2. Click **Picture** .... P
3. Click **From File** .... F

   OR

   Click (**Insert Picture From File** button) on Drawing toolbar.
4. Click **Look in** arrow .... Alt+I
5. Select drive or folder.
   - ✓ *If necessary, double-click folder name.*
6. Click picture file.
7. Click **Insert** .... Alt+S

Resize Inserted Picture

1. Click **Format**.............. Alt+O
2. Click **Properties** .... T

   OR

   Double-click picture.
3. Select **Specify size** check box.
4. Set Width and Height measurements.
   - ✓ *To maintain current ratio of width to height, set only a Width or Height measurement.*

Resample Picture

- Click (**Picture Actions** box) at bottom right of resized picture.
  - Click *Only Modify Size Attributes* to change size.
  - Click *Resample Picture To Match Size to resample.*

Save Picture in Web

1. Click **File**..................... Alt+F
2. Click **Save** .... S

   OR

   Click (**Save** button) on Standard toolbar.
3. To rename embedded picture, click Rename and type new name.
4. To change folder location:
   a. Click Change Folder... .
   b. Double-click images folder to open it.
   c. Click OK .... Enter

Insert Background Image

1. Click **Format**............... Alt+O
2. Click **Background**.............. K
3. Select **Background picture** check box .... Alt+I
4. Click Browse... .
5. Select drive and folder where background picture is located.
6. Click picture file.
7. Click Open ..... Alt+O

Modify Background Image

- Use tools on Pictures toolbar to modify image:
  - To lighten colors, click (**More Brightness** button) on Pictures toolbar.
  - To wash out colors, click (**Color** button) on Pictures toolbar and then click **Wash Out**.

Import, Rename, and Move Picture File

1. To import picture:
   a. Click **File** .... Alt+F
   b. Click **Import** .... M
   c. Click  Add File... .
   d. Select drive and folder of file to be imported.
   e. Click file to import.
   f. Click Open .

      Additional files may be selected and added to the Import dialog box.
   g. Click OK .... Enter
2. To rename file:
   a. Switch to Folders view.
   b. Click once on file name to select.
   c. Click again on file name.
   d. Type the new file name to replace original name, including extension.
   e. Click outside file name to complete the change.
3. To move file into folder:
   a. In Folders view, click the file to select it.
   b. Drag file to folder in Folder List or in the Contents pane of Folders view.

Exercise Directions

1. Start FrontPage 2003.
2. Open **Conservatory**.
3. Import **PC030015.jpg** from the Data folder.
4. Rename the file **background.jpg** and drag the file into the images folder.
   ✓ *Don't forget to include the jpg extension when you rename the file.*
5. Open **index.htm**.
6. Apply **background.jpg** as a background picture.
7. The background picture obscures the text. Display the Pictures toolbar, click the Color button on the toolbar, and choose the Wash Out option.
   ✓ *To display the Pictures toolbar, right-click any toolbar and select Pictures or click View>Toolbars>Pictures.*
8. Save the Web page, making sure **background.jpg** is saved in the images folder.
9. Open **holiday.htm**.
10. Apply the **background.jpg** file to the current page. Save and close the page.
11. Open **spring.htm** and position the insertion point to the left of the main heading.
12. Insert the **spring.jpg** picture from the Data files. Specify a size of 200 pixels wide, and then choose to resample the picture.
13. Deselect the picture, and then press the **Enter** key to move the heading below the picture.
14. Save the page, making sure the picture is saved in the images folder. Close the page.
15. Activate **index.htm**. Delete the first letter (*S*) in the main heading.
16. Search in the Clip Art task pane for *alphabets* or *bows* and insert a decorative letter *S* from the search results.
    ✓ *The search may take some time to locate desired clips.*
    ✓ *If your search does not find the decorative letter shown in the illustration on page 72, choose another letter style or restore the letter you deleted and insert any flower picture.*
17. Specify a size of 70 pixels high for the clip art and resample the picture.
    ✓ *Note the white space that surrounds the clip art picture. In the next exercise, you will learn how to make this color transparent so the background appears around the letter.*
18. Save the embedded clip art picture in the images folder with the new name **letter.jpg**.
    ✓ *Be sure to save the picture as a JPG rather than a GIF picture.*
19. Open **desert.htm**.
20. Position the insertion point to the left of the first paragraph of text. Insert the **cactus.jpg** picture from the Data files.
21. Specify a size of 175 pixels wide and apply the Right text wrapping style. Resample the picture.
22. Save the page, making sure the picture is saved in the images folder.
23. Preview **index.htm** in the browser. Your page should look similar to Illustration A.
24. Close the browser.
25. Close the Web site.
26. Exit FrontPage 2003.

Illustration A

The Summers Conservatory is one of Lexington's most popular park sites. It is named in honor of Katherine E. Summers, who first suggested in 1907 that the Lexington Park Board build a public conservatory and worked tirelessly to fund the project. The central court of the current Conservatory building was completed in 1919, and the Desert House and Tropical Room were added in 1922.

The Summers Conservatory hosts a number of events and displays throughout the year. One of the most interesting is the Butterfly Extravaganza, which takes place in late spring. Thousands of butterflies are released within the Conservatory to mingle freely with visitors—an entrancing site!

Shows throughout the year highlight seasonal flowers and foliage arranged according to themes that differ from year to year. These shows can take up to two full weeks to set up and always include hundreds of plants. The seasonal shows take place in spring (March - April), summer (June - August), and fall (September - November)

The annual Holiday Show is a special seasonal show that brings visitors from the entire three-state area. Hundreds of poinsettias, cyclamens, ferns, and other seasonal plants make a lush display that contrasts richly with the winter scene beyond the greenhouse windows. Visitors of all ages enjoy the toy trains and antique music boxes on display.

On Your Own

1. Start FrontPage 2003.
2. Open **Refuge**.
3. Locate a suitable background picture from Office 2003's Stationery files and apply it to **index.htm**.
   - ✓ *Navigate to Program Files>Common Files>Microsoft Shared>Stationery.*
4. Save the background picture with a new name to the images folder.
5. Modify the background picture as necessary to ensure text is easy to read.
6. Apply the same background picture to **visiting.htm**.
7. On **index.htm**, insert **eagle.jpg** from the Data folder above the main heading. Choose a suitable size for the picture.
8. Add a text box below the picture with the following information: **Photo: Lee Emery/USFWS**. Add an appropriate border and fill and change the font size and style if desired to improve the appearance of the text.
9. Insert a black and white clip art picture of an eagle to the left of the first paragraph of text. Save the picture as a JPG file and wrap text at the right side of the picture.
10. Add at least two additional photos of eagles to the Web, one on **index.htm** and one at the top of **visiting.htm**.
    - ✓ *To find photos of eagles, deselect all but the Photographs option in the Results should be down list.*
11. Specify appropriate sizes and wrapping styles for the pictures and save them with appropriate names.
12. Preview the **index.htm** page in the browser.
13. Close the browser.
14. Close the Web site.
15. Exit FrontPage 2003.
16. Discuss copyright laws and issues as they relate to resources on the Internet and on an intranet.

Exercise 10

◆ **Change Picture Attributes** ◆ **Supply Alternative Text**
◆ **Create Thumbnail** ◆ **Create Hotspot (Image Map)**
◆ **Enter Text Over Picture**

On the Job

Picture attributes can be changed to modify the picture's appearance. Webmasters can make colors transparent to allow a background to display and add borders and beveled edges to pictures. Web authors can use thumbnail pictures and hotspots on pictures to create links between pages. Entering text on top of a picture gives more information about the picture or link.

In this exercise, you will continue to work on the Summers Conservatory's Web site. You will change attributes of several pictures in the Web site, add borders and resize pictures, create a thumbnail, and create hotspots (image maps) in several different shapes. Finally, you will enter text over a picture.

Terms

hotspot (image map)
Area of a picture formatted as a hyperlink. Clicking anywhere in the area opens the target page. Hotspots can be rectangular, circular, or polygonal in shape.

thumbnail
A small version of a picture automatically formatted as a hyperlink to a larger version of the picture.

Notes

Change Picture Attributes

- Once inserted in a Web site, a picture's attributes can be changed to modify the appearance of the picture.
- The Pictures toolbar contains a number of tools that can be used to change picture attributes. Some of these tools are discussed in this exercise.
- Attributes can also be changed in the Picture Properties dialog box. Use this dialog box to:
  - Apply a wrapping style.
  - Specify a vertical alignment option and the amount of white space around the picture.
  - Control border width.
  - Specify exact size.
- If a change to picture attributes gives an unexpected or unwanted result, use the Restore button on the Pictures toolbar or the Undo button to restore original formats.

  ✓ *The Restore button restores the picture to its appearance at the time it is first inserted. The Undo button reverses changes one at a time.*

Change Picture Format

- Some modifications to a picture require the picture to be a GIF.
- For example, a Web designer can make a color in a GIF picture transparent, so the background appears instead of that color.

- If the designer attempts to modify a JPG picture in a way that only a GIF can be modified, FrontPage asks if the picture should be converted to GIF format (see illustration below).

FrontPage offers to change picture format

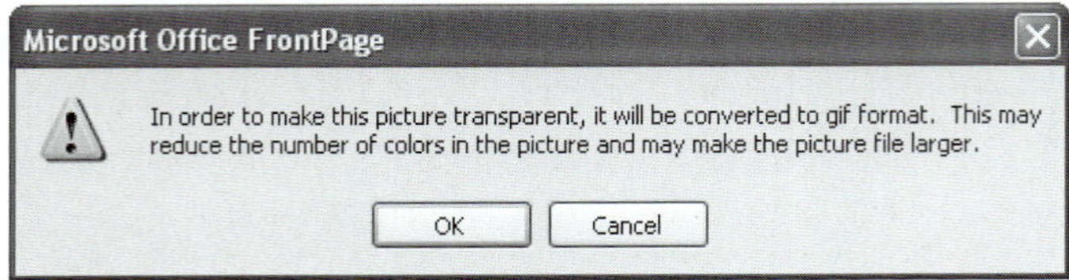

- Web designers can also change the picture format by:
  - Clicking the General tab in the Picture Properties dialog box and clicking the Picture File Type button.
  - Clicking the Picture File Type button in the Save Embedded Files dialog box.
- Clicking the Picture File Type button in either location opens the Picture File Type dialog box (see illustration below). This dialog box provides guidance on which format is best for particular types of pictures.

Picture File Type dialog box

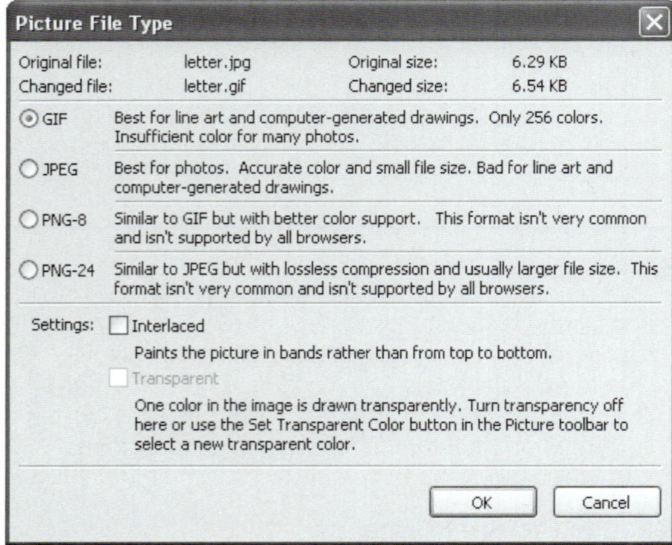

- If the author changes the file type, as has been done in the illustration above, FrontPage shows the changed file type and changed file size.

Set Transparent Color

- Clip art pictures are generally surrounded by white space that is not apparent when the pictures are inserted on a default white background.
- If a picture is inserted on a color or picture background, however, the white area stands out.
- This white area can be eliminated by making the color transparent so the background shows through.
- A picture must be in GIF (or PNG) format before one of its colors can be made transparent.
- To make a color transparent, use the Set Transparent Color button on the Pictures toolbar.

Add Picture Border

- Borders give pictures clean, sharp edges that contrast well with any background.
- Use the Picture Properties dialog box to apply a picture border.

  ✓ *The Borders and Shading command on the Format menu does not control picture borders. It controls paragraph borders and shading.*

- By default, picture border width is set at 0 in the Picture Properties dialog box.
- To add a visible border to the picture, change the setting for the border to a number. The higher the number, the wider the border.
- FrontPage picture borders are black, unless the picture is being used as a hyperlink. When used as a hyperlink, the border is the same color used to identify hyperlinks (bright blue by default).
- Another way to add a border to a picture is to use the Bevel button on the Pictures toolbar.
- Adding a beveled edge to a picture gives it a three-dimensional look (see illustration below).

Bevel edge applied to a picture

✓ *Clicking the Bevel button additional times after the first time successively lightens the top and left side of the bevel edge and darkens the bottom and right side of the bevel edge.*

- When the author changes picture attributes (such as adding a border or changing format), FrontPage will prompt the author to overwrite the existing picture in the images folder the next time the Web page is saved.

Resampling and File Size

- The Web designer must remember that pictures add to the size of a Web and affect its download time.
- Designers can keep download time at a minimum by reducing the size of large pictures.
- The Picture Actions box that displays when an author resizes a picture is one way to maintain control of file size. A picture usually has a smaller file size after resampling.
- An author can also use the Resample button on the Pictures toolbar after making a sizing change.
- To see the impact of resampling, watch the status bar, which shows the download time for the current page.

Supply Alternative Text

- Even when resized or resampled, the file size of some Web pictures may remain large enough to slow downloading of a page.
- Designers can specify alternative text that displays while the page is loading in the location where the picture will appear (see illustration below).

Alternative text in place of picture

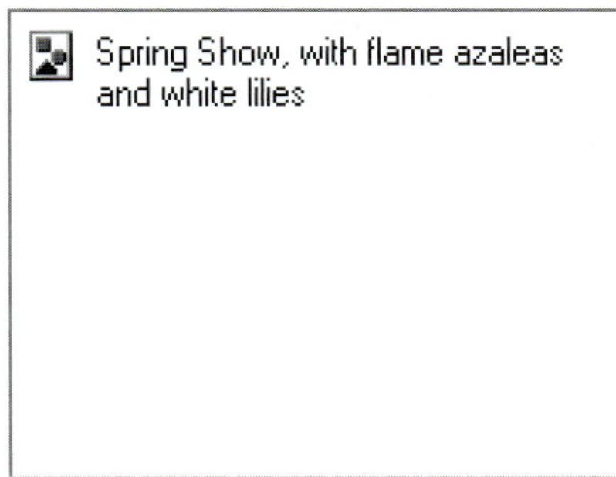

- Some Web surfers turn off the display of pictures in their browsers to load pages more quickly. Alternative text alerts viewers to the subject of a picture so they can display it if desired.
- Alternative text is also important for *accessibility*. Visually impaired Web users rely on alternative text to tell them how a Web page is illustrated.

  ✓ *You will learn more about accessibility issues in Lesson 10.*

- Supply alternative text using the Picture Properties dialog box (see illustration below). The General tab in this dialog box also allows the designer to supply a lower-resolution version of a picture.

Supply alternate text in the Picture Properties dialog box

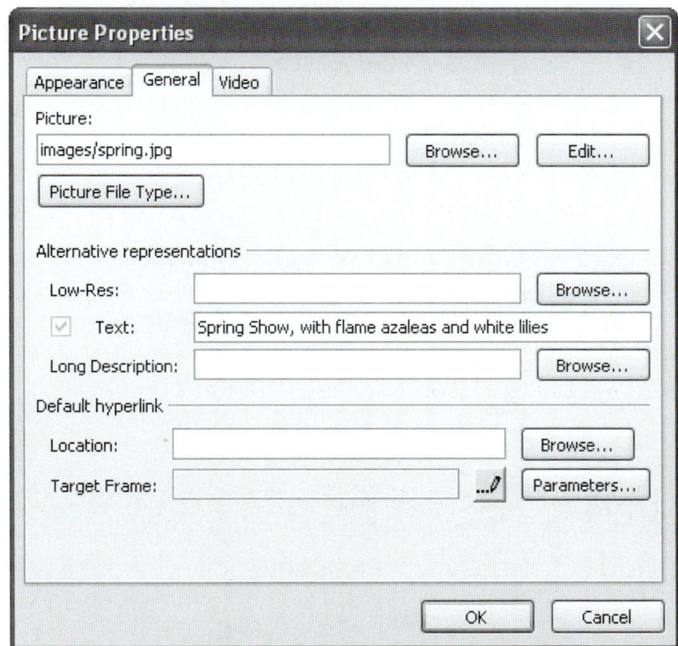

Code Cues

The <img> tag is used to insert and control the appearance of a picture in HTML code. Use the border attribute to specify a border value in pixels, the src attribute to specify the location of the picture file, the width and height attributes to control picture size, and the alt attribute to specify alternative text.

Create Thumbnail

- A **thumbnail** is a small version of a picture automatically formatted as a hyperlink to a larger version of the picture.
- Using thumbnails keeps download times to a minimum because Web site visitors do not have to wait for a large picture on a Web page to download.

- Visitors can click the thumbnail if desired to see the page containing the larger version.

  ✓ *After opening the larger version, click the Back button in the browser to return to the page containing the thumbnail.*

- The larger version of the picture may be on a page by itself or may display on a page with text.
- To create a thumbnail, use the Auto Thumbnail button on the Pictures toolbar.
- FrontPage automatically reduces the size of the selected picture and applies the default hyperlink color border (see illustration below).

Thumbnail on Web page

The annual Holiday Show is a special seasonal show that brings visitors from the entire three-state area. Hundreds of poinsettias, cyclamens, ferns, and other seasonal plants make a lush display that contrast richly with the winter scene beyond the greenhouse windows. Visitors of all ages enjoy the toy trains and antique music boxes on display.

- The picture used to create the thumbnail will display at its full size in the browser (or in Preview Page view) when the thumbnail is clicked.
- To control the size of the larger version, size it in a program such as a photo editor before importing or inserting it in FrontPage.
- The author can also control picture size by inserting the picture on a page, sizing it, and then creating a hyperlink from the thumbnail to the page containing the larger version.

  ✓ *To modify display options for thumbnails, click Tools>Page Options and select the AutoThumbnail tab. Authors can change default size and border style for thumbnails.*

Create Hotspot (Image Map)

- Another way to create a hyperlink using a picture is to create a **hotspot (image map)**. A hotspot is a region of a picture formatted as a hyperlink.
- To insert a hotspot, use one of the three hotspot shapes on the Pictures toolbar. These shapes allow the user to draw the hotspot region on the picture (see illustration below).

Hotspot drawn on a picture

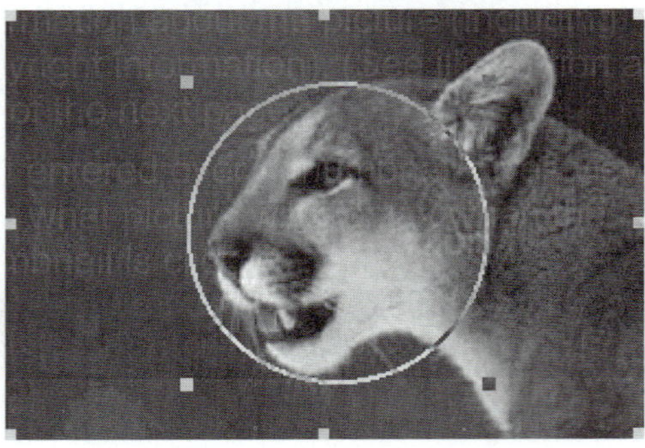

- After the hotspot shape has been drawn, FrontPage automatically opens the Insert Hyperlink dialog box so the Web author can create the hyperlink.

  ✓ *It is a good idea to create a ScreenTip as well so Web site visitors can identify the hotspot on the picture.*

- Modify hotspot shapes by dragging a corner handle of the hotspot.
- The Highlight Hotspots button on the Pictures toolbar is useful for hiding the picture that contains a hotspot and displaying only the hotspot.
- Use this button to confirm hotspot shape and position when the picture content makes it difficult to see the hotspot.

Enter Text Over Picture

- The Text button on the Picture toolbar allows the Web author to insert a text box on top of a picture or thumbnail.
- Enter text over a picture to give more information about the picture (including copyright information). (See illustration at the top of the next page.)
- Text entered over a thumbnail gives viewers an idea what picture will display when the thumbnail is clicked.

Text entered on picture gives additional information

- A picture must be in GIF format before the author can enter text over it.
  ✓ *Changing a picture's format to GIF can cause loss of quality, so think carefully before deciding to add text to a picture.*
- Format text over a picture with fonts, sizes, styles, and colors to make it stand out on the picture. The author can also change alignment.
- White or light-colored text is often necessary to provide good contrast with a thumbnail. It is also possible to wash out a thumbnail picture like any other picture to make text more readable.

Procedures

Change Picture Format

1. Double-click picture to open Picture Properties dialog box.
2. Click **General** tab.
3. Click **Picture File Type** button.

   OR

   Click **Picture File Type** button in Save Embedded Files dialog box when saving picture for first time.
4. Click **JPEG** or **GIF** option button in Picture File Type dialog box.
5. Select additional options if desired.

   ✓ *The Picture File Type dialog box includes useful information about choosing formats and additional modifications for each format.*

Set Transparent Color

1. Select picture by clicking once.
2. Click (**Set Transparent Color** button) on Pictures toolbar.
3. If FrontPage prompts to change the format to GIF, click OK .... Enter
4. Use pointer to click on color to be made transparent.

Add Picture Border

1. Select picture by clicking once.
2. Click **Format** .... Alt+O
3. Click **Properties** .... T

   OR

   Double-click picture.

In Picture Properties dialog box

4. Change **Border thickness** from 0 to a number.

   ✓ *The higher the number, the thicker the border.*

OR

1. Select picture by clicking once.
2. Click (**Bevel** button) on Pictures toolbar.

   ✓ *Click additional times to increase contrast of bevel border.*

Resize and Resample

1. Resize picture using Picture Properties dialog box or by dragging handles.
2. Click (**Resample** button) on Pictures toolbar.

OR

- Click Picture Actions box below resized picture.
  - Click Only Modify Size Attributes to change size.
  - Click Resample Picture To Match Size to resample.

Supply Alternative Text

1. Select picture by clicking once.
2. Click **Format** .... Alt+O
3. Click **Properties** .... T

   OR

   Double-click picture.

In Picture Properties dialog box

4. Click **General** tab.
5. Type alternative text in Text box in Alternative representations area.

Create Thumbnail

1. Insert picture on page.
2. Click (**Auto Thumbnail** button) on Pictures toolbar.
3. If full-size picture has been inserted on a page different from the page containing the thumbnail:
   a. Click (**Hyperlink** button) on Standard toolbar.
   b. Create the hyperlink to the page containing the full-size picture.

Create Hotspot (Image Map)

1. Select picture by clicking once.
2. Click:
   - (**Rectangular Hotspot** button) on Pictures toolbar.
   - (**Circular Hotspot** button) on Pictures toolbar.

     ✓ *Position pointer where center of circle will be and then drag outward to create hotspot.*
   - (**Polygonal Hotspot** button) on Pictures toolbar.

     ✓ *Click pointer to begin shape and click for each change of direction. Double-click to end shape.*
3. Select target of hotspot in Insert Hyperlink dialog box.

Enter Text Over Picture

1. Select picture by clicking once.
2. Click (**Text** button) on Pictures toolbar.
3. Type text.

4. To format text:
   c. Click on text twice, slowly to position an insertion point.
   d. Select text with pointer and apply new font, style, size, or color.
5. To move text, click on text once to select it, then drag it to new location within picture.
6. To align text, click on text once to select it, then click desired alignment button on Formatting toolbar.

Exercise Directions

1. Start FrontPage 2003.
2. Open **Conservatory**.
3. Open **index.htm**.
4. Make the white color that surrounds the clip art letter transparent.
   ✓ *FrontPage will prompt you to change the format of the picture so you can make the color transparent.*
5. Open **desert.htm**.
6. Apply a border of **3** to the picture.
7. Insert the picture **desert.jpg** from the Data files to the left of the page's major heading.
8. Resize the picture to be 100 pixels wide.
   ✓ *Notice the download time at the right side of the status bar.*
9. Resample the picture and notice how the download time changes.
10. Create a circular hotspot about the size of the cactus in this picture.
11. Link the hotspot to **index.htm** and create a ScreenTip for the link that reads **Home Page**.
12. Open **holiday.htm**.
13. Insert the picture **holiday.jpg** from the Data files at the top of the page to the left of the main heading. Specify a size of 400 pixels wide. Resample the picture.
14. Click to the right of the picture and press the **Enter** key to move the heading below the picture.
15. Supply the alternative text **Winter Holiday Display** for the picture.
16. Reduce the width of the picture about an inch by dragging the bottom-right corner handle upward and inward. Use the Resample button on the Pictures toolbar to resample the picture.
17. Apply a beveled edge to the picture. The beveled edge does not look attractive. Undo this change and apply a border with a thickness of **2**.
18. Create a rectangular hotspot somewhere within the picture and link it to **index.htm** with an appropriate ScreenTip.
19. Open **spring.htm**.
20. Supply alternative text for the picture that reads **Spring Show, with flame azaleas and white lilies**.
21. Create a rectangular hotspot in the picture that links to **index.htm** with an appropriate ScreenTip.
22. Activate **index.htm**.
23. At the bottom of the page, insert **holiday.jpg**.
    ✓ *To save time, you can open the images folder in the Folder List by clicking its plus button and then drag the picture name to the page.*
24. Create a thumbnail from this picture and link it to **holiday.htm**. (If you dragged the picture from the images folder, edit the current link so that the thumbnail links to the correct page.)
25. Press **Spacebar** five times and insert **cactus.jpg**.
26. Create a thumbnail from this picture and link it to **desert.htm**.
27. Press **Spacebar** five times and insert **spring.jpg**.
28. Create a thumbnail from this picture and link it to **spring.htm**.
29. Add text reading **Holiday Show** to the **holiday.jpg** thumbnail, **Desert House** to the **cactus.jpg** thumbnail, and **Spring Show** to the **spring.jpg** thumbnail. Format the text so it is easy to read.
30. Save all pictures in the images folder.
31. Preview the Web in the browser, checking all hyperlinks. The **desert.htm** page should look similar to Illustration A.
32. Close the browser.
33. Close the Web site.
34. Exit FrontPage 2003.

Illustration A

Desert House

The Conservatory's Desert House showcases cacti, succulents, and other species that prefer dry environments and can store water for long periods of time. The Desert House's dry conditions and the cool winters and hot summers in our area encourage many Desert House plants to bloom in colorful profusion in the spring.

The Desert House showcases common species of succulents, including yuccas, agaves, aloes, and crassulas (Jade plants), some of which attain very interesting shapes. Cactus species include the golden barrel cactus, "prickly pear" cactus, and many other spiky wonders.

On Your Own

1. Start FrontPage 2003.
2. Open **Refuge**.
3. Open **index.htm**.
4. Make the white background of the eagle clip art picture transparent.
5. Change the format of one of the pictures on this page to GIF.
6. Apply suitable borders to the pictures above the main headings on **index.htm** and **visiting.htm**.
7. Create a polygonal hotspot on the picture that links to **index.htm**. Supply an appropriate ScreenTip.
8. On **index.htm**, create a thumbnail at the bottom of the page using the picture that displays on **visiting.htm** and link it to that page.

   ✓ *You may need to remove the hotspot from the copy of the picture on index.htm before you can make it into a thumbnail.*
9. Add text on or beside the thumbnail to indicate that clicking it will take the visitor to the **visiting.htm** page.
10. Copy the text in the text box below the picture at the top of **index.htm**.
11. Paste the copied text on the picture and format it so it appears clearly in the lower-right corner of the picture.
12. Delete the text box below the picture and any extra space above the main heading.
13. Preview the Web site in the browser and check links.
14. Close the browser.
15. Close the Web site.
16. Exit FrontPage 2003.

Exercise 11

◆ **Insert Video Clip** ◆ **Use Rulers and Grid**
◆ **Insert Digitized Photo (from Digital Camera or Scanner)**
◆ **Modify Web Page Layout (Absolute Positioning)**

On the Job

FrontPage allows the Web author to add a video to a Web page and control how the video plays when the page is opened. Supported video formats include AVI, MPEG, and QuickTime. Authors can also insert pictures directly from a digital camera or scanner. Pictures and text can be placed at exact, or absolute, locations on a page so they are not affected by page flow. Use FrontPage's rulers and grid to help with object positioning.

In this exercise, you will work on a Web site for Ross Environmental Action, a citizens' action group focused on cleanup of a federal Superfund site. You will add a video to the site and insert pictures created with a digital camera and scanner. Finally, you will position text and pictures at exact locations using rulers and absolute positioning.

Terms

absolute positioning
Controlling the exact location of text and pictures on a Web page by specifying coordinates on the page.

AVI (Video for Windows)
A format developed by Microsoft for storing and playing video data. Not adequate for full-length videos, but requires no special hardware to play.

MPEG (Moving Picture Experts Group)
A standard video format that achieves a high compression rate by storing only changes from frame to frame of the video; pronounced "em-peg."

QuickTime
A software system developed by Apple Computer that handles many types of multimedia files on both PC and Mac platforms.

Notes

Insert Video Clip

- A video clip adds special visual appeal to a Web site.
- Videos support or expand on the text information on a page in a dynamic way.
- Because video files can be large, video clips used on Web pages are usually short. Keeping the clip short minimizes download time.
- FrontPage supports the following video formats:
  - **AVI**. This format, properly termed Video for Windows, has fairly low resolution and 30 frames per second, but does not require special hardware to play.
  - **MPEG**. The MPEG format has higher resolution than AVI and provides slightly better quality (almost as good as a standard VCR video). MPEG files require special hardware or software to decode.

- **QuickTime**. This software application was created for Macintosh systems but can be run on all computers that have the proper drivers. QuickTime handles multimedia files of all types, including video, audio, and animation.

- To insert a video clip on a Web page, use the Insert>Picture>Video command on the menu bar.
- After the designer inserts the video clip, FrontPage displays the first frame of the clip or a placeholder on the page. The placeholder or the video image can be resized to change the size at which the video clip will display (see illustration below).

Video clip placeholder on page

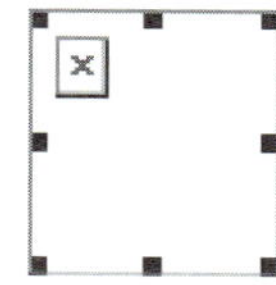

- Use the Video tab on the Picture Properties dialog box (see illustration below) to specify:
  - The video source.
  - How many times the video will play (loop) and the delay between loops.
  - Whether the video will start when the Web page opens or when the mouse pointer is placed on the video.

Video tab allows user to format video

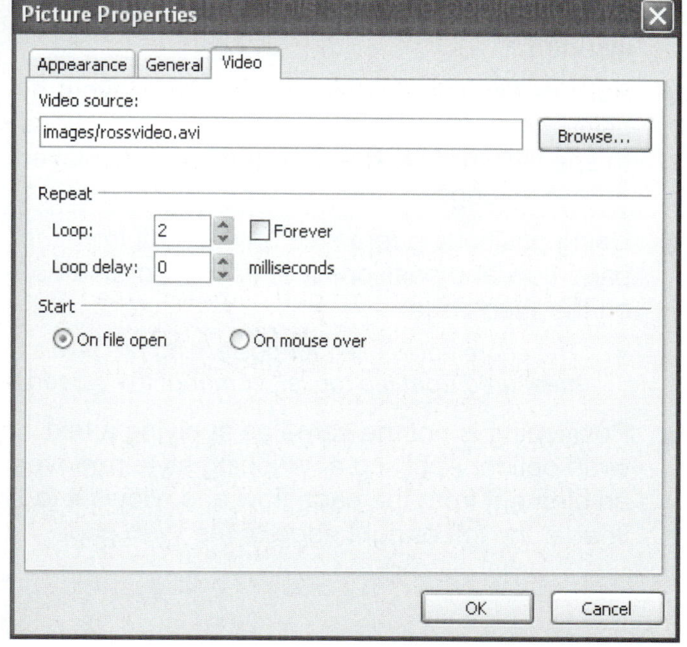

- Video clips do not play in Page view. To preview a video clip, view the page in the browser.
- Video clips, like pictures, are saved as embedded files in the Web site.

Use Rulers and Grid

- While a Webmaster can easily resize a video or other picture by specifying width and height measurements in the Picture Properties dialog box, this process may require some trial and error to achieve a size that looks good on the page.
- FrontPage's rulers can help an author size objects fairly precisely without having to use the Picture Properties dialog box.
- Display rulers using the View>Ruler and Grid>Show Ruler command on the menu bar. FrontPage displays a vertical and horizontal ruler with measurement units in pixels by default (see illustration below).

Default rulers measure in pixels

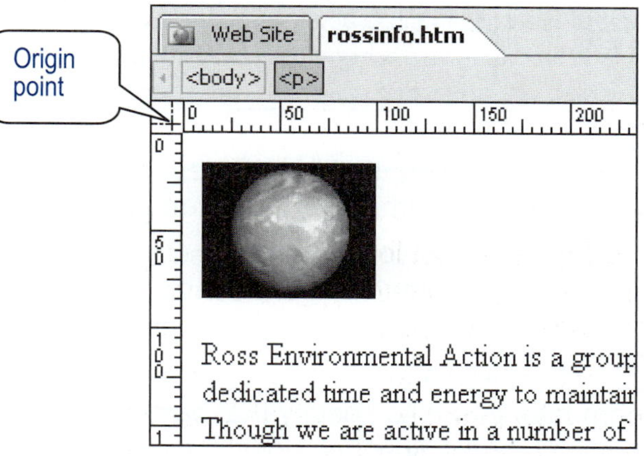

- By default, the rulers begin measuring at 0,0 in the top-left corner of the screen. Drag the origin point to reset the rulers to measure from 0 at any location on the page, or use the Set Origin From Selection command on the View>Ruler and Grid submenu to start the ruler origins from a selected object.

  ✓ *Reset the origin by double-clicking the origin point or using the Reset Origin command on the View>Ruler and Grid submenu.*

- An author can change the units of measure on the rulers by choosing the View>Rulers and Grid>Configure command on the menu bar.

- This command opens the Ruler and Grid tab of the Page Options dialog box. Besides the default pixels, the rulers can be set to measure in inches, centimeters, or points.
- As the mouse pointer moves on the page, dashed lines move on the rulers to show the position of the pointer.
- FrontPage also offers a grid feature that applies regularly spaced grid lines over the page to help an author position objects on the page (see illustration below).

Grid lines superimposed on the page

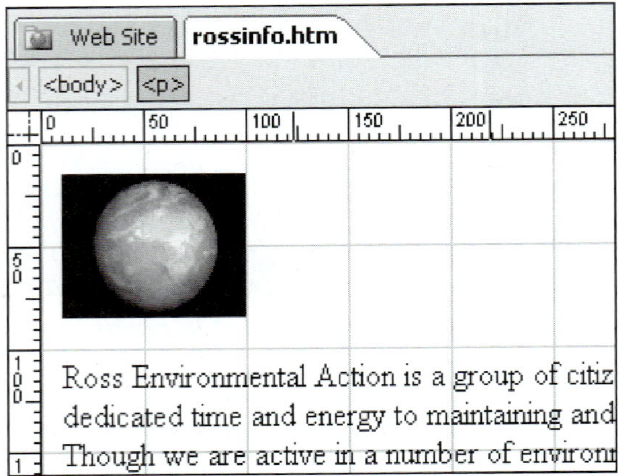

- Display the grid using the View>Ruler and Grid>Show Grid command on the menu bar.
- The grid can be configured using the View>Ruler and Grid>Configure command on the menu bar. Change grid spacing, line style, or line color.
- A Webmaster can also specify that objects snap to the grid to make absolute positioning easier. (Absolute positioning is covered later in this exercise.) Adjust the snapping distance using the View>Ruler and Grid>Configure command.
- To hide the rulers and grid, use the View>Ruler and Grid>Show Ruler or Show Grid command. To restore all default settings for rulers and grid, click the Reset Defaults button on the Ruler and Grid tab of the Page Options dialog box.

Insert Digitized Photo (from Digital Camera or Scanner)

- FrontPage allows a Web designer to insert a picture directly from a scanner or digital camera.
- The Insert>Picture>From Scanner or Camera command on the menu bar gives the author access to a scanner or digital camera, if available.
  - When a scanner is attached to the computer running FrontPage, the author can start and control aspects of the scan from within FrontPage.
  - When a digital camera is attached to the computer, the author can access the camera's storage medium to upload pictures to the current Web site.
- The Insert Picture from Scanner or Camera dialog box lets the Webmaster add pictures directly to the Clip Organizer so they will be available for later use (see illustration below).

Insert a digitized picture from scanner or camera

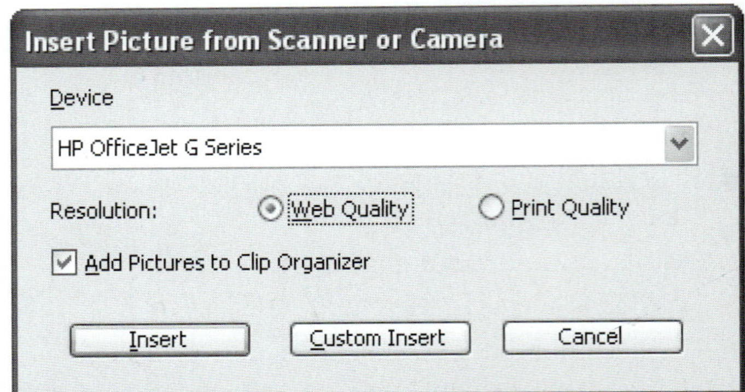

Modify Web Page Layout (Absolute Positioning)

- Text and pictures on a Web page usually appear sequentially in the order they were inserted.
- Authors can modify default Web-page layout by using FrontPage **absolute positioning** options to specify where text and pictures are displayed on a Web page.
- Using positioning removes an element from the page flow and positions it at exact coordinates on the Web page.

  ✓ *The coordinates used for positioning are pixels measured from the top left corner of the screen.*

- Positioning is not the same as applying a text wrap option. Applying a wrapping style removes an element from the page flow and allows it to float at the left or right edge of the Web page.

- An absolutely positioned element appears at the same location on the Web page no matter what browser is used to display it.
  ✓ *Differing screen resolutions can make absolutely positioned text and pictures appear to be in different locations, but the pixel coordinates will be correct.*
- When a picture is positioned absolutely, text will not wrap around it. Instead, text runs behind or on top of the picture.
- To prevent paragraph text from running over or behind a picture, the text can also be positioned absolutely.
- To position a paragraph of text or a picture:
  - Select the paragraph or picture.
  - Click the Position Absolutely button on the Pictures toolbar.
- In FrontPage 2003, absolute positioning is handled using *layers*. When a designer clicks the Position Absolutely button, FrontPage inserts the text or picture in a layer.
- The layer has a blue border and a tab at the top left corner with the default name <No ID>.
  ✓ *To change the layer name, double-click the name tab to open the Layers task pane.*
- To position the layer, drag it to the desired location by its name tab.
- To resize the layer, drag a side or corner handle, just as when resizing a picture.
- To fine-tune position or size, display the Positioning toolbar. As shown in the illustration below, this toolbar allows a Web designer to specify Left, Top, Right, or Bottom coordinates as well as the width and height of the paragraph or picture.

Code Cues

Text or a picture positioned absolutely appears within div tags. The div tags allow a user to specify a style for a block (or division) of text or a picture. The HTML code for the absolutely positioned paragraph below, for example, is:

```
<div style="position: absolute; z-index: 2; top: 70px; left: 30px; width: 230px; height:105px">Here is a picture...</div>
```

- After a paragraph of text has been positioned absolutely, existing text or text added to a Web page might move behind the positioned paragraph. This text can be returned to its proper location by inserting blank paragraphs to move the text below the positioned paragraph.
  ✓ *If necessary, drag the positioned paragraph out of the way to insert the blank paragraphs.*
- Older browsers may not display absolutely positioned or layer elements properly. For best display results on a wide variety of browsers, use a layout table to position elements rather than absolute positioning.
  ✓ *You will learn how to use a table to control page layout in Lesson 3, Exercise 14.*
  ✓ *You will learn more about using layers in Lesson 4, Exercise 24.*

Text and a picture positioned absolutely on page

Procedures

Insert Video Clip

1. Click **Insert** .... Alt+I
2. Click **Picture** .... P
3. Click **Video** V
4. Click **Look in** arrow .... Alt+I
5. Select drive or folder.
   ✓ *If necessary, double-click folder name.*
6. Click video file.
7. Click Open ..... Alt+O
8. To resize video, click video placeholder and drag corner handle.
9. To format video:
   Double-click video placeholder.
   OR
   a. Right-click placeholder and click **Picture Properties** on shortcut menu.
   b. Click **Video** tab and select:
      - Number of times to loop.
      - Whether to start video when page opens or when mouse pointer is placed on video.

Use Rulers

Show or hide rulers

1. Click **View** .... Alt+I
2. Click **Ruler and Grid** .... U
3. Click **Show Ruler** .... R

Change ruler unit of measure

1. Click **View** .... Alt+I
2. Click **Ruler and Grid** .... U
3. Click **Configure** C
4. Click **Ruler and Grid Units** down arrow and click new unit of measure.
5. Click ruler origin point.
6. Drag to new location to set origins (0,0)

OR

1. Select object from which to set origins.
2. Click **View** .... Alt+I
3. Click **Ruler and Grid** .... U
4. Click **Set Origin From Selection** .... S

Reset origin

- Double-click origin point where vertical and horizontal rulers meet.

OR

1. Click **View** .... Alt+I
2. Click **Ruler and Grid** .... U
3. Click **Reset Origin** .... O

Use Grid

Show or hide grid

1. Click **View** .... Alt+I
2. Click **Ruler and Grid** .... U
3. Click **Show Grid** .... G

Change grid properties

1. Click **View** .... Alt+I
2. Click **Ruler and Grid** .... U
3. Click **Configure** C
4. Click **Spacing** spin arrows to adjust grid spacing.
5. Click **Line style** down arrow to select new line style.
6. Click **Line color** down arrow to display color palette.

To snap objects to grid or turn off snapping

1. Click **View** .... Alt+I
2. Click **Ruler and Grid** .... U
3. Click **Snap to Grid** .... N

Insert Digitized Photo from Scanner or Camera

1. Attach scanner or camera to computer using proper cable.
2. Click **Insert** .... Alt+I
3. Click **Picture** .... P
4. Click **From Scanner or Camera** .... S
5. Select resolution, if applicable.
6. Click **Insert** or **Custom Insert** to start scanner or display stored pictures.

Use Absolute Positioning

1. Select paragraph or picture to position.
2. Click (**Position Absolutely** button) on Pictures toolbar.
3. Drag layer to desired location, or drag handles of layer to size paragraph and position text.
4. To fine-tune position:
   a. Right-click any toolbar and select **Positioning** to display Positioning toolbar.
   b. Enter new coordinates for Left, Top, Right, Bottom, Width, and Height values.

Exercise Directions

1. Start FrontPage 2003.
2. Open **Ross**.
3. Open **index.htm**.
4. Turn on rulers and grid, and choose to snap objects to the grid.
5. Click to the left of the paragraph of text on this page and insert the **rossfinal.jpg** digital picture from the Data files.
6. Use the horizontal ruler to help you resize the picture to be about 270 pixels wide (drag the bottom right corner diagonally inward to maintain the correct proportion of width and height), and resample.
7. Click to the right of the picture and press **Enter** to move the paragraph below the picture.
8. Select the picture and use absolute positioning to position the upper-left corner of the picture at 100 pixels on the horizontal ruler and 150 pixels on the vertical ruler.
9. Select the paragraph of text and the hyperlinks below the paragraph and use absolute positioning to position the text and links with a Top measurement of 150px and a left measurement of 400px on the Positioning toolbar.
10. Use the Positioning toolbar to make the paragraph 270 pixels wide and 120 pixels high.
11. Save changes and store the new picture in the images folder.
12. Open **rossinfo.htm**.
13. In the blank space at the top of the page, insert the **rossvideo.avi** video.
14. Modify the video size so the right edge of the video is at the 100 pixel mark on the horizontal ruler.
15. Specify that the video loop 2 times and begin playing when the page is opened.
    ✓ *Set video properties in the Picture Properties dialog box.*
16. Preview the video in the browser.
17. Ross Environmental Action wants to use their letterhead as a heading on the Web page.
    - If you have a scanner attached to your computer or network, scan the letterhead in Illustration A and insert it below the video clip.
    - If you do not have a scanner, use **heading.gif**, which has been scanned for you.
18. Use absolute positioning to position the letterhead GIF to the right of the video clip. Set coordinates of Left 100 and Top 6 in the Positioning toolbar.
19. Preview the **index.htm** page in the browser to see the absolute positioning of picture and text. Click the Ross Environmental Action link to display the **rossinfo.html** page. The first part of the page should look similar to Illustration B.
20. Close the browser.
21. Close the Web site.
22. Exit FrontPage 2003.

Illustration A

Ross Environmental Action

Illustration B

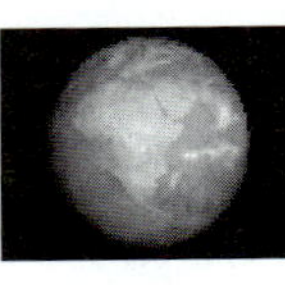

Ross Environmental Action

Ross Environmental Action is a group of citizens living and working in the Ross area who have dedicated time and energy to maintaining and restoring the environment of southwestern Ohio. Though we are active in a number of environmental causes, our current chief focus is the environmental remediation at Ross Feed Materials Production Center.

For over 30 years, the Ross Feed Materials Production Center (RFMPC) produced high-grade uranium products for our country's defense program. Production began in the early 1950s and continued until the late 1980s. At that time, the process of environmental remediation began.

Environmental remediation is a multistage process. The following diagram briefly outlines the process. Completed stages are shown with crosshatching.

On Your Own

1. Start FrontPage 2003.
2. Open **Refuge**. Display the rulers and grid.
3. Add a new Web page to the site named **pictures.htm** with the page title **Eagle Images**.
4. Apply the same background as on **index.htm** and insert an appropriate title for a Web page that contains pictures of eagles.
5. Insert the following text below the heading: **Eagles are among our most majestic birds. They soar above the water in search of the fish that they feed on. They can pluck a fish from the water without slowing.**
6. Insert the **soaring.mpeg** video clip below the paragraph. Size the video placeholder appropriately and set the video to play once when the mouse pointer rests on it.
7. Use absolute positioning to place the paragraph and the video clip side by side, with the video clip on the right and the paragraph on the left.
8. Insert blank paragraphs beneath the absolutely positioned paragraph to bring the insertion point below the positioned paragraph.
   ✓ *You might need to move the positioned paragraph out of the way to insert the blank paragraphs.*
9. If your computer has a scanner attached, scan a picture of an eagle from any source and insert it on the **pictures.htm** page with a short paragraph describing the picture.
10. If you do not have access to a scanner, locate a picture of an eagle from a Web site such as that of the US Fish and Wildlife Service (www.fws.gov) and paste it on the **pictures.htm** page with a short paragraph describing the picture.
    ✓ *If you copy a picture from a Web site, add an appropriate credit notice on or below the picture, such as Photo: George Kennedy/USFWS.*
11. Add navigation bars to each page of the Web.
12. Preview the Web in the browser.
13. Close the browser and the Web site.
14. Exit FrontPage 2003.

Exercise 12

◆ **Create Graphic Image (AutoShapes)**
◆ **Insert Flash Animation** ◆ **Create Photo Gallery**

On the Job

The Office drawing tools include a number of predrawn AutoShapes the user can employ to create more sophisticated drawings or quickly insert standard shapes on a Web page. FrontPage 2003 makes it easy to insert a Macromedia Flash animation on a page to create interactive or dynamic pages. FrontPage's Photo Gallery feature lets an author position a number of pictures on a Web page without having to use a table or position each picture absolutely.

In this exercise, you will continue to work with the Ross Environmental Action Web site. You will add a flowchart created from AutoShapes, insert a Flash animation on the home page, and insert a Photo Gallery showing pictures of wetland construction at the Ross site.

Terms

animation
File created in a program such as Macromedia Flash in which object movement is controlled in a series of frames.

AutoShapes
Predrawn graphic shapes in several categories, including lines, common shapes, block arrows, flowchart shapes, and stars and banners. AutoShapes are inserted the same way as any drawing object.

component
A program written to perform a specific action in a FrontPage Web.

Photo Gallery
FrontPage feature that allows an author to add multiple thumbnail images to a Web page in a variety of layouts. The Photo Gallery thumbnails display larger versions of pictures and captions when clicked.

Notes

Create Graphic Image (AutoShapes)

- **AutoShapes** are predrawn graphic shapes such as rectangles, triangles, arrows, flowchart symbols, and stars that can be inserted as easily as a drawing object.
- Display the AutoShape categories by clicking the AutoShapes button on the Drawing toolbar (see illustration in next column). Then click the category name to display a palette of shapes for that category.

AutoShapes menu

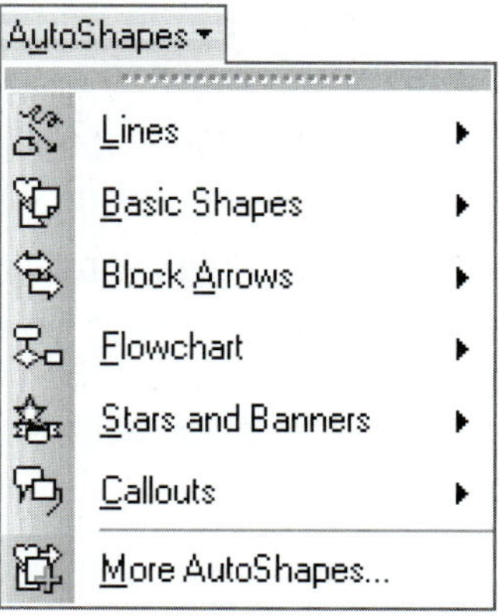

- To speed work, drag the AutoShapes menu away from the Drawing toolbar to float on the page. Each category palette can also be dragged away from the AutoShapes menu to float on the page (see illustration below).

Block Arrows floating palette

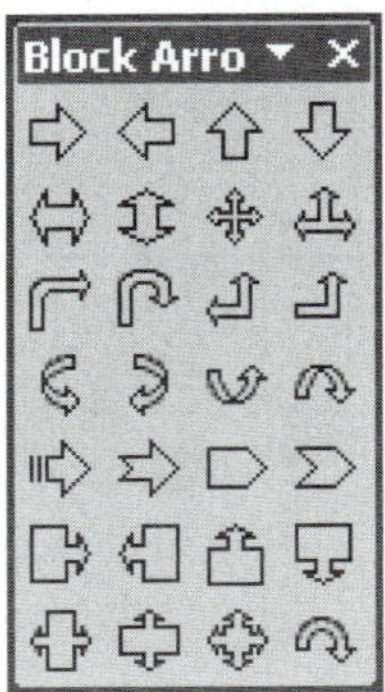

- The Web author should insert AutoShapes within a drawing canvas to ensure they will display correctly in a browser.
- To insert an AutoShape, select the desired shape on a palette, and then use the crosshair pointer to draw the shape.
- AutoShapes can be formatted the same way drawing objects are formatted:
  - Resize an AutoShape by dragging selection handles. Drag the yellow diamond (if one appears for the shape) to adjust the shape. Drag the green rotate handle to rotate the shape on a central axis.
  - Move an AutoShape by dragging it with the four-headed pointer.
  - Group AutoShapes using the Group command on the Draw menu.
  - Add text to an AutoShape by right-clicking the shape and selecting Add Text from the shortcut menu.
  - Fill an AutoShape using the Fill Color button on the Drawing toolbar to add a color, gradient, texture, or pattern.

  ✓ *To add gradients, textures, or patterns, click Fill Effects on the Fill Color palette.*
- When creating a complex drawing with AutoShapes (or other drawing objects), use the Align or Distribute command on the Draw menu to make sure objects align with each other or are distributed evenly.

Insert Flash Animation

- Webmasters use **animations** to add interactive or dynamic elements to Web pages. An animation can simply provide visual interest or can perform important work on a Web page.
- For example, a Webmaster can create animations that teach language skills, show geometric functions, or explain spatial concepts such as rotation and flipping.
- One of the most popular programs for creating Web animation is Macromedia Flash. FrontPage 2003 now allows an author to easily insert a Flash animation using the Insert>Picture>Flash command on the menu bar.

  ✓ *You must locate and insert the Flash .swf file, not the Flash .fla file.*
- Inserting an animation is similar to inserting a video. FrontPage supplies a placeholder for the animation, as shown in the illustration below.

Flash animation placeholder

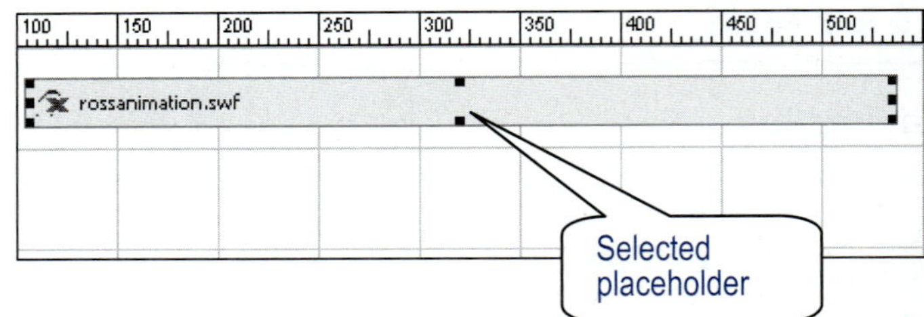

- The placeholder can be resized as desired by dragging selection handles. Check size in Preview view or by previewing the page in the browser.
- To change size more precisely or to modify other properties, double-click the inserted animation to open the Movie in Flash Format Properties dialog box (see illustration at top of next page).
- On the Appearance tab, an author can specify quality, scale, background color, and alignment for the animation. Use Layout options to fine-tune alignment and spacing and add a border. Use Size options to specify exact width and height in pixels or a percent of the original size.

Movie in Flash Format Properties dialog box

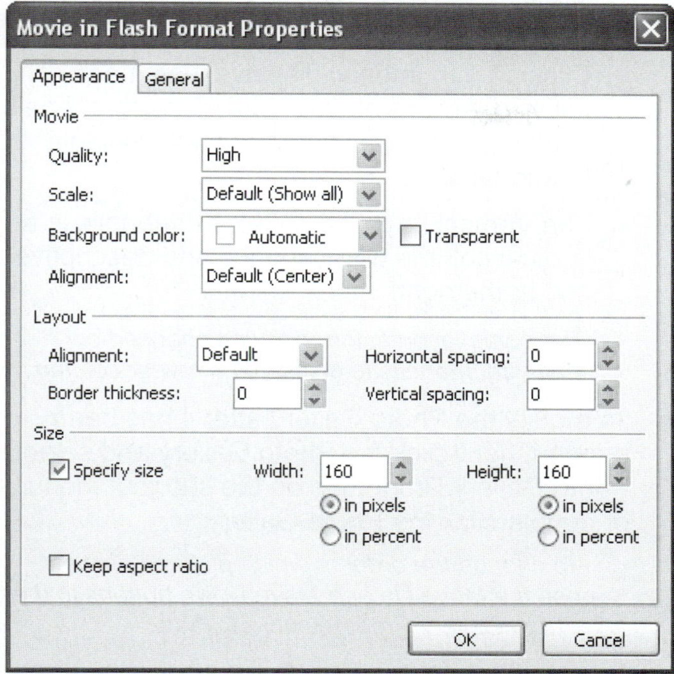

- Click the General tab in this dialog box to specify name and path to the animation. An author can also control playback options such as automatically playing and looping.

Create Photo Gallery

- FrontPage's **Photo Gallery** allows the Webmaster to create an attractive arrangement of picture thumbnails on a page without the fuss of positioning them.
- FrontPage automates the process of inserting pictures for the Photo Gallery. To insert a new gallery, click the Insert>Picture>New Photo Gallery command on the menu bar.
- Captions and descriptive text can be added for each thumbnail (see illustration below). The caption appears below or to the right of the thumbnail, or appears in a ScreenTip.

Adding pictures and captions to a Photo Gallery

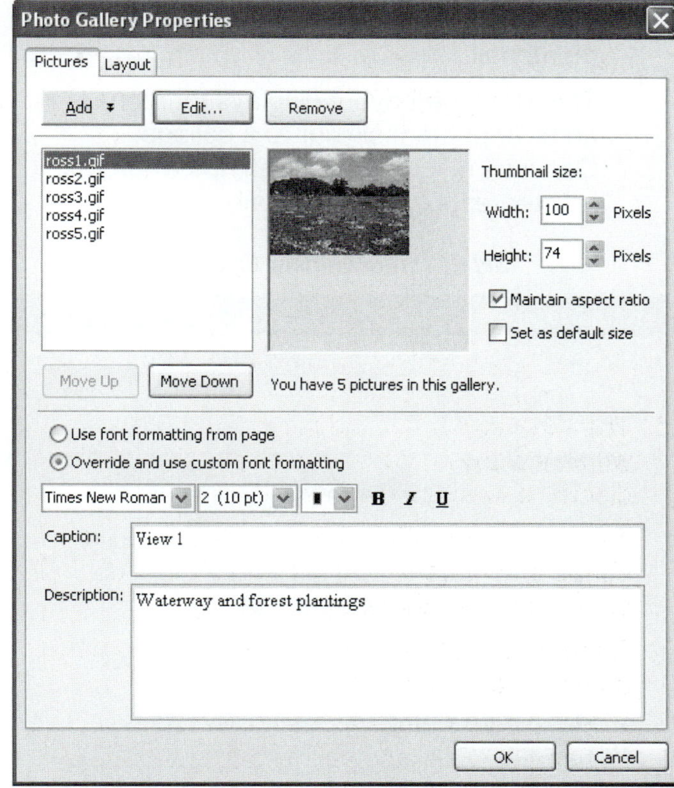

- The designer can use the page's font formatting or choose different font, font size, color, and font style for both captions and descriptive text.
- Use the thumbnail size boxes to control the width and height of each thumbnail that appears in the gallery, or set a default size for all thumbnails.

- After the pictures have been added in the Photo Gallery Properties dialog box, click the Layout tab to select a layout for the thumbnails (see illustration below).
  - The Horizontal Layout (the default) displays thumbnails horizontally across the page, with captions and descriptive text below each thumbnail.
  - The Montage Layout displays thumbnails in an arrangement similar to a collage. Captions display as ScreenTips when the pointer rests on a thumbnail.

Select Photo Gallery layout

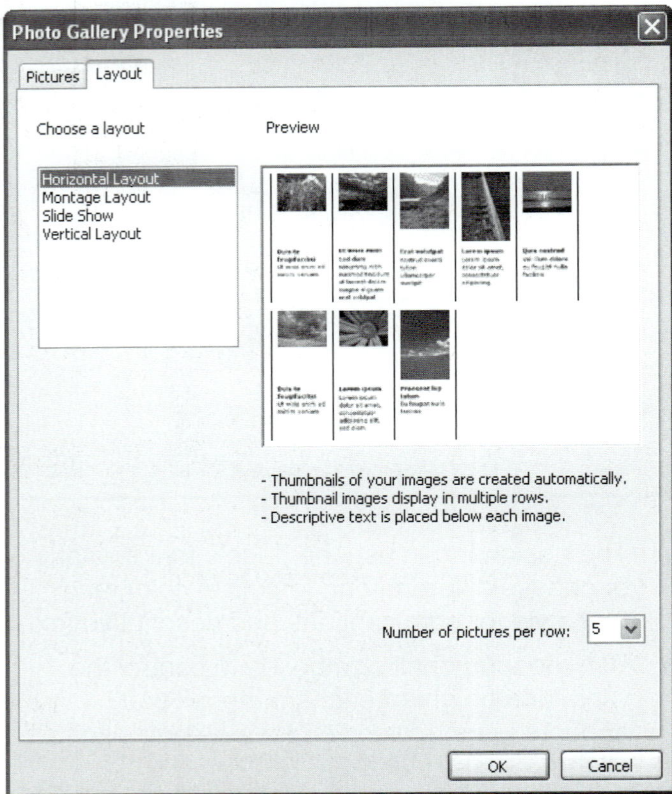

  - The Slide Show Layout displays thumbnails in a horizontal row above an expanded image and its caption and descriptive text. Clicking a thumbnail displays that image at full size. Arrows at each end of the thumbnail row let the user scroll through all available thumbnails.
  - The Vertical Layout displays thumbnails in a vertical column with captions and descriptive text to the right.

  ✓ *For some layouts, the user can choose how many thumbnails to display in a row or column.*

- To modify the Photo Gallery after it has been created, right-click the Photo Gallery and select Photo Gallery Properties on the shortcut menu, or double-click the Photo Gallery.

  ✓ *To change the order in which pictures display, use the Move Up and Move Down buttons in the Photo Gallery Properties dialog box.*

- A Photo Gallery is a FrontPage **component**. A component is a program that performs a specific action on a FrontPage Web page.
- FrontPage includes many components designed to create and format page elements.
- When the pointer rests on a component in Page view, the pointer shape changes to indicate the presence of the component and a ScreenTip displays with the name of the component (see illustration below).

Component pointer shape

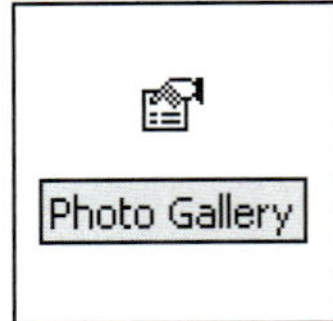

✓ *You will learn more about inserting and formatting FrontPage components in later exercises.*

Procedures

Create Graphic Image (AutoShapes)

1. Display Drawing toolbar if necessary.
2. Click **AutoShapes** .... Alt+U
3. Select AutoShape category:
   - **Lines** L
   - **Basic Shapes** .... B
   - **Block Arrows** .... A
   - **Flowchart** .... F
   - **Stars and Banners** .... S
   - **Callouts** C
4. Select desired shape on category palette.
   ✓ *To see a shape's name, rest the pointer on it to display a ScreenTip.*
5. Drag crosshair pointer in Web page to create object.

Modify AutoShape

1. Add color to shape:
   - (**Fill Color** button) on Drawing toolbar.
     ✓ *Click down arrow to choose from palette or select More Fill Colors or Fill Effects.*
   - (**Line Color** button) on Drawing toolbar.
     ✓ *Click down arrow to choose from palette or select More Line Colors or Patterned Lines.*
2. Group AutoShapes:
   a. Click first shape, hold Shift, and click additional shapes.
   b. Click **Draw** menu on Drawing toolbar ...... Alt+R
   c. Click **Group** .... G
3. Add text to an AutoShape:
   a. Right-click AutoShape.
   b. Click **Add Text** X
4. Align AutoShapes:
   a. Click first shape to align, hold Shift, and click other shapes to align.
   b. Click **Draw** menu on Drawing toolbar ...... Alt+R
   c. Click **Align or Distribute** .... A
   d. Choose alignment option.
5. Copy AutoShapes:
   a. Select shape.
   b. Click (**Copy** button) on Standard toolbar.
   c. Deselect shape.
   d. Click (**Paste** button) on Standard toolbar.

Insert Flash Animation

1. Click on page at location to insert animation.
2. Click **Insert** .... Alt+I
3. Click **Picture** .... P
4. Click **Movie in Flash Format** L
5. Click **Look in** arrow ..... Alt+I
6. Select drive or folder.
   ✓ *If necessary, double-click folder name.*
7. Click animation file.
   ✓ *The file must have the .swf format.*
8. Click Insert ..... Alt+S
9. To resize video, click video placeholder and drag corner handle.
10. To format video:
    Double-click video placeholder.
    OR
    - Right-click placeholder and click **Movie in Flash Properties** on shortcut menu.
    - On Appearance tab, specify quality, scale, background color, alignment, border, spacing, or size.
    - Click **General** tab to specify name, location, autoplay, and loop options.

Create Photo Gallery

1. Click **Insert** .... Alt+I
2. Click **Picture** .... P
3. Click **New Photo Gallery** .... P
4. Click **Add** .... Alt+A
5. Click **Pictures from Files** ... F
   OR
   Click Pictures from Scanner or Cameras .... S
6. Click **Look in** arrow .... Alt+I
7. Select drive or folder.
   ✓ *If necessary, double-click folder name.*
8. Click picture file.
9. Click Open ..... Alt+O
   ✓ *Repeat to insert additional pictures in the Photo Gallery.*
10. Add caption and/or descriptive text for each picture.
11. Click **Layout** tab and choose layout.
12. Click OK .... Enter
13. Modify Photo Gallery by double-clicking Photo Gallery.
    OR
    Right-click Photo Gallery and select **Photo Gallery Properties** .... O

Exercise Directions

1. Start FrontPage 2003.
2. Open **Ross**.
3. Open **index.htm**. If necessary, display rulers and grid.
4. Hide the Folder List to allow more room for the Web page.
5. Click at the top of the page. The insertion point should be centered.
6. Insert the **rossanimation.swf** file from the Data folder.
7. Resize the animation placeholder as follows:
   - Drag the left side selection handle to the left to the 150 mark on the horizontal ruler.
   - Drag the bottom selection handle down to just above the picture and text.
   - Check size in the Flash Properties dialog box. Width should be about 427 and height about 117.
8. Click the General tab in the Movie in Flash Format Properties dialog box and deselect the Loop option.
9. Save the page (save the flash file in the images folder) and preview the animation in the browser.
10. Open **rossinfo.htm**.
11. Insert a new drawing canvas below the third paragraph and enlarge it by dragging the right side to the full width of the text (about 700 on the horizontal ruler).

    ✓ *To insert a new drawing canvas, click the Insert>Picture>New Drawing command on the menu bar.*
12. Insert the flowchart shown in Illustration A:
    - Use the Process and Terminator shapes from the Flowchart AutoShape palette and the Right Arrow shape from the Block Arrows palette. Use the grid to help you size and position the objects.
    - Reduce the internal margins of the Process and Terminator rectangles to fit text more easily. (Use the Text Box tab in the Format AutoShape dialog box to change margins.)
    - After inserting all shapes and text, select all the shapes and use the Distribute Horizontally option to make sure the shapes are evenly spaced.
    - Use the Align Middle option to make sure the shapes align with each other.
13. Fill the arrows with a light color fill.
14. Fill the first three boxes with a crosshatch pattern that consists of a white background and a darker foreground color.

    ✓ *Make sure the text is still readable after the pattern has been applied.*
15. Fill the last two boxes with a color fill.
16. Use the Fit command on the Drawing Canvas toolbar to fit the canvas around the drawing. (You may need to move the next paragraph back below the drawing.)
17. Open **gallery.htm.**
18. Below the first paragraph, insert a Photo Gallery that uses pictures **ross1.gif**, **ross2.gif**, **ross3.gif**, **ross4.gif**, and **ross5.gif** from the Data files. Add the following captions and descriptions in 10 point Times New Roman font:

Caption	**Description**
View 1	Waterway and forest plantings
View 2	Waterway basin seeded and mulched
View 3	Wet forest, prairie, and meadow plantings
View 4	Deep water and waterway plantings
View 5	Forest plantings and mulch for fall plantings

19. Apply the Slide Show layout.
20. Preview the Web in the browser. The **rossinfo.htm** page should look similar to Illustration B and the **gallery.htm** page should look similar to Illustration C.
21. Test the thumbnails in the Photo Gallery to make sure captions and descriptions are correct.

    ✓ *Make sure all pictures are stored in the images folder.*
22. Close the browser.
23. Close the Web site.
24. Exit FrontPage 2003.

Illustration A

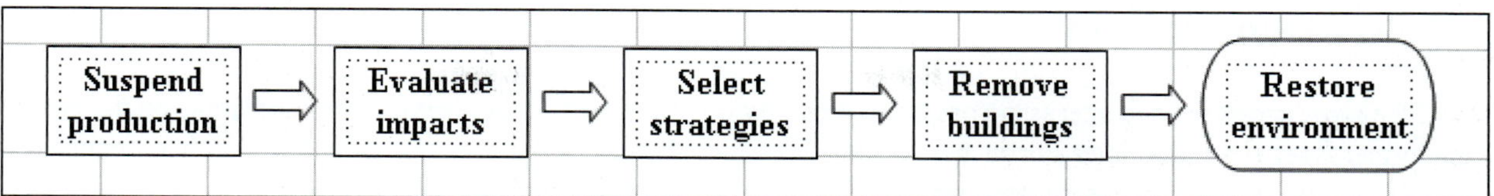

Illustration B

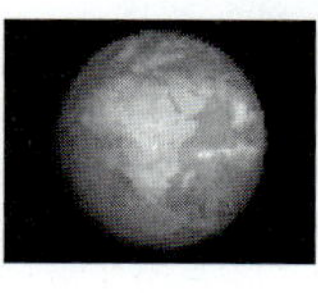

Ross Environmental Action

Ross Environmental Action is a group of citizens living and working in the Ross area who have dedicated time and energy to maintaining and restoring the environment of southwestern Ohio. Though we are active in a number of environmental causes, our current chief focus is the environmental remediation at Ross Feed Materials Production Center.

For over 30 years, the Ross Feed Materials Production Center (RFMPC) produced high-grade uranium products for our country's defense program. Production began in the early 1950s and continued until the late 1980s. At that time, the process of environmental remediation began.

Environmental remediation is a multistage process. The following diagram briefly outlines the process. Completed stages are shown with crosshatching.

Illustration C

Remediation Gallery

One of the most important and interesting projects underway is the planning and creation of wetland areas on the grounds of the former Ross Feed Materials Production Center. Wetlands are vital in our area for controlling flooding, removing pollutants, and providing habitat for many species of birds, small mammals, and amphibians.

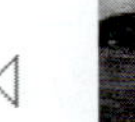      

View 1

Waterway and forest plantings

[Introduction] [Ross Environmental Action] [Gallery]

On Your Own

1. Start FrontPage 2003.
2. Open **Refuge**.
3. Open **index.htm**.
4. Cut the text you inserted next to the thumbnail at the bottom of the page.
5. Insert an AutoShape arrow in a drawing canvas to the right of the thumbnail at the bottom of the page pointing to the thumbnail.
6. Paste the text you copied into the AutoShape. Fill the arrow with an appropriate color.
7. Delete the eagle clip art next to the first paragraph of text.
8. Click just to the left of the main heading (*Roaring River Eagle Refuge*) and insert the **refugeanimation.swf** file from the Data files.
9. Apply right alignment to move the animation to the right side of the page. Drag the bottom middle selection handle down to make the eagle fly further. Check the effect in Preview view and adjust as necessary.
10. Set the animation background to transparent and set the animation not to loop.
11. Open **visiting.htm**.
12. Create an AutoShape that informs viewers they can save money by buying an annual membership and position it near the next-to-last paragraph.
13. Fill the AutoShape with a color or pattern.
14. Open **pictures.htm**.
15. Modify the last paragraph of text to be a general remark about eagles. Delete the last picture.
16. Create a Photo Gallery that uses the picture you removed plus additional pictures from clip art files or the Internet. Where necessary, give copyright credit in the caption for the picture.
17. Choose an appropriate layout for the Photo Gallery.
18. Preview the Web site in the browser.
19. Close the browser and the Web site.
20. Exit FrontPage 2003.

Exercise 13

◆ **Critical Thinking** ◆ **Challenge**

In this exercise, you will work on the new Web site of the Deep Creek Inn, a resort hotel and conference center located in the Midwest. You will add graphic elements such as backgrounds, pictures, drawings, an animation, and a video clip to make the site attractive to potential visitors.

Exercise Directions

1. Start FrontPage 2003.
2. Open **Deepcreek**.
3. Open **index.htm**. Display rulers and grid if desired.
4. Use a stationery background or search for a clip art picture that can be used as a background. If necessary, wash out the background so it does not obscure the text.
   ✓ *Search for background in the clip art files. Locate stationery backgrounds at Program Files>Common Files>Microsoft Shared>Stationery.*
5. Save the background picture as **background.jpg** in the images folder.
   ✓ *Save the page, and in the Save Embedded Files dialog box click the Rename button and type the new file name, being sure to include the .jpg extension. Confirm that the background picture will be stored in the images folder, and click OK.*
6. Apply the same background on the **wonders.htm** page.
7. Apply a light-colored background color on the **directions.htm** page. You may want to customize a color to match the background picture you selected for the other two pages.
8. Insert horizontal lines below the navigation bars on each page. Choose an appropriate color and width for the lines.
9. Replace the heading on **index.htm** with a WordArt graphic. Choose an appropriate style and modify the color if necessary.
10. Insert the **lake1.jpg** picture next to the heading on **index.htm**. Resize the picture appropriately. Add a border to the picture and apply a left wrapping style so the heading and links appear to the right of the picture.
11. Click to the left of the first paragraph of text and insert **deepanimation.swf**. Apply right alignment.
12. Specify a transparent background and set a size of about 190 wide by 290 high. Deselect the Loop option.
13. On **directions.htm**, click to the left of the *From Cincinnati* heading and insert a clip art picture of Ohio. Size the picture appropriately and wrap text at the right side of the picture.
    ✓ *Search for* Ohio.
14. If a white background surrounds the picture, change the picture format and make the white color transparent.
15. Create the map shown in Illustration A at the bottom of **directions.htm** using drawing tools and AutoShapes. Fill the star and the text boxes with appropriate colors. Add a border and center the drawing.
    ✓ *Hint: Use the Curve AutoShape to draw the curved line.*
16. On **index.htm**, insert the Ohio clip art picture in the blank paragraph above the copyright notice and create a thumbnail that links to the **directions.htm** page. The thumbnail should be left-aligned.
17. Import **P8160.jpg**. Rename the file **tree.jpg** and move it to the images folder.
18. Insert **tree.jpg** to create another thumbnail a few spaces to the right of the first thumbnail. Link the thumbnail to the **wonders.htm** page.

19. Adjust the sizes of the two thumbnails to be roughly the same height. You may also want to use the Crop tool on the Picture toolbar to crop the **tree.jpg** thumbnail to match the width of the other thumbnail.
20. Add text over the Ohio thumbnail that reads **Getting Here**. Choose an appropriate color for the text.
21. Add text over the second thumbnail that reads **Images**.
    ✓ *If necessary, wash out the thumbnail pictures to make the text easier to read.*
22. On **directions.htm**, insert **lake2.jpg** above the main heading. Resize the picture to 200 pixels wide and resample it. Add a border around the picture.
23. Create a hotspot in the middle of the picture that links to **index.htm**. Add an appropriate ScreenTip.
24. Copy the picture and paste it above the heading on **wonders.htm**.
25. On **wonders.htm**, center the last paragraph on the page and then create a Photo Gallery below the centered paragraph. Use **tree.jpg** from the images folder and **butterfly.jpg**, **cliff.jpg**, **flower.jpg**, **pool.jpg**, **trail.jpg**, and **waterfall.jpg** from the Data files. Use a layout of your choice. It is not necessary to create captions.
26. On **wonders.htm**, select the first paragraph on the page (*The Deep Creek Inn is located . . .*) and apply absolute positioning. Reduce the width of the paragraph and center it above the last paragraph on the page to give a more attractive appearance to the page.
    ✓ *You may want to turn on the ruler and grid to help you adjust the width and placement of the positioned paragraph. You will need to add blank paragraphs above the last paragraph on the page to fit the positioned paragraph above it.*
27. Center the text in the absolutely positioned paragraph.
28. Save all changes. Preview the Web site in the browser. Check all links.
29. Close the browser.
30. Close the Web Site.
31. Exit FrontPage 2003.

Illustration A

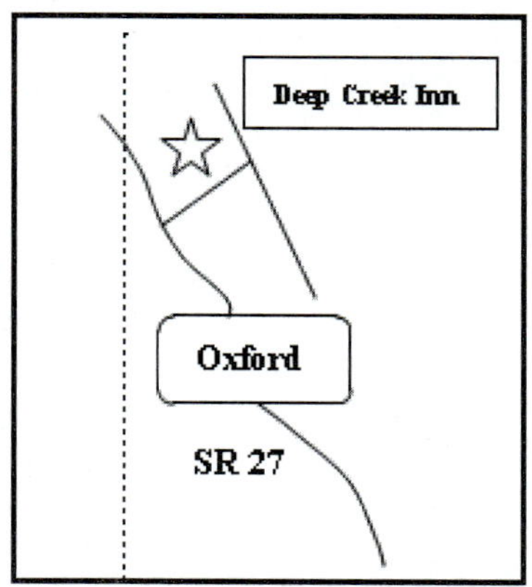

Challenge Exercise

1. Go online and find sites that offer image files, clip art, and video files for use.
2. Add a page titled **GraphicsResources** to the Web site you created in the first Challenge exercise (page 54) and set up a list of links to these pages for future reference. Make sure to cite these sources and list conditions of use.
3. Use a Draw or Paint program to create your own simple graphics that you could insert in a Web site created in this lesson or Lesson 1.

   ✓ *Use the Help feature available in these programs as necessary, or go online to find documentation that will help you create your own graphics.*
4. If you have a digital camera, take a picture that would fit thematically into a Web site created in this lesson or Lesson 1 and insert it into the Web.
5. Research a program that would allow you to create video, such as Macromedia Director or Flash. If such a program is available to you, attempt to create your own video.

   ✓ *Use Help or go online to find documentation on how to use these programs.*
6. Write a short procedure for how you created or would create your own video.

LESSON 3

Create Tables in FrontPage 2003

Exercise 14

◆ Structure Web Page with Table ◆ Create Layout Table
◆ Select and Resize Layout Table and Cells
◆ Trace a Web Page Layout ◆ Enter Text (Table)
◆ Insert Picture (Table)

On the Job

Web designers can use tables on Web pages to organize information or structure the entire Web page layout. Using a layout table allows the author to control text and pictures in ways that would otherwise require considerable effort. Authors can create a layout table using the Layout Tables and Cells task pane. Resize the table and cells as desired to fit text, pictures, and other objects. FrontPage 2003 allows an author to trace a layout from an illustration to speed Web page creation.

In this exercise, you will create a layout table by tracing an artist's sketch of a Web page for a family reunion Web site. You will create the table and its cells, modify cell sizes and positions, and enter text and a picture.

Terms

cell
In a table, the area where a column and a row intersect.

column
In a table, cells that run vertically down the table.

row
In a table, cells that run horizontally across the table.

spacer
A GIF stored in the Web used to create spaces between layout table cells.

Notes

Structure Web Page with Table

- Creating a sophisticated Web page layout can require careful positioning of text and pictures.
- Some older browsers will not correctly display positioned text and pictures.
- To achieve an interesting layout that will be viewable on most browsers, use a table to control the position of text and pictures.
- A table supplies a grid of **cells** within which the Web author can enter text or graphics.
- By changing sizes and alignments of text within individual cells, the author can create a layout that would otherwise require absolute positioning of a number of paragraphs.
  ✓ *Using a table can ensure that pictures display right next to related text, rather than floating near the text at the left or right margin.*
- FrontPage 2003 allows an author to create two distinct types of tables: data tables and layout tables.

- A data table supplies a regular grid of **columns** and **rows**. Columns run vertically down the table. Rows run horizontally across the table. Data tables are used primarily to organize information, as shown in the sample below.

Data table

Item	Description	Stock Price
71986F	Speedo Prism	$51.00
71987F	Speedo Zig Zag	$51.00
71986F	Speedo Splice	$48.00

- A layout table does not have to display a regular grid of columns and rows. Instead, a layout table is composed of layout cells that can appear anywhere within the table outline, as shown below.

Layout table

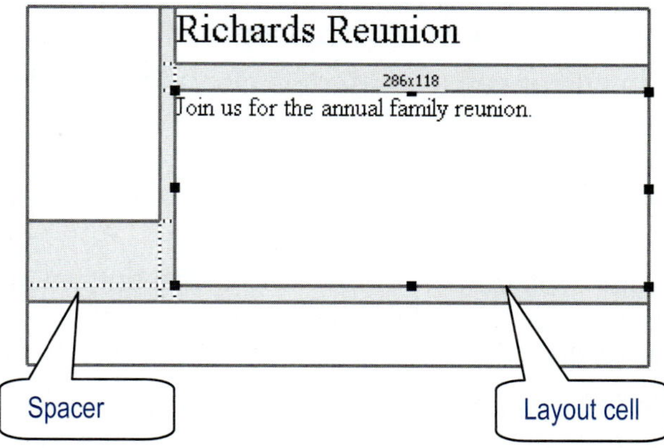

- Though an author doesn't have to create a specified number of rows and columns with a layout table, FrontPage maintains a grid structure using **spacers** such as the one identified in the illustration above.
- This exercise and Exercise 15 concentrate on creating and formatting layout tables. Exercise 16 begins the discussion of data tables.

Create Layout Table

- Create a layout table using the Layout Tables and Cells task pane, shown at the top of the next column. To display the task pane, use the Table>Layout Tables and Cells command on the menu bar.
- At the bottom of this task pane is a Show when creating a new page check box. When this box is selected, the Layout Tables and Cells task pane displays each time an author creates a new page in a Web.

Layout Tables and Cells task pane

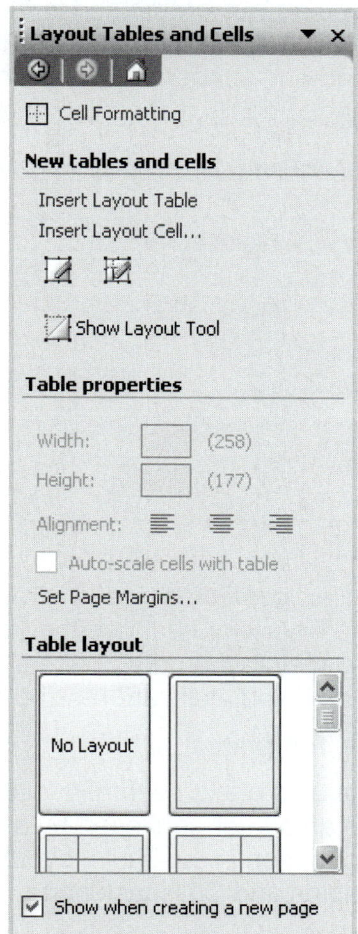

Insert Layout Table

- First, create the layout table:
  - Click Insert Layout Table on the task pane to insert a default-sized layout table 450 pixels square.
  - Click the Draw Layout Table button on the task pane to draw the layout table as desired.
- A layout table has a green border. Size tags appear on each side of the table border to display the exact pixel length of the side.

Insert Layout Cells

- Next, draw the cells in the table using the Draw Layout Cell button on the task pane. Each layout cell has a blue border with selection handles and a size tab at the top giving the width and height measurement for the cell.

- Along with the first layout cell, FrontPage inserts spacers to create a grid in the table, as shown below. Layout cells have a white background and spacers a pale yellow background to easily distinguish between them.

Layout cell and spacers inserted in table

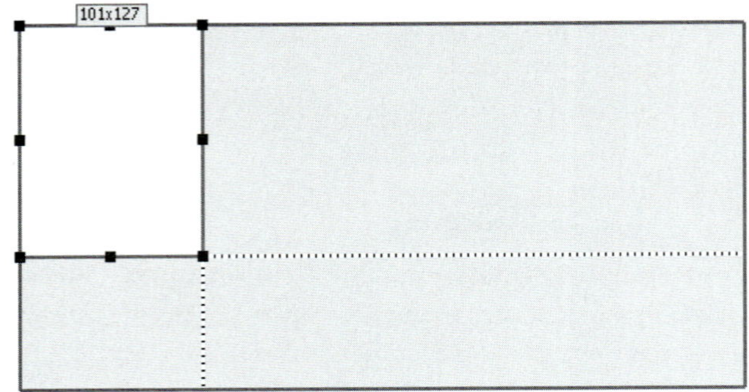

- As the author continues to add layout cells, FrontPage inserts or changes the size of spacers to maintain a grid. Spacers are also changed as layout cells are resized.

Layout Table Templates

- FrontPage also offers several layout table templates an author can insert by simply clicking an option in the Table layout list in the Layout Tables and Cells task pane.
- Choosing one of these default layouts can save time and experimentation in turning out a sophisticated page layout.

Select and Resize Layout Table and Cells

- Select the layout table by clicking anywhere on the outside (green) border of the table to display selection handles and size tabs.
- To adjust the size of the layout table, drag the sides by selection handles, or specify an exact size in the Layout Tables and Cells task pane's Width and Height boxes. Align the table in the page using the task pane's alignment buttons.
- Select a layout cell by clicking on its border to display selection handles and size tab.
- When finished sizing a table's cells, you can click the Show Layout Tool button on the Layout Tables and Cells task pane to turn off the green cell and table borders and the size tabs.
- To modify cell size, drag a side by a selection handle. Or, double-click the size tab on the cell to open the Cell Formatting task pane and specify cell width and height.
- An author can also adjust column widths and properties using shortcut menus. When the layout table is selected, width and height measurements display for each cell. Clicking one of these size tags displays a shortcut menu as shown below.

Resizing options for a cell

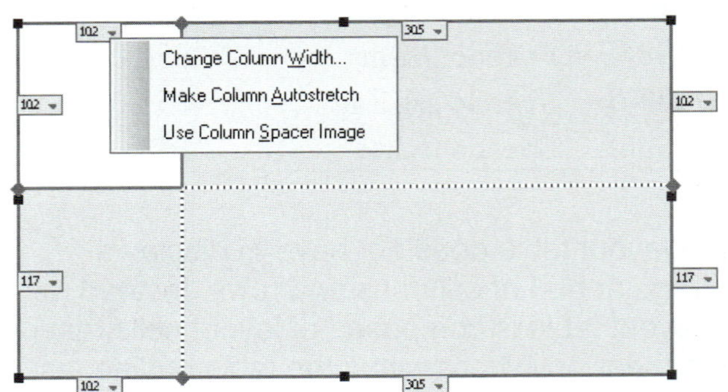

- Click Change Column Width (or Row Height) to display a dialog box that allows the author to specify an exact width or height.
- An author can also use this menu to apply the Autostretch property to a row or column.
- An Autostretch row or column adjusts according to the window size of the browser, while other columns or rows in the table remain at a fixed width. A blue border is added to the bottom of a column or the side of a row formatted to Autostretch.
- In the example at below, the right column is set to Autostretch, so it will adjust as necessary in a browser, while the left column will always be 125 pixels wide.

Autostretch column can adjust

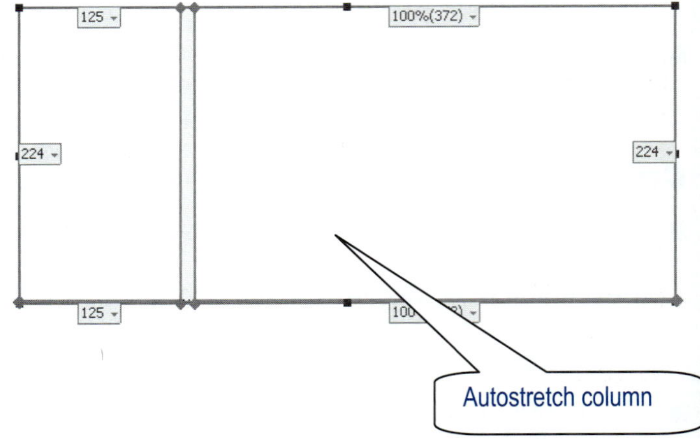

Trace a Web Page Layout

- In FrontPage 2003, an author can use a tracing image to help create a Web page layout. The tracing image displays on the page so the Webmaster can use it as a guide for laying out page elements.
- In the illustration below, for example, an author is creating a layout table based on an artist's Web page concept.

Tracing image used as basis for layout table

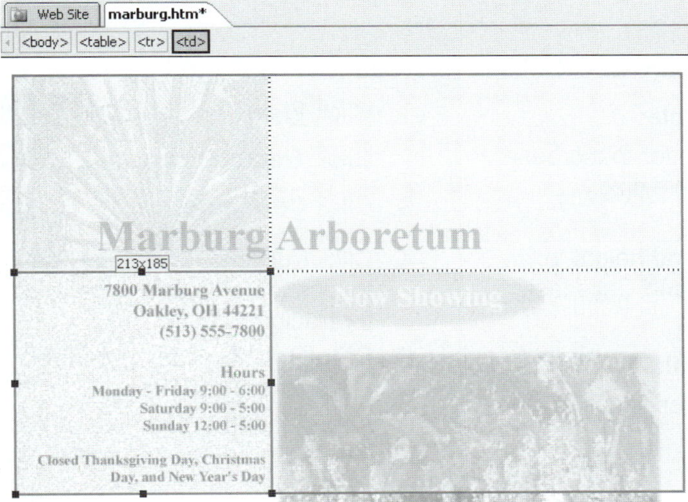

- Use the View>Tracing Image>Configure command on the menu bar to open the Image Tracing dialog box shown below. Use this dialog box to specify the image to be used for tracing and control the degree of transparency of the image.

Image Tracing dialog box

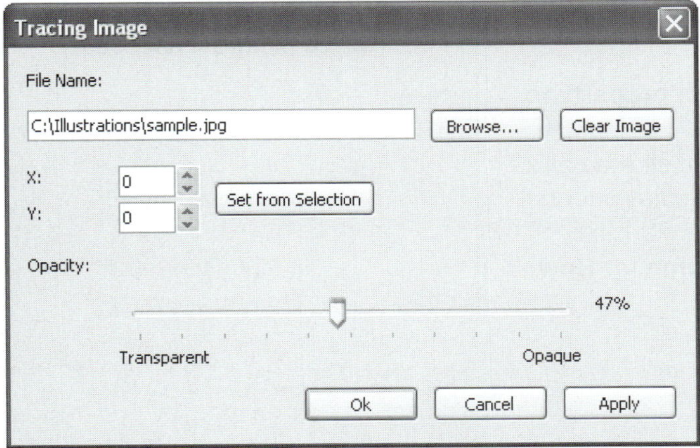

✓ *The tracing image is saved in the Web just like any other picture.*

- An author can also use X and Y coordinates to set the top-left corner of the image as desired to align with other page elements.
- Click the Apply button to see the image in the page while keeping the dialog box open for further adjustments.
- The tracing image doesn't display in the browser. The author can hide the image when through using it by clicking the View>Tracing Image>Show Image command on the menu bar.

Enter Text (Table)

- After creating the layout table and cells, an author can insert text by simply clicking in any cell and typing.

  ✓ *When not selected, the table and its cells are surrounded by dotted lines.*

- If the cell entry is longer than the cell size, text automatically wraps within the cell.
- Pressing the Enter key starts a new paragraph in a table cell.

  ✓ *Paragraphs within a table cell have the same default space after them as in regular Web page text.*

- Text in table cells can be formatted just like any other text on a Web page with styles, fonts, font sizes, font styles, colors, and alignments.
- To see more accurately what a table will look like in the browser, hide the Folder List while working with the table in FrontPage.

Insert Picture (Table)

- One of the chief reasons to use a layout table for page layout is the ability to position pictures easily.
- For example, an author can insert a picture in the center column of a three-column table with text in the left and right columns (see illustration at right).
- Setting up a layout like this without a table would require absolute positioning of the picture and both paragraphs of text.

Picture inserted in table cell

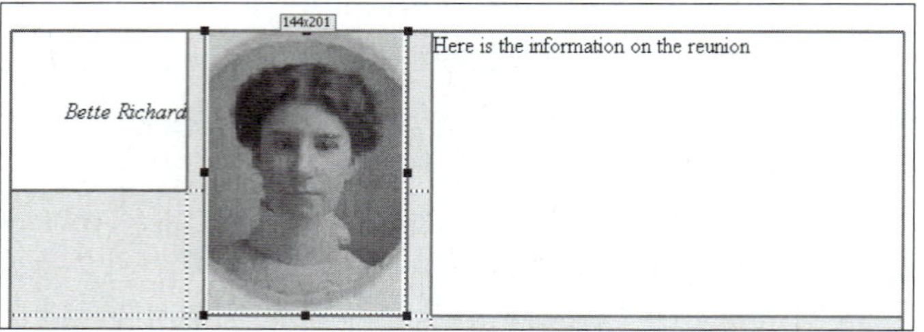

- Insert pictures in table cells the same way they are inserted on a Web page. Click in a table cell and insert clip art or a picture file.
- The inserted picture may need to be resized as when inserted directly on a Web page. The table cell automatically expands to accommodate the picture.

Procedures

Insert Layout Table

1. Click **Table** .... Alt+A
2. Click **Layout Tables and Cells** .... B
3. Click **Insert Layout Table** link in Layout Tables and Cells task pane to insert default layout table.

   OR

   Click (**Draw Layout Table** button) and draw layout table to desired size.

   OR

   Click layout table template from Table Layout list in task pane.

Insert Layout Cells

1. Click (**Draw Layout Cell**)
2. Draw cell anywhere in layout table.

Select Layout Table and Cells

To select layout table:

- Click outside border of table to display green border and sizing handles.

To select layout cell:

- Click border of cell to display blue border and sizing handles.

Resize Layout Table and Cells

To resize layout table:

- Drag green border to increase or decrease table size.

OR

- Specify width and height in Layout Tables and Cells task pane.

To resize layout cell:

- Drag blue border of cell to change size.

OR

- Double-click cell's size tab to display Cell Formatting task pane and specify width and height.

OR

1. Select table, then click a cell's down arrow to display shortcut menu.
2. Click **Change Column Width** (or **Row Height**).
3. Specify exact column width or height.

To apply Autostretch property to cell:

1. Select table, then click a cell's down arrow to display shortcut menu.
2. Click **Make Column** (or **Row**) **Autostretch**.

Trace a Web Page Layout

1. Click **View** .... Alt+V
2. Click **Tracing Image** .... M
3. Click **Configure** C
4. Click Browse... and navigate to location of image to be used for tracing.
5. Drag Opacity slider to control transparency of image.
6. Adjust X and Y coordinates as necessary to position image on page.

Enter Text (Table)

1. Begin typing in first table cell.
2. To create new paragraph in cell, press Enter.

Insert Picture (Table)

1. Position insertion point in cell where picture will be inserted.
2. Insert clip art picture, picture from file, or drawing object.
3. Resize picture if necessary.

Exercise Directions

1. Start FrontPage 2003.
2. Open **Reunion**.
3. Open **index.htm** and hide the Folder List.
4. Display a tracing image for the page: in the Image Tracing dialog box, browse to find the **trace.jpg** file.
5. Set opacity to 50%. Set the X coordinate for the tracing image to 9 and the Y coordinate to 16.
   ✓ *Click the Apply button. If these coordinates don't result in the title of the tracing image lining up fairly well with the existing title on the page, adjust the coordinates.*
6. You will create a layout table using only the boxes below the title and links. Starting at the upper-left corner of the *picture caption here* box on the tracing image, use the pencil pointer to drag the layout table border around the outside of the five layout boxes in the tracing image, ending at the lower-right corner of the *Maine laugh of the year* box. The table should be approximately 625 by 380 pixels.
   ✓ *You may want to draw as much of the table as you can in the current page width, then close the Layout Tables and Cells task pane and adjust the table size.*
7. Draw the layout cells using the tracing image's boxes as a guide. You should have five cells: three along the top of the table, one at the left center, and one at the right bottom.
   ✓ *Do not create a layout cell for the links, even though they are enclosed in a box on the tracing image.*
8. Hide the tracing image.
9. In the first cell at the top left, type the following text: **Bette Richard, nee Hall. Enlargement from a locket passed down in the Richard family.**
10. Apply italic font style to the text.
11. In the second cell in the first row, insert the picture **bette.jpg** from the Data folder.
12. Resize the picture to 150 pixels wide and resample the picture.
13. In the third cell of the first row, insert the text shown in Illustration A.
14. In the left-center cell, insert the following paragraph:
    If you have information for the Richard Record, a compendium of gossip and bragging by Richards round the world, please submit it using the form on the Activities page.
15. In the bottom-right cell, insert the following text (boldface the title, as shown):
    Maine Laugh of the Year:
    A young in-law definitely not from Down East told one of her patients on the psych ward that she was married to a "Mainiac." (He laughed.)
16. Center the text.
17. Modify the table structure as follows. (Look at Illustration B to help you adjust the table.)
    - Adjust the layout table's width to 650 pixels.
    - Make the first cell, which contains the figure caption, the same height as the picture cell.
    - If the picture cell width has changed, adjust the picture size to fit it exactly.
    - Adjust the width of the widest cell in the top row to reach the right edge of the table. Adjust the height of this cell to be the same height as the picture cell.
    - Select the Richards Record cell and move it up slightly if necessary so the space between this cell and the picture is about the same as the space between the caption and the picture in the top row of the table (about 13 pixels).
    - Move the bottom-right cell up so the top of the cell is even with the bottom of the Richards Record cell, and expand the cell width to meet the right edge of the table.
    - Adjust the height of the table to eliminate the space below the last cell.
18. Preview the Web in the browser.
19. Close the browser.
20. Close the Web site.
21. Exit FrontPage 2003.

Illustration A

Join us this summer for the twentieth annual Richard Family Reunion. Richards from all over the New England area as well as the rest of the country and around the world will gather in Rumford, Maine, the weekend following Independence Day.

The dates for this year's reunion are July 6 and 7. Plan to make your reservations early, using information on the Lodging page. Remember that you might be able to find emergency lodging with one of your Richard or Hall cousins, but those beds fill up fast!

Illustration B

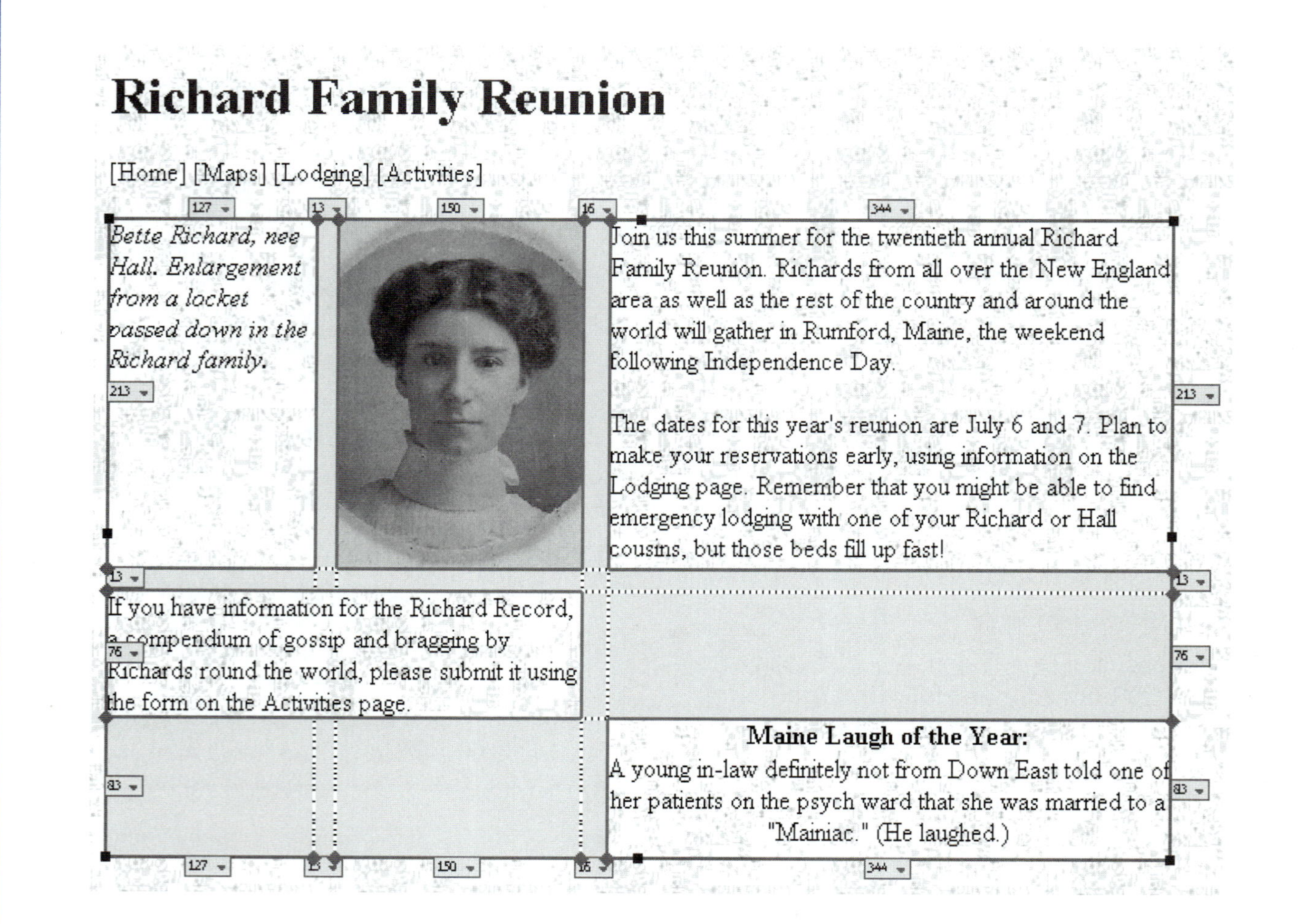

On Your Own

1. Start FrontPage 2003.
2. Start FrontPage 2003.
3. Create a Web site for a reunion or gathering of your family. Give the Web site an appropriate name.
4. Use a layout table to create a layout on the **index.htm** page.

   ✓ *If you have access to a scanner, you may want to create a layout on paper first, scan the layout, and use it as a tracing image.*

5. Insert text in table cells related to the family gathering.
6. Insert a picture related to the family gathering in one table cell.

   ✓ *If you have access to a scanner, scan a family picture to insert on the Web, or use appropriate clip art.*

7. Resize the table and its cells as necessary to fit text and the picture.
8. Preview your Web site in the browser and then make any modifications necessary.
9. Close the browser and the Web site.
10. Close FrontPage 2003.

Exercise 15

◆ **Change Layout Cell Properties**
◆ **Format Layout Cells**
◆ **Modify Table Background**

On the Job

The Web author can change cell properties and formats to improve the appearance of a layout table. Change the vertical alignment of text within a cell to align text at the top or bottom of the cell. Adjust spacing within cells to prevent cell data from appearing crowded. Modify cell borders and background colors to draw attention to a particular cell, or apply a shadow or corner effect. An author can also add a background to an entire table.

In this exercise, you will continue to work on the Richard family reunion Web site. You will change vertical and horizontal alignment of text, adjust cell padding, and apply border, background, shadow, and corner formats. Finally, you will change the background color for the table.

Terms

cell padding
Space added between a cell border and the text within the cell.

Notes

Change Layout Cell Properties

- When working with a layout table, a Webmaster can use FrontPage 2003's Cell Formatting Task pane to make a number of property and format changes.
- To open the Cell Formatting Task pane, double-click a cell in a layout table, or display the Layout Tables and Cells Task pane and click the Cell Formatting link at the top of the Task pane.
- The Cell Formatting Task pane (see illustration at top of next page) has links at the top of the pane to jump to different sections of the pane. A scroll bar appears at the bottom of the pane. Place the mouse pointer over the scroll bar to move down in the pane.

  ✓ *After the pane scrolls down, a scroll bar appears at the top of the pane to allow the user to scroll back up.*

  ✓ *The scroll bar may not appear if the monitor is large enough to display the whole Task pane.*

Text Alignment (Table Cells)

- Text in a table can be aligned not only horizontally (Left, Right, Center, and Justify) but also vertically (Top, Middle, and Bottom).
- Use the Formatting toolbar alignment buttons to change horizontal alignment.
- Use the VAlign drop-down list in the Cell Formatting Task pane to change vertical alignment.

Adjust Cell Padding and Margins

- By default, FrontPage adds no extra space between a cell's border and the text within the cell.

Cell Formatting Task pane

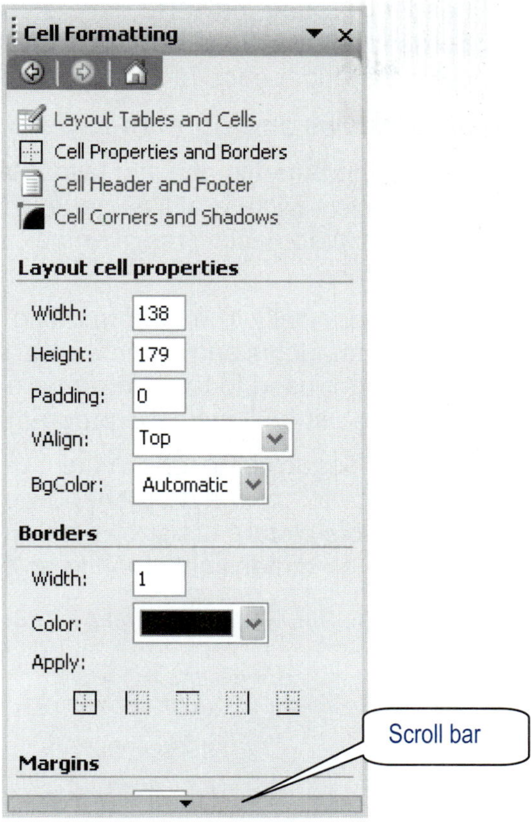

- When a table displays cell borders, this default cell spacing can result in a crowded look and sometimes makes text in a table difficult to read.
- One way to adjust space between text and cell border is to apply a **cell padding** value in the Cell Formatting Task pane. Increasing cell padding adds space between the cell border and the text.
- The illustration at the top of the next column shows the difference between a cell with 0 padding (at left) and the same cell with a padding of 10 (at right).
- If there is enough room in the cell for cell content to reflow, as in the illustration at the top of the next column, cell size doesn't change when padding is added. If the cell is already very full, adding padding will change the cell's height as text is moved to accommodate the padding.
- Another way to adjust spacing between cell content and cell borders is to specify margin settings in the Cell Formatting Task pane.
- Using the margin settings allows a Webmaster to specify a side of the cell (left, top, right, bottom) to add space.

Cell padding applied to a cell

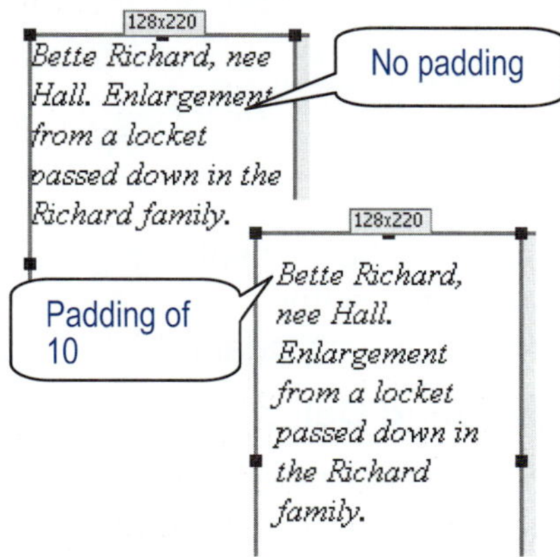

- Specifying a margin almost always changes the size of the cell, so an author may then have to adjust the table size (and possibly other cell sizes) to maintain the desired grid.

Format Layout Cells

- The Cell Formatting Task pane offers a number of ways to format layout cells
  - Specify one or more borders for a cell, in a desired color and weight.
  - Choose a background color for a cell.
  - Apply header and/or footer bars to a cell.
  - Apply a shadow effect to a cell.
  - Apply rounded corners or custom corner effects to a cell.

Apply Cell Borders

- By default, a FrontPage layout table has no borders, but an author can apply one or more borders to draw attention to a particular cell.
- Use the Borders section of the Cell Formatting Task pane (see illustration at top of next page) to apply borders.
- Type a width value, choose a color from the Color palette, and then click one or more icons to apply the border to specific sides of the cell or header or footer.

  ✓ *Click More Colors on the color palette to choose colors other than those shown in the palette.*

- To remove the border, deselect the selected icons that indicate where the border is applied.

Border options in Task pane

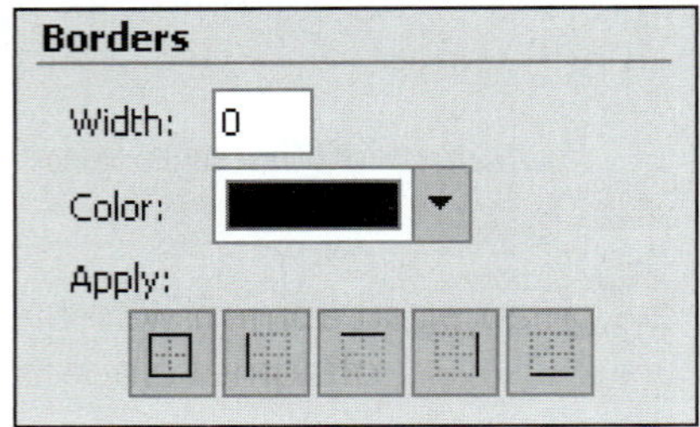

- When changing border settings, such as color or thickness, the author must reapply the border to the cell by clicking again the location icons.

Apply Background Color to Cells

- For a bolder form of cell emphasis, an author can apply a background color to a cell using the Cell Formatting Task pane.
- Select the cell, click the BgColor down arrow, and choose a color from the color palette.

  ✓ *An author must make sure text is readable against a background color. It may be necessary to change the text color to improve readability.*

Apply Header and/or Footer to Cells

- Another way to draw attention to a specific cell in a table is to apply a header or footer to it using the Cell Formatting Task pane.
- Headers and footers are heavy color bars that can be applied to the top (header) and bottom (footer) of a table cell (see illustration below).

Header and footer applied to a cell

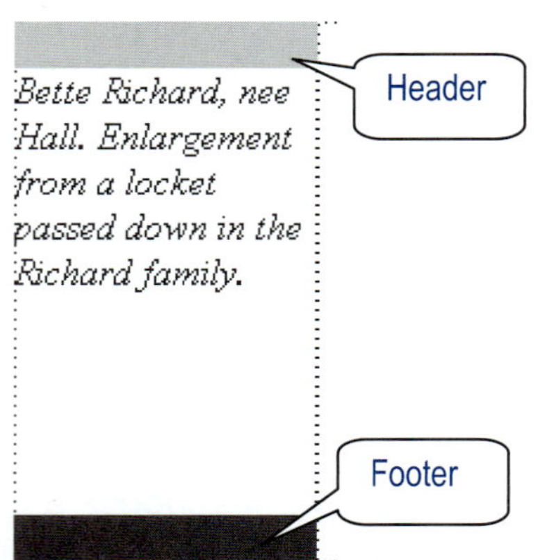

- Select either Show header or Show footer (or both) in the Cell Formatting Task pane, and then specify color, height, and padding, if desired.

- A designer can also specify a border for the header or footer may also have a border. The border appears at the bottom of the header color bar and the top of the footer color bar.

Apply Shadows and Corners to Cells

- One of the benefits of using layout table features to structure a Web page is the fine control a Webmaster has over the table's appearance.
- This is especially true for formatting options such as shadows and corners that a Webmaster used to have to prepare outside FrontPage in an illustration program.
- Use the Shadows options in the Cell Formatting Task pane to apply a drop-shadow effect to a cell or table picture (as shown below). Shadows add a three-dimensional look to an object.

Shadow applied to a table picture

- Select a cell (or a picture within a cell), specify values for size of the shadow (its width) and softness of the shadow (how it fades into the background), and choose a color for the shadow. Then select a shadow style.

  ✓ *FrontPage adds MsoPnl_sh image files that contain settings for shadows when the page is saved.*

- Using the Corners options in the Cell Formatting Task pane, an author can apply a rounded corner to any or all corners of a cell (see illustration at the top of the next page).
- Select the cell, choose a corner and border color (borders connect corners at the top and bottom of the cell), and then select corner width and height.
- Then choose the corners to apply from the icons in the Task pane.

Cell with rounded corners

If you have information for the Richard Record, a compendium of gossip and bragging by Richards around the world, please submit it using the form on the Activities page.

✓ *FrontPage adds MsoPnl_Cnr files to the Web site when the page is saved.*

- Besides creating rounded corners for a cell, an author can specify a graphic to appear in the corners of the cell.
- Click the Use custom image option in the Corners section of the Cell Formatting Task pane and then browser to the location of the custom image.
- Graphics appear in the specified corners as shown below.

Graphics used for corners

If you have information for the Richard Record, a compendium of gossip and bragging by Richards around the world, please submit it using the form on the Activities page.

- The border between the corner images defaults to black. To change the border color, select a new header or footer color.

Modify Table Background

- If the page on which the table is inserted has a background picture, the table also displays that background. This can sometimes make the table text difficult to read.
- To improve readability, background color can be changed for an entire table using the Table Properties dialog box (see illustration at the top of the next column).
- Select a new background color for the table or cell using the Background drop-down palette.

Table Properties dialog box

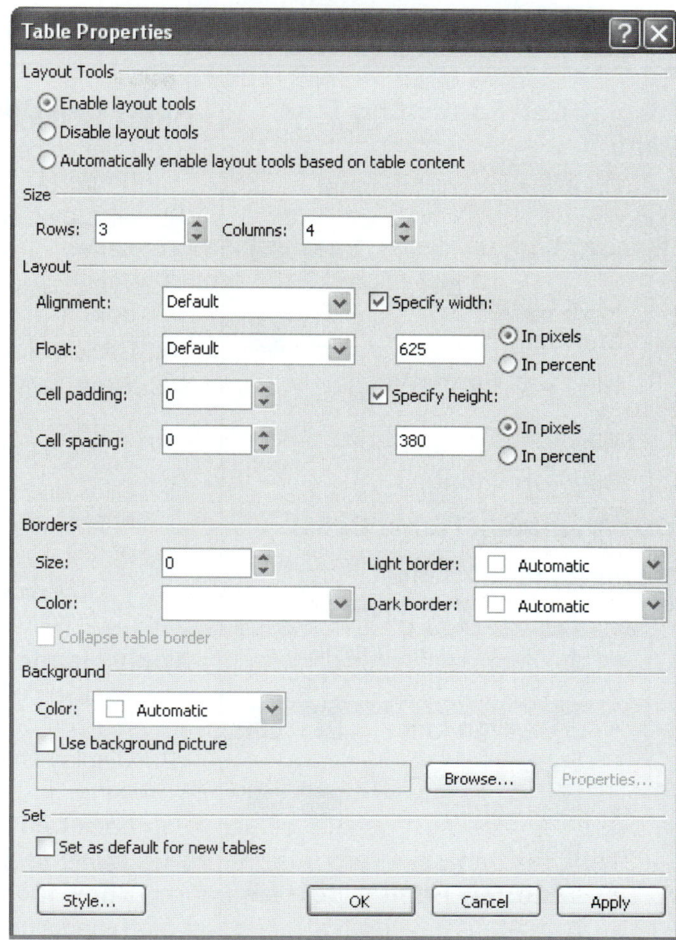

✓ *Click the More Colors option to see additional colors.*

- A picture can also be used as a background for a table or a cell. Choose the *Use background picture* check box and browse to the location of the picture file.
- The default background color is white. White displays as the Automatic choice in the Background color palette even when the page's background picture is obviously displayed in the table.
- To make sure the white background appears in the table, it may be necessary to click More Colors on the Background color palette and select the white color in the More Colors dialog box.

✓ *You will work more with the Table Properties dialog box in the next exercise.*

Procedures

Display Cell Formatting Task Pane

- Double-click cell to format.

OR

1. Click **Table** .... Alt+A
2. Click **Layout Tables and Cells** .... B
3. Click **Cell Formatting** link.

   OR

   Right-click in table and click **Cell Formatting**.

Text Alignment (Table Cells)

Set horizontal alignment

1. Click in cell to be modified.
2. Click horizontal alignment option on Formatting toolbar:
   - (**Align Left** .... Ctrl+L button).
   - (**Center** .... Ctrl+E button).
   - (**Align Right**..... Ctrl+R button).
   - (**Justify** button)

Set vertical alignment

1. Click in cell to be modified.
2. Display Cell Formatting Task pane.
3. Click **VAlign** down arrow and select alignment.

Adjust Cell Padding

1. Click in cell to be modified.
2. Display Cell Formatting Task pane.
3. Type padding value in **Padding** box.
4. Press Enter.

Set Margins

1. Click in cell to be modified.
2. Display Cell Formatting Task pane.
3. Type values in **Left**, **Top**, **Right**, and/or **Bottom** boxes.
4. Press Enter.

Apply Cell Borders

1. Click in cell to receive border(s).
2. Display Cell Formatting Task pane.
3. Type value in Borders **Width** box.
4. Click **Color** down arrow and select color from palette.

   ✓ *Click More Colors to open More Colors dialog box.*
5. Click one or more buttons to apply border to specific sides of cell.

   ✓ *To remove border, click same button(s) again.*

Apply Header/Footer to Cell

1. Click in cell that will display header/footer.
2. Display Cell Formatting Task pane.
3. Click **Cell Header and Footer**.
4. Select **Show header** and/or **Show footer** check box.
5. Type value for **Padding** if desired.
6. Type value for **Height** if desired.
7. Click **BgColor** down arrow and select color from palette.
8. Select border color and width if desired.
9. Press Enter.

Apply Background Color to Cells

1. Click in cell to be modified.
2. Display Cell Formatting Task pane.
3. Click **BgColor** down arrow and select color from palette.

Apply Shadows to Cells

1. Click in cell to receive shadow.
2. Display Cell Formatting Task pane.
3. Click **Cell Corners and Shadows**.
4. Type value for width of shadow in **Width** box.
5. Type value for softness of shadow in **Softness** box.
6. Click **Color** down arrow and select color from palette.
7. Select desired shadow style button.

Apply Corners to Cells

1. Click in cell to receive corners.
2. Display Cell Formatting Task pane.
3. Click **Cell Corners and Shadows**.
4. Click **Color** down arrow and select color from palette.
5. Click **Border color** down arrow and select color from palette.
6. Type values for width and height.

   OR

   Click **Use custom image** and select graphic file for corners.
7. Select corner(s) to apply curve to.

Modify Table Background

1. Click **Table** .... Alt+A
2. Click **Table Properties**........ R
3. Click **Table**.

   OR

   Right-click in cell and click **Table Properties** .... B
4. Click **Background** down arrow and select background color.

   OR

   - Click in Use background picture check box.
   - Click Browse... to locate picture file.

Exercise Directions

1. Start FrontPage 2003.
2. Open **Reunion**.
3. Open **index.htm**.

   ✓ *You might need to display the Folder List to open the Web page. Hide the Folder List again after opening the Web page.*
4. Change the horizontal alignment of the first table cell to Right and the vertical alignment to Middle.
5. Create a header for this cell as follows:
   - Choose to apply a header.
   - In the BgColor palette, click **More Colors**.
   - In the More Colors dialog box, locate the current hex value in the top-right corner of the dialog box and insert the following hex value:

     Hex={DF,B9,BD}
   - Click **OK** to add this custom color to the Web site and apply the header.
6. Select the cell that contains the picture.
7. Create a shadow for the picture as follows:
   - Select the new salmon color you added to the color palette in step 5.
   - Specify a width of 10 and a softness of 50 if necessary.
   - Select the first shadow style to apply the shadow to the bottom and right sides of the picture.
   - If necessary, adjust the picture size so there is no white space between the picture and the shadow. Resample the picture if you change its size.
8. Save changes and store the MsoPnl_sh files in the images folder.
9. Select the Richard Record cell and change its height to about 115. Change cell padding to 3.
10. Change the cell's background color to the maroon in the Document Colors section of the color palette (the same color as the main heading on the page).
11. Change the color of text in the cell to white.
12. Apply round corners to this cell, using the values of 10 for width and height. Specify the document maroon for both corners and borders.
13. Click in the Maine Laugh of the Year cell and apply a 4-pixel border to the top of the cell, using the document's maroon color.
14. Apply a white background to the entire table.

    ✓ *You might need to use the white color in the More Colors dialog box.*
15. Preview the page in the browser after saving all formatting files in the images folder.
16. Make the following adjustments to the table:
    - The all-white table is not visually interesting. Remove the background formatting from the entire table.
    - The photo caption would look better at the top of the cell. Change vertical alignment back to Top.
    - Select the table and then click the size tab at the top of the widest cell at the top of the table (the cell giving information about the reunion). Make this an Autostretch column.
    - Make any other adjustments to alignment and spacing you think necessary.
17. Preview the Web page in the browser. Your page should look similar to Illustration A.
18. Close the browser.
19. Close the Web site.
20. Exit FrontPage 2003.

Illustration A

Richard Family Reunion

[Home] [Maps] [Lodging] [Activities]

Bette Richard, nee Hall. Enlargement from a locket passed down in the Richard family.

Join us this summer for the twentieth annual Richard Family Reunion. Richards from all over the New England area as well as the rest of the country and around the world will gather in Rumford, Maine, the weekend following Independence Day.

The dates for this year's reunion are July 6 and 7. Plan to make your reservations early, using information on the Lodging page. Remember that you might be able to find emergency lodging with one of your Richard or Hall cousins, but those beds fill up fast!

If you have information for the Richard Record, a compendium of gossip and bragging by Richards round the world, please submit it using the form on the Activities page.

Maine Laugh of the Year:
A young in-law definitely not from Down East told one of her patients on the psych ward that she was married to a "Mainiac." (He laughed.)

On Your Own

1. Start FrontPage 2003.
2. Open the Web site you created in Exercise 14.
3. Change vertical and horizontal alignments as necessary to improve the appearance of the table.
4. Adjust cell padding if necessary to avoid a crowded look.
5. Change the background color of the entire table or individual cells in the table.
6. Add borders to cells if appropriate to emphasize them.
7. Apply special formatting such as a header or footer, shadow, or curves to one or more cells.
8. Preview the Web site in the browser.
9. Close the browser.
10. Close the Web site.
11. Exit FrontPage 2003.

Exercise 16

◆ Create Data Table ◆ Change Data Table Properties
◆ Modify Cell Properties ◆ Change Data Table or Cell Background

On the Job

Create a data table to organize information on a Web page. Data tables can be modified and formatted using the Table and Cell Properties dialog boxes to change table size and alignment, text alignment, border options, and backgrounds.

In this exercise, you will work with a table on Fast Finish Swimwear's new Web site. You will create a table, enter data, and change table and cell properties to format the new table.

Terms

cell spacing
Spacing between cells in a table.

Notes

Create Data Table

- Recall from Exercise 14 that FrontPage authors can create two types of tables: layout tables (to control page layout) and data tables (to organize information on a Web page).
- A data table is formed of a regular grid of columns and rows that intersect to create cells.
- Create a data table quickly using default settings by clicking the Insert Table button on the Standard toolbar and dragging across the number of columns and rows desired.
- FrontPage inserts a default table that spans the entire width of the page (see illustration below).

Default table in Web page

Online ordering is currently under construction, so to order any of the products on this site, call Fast Finish Swimwear at (614) 555-2100. Be sure to check the Sale Table below for off-season bargains and overstocks.

- To control table settings as the table is created, use the Table>Insert>Table command on the menu bar.
- In the Insert Table dialog box (see illustration at top of next page), choose:
  - Number of rows and columns for the table.
  - Alignment for table cells (the default is left alignment).
  - Width and height of the table in percent of page width or in pixels.
  - Cell padding and spacing (the amount of space between the cell border and text and between cells).
  - Border size and color.

  To eliminate borders, set Border size to 0.

  - Background color or picture.

  ✓ *Table properties can be changed after a table has been created using the Table Properties dialog box, which looks very similar to the Insert Table dialog box.*

Insert Table dialog box

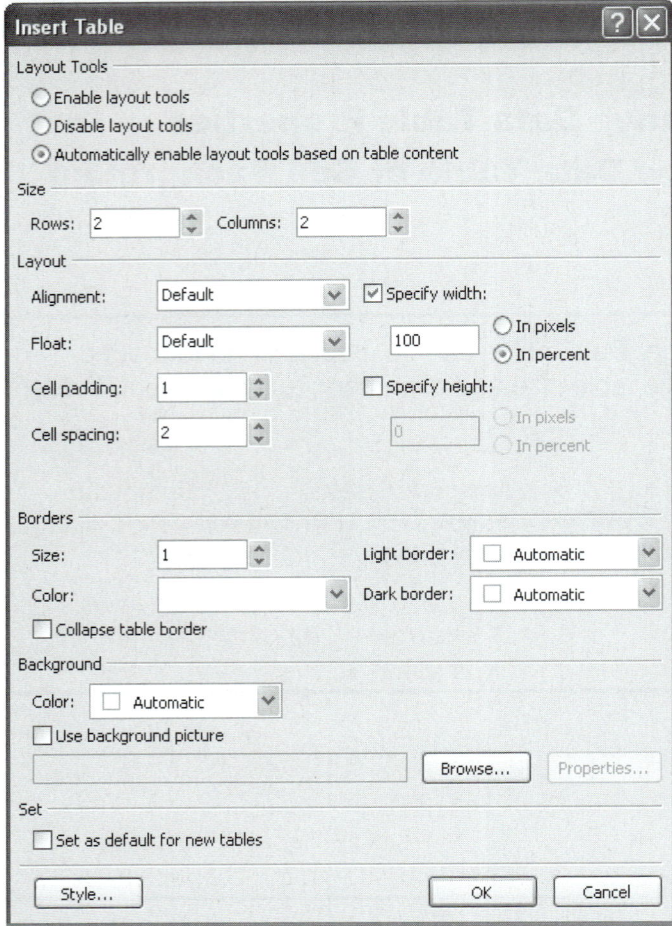

■ An insertion point displays in the first cell of the table. Enter text by typing in the cell and then using Tab or an arrow key to move to the next cell.

✓ *An author can format text and insert pictures in a data table's cells just as in a layout table.*

Resize Columns and Rows

■ By default, FrontPage makes all columns the same width and all rows the same height. As text is entered, columns resize to fit data more closely.

■ An author can also manually adjust column width and row height (see illustration below).

Drag a border to enlarge or reduce column width

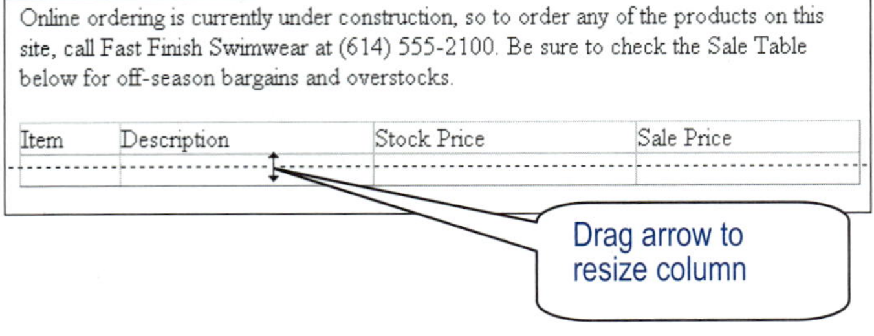

■ The easiest way to adjust column width or row height is to position the mouse pointer on a column or row border and, when the pointer becomes a two-headed arrow (see illustration at bottom of previous column), drag the border to enlarge or reduce the size of the column or row.

■ Row height or column width can also be specified in pixel measurements using the Specify width or Specify height boxes in the Cell Properties dialog box.

✓ *When the author changes a cell's width, all cells in the same column change to the new width. When the author changes a cell's height, all cells in the same row change to the new height.*

■ In a default table that runs the width of the page, as one column is resized, others also change size to maintain the default table width.

Select Cells

■ Some table modifications require columns, rows, or the entire table to be selected.

■ To select cells in columns or rows:

- Use the Table>Select command on the menu bar and choose Table, Column, Row, or Cell.
- Drag over the cells with the pointer.
- Position the pointer just above a column or to the left of a row and click with the solid black arrow pointer (see illustration below).

Select an entire column

> **Code Cues**
>
> Use the Quick Code Selector to help you select the portion of the table you want. The <table> tag selects the entire table. The <tr> tag selects the row in which the insertion point current appears. The <td> tag selects the current cell.

Change Data Table Properties

■ After a table has been created and text or other objects have been entered, it may be necessary to change table properties.

- An author can, for example, change the table's size, change its alignment on the page, set cell spacing or padding values, modify borders, or change the table background.
- To open the Table Properties dialog box:
  - Click in the cell to format and use the Table>Table Properties>Table command on the menu bar.
  - Right-click in the table and click Table Properties on the shortcut menu.

Change Data Table Size

- By default, a new table spans the entire page width; that is, its width is 100 percent of the page width.
- Not all tables need to be as wide as the page, however. Use the Table Properties dialog box to specify table width.
  - Enter a percent less than 100 to size the table relative to page width.
  - Select the Pixel option button and enter a pixel width to specify an absolute table width.
- A resized table might not look attractive when viewed in FrontPage, because FrontPage's Page view is not as wide as a browser's page.
- To verify sizing changes, preview the table in the browser.

  ✓ *Remember to save each change before previewing in the browser to see the latest version of the page.*

  ✓ *It is not necessary to click the Preview in Browser button each time the same page is viewed. Leave the browser window open and click the Refresh button to see the latest version of the page.*

Change Data Table Alignment

- A Web designer can align a table that is not as wide as the page horizontally at the left, center, or right of the Web page.
- Specify alignment in the Table Properties dialog box.
- It is also possible to apply a Float option of Left or Right to allow text to wrap around the table (see illustration below). For this option to work correctly, the table width must be set in pixels rather than in percent of page width.

Wrap text around a floating table

Silk-screened Bags	
24 - 48 bags	$27.95 ea
48 or more	$24.95 ea

Give your team a winning attitude by providing them with team accessories from Fast Finish Swimwear. We offer caps, bags, parkas and other warm-ups, sweatshirts and T-shirts, towels, and even team banners. All of these items can be customized with your team's name or logo, or with the names of individual swimmers.

✓ *For best appearance, do not wrap text around a table that is half the page width or wider. This feature is best used with smaller tables.*

Adjust Cell Spacing and Padding in Data Table

- By default, FrontPage adds no extra space between cells or between a cell's border and the text within the cell.
- In a data table, this default cell spacing can result in a crowded look and sometimes makes text in a table difficult to read.
- Adjust **cell spacing** and cell padding in the Table Properties dialog box. Increasing cell padding adds space between the cell border and the text.

Modify Data Table Borders

- Use the Table Properties dialog box to modify borders for an entire table.
- Insert a higher number in the Size spin box to make the table outline heavier.

  ✓ *Changing the Size number affects only the outline. Cell borders within the table remain at the default 1-pixel width.*
- Set the border size to 0 to remove all borders in the table.

  ✓ *The table borders are replaced by dotted outlines that do not display in the browser.*
- Use the Color drop-down palette to change the color of all borders in the table (the table's outline as well as the borders around cells).
- For a three-dimensional border effect, choose different colors from the Light border and Dark border palettes.
  - The top and left sides of the table outline use the light border color.
  - The bottom and right sides of the table outline use the dark border color.
  - Cell borders within the table use the light border color.
  - To give cell borders within the table a three-dimensional look, make sure the *Collapse table border* check box is deselected.

Modify Cell Properties

- As for a layout table, data tables allow the author to make a number of changes to cell properties.
- The Web author can:
  - Specify horizontal and vertical text alignment.
  - Specify cell width or height.
  - Select the Header cell check box to add emphasis (bold formatting) to a cell.
  - Select the No wrap check box to prevent text from wrapping in a cell.
  - Change cell border color.
  - Change cell background color or specify a background picture for the cell.
- Changes to data table cells are made in the Cell Properties dialog box (see illustration below).

Cell Properties dialog box

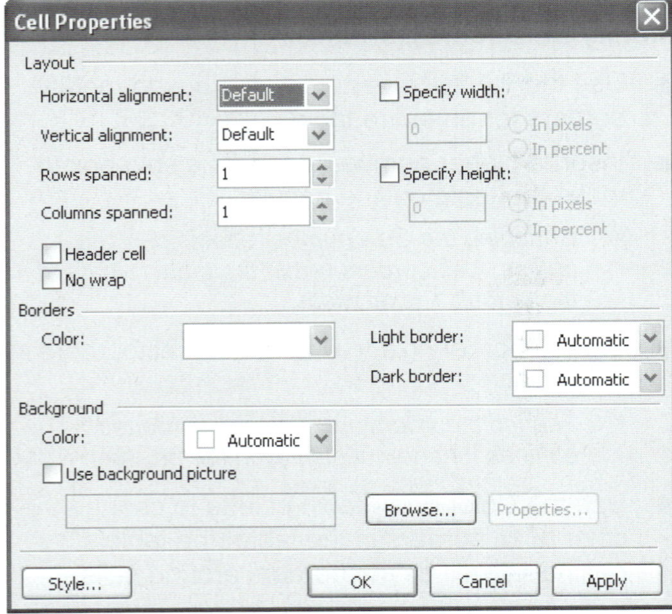

- To open the Cell Properties dialog box:
  - Click in the cell to format and use the Table>Table Properties>Cell command on the menu bar.
  - Right-click in the cell to format and click Cell Properties on the shortcut menu.

Change Text Alignment in Data Table

- Text in a table can be aligned not only horizontally (Left, Right, Center, and Justify) but also vertically (Top, Middle, Baseline, and Bottom).
- Use the Formatting toolbar alignment buttons to change horizontal alignment.
- Use the Cell Properties dialog box to change vertical alignment or horizontal alignment.

  ✓ *To save time, use the Cell Properties dialog box to make all cell alignment changes at once.*

Modify Data Table Cell Borders

- Use the Cell Properties dialog box to modify borders of individual cells.
- Use the Color palette to change the color of the current cell's borders.
- Individual cells can be formatted with light and dark borders to give a three-dimensional effect.
- Creating a border around a single cell of a table sometimes requires the author to apply borders to portions of other cells.
- The Format>Borders and Shading command on the menu bar can be used to apply a border to an individual cell, to an entire table, or to any text paragraph on a Web page.
- The Borders and Shading dialog box (see illustration below) allows the Web author to choose a border style, color, and width and apply the border to any side of the cell, table, or paragraph.

Borders and Shading dialog box

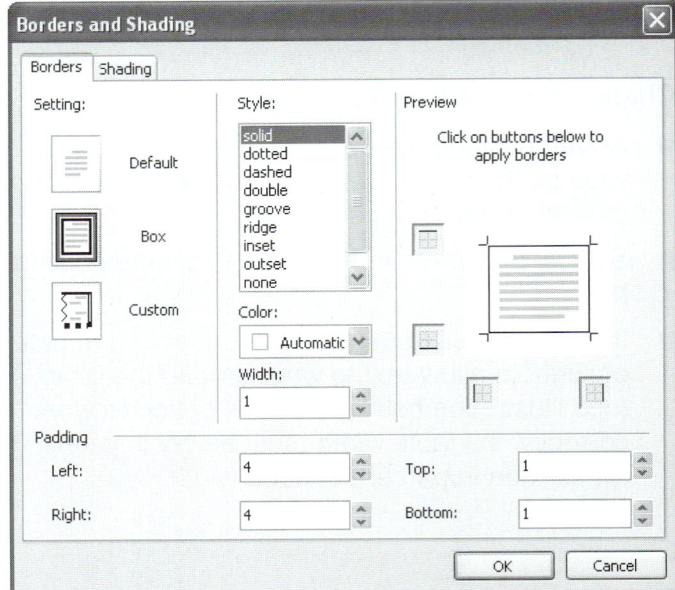

- If a table cell has more than one paragraph, all paragraphs must be selected before the border is applied, or it will apply only to the paragraph where the insertion point is located.
- To apply a border to a table using the Borders and Shading dialog box, first select the entire table. Only the table outline will be formatted with the border style.
  - ✓ *Select the table using the Table>Select>Table command on the menu bar.*
- A border applied using the Borders and Shading dialog box has sizing handles like a drawing object. Adjusting these handles may cause the text within the border object to shift position.

Change Data Table or Cell Background

- As for a layout table, a data table is by default transparent, allowing the page background to show through.
- Change background color for an entire data table or any cell using the Background Color palette in either the Table Properties or Cell Properties dialog box.
- Select a new background color for the table or cell using the Background Color drop-down palette.
  - ✓ *Click the More Colors option to see additional colors.*
- A data table can also have a picture background. Choose the *Use background picture* check box and browse to the location of the picture file to fill the table or cell.

Procedures

Create Data Table

1. Click  (**Insert Table** button) on Standard toolbar.
2. Drag across palette to select number of columns and rows.

OR

1. Click **Table** .... Alt+A
2. Click **Insert** I
3. Click **Table** .... T
4. Select number of rows and columns and choose other formats if desired.

Resize Columns and Rows

1. Position pointer on column or row border.
2. Use double-headed arrow to drag border to increase or reduce size of column or row.

OR

1. Click in any cell of column or row to resize.
2. Click **Table** .... Alt+A
3. Click **Table Properties** .... R
4. Click **Cell** .... E

   OR

   Right-click in cell and click **Cell Properties** .... R
5. Select **Specify width** or **Specify height** check box.
6. Type exact pixel or percent width or height for column or row.

Select Cells

1. Click in any cell of column or row.
2. Click **Table** .... Alt+A
3. Click **Select** C
4. Click **Table**, **Column**, **Row**, or **Cell**.

   OR

   Drag over cells to select.

   OR

   Position pointer just above column or just to left of row and click to select entire column or row.

Change Data Table Size

1. Click anywhere in table.
2. Click **Table** .... Alt+A
3. Click **Table Properties** .... R
4. Click **Table** .... T

   OR

   Right-click in table and click **Table Properties** .... B
5. Click **In pixels** or **In percent** option button.
6. Type desired width measurement.

Change Data Table Alignment

1. Click anywhere in table.
2. Click **Table** .... Alt+A
3. Click **Table Properties** .... R
4. Click **Table** .... T

   OR

   Right-click in table and click **Table Properties** .... B
5. Click **Alignment** down arrow and select **Left**, **Right**, or **Center** alignment.
6. If desired, click **Float** down arrow and select **Left** or **Right** to wrap text to right or left of table.

Adjust Cell Spacing and Padding in Data Table

1. Click **Table** .... Alt+A
2. Click **Table Properties** .... R

3. Click **Table** .... T

   OR

   Right-click in cell and click **Table Properties** .... B
4. Set new value in **Cell padding** spin box and/or **Cell spacing** spin box.

Modify Data Table Borders

1. Click **Table** .... Alt+A
2. Click **Table Properties** .... R
3. Click **Table** .... T

   OR

   Right-click in cell and click **Table Properties** .... B
4. Set new value in **Size** text box.
5. Click **Color** down arrow and select new border color.
6. To set three-dimensional looking borders:
   a. Click **Light border** down arrow and select color for top and left border.
   b. Click **Dark border** and select color for bottom and right border.

Change Text Alignment in Data Table

1. Click in cell to be modified.
2. Click horizontal alignment option on Formatting toolbar:
   - (**Align Left** .... Ctrl+L button).
   - (**Center** .... Ctrl+E button).
   - (**Align Right**..... Ctrl+R button).
   - (**Justify** button)

OR

1. Click **Table** .... Alt+A
2. Click **Table Properties** .... R
3. Click **Cell** .... E

   OR

   Right-click in cell and click **Cell Properties** .... R
4. Click **Horizontal alignment** down arrow and select alignment.
5. Click **Vertical alignment** down arrow and select alignment.

Modify Data Table Cell Borders

1. Click **Table** .... Alt+A
2. Click **Table Properties** .... R
3. Click **Cell** .... E

   OR

   Right-click in cell and click **Cell Properties** .... R
4. Click **Color** down arrow and select new border color.
5. To set three-dimensional looking borders:
   a. Click **Light border** down arrow and select color for top and left border.
   b. Click **Dark border** and select color for bottom and right border.

Use Borders and Shading

1. Click in cell or paragraph, or select multiple paragraphs or entire table.
2. Click **Format** .... Alt+O
3. Click **Borders and Shading** .... B
4. Select Style for border.
5. Select Color for border.
6. Select Width for border.
7. Click on preview paragraph to set each side of border.

Change Data Table or Cell Background

1. Click **Table** .... Alt+A
2. Click **Table Properties**........ R
3. Click **Table** or **Cell**.

   OR

   Right-click in cell and click **Table Properties** or **Cell Properties** on shortcut menu.
4. Click **Background Color** down arrow and select background color.

   ✓ *Click More Colors to open More Colors dialog box.*

   OR

   Click in **Use background picture** check box.
5. Click Browse... to locate picture file.

Exercise Directions

1. Start FrontPage 2003.
2. Open **Fastfinish**.
3. Open **index.htm**.
4. Scroll to the bottom of this page and click below the last paragraph.
5. Insert a new data table with four columns and two rows.
6. Insert the data shown in Illustration A below. After you complete the second row of table data, press Tab to create a new row and continue typing.
7. Specify a width for the table of 75 percent of page width.
8. Center the table in the Web page.
9. Save changes and preview the table to make sure each entry fits on a single line.
   ✓ *Leave the browser open.*
10. In FrontPage, center the column headings and center the values in the Stock Price and Sale Price columns.
11. Boldface the column heads.
12. Increase the height of the first row of the table to 25 pixels and change vertical alignment in these cells to Bottom.
13. Fill the entire table with a white background.
14. Change the table borders to Navy.
15. Change the background color of the first row of cells to Navy, and then change the text color to white.
16. Save changes and refresh the view in the browser. Your table should look similar to the one shown in Illustration B.
17. Change cell padding for the table to 2. Check the table in the browser again.
18. Close the browser.
19. Close the Web site.
20. Exit FrontPage 2003.

Illustration A

Item	Description	Stock Price	Sale Price
71986F	Speedo Prism	$51.00	$43.50
71987F	Speedo Zig Zag		
71988F	Speedo Splice		
20111F	Tyr Streamline	$53.00	$45.50
20114F	Tyr Tetris		
20115F	Tyr Mini Floral		
70585M	Speedo Shattered	$27.00	$21.50
70587M	Speedo Flames		
70588M	Speedo Seagulls		
72800	Sprint Goggles	$6.50	$4.00
72801	Relay Goggles		
72802	Optical Goggles	$18.50	$14.50
22332	Raceflex Goggles	$12.00	$8.50
22334	Splitstream Goggles		
22338	Velocity Goggles		

Illustration B

Item	Description	Stock Price	Sale Price
71986F	Speedo Prism	$51.00	$43.50
71987F	Speedo Zig Zag		
71988F	Speedo Splice		
20111F	Tyr Streamline	$53.00	$45.50
20114F	Tyr Tetris		
20115F	Tyr Mini Floral		
70585M	Speedo Shattered	$27.00	$21.50
70587M	Speedo Flames		
70588M	Speedo Seagulls		
72800	Sprint Goggles	$6.50	$4.00
72801	Relay Goggles		
72802	Optical Goggles	$18.50	$14.50
22332	Raceflex Goggles	$12.00	$8.50
22334	Splitstream Goggles		
22338	Velocity Goggles		

On Your Own

1. Start FrontPage 2003.
2. Open **Management**.
3. Open **index.htm**.
4. Insert a blank paragraph above the *Course Guidelines* heading and insert the first table shown in Illustration C, below.
5. Change cell padding for the table to 3.
6. Reduce the table to an appropriate width and center it. Make sure each entry fits on a single line.
7. Insert the second table in Illustration C below the *Grading Information* heading.
8. Resize the table using a pixel width and float the table at the right edge of the page.
9. Change text alignments as desired to improve the table's appearance.
10. Change border and background options as desired to make the tables stand out on the page.
11. Preview the Web page in the browser. Make any necessary changes to the formats.
12. Close the browser.
13. Close the Web site.
14. Exit FrontPage 2003.

Illustration C

Contact Information:	Fall	Winter
Office	Fellows 210	
Office hours	MWF 10:00-12:00	
Messages	555-3202	
E-mail	slevy@centralu.edu	

Tests	70 points (%)
Typed written assignments	15
Participation	10
Presentation	7

Exercise 17

◆ Use Fill Commands ◆ Insert Table Caption
◆ Use AutoFit to Contents ◆ Apply Table AutoFormat

On the Job

A Web author can use FrontPage's Fill commands to quickly enter identical data in table cells, as in a spreadsheet. The author can add a table caption to a table and fit the table columns automatically to the contents. Apply a number of formats to the table automatically using the AutoFormat command.

In this exercise, you continue to work with a table on Fast Finish Swimwear's Web site. You will use the Fill command to enter data, add a caption, try AutoFitting the table to its contents, and finally format the table with an AutoFormat.

Terms

AutoFormat
FrontPage feature that automatically formats a table with fonts, font styles, alignments, colors, and border and shading options.

caption
A descriptive word or phrase that identifies the content of a table or figure.

Notes

Use Fill Commands

- Tables that store related information often include similar or identical data in a number of cells.
- To save time in entering identical data, use FrontPage's Fill commands.
- The Fill command copies data from one cell to other empty cells. Data can be filled down or to the right.
- To use the Fill commands, select the data to be used as fill as well as the empty cells to fill, and then click Table>Fill>Down or Table>Fill>Right.
- The selected data immediately fills the selected empty cells (see illustration at the top of the next column).

Select the data to use as fill and the empty cells

	Stock Price	Sale Price
	$51.00	$43.50

✓ *More than one column or row of data can be filled at one time, as shown in the illustration above.*

Insert Table Caption

- A **caption** is a word or phrase that identifies the content of a table or figure.
- Use the Table>Insert>Caption command on the menu bar to create a table caption.

- Issuing this command centers the insertion point above the table so the user can type the caption.
- A caption can be formatted like any other text by changing its style, font, font style and size, color, and alignment.
- A caption's properties are limited to placement at the top or bottom of the table (see illustration below).

Caption Properties dialog box

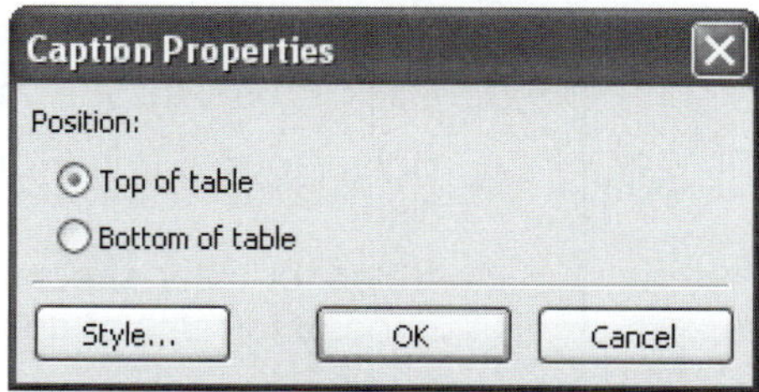

Use AutoFit to Contents

- By default, FrontPage data tables allow a generous amount of white space to make table data easier to read.
- In some circumstances, an author may want to eliminate any unnecessary white space.
- Use the Table>AutoFit to Contents command on the menu bar to fit columns to the width of the longest entry in each column.
- The illustration below shows part of a table that has been AutoFit to its contents. Note that each column is only as wide as the longest entry in the column.

Table that has been AutoFit

Item	Description	Stock Price	Sale Price
71986F	Speedo Prism	$51.00	$43.50
71987F	Speedo Zig Zag		
71988F	Speedo Splice		
20111F	Tyr Streamline	$53.00	$45.50
20114F	Tyr Tetris		
20115F	Tyr Mini Floral		
70585M	Speedo Shattered	$27.00	$21.50
70587M	Speedo Flames		
70588M	Speedo Seagulls		

- When using AutoFit to Contents, it is advisable for readability to provide some cell spacing or padding.

Apply Table AutoFormat

- Other Microsoft Office applications such as Word and Excel have long featured **AutoFormats**, formatting schemes that apply fonts, alignments, font styles, and fill and border options to tables.
- FrontPage 2003 also offers AutoFormats to format Web tables.
- Apply an AutoFormat by clicking the Table>Table AutoFormat command on the menu bar. Choose one of over 30 AutoFormat styles from the Table AutoFormat dialog box (see illustration below).

Table AutoFormat dialog box

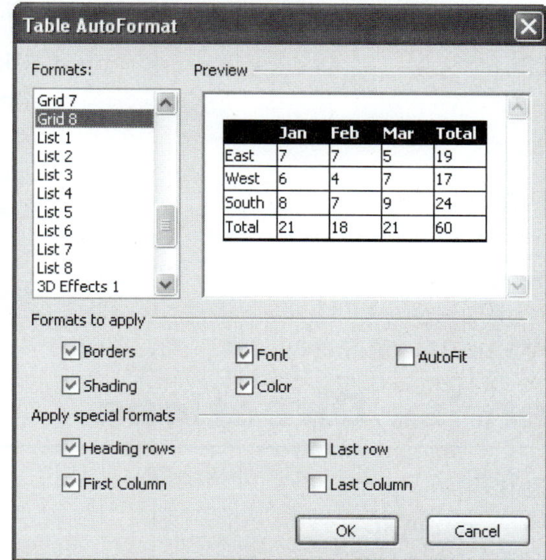

- Using an AutoFormat can save a considerable amount of formatting time and give a table a professional look.
- The Web designer can customize the AutoFormat to match the data in a specific table by selecting or clearing check boxes in the Table AutoFormat dialog box:
  - Choose whether to apply the AutoFormat's borders, shading, fonts, or colors.
  - Select the AutoFit check box to fit column width to each column's widest entry.
  - Choose areas of the table to apply special emphasis such as bold or bold italic. For example, special formatting can be applied to headings or to the last row of a table that contains totals.
- Formats applied by an AutoFormat can be further modified if desired.

Procedures

Use Fill Commands

1. Select data to use as fill and cells to fill with that data.
2. Click **Table** .... Alt + A
3. Click **Fill** L
4. Click **Down** .... D

   OR

   Click **Right** .... R

   ✓ *More than one column or row can be filled at the same time.*

Insert Table Caption

1. Click anywhere in table.
2. Click **Table** .... Alt + A
3. Click **Insert** I
4. Click **Caption** .... A
5. Begin typing caption at insertion point above table.
6. Change placement of caption:
   a. Click in caption.
   b. Click **Table** .... Alt + A
   c. Click **Table Properties** ... R
   d. Click **Caption** .... O

      OR

      Right-click in caption and click

      Caption Properties .... O
   e. Select **Top of table** or **Bottom of table**.

Use AutoFit to Contents

1. Click anywhere in table.
2. Click **Table** .... Alt + A
3. Click **AutoFit to Contents** .. A

Apply Table AutoFormat

1. Click anywhere in table.
2. Click **Table** .... Alt + A
3. Click **Table AutoFormat** ..... F
4. Select format from **Formats** list.
5. Select or clear check boxes to choose formats or special emphasis.

Exercise Directions

1. Start FrontPage 2003.
2. Open **Fastfinish**.
3. Open **index.htm**.
4. Scroll to display the table on this Web page if necessary.
5. The Stock Price and Sale Price columns contain a number of gaps. Use the value in the cell above each group of empty cells to fill the empty cells.

   ✓ *To save time, select values in both the Stock Price and Sale Price columns and fill down both columns at once.*
6. Add a caption to the top of the table that reads **Sale Table**.
7. Apply the Heading 3 style to the caption.
8. AutoFit the contents of the table and preview the result in the browser.

   ✓ *Leave the browser open.*
9. AutoFit doesn't seem appropriate for this table. Return to FrontPage and undo the AutoFit.
10. Apply the **Subtle 1** AutoFormat to the table, deselecting the first column emphasis.
11. Select text in the first row of the table and change the font color back to black.
12. Save changes and refresh the view in the browser. Your table should look similar to the one shown in Illustration A.
13. Close the browser.
14. Close the Web site.
15. Exit FrontPage 2003.

Illustration A

Sale Table

Item	Description	Stock Price	Sale Price
71986F	Speedo Prism	$51.00	$43.50
71987F	Speedo Zig Zag	$51.00	$43.50
71988F	Speedo Splice	$51.00	$43.50
20111F	Tyr Streamline	$53.00	$45.50
20114F	Tyr Tetris	$53.00	$45.50
20115F	Tyr Mini Floral	$53.00	$45.50
70585M	Speedo Shattered	$27.00	$21.50
70587M	Speedo Flames	$27.00	$21.50
70588M	Speedo Seagulls	$27.00	$21.50
72800	Sprint Goggles	$6.50	$4.00
72801	Relay Goggles	$6.50	$4.00
72802	Optical Goggles	$18.50	$14.50
22332	Raceflex Goggles	$12.00	$8.50
22334	Splitstream Goggles	$12.00	$8.50
22338	Velocity Goggles	$12.00	$8.50

On Your Own

1. Start FrontPage 2003.
2. Open **Management**.
3. Open **index.htm**.
4. Display the first table on the Web page, if necessary.
5. Use the Fill Right command to fill blank cells in the table using data to the left of the blank cells.
   - ✓ *To save time, select all contact info in the Fall column and fill right.*
6. AutoFit this table to its contents.
7. Display the second table on the page.
8. Insert an appropriate caption for the floating table.
9. Preview the Web page in the browser.
10. Close the browser.
11. Close the Web site.
12. Exit FrontPage 2003.

Exercise 18

◆ Change Table Structure ◆ Split Table
◆ Split Cells ◆ Merge Cells ◆ Create Nested Table

On the Job

Table structure can be changed at any time, even after text has been entered. New columns and rows can be inserted in the table, and existing columns and rows can be deleted. Long tables that contain groups of related information can be split into separate tables. Individual cells or groups of cells can be split to divide them into additional columns or rows or merged to create cells that span rows or columns. A new table can be inserted in a cell of an existing table to create a nested table.

In this exercise, you will continue working with the tables in the Fast Finish Swimwear Web site. You will insert and delete columns and rows, split a long table into separate tables, split and merge cells, and finally create nested tables in an existing table.

Terms

merge
In a table, combine two or more cells to create one larger cell.

nested table
A table created within one cell of an existing table.

Notes

Change Table Structure

- Even after planning carefully, a Web designer might need to restructure a table after its creation.
- Changing table structure includes inserting new columns and rows to accommodate new information and deleting existing columns and rows when they are no longer necessary.
- FrontPage's Tables toolbar supplies a number of tools that can be used to work with tables (see illustration at the top of the next page).

✓ *Display the Tables toolbar by clicking View>Toolbars>Tables or by right-clicking any toolbar and selecting Tables.*

- Use the Tables toolbar's tools to draw a table structure, insert a row or column, delete cells, merge or split cells, apply vertical alignment options to cell text, distribute rows or columns evenly, add a color fill, apply an AutoFormat, or fill down or right.

✓ *These features are also available on the Table menu, but they can be accessed more conveniently from the Tables toolbar.*

Tables toolbar

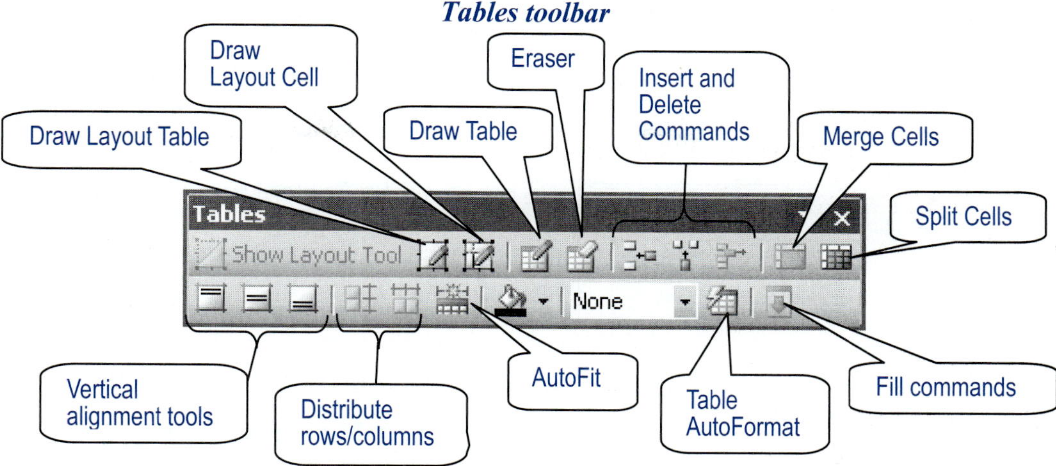

Insert Columns and Rows

- Use the Insert Rows or Insert Columns button on the Tables toolbar to quickly insert a row or column in a table.
- The Insert Rows button inserts a new row above the row that contains the insertion point.
- The Insert Columns button inserts a new column to the left of the column that contains the insertion point.
- Use the Table>Insert>Rows or Columns command on the menu bar for more control over where new rows and columns are inserted.
- In the Insert Rows or Columns dialog box (see illustration below), select the Rows or Columns option button and then specify:
  - How many new rows or columns to insert.
  - Whether a new row will be inserted above or below the current row.
  - Whether a new column will be inserted to the left or right of the current column.

Specify placement of new row or column

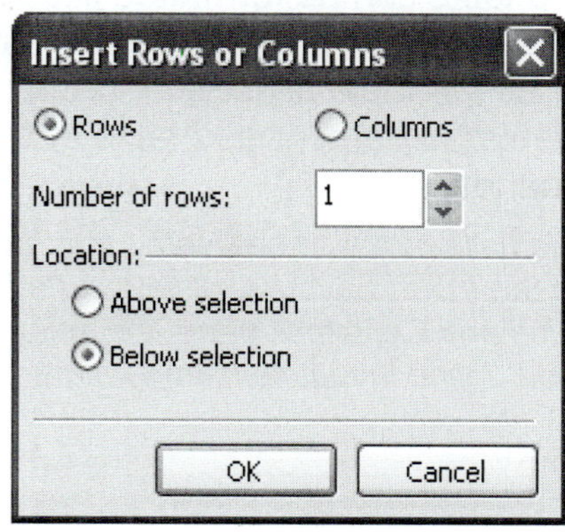

✓ *Location options in the Insert Rows or Columns dialog box change depending on whether Rows or Columns is selected.*

Delete Columns and Rows

- Before a column or row can be deleted, it must be selected.

  ✓ *Review how to select a row or column in Exercise 16.*
- With a column or row selected, click the Delete Cells button on the Tables toolbar or use the Table>Delete Cells command on the menu bar.
- When a row or column is deleted, other rows and columns shift up or to the left to fill the space.
- The Delete Cells button or command must be used to change table structure. Using the Delete key will merely remove text from selected cells.

Split Table

- FrontPage offers a restructuring command called Split Table that allows the Web author to separate one large table into several smaller tables (see illustration on the following page).
- A table can be split only horizontally. The split occurs above the row that contains the insertion point.
- The splitting process inserts a blank paragraph between split tables so it is easy to add a caption or explanatory text.

Split a table into two or more smaller tables

Fall	Fitness	Easy Aerobics
Fall	Fitness	Introductory Weights
Fall	Fine Arts	Music Appreciation
Fall	Crafts	Beginning Pottery
Fall	Fitnes	
Winter	Fitnes	
Winter	Fine A	
Winter	Fine A	
Winter	Crafts	
Winter	Fitnes	

Fall	Fitness	Easy Aerobics
Fall	Fitness	Introductory Weights
Fall	Fine Arts	Music Appreciation
Fall	Crafts	Beginning Pottery
Fall	Fitness	Intermediate Yoga

Winter	Fitness	Body Sculpting
Winter	Fine Arts	Great Masters
Winter	Fine Arts	Drama
Winter	Crafts	Intermediate Basketry
Winter	Fitness	Intermediate Weights

Split Cells

- A Web designer can split cells in a table to form two or more rows or columns within the cell.
- To split a cell, click in the cell and use:
  - The Split Cells button on the Tables toolbar.
  - The Table>Split Cells command on the menu bar.
- In the Split Cells dialog box (see illustration below), choose whether to split the cell into rows or columns and specify the number of rows or columns to create.

Split Cells dialog box

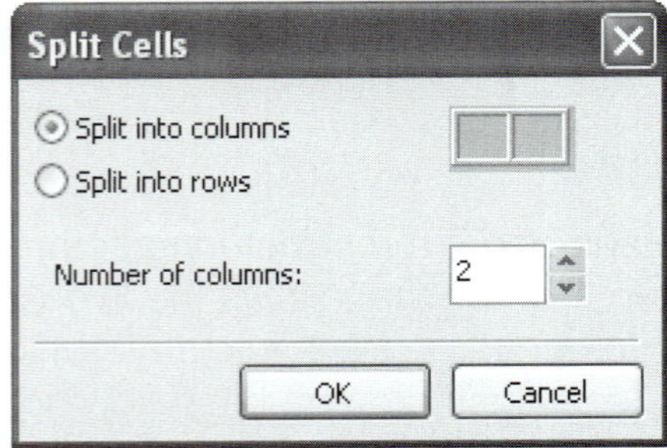

Merge Cells

- Cells in a table may be **merged** to create a single larger cell to hold text or a picture (see illustration below).

Four columns merged to create one cell

Dolfin Bolt Solid	$25.00/$15.00	$20.00/$12.00	Red, Green, Royal, Maroon, Navy
Nike Solid	$44.00/$23.00	$35.20/$18.40	Royal, Navy, Black

- Cells can be merged either horizontally or vertically.
- To merge cells, select the cells and use
  - The Merge Cells button on the Tables toolbar.
  - The Table>Merge Cells command on the menu bar.
- By default, text entered in a merged cell has left alignment and is centered vertically in the cell. Both vertical and horizontal alignment can be changed in the Cell Properties dialog box.

Create Nested Table

- Another way to pack more information into a table is to create a **nested table**. A nested table is a table created within a cell of an existing table (see illustration below).

Table nested within table cell

<table><tr><td>Fall</td><td>Fitness</td><td>Easy Aerobics<table><tr><td>Monday</td><td>7:00 - 8:00</td></tr><tr><td>Thursday</td><td>7:30 - 8:30</td></tr></table></td></tr></table>

- Create a nested table the same way any other table is created. With the insertion point in a table cell:
  - Click the Insert Table toolbar button and drag to select rows and columns.
  - Click the Table>Insert>Table command on the menu bar and specify number of rows and columns.
- The new table structure appears within the table cell, complete with table and cell borders.
- Enter text in a nested table just as in any other table.
- A nested table can be formatted like any other table: resize columns or rows, merge cells, change text or table alignment, remove or adjust table borders, or add table or cell backgrounds.

✓ *Table cells can also be nested in a layout table. Use the Insert Layout Cell link in the Layout Tables and Cells task pane and select the Inline option. Inline layout cells have a green border.*

Procedures

Insert Columns or Rows

1. Click **Table** .... Alt + A
2. Click **Insert** I
3. Click **Rows or Columns** ..... N
4. Click **Rows** or **Columns** option button.
5. Specify number of rows or columns to insert.
6. Select **Above selection** or **Below selection** for rows.

   OR

   Select **Left of selection** or **Right of selection** for columns.

OR

1. Click (**Insert Rows** button) on Tables toolbar to insert a row above the row that contains the insertion point.
2. Click (**Insert Columns** button) on Tables toolbar to insert a column to the left of the column that contains the insertion point.

Delete Columns or Rows

1. Select row or column to delete:
   a. Position insertion point just above the column or just to the left of the row until the solid black selection arrow appears.
   b. Click to select column or row.
2. Click **Table** .... Alt + A
3. Click **Delete Columns/Rows** .... D

   OR

   Click (**Delete Cells** button) on Tables toolbar.

Split Table

1. Click in table row that will be the first row in the new table.
2. Click **Table** .... Alt + A
3. Click **Split Table** .... T

Split Cells

1. Click in cell to split.
2. Click **Table** .... Alt + A
3. Click **Split Cells** .... P

   OR

   Click (**Split Cells** button) on Tables toolbar.

Merge Cells

1. Select cells to merge.
2. Click **Table** .... Alt + A
3. Click **Merge Cells** .... M

   OR

   Click (**Merge Cells** button) on Tables toolbar.

Create Nested Table

1. Click in cell where nested table is to be inserted.
2. Click **Table** .... Alt + A
3. Click **Insert** I
4. Click **Table** .... T
5. Select number of rows and columns and choose other formats if desired.

OR

1. Click (**Insert Table** button) on Standard toolbar.
2. Drag across palette to select number of columns and rows.

Exercise Directions

1. Start FrontPage 2003.
2. Open **Fastfinish**.
3. Open **teams.htm**.
4. Fast Finish no longer carries Nike suits. Delete the last row of the table on this page.
5. Insert a new row below the Speedo Aquablade Female row.
6. In the new row, type **Speedo Aquablade Male**.
7. Delete the *Embroidery* column.
8. Insert a new column in the same location and name it **Colors**. Boldface the column heading.
9. Insert the color information shown in Illustration A for the swimsuits. (Be sure to use Fill when possible to save time.)
10. After entering information in the last Colors cell, press Tab to create a new row at the bottom of the table.
11. Merge cells in this row to create one wide cell.
12. In the merged cell, type **Embroidery $4.50.** Center and boldface the entry.

13. Split the *Price* cell into two rows.
14. In the new split row below *Price*, type **Male/Female** and boldface the entry.
15. Split the *Price 12+* cell into two rows and type **Male/Female** in the new split row. Boldface the entry.
16. In the blank *Price* cell for the Speedo Aquablade Female suit, create a nested table with two rows and two columns. (See Illustration B for the finished version of this table.)
17. Insert the following information in the nested table:

    High neck **$89.00**

    Reg cut **$81.00**

18. Create an identical nested table in the blank *Price 12+* cell.

    ✓ *To save time, select the nested table (Table>Select>Table), copy the table, and paste it in the blank cell.*

19. Insert the following *Price 12+* information for the Female Aquablade:

    High neck **$71.20**

    Reg cut **$64.80**

20. Create nested tables for the Male Aquablade suits using the following information:

    Price

    Leg suit $89.00

    Racer $36.00

    Price 12+

    Leg suit $71.20

    Racer $28.80

21. Format the nested tables as follows:
    - Remove the table borders for all nested tables.
    - Boldface the suit descriptions.
    - Center the prices.
    - Apply a light color background to the suit description cells.
22. Adjust the table width by dragging column borders and/or resizing the table width to display data attractively with a minimum of run-over lines.
23. Split the table to create separate tables for Tyr suits and Dolfin suits.
24. Preview the Web page in the browser.
25. Close the browser.
26. Close the Web site.
27. Exit FrontPage 2003.

Illustration A

Description	Price	Price/12+	Colors
Speedo Aquablade Female			Royal, Navy, Black
Speedo Aquablade Male			Royal, Navy, Black
Speedo Team Solid	$46.00/$23.50	$36.80/$18.80	Sapphire, Navy, Black
Speedo Solid	$46.00/$24.00	$36.80/$19.20	Sapphire, Navy, Black
Speedo Aqua Drop	$49.00/$26.00	$39.20/$20.80	Green, Blue, Red, Purple
Speedo Seagulls	$57.00/$29.00	$45.60/$23.20	Green, Blue, Red, Purple
Tyr Swirl	$53.00/$27.00	$42.40/$21.60	Green, Blue, Burgundy, Purple
Tyr Pulsar	$46.00/$23.50	$36.80/$18.80	Green, Royal, Burgundy, Black
Tyr Varsity Splice	$46.00/$25.00	$36.80/$20.00	Green, Royal, Navy, Black
Tyr Team Solid	$39.00/$22.00	$31.20/$17.60	Green, Royal, Burgundy, Black
Tyr Powerflow	$60.00/$31.00	$48.00/$24.80	Green, Royal, Navy, Black
Dolfin Team Solid	$33.00/$17.50	$26.40/$14.00	Red, Green, Royal, Maroon, Navy
Dolfin Bolt Solid	$25.00/$15.00	$20.00/$12.00	Royal, Navy, Black

Illustration B

Description	Price		Price 12+		Colors
	Male/Female		Male/Female		
Speedo Aquablade Female	**High neck** **Reg cut**	$89.00 $81.00	**High neck** **Reg cut**	$71.20 $64.80	Royal, Navy, Black
Speedo Aquablade Male	**Leg suit** **Racer**	$89.00 $36.00	**Leg suit** **Racer**	$71.20 $28.80	Royal, Navy, Black
Speedo Team Solid	$46.00/$23.50		$36.80/$18.80		Sapphire, Navy, Black
Speedo Solid	$46.00/$24.00		$36.80/$19.20		Sapphire, Navy, Black
Speedo Aqua Drop	$49.00/$26.00		$39.20/$20.80		Green, Blue, Red, Purple
Speedo Seagulls	$57.00/$29.00		$45.60/$23.20		Green, Blue, Red, Purple

On Your Own

1. Start FrontPage 2003.
2. Open **Management**.
3. Open **index.htm**.
4. Insert a new column to the right of the *Winter* column and give it the heading **Spring**. Boldface the heading.
5. Dr. Levy's office will be in **Burrows 125** for the Spring quarter. Fill all other information right, except for the Messages number.
6. Split the *Fall*, *Winter*, and *Spring* cells into two rows.
7. Move *Fall*, *Winter*, and *Spring* down into the bottom portion of the split cells and merge the three top split cells into one cell.
8. In the merged cell, type **2006 Academic Year**. Center and boldface the text.
9. Delete the Messages number in the *Fall* column. Create a nested table in the cell that contains the following information:

   Phone **555-3202**

   V-mail **555-4659**
10. Insert the same nested table for Winter and Spring, but change the Phone number for Spring to 555-1809.
11. Format the nested tables to make information attractive and easy to read.
12. Add a row to the bottom of the second table on the page. Insert the following information:

    Total **102**
13. Open **schedule.htm**.
14. Delete the column that contains the abbreviated days of the week.
15. Apply the same table formats you used for the other tables, and then split the table to separate it by months.
16. Preview the Web site in the browser.
17. Close the browser.
18. Close the Web site.
19. Exit FrontPage 2003.

Exercise 19

◆ **Critical Thinking** ◆ **Challenge**

In this exercise, you will work on the new Web site of the East Fork Riding Center. You will use a table to lay out the home page and format other tables on the site using alignments, border options, backgrounds, and AutoFormats. You will insert several pictures, insert and delete columns and rows, merge and split cells, and split a table.

Exercise Directions

1. Start FrontPage 2003.
2. Open **Eastfork**.
3. Open **index.htm**.
4. Create a layout table to organize this page's layout. Use the information in **riding.doc** in the Data folder for the page's text.
5. Insert one or more clip art pictures or photos of horses or riders on the page as illustration.
   - ✓ *Adjust layout cells as desired to position text and pictures attractively. Adjust horizontal and vertical text alignments as desired.*
6. Apply shadows, corners, headers, backgrounds, and/or borders as desired to improve the page's appearance.
7. In the last paragraph table cell, nest the data table shown in Illustration A.
8. Modify borders and table and cell backgrounds for the nested table as desired to emphasize the information.
9. Open **lessons.htm**.
10. Below the text, create the data table shown in Illustration B. Use Fill commands to speed data entry.
11. Split the column below the *Payment Plan* heading into two columns. (Do not split the *Payment Plan* cell.)
12. In the new column, enter the following payments: For Monday, $82.50; for Tuesday through Friday, $99.00; for Saturday, $82.50; and for Sunday, $66.00.
    - ✓ *Use Fill Right to enter the $99.00 values.*
13. Adjust the table width and center the table in the page.
14. Apply an AutoFormat to the table and adjust formats as necessary to present data clearly.
15. Open **calendar.htm**.
16. Delete the first column of the table.
17. Delete the row that contains information for an event that takes place on October 28.
18. Insert a row with the following information:

    April 15 **Vet visit - no classes**
19. Apply the same AutoFormat you used for the previous table. Adjust formats as necessary to present data attractively.
20. Split the table so that each new table begins with the first day of a semester (Winter, Spring, Summer, and Fall).
21. Create a caption for each table to indicate which semester's events appear in the table.
22. Adjust each semester table width to avoid extra space in each column and center the table in the page.
23. Save all changes. Preview the Web in the browser. Check all links.
24. Close the browser.
25. Close the Web site.
26. Exit FrontPage 2003.

Illustration A

Appropriate Footwear	
English	Hunt boot, paddock shoe
Western	Roper, traditional cowboy boot
Either	Riding "gym" shoe with heel and light tread
Overall	Small heel to prevent foot slipping through stirrup; heavy enough to provide protection if stepped on

Illustration B

Riding Day	Total Payment	Payment Plan
Monday	$181.50	$99.00
Tuesday	$198.00	$99.00
Wednesday	$198.00	$99.00
Thursday	$198.00	$99.00
Friday	$198.00	$99.00
Saturday	$165.00	$82.50
Sunday	$148.50	$82.50

Challenge Exercise

1. Break into groups of three or four based on a core course that all of you have in common (English, math, history, science, etc.).
2. As a group, you will create a Web site that is related to a topic that you have discussed in that course, making sure to use tables in the layout of your site.
   - ✓ *For example, you could do further research into the author of a book you are reading in an English course, and your Web site could include a brief biography of the author and links to further information about the author and his or her work. In history, if you are studying a certain event in one country, find out what is happening in other parts of the world at the same time. Or, if you are studying political events, find out what was happening socially, culturally, scientifically, or economically during that same time period.*
   - ✓ *As always, cite any sources that you use.*
3. Before you begin, compile a list of tasks that have to be done to create the Web site. Decide what role(s) each person will play (i.e., research, writing up information, leading the group, designing the Web site, entering information) and an approximate timeline for how long each task should take.
4. Exchange e-mail addresses so you can exchange information, discuss progress, and revise your timeline as necessary.
   - ✓ *If you exchange any files via e-mail, remember to scan the files with antivirus software before opening them.*
5. When the Web site is completed, use the list you created on page 10 to evaluate your site, both in appearance and function. Revise the Web as necessary.
6. Check your work against the list of tasks you created in step 3. Was each task met? Did the task take more or less work and/or time than anticipated?

LESSON 4

Frames, Layers, and Special Effects

Exercise 20

◆ About Frames Pages ◆ Create Frames Page
◆ Set Initial Pages ◆ Create New Web Page (Frames)
◆ Link within Frames Page

On the Job

A frames page is used to organize several different Web pages within a single page. Use a FrontPage template to create a frames page and then specify what pages will open in each frame of the frames page. New Web pages can also be created from within a frames page. Links can be used to control the display of pages in a frames page.

In this exercise, you will work on your friend Clair's Web site. You will create a frames page to display information about Clair's new personal coaching business, set initial pages to open in each frame, and create a new page for a particular frame. Finally, you will set up the hyperlinks that link pages within the frames page.

Terms

frames page (frameset)
A single Web page that provides a structure for displaying several Web pages.

initial page
The page that will open in a frame when the *frames page* opens in a browser.

target frame
The frame in a *frames page* in which a linked page will open.

Notes

About Frames Pages

- A **frames page** (also called a **frameset**) is a Web page divided into two or more frames, each of which contains a separate Web page.
- A common frames page configuration is to have the page title in a banner frame, hyperlinks in a contents frame, and a main frame that displays pages when links are clicked in the contents frame.
- Frames pages are useful because some frames can remain on the screen at all times (such as the page title and contents links) while the content of the main frame changes.
- The frames page itself contains no text or other content. A frames page is simply a container for the frames that display specific pages.
- Not all browsers support frames pages. While recent browser versions will display frames correctly, earlier versions might not.
  - ✓ *Some Web sites provide both frame and nonframe versions of pages to support a wide variety of browsers.*
  - ✓ *Many Web designers have moved away from frames pages in favor of using tables and other formatting options to lay out pages, but there are still many sites on the Web that use frames pages successfully.*

Create Frames Page

- Create a frames page using one of FrontPage's frames page templates.
- Click the More page templates link in the New task pane to display the Page Templates dialog box.
- The Frames Pages tab in the Page Templates dialog box displays available frames page templates.
- Click a template to see a preview of the frame layout for that frames page.
- A new frames page should be saved before pages are inserted in the frames. Frames pages have names and page titles just like other Web pages.
- The Save As dialog box for a frames page shows a heavy border page outline that signifies the frames page itself (not one of its frames) is being saved (see illustration below).

Save As dialog box for a frames page

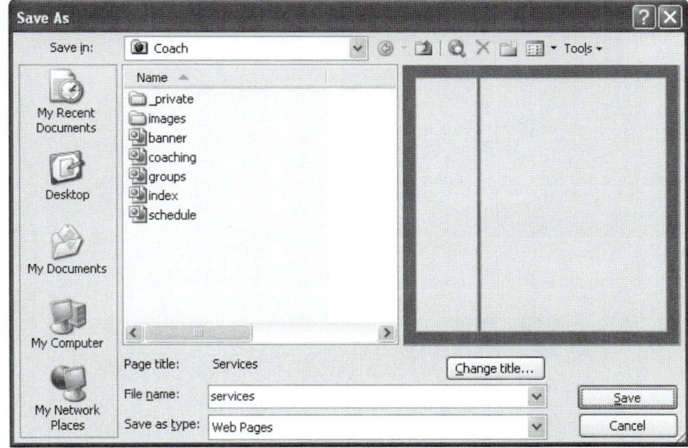

- A new button, No Frames, appears at the bottom of the frames page in Page view. Click the No Frames button to see the page that will display if a browser that does not support frames tries to open the page.
  ✓ *FrontPage creates this page automatically with every frames page. This message can be customized if desired and a link provided to a nonframes page.*
- As when working with a full-page table, it can be helpful when working with a frames page to hide the Folder List in order to provide more room for the frames to display.

Set Initial Pages

- A new frames page displays two buttons in each frame, giving the user options to set the initial page or create a new page in the frame (see illustration below).

New frames page with no content

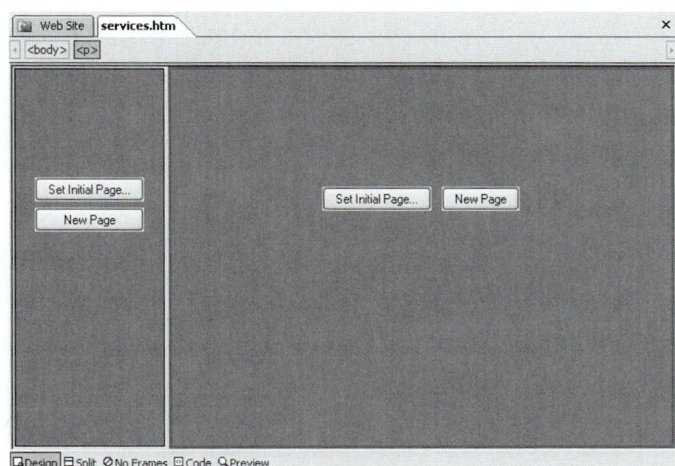

- A frame's **initial page** is the page that opens in the frame when the frames page itself is opened in a browser.
- Click the Set Initial Page button in a frame to open the Insert Hyperlink dialog box.
  ✓ *Setting an initial page is equivalent to creating a link between the frame and the initial page.*
- The initial page can be a page in the current Web site or a page from another location. Use the Insert Hyperlink dialog box to select or locate the initial page.
- As soon as the initial page is selected in the Insert Hyperlink dialog box, the page displays in the frame.
- Most frames will display a scrollbar if the page's content exceeds the FrontPage or the browser window size.
  ✓ *Banner frames by default do not display scrollbars.*

Create New Web Page (Frames)

- The New Page button in a frame gives the user the option of creating a new Web page from within the frame.
- Clicking the New Page button in a frame opens a new page in that frame and surrounds the frame with a dark blue outline to indicate the frame is active.
  ✓ *Text or other formatting can be entered or applied only in the active frame.*

- Enter text in the new page just as on any Web page.
- Save a page created within a frame using the File>Save or Save As command or the Save toolbar button.
- A page created within a frame can also be saved using the Frames>Save Page or Save Page As commands on the menu bar.
- When a page created within a frame is saved, the Save As dialog box displays a representation of the frame being saved, as shown below.

Saving a frame within a frames page

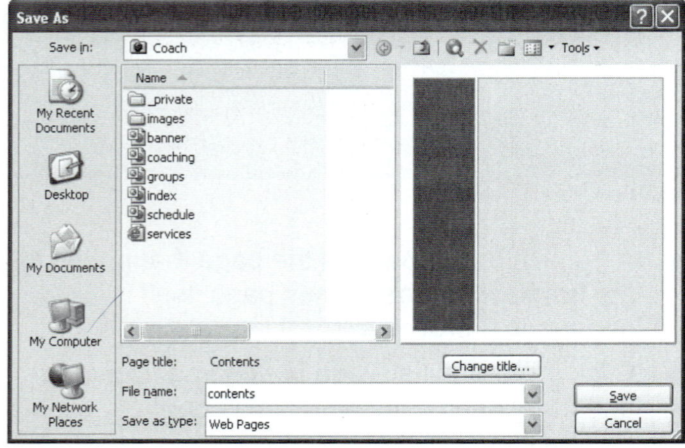

✓ *Compare the illustration above (saving a frame) with the illustration on page 139 (saving a frames page).*

- A page created within a frame is stored in the Web site just like any other page created in Page view.
- When working with a page displayed in a relatively small frame, the user may be distracted by many runover lines.
- To make it easier to develop the page's content, use the Frames>Open Page in New Window command on the menu bar to display the page in its own window.

  ✓ *Close the new window to return to the frames page.*

Link within Frames Page

- As mentioned at the beginning of this exercise, a common frames page layout supplies hyperlinks in one frame that activate pages in another frame.
- Hyperlinks from one frame to another frame must specify which frame the target page will open in. This frame is called the **target frame**.
- To specify the target frame when setting up the link, click the Insert Hyperlink button on the Standard toolbar, and then click Target Frame button in the Insert Hyperlink dialog box.
- The Target Frame dialog box (see below) supplies a preview of the frames page. Select the target frame by clicking a frame on the preview.

Select the target frame for a linked page

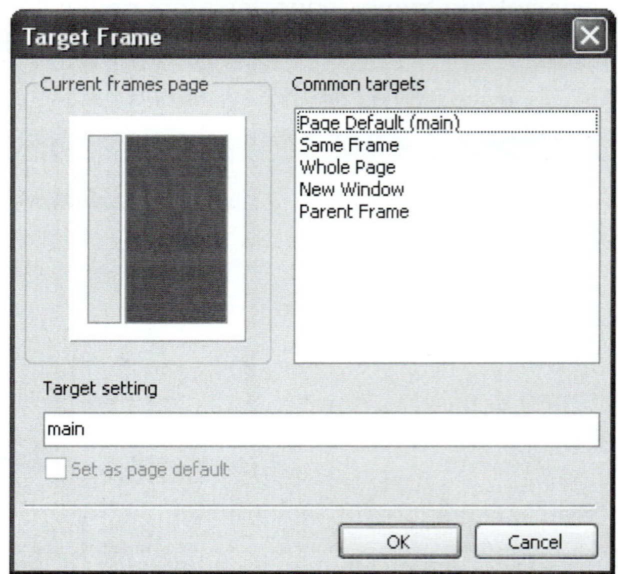

- Frames pages created using templates supply names for each frame. For example, the Contents frames page template has two frames: the narrower left frame is named *contents* and the larger right frame is named *main*.
- In the illustration above, clicking in the larger frame of the preview tells FrontPage to open the linked page in the main frame, as indicated in the Target setting box.

  ✓ *You will work with some of the other common targets in the next exercise when you link the frames page to the home page.*

Procedures

Create Frames Page

1. Click **File** .... Alt+F
2. Click **New** .... N
3. Click **More page templates** in Task Pane.

   OR

   Click **Create a new normal page** button's down arrow and click **Page** .... P
4. Click **Frames Pages** tab.
5. Select frame page template.
6. Save a frames page:
   a. Click **File** .... Alt+F
   b. Click **Save As** .... A

      OR

      Click (**Save** button).
   c. Name page and change page title.

      ✓ *Make sure Save As dialog box shows outline of frames page.*

Set Initial Pages

1. In new frames page, click in desired frame to activate it.

   ✓ *A dark blue outline surrounds the active frame.*
2. Click **Set Initial Page** button I
3. In Insert Hyperlink dialog box, select or browse to location of page to open.

Create New Web Page (Frames)

1. In new frames page, click in desired frame to activate it.

   ✓ *A dark blue outline surrounds the active frame.*
2. Click New Page **New Page** button .... N
3. Begin typing in frame to add content to page.
4. Save new page:
   a. Click **File** .... Alt+F
   b. Click **Save As** .... A

      OR

      - Click (**Save** button).

      OR

      - Click **Frames** .... Alt+R
      - Click **Save Page** .... S or **Save Page As** ...... A
   c. Name page and change page title.

      ✓ *Make sure Save As dialog box shows shape of current frame.*

Link within Frames Page *(Ctrl+K)*

1. Select text or graphic for link.
2. Click **Insert** .... Alt+I
3. Click **Hyperlink** I

   OR

   Click (**Insert Hyperlink** button).
4. Select or browse to location of page to open.
5. Click Target Frame... **Target Frame** button .... Alt+G
6. Click in frame where target page should open.

Exercise Directions

1. Start FrontPage 2003.
2. Open **Coach**.
3. Create a new frames page using the Banner and Contents template.
4. Save the frames page as **info.htm** with the page title **Coaching Information**.
5. Click the **Set Initial Page** button in the top (banner) frame. Set **banner.htm** as the initial page for this frame.
   - ✓ *The banner frame may not entirely display the contents of the banner.htm page. You will resize the banner frame in the next exercise.*
6. Set **coaching.htm** as the initial page for the largest remaining frame (the main frame).
7. Click the **New Page** button in the remaining frame (the contents frame).
8. In the contents frame, type the following paragraphs:

   What Is Coaching?

   Coaching Groups

   Schedules and Fees
9. Apply the Heading 4 style to the three paragraphs.
10. Save the page within the frame as **contents.htm** with the page title **Contents**.
11. Create a hyperlink from the *What Is Coaching?* heading in the contents pane to **coaching.htm**. The page should open in the main frame.
12. Create hyperlinks from the *Coaching Groups* and *Schedules and Fees* headings to **groups.htm** and **schedule.htm**. Both pages should be set to open in the main frame.
13. View the HTML code for the frames page and identify the code that prevents the banner frame from displaying scroll bars.
14. Preview the Web page in the browser and check the links. Your page should look similar to the one shown in Illustration A.
15. Close the browser.
16. Close the Web site.
17. Exit FrontPage 2003.

Illustration A

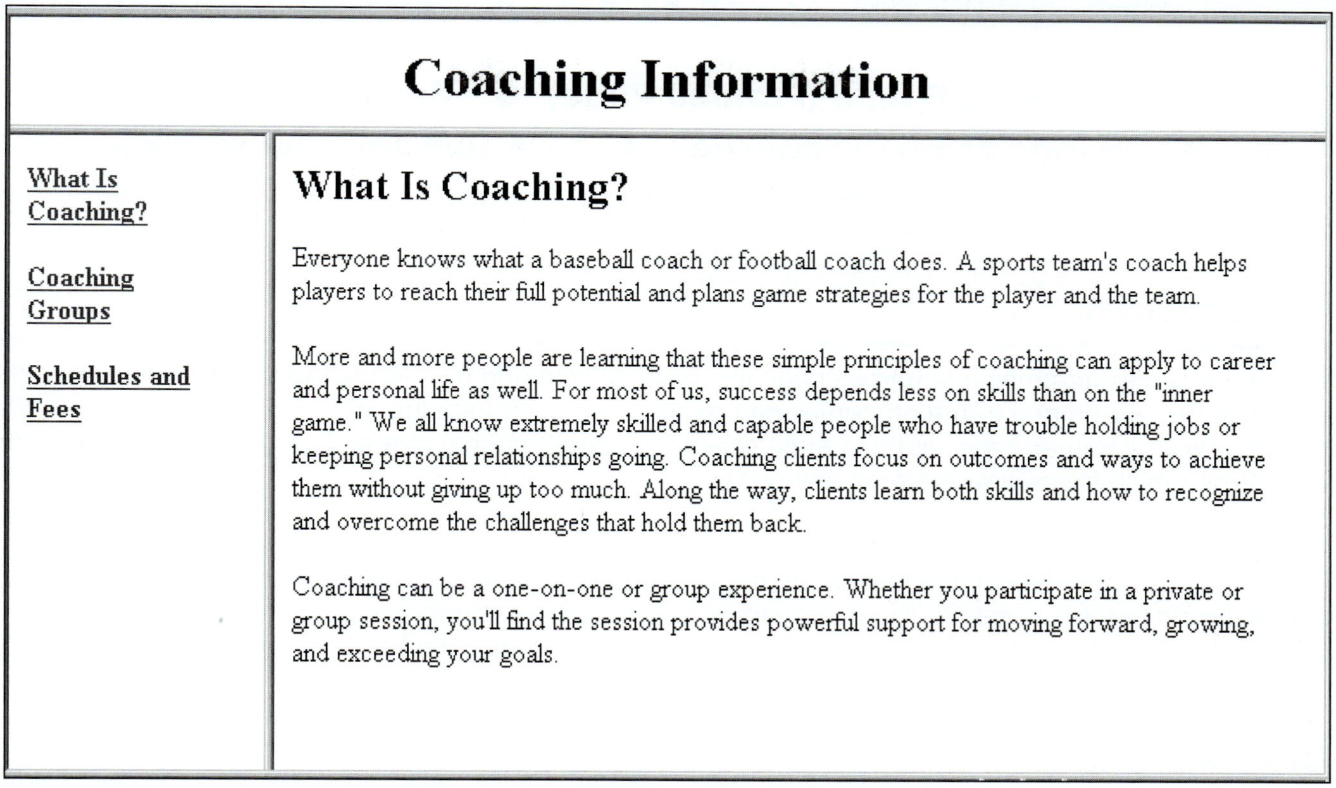

Coaching Information

What Is Coaching?

Coaching Groups

Schedules and Fees

What Is Coaching?

Everyone knows what a baseball coach or football coach does. A sports team's coach helps players to reach their full potential and plans game strategies for the player and the team.

More and more people are learning that these simple principles of coaching can apply to career and personal life as well. For most of us, success depends less on skills than on the "inner game." We all know extremely skilled and capable people who have trouble holding jobs or keeping personal relationships going. Coaching clients focus on outcomes and ways to achieve them without giving up too much. Along the way, clients learn both skills and how to recognize and overcome the challenges that hold them back.

Coaching can be a one-on-one or group experience. Whether you participate in a private or group session, you'll find the session provides powerful support for moving forward, growing, and exceeding your goals.

On Your Own

1. Start FrontPage 2003.
2. Spend a few moments thinking about special skills or knowledge you possess that you could share with others.
   ✓ *For example, soccer, baseball, basketball, or skating skills; knowledge of languages; music or art talents; crafts or gaming experience.*
3. Create a Web site similar to the one you worked with in this exercise in which you offer yourself as a coach for people wanting to learn your skills. Name the Web site **OYO20**,
4. On the **index.htm** page, give a brief introduction to the skills you intend to coach and tell something about yourself and your experience.
   ✓ *Insert clip art if you can find appropriate pictures.*
5. Create at least two pages to be used in a frames page giving more information about your coaching topic. One page should cover reasons why a person would want to master your skills. Another page should discuss fees and other requirements.
6. Create a frames page using a frames page template. Create pages as necessary for a banner or contents.
7. Set initial pages and insert links to open your information pages in the main frame.
8. Preview your Web site in the browser and then make any modifications necessary.
9. Close the browser and the Web site.
10. Close FrontPage 2003.

Exercise 21

◆ **Add New Frame (Frames Page)** ◆ **Modify Frame Size**
◆ **Change Frame Properties** ◆ **Link to/from Frames Page**
◆ **Insert Inline Frame**

On the Job

Web authors can split frames in a frames page like table cells to add new frames to the frames page. Frames can be resized and frame properties can be modified to change the way each frame displays. When linking to or from a frames page, authors must select the correct page name and target frame. Authors can insert a single inline frame anywhere on any page.

In this exercise, you will continue to work on the Coach Web site. You will add a new frame to the frames page, adjust frame sizes, modify frame properties to improve the appearance of the page, and link the frames page to and from the home page. Finally, you will insert an inline frame on the home page.

Terms

inline frame
FrontPage 2003 feature that allows the author to insert a frame on any Web page (not just within a frames page).

Notes

Add New Frame (Frames Page)

- New frames can be added to a frames page at any time after the page has been created.
- Adding a frame really means splitting an existing frame, so new frames can be added only within existing frames.
  - ✓ *It is not possible, for example, to create a new frame that spans existing frames as a banner frame does.*
- To add a new frame, first select the frame that will be split by clicking in the frame. Then:
  - Click on a frame border (the dark blue outline), hold the Ctrl key, and drag to split the frame.
  - Click the Frames>Split Frame command on the menu bar and choose whether to split the frame into rows or columns.
- The new frame contains Set Initial Page and New Page buttons just as does any new frames page (see illustration below).

Add a new frame by splitting an existing frame

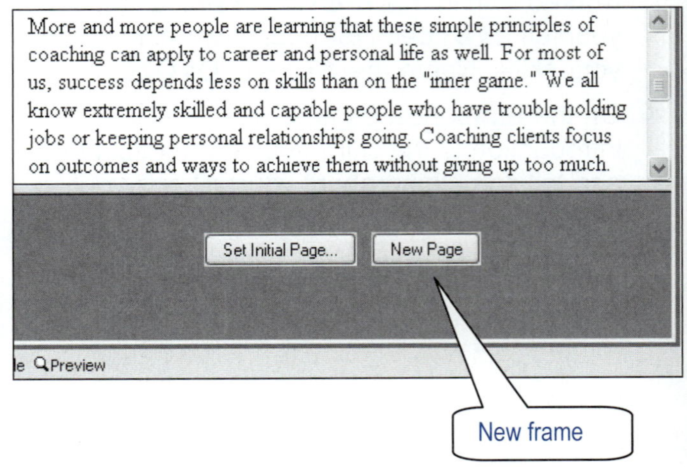

- A new frame takes its name from the frame in which it was created. A frame created within the main frame will be named main1.
- The frame's name can be changed in the Frame Properties dialog box.
- A new frame (or any other frame) can be deleted by selecting the frame and using the Frames>Delete Frame command on the menu bar.

Modify Frame Size

- A frames page template sets default sizes for each frame in the page, but these sizes can be adjusted if necessary.
- Adjust a frame's size by positioning the mouse pointer on a frame's border so that it becomes a two-headed arrow (see illustration below).
- Drag the border to resize the frame.

Resize a frame by dragging its border

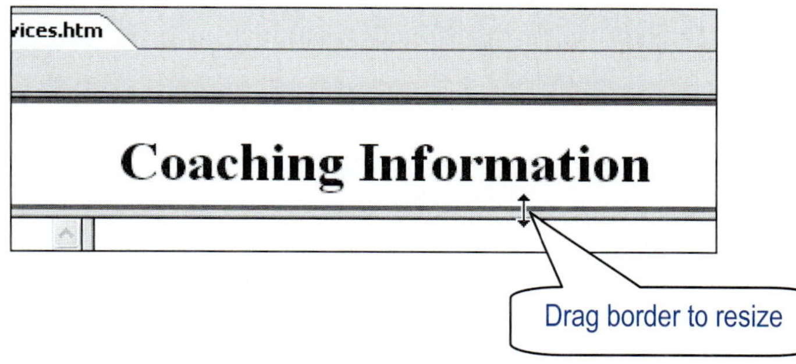

✓ *A frame can also be resized to exact dimensions in the Frame Properties dialog box.*

Change Frame Properties

- A Web designer can change properties for each frame in a frames page.
- Display the Frame Properties dialog box for a frame by:
  - Clicking in the frame to select it and using the Frames>Frame Properties command on the menu bar.
  - Right-clicking in a frame and then clicking Frame Properties on the shortcut menu.
- The Frame Properties dialog box (see illustration in next column) allows the designer to:
  - Change the frame's name or initial page.
  - Supply a long description of the frame and a title for it.

Frame Properties dialog box

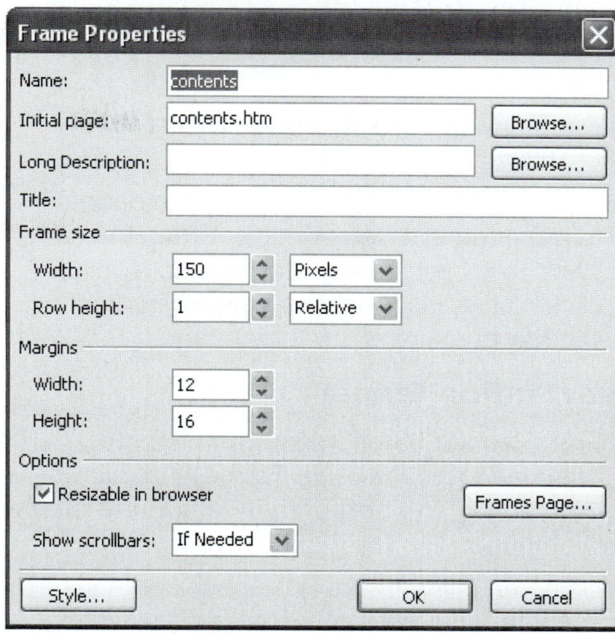

  - Change the frame's width or height relative to other frames, as a percentage of the browser window, or in pixels.
  - Set margin width or height to change the amount of space between the frame's text and its borders.
  - Specify whether a frame can be resized in the browser.
  - Choose whether to display scrollbars.
  - Change properties for the entire frames page. Clicking the Frames Page button opens the Frames tab in the Page Properties dialog box to allow the Web author to change spacing between frames or hide frame borders.
- It is also possible to change the look of a frames page by changing page properties for each page in a frame.
- For example, change page backgrounds of one or more frames for a visually interesting look.

Link to/from Frames Page

- When linking from an existing page to a frames page, the author must be sure to select the frames page name for the link, *not* any of the pages displayed in frames.
- When linking from a frames page to another page, the author must specify the correct target frame for the target page, just as when linking within a frames page.

- To make sure the target page does not open in one of the frames page's frames, choose the Whole Page target in the Target Frame dialog box.
  - ✓ *This target setting replaces the entire frames page with the target page.*
- A Web designer might also want to open a target page in a new window. When the New Window target setting is applied to a link, clicking the link launches a new browser window containing the target page

Insert Inline Frame

- FrontPage 2003 offers an **inline frame** command (Insert>Inline Frame) that allows the Web author to insert a frame anywhere on any Web page.
- Using an inline frame is a good way to insert supplemental information on a page without greatly changing the current layout.
- An inline frame displays scrollbars if initial page depth exceeds the inline frame size, so the frame can be relatively small in relation to the page in which it is inserted.
- A new inline frame displays at the insertion point and contains the familiar Set Initial Page and New Page buttons to allow the user to insert the frame's content. (See illustration below.)
- Inline frames can be modified like inline pictures: Change frame alignment using the Formatting toolbar's alignment buttons. Change frame size by dragging a selection handle.

Inline frame inserted on a page

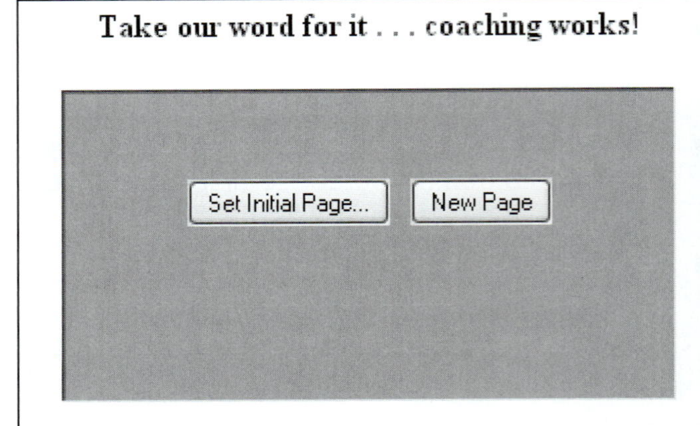

Procedures

Add New Frame

1. Click in the frame to split to select it.
2. Click **Frames** .... Alt+R
3. Click **Split Frame**................ F
4. Specify whether to split the frame into rows or columns.

OR

1. Click in the frame to select it.
2. Position the pointer on the frame border (the dark blue outline).
3. Hold Ctrl and drag the border to create the new frame.

Delete Frame

1. Click in the frame to delete.
2. Click **Frames** .... Alt+R
3. Click **Delete Frame**............. D

Modify Frame Size

1. Position the insertion point on the frame border so it becomes a two-headed arrow.
2. Drag the border to adjust the frame to the desired size.

OR

1. Click in frame to modify.
2. Click **Frames** .... Alt+R
3. Click **Frame Properties** ...... P

   OR

   Right-click in frame and click **Frame Properties** .... P
4. Specify new sizes in the **Width** and **Height** spin boxes.

Change Frame Properties

1. Click in frame to modify.
2. Click **Frames** .... Alt+R
3. Click **Frame Properties** ...... P

   OR

   Right-click in frame and click **Frame Properties** .... P
4. Change frame properties as follows:
   - Change name or initial page for frame.
   - Supply a long description of the current frame.
   - Change width or height of frame relative to other frames, as percentage of page width, or as pixel measurement.
   - Change margins between frame text and frame borders.
   - Allow or prevent frame resizing in browser.
   - Specify whether scrollbars will be displayed **If Needed**, **Never**, or **Always**.
5. Click Frames Page... to change properties for the entire frames page:
   - Change spacing between frames.
   - Show or hide frame borders.

Link to/from Frames Page

To link to a frames page

- Set the frames page as the target page.

  ✓ *Do not set one of the frame's pages as the target, or the frames page structure will not appear.*

To link from a frames page

1. Select text or graphic for the link.
2. Click **Insert** .... Alt+I
3. Click **Hyperlink** I

   OR

   Click (**Insert Hyperlink** .... Ctrl+K button) on Standard toolbar.
4. Select or browse to location of page to open.
5. Click Target Frame... .... Alt+G
6. Click **Whole Page** target option to replace frames page with target page.

Insert Inline Frame

1. Position insertion point where inline frame should appear.

   Apply alignment option at this point if desired.
2. Click **Insert** .... Alt+I
3. Click **Inline Frame** .... E
4. To modify inline frame:
   - Apply alignment to center, left align, or right align frame.
   - Drag selection handle to resize.

Exercise Directions

1. Start FrontPage 2003.
2. Open **Coach**
3. Open **info.htm**.
4. Resize the banner frame (the frame at the top of the Web page) to display the horizontal rule and navigation bar.
5. Create a new frame at the bottom of the contents frame (the narrower frame below the banner frame).
6. Create a new Web page within the new frame and insert the following paragraph in the new page:

   Try a FREE hour of coaching! Contact Clair for more information.
7. Create a mailto link from the words *Contact Clair* and specify the e-mail address **clairmcd@mcd.net**.
8. Save the Web page as **trial.htm** with the page title **Trial Offer**.
9. Change the frame's name from contents1 to **trial**.
10. Adjust the width of the contents frame so that each link displays on one line. If necessary, adjust the height of the new frame to display all text.
11. Hide the frames page borders. (In the Frame Properties dialog box, click the Frames Page button and deselect Show Borders.)
12. Click in the contents frame and change the page background to the same color used for the horizontal rule in the banner frame.

    ✓ *Right-click the rule and check the rule's properties to determine the correct color.*
13. If desired, also change hyperlink colors to contrast better with the new background color.
14. Link *Home* in the banner's navigation bar to **index.htm**.

    ✓ *Don't forget to set the correct target frame.*
15. Open **index.htm**.
16. Import the **responses.htm** Web page from the Data folder into the current Web.

    ✓ *Use the File>Import command on the menu bar.*
17. On **index.htm**, position the insertion point after the last word in the last text paragraph above the horizontal rule.
18. Press the **Enter** key and type **Take our word for it . . . coaching works!**
19. Apply center alignment to this new paragraph, and then press the **Enter** key again.
20. Insert an inline frame.
21. Set **responses.htm** as the initial page for the inline frame.
22. Link *Coaching Information* in the navigation bar to the **info.htm** frames page. Adjust the width of the frame as necessary.
23. Save all changes and preview the Web in the browser. Test the links. The frames page should look similar to the one shown in Illustration A.
24. Close the browser.
25. Close the Web site.
26. Exit FrontPage 2003.

Illustration A

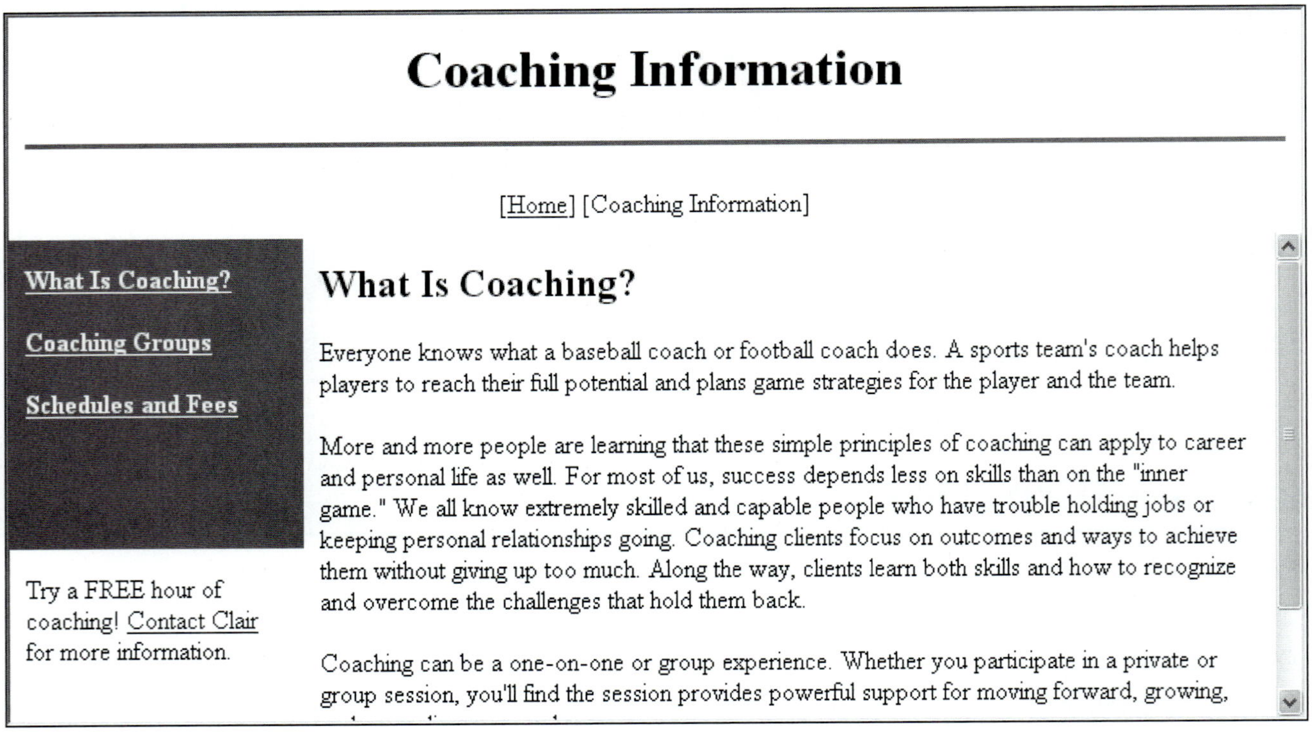

Coaching Information

[Home] [Coaching Information]

What Is Coaching?

Coaching Groups

Schedules and Fees

Try a FREE hour of coaching! Contact Clair for more information.

What Is Coaching?

Everyone knows what a baseball coach or football coach does. A sports team's coach helps players to reach their full potential and plans game strategies for the player and the team.

More and more people are learning that these simple principles of coaching can apply to career and personal life as well. For most of us, success depends less on skills than on the "inner game." We all know extremely skilled and capable people who have trouble holding jobs or keeping personal relationships going. Coaching clients focus on outcomes and ways to achieve them without giving up too much. Along the way, clients learn both skills and how to recognize and overcome the challenges that hold them back.

Coaching can be a one-on-one or group experience. Whether you participate in a private or group session, you'll find the session provides powerful support for moving forward, growing,

On Your Own

1. Start FrontPage 2003.
2. Open the Web site you created in the last exercise.
3. Add a new frame to one of the frames in your frames page and create a new page in the frame.
4. Add text to the new page that offers new clients a discount rate if they contact you by a specific date.
5. Insert a mailto link to your e-mail address if you have one.
6. Save the new page and change the new frame's name.
7. Adjust frame sizes as necessary to accommodate all text.
8. Change other frame or page properties to emphasize the frames in the frames page.
9. Create navigation bars, if necessary, and link the frames page and the home page.
10. Insert an inline frame on the home page. Create a new page in the frame that lists satisfied clients and the nice things they have to say about your coaching methods.
11. Preview the Web site in the browser and check all links.
12. Close the browser.
13. Close the Web site.
14. Exit FrontPage 2003.

Exercise 22

◆ **Insert Background Sound**
◆ **About Dynamic Effects Components**
◆ **Create Interactive Button** ◆ **Insert Marquee**

On the Job

FrontPage authors can add a number of special effects to Webs to make them more interesting. Authors can add a background sound that begins playing when the page opens. FrontPage's dynamic effects components let the author add a marquee (text that scrolls across a page) and interactive buttons (graphic buttons that change appearance as a visitor uses them).

Your friend Annie runs a bird-sitting business to watch birds while their owners are away. In this exercise, you will add special effects to Annie's Parrot Vacations Web site. You will insert a background sound, add a marquee to the home page, and create interactive buttons for navigation.

Terms

AU (Audio File Format)
A standard audio file format developed by Sun and NeXt. The file name extension for AU files is *.au*.

component
A program written to perform a specific action on a FrontPage Web page.

interactive button
A graphic button that can be used for links or other scripts and automatically changes appearance depending on state.

marquee
A FrontPage component that scrolls text across a Web page.

MIDI (Musical Instrument Digital Interface)
A standard audio file format that synthesizes music played on an instrument or keyboard. The file name extension for MIDI files is *.mid*.

WAV (Waveform Audio File Format)
A standard audio file format developed by Microsoft. The file name extension for WAV files is *.wav*.

Notes

Insert Background Sound

- Add special impact to a Web site by inserting a background sound for a Web page.
- The sound formats used most frequently for Web pages are:
  - **AU**. This audio format was developed by NeXt and Sun and can be used on most computers. An AU file can reproduce any sound. AU files can be quite large even if the actual sound played is short.
  - **MIDI**. The MIDI audio format consists of specific musical instructions rather than a recording. MIDI files are thus smaller than AU and WAV files.
  - **WAV**. The WAV format was developed for Windows computers by Microsoft. Like AU files, WAV files can be played on a wide variety of computers. WAV files are sound recordings that can be large even if the sound played is short.

- Use the File>Properties command on the menu bar to open the Page Properties dialog box and then type the path to the background sound file or use the Browse button to locate the file.
- The background sound file is a property of the Web page that is active when the sound is set. Usually, background sounds are set for the home page of a Web site, but sound can be added to any page in a Web site.
- Sound files can be set to loop forever or to loop a specified number of times.

  ✓ *As a general rule, set a sound file to loop one or two times. Sounds that may be interesting or amusing the first time they are heard can become wearing if they continue indefinitely.*

- Background sounds do not play in Page view. To hear the background sound, use Page Preview or preview the page in the browser.

  ✓ *The background sound will play each time the Web page is opened or refreshed.*

- A background sound plays in the browser only as long as its Web page is displayed. The sound stops when a new page from the Web site is displayed.
- Sound files are embedded files like pictures. When saving a page after inserting a sound file, the Web author must specify a location to store the sound file.

  ✓ *Create a new folder to store sounds or store them in the images folder.*

About Dynamic Effects Components

- FrontPage includes a large variety of **components**, programs written to perform specific tasks in a FrontPage Web site.
- To choose a component to add to a Web site, use the Insert>Web Component command on the menu bar to open the Insert Web Component dialog box (see illustration at the top of the next column).
- The left pane of the Insert Web Component dialog box lists component types. The right pane lists specific components or effects for that type.
- This exercise covers two components from the Dynamic Effects category. Dynamic effects components add movement or other visual effects to objects or text in the Web.

Insert Web Component dialog box

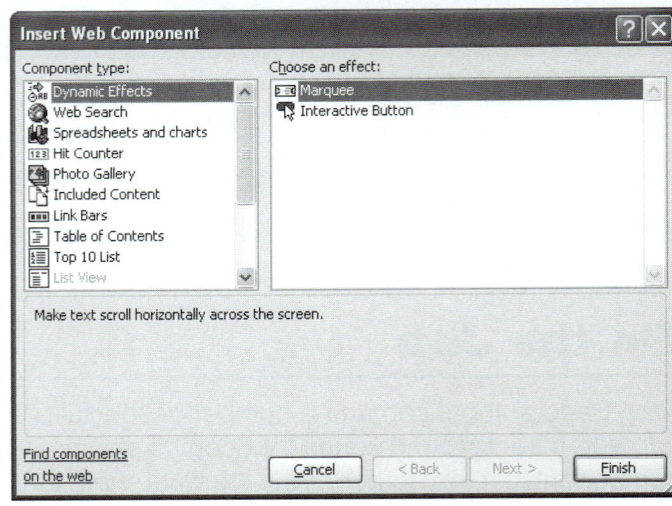

Create Interactive Button

- An **interactive button** is a graphic button that can be used for links or other script actions and formatted with special visual effects.
- Interactive buttons are new in FrontPage 2003. They allow an author to insert sophisticated design elements without having to create them in an illustration program.
- Interactive buttons change their appearance depending on the actions of the Web user, which is the reason they are called *interactive*. The button's default appearance is evident as a page loads. Another appearance displays when the mouse pointer hovers over the button, and a third displays when the button is clicked.

  ✓ *You will learn more about the scripts that control these changes of appearance in Exercise 25 of this lesson.*

- Insert an interactive button by clicking the Insert>Web Component command on the menu bar and then selecting the Interactive Button dynamic effect.
- In the Interactive Buttons dialog box (see illustration at the top of the next page):
  - Choose a button style from the Buttons list.

    ✓ *Move the mouse over the button in the Preview area to see how it changes formats.*

  - Insert the text that will appear on the button and specify the page the button will link to.

Interactive Buttons dialog box

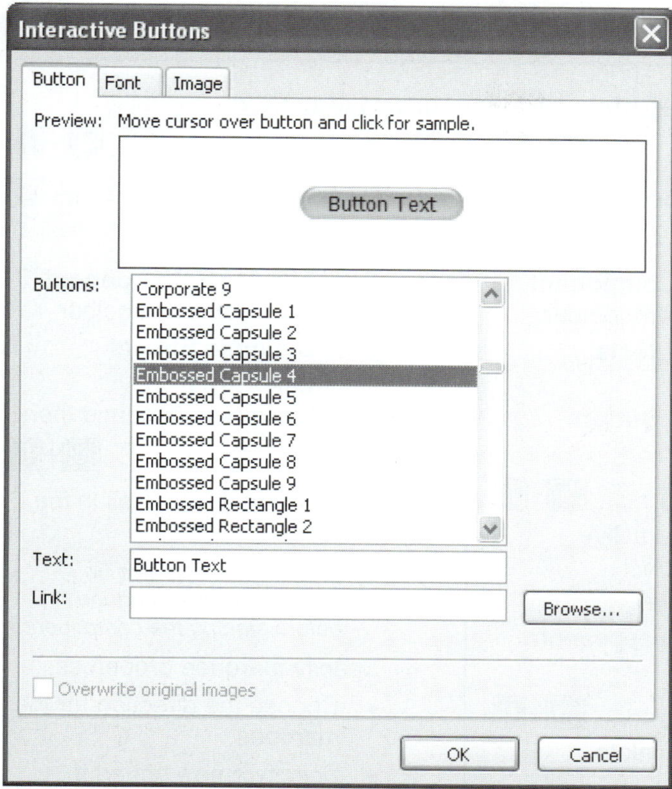

- To further customize the interactive button, use the Font and Image tabs in the Interactive Buttons dialog box.
  - On the Font tab, change the font, style, and size of the button's text, as well as choose the color of text for the default, hover, and clicked states of the button. A user can also select horizontal and vertical alignment options for the text.
  - On the Image tab, adjust the width and/or height of the button and select background options for the button. An author can also choose on this tab which button appearances to create.
- After a Web designer has selected interactive button options, FrontPage adds the selected button appearances to the Web site. These graphics should be stored in the images folder with other Web images.
- Like other dynamic effects, interactive button effects are visible only in Page Preview or in the browser.
- To change an interactive button's properties, simply double-click it in Page view to open the Interactive Buttons dialog box again.

Insert Marquee

- A **marquee** is a FrontPage component that scrolls text across a Web page.
- Marquees can be used to deliver a special message or display a company slogan.
- Insert a marquee by clicking the Insert>Web Component command on the menu bar and then selecting the Marquee dynamic effect.
- Use the Marquee Properties dialog box (see illustration below) to insert the marquee text and choose options for displaying the marquee:
  - Choose the direction the text will scroll, the speed at which it will scroll, and whether it scrolls, slides into place, or alternates from side to side on the page.
  - Specify the height and width of the text box that contains the scrolling text
  - Select a background color for the text box that contains the scrolling text.

    ✓ *If the page has a background picture, use the Automatic option in the Background color palette to make the text box transparent.*

Marquee Properties dialog box

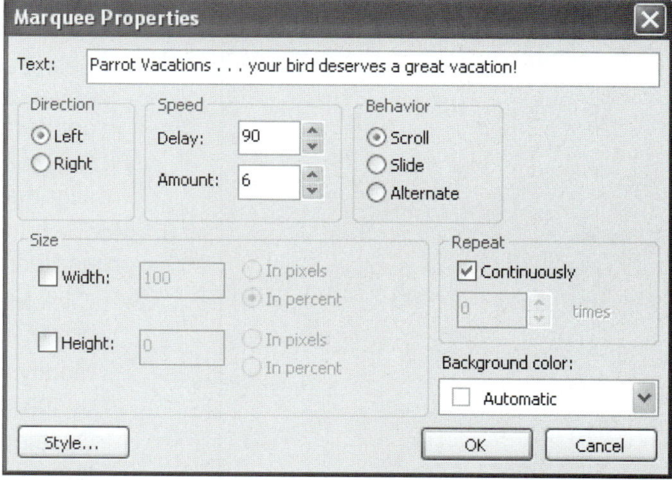

- Indicate how many times the text will scroll.
- Use the Style button in the lower-left corner of the Marquee Properties dialog box to format the marquee text.
- Clicking this button opens the Modify Style dialog box. Click the Format button in this dialog box and then select Font from the drop-down menu to change text formats.

Procedures

Insert Background Sound

1. Click **File** .... Alt+F
2. Click **Properties** .... R
3. Click Browse... .... Alt+B and locate sound file.
4. Clear the check mark from the **Forever** check box, if desired, and insert a number in the **Loop** spin box to control number of times sound file will play.

Create Interactive Button

1. Click **Insert** .... Alt+I
2. Click **Web Component** C

   OR

   Click (**Web Component** button) on Standard toolbar.
3. Click **Dynamic Effects** component type.
4. Click **Interactive Button** effect.
5. Click Finish .... Alt+F to display the Interactive Buttons dialog box.
6. Select button style.
7. Type text that will appear on the button.
8. Click Browse... .... Alt+B and select file to link to.
9. Modify button text properties: Click **Font** tab in dialog box.
   - Select new font, change font style, or size.
   - Select color for original, hover, or pressed appearance.
   - Select horizontal or vertical alignment option.
10. Modify button image properties:
    - Click **Image** tab in dialog box.
    - Modify width or height of button
    - Deselect appearances if all three will not be used.
    - Select background color to surround buttons or choose transparent background.

Insert Marquee

1. Click **Insert** .... Alt+I
2. Click **Web Component** C

   OR

   Click (**Web Component** button) on Standard toolbar.
3. Click **Dynamic Effects** component style.
4. Click **Marquee** effect and then click Finish .... Alt+F
5. Type text that will scroll in the marquee text box.

   ✓ *Existing text can also be selected for the marquee before starting the component.*
6. Specify marquee properties:
   - Choose the direction for the marquee.
   - Specify a new speed if desired.
   - Select the behavior of the marquee text:
     - **Scroll** moves continuously across the page.
     - **Slide** moves from one side of the page to the other and stops.
     - **Alternate** moves from one side of the page to the other continuously.
   - Specify how many times to scroll.
   - Specify marquee text box background color.
7. Format marquee text:

   a. Click Style... ... Alt+Y to open Modify Style dialog box.

   b. Click Format ▾ Alt+O and click **Font** to change font, font style, size, and color.

Exercise Directions

1. Start FrontPage 2003.
2. Open **Parrot**.
3. Open **index.htm**.
4. Insert the sound file **finches.wav** from the Data folder as a background sound for the Web page.
5. Set the sound file to play twice.
6. Save the Web page and store the sound file in the images folder.
7. Position the insertion point after the main head on the page and press Enter to insert a new, blank paragraph.
8. In the new paragraph, insert the Soft Rectangle 3 interactive button. Type the button text **Nutrition** and link the button to the **nutrition.htm** page.
9. Make the following changes to the button's text properties:
   - Change the font style to Bold.
   - Change the hover font color to Blue.
10. Save the page, storing the button images in the images folder.
11. Click to the right of the new interactive button, if necessary, and press **Spacebar** five times.
12. Insert another interactive button with the same properties. Use **Rates** for the button text and link the button to **rates.htm**.
13. On **index.htm**, click below the last paragraph and insert a marquee that uses the text **Parrot Vacations . . . your bird deserves a great vacation!**
14. Click the **Style** button in the Marquee Properties dialog box and change the font style of the marquee text to bold. Change the text color to the same dark blue color used in the heading on this page.

    ✓ *After clicking Style, click Format in the Modify Style dialog box, and then click Font on the drop-down menu.*
15. Save all changes and preview the Web in the browser. Check all links and view the marquee in action. The **index.htm** page should look similar to Illustration A.
16. Close the browser.
17. Close the Web site.
18. Exit FrontPage 2003.

Illustration A

Parrot Vacations

Rates

Welcome to Parrot Vacations!

Here at Parrot Vacations, we think your birds should have as good a time as you do when you go on vacation. We nurture your birds in a cheerful, bird-oriented home setting. Our priorities are your bird's safety, good nutrition, and loving attention. Your bird will have a great vacation no matter how short or long your trip.

Some bird sitting services offer to "visit" your bird while you're away and feed it. That means your bird probably gets 15 minutes of attention per day. Other services will take your bird to a large facility such as a pet store where nothing is familiar and your bird may be only one of hundreds.

At Parrot Vacations, your bird will become a member of the family. All birds get lots of shoulder time and out-of-cage time. Perches are installed from wall to wall across some rooms and festooned with colorful spirals and wooden and Lucite toys. Birds enjoy the view through large windows and skylights.

Before bringing your bird to Parrot Vacations, you must have your bird checked by your vet. Only birds with a clean bill of health are permitted. We will use our judgment about letting your bird interact with other birds. Usually all boarding birds enjoy (or at least tolerate) each other. Sometimes they even teach each other new words!

Parrot Vacations . . . your bird deserves a great vacation!

On Your Own

1. Start FrontPage 2003.
2. Open **Winter**.
3. Open **index.htm**.
4. Locate a suitable file to insert as a background sound. Search for music on your system or on the Web, download a file if necessary, and then insert it as the background sound.
5. On **index.htm**, insert below the last paragraph of text before the horizontal line an interactive button that links to the **zoo.htm** page. Select an appropriate button style and modify properties as desired.
6. Open **zoo.htm**.
7. At the bottom of the page, create a marquee with the following text:

   Holiday Lights November 20 through January 6
8. Format the marquee text as desired.
9. Preview the Web in the browser. Test all links.
10. Close the browser and the Web site.
11. Exit FrontPage 2003.

Exercise 23

◆ Create Page Transition ◆ About Dynamic HTML Effects
◆ Text Animation ◆ Picture Animation
◆ Use DHTML to Apply Formatting

On the Job

FrontPage offers several additional dynamic features. Page transitions display a special effect when a page is loaded or refreshed. Apply text or picture animation to cause a paragraph or picture to take a specific action, such as flying in from the right, when cued by the page load or the mouse. A dynamic effect can also be applied to display text formatting when cued by the mouse pointer.

In this exercise, you will continue to work on the Parrot Vacations Web site. You will add page transitions and animate text and a picture. Finally, you will use dynamic HTML settings in a paragraph to display specific formatting when the mouse pointer rests on the paragraph.

Terms

dynamic HTML
HTML code that instructs a browser to animate text or other objects on a page.

Java
A programming language widely used to create programs that run within a Web page.

transition effect
A special effect that displays when one object (such as a Web page or image) replaces another.

Notes

Create Page Transition

- One way to add visual interest to a page is to apply a **transition effect**.
- A transition effect can be set to occur when the Web visitor opens or closes a page or enters or exits the Web site.
- Set a page transition using the Format>Page Transition command on the menu bar.
- In the Page Transitions dialog box (see illustration in next column), choose one of the 25 effects, set a duration for the effect, and specify the event that will trigger the effect.

Page Transitions dialog box

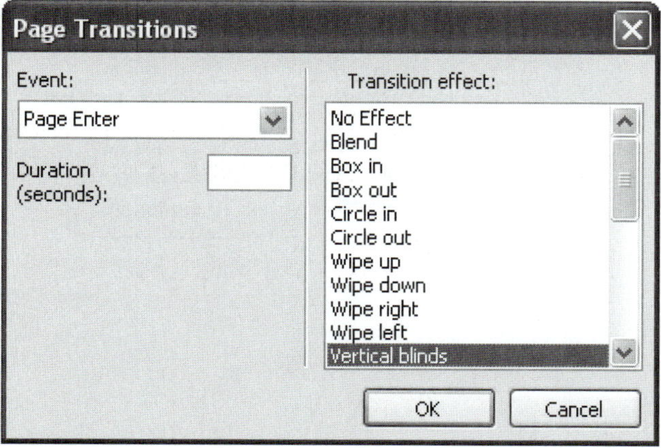

✓ *Different transition effects can be set for opening and closing the same page.*

About Dynamic HTML Effects

- Animation and other effects can be applied to specific page elements using **dynamic HTML**, HTML coding that instructs the browser to animate text or images on a page.
- Dynamic HTML (or DHTML) code is contained within the page and does not require any information from a server. Thus, DHTML effects download and display promptly.
- To create a DHTML effect, use the DHTML Effects toolbar.
- When applying DHTML effects, the author can choose from four events to trigger the effects:
  - Click (displays the effect when a visitor clicks on the text or picture).
  - Double-click (displays the effect when a visitor double-clicks the text or picture).
  - Mouse over (displays the effect when the mouse rests on the text or picture).
  - Page load (displays the effect automatically when the page opens in the browser).
- DHTML effects work correctly only in Internet Explorer 5.0 and later versions, and some recent versions of Netscape Navigator.
- Some dynamic effects will not display on pages that have scripts, such as those necessary to control interactive buttons.
- Page transitions will not display on pages that also have dynamic HTML effects.
- Animating text or a picture adds the animate.js Java script to the Web's Folder List. **Java** is an application that runs programs within Web pages.
- FrontPage 2003 offers a new feature, behaviors, that allows an author to easily create scripts for additional interactive effects.

  ✓ *Behaviors are covered in Exercise 25.*

Text Animation

- A Web designer can animate a paragraph of text using DHTML effects to add special zip to a Web page.
- To animate text, display the DHTML Effects toolbar, choose the event to trigger the animation, select the effect, and specify other settings that affect the display of the animated text.

  ✓ *Other settings include direction from which the text will appear and how the text will appear. For example, text can be displayed all at once or one word at a time.*
- The effects that can be applied to text differ according to the triggering event. The Page load event, for example, lets the user choose from eight effects, while the Mouse over event gives the author only one effect option.
- Text that has a DHTML effect applied displays light-blue shading to remind the author an effect has been applied (see illustration below).

  ✓ *Turn off this shading if desired by clicking the Highlight Dynamic HTML Effects button on the DHTML Effects toolbar.*

Animating a text heading using the DHTML Effects toolbar

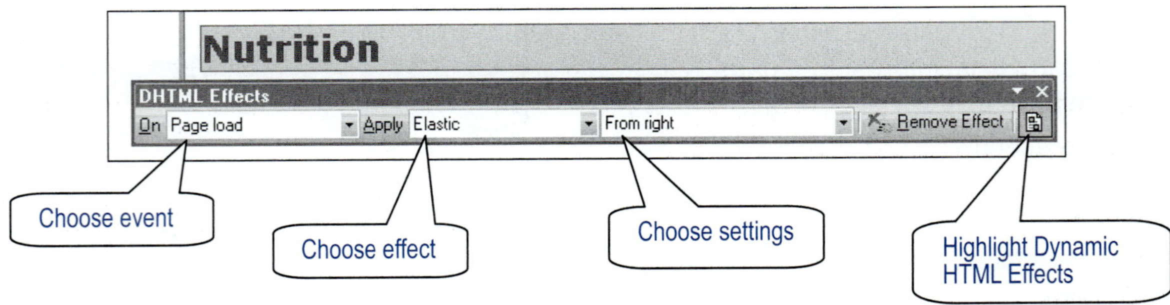

- Remove an effect by clicking in the paragraph that has been animated, displaying the DHTML Effects toolbar, and clicking the Remove Effect button.

Picture Animation

- Pictures can be animated in the same way as text.
- Click a picture to select it, and then display the DHTML Effects toolbar.
- As for text, select the event, the effect, and other settings for the effect.
- Pictures with animation effects applied usually (but not always) display light-blue shading like that for animated text.
- An interesting effect offered for the Click and Mouse over events is Swap Picture. Use this effect to switch between two pictures at the click of the mouse or when the mouse pointer rests on a picture.

  ✓ *Another way to swap pictures is to use dynamic HTML scripting, discussed in Exercise 25.*

Use DHTML to Apply Formatting

- DHTML can also be used to apply formatting to text automatically when prompted by a click, double-click, or mouse over.
- Formatting applied in this way makes a paragraph stand out from surrounding text (see illustration below).
- To format text using DHTML, click in the paragraph to format and display the DHTML Effects toolbar.
- Select the Click, Double click, or Mouse over event and then apply the Formatting effect.
- The third drop-down list in the DHTML Effects toolbar then lists two options: Choose Border and Choose Font.
- Use these options to apply border, shading, and font formatting to the text.

  ✓ *Formatting can be applied only to an entire paragraph, not to single words or phrases.*

  ✓ *For more control over DHTML formatting, use behaviors, covered in Exercise 25.*

Different formatting displays on mouse over

All birds get a morning "buffet" of fruits, vegetables, grains, and pasta. Pellets are available all day long, along with plenty of fresh water. At dinnertime, birds are provided with seeds, nuts, and dried fruits.

All fruits and vegetables are organically grown.

Procedures

Create Page Transition

1. Click **Format** .... Alt+O
2. Click **Page Transition** .... A
3. Select event to trigger transition.
4. Select transition effect.
5. Specify duration of effect.

Text Animation

1. Click in paragraph of text to animate.

Display the DHTML Effects toolbar

2. Click **View** .... Alt+V
3. Click **Toolbars** .... T
4. Click **DHTML Effects**.

On DHTML Effects toolbar

5. Click **On** down arrow and choose triggering event.
6. Click **Apply** down arrow and choose animation effect.
7. Click down arrow of third option in toolbar if applicable to specify additional settings.

Picture Animation

1. Click picture to animate to select it.

Display the DHTML Effects toolbar

2. Click **View** .... Alt+V
3. Click **Toolbars** .... T
4. Click **DHTML Effects**.

On DHTML Effects toolbar

5. Click **On** down arrow and choose triggering event.
6. Click **Apply** down arrow and choose animation effect.
7. Click down arrow of third option in toolbar if applicable to specify additional settings.

Remove Animation Effect

1. Click in paragraph or picture that has effect applied.
2. Display DHTML Effects toolbar.
3. Click Remove Effect button on DHTML Effects toolbar.

Use DHTML to Apply Formatting

1. Click in paragraph to format.

Display the DHTML Effects toolbar

2. Click **View** .... Alt+V
3. Click **Toolbars** .... T
4. Click **DHTML Effects**.

On DHTML Effects toolbar

5. Click **On** down arrow and choose **Click**, **Double click**, or **Mouse over**.
6. Click **Apply** down arrow and choose **Formatting**.
7. Click **Choose Border** and select border and shading options.
8. Click **Choose Font** and select font, size, style, and color options.

Exercise Directions

1. Start FrontPage 2003.
2. Open **Parrot**.
3. Open **nutrition.htm**.
4. Click anywhere in the *Nutrition* heading and apply the Fly in effect on Page load. Specify that the paragraph will fly in from the top-right.
5. Click in the last paragraph on the page and center it.
6. Use DHTML to format the paragraph on Mouse over as follows:
   - Insert 2 pixel borders above and below the paragraph using the gold color used for the horizontal rule on the **index.htm** page (Hex=FF,CC,00 in the More Colors dialog box).
   - Apply bold formatting to the text using the document's blue color.
7. Open **index.htm**.
8. Use the DHTML Swap Picture effect to switch the picture on this page on Mouse over with **cockatoo2.jpg** from the images folder.
   ✓ *You may get a warning about scripts on the page interfering with the effect, but it should work in the browser.*
9. Open **rates.htm**.
10. Apply a transition to this page.
11. Preview the Web site in the browser.
12. Close the browser.
13. Close the Web site.
14. Exit FrontPage 2003.

On Your Own

1. Start FrontPage 2003.
2. Open **Winter**.
3. Open **zoo.htm**.
4. Insert **peacock.jpg** below the navigation bar. (Do not wrap text around the picture.)
5. Apply the Fly in effect to this picture to occur when the page loads. Choose an appropriate direction for the flight.
6. Use DHTML to apply formatting to the last text paragraph on the page. Choose appropriate borders or shading and font formatting for the paragraph.
7. Apply a page transition to this page.
8. Preview the Web in the browser.
9. Close the browser and the Web site.
10. Exit FrontPage 2003.

Exercise 24

◆ About Layers ◆ Insert Layers
◆ Size and Position Layers ◆ Change Layer Properties
◆ Insert Layer Content ◆ Manipulate Layers

On the Job

FrontPage 2003's new layers support allows an author to create layers on a page to control position and behavior of text, pictures, and other objects. Insert or draw a layer and then size and position it as desired. Change layer properties such as borders and shading to emphasize layers. Insert in a layer any content that can be inserted on a page, including animations. Use the Layers task pane to control layer order and visibility.

In this exercise, you will begin fine-tuning an already-started Web site for Sitwell's Coffee House. You will create layers to hold text and pictures, insert the content, adjust layer size and position, and change layer properties. Finally, you will adjust layer order and nest layers to improve the appearance of the page.

Terms

layer
A container for text, pictures, or other elements that can be sized and positioned precisely.

Z-order
Stacking order of layers on a page; 1 is at the bottom of the stack.

Notes

About Layers

- You learned In the previous lesson how to control page layout using layout tables, which make it easy to place content in cells anywhere on a page.
- FrontPage 2003 offers a new way to control Web page content using layers.
- A **layer** is a container for Web page content. Any content that can be inserted on a Web page can be inserted into a layer.
- The illustration below, for example, shows a layer that will become a pop-out menu containing links to pages in a Web.

Menu layer next to interactive button

- Using layers to control page layout has some advantages over other methods:
  - Layers can be drawn anywhere on a page, without having to first insert a layout table.
  - Layers can be adjusted to any size, and layers are independent of one another, so there is no layout grid to deal with.
  - Layers can overlay one another for interesting visual effects.
  - Layer visibility can be controlled by dynamic HTML scripts so layers appear or disappear as a visitor interacts with a page.

✓ *Exercise 25 discusses dynamic HTML scripts.*

Code Cues

Layer <div> tags can include a number of attributes, such as id (which requires the layer name as a value) and style (which includes information on size, visibility, and stacking order).

Insert Layers

- An author can insert a layer in several ways:
  - Use the Insert>Layer command on the menu bar to insert a default-sized layer on the page.
  - Display the Layers task pane and click the Insert Layer button to insert a default-sized layer.
  - Click the Draw Layer button on the Layers task pane to draw a layer to a desired size.
- Draw a layer the same way as drawing an object such as a rectangle.
- A new layer displays with a heavy blue border and selection handles. A tab in the upper-left corner of the layer displays the layer's name (see illustration below). By default, layers are numbered consecutively as they are inserted.

New layer shows default name

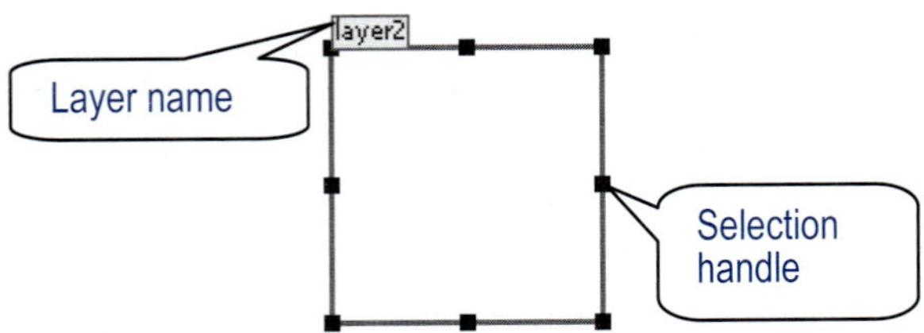

Size and Position Layers

- Regardless of how the layer is inserted, it can easily be resized and repositioned.
- Drag any selection handle to adjust the size of the layer.
- To reposition a layer, move the mouse pointer over the layer border until it becomes a four-headed arrow. Then drag the layer to a new position (see illustration below).

Drag a layer to a new position

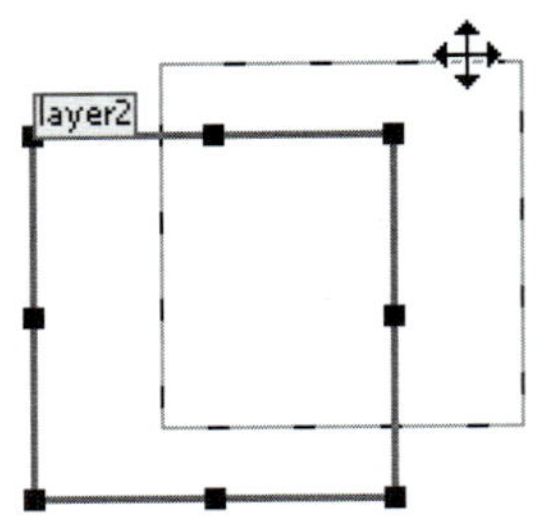

- Sizing and positioning by dragging are often adequate ways of adjusting layers, but in some cases an author may require more precision.
- To size and position a layer precisely, double-click the layer border to display the Layers task pane and then click Positioning at the bottom of the pane. The Position dialog box opens, as shown below.

Position dialog box

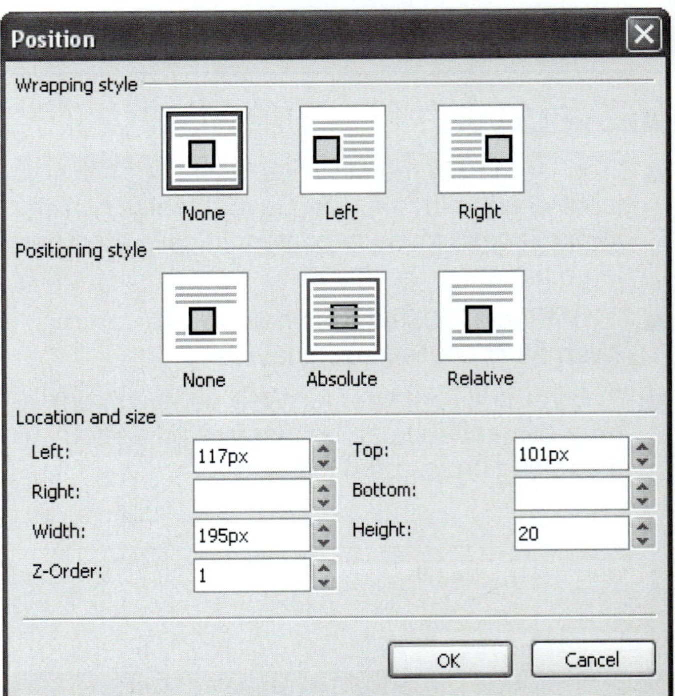

- Here a Webmaster can specify the width and height of the layer as well as its precise coordinates. The Left value is the distance in pixels from the left edge of the page. The Top value is the distance in pixels from the top of the page.

  ✓ *In some cases, it may make more sense to position a layer with reference to the bottom right of the page using the Right and Bottom values.*

- An author can also specify the Z-order of the selected layer to determine its stacking order. Z-order is discussed in more detail later in the exercise.
- Note that a Webmaster can also specify a wrapping style and a positioning style. Choosing the None positioning style eliminates free positioning so the layer becomes static like a drawing object.

Change Layer Properties

- Besides changing size and position, a Webmaster can make several other changes to layer properties: rename the layer and apply borders and shading.

Rename Layer

- One of the most useful of these changes is to rename a layer. As indicated earlier, layers are given consecutive numbers by default.
- On a page with several layers, these default names may become confusing. Replace the default names with names that reflect the layer's content to make it easier to work with the layers.
- To rename a layer, use the Layers task pane. Double-click the default layer name to select it (see illustration below) and then type a new layer name.

Rename a layer

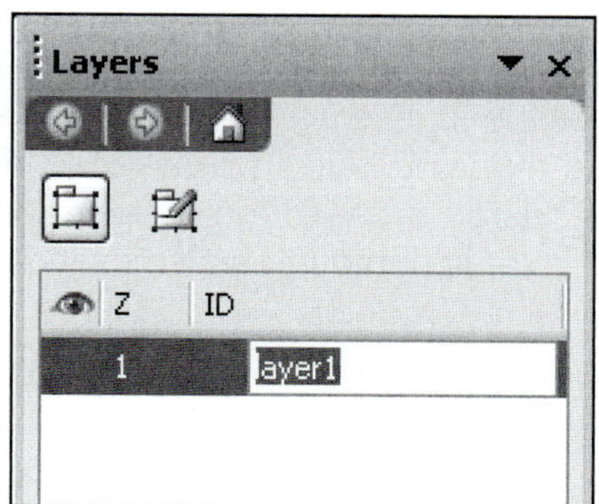

- The new layer name appears in the name tab at the top left corner of the layer.

Apply Borders and Shading to Layers

- To make a layer stand out on the page, change border and shading properties. With the layer selected, click Borders and Shading at the bottom of the Layers task pane.
- The Borders and Shading dialog box opens. Use the Borders tab to select a border style, color, and weight, just as for any paragraph or table cell.

  ✓ *Note the padding options on this tab. Apply padding as in a table to avoid crowding layer text with the applied border.*

- The Shading tab (see illustration below) allows an author to specify both the background color for the layer and the foreground color for the layer's text.

Apply layer background with Shading tab

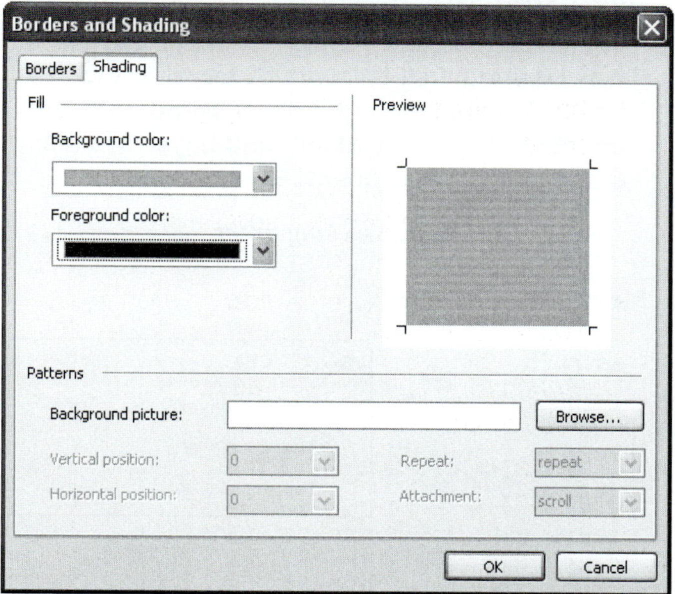

Insert Layer Content

- As mentioned earlier, you can insert into a layer any content that can be placed on a Web page.
- To insert text, select the layer. An insertion point begins blinking in the upper-left corner of the layer and the author can simply begin typing.
- Text can also be inserted by copying it and pasting it at the layer's insertion point.

- Likewise, pictures and other objects can be inserted at the insertion point in the layer just as on a Web page.
  ✓ *If a picture is larger than the layer, the layer will resize to accommodate the picture.*

Manipulate Layers

- Once layers have been inserted on a page, an author can manipulate them in various ways to modify page appearance.
- An author can change stacking order to control layer display, control layer visibility, and even nest one layer within another.

Change Layer Stacking Order

- As an author adds layers to a page, they display in reverse order in the Layers task pane. The first layer inserted is at the bottom of the list. Subsequent layers stack on top of the first layer, and the last layer inserted is at the top of the Layers list.
- In the illustration below, for example, Layer 1 was inserted first, followed by Layer 2 and Layer 3. Note that Layer 3 is stacked on top of the other two layers at left, and Layer 3 is the first item in the Layers list at right.

Layer stacking order

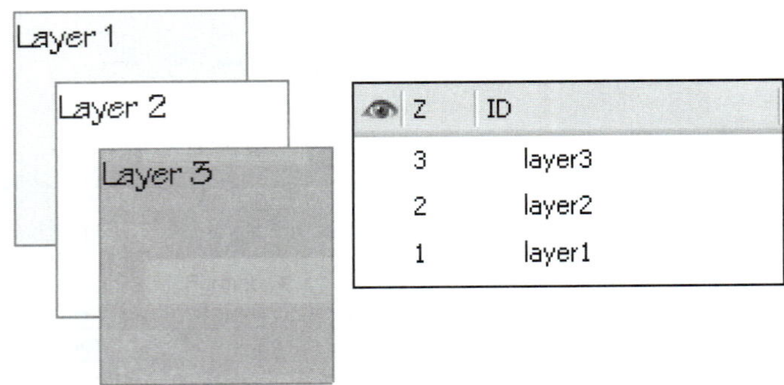

- It is frequently necessary to adjust stacking order to prevent one layer from obscuring the contents of another or to control page appearance.
- Change stacking order by changing a layer's **Z-order** number. The Z-order number displays in the Z column in the Layers task pane. The higher the Z-order number, the nearer the layer is to the top of the stack.
- To adjust the number, double-click it and type a new number.
- More than one layer can have the same Z-order number.
- It is also possible to simply drag a layer in the Layers task pane list upward or downward to change its order in the list.
- In the illustration below, for example, layer1 is being dragged above layer3. After the layer is dropped, layer1 receives a new Z-order number, 4, and displays at the front of the stack.

Drag a layer to change stacking order

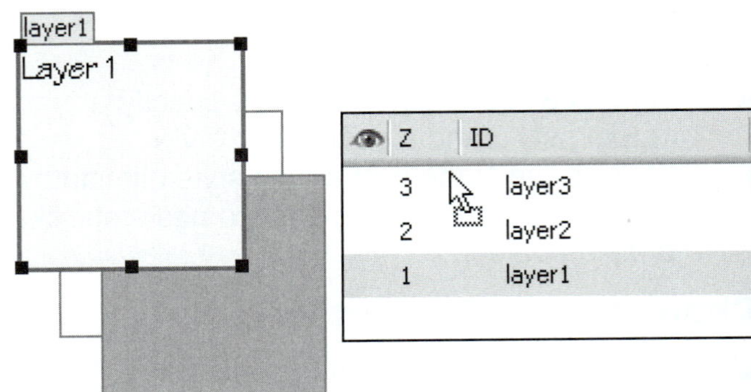

Change Layer Visibility

- By default, all new layers are visible on the page. An author may, however, wish to hide one or more layers to make it easy to work on other parts of the page.
- Control visibility using the Layer Visibility column of the Layers task pane. When an open eye displays in this column, a layer is visible.
- To hide a column, click on the open eye until it shuts. The layer is then hidden from view, but is still present in the Web.
  ✓ *Hidden layers do not display in the browser.*
- Visibility can also be set by right-clicking a layer in the Layers task pane and clicking one of the options on the shortcut menu.

Nest Layers

- It is possible to insert a layer within a layer. This is called a nested layer. The layer in which a layer is nested is called the *parent* layer. The nested layer is sometimes also called the *child* layer.
- Nested layers can be moved as one unit, which can save time in a complex layout.

- To nest a layer, drag the child layer in the Layers task pane on top of the parent layer. The child layer then appears indented below the parent layer, as shown in the illustration below.

Nesting a layer

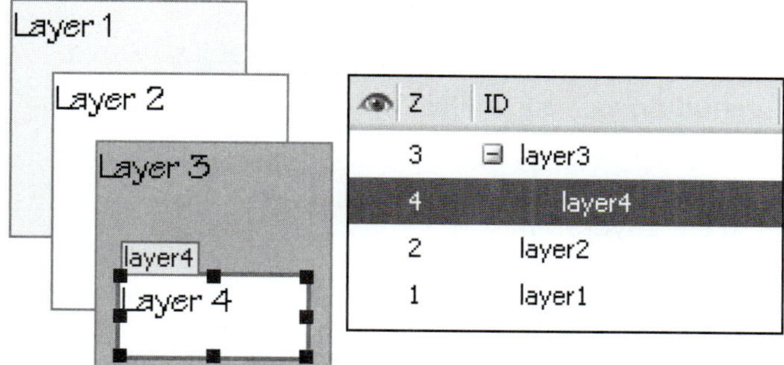

- Note the minus sign that appears to the left of the layer3 name in the layers list. This sign indicates that the parent layer has been expanded to display the child layer.
- Click the minus sign to change it to a plus sign and collapse the display. This enables an author to work with both the parent and nested layer as a single unit.

Procedures

Insert Layers

1. Click **Insert** .... Alt+I
2. Click **Layer** .... Y

   OR

   Display Layers task pane:

   a. Click **View**.............. Alt+I

   b. Click **Task Pane** .... K

   c. Click **Other Task Panes** down arrow on task pane.

   d. Click **Layers**.
3. Click [icon] to insert default-sized layer.
4. Click [icon] to display drawing pointer and draw layer to desired size.

Size and Position Layers

By dragging

1. Click layer border to select layer.
2. Resize by placing mouse pointer on sizing handle to display double-pointed arrow and dragging.
3. Position by placing mouse pointer anywhere on border to display four-headed arrow and then drag to new location.

Size and position absolutely

1. Double-click layer border to select it and open Layers task pane, if necessary.
2. Click **Positioning** at bottom of Layers task pane.
3. Specify absolute position values in **Left** and **Top** or **Right** and **Bottom** boxes.
4. Specify exact size in **Width** and **Height** boxes.

Rename Layer

1. Double-click layer to select it and open Layers task pane, if necessary.

In Layers task pane

2. Double-click default layer name.
3. Type new name.

Apply Borders and Shading to Layers

1. Double-click layer to select it and open Layers task pane, if necessary.
2. Click **Borders and Shading** at bottom of Layers task pane.
3. Click **Borders** tab to apply a border:

   a. Select border style.

   b. Click **Color** down arrow and select color from palette, or create custom color.

   c. Click **Width** spin buttons to select border weight.

   d. Click border icons to apply selected border style to preview.

   e. Specify padding values if desired.
4. Click **Shading** tab to apply shading:

   a. Click **Background color** down arrow and select shading color from palette, or create custom color.

   b. Click **Foreground color** down arrow and select text color from palette, or create custom color.

Insert Layer Content

Insert text

- Select layer if necessary and begin typing at insertion point.

OR

- Paste copied text at insertion point.

OR

Insert picture or other element

1. Select layer to display insertion point.
2. Use regular menu command (such as Insert>Picture>From File) to insert element.
3. Adjust layer size as necessary to fit object.

Change Layer Stacking Order

In Layers task pane

1. Click layer name to select layer.
2. Drag layer to desired position in layers list.

OR

1. Double-click Z-order number in layer to change.
2. Type new Z-order number.
   ✓ *The higher the number, the closer to the top of the stacking order.*

Change Layer Visibility

In Layers task pane, to hide layer

1. Click in (**Layer Visibility**) column for layer until "eye" closes.
2. Click outside Layers task pane to complete operation.

To make hidden layer visible

- Click (**Layer Visibility**) to remove closed eye.

OR

- Right-click a layer in the Layers task pane and click a visibility option.

Nest Layers

In Layers task pane

1. Click layer that will become child layer to select it.
2. Drag child layer on top of parent layer.

To unnest layers

- Drag child layer just above parent layer.

Exercise Directions

1. Start FrontPage 2003.
2. Open **Coffee**.
3. Open **index.htm**. Hide the Folder List.
4. Draw a new layer to the right of the *Information* interactive button. The layer should be about 195 by 20 pixels. The top of the layer should align with the top of the interactive button.
5. Rename the layer **info**.
6. Click in the info layer, change the font to Architect, press **Spacebar** twice, and type **About Us | Hours | Location**.
   ✓ *If you don't have Architect, select another sans serif font.*
7. If necessary, adjust the layer size to display all text on a single line.
8. Apply border and shading as follows:
   - Click More Colors in the Shading tab's Background color palette and specify the value Hex={FF,F2,DE}. This is a cream color you will use several times in the Web site.
   - Apply a 1-pt Maroon solid border to the top of the layer only.
9. Link *About Us* to **about.htm** and *Hours* to **hours.htm**.
   ✓ *For now, you will create only this pop-out menu, but your design calls for another pop-out menu for the* Entertainment *button.*
10. Hide the info layer, as you're done with it for the moment.
11. Use the Cut button to cut the first paragraph of text on the page.
12. Insert a new layer below the interactive buttons and paste the cut text into it. Resize the layer to about 318 by 158 pixels, and rename the layer as **shadowtext**.
13. Hide this layer for the time being.
14. Draw a new layer in about the same location as the shadowtext layer and size it about 305 by 190 pixels. Name the layer **shadow**.
15. Insert in the shadow layer **shadowlayer.jpg** from the Data folder. Save the page to store the picture in the images folder.
16. Make the shadowtext layer visible and nest it in the shadow layer.
    ✓ *The shadowtext layer may move on the page after you nest it. This is normal.*

17. Drag the shadowtext layer on top of the shadow layer on the page, so the text sits on the shadowed rectangle.

    ✓ *If you have trouble getting the text to position on the graphic, change the Z-order for both layers to 2.*

18. Move the shadow layer (the nested layer should move with it) to Left 2px and Top 215px then hide both layers so you can continue to work on the page.
19. Draw a new layer 188 pixels wide by 250 pixels high. Position the layer to the right of the page title, at 357px by 15px. Name the new layer **pix**.
20. Insert in the pix layer the **cup.jpg** graphic stored in the images folder.
21. Insert three more layers to hold the remaining paragraphs of text on the page.
22. For the first remaining paragraph (*Looking for more…*) format as follows:
    - Name the layer **jump**.
    - Size the layer to about 360 by 130 pixels.
    - Position the layer at 290px by 355px.
    - Shade the layer with the cream color you used earlier, and apply a border style such as Outset. You can adjust border colors as desired and add 2px padding at top, left, and right.
23. For the blurb from *City Beat*, format as follows:
    - Name the layer **beat**.
    - Size the layer to 100 by 130 pixels. Center the text in the layer.
    - Shade the layer with Maroon and change its text to white.
    - Position the layer at 115px by 405px.
24. For the blurb from the *Richmond Post*:
    - Name the layer **post**.
    - Size the layer to 260 by 85 pixels.
    - Position the layer at 425px by 261px.
    - Apply the same shading and text formats as for the beat layer.
25. Create one last layer to hold the Flash animation on the page:
    - Name the layer **flash**.
    - Move the Flash animation into the layer.
    - Resize the animation to 170 by 137. (Deselect the Keep aspect ratio check box to resize to these measurements.)
    - Deselect the Loop option on the General tab.
    - Size the layer to 194 by 154 pixels.
    - Position the layer at 536px by 82px.
26. Make all layers visible.
27. Preview the Web in the browser. Your screen should look similar to Illustration A. Make any necessary adjustments to layer position or stacking order to achieve a similar layout.

    ✓ *Be sure to test the links on your pop-out menu and the Coffee Menu interactive button. The Entertainment button has no active links.*

28. Close the browser.
29. Close the Web site.
30. Exit FrontPage 2003.

Illustration A

On Your Own

1. Start FrontPage 2003.
2. Open **Winter**.
3. Open **index.htm**.
4. Insert layers to hold the text and picture on this page. You can decide how much text to insert in each layer.
5. Position the layers in a pleasing layout.
6. Format the layers as desired with borders and shading.

   ✓ *If you have access to a graphic design program, you may want to create objects with special fill effects such as gradients or shadows to insert in the layers, then nest text over them, as you did in the exercise.*
7. Adjust stacking order as necessary to display layers attractively.
8. Preview the Web site in the browser.
9. Close the browser and the Web site.
10. Exit FrontPage 2003.

Exercise 25

◆ **About Behaviors** ◆ **Attach Action to an Object**
◆ **Modify Events and Actions** ◆ **FrontPage Behaviors**

On the Job

FrontPage 2003's new behaviors make it possible to create sophisticated actions without having to write a single line of code. Select an object, choose an action to apply to it, supply necessary information for the script, and then specify an event that will cause the script to run. FrontPage includes many actions to choose from, including behaviors that change properties, open browser windows, swap images, and so on.

In this exercise, you will continue working on the Sitwell's Coffee House Web site. You will apply a number of different actions to objects in the Web to provide a true interactive experience for Web visitors.

Terms

action
Java script that performs a specific task such as opening a window or changing text properties when prompted by an *event*.

event
Operation such as a mouse click or key press that causes an *action* to run.

jump menu
List of links in the form of a drop-down menu.

Notes

About Behaviors

- Behaviors are new in FrontPage 2003. This feature allows authors who have no script-writing experience to attach prewritten scripts to objects to perform a variety of tasks, including:
  - Changing text formatting.
  - Controlling layer visibility.
  - Opening a new browser window containing a related Web page.
  - Creating a jump menu to display links in a drop-down menu format.
  - Swapping images.
- Using behaviors can give a Web site a more professional look and feel by providing interactive features important to Web site users.

  ✓ *You have already used dynamic HTML scripting when inserting interactive buttons.*

Attach Action to Object

- Insert an **action** on a Web page by following a few simple steps:
  - Select the object to which the script will be attached.
  - Select the action to attach.
  - Supply information for the script.
  - Specify the operation that will cause the action to run.

Select Object to Attach Script To

- An action can be attached to an entire page, to a paragraph, to a link, to a picture—even to a single cell of a table.
- On a simple page, it is an easy task to click an object to select it.

- On more complex pages, it is helpful to use the Quick Tag Selector at the top of the page to select the appropriate tag.
- In the illustration below, for example, the author wants to select the last cell in the table. Clicking the <td> tag in the Quick Tag Selector highlights the correct cell.

Use Quick Tag Selector to select object

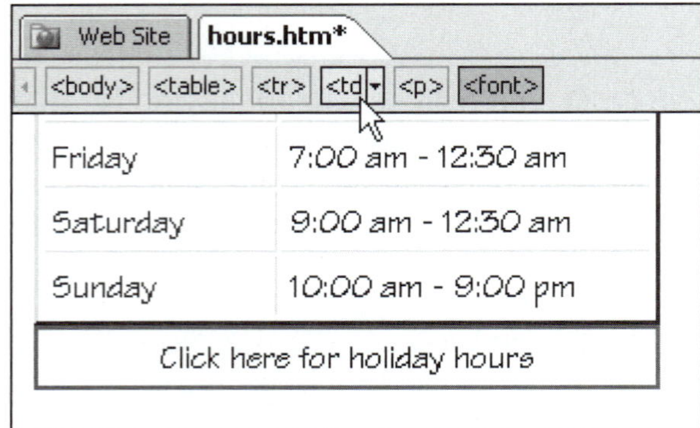

Select Action to Attach

- Use the Behaviors task pane to select and work with behaviors.
- Click the Format>Behaviors command on the menu bar to open the Behaviors task pane.
- To choose the action to attach, click the Insert button in the task pane to display a list of action options.
- Options can vary according to the object that has been selected. For example, if a picture has been selected, the Jump Menu action is not available for use.

Provide Information for Behavior

- After an author selects an action, a dialog box opens to allow the author to provide the information that behavior needs.
- The dialog box changes according to the action. The Change Property dialog box shown at the top of the next column, for example, allows the Webmaster to change font, position, borders, and visibility properties for a selected object.

Change Property dialog box

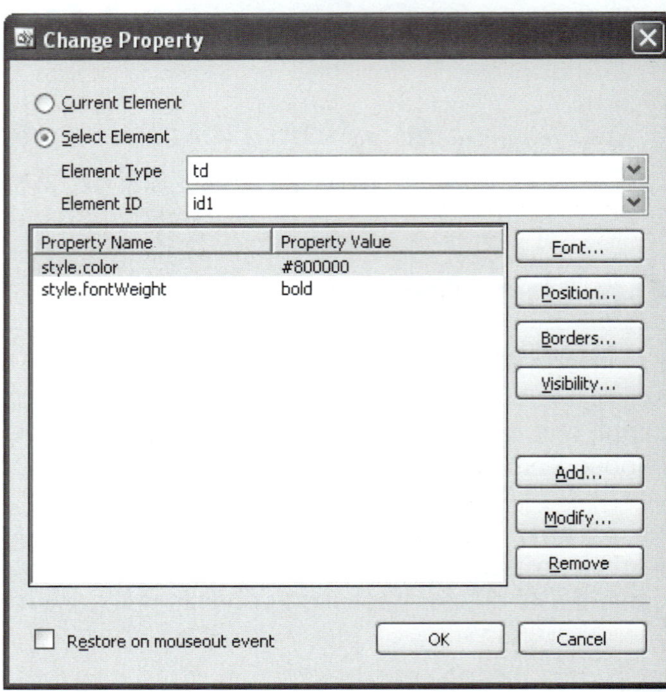

Specify Event

- After an author has supplied necessary information, FrontPage adds the action to the Behaviors task pane. The Action column of the task pane shows the action, and the Event column shows the **event** that will trigger the action.
- FrontPage supplies a default event for each action, but it may not be the one the author wants. Click the event's down arrow to display a list of other events available for the action.
- FrontPage has a wide variety of events with names that may be confusing for the first-time user. Some of the more common are described below.

Event	Event occurs when
onclick	User clicks object
ondblclick	User double-clicks object
onload	Page or image finishes loading
onmousedown	Mouse button is pressed
onmouseout	Mouse pointer is moved away
onmouseover	Mouse pointer is over object
onmouseup	Mouse button is released
onunload	User leaves a page

Modify Events and Actions

- Previewing is a must when working with actions. If the action doesn't work as desired, an author can easily modify both actions and events from the Behaviors task pane.
- Double-click an action in the task pane to open its dialog box for modifications. Click the event down arrow to select a new triggering event.
- An author can also simply remove the action by selecting it in the task pane and clicking the Delete button.
- Deleting the action in the task pane doesn't usually delete it from the page code. To remove all traces of the action, use Split or Code view to locate the code in the <head> portion of the page and delete it manually.

FrontPage Behaviors

- FrontPage 2003 offers 18 actions an author can attach to various page elements. For complete information on all of these actions, consult FrontPage's Help files.
- The sections below discuss some of the more common actions that an author can use to add functionality to a Web.

Change Property

- The Change Property action can be used to change a number of properties for a selected object. Use this action, for example, to apply text formatting, add a border to an object, change object position, or change layer visibility.
- The biggest challenge in using this action is to properly select the element whose properties are to be changed.
- The Change Property dialog box allows an author to apply changes to the currently selected element or to select an element from within the dialog box.
- Use the Element Type list to select the HTML tag of the desired element. The Element ID list allows an author to select a specific element if more than one is present on a page.
- For example, to select a specific layer, choose the <div> tag in the Element Type list and then choose the layer name in the Element ID list.
- Once the correct element has been selected, use the Font, Position, Borders, and Visibility buttons as necessary to change the element's properties.
- Select the Restore on mouseout event check box in the Change Property dialog box to restore original properties once the mouse is moved away from the object.

Jump Menu

- A **jump menu** is a drop-down list of links (see illustration below). A visitor can click any of the items on the menu to jump to that link's target. Jump menus are efficient ways to group links on a page.

Jump menu

- To set up a jump menu, use the Jump Menu action to open the Jump Menu dialog box. Here the author can add items to the menu.
- Menu items require a choice name (the name that will display in the menu) and a value (the URL of the target page) (see illustration below).

Add choices to the menu

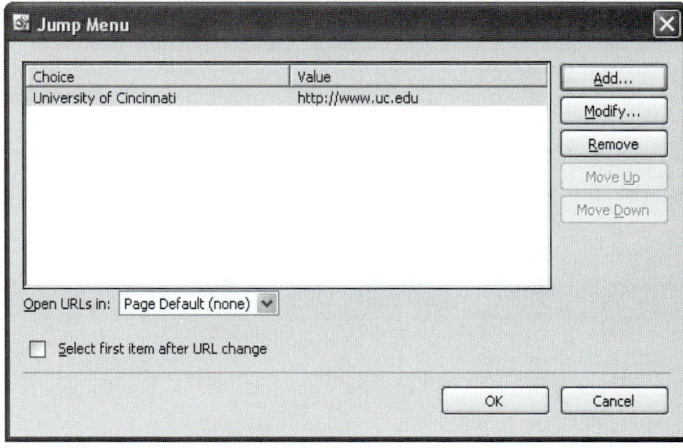

✓ *Note that the URL must be an absolute URL, with the http protocol as well as the complete path.*

- The Webmaster can choose whether to open target pages in the current page or in a new browser window.
- After several choices have been added, an author can use the Move Up or Move Down button to rearrange the list. Click the Modify button to change a particular choice, or the Remove button to delete a choice.

Open Browser Window

- The Open Browser Window action opens a new browser window containing a designated Web page when the specified event occurs.
- This action is a good way to display information related to a page without forcing the visitor to jump away from the original page.
- In the illustration below, for example, the Sitwell's Holiday Hours window opens when a visitor clicks the *Click here for holiday hours* option below the table.

Opened browser window

- Specify the settings for this action in the Open Browser Window dialog box (see below).

Open Browser Window dialog box

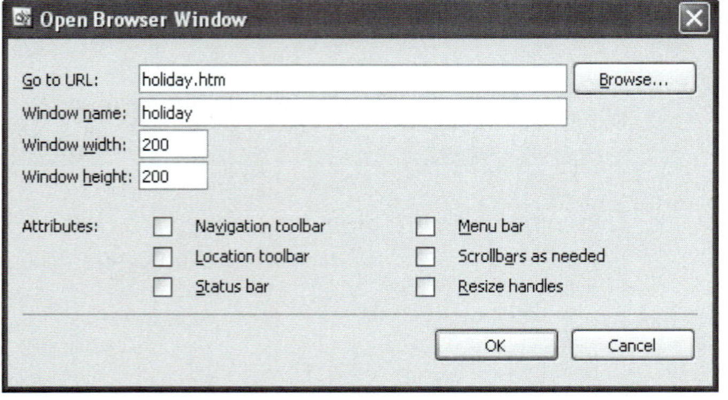

- Here the Webmaster can specify the URL of the page that will open in the new browser window and supply a name for the window.

  ✓ *The window name is not the same as the window title, which will display in the window's title bar. The window name is used in the Java code to identify the new browser window.*

- The Webmaster has a number of options for formatting the browser window: he or she can specify width and height and attributes such as whether the new window will have toolbars, a menu bar, scrollbars, or a resize handle.

Swap Image

- Recall that you have already learned to swap pictures using a dynamic HTML effect. The behavior Swap Image action works much the same way.
- In the Swap Image action's dialog box, select the original image and then specify the swap image (see below).

Swap Image dialog box

  ✓ *An author can set up more than one image to swap using this dialog box.*

- Clicking the Restore on mouseout event check box at the lower-left corner of this dialog box automatically attaches the Swap Image Restore action. This action swaps the images back so the original one displays again when the mouse is moved away from the image.

Procedures

Attach Action to Object

1. Select object to attach action to.

   ✓ *Use Quick Tag Selector for best results.*

Display Behaviors task pane

2. Click **Format**................ Alt+Y
3. Click **Behaviors**.................. V
4. Click Insert ▾ in Behaviors task pane.
5. Select action from Insert menu.
6. Supply information required for action.
7. Click the event name and then the events down arrow for action if necessary to specify different event.

Modify Events and Actions

In Behaviors task pane

- Double-click action to open its dialog box and make adjustments.
- Click the event's down arrow for an action to select a different event.
- Click action to select it and click Delete to remove action entirely.

  ✓ *It may be necessary to remove script manually in Code or Split view.*

Change Text Properties

1. Select paragraph to which new text properties will apply.
2. Display Behaviors task pane and select Change Property action.

   ✓ *See above for instructions on attaching action to object.*

In Change Property dialog box

3. Verify that correct tag displays in **Element Type** box.
4. Change text properties:
   - Click Font... . Alt+F to specify font options.
   - Click Position... . Alt+P to position selected paragraph.
   - Click Borders... . Alt+B to specify border options.

Change Layer Visibility Properties

1. Select object or tag that controls layer visibility.
2. Display Behaviors task pane and select Change Property action.

In Change Property dialog box

3. Click **Select Element**.. Alt+S option.
4. Click **Element Type** drop-down list and select **div**.
5. Click **Element ID** drop-down list and select layer name.
6. Click Visibility... ...... Alt+V and select desired visibility property.

Jump Menu Action

1. Position insertion point in paragraph where jump menu will display.
2. Display Behaviors task pane and select Jump Menu action.

In Jump Menu dialog box

3. Click Add... ...... Alt+A
4. Type **Choice** text (actual menu item).
5. Type **Value** URL (address of choice target).

   OR

   Click Browse... .... Alt+B and navigate to URL to get its address.
6. Click OK.
7. Click **Open URLs in** drop-down list and specify **New Window** to open target in new window.
8. Adjust items on menu using Move Up or Move Down button.

Open Browser Window Action

1. Select object that will control action.
2. Display Behaviors task pane and select Open Browser Window action.

In Open Browser Window dialog box

3. Type name/path of target page.

   OR

   Click Browse... .... Alt+B and navigate to target page.
4. Type name for window (no spaces between words).
5. Specify width and height of window.
6. Select additional attributes for window.

Swap Image Action

1. Select original image.
2. Display Behaviors task pane and select Swap Image action.

In Swap Images dialog box

3. Select original image, if necessary, in image list.
4. Type name of swap image in Swap Image URL box

   OR

   Click Browse... .... Alt+B and navigate to swap image.

Swap Image Restore Action

1. Display Behaviors task pane and select Swap Image Restore action.
2. Click OK to insert action.

   OR

   Select **Restore on mouseout event**.......................... Alt+R check box in Swap Images dialog box.

Exercise Directions

1. Start FrontPage 2003.
2. Open **Coffee**.
3. Open **index.htm**. Hide the Folder List, if necessary.

   ✓ *Your first task is to script the info layer. Recall that this will be a pop-out menu that will display when a visitor clicks the Information interactive button. You don't want the menu to appear on the page until the button is clicked, so you will attach an action to the page to hide this layer only when the page loads.*

4. Use the Quick Tag Selector to select the <body> tag for the page. (The entire page is selected.)
5. Display the Behaviors task pane. Note that there is already one behavior listed: Preload images. Specify the Change Property action. Supply the following information for the script:
   - Click the **Select Element** option.
   - If necessary, specify the **<div>** tag in the Element Type list.
   - If necessary, select the **info** layer in the Element ID list.
   - Click the **Visibility** button and select the **Hidden** option.
   - Note that FrontPage automatically selects the onload event, which is correct in this case.
6. Check to make sure the action works: save the page and preview it in the browser. The info layer should not display when the page opens.

   ✓ *Now you need to attach an action to the Information button that will make the hidden layer visible when a visitor clicks the interactive button.*

7. Click the *Information* interactive button to select it. Note that four actions already appear in the Behaviors task pane for this button. (These actions control the three button appearances.)
8. Specify the Change Property action. Select **Select** Element option, the info **<div>** tag, and the **info** tag, as in step 5, and select the **Visible** Visibility option. FrontPage adds an onclick event to the list, which is correct.
9. Save the page and refresh the browser, if desired, to test the action: click the Information button to see the menu pop out to the right.
10. For more visual interest on the page, swap the cup picture with a photo as follows:
    - Select the cup image and specify the Swap Image action.
    - In the Swap Images dialog box, select **cup.jpg**. Use the Browse button to locate the **oval.jpg** image in the Web site's images folder.
    - Select the Restore on mouseout event check box.
11. Insert a jump menu in the layer that begins *Looking for more information ...* as follows:
    - Click at the end of the text and press **Enter** to create a new paragraph. Apply center alignment.
    - Specify the Jump Menu action for this paragraph.
    - Add menu choices as follows. If you know the Web addresses of a movie theater or book store in your area, supply the correct URLs along with the jump menu choice.

      New Times Books
      http://www.prenticehall.com

      Village Theatre
      http://www.imdb.com

      University of Cincinnati
      http://www.uc.edu
    - Specify that the target pages will open in a new browser window.
12. Save changes to the page and test all actions. Your page should look like Illustration A after you have tried the actions.

    ✓ *You may find that your first jump menu choice won't work until after you have tried other choices.*

13. Open **hours.htm**.
14. Select the last cell in the table using the Quick Selector's <td> tag.
15. Change text properties as follows:
    - Specify the Change Property action.
    - Accept the Current Element option.
    - Click **Font**. Change the style to Bold and the font color to Maroon.
    - Click **Borders**. Specify a 2-pt Maroon border on the bottom only.
    - Select the Restore on mouseout event check box.
    - Specify the onmouseover event, if necessary.
16. Now you need to add another action that will open a window when a visitor clicks the text you have just formatted:
    - With the same <td> tag selected, specify the Open Browser Window action.

- Browse to the **holiday.htm** page in the current Web.
- Name the window **holiday**.
- Specify a window size of 200 pixels wide by 220 pixels high.
- Make sure the onclick event is applied to this action.

17. Test the actions on this page in the browser. Make any necessary adjustments to the actions.
18. Close the browser.
19. Close the Web site.
20. Exit FrontPage 2003.

Illustration A

On Your Own

1. Start FrontPage 2003.
2. Open any Web site you have created previously in this course.
   ✓ *Or, you may want to continue working on the Coffee Web site.*
3. Practice applying actions to elements in the site. You may want to do some research on actions you haven't yet used and try applying them. For example:
   - Use the Play Sound action to play a sound when a page opens or closes (for example, add a jingle bell sound to the **holiday.htm** page in the Coffee Web site).
   - Use the Popup Message action to create a warning box for an element.
   - Use the Set Text of Status Bar action to supply further information about an element in the status bar.
4. Try a number of event options so you get a good feel for how they control actions.
5. Test your actions as you create them and modify actions and events as necessary to work properly.
6. Close the browser and the Web site.
7. Exit FrontPage 2003.

Exercise 26

◆ **Critical Thinking** ◆ **Challenge**

In this exercise, you will work on the newly constructed Columbia Savings Web site. You will add and format a frames page with information on the bank's services. You will add layers to the home page controlled by behaviors. You will also jazz up the Web site with a number of animations and special effects such as a background sound, a marquee, and interactive buttons.

Exercise Directions

1. Start FrontPage 2003.
2. Open **Bank**.
3. Open **index.htm**.
4. Locate an appropriate background music file for the Web. Choose how many times to play it and store it in the images folder.
   ✓ *Search for music on your system or on the Web, download a file if necessary, and then insert it as the background sound.*
5. Close the Folder List and display the Layers task pane. Note that the page has three layers. Two layers (services and loans) are stacked on top of each other to the right of the interactive buttons. You will first complete work on the layers, then link them to the interactive buttons.
6. Complete the interactive layers as follows:
   - Select the aboutus layer and adjust its dimensions to 290 by 100 pixels and positioning to Left 123px and Top 147px. You should now have three layers stacked on top of each other, though only the top one is visible.
   - Apply border and shading formatting to the aboutus layer similar to those for the other two layers, using a shading color of your choice.
7. Attach behaviors and link the layers to the interactive buttons:
   - Change the visibility of each of these layers so they will not display when the page loads. (You will have to change the visibility property for each layer separately.)
   - Attach each layer to its proper interactive button so that when a visitor clicks the button, the correct layer opens.
   - Attach a Change Property action to each layer so that it will be hidden when a visitor clicks on the layer.
     ✓ *Select each layer in the Layers task pane, then click Behaviors at the bottom of the Layers task pane (under See also) to open the Behaviors task pane to attach the action.*
8. To let visitors know they can close a layer by clicking it, insert another layer below the layer stack with the instruction **Click box to close it.** Format this layer as desired.
9. Click in the text at the bottom of the page, *Click for Current Columbia CD Offerings*. Modify the text properties as follows:
   - Change the properties of this text to emphasize it when a visitor places the mouse over the text.
   - Then attach an action to the text that opens a browser window when the text is clicked. The browser window should contain **cd.htm**. Adjust the browser window size to fit the table attractively.
10. Test all actions on this page and make any necessary adjustments.
11. Open **checking.htm**, **savings.htm**, and **smartcard.htm**.
12. Apply a text animation effect to the first heading on each of these pages. Save and close the pages.
13. Create a new frames page in the site as follows:
    - Create the frames page using the Banner and Contents template. Name the page **services.htm** and give it the page title **Services**.

- Set **checking.htm** as the initial page in the main frame.
- Create a new page in the banner frame and name it **banner.htm** with the page title **Banner**.
- Insert the heading **Services**. Apply the Heading 2 style and change the text color to Gray.
- Use the **background.jpg** file from the images folder for the banner background.
- Create a new page in the contents frame and name it **contents.htm** with the page title **Contents**. Apply the **background.jpg** background.

14. Insert the following paragraphs as a vertical list:

    Checking Accounts

    Savings Accounts

    Smart Card

15. Format the paragraphs as desired and link them to **checking.htm**, **savings.htm**, and **smartcard.htm**.
16. Hide the frame borders for the frames page.
17. Create a new frame within the contents frame and insert three interactive buttons the same style as those used on **index.htm**. Link the buttons to **index.htm**, **aboutus.htm**, and **loan.htm**. Use the same background picture as for the banner and contents frames if desired.

    ✓ *Don't forget to set the correct target page.*

18. Save the new frame page as **nav.htm** with the page title **Buttons**. Hide the frame border, if necessary.
19. Open **aboutus.htm**.
20. Swap the picture of bills with **coins.jpg** in the images folder with the onmouseover event. (Use any DHTML option for swapping images.)
21. Insert three interactive buttons in the table cell below the main heading to link to **index.htm**, **loan.htm**, and **services.htm**. Format the buttons as desired.
22. Open **loan.htm**.
23. At the bottom of the page, insert a marquee that reads:

    Current conventional loans from 5.75%

24. Format the marquee as desired.

    ✓ *To allow the background picture to display around the moving text, choose Automatic on the Background color palette in the Marquee Properties dialog box.*

25. Insert interactive buttons below the main heading to link to **index.htm**, **aboutus.htm**, and **services.htm**.
26. Open **index.htm**.
27. Preview the Web in the browser. Check all links and animations. Your frames page should look similar to Illustration A.
28. Close the browser.
29. Close the Web site.
30. Exit FrontPage 2003.

Illustration A

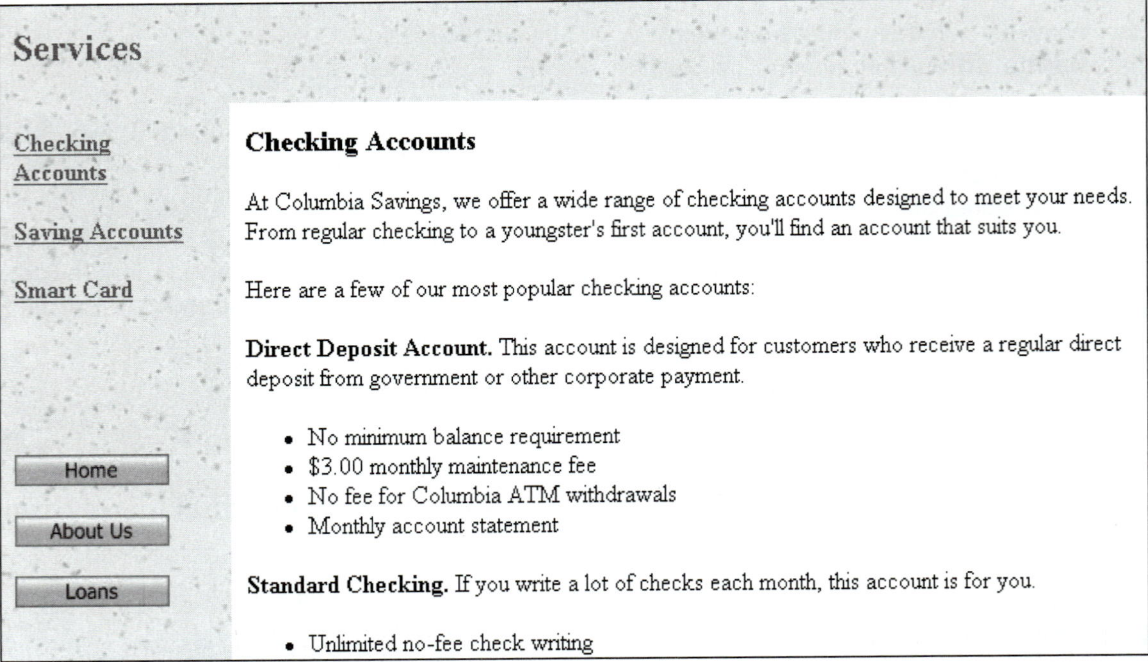

Challenge Exercise

1. Search the Internet for sites that contain sound files for use. Add a page titled **SoundResources** to the **Resources** Web site you created on page 54 to contain links to the sites that you found.
2. Find particular sound files that would fit in Web sites that you have created thus far in this course. Save them to a folder on your own computer, or to a network folder that everyone in the class can access. As always, respect copyright and terms of use.
3. If you have a voice/sound recorder, make your own sound files to add to this shared folder and to the Web sites created thus far.
4. Write out short, step-by-step instructions on how you created your own sound files.
5. Search for free scripting additions (such as Javascript, Java applets, or CGI scripts) on the Web. Read FrontPage's Help files and any online documentation you can find on how you would incorporate these elements in your Web sites.

LESSON 5

Advanced Web Formatting: Dynamic Templates, Themes, and Styles

Exercise 27

◆ **About Dynamic Web Templates** ◆ **Create New Template**
◆ **Attach Dynamic Web Template to New Page**
◆ **Work with Editable Areas** ◆ **Modify Template and Update Pages**

On the Job

FrontPage 2003's dynamic Web templates allow a user to set up a template for pages that contain similar or identical material. On the template page, specify areas that an author can edit on each page. Other regions become uneditable to preserve text and other elements that stay the same on each page. Attach the template to new pages and then complete the page by changing editable areas. When the template is changed, all pages attached to it automatically update.

In this exercise, you will create a dynamic Web template for a new Web site for Richmond Tech. You will establish editable areas and then attach the template to several new pages that cover some of Tech's sports programs. After modifying the template, you will observe how the pages that use the template automatically reflect the changes.

Terms

dynamic Web template
A page on which an author can specify regions that can be edited, with all other regions locked to prevent changes.

editable region
Region on a dynamic Web template page that an author can edit by adding new text, images, or other Web page elements.

noneditable region
An area on a dynamic Web template page that cannot be changed.

Notes

About Dynamic Web Templates

- You have already worked with several FrontPage templates. Templates supply a standard structure for a page that saves an author time in creating a layout.
- FrontPage 2003 includes a new feature, dynamic Web templates, that allows an author to create repetitive pages in a Web site quickly, easily, and accurately.
- A **dynamic Web template** is a page that contains areas an author can edit on each new page, as well as areas that cannot be edited.
- This makes it easy to insert information that is unique to a particular page while preserving information that stays the same from page to page.
- An author can decide which pages are attached to the template. If the template is changed, all pages attached to it also change.

Create New Template

- Create a dynamic Web template the same way as any other page. A template can be organized using a layout table, for example, and can contain any text or images that can be placed on a regular page.
- To save a page as a dynamic Web template, use the Dynamic Web Template (*.dwt) file type in the Save As dialog box (see illustration below).
- Selecting this file type gives the template file a .dwt extension that makes it easy to locate in the Web site's files.

Save page as dynamic Web template

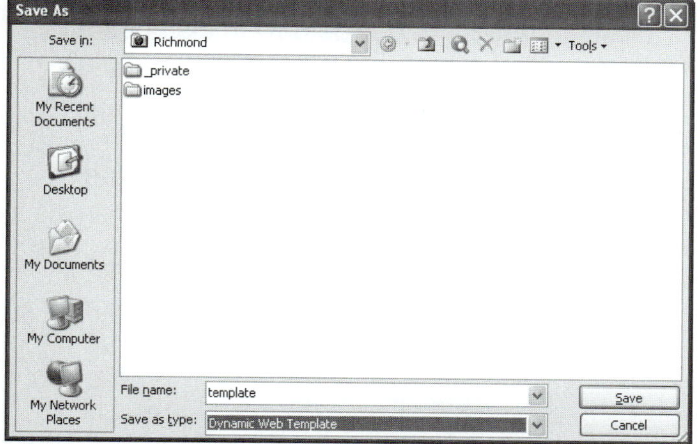

- Once the page layout is complete, the author must decide which areas of the page will be editable on each new page that uses the template.
- An area that can be changed on a new page is called an **editable region**. An area that cannot be edited is called a **noneditable region**.
- Editable regions are marked by light yellow outlines and tabs that give the name of the region.
- The illustration below shows a new page that has been attached to a dynamic Web template. Note the tabs and outlines that define each editable region.

Page attached to a dynamic Web template with editable and noneditable regions

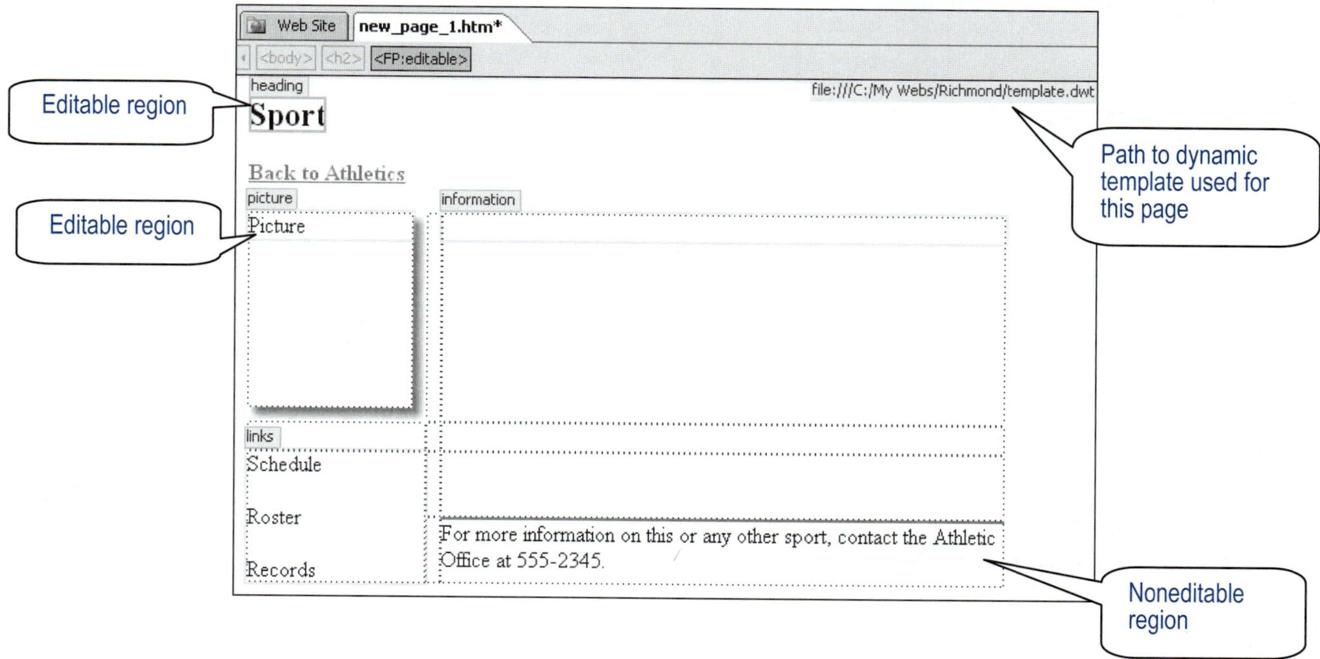

- The template used for the new page shown in the previous illustration includes four editable regions that can be used to enter the specific sport name, a picture of the sport, information about the sport, and links to more information.
- The template also includes two noneditable regions: the link back to the Athletics page and the *For more information* paragraph at the bottom of the layout table cannot be edited on this page.

  ✓ *Noneditable areas can be edited on the original template page only.*

Manage Editable Areas

- The Webmaster must designate each area of the template page that will be editable.
- Select the text, image, table cell, or other element that is to be editable and then:
  - Click the Format>Dynamic Web Template>Manage Editable Regions command on the menu bar.
  - Right-click and select Manage Editable Regions from the shortcut menu.
- Either command opens the Editable Regions dialog box (see below). Type a name for the editable region and click the Add button to add it to the list of regions.

Manage Editable Regions dialog box

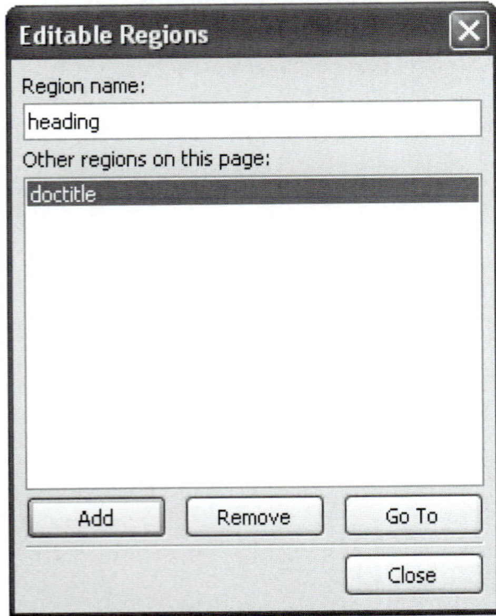

- Use this dialog box also to rename a region or to remove it from the page. On a complex page, the Goto button can help the user locate a specific region.

Attach Dynamic Web Template to New Page

- Once the template page is complete and the editable regions have been specified, the template is ready for use with new pages.
- To attach a template to a new page, use the Format>Dynamic Web Template>Attach Dynamic Web Template.
- The Attach Dynamic Web Template dialog box opens to allow the author to locate the template page.
- The new page displays all editable and noneditable regions, just as on the template.
- A dynamic Web template can also be attached to an existing page. In this case, FrontPage will ask the author to decide how to distribute the current page content among editable regions.
- In the dialog box shown below, for example, FrontPage suggests that all content in the body of the page (between the <body> tags) be included in the header editable region.

Deciding where existing content should go

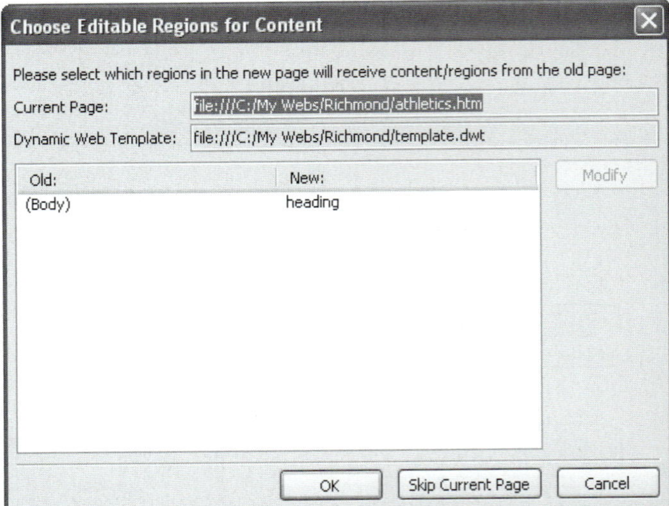

- The author can select the entry and click the Modify button to specify another editable region for the existing content.

> **Code Cues**
>
> If you look at the code of a page that has an attached template in Split or Code view, you'll see that FrontPage shades all portions of the code with light yellow to indicate what is controlled by the template. Only text you insert in editable areas is not shaded.

Work with Editable Areas

- Working with editable areas on a new page is simple. Click in the editable area and select placeholder text, if necessary. Then type new text or insert a graphic or other element just as on any page.
- Editable areas usually have some flexibility to accommodate text and images. Table cells, for example, will expand as necessary to hold content. Image sizes can be adjusted as on any page to fit the layout.

Modify Template and Update Pages

- The real value in using a dynamic Web template is the ease with which an author can manage changes to all pages attached to a template.
- An author can make changes to a single page, the template, that can then automatically be made to other pages.
- After changing the template, FrontPage displays the information box shown below when the author saves changes to the template.

FrontPage asks to update pages

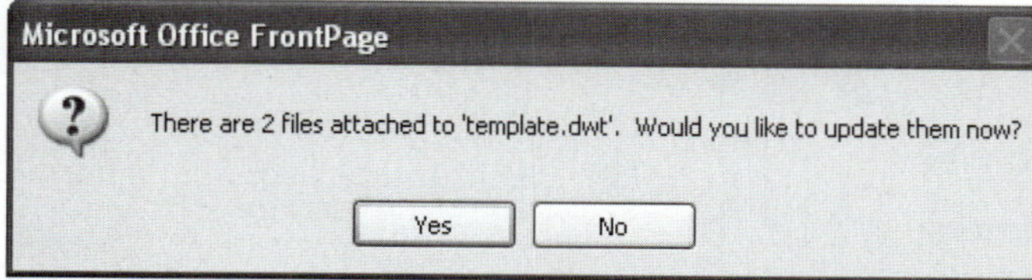

- Clicking Yes in this information box automatically updates pages attached to the template and displays a confirmation box to let the author know how many files have been updated.
- Clicking the Show log check box in the confirmation box gives further detail on the changes made, as shown at the top of the next column.
- An author can also click No to choose not to update. This is an appropriate choice when an author is making a number of changes to a template and wants to save without updating.

FrontPage confirms changes made to attached files

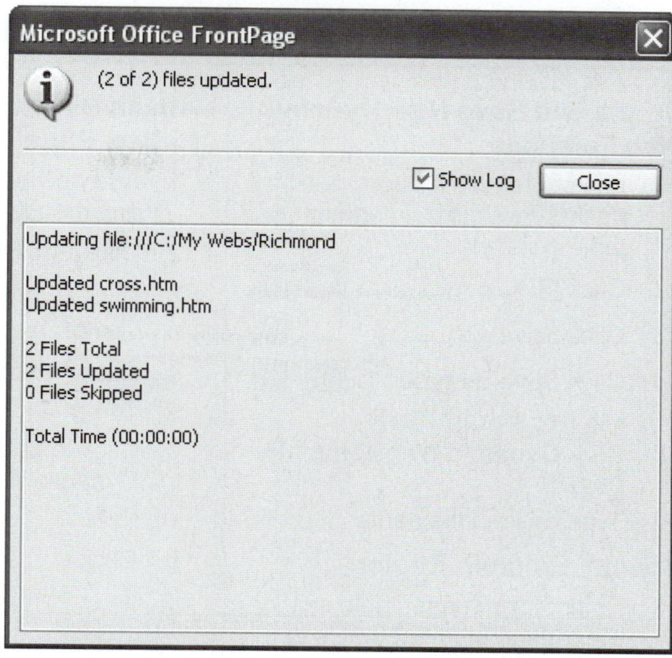

- If an author chooses not to update automatically, he or she can use the Format>Dynamic Web Template>Update Selected Page command on the menu bar to update the current page when desired.
- Some changes made to the template may not automatically display in attached pages. For example, changes made to the format of editable areas may not display.
- All changes made to noneditable areas will display, however, as will structural changes such as the addition of new editable or noneditable areas.
- If desired, an author can also detach a page from a template. Click the Format>Dynamic Web Template>Detach from Dynamic Web Template command on the menu bar to detach a page.
- When detached, the page maintains all template formatting, but it can no longer be updated from the template when the template changes.

Procedures

Create and Save New Dynamic Web Template

1. Lay out template page as desired, with text, images, table cells, etc.
2. Click **File** .... Alt+F
3. Click **Save As** .... A
4. Click **Save as type** ..... Alt+T list.
5. Click **Dynamic Web Template (*.dwt)**.
6. Type desired file name.

Specify Editable Region

1. Select text, image, table cell, or other page element that is to be editable on new pages.
2. Click **Format** .... Alt+O
3. Click **Dynamic Web Template** .... W
4. Click **Manage Editable Regions** .... M

   OR

   Right-click selection and click **Manage Editable Regions**.
5. Type name for editable region.
6. Click Add .... Alt+A
7. Click Close .... Alt+C

Attach Dynamic Web Template to New Page

1. Add new page to Web using any means.
2. Click **Format** .... Alt+O
3. Click **Dynamic Web Template** .... W
4. Click **Attach Dynamic Web Template** .... A
5. Click template file in Attach Dynamic Web Template dialog box.
6. Click Open ..... Alt+O
7. Click Close to accept the update of the new page.

Modify Dynamic Web Template

1. Open template page.
2. Modify content or format of noneditable regions, or rename or delete editable regions:
   a. Click **Format** .... Alt+O
   b. Click **Dynamic Web Template** .... W
   c. Click **Manage Editable Regions**.

      OR

      Right-click selection and click **Manage Editable Regions**.
   d. Select region name, type new name, and click Rename.

      OR

      Select region name and click Remove to delete editable area.

Update Attached Pages

1. After making changes to template page, click (**Save** button).
2. When prompted to update attached pages, click Yes to automatically update all attached pages.

   OR

   Click No to update manually at a later time.
3. To update manually:
   a. Click **Format** .... Alt+O
   b. Click **Dynamic Web Template** .... W
   c. Click **Update Selected Page** .... U
4. To detach page from template:
   a. Click **Format** .... Alt+O
   b. Click **Dynamic Web Template** .... W
   c. Click **Detach from Dynamic Web Template** .... D

Exercise Directions

1. Start FrontPage 2003.
2. Open **Richmond**.
3. Open **template.htm**. This page will be used to create the dynamic Web template.
4. Save the page as **template.dwt** in the current Web site.
5. Select the heading *Sport* at the top of the page and create from it an editable region named **heading**.
6. Select the table cell with the drop shadow and create an editable region named **picture**.
7. Select the wide table cell to the right of the picture cell and create an editable region named **information**.
8. Select the table cell below the picture cell that currently contains three lines of text and create an editable region named **links**.
9. Save **template.dwt**.
10. Add a new page to the Web site and save it as **cross.htm** with the page title **Cross Country**.
11. Attach the **template.dwt** template to the new page. Notice the editable regions. Place the mouse pointer over the link at the top of the page to see that you are unable to select or change it because it's a noneditable region.
12. Edit the **cross.htm** page as follows:
    - Change the *Sport* heading at the top of the page to **Cross Country**.
    - Delete the *Picture* placeholder in the picture editable region and insert the **cross.jpg** image from the images folder in the Web site.
    - Insert the following text in the information editable region.

      Head Coach: Brian Wilcox

      Assistant Coaches: Emily Jordan, Tom Guttierez

      The Cross Country team meets for practice Monday through Friday, from 3:30 to 5:30, at the outdoor track.
13. Save changes and preview the page in the browser.
14. Add another new page to the Web site and save it as **swimming.htm** with the page title **Swimming**.
15. Attach the template.dwt template to the new page and edit the page as follows:
    - Change the *Sport* heading to **Swimming**.
    - Insert the **swimming.jpg** image from the images folder into the picture editable region.
    - Add the following text to the information editable region.

      Head Coach: Stephanie Willis

      Assistant Coaches: Jake Pohl, Marcy Gordon, Rafe Florez

      The Tech Titans swim team finished a very respectable third in state competition as a result of the fabulous kick of the men's Freestyle Relay team. Join us for winter swimming at Titan Natatorium, 3:00 to 5:30 Monday through Friday.
16. Save changes and preview the page.
17. Make **template.dwt** active and modify the template as follows:
    - Change the color of the link at the top of the page to Gray and boldface the link.
    - Insert a 2-pixel gray border to the top of the table cell that contains information about contacting the Athletic Office.
    - Open **index.htm** and copy the update and copyright information from the bottom of the page.
    - Paste this information below the table on **template.dwt** and change the text of the first line to read **Page last updated March 31, 2004.**
18. Save changes to template.dwt and choose to update the two attached pages.
19. View each page to see the changes. Save and close all open pages.
20. Open **athletics.htm**. Link *Cross Country* in the table to **cross.htm** and *Swimming to* **swimming.htm**. Save changes.
21. Preview the Web in the browser and check the links and the template pages. The **swimming.htm** page should look similar to the one shown in Illustration A.
22. Close the browser.
23. Close the Web site.
24. Exit FrontPage 2003.

Illustration A

Swimming

Back to Athletics

Head Coach: Stephanie Willis

Assistant Coaches: Jake Pohl, Marcy Gordon, Rafe Florez

The Tech Titans swim team finished a very respectable third in state competition as a result of the fabulous kick of the men's Freestyle Relay team. Join us for winter swimming at Titan Natatorium, 3:00 to 5:30 Monday through Friday.

Schedule

Roster

Records

For more information on this or any other sport, contact the Athletic Office at 555-2345.

Page last updated March 31, 2004.
Copyright © Richmond Tech.

On Your Own

1. Start FrontPage 2003.
2. Review some of the Web sites you have created so far in this course, either in main exercises or On Your Own exercises.
3. Identify a Web site that might require several pages with similar content that could be created using a dynamic Web template.
4. Create the template and save it in the Web site.
5. Identify editable regions and give them appropriate names.
6. Create several new pages and attach the template to them.
7. Fill in unique information on each page.
8. Modify the template as necessary to improve the look of the pages and update all attached pages.
9. Preview the Web site in the browser.
10. Close the browser and the Web site.
11. Close FrontPage 2003.

Exercise 28

◆ **About Themes** ◆ **Apply Theme**
◆ **Customize Theme** ◆ **Create New Theme**

On the Job

Use a FrontPage theme to apply a number of formatting options at one time to a page or entire Web. Themes supply backgrounds, font and color formatting, and graphic elements such as bullets and rules. A theme can be customized to change colors, graphic elements, and fonts. A Webmaster can also create a new theme from scratch using the same tools as for customizing a theme.

In this exercise, you will work on the Churchill Garden Centers Web site. You will format the site with a theme, customize the theme, and then apply the customized theme to the Web site.

Terms

theme
A collection of graphic elements and formats that can be applied to a Web site to modify Web page elements such as backgrounds, headings and other text, rules, and bullets.

Notes

About Themes

- A **theme** is a collection of graphic elements and formats that can be applied to a Web site to provide a consistent and professional-looking appearance.
- A theme can supply an interesting background graphic, graphic buttons and bullets, fonts and font styles, font colors, and horizontal rules and table borders.
  - ✓ *Graphic buttons are used in FrontPage link bars, navigation buttons controlled by FrontPage. You will learn more about inserting link bars in Lesson 6, Exercise 33.*
- FrontPage 2003 has added a number of new themes to its extensive list, as well as updated familiar themes from past versions. The Web designer can choose from over 70 different themes.
  - ✓ *Only a portion of these themes are installed via a default installation, but the remaining themes can be easily installed from the Theme task pane.*
- Previous FrontPage versions created themes using HTML coding. In FrontPage 2003, themes are applied using *cascading style sheets*. Cascading style sheet (CSS) themes result in more streamlined code for each page using a theme.
  - ✓ *You will learn more about cascading style sheets in Exercise 30.*
  - ✓ *Themes in Webs created in earlier versions of FrontPage will still display correctly in FrontPage 2003.*
- FrontPage's themes vary from extremely informal to highly professional. When choosing a theme for a Web site, consider the site's subject matter as well as its intended audience.

Apply Theme

- Choose a theme to apply in the Theme task pane. To open the Theme task pane, use the Format>Theme command on the menu bar.
- The Theme task pane (see illustration below) displays the Web's default theme, recently used themes, and available themes.

Choose a theme in the Theme task pane

- Three check boxes in the Theme task pane let the author change some theme formatting options:
  - Select the Vivid colors check box to change some theme colors to more vibrant colors.
  - Select the Active graphics check box to apply graphic elements, such as buttons, that will be animated when viewed in the browser.
  - Select the Background picture check box to insert the background picture shown in the sample.

    ✓ *Clearing this check box substitutes a plain white or color background.*

- Apply a theme to the current page by clicking it in the Theme task pane. A theme can also be designated as the Web site's default theme, which will apply it to all pages currently in the Web site.
- Designate a theme as the default by positioning the mouse pointer on the theme to display a down arrow. Click the arrow to open a shortcut menu and select *Apply as default theme*.

  ✓ *After an author designates a theme as the default theme for the Web site, it appears in the Web site default theme section of the task pane.*

- When the Web author applies a theme to a Web site that already contains text, headings, and other elements, the theme immediately formats all text and elements with its designs.
- After a theme has been designated as the default, any new page added to the site will automatically use that theme.
- Different themes may be used for different pages in a Web site to emphasize specific pages. It is also acceptable to apply a theme to some pages while leaving others unformatted for emphasis.
- Remove a theme from a page or a Web site by opening the Theme task pane and selecting (No theme) in the theme list.

Code Cues

You can find the theme of a FrontPage Web page in code by looking for a meta tag that has *Microsoft Theme* as the value for the name attribute and the theme name as the value for the content attribute. For example:
<meta name="Microsoft Theme" content="nature 1011"

Customize Theme

- All elements of a theme have been designed to work together and complement each other.
- The Web designer can, however, customize a theme to change specific elements such as colors of headings or text, images used for buttons and other graphic elements, and fonts of text and headings.

- To customize a theme, display the theme's shortcut menu and select Customize. The Customize Theme dialog box opens, as shown at the top of the next page.

Customize Theme dialog box

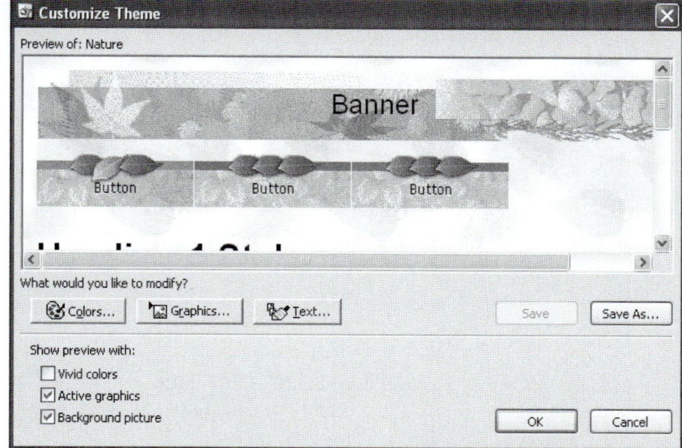

- The dialog box displays samples of the theme's format with Colors, Graphics, and Text buttons, as well as a Save and Save As button.
- Click the Colors, Graphics, or Text button to change the Customize Theme dialog box so it displays tools for modifying the theme. Tools displayed depend on which button was clicked.
- After customizing a theme, the author should save the theme with a new name to avoid overwriting default theme formats.

  ✓ *A customized theme can be applied to one page or all pages of a Web, just like any other theme.*

Change Theme Colors

- FrontPage allows the author to change the color of any theme element, such as headings, hyperlinks, and text.
- To change theme colors, click the Colors button in the Customize Theme dialog box.
- The Customize Theme dialog box displays three tabs for modifying colors (see illustration below).
  - The Color Schemes tab lists color schemes for all themes. Change the current scheme to another scheme by clicking the new scheme.

    ✓ *The blocks to the right of a color scheme's name display in order the colors for Heading 2, Heading 1, background, text, and hyperlink.*

  - The Color Wheel tab lets the author change the brightness of the colors in the current color scheme.
  - The Custom tab lets the author select a specific item from a list and change the color of that item using a familiar color palette.

    ✓ *The Preview shows new colors for theme elements as they are changed.*

Modify color for a theme element

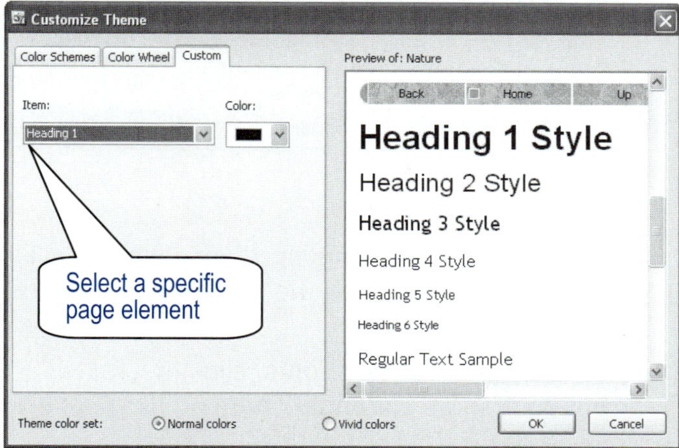

Change Theme Graphics

- Each theme provides a number of graphic images to be used for various kinds of buttons, bullets, and, sometimes, a background picture.
- The Web author can supply custom images for any of these graphic elements.

  ✓ *For example, a company could use its graphic logo as buttons on a Web page or as a Web page background.*

- To modify a theme's graphics, click the Graphics button in the Customize Theme dialog box.

- The Customize Theme dialog box (see illustration below) provides a drop-down list of graphic elements and a Picture tab that can be used to browse to the location of a new image file.
- The Preview shows how new graphic images will look in the current theme.

Modify a theme's graphics

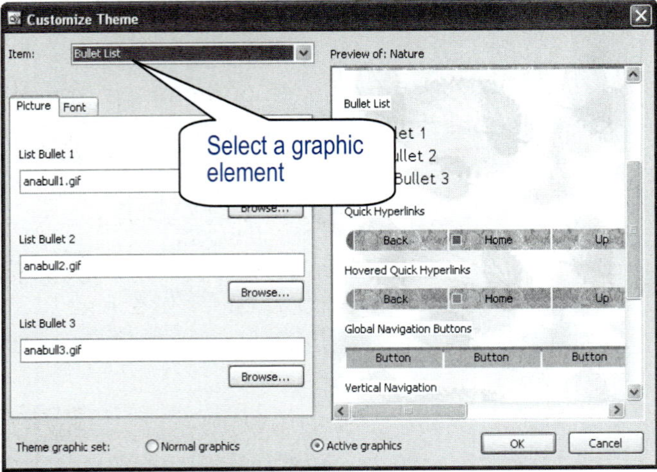

Change Theme Fonts

- A theme supplies fonts and font styles for all text elements such as the body text, headings, and links.
- To change a theme's fonts, click the Text button in the Customize Theme dialog box.
- The Customize Theme dialog box (see illustration at the top of the next page) supplies a drop-down list of text elements and a font list that can be used to select a new font for an element.
- The Preview shows new fonts as they are selected.
- Keep in mind that, as in any document, a Web page looks best if it uses only a few fonts. A good rule of thumb is one font for headings and another font for body text and links.
- If an author desires more variety in the look of the page, he or she can change the size or style of a font. For example, if a Web page requires figure or table captions, use the same font as for headings in a smaller size or different font style.

Modify font of a theme text element

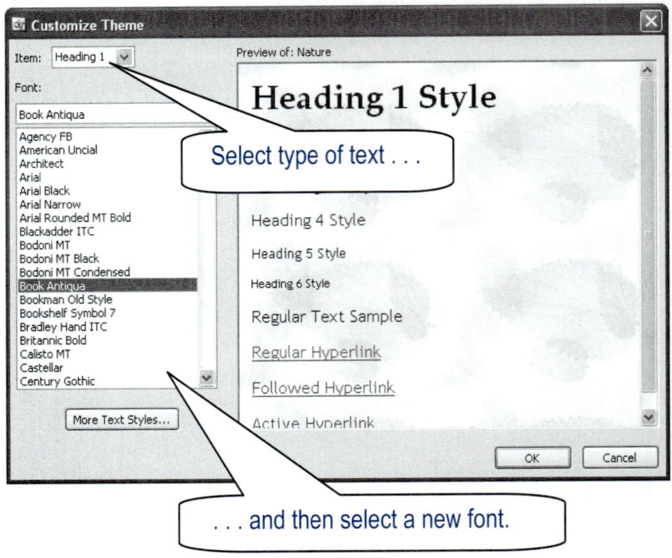

Create New Theme

- An author can also create a new theme from scratch using the Customize Theme dialog box.
- Click the *Create new theme* link at the bottom of the Theme task pane to open a Customize Theme dialog box that looks like the illustration below.

Create a new theme in the Customize Theme dialog box

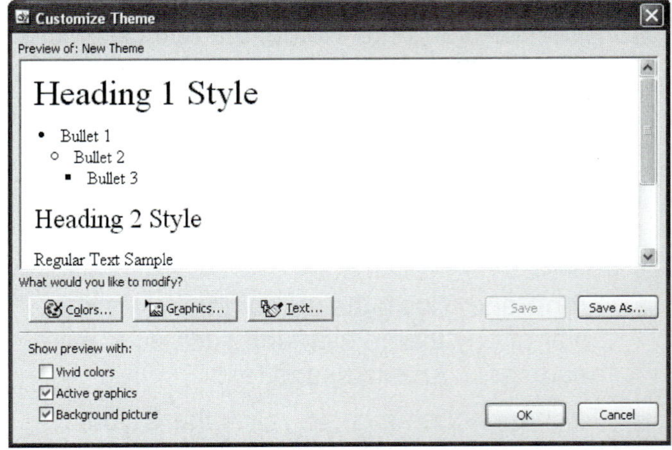

- Use the Colors, Graphics, and Text buttons to make choices for the new theme, just as when customizing a theme. Then save the theme with a descriptive name to add it to the list of themes displayed in the Theme task pane.
- Another way to apply global formatting to a Web is to create a cascading style sheet that can then be attached to specific pages in the Web. This subject is covered in Exercise 30.

Procedures

Apply Theme

1. Click **Format** .... Alt+O
2. Click **Theme** .... H
3. Select theme in Theme task pane.
4. Select or clear check boxes for:
   - Vivid colors
   - Active graphics
   - Background picture
5. Click theme thumbnail to apply to current page only.

   OR

   Make theme the Web site default:

   a. Position mouse pointer on theme thumbnail in task pane to display down arrow.

   b. Click down arrow to display shortcut menu.

   c. Click **Apply as default theme** .... A

Remove Theme

1. Click **Format** .... Alt+O
2. Click **Theme** .... H
3. Select **(No Theme)** in Theme task pane.

Change Theme Color

1. Click **Format** .... Alt+O
2. Click **Theme** .... H
3. Display down arrow on theme thumbnail.
4. Click down arrow to display shortcut menu.
5. Click **Customize** C
6. Click [Colors...] ...... Alt+O

On Color Scheme tab in Customize Theme dialog box

7. Click new color scheme in color schemes list.

On Color Wheel tab in Customize Theme dialog box

8. Move slider left or right to darken or brighten colors.

On Custom tab in Customize Theme dialog box

9. Change color of a single element:

   a. Click **Item** down arrow and click item to change.

   b. Click **Color** down arrow and select color from palette, or click **More Colors** .... M

Save Customized Theme with New Name

In Customize Theme dialog box

1. Click [Save As...] .... Alt+A
2. In Save Theme dialog box, accept default name or supply new one.

   ✓ *Do NOT click Save button after modifying a theme. This will overwrite default theme styles with modifications.*

Change Theme Graphics

1. Click **Format** .... Alt+O
2. Click **Theme** .... H
3. Display down arrow on theme thumbnail.
4. Click down arrow to display shortcut menu.
5. Click **Customize** C
6. Click [Graphics...] ... Alt+R
7. Click **Item** down arrow and select graphic element.
8. Click [Browse...] .... Alt+R to locate image to use for element.

Change Theme Fonts

1. Click **Format** .... Alt+O
2. Click **Theme** .... H
3. Display down arrow on theme thumbnail.
4. Click down arrow to display shortcut menu.
5. Click **Customize** C
6. Click [Text...] .... Alt+T
7. Click **Item** down arrow and select text element.
8. Click desired font in font list.

Create New Theme

1. Click **Create new theme** link at bottom of Theme task pane.
2. Click [Colors...], [Graphics...], and [Text...] buttons to specify theme elements.
3. Click [Save] .... Alt+S
4. In Save Theme dialog box, accept default name or supply new one.

Exercise Directions

1. Start FrontPage 2003.
2. Open **Gardens**.
3. Open **index.htm**.
4. Apply the **Nature** theme to the selected Web page. If necessary, clear the Vivid colors check box and select the Active graphics and Background picture check boxes.
5. Scroll down the **index.htm** page and note the changes the theme has made in text font and color, table borders, and the horizontal rule. The page also has a graphic background.
6. Open **history.htm** and **inventories.htm**.
7. Make the **Nature** theme the default theme for the entire Web site.
8. View the changes the theme has made on the **history.htm** and **inventories.htm** Web pages.
9. Activate **index.htm**.
10. Customize the theme as follows. (Choose to customize the version in the themes list, not the version in the Web site default area of the task pane.)
    - Change the Heading 1 font to Footlight MT Light.

      ✓ *If Footlight MT Light is not found, choose another font.*
    - Change the Heading 1 color to Green and choose a brown color for Heading 2.
    - Change the Followed Hyperlink color to the same brown you chose for Heading 2.

      ✓ *Do NOT save changes at this point. Go on to the next step to save the theme as a copy.*
11. Use the **Save As** button to save the modifications you have made with the name **Copy of Nature**.
12. Apply your customized theme to the entire Web site.

    ✓ *You may have to apply the custom theme a second time to the index.htm page to see changes.*
13. Preview the Web site in the browser and check the links. The top of the **index.htm** page should look similar to the one shown in Illustration A.

    ✓ *Notice how the leaves used for the bullets change color. This results from choosing Active graphics in the Theme dialog box.*
14. Close the browser.
15. Close the Web site.
16. Exit FrontPage 2003.

Illustration A

Churchill Garden Centers

[Home] [History] [Inventories] [Specials] [Garden Links]

Welcome to the Churchill Garden Centers Web site! Churchill's has served the Tri-State area for four generations.

Churchill Garden Centers offers the widest selection of perennials, annuals, and nursery plants of any garden store in the area. We also carry many other garden accessories, such as teak benches, decorative planters from tiny to enormous, wind chimes, fountains, and bird baths and feeders.

Take a tour of our site to learn our history and browse a selection of our current inventory. Check the Specials page to see what plants or other items we're featuring this week. Then come visit one of our Garden Centers to see what everyone's talking about.

Garden Center Locations

On Your Own

1. Start FrontPage 2003.
2. Open **Cats**.
3. Open **index.htm**.
4. Apply a theme of your choice to the Web page and then view the results. Or, create a new theme from scratch, using the **alley.gif** file from the Data folder as the theme's background picture.
5. Apply the theme to all pages in the Web site.
6. Change the font of Heading 1, Heading 2, and Heading 3 to a new font.
7. Change the theme's color scheme or change the colors of the three heading styles individually.
8. Save the customized theme with an appropriate name.
9. Preview the Web site in the browser.
10. Make any necessary changes to theme elements.
11. Close the browser and the Web site.
12. Close FrontPage 2003.

Exercise 29

◆ **Review Styles** ◆ **Modify HTML Style**
◆ **Create New Style**

On the Job

FrontPage's styles are HTML text and paragraph formats that have been named for easy application to Web page elements. HTML styles can be modified to change font, alignment, font style, and color. All paragraphs formatted with a particular style will automatically display changes made to the style. A Web designer can create new styles to apply specific formatting to text.

In this exercise, you will continue to work with the Gardens Web site. You will add a new page to the site and modify existing HTML styles on the page. Finally, you will create a new style for the page.

Terms

HTML style
Formats attached to standard HTML tags. For example, the default <h1> HTML style is 24-point Times New Roman bold.

user-defined style
A standard HTML style that has been modified or a style that has been created by a Web author.

Notes

Review Styles

- Recall that a *style* is a set of formats for particular kinds of text, such as headings, body text, or bulleted or numbered lists.
- FrontPage supplies a name for each style that tells what kind of text the style is meant to format.
- Each style name has an HTML tag equivalent. When a style is applied to text, FrontPage automatically codes the text with the correct HTML tags.

Modify HTML Style

- The default styles available for a Web are called **HTML styles**.
- HTML styles are listed in the Style dialog box (see illustration in next column) according to their HTML tag names.

Style dialog box

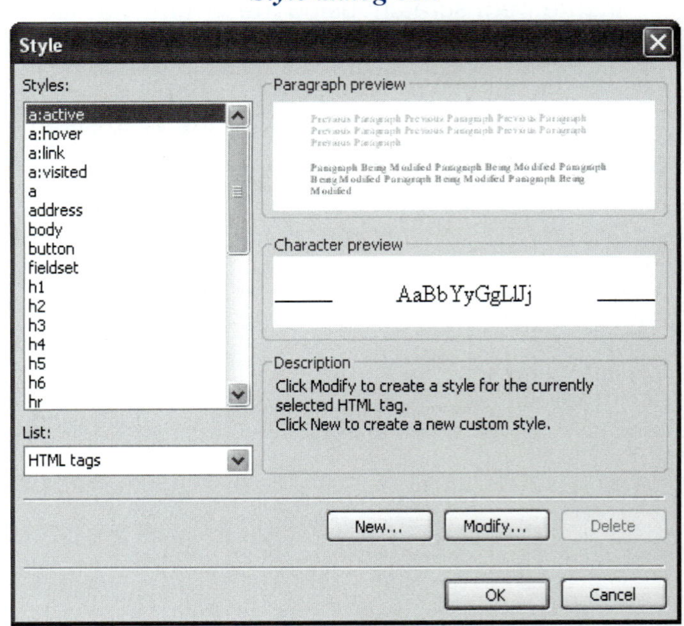

✓ *The HTML Styles list requires some knowledge of HTML tags. Recall that <a> is the opening tag for a hyperlink, for example, and <h1> is the tag for a first-order heading (Heading 1).*

- Unlike the Style dialog box in a program such as Word, the FrontPage Style dialog box does not identify the formats that make up a standard HTML style.
- For example, clicking the <h1> style in the Styles list does not tell the Web author that the default formats for the <h1> heading are 24-point, bold, Times New Roman, black, and left alignment.
- The author can change the default formats for an HTML style in the Style dialog box. To open the Style dialog box, use the Format>Style command on the menu bar.
- Modify an HTML style by clicking the style in the Styles list and then clicking the Modify button.
- The Modify Style dialog box (see illustration below) lets the user supply a new name for the style if desired. Click the Format button to display a drop-down menu with commands for Font, Paragraph, Border, Numbering, and Position.

Modify Style dialog box

Modify Style
Name (selector): h2
Style type: Paragraph
Preview
Description
color: #800000; font-weight: bold
Format OK Cancel

- As changes are made to the style, the Preview area displays the formats and the Description area describes the new formats.

- After an author has modified an HTML style, FrontPage adds it to the list of **user-defined styles** for that page (see illustration below). User-defined styles are styles that have been modified or created on the Web page.

User-defined style list for a Web page

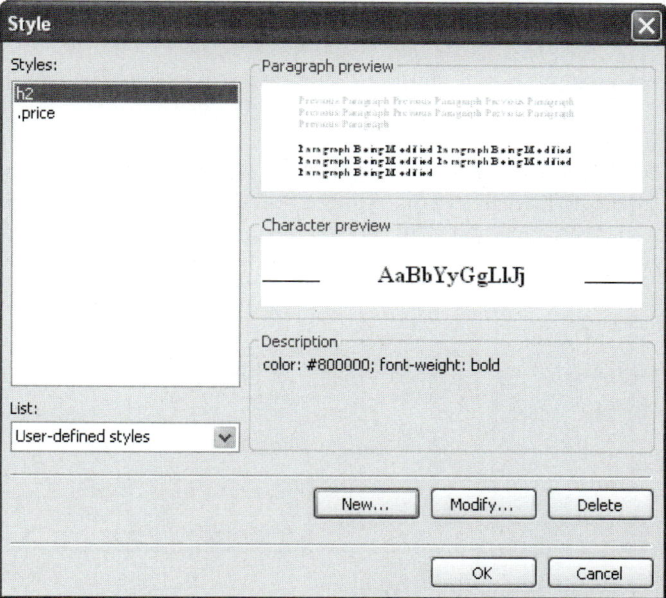

- When a style is modified, all paragraphs on the page formatted with that style automatically update with the new formats.
- Modifications to HTML styles affect only the current page. Changes made to the <h1> style on the index page, for instance, will not appear on other pages in the Web site that use the <h1> style.

✓ *To create styles that can be applied easily to all pages in a Web site, use a cascading style sheet. You will learn about cascading style sheets in Exercise 30.*

- Styles supplied by themes take precedence over most user-defined styles. For this reason, the Web designer will not be able to modify some styles such as headings on pages formatted with a theme.

✓ *It is possible, however, to modify other styles, such as those for Normal text, or add formatting such as borders and alignment to theme styles.*

Create New Style

- Web authors can also create a new style from scratch. Use the New button in the Style dialog box to open the New Style dialog box.

- Supply a name for the new style (see illustration below) and click the Format button to display the drop-down menu with Font, Paragraph, Border, Numbering, and Position commands.

New Style dialog box

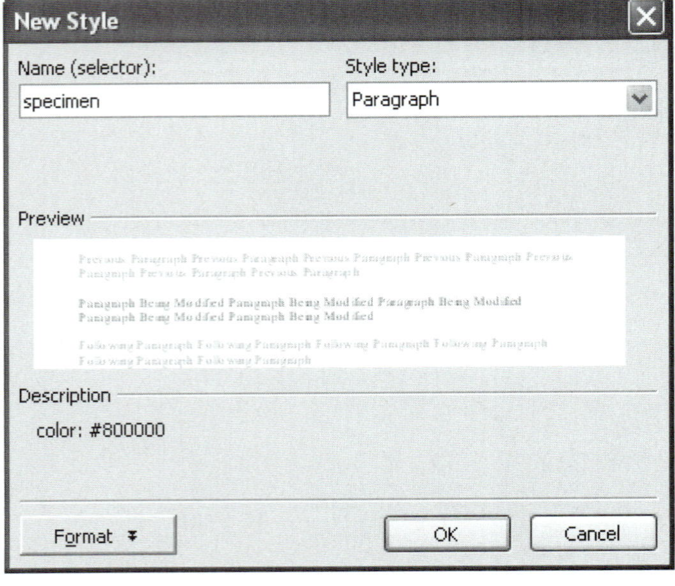

- New styles are displayed on the User-defined styles list. The style name is preceded by a period: .price, for example.
- The new style name appears in the Style drop-down list on the Formatting toolbar.
- To apply a style to text, click in the paragraph to format, display the Style list on the Formatting toolbar, and select the style.
- User-defined styles may be modified at any time. Select the style from the User-defined styles list in the Style dialog box and click the Modify button.

Code Cues

HTML information for user-defined styles is stored in the heading portion of a Web page between <style> </style> tags.

Procedures

Modify HTML Style

1. Click **Format** .... Alt+O
2. Click **Style** .... S
3. Click style name in **Styles** list.
4. Click Modify... .... Alt+M
5. Type new name for style if desired.
6. Click Format ..... Alt+O
7. Choose:
   - **Font** to change font, font style, font size, color.
   - **Paragraph** to change alignment or indents.
   - **Border** to add a border or shading.
   - **Numbering** to format as a bulleted or numbered item.
   - **Position** to apply wrapping style or absolute position option.

Create New Style

1. Click **Format** .... Alt+O
2. Click **Style** .... S
3. Click New... .... Alt+N
4. Type new name for style.
5. Click Format ..... Alt+O
6. Choose:
   - **Font** to change font, font style, font size, color.
   - **Paragraph** to change alignment.
   - **Border** to add a border or shading.
   - **Numbering** to format as a bulleted or numbered item.
   - **Position** to apply wrapping style or absolute position option.

Modify User-Defined Style

1. Click **Format** .... Alt+O
2. Click **Style** .... S
3. Click **List** down arrow and select **User-defined styles** if necessary.
4. Click style name in **Styles** list.
5. Click Modify... .
6. Type new name for style if desired.
7. Click Format and modify formats as necessary.

Apply Style

1. Click in paragraph to format.
2. Click **Style** list on Formatting toolbar.
3. Select desired style.

Exercise Directions

1. Start FrontPage 2003.
2. Open **Gardens**.
3. Import **specials.htm** from the Data folder.
   - ✓ *Because this page is imported, it doesn't pick up the theme applied to the rest of the pages in the Web site.*
4. To emphasize that this is a special page in the Web site, do not apply the Web site's theme to it.
5. On **specials.htm**, modify the <h1> HTML style to have the same font and color you applied to the Heading 1 text on the other pages in the Web site.
6. Modify the <h2> HTML style to have the same color you applied to the Heading 2 text on the index.htm.
   - ✓ *Scroll down and note that both Heading 2 headings have been updated with the new color.*
7. Click in the first specimen name (*Crimson Pygmy Barberry*) in the table below the *Shrubs* heading.
8. Create a new style named **specimen** that formats the font in bold with a dark red color.
9. Apply this new style to all specimen names in the two tables (*Crimson Pygmy Barberry, Gold Coast Juniper, Winter King Hawthorn,* and *Canada Red Cherry*).
10. Click in the price for the Crimson Pygmy Barberry.
11. Create another new style named **price** that boldfaces and right-aligns the price.
12. Apply the new style to all prices on the page.
13. Link the **specials.htm** page to the remaining pages in the Web site using the navigation bar at the top of the page.
    - ✓ *You don't have to create a link for Specials or Garden Links. You will create the Garden Links page in the next exercise.*
14. Preview the Web site in the browser and check formatting and links. The **specials.htm** Web page should look similar to Illustration A.
15. Close the browser.
16. Close the Web site.
17. Exit FrontPage 2003.

Illustration A

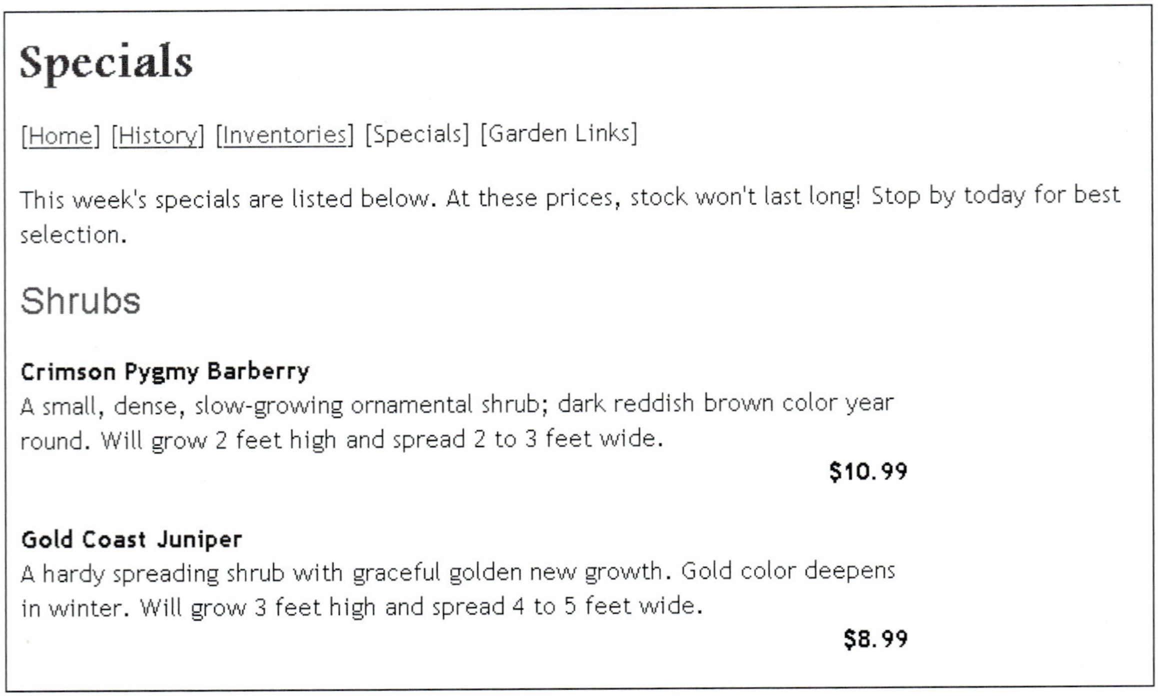

Specials

[Home] [History] [Inventories] [Specials] [Garden Links]

This week's specials are listed below. At these prices, stock won't last long! Stop by today for best selection.

Shrubs

Crimson Pygmy Barberry
A small, dense, slow-growing ornamental shrub; dark reddish brown color year round. Will grow 2 feet high and spread 2 to 3 feet wide.

$10.99

Gold Coast Juniper
A hardy spreading shrub with graceful golden new growth. Gold color deepens in winter. Will grow 3 feet high and spread 4 to 5 feet wide.

$8.99

On Your Own

1. Start FrontPage 2003.
2. Open **Cats**.
3. Import **FAQs.htm** from the Data folder.
4. On **FAQs.htm**, modify the <h2> HTML style to have the same font and color you applied to the Heading 2 text on the other pages in the Web site.
5. Modify the <h4> HTML style as desired to make the headings stand out on the Web page.
6. Click in the first explanatory paragraph on the Web page and create a new style for the paragraph. Change the font, alignment, or any other format to make the paragraph stand out.
7. Apply the new style to the other explanatory paragraphs on the Web page.
8. Update the links on the **FAQs.htm** Web page and add links to the page from the other pages in the Web site.
9. Preview the Web site in the browser. Check styles and links and make any necessary changes.
10. Close the browser.
11. Close the Web site.
12. Exit FrontPage 2003.

Exercise 30

◆ More About Styles ◆ Create Cascading Style Sheet (CSS) ◆ Save Cascading Style Sheet ◆ Link Cascading Style Sheet ◆ Modify Cascading Style Sheet

On the Job

By default, styles apply to a single page in a Web site. To apply styles across all pages of a site, the author can create a cascading (or external) style sheet. The cascading style sheet supplies styles that can be used by all pages in a Web site. FrontPage supplies some external style sheets as page templates for quick formatting.

In this exercise, you will continue to work with the Gardens Web site. You will create a cascading style sheet to apply changes to all pages in the Web site and use a style sheet template to apply styles to a single page.

Terms

cascading (external) style sheet
A style sheet saved as a file in a Web site that can be linked to one or all pages in the site.

embedded style sheet
A style sheet saved in the head portion of a specific Web page.

inline style
A style applied to a single page element such as a heading or paragraph of text.

Notes

More About Styles

- So far in this course, you have learned about two types of FrontPage styles:
  - **Inline styles** are styles applied to a single page element, such as when a Web author changes the format of a single heading on a Web page.

    ✓ *An inline style change appears within the HTML tag for a Web page element.*

  - An author creates an **embedded style sheet** when styles are changed for an entire Web page; for example, when the author changes the <h2> HTML style for a Web page.

    ✓ *An embedded style sheet appears in the head portion of the HTML coding for a Web page.*

- Inline and embedded styles affect only the current Web page and cannot be applied to other pages in the same Web site without recreating the changes on each page.
- To apply styles across an entire Web site, the user can create a cascading style sheet.
- A cascading style sheet can be used to make changes to pages already formatted with a theme.

Create Cascading Style Sheet (CSS)

- A **cascading style sheet (CSS)** is actually a template that contains style formatting for Web page elements.
- Because a cascading style sheet is saved as a separate page in a Web site rather than within a specific Web page, it is also called an **external style sheet**.
- An author can add a cascading style sheet to a Web site in one of two ways:
  - Use one of FrontPage's Style Sheet templates from the Page Templates dialog box.
  - Create the cascading style sheet from scratch in a blank Web page.
- FrontPage's Style Sheet templates are similar (but not identical) to some of FrontPage's themes (see illustration below).

Style Sheet templates

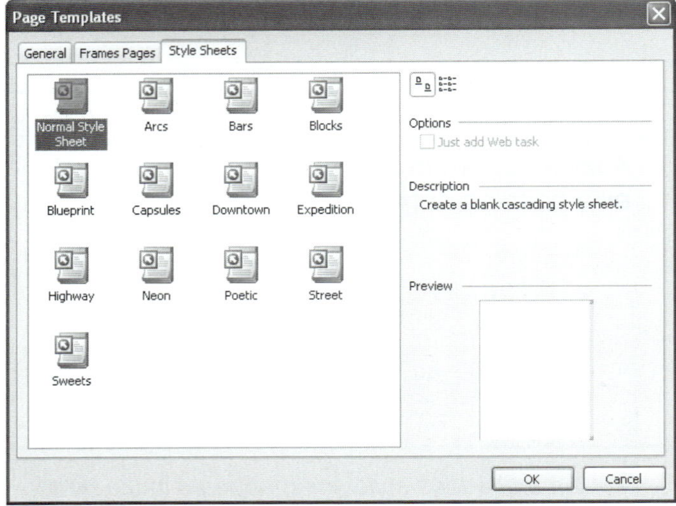

- Previews of the Style Sheet formats are not available, but the Description section details fonts and text and background colors.
- After the Web author chooses a Style Sheet template, it appears in the Web site as a page with a default new page name.
- Creating a cascading style sheet from scratch can be a bit more involved.
- The cascading style sheet must be created using a *blank* page that contains no text and is not formatted with a theme.
- Use the Style dialog box to modify HTML styles in the blank page or create new styles.

Save Cascading Style Sheet

- A Web designer must save a cascading style sheet with the .css extension for FrontPage to recognize it as a style sheet.
- When creating a cascading style sheet from scratch, specify the CSS Files (*.css) file type (see illustration below).

Save a cascading style sheet

- Style Sheet templates automatically supply this extension when the template is saved with a new name.
- Cascading style sheets appear in the Folder List along with the other pages in the Web site.

Link Cascading Style Sheet

- A cascading style sheet does not take effect until it is linked to a page or pages in the Web site.
- Link a cascading style sheet to a Web page using the Format>Style Sheet Links command on the menu bar.
- In the Link Style Sheet dialog box (see illustration at the top of the next page), choose whether to apply the style sheet to the current page or all pages in the Web site and then use the Add button to locate the style sheet.
- A style sheet link can be removed by clicking the style sheet in the Link Style Sheet dialog box and clicking Remove.
- Style changes applied to standard HTML styles such as headings and body text update as soon as the style sheet is linked to the current page or all pages.

Link Style Sheet dialog box

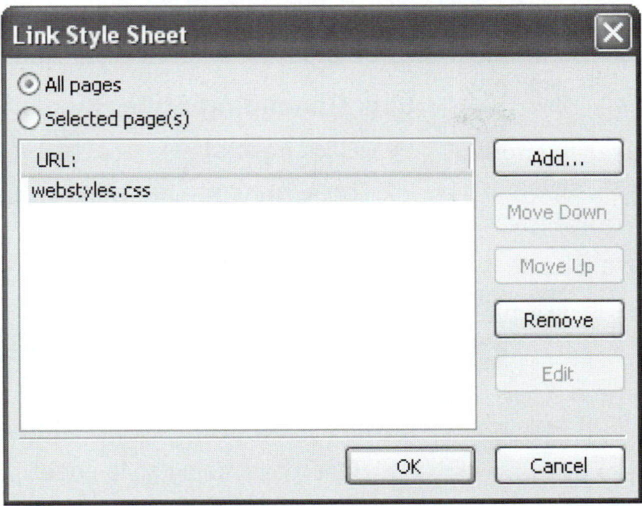

- New styles for specific page elements appear on the Style drop-down menu on the current Web page or all Web pages and can be applied from that menu.
  - ✓ *It may be necessary to search among a number of .ms and .user styles to find the new style.*
- An author can create and save more than one cascading style sheet for a Web site and link different style sheets to individual pages in the Web site.
  - ✓ *Only one style sheet can be active at a time, even though more than one may appear in the Link Style Sheet dialog box.*

Modify Cascading Style Sheet

- A Web author can open a cascading style sheet in FrontPage for further modification. Style coding is contained within braces ({ }).
- After a cascading style sheet has been saved, its HTML coding displays on the page, as shown in the illustration at the top of the next column.

Cascading style sheet displays codes after saving

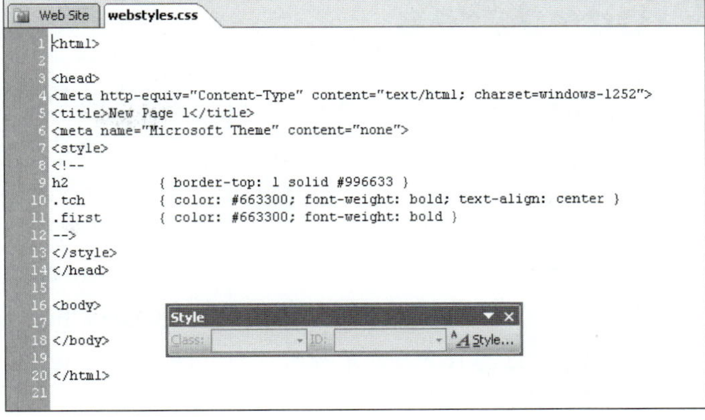

- A style sheet created from a Style Sheet template contains only the style coding (see illustration below). Each style has an opening brace ({), style formatting information, and a closing brace (}).

Style information for a Style Sheet template

Web Site | linkstyles.css

```
a:link
{
    color: rgb(51,153,255);
}
a:visited
{
    color: rgb(51,102,204);
}
a:active
{
    color: rgb(255,153,0);
}
table
{
    table-border-color-light: rgb(255,204,102);
    table-border-color-dark: rgb(204,153,102);
}
body
{
    font-family: Verdana, Arial, Helvetica;
    background-color: rgb(255,255,204);
    color: rgb(102,102,51);
}

h1
{
    font-family: Times New Roman, Times;
    color: #996600;
```

Style | Class: | ID: | Style...

- For both types of style sheets, FrontPage displays a Style toolbar with a Style button that opens the Style dialog box.
- An author can either modify the style sheet's HTML code right on the page, or click the Style button and modify the style in the Style dialog box.

Procedures

Insert Style Sheet Template

1. Click **File** .... Alt+F
2. Click **New** .... N
3. Click **More page templates** in task pane.

   OR

   a. Click (**Create a new normal page** button) down arrow.

   b. Click **Page** .... P
4. Click **Style Sheets** tab in Page Templates dialog box.
5. Select Style Sheet template.

Create Cascading Style Sheet

1. Insert new, blank page in Web site.

   ✓ *If necessary, remove theme from blank page. Do NOT type any text in page.*
2. Click **Format**............... Alt+O
3. Click **Style** .... S
4. Modify existing HTML styles or create new styles as desired.

Save Cascading Style Sheet

1. Click **File**..................... Alt+F
2. Click **Save As** .... A

   OR

   Click (**Save** .... Ctrl+S button) on Standard toolbar.
3. Name page and supply new page title if desired.
4. Click **Save as type** down arrow and choose **CSS Files (*.css)**.

   ✓ *Style Sheet templates are automatically formatted as HyperText Style Sheets.*

Link Cascading Style Sheet

1. Click **Format** .... Alt+O
2. Click **Style Sheet Links** ...... Y
3. Choose to apply the style sheet to the selected page or all pages.
4. Click Add... .... Alt+D and select the style sheet file.

Modify Cascading Style Sheet

1. Open cascading style sheet page in Page view.
2. Modify HTML code directly on the page.

OR

1. Click Style... .... Alt+S button on page to open Style dialog box.
2. Modify styles as directed in Exercise 29.

Exercise Directions

1. Start FrontPage 2003.
2. Open **Gardens**.
3. Create a new cascading style sheet that contains the following formatting:

   ✓ *Don't forget to remove the theme from the blank page you use to create the style sheet.*

   - Modify the <h2> HTML style to have a brown border with a weight of 1 above the heading. Use the same color of brown as the heading.
   - Create a new style named **first** (to be used on the first paragraph of each page) that applies bold formatting and a dark brown color.
   - Create a new style named **tch** (to be applied to the table column heads) that applies bold formatting, a dark brown color, and center alignment.
4. Save the new style sheet as **webstyles.css**.
5. Close the **webstyles.css** page.
6. Link the **webstyles.css** style sheet to all pages in the Web.

   ✓ *Click Continue if FrontPage tells you it will review all style sheet links in the Web site.*
7. Apply the **first** style to the first text paragraph on each page in the Web.
8. Apply the **tch** style to the column headings in the tables on the **index.htm** and **inventories.htm** pages.
9. Import **links.htm** from the Data folder and open the page.
10. To make this page stand out in the Web, you will format it using a Style Sheet template. Insert the **Arcs** Style Sheet template and name it **linkstyles.css**.
11. Activate **links.htm** and link the **linkstyles.css** style sheet to this page only.
12. To match colors on this page more closely to the rest of the Web, activate **linkstyles.css** and make the following changes to heading colors:

    <h1> color: #996600

    <h3> color: #009933

    ✓ *You can modify the HTML code directly or make changes using the Style dialog box.*

13. Update navigation bars on all pages.
14. Save all changes and preview the Web site in the browser. The **links.htm** page should look similar to Illustration A.
15. Close the browser.
16. Close the Web site.
17. Exit FrontPage 2003.

Illustration A

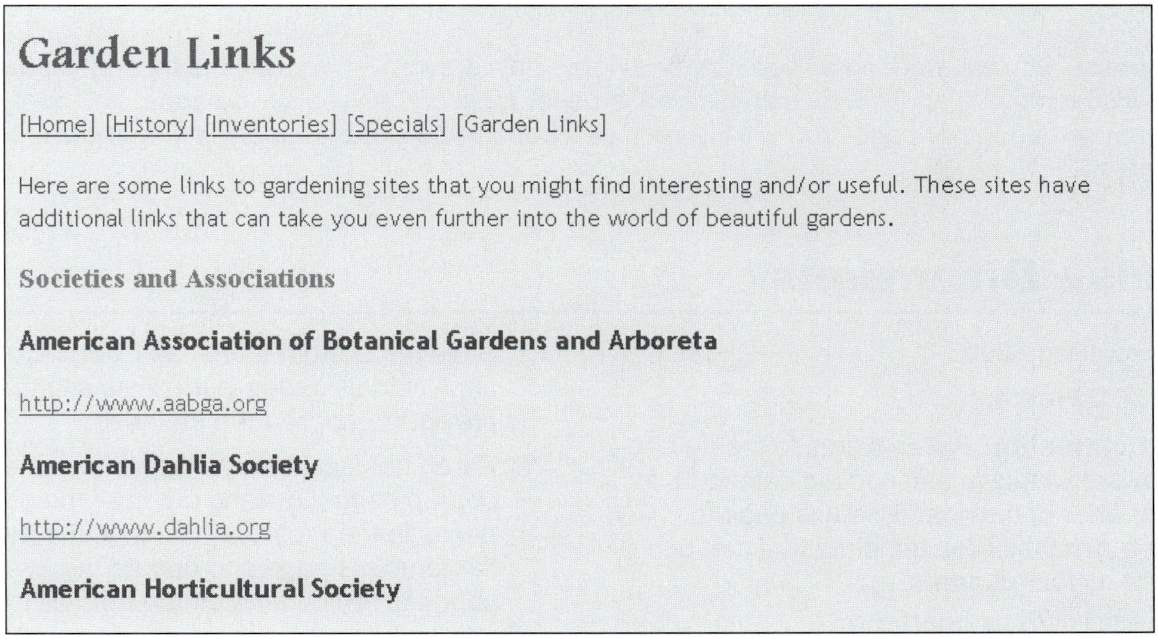

Garden Links

[Home] [History] [Inventories] [Specials] [Garden Links]

Here are some links to gardening sites that you might find interesting and/or useful. These sites have additional links that can take you even further into the world of beautiful gardens.

Societies and Associations

American Association of Botanical Gardens and Arboreta

http://www.aabga.org

American Dahlia Society

http://www.dahlia.org

American Horticultural Society

On Your Own

1. Start FrontPage 2003.
2. Open **Cats**.
3. Create a new cascading style sheet that contains the following formatting:
   - Modify the <h4> HTML style to have a border at the top of the heading in the same color as the heading.
   - Create a new style named **cap** (to be used for the paragraph next to the two photos in the Web) that has bold, right-aligned formatting with a border at the top of the paragraph.
4. Save the style sheet as **styles.css** and close the page.
5. Link the **styles.css** style sheet to all pages in the Web site.
6. Apply the **cap** style to the first paragraph on the **index.htm** page and the last paragraph on the **contributions.htm** page.
7. The **cap** style text looks too big. Open **styles.css** and insert the following code for the **cap** style, following the space after the opening brace:

   font-size: 10pt;

   ✓ *Make sure you insert a space after font-size: 10pt; to correctly space the code.*
8. Preview the Web site in the browser and check the new heading style and the caption style.
9. Close the browser and the Web site.
10. Exit FrontPage 2003.

Exercise 31

◆ Critical Thinking ◆ Challenge

In this exercise, you will work on a Web site for a home daycare center. You will create pages based on a dynamic Web template, apply and customize a theme for most of the Web site's pages, and apply a Style Sheet template to another page. You will create a cascading style sheet to apply final formatting touches to the Web site.

Exercise Directions

1. Start FrontPage 2003.
2. Open **Daycare**.
3. Open **quarter.htm**. Karen wants to create pop-up browser windows that contain calendars for each quarter of the year. Use this page to create a dynamic Web template that can be used for all four quarters:
   - Save the page as **quarter.dwt**.
   - Create an editable region from the *Quarter* heading with an appropriate name.
   - Specify that the entire table is an editable region and give it an appropriate name.
4. Create four new pages named **winter.htm**, **spring.htm**, **summer.htm**, and **fall.htm**.
5. Attach the **quarter.dwt** template to each page. Change the quarter name at the top of each page to match the file name. (That is, change *Quarter* to **Winter** in **winter.htm**.)
6. Insert the information shown in Illustration A on the appropriate pages.
7. Apply the **Poetic** theme to **index.htm**, **calendar.htm**, **options.htm**, **policies.htm**, **quarter.dwt**, and **whatsnew.htm**. When asked if you want to update the pages attached to the dynamic Web template, click **Yes**.
8. Customize the theme to change the Heading 3 color to a dark red and the body text to black.

   ✓ *Choose the black color in the color palette, not Automatic.*

9. Change the graphic symbol used for the bullet list to **ballbullet.gif** from the Data folder.

   ✓ *You need to modify only List Bullet 1. Leave the other bullet files as they are.*

10. Save the custom theme as **Poetic Copy** and apply it to all pages in the Web site that you previously applied the theme to.
11. Karen has decided she wants the calendar pop-up pages to stand out from the other pages in the Web site. Remove the theme on the template page and update the attached pages to remove the theme from all four.
12. Modify the <body> HTML style on the **quarter.dwt** page to use Book Antiqua, so these pages will match the themed pages. (Update the attached pages after making this change.)
13. Create a cascading style sheet that contains two new styles:
    - Create a style to be used on the quarter calendar pages to format the table column headings. Give the style an appropriate name and use font, font style, and color formatting.
    - Create a second style to use to format the days Karen is closed on the quarter calendar pages. Chose bold and red formatting.
14. Save the cascading style sheet as **styles.css** and link it to all pages in the Web site.
15. Open the four calendar quarter pages and apply the new table column headings style to the column headings for each table. Apply the bold red style to the dates in the second column of each table and the word *Closed* in the third column for the days Karen is closed.

    ✓ *If you don't see the new styles available in the Style list, reattach the cascading style sheet to the quarter.dwt page and update attached pages.*

16. Karen would also like the **whatsnew.htm** page to look somewhat different from the other pages to emphasize the page. Remove the theme from this page.
17. Insert the **Poetic** Style Sheet and save it as **newstyle.css**.
18. Link the **newstyle.css** style sheet to **whatsnew.htm**.
    - ✓ *In the Link Style Sheet dialog box, click styles.css and then click the Remove button before adding the newstyle.css style sheet.*
19. Create the appropriate hyperlinks on each page of the Web.
20. Add behaviors to each button on the **calendar.htm** page that opens a browser window to display the correct calendar quarter page. Test the page to make sure the browser window is large enough for each quarter page.
21. Preview the Web site in the browser. Check all links. The **index.htm** page should look similar to Illustration B.
22. Close the browser.
23. Close the Web site.
24. Exit FrontPage 2003.

Illustration A

Winter

Month	Day(s)	Daycare Status
January	January 1 and 2	Closed
	January 15 (M.L. King Day)	Full day provided
February	February 16 (President's Day)	Full day provided

Spring

Month	Day(s)	Daycare Status
April	April 12 -16 (Easter break)	Full days provided
May	May 3 - 7	Closed
	May 31 (Memorial Day)	Closed
June	June 7	Start summer full time

Summer

Month	Day(s)	Daycare Status
July	July 4	Closed
	July 26 - 30	Closed
August	August 30	Start school schedule
September	September 6 (Labor Day)	Closed

Fall

Month	Day(s)	Daycare Status
October	October 11 (Columbus Day)	Full day provided
November	November 11 (Veterans' Day)	Full day provided
	November 25 and 26	Closed
December	December 24 and 27	Closed

Illustration B

Karen's Home Daycare

[Home] [Calendar] [Care Options] [Policies] [What's New]

Welcome to the Web site of Karen's Home Daycare. Karen's provides affordable daycare options for your children aged 6 months to 10 years.

Karen's Home Daycare is family-style childcare in a large Victorian home in the Clifton Gaslight district, convenient to city parks, the library, and the Zoo. Karen Grantham, the chief caregiver, began the daycare business in 1989 while caring for her first child. She brings considerable parenting experience and twenty years of disaster control to Karen's Home Daycare.

Services

Karen's Home Daycare offers:

- Before- and after-school care in the Clifton area.
- Transportation to and from local schools.
- Full- and part-time care.

Challenge Exercise

1. In groups of three or four, find a local volunteer organization (or a local branch of a national organization) that is in need of a Web site. Or, consider setting up a site for your school or a club.
2. Set out to design a Web site for this organization. Ask them to provide content (for example, text in Word format; an image of their logo, etc.) that you can put on the pages.
3. Before your group begins, create a list of technological tasks that you will follow in designing the Web site and set timelines for how long you think each task will take. Decide who will be responsible for which tasks.
4. Exchange your task specifications and timelines with another group and check for any obvious gaps to make sure you are not forgetting anything.
5. Talk to a person at the volunteer organization about what kind of image they are trying to portray. In creating the Web site, use either a customized theme or Cascading Style Sheets that fit the image that the volunteer organization wants to set forth.
6. Ask members of the organization, your peers in class, your teacher, and any professional Webmaster you know for advice on how to improve the design of your Web site. You may wish to print out sample pages of your Web site to show them.
7. When the site is done, compare your site against the design checklist created on page 10.
8. Look at your list of technological tasks. Was each one met successfully? Did it take more or less time than anticipated?
9. Write a short report on how you could improve the process to create a better product in the future.

LESSON 6

Web Development: Navigation Structures and Tasks

Exercise 32

◆ **Review Navigation View** ◆ **Create Navigation Structure**
◆ **Use Navigation View Tools** ◆ **Revise Navigation Structure**
◆ **Create Page Banner** ◆ **Change Page Title in Page Banner**

On the Job

A navigation structure shows how pages in a Web site are related to each other. A Web author creates a Web site's navigation structure in Navigation view by dragging Web pages from the Folder List in the navigation pane. The navigation structure can be modified by adding, moving, or removing pages. After a navigation structure is in place, the author can add visual interest to a page with a decorative page banner based on the page title.

In this exercise, you will work on a Web site for McKenzie's Salon. You will create a navigation structure for the site and then modify the navigation structure by adding and deleting Web pages. Finally, you will add and modify a page banner on the home page.

Terms

child pages
Web pages subordinate to a higher-level Web page in the navigation structure.

navigation structure
A graphical depiction of how pages in a Web site relate to each other.

page banner
A decorative heading that can be added to pages which are part of a navigation structure.

parent pages
Web pages that have subordinate Web pages below them in the navigation structure.

Notes

Review Navigation View

- Navigation view is the FrontPage view that displays a graphical representation of how pages in a Web site relate to each other.
- Navigation view consists of the Folder List and the blue-shaded Navigation pane.
- Navigation view is used to create and modify a Web site's **navigation structure**. The navigation structure, which looks like an organization chart, shows how pages are linked in the Web (see illustration on the following page).
- After pages have been added to the navigation structure in Navigation view, the Web designer can add components such as page banners and FrontPage navigation bars to pages in the Web site.

  ✓ *You will learn how to create FrontPage navigation bars in the next exercise.*

Create Navigation Structure

- By default, only a Web site's home page appears in Navigation view.
- To create a navigation structure, drag a Web page's file name from the Folder List to the appropriate position in the Navigation pane.

✓ *A shaded line displays to show how the new page will relate to existing pages.*

- For example, to add a subordinate Web page to the navigation structure, drag the page name below the home page.
- To add a page on the same level as another page, drag the page name beside the existing page.

✓ *Pages can easily be moved after being added to the structure by simply dragging them to a new position.*

- When complete, a navigation structure consists of several levels, with a level of pages below the home page and other pages below those pages (see illustration below).
- Pages subordinate to a page are **child pages**. In the illustration below, Employment, Salon Services, Spa Services, and Price List are child pages of Home Page.
- Pages that have subordinate pages below them are **parent pages**. In the Illustration below, Salon Prices is the parent page of Service List.

✓ *A page can be both a parent-level page and a child-level page if it displays below a higher-level page and above a lower-level page.*

Default Navigation view

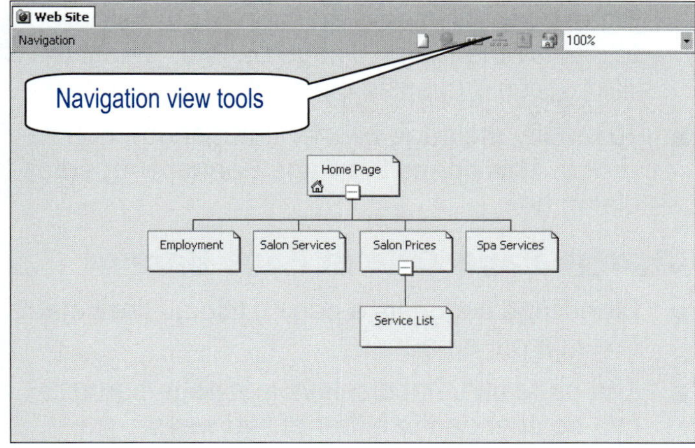

- The page names that display in the navigation structure are the page titles created when the pages were first saved.

✓ *These page titles can be changed in Navigation view. You will learn how to change them in the next exercise.*

- To open any page in the navigation structure in Page view, double-click the page.
- After a navigation structure has been established, it can be viewed in the Navigation pane of the Folder List by clicking Navigation at the bottom of the Folder List.

Use Navigation View Tools

- In FrontPage 2003, Navigation view includes some helpful tools at the top of the navigation pane (see illustration at the top of the next page).
  - Use the New Page button to insert a new page right in Navigation view.
  - Use the Add Existing Page button to open the Insert Hyperlink dialog box and select a page to add to the navigation structure.
  - The New Custom Link Bar button lets an author create a customized link bar.

    ✓ *You learn about custom link bars in Lesson 8, Exercise 43.*

  - The Included in Link Bars button lets an author specify pages to be included in the Web site's link bars.
  - The View Subtree Only button lets an author limit the display to a specific branch of the navigation structure.
  - Portrait/Landscape lets the author change the display from the default portrait to landscape.

Navigation view tools

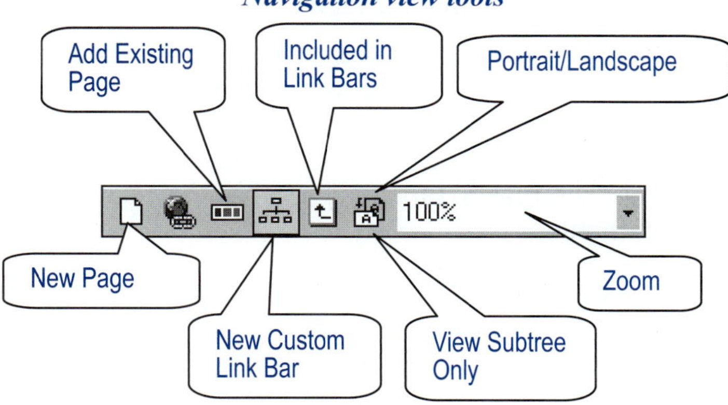

  - Use the Zoom box to specify a zoom percentage or select from a list of percentages to display the navigation structure.

Revise Navigation Structure

- After a Web author has created a navigation structure, the author can easily revise the structure by adding, removing, or moving pages.

- When deleting a page, the author can choose to remove it from the structure only or delete it from the Web site.
- Pages can be added to an existing structure by dragging them from the Folder List or using the Add Existing Page button from the Navigation tools.
- Additionally, entirely new Web pages can be created in Navigation view. Click a page in the structure and then click the New Page Navigation tool to create a child page of the selected page (see illustration below).

Add a new page to the navigation structure

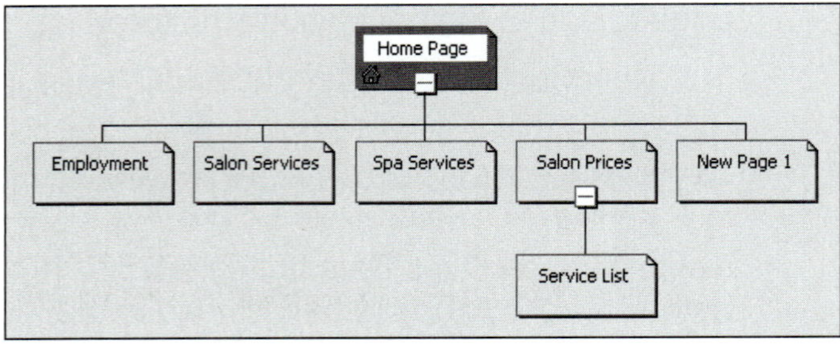

- Change the new page's page title in Navigation view by clicking it until it is highlighted and then typing a new name.
  ✓ *The page name changes to a version of the page title. To rename the page, use Folders view.*
- Move a page by clicking it and dragging it to a new location in the structure.
- The Navigation tools that control display can be helpful when revising a navigation structure. An author can choose to display only a branch of the structure, for example, as shown below, or display pages in landscape rather than portrait orientation.

Single branch of structure shown in landscape

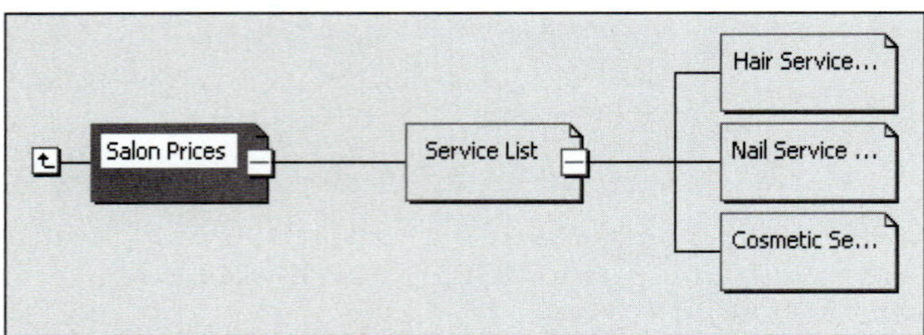

Create Page Banner

- Pages that have been added to a navigation structure can be formatted with **page banners**, decorative headings usually used as the main heading on a page (see illustration below).

Page banner for the Poetic theme

- Each theme supplies a page banner that coordinates with other theme formats.
  ✓ *A page banner can be applied on a page that has no theme applied, but it will look the same as a regular heading.*
- Insert a page banner quickly using the Insert>Page Banner command on the menu bar to display the Page Banner Properties dialog box.
- Page banners are FrontPage components and can also be inserted from the Insert Web Component dialog box. Click the Included Content component type to locate the Page Banner component.
- Choose to insert either picture or text in the Page Banner Properties dialog box. Select the Picture option when a theme has been applied to display the theme's page banner. Select the Text option to display the banner as plain text.
- To modify the page banner component, double-click it. This opens the Page Banner Properties dialog box.

Change Page Title in Page Banner

- FrontPage suggests a page's title as the default text in a page banner.
- The page title that displays in a page banner can be changed in either of two ways:
  - In Navigation view, change the page's title by clicking to select the existing title and then typing a new title.
  - In the Page Banner Properties dialog box, type a new page title in the Page banner text box (see illustration in the next column).

- Either of these options changes the page's page title in all views and in the HTML code for the page.

Change page title in page banner

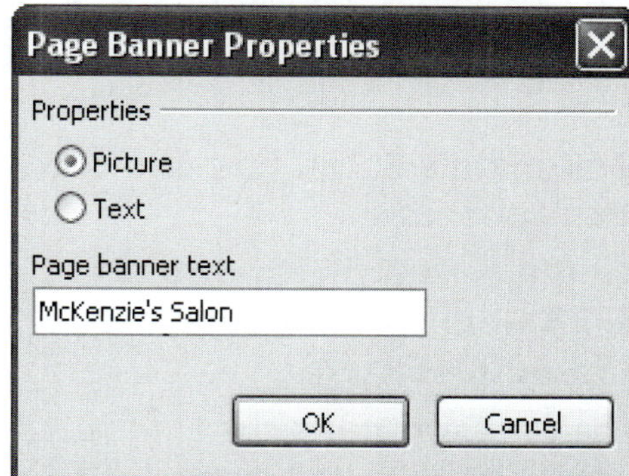

Procedures

Create Navigation Structure

1. Switch to Navigation view by clicking **Navigation** at bottom of Web Site pane.

   OR

   a. Click **View**............... Alt+V

   b. Click **Navigation** .... N
2. Click page's file name in Folder List and drag to Navigation pane.
3. Create a child page by dragging a page name below an existing page.
4. Create a page on the same level as an existing page by dragging the new page to the left or right of the existing page.

OR

1. Click (**Add Existing Page** button) in Navigation tools to open Insert Hyperlink dialog box.
2. Select page to add from list of Web site pages.

Create New Web Page in Navigation View

1. Click in the page that will be the parent page of the new page.
2. Click (**New Page** button) in Navigation tools.
3. Set page title:

   c. Click new page title twice to highlight it.

   d. Type new page title.
4. Rename the page if desired in Folders view.
5. Double-click the page to open it in Page view and add content.

View Single Branch of Navigation Structure

1. Click page that is top of branch.
2. Click (**View Subtree Only** button) in Navigation tools.
3. When finished viewing branch, click button again to display entire navigation structure.

Change Navigation Structure Orientation

1. Click top page of structure.
2. Click (**Portrait/Landscape** button) in Navigation tools.

Delete Page from Navigation Structure

1. Click page to delete to select it.
2. Click **Edit**..................... Alt+E
3. Click **Delete**........................ D

   OR

   Right-click page and select **Delete**................................ D
4. Choose **Remove page from the navigation structure** or **Delete this page from the Web**.

Create Page Banner

On page that has been added to navigation structure

1. Click **Insert** .... Alt+I
2. Click **Page Banner** .... N

   OR

   a. Click Web Component ... C

   b. Click **Included Content** component and select **Page Banner**.

   c. Click Finish ... Alt+F
3. Select **Picture** or **Text** option.
4. Double-click page banner component on page to modify it.

Change Page Title in Page Banner

1. Switch to Navigation view.
2. Click page title to change until it becomes highlighted.
3. Type new page title.

OR

1. Double-click page banner component.
2. In Page Banner Properties dialog box, type new title in Page banner text box.

Exercise Directions

1. Start FrontPage 2003.
2. Open **Salon**.
3. Switch to Navigation view.
4. Drag the **spa.htm** page into the Navigation pane below the Home Page. (When it displays in the navigation structure, the page will be identified by its title, Spa Services.)
5. Drag the **employment.htm** page into the Navigation pane below the Home Page and to the right of the Spa Services page.
6. Add the **salon.htm** page to the right of the Employment page.
7. Add the **prices.htm** page to the right of the Salon Services page.
8. Add the **banner.htm** page as a child page below Salon Prices.
9. Add **hairprices.htm**, **nailprices.htm**, and **cosmeticprices.htm** as child pages below the Service List page.
10. Move the Spa Services page to the right of the Salon Services page.
11. Create a new page as a child page of the Home Page. Change the page's title to **Find Us**.

    ✓ *You will rename the page itself in step 15.*

12. Open the Find Us page in Page view. Apply the **Canvas** theme with vivid colors.
13. Insert the Heading 1 heading **Locations**.
14. Press **Enter** twice and enter the following text:

    ✓ *Use the <br> tag in the address information (Shift+Enter) to avoid paragraph spacing around these lines. Insert the first <br> tag after* Kenilworth Galleria *and the last one after* 5300 Shaker Lane as shown below.

    **McKenzie's Salon has two convenient locations:
**

    **Kenilworth Galleria
**
    **6728 Kenilworth Boulevard
**
    555-3000<Enter>

    **Shaker Commons
**
    **5300 Shaker Lane
**
    555-3001<Enter>

    Both locations are open Monday through Friday from 9:00 to 9:00 and Saturday 9:00 to 5:00.

15. Rename the page in Folders view as **location.htm**.
16. Open **index.htm**.
17. Delete the current main head on **index.htm** and insert a page banner as a picture.
18. Change the page title in the page banner to **McKenzie's Salon**.
19. Switch back to Navigation view and delete the Employment page from the structure.
20. Display the structure in landscape view.
21. Your Navigation pane should look like the one in Illustration A.
22. Close the Web site.
23. Exit FrontPage 2003.

Illustration A

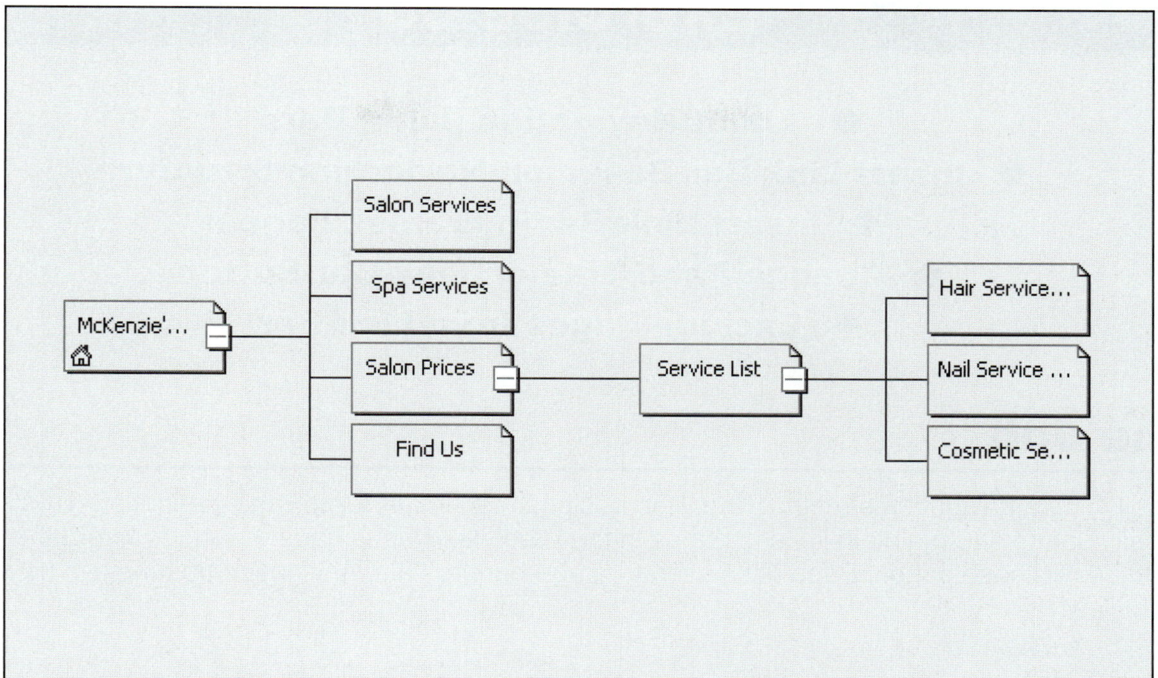

On Your Own

1. Start FrontPage 2003.
2. Open **Club**.
3. Create a navigation structure for the Web as follows:
   - Add **aboutus.htm**, **joining.htm**, **favorites.htm**, and **tips.htm** as child pages of the Home Page.
   - Add **credit.htm** as a child page of Joining.
   - Add **banner.htm** as a child page of Favorites.
   - Add **china.htm**, **egypt.htm**, and **london.htm** as child pages of Travel Sampler.
4. Create a new child page of the Home Page with the page title **What's New**.
5. Open the What's New page and apply the **Passport** theme with vivid colors.
6. Insert the Heading 1 heading **What's New?**
7. Insert the following text:

   Coming soon to the Hyde Park Travel Club Web site:
   - **Online membership registration.**
   - **Online previews of scheduled trips.**
   - **Reviews of previous trips with photo galleries.**
8. Change the new page's file name to **whatsnew.htm**.
9. Open **index.htm**. Delete the current main heading on this page and insert a picture page banner in its place.
10. Close the Web site.
11. Exit FrontPage 2003.

Exercise 33

- ◆ About Navigation (Link) Bars
- ◆ Insert Link Bar Based on Navigation Structure
- ◆ Insert Link Bar in Frames Page
- ◆ Change Page Title on Link Bar Button
- ◆ Exclude Pages from Link Bar

On the Job

After establishing a navigation structure, the Web designer can insert FrontPage navigation (link) bars that automatically set up and maintain links to pages in the Web site. Pages can be excluded from the link bar to prevent access to those pages. Page titles used for page banners and navigation buttons can be modified in Navigation view.

In this exercise, you will continue to work with the Salon Web site. Now that you have created a navigation structure, you will add FrontPage link bars to each page, including the site's frames page. You will also change page titles for navigation buttons.

Terms

link bar
A FrontPage component that creates a navigation bar based on a navigation structure and updates the bar as the structure changes.

Notes

About Navigation (Link) Bars

- Throughout the course so far, you have worked with *user-defined navigation bars*. The Web designer creates user-defined navigation bars, usually horizontal lists of hyperlinks that link a Web site's pages.
- Inserting a user-defined navigation bar on each page in a Web site can involve a lot of work, even if the bar is copied from page to page.
- When the author adds a new page to a Web site, he or she must create or copy a navigation bar and modify its links for the new page.
- If the author deletes a page from the Web site, he or she must remove the deleted page's link from each page's navigation bar.
- Fortunately, FrontPage has a solution to this situation. Once a navigation structure has been established in a Web site, the author can insert a FrontPage link bar.
- A **link bar** is a FrontPage component that creates a navigation bar with links to the types of pages the author specifies.
- As the Web designer adds or removes pages from the navigation structure, link bars based on that structure are automatically updated.
- On pages formatted with a theme, the link bar buttons are graphic objects that add visual interest to the page.

Insert Link Bar Based on Navigation Structure

- Insert a FrontPage link bar component from the Insert Web Component dialog box.
- Use the Insert>Navigation command on the menu bar to open the dialog box with the Link Bars component type already selected (see illustration below).

Insert a link bar component

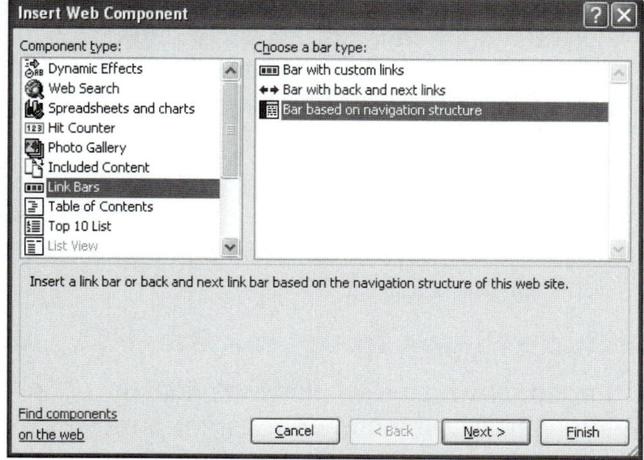

- The Link Bars component type offers three link bar options:
  - Bar with custom links.
  - Bar with back and next links.
  - Bar based on navigation structure.
- The first two options allow the user to create link bars by simply specifying the links and thus do not require a navigation structure.

  ✓ *You will create a custom link bar in Lesson 8, Exercise 43.*
- The link bar based on the navigation structure is the most commonly used type of link bar, and also the easiest to insert.
- After choosing this option, the author can select a theme for the buttons that will appear in the link bar and choose whether the buttons will appear in a horizontal or vertical row.

  ✓ *The author can choose the buttons of a theme different from the one currently applied.*
- The Web designer must then choose what links to include in the link bar. The Link Bar Properties dialog box (see illustration at the top of the next column) includes six link options and two check boxes for adding home page and parent page links to the link bar.

Link Bar Properties dialog box

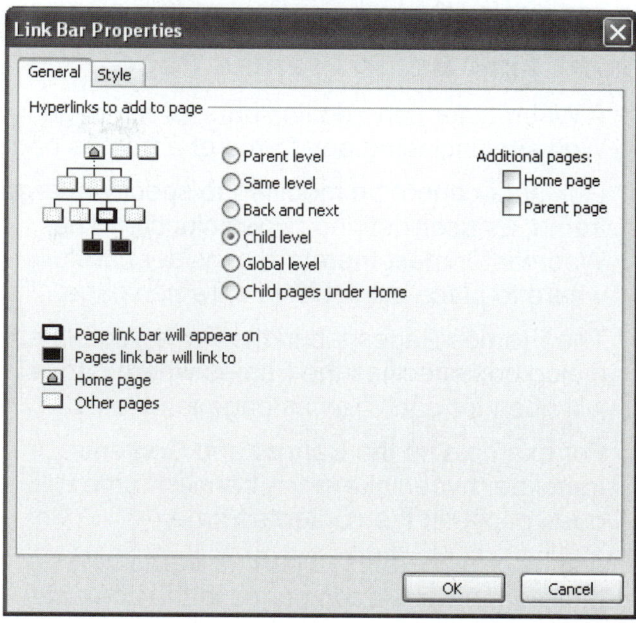

- The six options create links as follows:

Option	Explanation
Parent level	Link bar includes a button for the parent page and all other pages on that level.
Same level	Link bar includes buttons for all pages at the same level as the current page.
Back and next	Link bar includes Back and Next buttons for all pages at the same level as the current page.
Child level	Link bar includes buttons for all child pages of the current page.
Global level	Link bar includes buttons for all top-level pages in the Web, such as the home page.
Child pages under Home	Link bar includes buttons for all of the home page's child pages.

✓ *The sample navigation structure in the dialog box changes as each option is selected to show the author which pages will be included in the link bar for that option.*

- If the author chooses an incorrect option (the Same level option, for example, when the current page is the only one at that level), FrontPage will display a message on the Web page requesting that the author modify the link bar properties to correctly display the link bar.

- Modify a link bar component by double-clicking it to display the Link Bar Properties dialog box.

Insert Link Bar in Frames Page

- A Webmaster can add link bars to any page in a Web site, including any frame of a frames page.
- Link bars cannot be modified to specify a target frame, as user-defined hyperlinks can. The Webmaster must therefore consider carefully where to place a link bar in a frames page.
- The Frames Pages tab in the Page Templates dialog box specifies the frames where pages will open for each frames page template.
- For example, in the Banner and Contents template, hyperlinks in the banner frame will open pages in the contents frame.
- A link bar placed in the banner frame will therefore always open pages in the contents frame.
- To open pages in the main frame of a Banner and Contents frames page, the Webmaster must place the link bar in the contents frame.
- Setting up a link back to the home page can also be a challenge in a frames page.
- Because the Webmaster cannot customize a link bar link to the home page to specify the Whole Page option, links to the home page are best placed elsewhere on a frames page using a user-defined hyperlink for which the target frame can be set.

Change Page Title on Link Bar Button

- FrontPage uses a Web page's page title on a link bar button.
- However, a page title might be too long to display attractively on a link bar button (see illustration below).

Page titles are too long for link bar buttons

- A Web author can easily change page titles in Navigation view. Click the page title in the navigation structure to highlight it, and then type the new page title.
- Changes made to page titles in Navigation view change the Web page's page title, and the new page title displays in all views and in the HTML code for the page.

Exclude Pages from Link Bar

- Pages may be included in a navigation structure that the author does not want to appear on the link bar.
- The author can exclude such pages from the link bar by right-clicking on the page in Navigation view and deselecting the Included in Link Bars command on the shortcut menu.
- Or, the author can click a page in the navigation structure and then click the Included in Link Bars Navigation tool.
- The excluded page remains in the navigation structure, but neither it nor any child pages below it will appear on a link bar.
- An excluded page can be included again in link bars by following the same procedure.

Procedures

Insert Link Bar Based on Navigation Structure

On page that has been added to navigation structure

1. Click **Insert** .... Alt+I
2. Click **Navigation** V
3. Click **Bar based on navigation structure**.
4. Click **Next** button .... Alt+N
5. Choose style for link bar and click **Next** button.......... Alt+N
6. Choose orientation for link bar and click Finish ... Alt+F
7. Choose hyperlinks to add to link bar.
8. Double-click link bar component on page to modify it.

Insert Link Bar in Frames Page

1. Determine how pages will open in a frames page by clicking **Frames Pages** tab in Page Templates dialog box.
2. Select desired frames page template and read description of links and frames.

3. Insert link bars according to this description. For example:
   - A link bar in the banner frame of a Banner and Contents frames page opens pages in the contents frame.
   - A link bar in the header frame of a Header frames page opens pages in the main frame.
4. Add a link to the home page elsewhere on the frames page with a user-defined link that specifies the Whole Page target frame.

Change Page Title on Link Bar Button

1. Switch to Navigation view.
2. Click page title to change until it becomes highlighted.
3. Type new page title.

Exclude Pages from Link Bar

1. Right-click page to exclude in Navigation view.
2. Click **Included in Link Bars**............................ 

OR

1. Click page to exclude in Navigation view.
2. Click (**Included in Link Bars** button) in Navigation tools.

   ✓ *Follow same procedure to include an excluded page in link bar.*

Exercise Directions

1. Start FrontPage 2003.
2. Open **Salon**.
3. Open **index.htm**.
4. Below the main heading, insert a link bar based on the Web site's navigation structure. Choose to display links for child pages.

   ✓ *Accept the default style and orientation for all link bars you create in this exercise.*

5. Open **salon.htm**. Insert a link bar below the main heading that contains links to same-level pages and the home page.
6. Insert the same link bar on **spa.htm** and **location.htm**.
7. Open **prices.htm**.
8. Insert a link bar below the heading in the banner frame with links to child pages.

   ✓ *Adjust the frame height to display the link bar.*

9. Import the **certificates.htm** page from the Data folder.
10. Switch to Navigation view, and change the Navigation view to portrait, if necessary. Add the **certificates.htm** page to the navigation structure to the left of Salon Services.
11. Exclude the Spa Services page from the link bars. (There is not enough information on this page yet to make it useful.)
12. Open the **certificates.htm** Web page. Apply the **Canvas** theme with vivid colors and add a link bar with same-level and home-page links below the main heading.

    ✓ *Notice that FrontPage automatically removes the excluded page and adds the new Web page to the link bar.*

13. Activate **prices.htm**. Notice that the page titles in the link buttons are too long.
14. In Navigation view, remove the word *Service* from the *Hair Service Prices, Nail Service Prices,* and *Cosmetic Service Prices* pages.
15. Save all changes and preview the Web site in the browser. Check all links (particularly on the frames page). Your home page should look similar to Illustration A.
16. Close the browser.
17. Close the Web site.
18. Exit FrontPage 2003.

Illustration A

McKenzie's Salon

Salon Services Salon Prices Find Us

Welcome to McKenzie's Salon! Bored with your current look? Come to McKenzie's and let our artists create a new look that expresses your inner self.

At McKenzie's, we approach every new client as a blank canvas. We listen to your ideas and discuss with you what you want to see when you look in a mirror. You'll never be surprised by the end result of any of our services.

McKenzie's has always had a reputation for excellent service. Our new locations give us the chance to really pamper our clients. You'll leave McKenzie's rejuvenated and confident that you look your best.

A Full-Service Salon

On Your Own

1. Start FrontPage 2003.
2. Open **Club**.
3. Open **index.htm**.
4. Below the main heading, insert a link bar based on the Web's navigation structure. Choose to display links for child pages.
5. Open the **aboutus.htm**, **joining.htm**, and **whatsnew.htm** pages.
6. Insert link bars on these pages with same-level links and links to the home page. Save and close each page.
7. Open **china.htm** and insert a link bar based on the navigation structure above the heading. Use the Back and next link option.
8. Open **egypt.htm** and **london.htm** and insert the same Back and next link bar. Save and close each page.
9. The page title on the **aboutus.htm** page is too long to fit in the navigation buttons. Change the page title to **About Us**.
10. The Travel Tips page does not have enough information yet to be useful. Exclude it from the link bars at this time.
11. Insert a new Web page as a child page of the home page. Give it the page title **Next Meeting**.
12. Open the new Web page and apply the **Passport** theme with vivid colors.
13. Insert the Heading 1 heading **Next Meeting**.
14. Insert a link bar based on the navigation structure below the heading with links to same-level pages and the home page.
15. Insert a paragraph of text indicating that the next meeting is two weeks from the current date at 7:30 p.m. in Room 27 of the Hyde Park Community Center.
16. Rename the page **nextmeeting.htm**.
17. Save all changes and preview the Web site. Test all link bars.
18. Close the browser.
19. Close the Web site.
20. Exit FrontPage 2003.

Exercise 34

◆ About Shared Borders ◆ Turn On Shared Borders
◆ Insert Link Bar in Border ◆ Insert Date in Border
◆ Customize Shared Borders ◆ Turn Off Shared Borders

On the Job

FrontPage's shared borders feature sets up regions on all pages in a Web site to contain identical content such as link bars, a date, or other text. Authors can apply shared borders at the top, left, right, and/or bottom of the page. Authors can customize a shared border to stand out from the page or turn off a border for a single page without affecting borders on other pages.

In this exercise, you will work on a Web site in progress, the Computer Tutor Web site at your technical college. You will turn on shared borders for all pages in the site, add link bars to the borders, and insert a date in a border. You will customize the shared borders and turn off a border on one page.

Terms

comment
Informative text associated with a component that tells the Web author how to edit or modify the component.

shared border
Region of a Web page that appears in the same place on each page of the Web site and is used to present common information on all pages.

Notes

About Shared Borders

- Web sites frequently display identical information on each page of the Web site.
- For example, a Web author might insert a copyright notice at the bottom of each Web page and insert link bars at the top of each page.
- FrontPage makes it easy for an author to set up **shared borders**, areas at the top, bottom, left, or right of each Web page where such information can be displayed.
- Using a shared border ensures that common information displays in the same location and with the same formatting on each page.
- Information placed in a shared border on any Web page will display identically in that border on other pages.
- When a Web designer changes information in any shared border, that information will automatically change on other pages which have that border.
- Shared borders can be applied only to pages that have been added to a navigation structure.

Turn On Shared Borders

- Turn on shared borders using the Format>Shared Borders command on the menu bar.
- The Shared Borders dialog box (see illustration at top of following page) lets the author choose:
  - Whether to insert the border on one or all Web pages.
  - Which borders to turn on.
  - Whether to insert navigation buttons (that is, a link bar) in the top, left, or right border.

Shared Borders dialog box

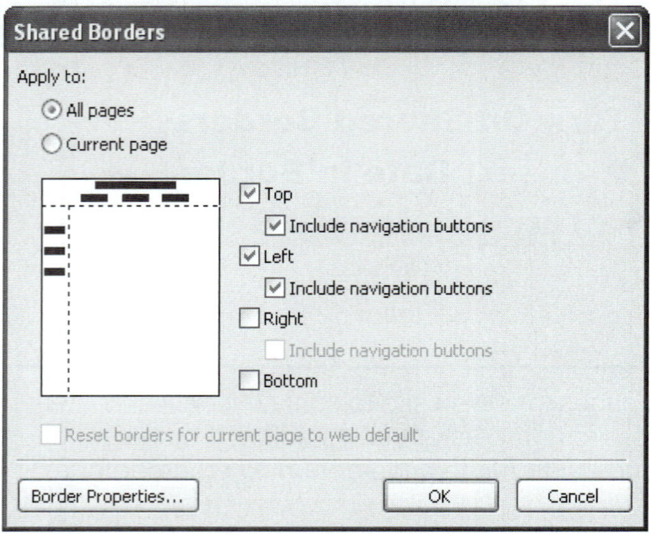

- As the author checks each border option in the dialog box, the sample page shows what the border will look like.
- Borders display on the page as follows:
  - The top shared border extends the entire width of the page at the top of the page.
  - The left shared border begins at the top of the page (or the bottom of the top border) and extends the depth of the page text or to the bottom border.
  - The right shared border begins at the top of the page (or the bottom of the top border) and extends the depth of the page text or to the bottom border.
  - The bottom shared border extends the entire width of the page at the bottom of the page.
- Any one or all of these borders can be applied to a Web site's pages.

Insert Link Bar in Border

- The Web designer can specify that navigation buttons display in the top, left, or right shared border.
- By default, the link bar inserted in the top shared border has buttons for same-level pages and the home page.
- The top border link bar of a child page also includes an Up button to take a site visitor back to the parent page.
- A link bar inserted in the left or right shared border has links for child pages.
- If a page does not have same-level or child-level pages in the navigation structure, the page displays a **comment** requesting the user to edit the link bar's properties (see illustration below).
  - ✓ *Editing the link bar in one page's shared border will change it in all other pages that have that same border.*
  - ✓ *Comments that appear in a shared border do not display in the browser.*
- Selecting the navigation buttons check box for the top shared border automatically inserts a page banner above the link bar (see illustration below).
  - ✓ *Note in the illustration below that no link bar displays on the home page because it does not have any same-level pages.*

Top and left shared borders with page banner and link bars

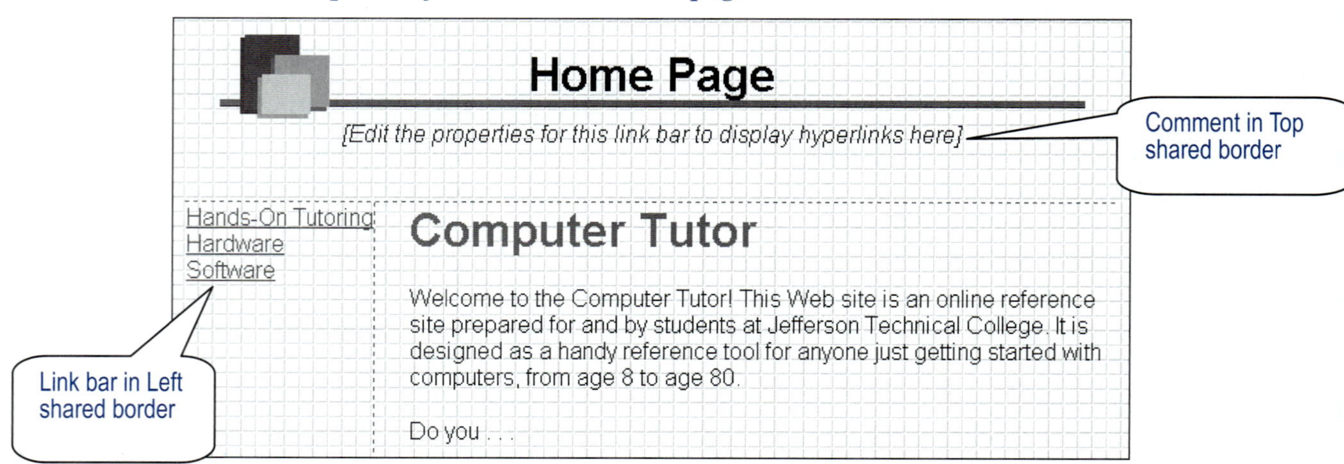

- By default, FrontPage displays the theme's navigation buttons in the top shared border (if a theme has been applied) and regular hyperlinks in the left or right shared border.
  - ✓ *Theme hyperlinks can be applied by editing the link bar in the left or right shared border.*

Code Cues

You can find information on a Web site's shared borders in code by looking for a meta tag that has *Microsoft Border* as the value for the name attribute and *t*, *l*, *r*, or *b* as the value for the content attribute. For example, a page with top and left shared borders has the following code:
<meta name="Microsoft Border" content="tl"

Insert Date in Border

- Web authors can include a Date and Time component in a Web page to show the last day or time a page was edited or updated.
- Insert the date and/or time using the Insert>Date and Time command on the menu bar.
- In the Date and Time dialog box, choose a display type:
  - Select the *Date this page was last edited* option to update the date and/or time each time the page is opened in FrontPage.
  - Select the *Date this page was last automatically updated* option to show the last date and/or time that the HTML content of a page was regenerated.
  - ✓ *These updates might not update as expected in FrontPage but will display correctly in the browser.*
- The author can choose from 20 different date formats and eight different time formats for the date and/or time from the Date and Time dialog box (see illustration below).

Date and Time dialog box

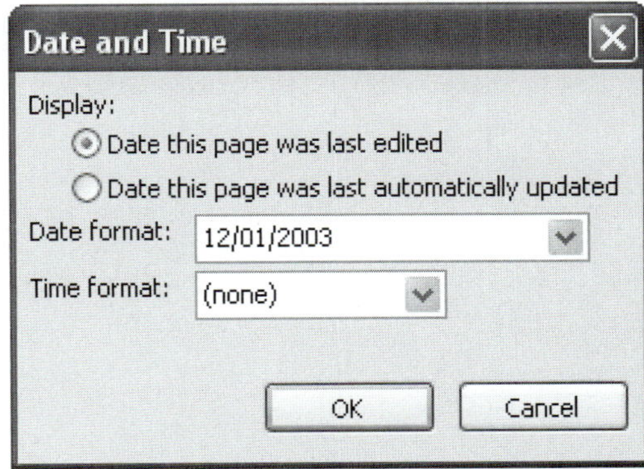

- Placing the Date and Time component in a shared border displays it on all pages that have that border and ensures that the date and/or time will update when a change is made to any page in the Web site.

Customize Shared Borders

- Web authors can customize shared borders in a number of ways:
  - Add a page element such as a horizontal rule to a top or bottom border.
  - Add color or a picture to any border using the Border Properties dialog box (see illustration below).

Border Properties dialog box

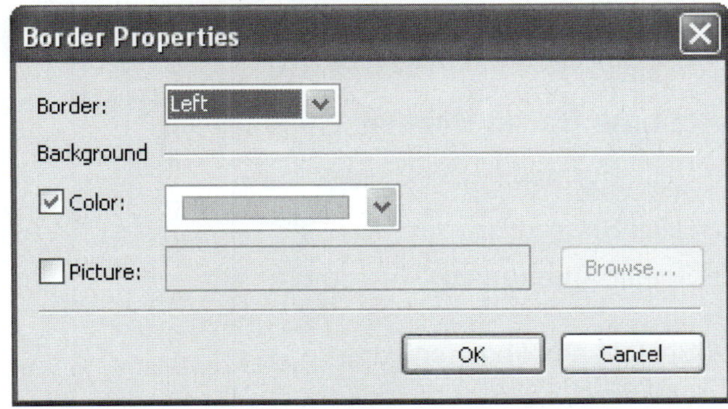

- Customizing changes made in any shared border will automatically be applied to all pages that have that border.

Turn Off Shared Borders

- In some Web sites, not all pages will need all shared borders. For example, in a Web site using left shared borders, a page that has no child pages will have no links in the left border.
- Any or all shared borders can be turned off for a single page by displaying the Shared Borders dialog box, selecting the Current page option, and clearing the check boxes for the border(s) to turn off.
- Shared borders can be turned off for the entire Web site by choosing the All pages option and clearing all check boxes.

Procedures

Turn On Shared Borders

1. Click **Format** .... Alt+O
2. Click **Shared Borders** .... D
   - ✓ *If Shared Borders is grayed out on the Format menu, click Page Options on the Tools menu, click the Authoring tab, and select Shared Borders.*
3. Select **All pages** or **Current page**.
4. Select check box for **Top**, **Left**, **Right**, and/or **Bottom** as desired.
   - ✓ *Any one or all check boxes may be selected.*

Insert Link Bar in Border

1. Click **Format** .... Alt+O
2. Click **Shared Borders** .... D
3. Select **All pages** or **Current page**.
4. Select check box for **Top**, **Left**, and/or **Right** border.
5. Select **Include navigation buttons** for any of these borders.
6. Add a link bar to an empty shared border:
   a. Select the empty border's comment.
   b. Click **Insert** .... Alt+I
   c. Click **Navigation**............ V
   d. Click **Bar based on navigation structure** and proceed with insertion of link bar.
      - ✓ *Inserting a link bar in any shared border will display the same link bar on other pages that have the same border.*

Insert Date in Border

1. Click in shared border to locate insertion point.
2. Click **Insert** .... Alt+I
3. Click **Date and Time** .... T
4. Select **Date this page was last edited** or **Date this page was last automatically updated**.
5. Click **Date format** down arrow and select date format.
6. Click **Time format** down arrow if desired and select time format.

Turn Off Shared Borders

1. Click **Format**................ Alt+O
2. Click **Shared Borders**......... D
3. Select **All pages** or **Current page**.
4. Clear any one or all border check boxes.

Customize Shared Borders

1. Click **Format** .... Alt+O
2. Click **Shared Borders** .... D
3. Click [Border Properties...] .. Alt+O

   OR

   Right-click in shared border and click **Shared Border Properties** .... P

In Border Properties dialog box

4. Click **Border** down arrow and select border to customize.
5. Select **Color** check box and click color palette down arrow to select new color for border.
6. Select **Picture** check box and click [Browse...] to locate picture in current Web site.
7. Customize shared border in other ways by adding a page element such as a horizontal rule to the border.

Exercise Directions

1. Start FrontPage 2003.
2. Open **Tutor** from the Data folder.
3. Open **index.htm**.
4. Turn on shared borders for all pages in the Web.
5. Select the Top and Left shared borders, and select navigation buttons for both borders.
6. Preview the Web site in the browser and test the link bars on each page.
7. Return to FrontPage and customize the left shared border to have a light gray color.
8. Change the page title of the **handson.htm** page to **Hands-On** in Navigation view to reduce the width of the left shared border.
9. On **index.htm**, click in the left shared border at the end of the last hyperlink in the link bar and press the **Enter** key three times.
10. Type **Last updated:** and format the text in a bold, bright color.
11. Press the **Enter** key and insert the date and time in the shared border.
    - Choose to display the date the page was last automatically updated.
    - Accept the default date format.
    - Select a time format that shows hours, minutes, and AM or PM.
12. Note the current time in the border.
13. The home page does not need a top shared border because there are no links to same-level or higher-level pages. Turn off the top shared border only on the **index.htm** page.
14. Re-insert a page banner as a picture on this page with the text **Computer Tutor**, and delete the Heading 1 *Computer Tutor* heading.
15. Refresh the view in the browser to see the changes to the **index.htm** page. The time in the left shared border should change to show the time the page was updated. Your home page should look similar to Illustration A.

    ✓ *The date and time will differ in your illustration.*
16. Close the browser.
17. Close the Web site.
18. Exit FrontPage 2003.

Illustration A

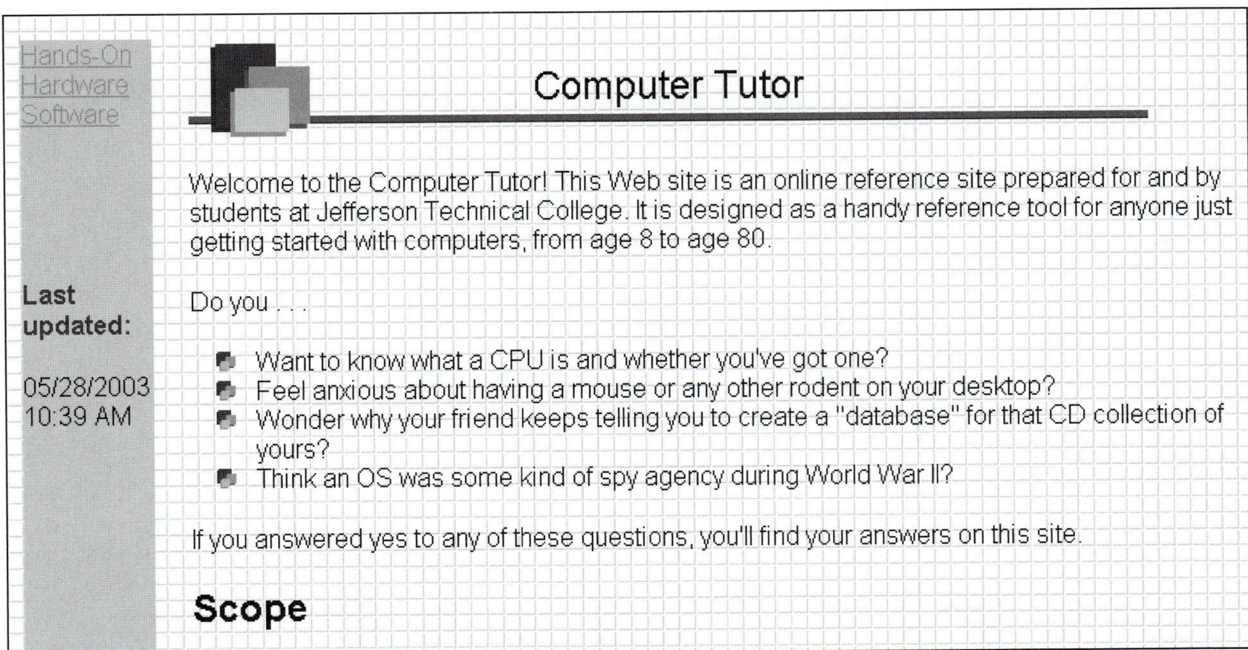

On Your Own

1. Start FrontPage 2003.
2. Open **Club**.
3. Open **credit.htm**. This Web page currently has no links to other pages.
4. Below the main heading, insert a link bar with links to the parent page and child level pages.
   - ✓ *Because the page has no child pages, only the Up navigation button will appear in the link bar, which is just what you want.*
5. Open **index.htm**.
6. Turn on left and top shared borders for all pages in the Web site. Specify navigation buttons only in the left shared border.
7. In the top shared border, specify a dark red color that matches the Heading 1 color.
8. Insert **Updated on** in the top shared border. Choose a color for the text that displays clearly on the background color.
9. Insert a date that will change when the page is automatically updated.
10. If desired, insert blank paragraphs above the hyperlinks in the left shared border to move them down next to the page's first paragraph of text.
    - ✓ *A blank paragraph could also be added above the page banner on the home page. Insert a blank paragraph and format it for the Normal style.*
11. Shared borders are unnecessary on the pages displayed in the frames page. Remove all shared borders from **china.htm**, **egypt.htm**, and **london.htm**.
12. Remove the left shared border from **banner.htm**.
13. The **index.htm** page now has two sets of links to child pages. Remove the link bar below the page banner.
    - ✓ *Click the link bar to select it and press Delete. Remove the blank paragraph that contained the link bar if desired.*
14. In the **favorites.htm** frames page, adjust the banner frame to display the link, if necessary.
15. Preview the Web site in the browser. Check all links.
16. Close the browser
17. Close the Web site.
18. Exit FrontPage 2003.

Exercise 35

◆ **Review Tasks View** ◆ **Add Task to Tasks List**
◆ **Modify Tasks List** ◆ **Start and Complete a Task**
◆ **Delete Task from Tasks List** ◆ **Show Task History**

On the Job

FrontPage's Tasks view helps authors organize and track tasks associated with creating a Web site. Authors can add tasks in any view, assign a task to a person or team, and give the task a priority. Tasks can be sorted and modified in Tasks view. After a task has been finished, an author can mark the task as complete or delete it. Completed tasks can be viewed again using the Show History command.

In this exercise, you will continue working with the Computer Tutor Web site. You will add tasks to the tasks list, sort tasks, and modify a task. After you finish several tasks, you will mark them as complete and delete one of them.

Terms

tasks list
List of tasks displayed in FrontPage's Tasks view.

Notes

Review Tasks View

- Creating a complex Web site of many pages may involve a number of people or teams and require hundreds of tasks.
- FrontPage's Tasks view organizes tasks by task, person assigned, priority, page associated with each task, and modified date (see illustration below).
- The tasks in the **tasks list** can be sorted or modified. After a task has been completed, it can be marked as completed and/or deleted.

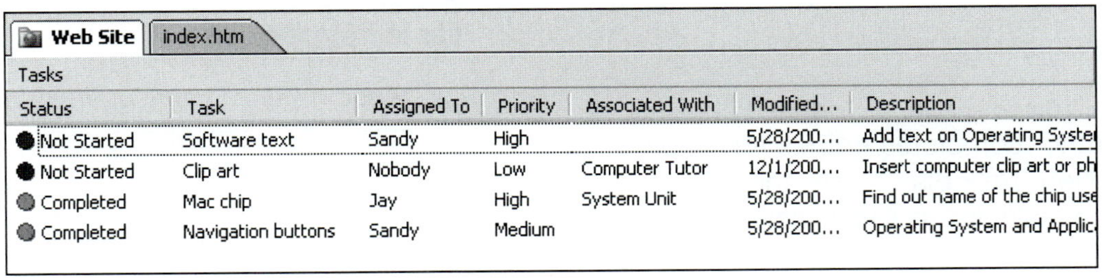

Tasks list in Tasks view

Web Site | index.htm

Tasks

Status	Task	Assigned To	Priority	Associated With	Modified...	Description
● Not Started	Software text	Sandy	High		5/28/200...	Add text on Operating Syste
● Not Started	Clip art	Nobody	Low	Computer Tutor	12/1/200...	Insert computer clip art or ph
● Completed	Mac chip	Jay	High	System Unit	5/28/200...	Find out name of the chip use
● Completed	Navigation buttons	Sandy	Medium		5/28/200...	Operating System and Applic

Add Task to Tasks List

- Tasks can be added to the tasks list while the author is working in any view or added directly in Tasks view.
  - In any view, use the Edit>Tasks>Add Task command on the menu bar.
  - In Tasks view, use the Edit>Tasks>Add Task command on the menu bar, or right-click and select Add Task from the shortcut menu.
- A Web designer can also add a task by selecting the *Just add Web task* check box in the Page Templates dialog box. FrontPage creates the Web page and also adds a task for finishing the Web page.
- Adding a task from Page view automatically associates the current page with the task. Select a page in Folders, Navigation, or Hyperlinks view to associate a task with the page. A task added in Tasks or Reports view does not have a page associated with it.
- The Add Task command opens the New Task dialog box (see illustration below). Here the user can specify a task name, assign the task to a person or team, set a priority for the task, and describe the task.

New Task dialog box

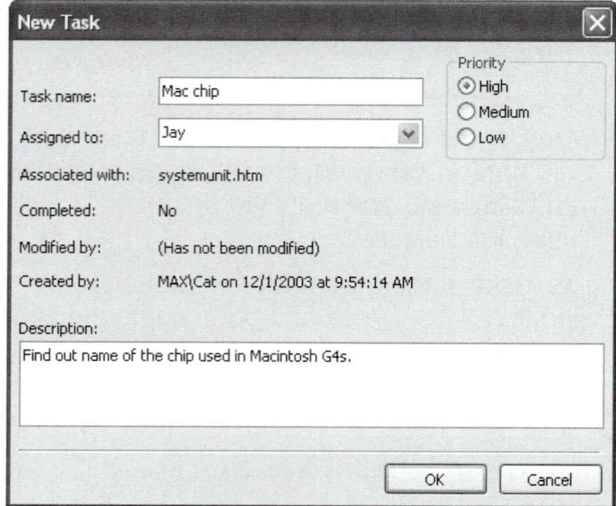

- After the author completes entries for a new task in the New Task dialog box, the task is added to the tasks list in Tasks view.

Modify Tasks List

- The tasks list in Tasks view organizes the information for each task into seven columns:

Column	Function
Status	Indicates current status of task
Task	Gives name of task
Assigned To	Shows name of team or person assigned to task
Priority	Specifies importance of task
Associated With	Lists page with which task is associated
Modified Date	Shows date and time task was modified
Description	Gives more information about task

- Click in any of the column headings to sort the tasks by that heading. For example, to place the tasks in alphabetical order by task name, click the Task column header.
  - ✓ *Clicking a header once orders items in ascending order (A to Z, 1 to 10). Clicking a second time reverses the order (Z to A, 10 to 1).*
- To increase a column's width to display more information, drag the border of the column heading.
- Modify a task in the tasks list by double-clicking or right-clicking it to open the Task Details dialog box, similar to the New Task dialog box.
- Change the task name, priority, assignment, or description in the Task Details dialog box.
- A task can also be modified right in the tasks list for certain columns.
- To select a new name in the Assigned To column, for example, click on the current name to display a drop-down list of names that have already been used (see illustration below). Assign the task to a new name by selecting the name from the list.

Change assigned name in the drop-down list

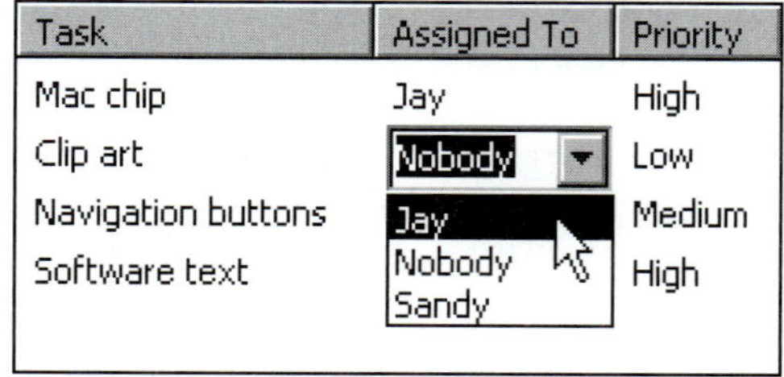

Start and Complete a Task

- If a task is associated with a page in the Web site, the Webmaster can start the task and open the page at the same time from Tasks view using the Edit>Tasks>Start Task command on the menu bar.
  - ✓ *Or right-click the task and select Start Task from the shortcut menu.*
- If a task is not associated with a page, the Start Task command is not available on the Edit>Tasks menu or the shortcut menu.
- When the task is finished, return to the tasks list in Tasks view to mark it complete.
- Mark a task complete using the Edit>Tasks>Mark Complete command on the menu bar, or right-click the task and select Mark Complete from the shortcut menu.
- The task's status changes immediately from Not Started, with a red bullet, to Completed, with a green bullet.
- When a page is opened from Tasks view as a task is started, FrontPage assumes the next time the page is saved that the task has been completed. FrontPage then asks the author if the task should be marked complete.

Delete Task from Tasks List

- Completed tasks can remain in the tasks list to provide a record of the work done on the Web site.
  - ✓ *Sort tasks by Status in reverse order to move the completed tasks to the bottom of the list, out of the way of other tasks that remain to be completed.*
- The author can also delete completed tasks to remove them from the tasks list.
- Delete a task using the Edit>Delete command on the menu bar, or right-click the task and select Delete Task from the shortcut menu.
- The Confirm Delete dialog box displays to allow the user to confirm or cancel the deletion.

Show Task History

- The Edit>Tasks menu contains another important command: Show History.
  - ✓ *This command is also available on the shortcut menu that displays when the right mouse button is clicked in Tasks view.*
- When this command is turned on, all tasks remain in view in Tasks view even after they are complete.
- When Show History is turned off (that is, not checked), completed tasks are removed from the tasks list when the author switches to another view, refreshes the Tasks view, or closes the Web site.
- If completed tasks are not displayed in Tasks view, simply turn on Show History to return them to the tasks list.

Procedures

Add Task to Tasks List

In any view

1. Open or select page with which task will be associated if possible.
   - ✓ *Specific pages cannot be selected in Reports or Tasks view.*
2. Click **Edit** .... Alt+E
3. Click **Tasks** .... K
4. Click **Add Task** .... A

   OR

   Right-click in Tasks pane in Tasks view and select **Add Task** .... A

In New Task dialog box

5. Type name in **Task name** text box.
6. Set priority as **High**, **Medium**, or **Low**.
7. Type name of team or person to handle the task in **Assigned to** text box, or choose the name from the drop-down list of available choices.
8. Type description of task in **Description** text box.

OR

In Page Templates dialog box

1. Select **Just add Web task** check box.
2. Save new Web page with name and page title.

Modify Tasks List

1. Sort tasks list by clicking in any column heading.
   - ✓ *Click once to sort in ascending order (A to Z, 1 to 10). Click twice to sort in descending order (Z to A, 10 to 1).*
2. Modify a task:
   a. Click task to be modified to select it.
   b. Click **Edit**................ Alt+E
   c. Click **Tasks**..................... K
   d. Click **Edit Task** .... E

   OR

   Right-click task and select **Edit Task**........................ E

   e. Change task name, priority, or description.

   OR

   Modify Assigned To or Priority in tasks list:

   f. Click **Assigned To** name or **Priority** to display drop-down list box.
   g. Click down arrow and select name or priority from list or type new name in **Assigned To** list box to add name to list.

Start and Complete a Task

If task is associated with a page

1. Click task to select it.
2. Click **Edit**..................... Alt+E
3. Click **Tasks** .... K
4. Click **Start Task** .... S

   OR

   Right-click task and select **Start Task** .... S
5. Associated page opens to allow task to be completed.
   - ✓ *If no page is associated with the task, complete the task on your own.*

Mark Task Complete

1. Click task to be marked to select it.
2. Click **Edit**..................... Alt+E
3. Click **Tasks** .... K
4. Click **Mark Complete**.......... M

   OR

   Right-click task and select **Mark Complete** .... M

Delete Task from Tasks List

1. Click task to be deleted to select it.
2. Click **Edit**..................... Alt+E
3. Click **Delete**......................... D

   OR

   Right-click task and select **Delete Task** .... D

Show Task History

1. Click **Edit**..................... Alt+E
2. Click **Tasks** .... K
3. Click **Show History** .... H

   OR

   Right-click in Tasks view and select **Show History**........... H

Exercise Directions

1. Start FrontPage 2003.
2. Open **Tutor**.
3. Open **index.htm**.
4. Create a new task associated with this Web page using the following information:

Task name:	**Clip art**
Priority:	**Low**
Assigned to:	**Nobody**
Description:	**Insert computer clip art or photo on this page.**

5. Open **systemunit.htm**.
6. Click in the paragraph that contains the blue, bracketed text *find out the latest chip for Macintosh G4s.*
7. Create a new task associated with this Web page:

Task name:	**Mac chip**
Priority:	**High**
Assigned to:	**Jay**
Description:	**Find out name of the chip used in Macintosh G4s.**

8. Switch to Tasks view and add a new task not associated with a Web page:

Task name:	**Navigation buttons**
Priority:	**Medium**
Assigned to:	**Sandy**
Description:	**Operating System and Application Software links are too long in left shared borders—reduce length.**

9. Add another new task in Tasks view:

Task name:	**Software text**
Priority:	**High**
Assigned to:	**Sandy**
Description:	**Add text on Operating System and Application Software pages.**

10. Sort the tasks from High priority to Low. Change the task with Low priority to Medium priority.
11. Sort the tasks by Assigned To name.
12. One task has not been assigned. Assign it to Jay.
13. Start the Mac chip task.
14. Jay has found the answer to this question. Delete the bracketed blue text, change the text color to Automatic, and insert the following text:

    the PowerPC G4 chip powers the latest Macintoshes.

15. Mark this task as complete.
16. Start the Clip art task.
17. Locate and insert an appropriate computer-related clip art graphic or photo on the **index.htm** page.
18. Mark this task as complete.
19. Adjust the length of the Operating System and Application Software page titles in Navigation view to **Operating** and **Applications**.
20. Mark this task as complete.
21. Delete the Clip art task, but leave the others in the tasks list. Your tasks list should resemble the one in Illustration A. (Your dates will differ.)
22. Switch to Folders view and then return to Tasks view. If your completed tasks do not appear, turn on Show History to restore the completed tasks to view.
23. Close the Web site.
24. Exit FrontPage 2003.

Illustration A

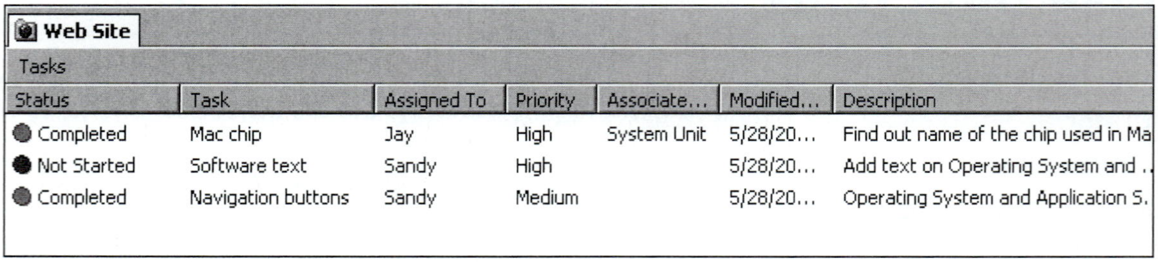

Web Site

Tasks

Status	Task	Assigned To	Priority	Associate...	Modified...	Description
Completed	Mac chip	Jay	High	System Unit	5/28/20...	Find out name of the chip used in Ma
Not Started	Software text	Sandy	High		5/28/20...	Add text on Operating System and ..
Completed	Navigation buttons	Sandy	Medium		5/28/20...	Operating System and Application S.

On Your Own

1. Start FrontPage 2003.
2. Open **Club**.
3. In the Page Templates dialog box, click the Normal Page template and click in the **Just add Web task** check box.
4. Name the page **paris.htm** with the Web-page title **Paris**.
5. In Tasks view, create the following tasks and assign them to yourself with appropriate priorities:
   - A task to finish the paris.htm page.
   - A task to add the page to the navigation structure to the right of the **london.htm** page.
   - A task to remove the shared borders from the Paris page.
   - A task to insert a heading and a photo on the Paris page. You also need to add several descriptive phrases about Paris, if you can.
   - A task to insert Back and Next navigation buttons on the Paris page.
   - A task to apply the Passport theme without vivid colors or background picture.
6. Change the Assigned To name for the finish paris.htm task to your name.
7. Sort the tasks list according to priority.
8. Start and complete each task according to priority.
9. Mark each task as complete as you finish it.
10. Keep all tasks in the tasks list for future reference if more favorites are added.
11. Close the Web site.
12. Exit FrontPage 2003.

Exercise 36

◆ **Critical Thinking** ◆ **Challenge**

In this exercise, you will work on a Web site for Summer Breeze Heating and Cooling. Pages have been created for the Web site, but the site needs a structure, link bars, and some additional pizzazz in the way of banners and shared borders. You will first create a task list for the chores you need to finish the Web site and then complete the tasks.

Exercise Directions

1. Start FrontPage 2003.
2. Open **Summer**.
3. Add the following tasks in Tasks or Page view with appropriate priorities and team members:
   - Create the navigation structure.
   - Insert new blank page for Contact from Navigation view.
   - Open **aboutus.htm** and create a task to insert link bars on this page, and on **employment.htm**, **store.htm**, and **testimonials.htm**.
   - Open **contents.htm** and add a task to create links to main frame pages.
   - In Tasks view, add a task to turn on shared borders with links in the left border.
4. You have decided not to add a link bar to **testimonials.htm**. Modify this task to remove mention of this page.
5. Create the navigation structure shown in Illustration A and then mark the navigation structure task as complete.
6. Make the following changes to the navigation structure:
   - Move Online Store to the right of Services.
   - Delete the Testimonials page from the structure but not from the Web site.
   - Add a new child page of About Summer Breeze with the page title **Contact Us**. Move the page to the left of Associations.
   - Change the page name to **contact.htm**.
7. Open the Contact Us page and insert the Heading 2 heading **Contact Us**. Insert the following information on the page. Format the text as desired.

   Summer Breeze Heating and Cooling

   Phone: 1-800-555-3600

   Fax: 1-800-555-3606

   Office hours are Monday through Friday 9:00 to 6:00.

   Closed Saturdays and Sundays.
8. Mark the task to create this page as complete.
9. Insert link bars based on the navigation structure on the child pages of the home page, except for the Services frames page. Use same-level and home page links.
10. Insert links on the **contents.htm** page that open its child pages. (Remember to set the correct target frame to open the child pages.)
11. Insert link bars on all other child pages that include same-level and parent links. Do not insert link bars on the pages that open in the main frame of **services.htm**.
12. Exclude the Employment page from the link bars.
13. Mark the link bar tasks complete.
14. Change the About Summer Breeze navigation buttons to **About Us**.
15. The Humidifier Products page title is also too long. Change it to **Humidifier**.

16. Insert a page banner on **index.htm** and change the page's page title to **Summer Breeze Heating and Cooling**.
17. Turn on Left and Right shared borders for all pages in the Web site. Insert navigation buttons in the left shared border.
18. Turn off shared borders for all pages that display in the **services.htm** frames page.
19. Customize the right shared border by deleting its comment and changing its background to one of the theme's colors.
20. Mark the shared borders task as complete.
21. Insert a date in the left shared border that will change when the page is updated.
22. Modify the position on the layers on **index.htm** as necessary to display text correctly.
23. Save all changes and preview the Web site in the browser. Check all links.
24. Close the browser.
25. Close the Web site.
26. Exit FrontPage 2003.

Illustration A

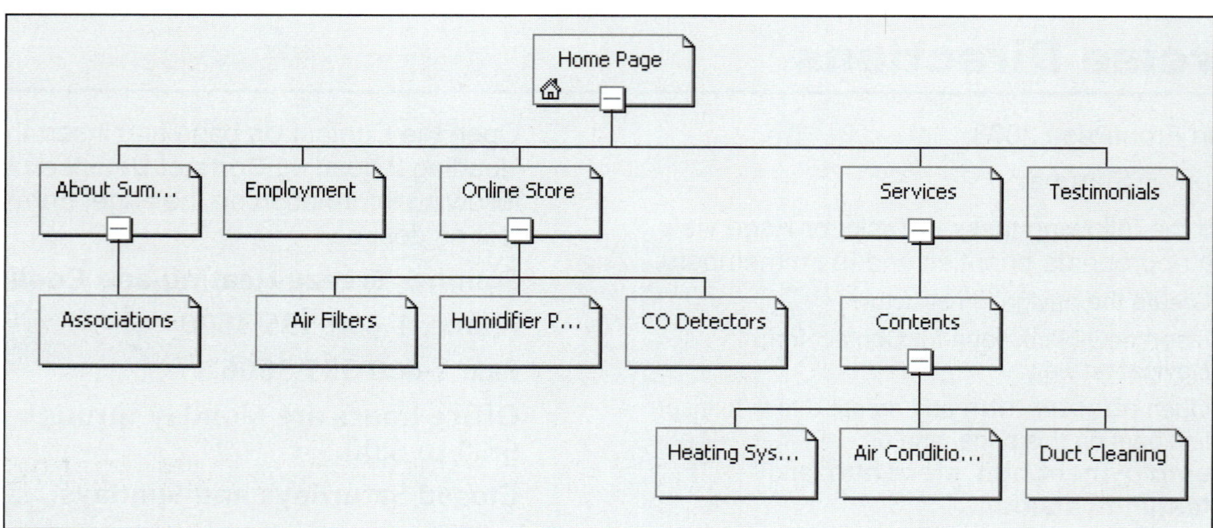

Challenge Exercise

1. Break into groups of five or six. Together, your goal will be to create a Web site that presents factual information about a local or national political, environmental, or economic issue.
2. Set a list of tasks that must be completed in the course of designing the Web site and a timeline for each task.
3. Decide who will be responsible for each task; as soon as the Web site is created, have one person enter that information in Tasks view.
4. Use other programs as necessary in creating the Web site: for example, use Word when you are creating content for the Web site and then import the file into FrontPage; use your e-mail program to exchange information with other members of your team, etc.

   ✓ *Remember to scan any files you exchange via e-mail for viruses.*

5. Use online resources, magazines, newspapers, and e-mail or in-person interviews to collect content information that you will use for the Web site. Remember to cite sources.

   ✓ *Evaluate the information you find carefully—is the author likely to be biased? Is the information current and up to date? Does it match with other sources that you have found?*

6. As the Web site progresses, update information in Tasks view to reflect your progress.
7. When the Web site is finished, have another group in your class evaluate your Web site.
8. Discuss as a group how you could improve the process of creating the Web site and setting out technological tasks.

LESSON 7

Web Site Publishing and Searching

Exercise 37

◆ About Publishing FrontPage Web Sites
◆ Using a Personal Web Server ◆ Insert Hit Counter
◆ Publish Web Site ◆ Optimize Published HTML

On the Job

Many FrontPage features and components are designed to work properly only when the Web site is published to a server. Web designers can publish to the server of an Internet service provider or to personal Web servers resident on their own computers. A new optimizing feature helps to reduce page size for faster downloading. The hit-counter component, which works correctly only when published, shows the number of visitors to a site.

In this exercise, you will work on a Web site for the Clifton Historic House Tour. This Web site is almost ready to be published. You will add a hit counter to the home page, optimize the site's HTML code, and then check the Web site by publishing it to a personal Web server.

Terms

disk-based Web site
A Web site whose pages are stored on a disk, such as a computer's hard disk.

FrontPage extensions
Programs and scripts that allow authoring in FrontPage and enable servers to display FrontPage components correctly.

FTP (File Transfer Protocol)
A communications protocol used to transfer files from one location to another.

hit counter
A FrontPage component that counts the number of visitors to a Web site.

HTTP (Hypertext Transfer Protocol)
The protocol that allows a browser and a server to communicate.

personal Web site server
A program on a computer that functions the same way as an Internet server, allowing the user to publish FrontPage Web sites locally.

publish
Copy a Web site's files to a server. The server may be a *personal Web server* or a server connected to the Internet.

server-based Web site
A Web site that has been published to any server.

WebDAV (Web-based Distributed Authoring and Versioning)
A protocol that allows for collaboration in editing and managing a remote Web site.

Notes

About Publishing FrontPage Web Sites

- Up to this point in this course, you have worked with **disk-based Web sites** that are stored on your computer's hard disk.
- Many of FrontPage's more advanced components and features require the author to **publish** the Web site to a server.
- Publishing is the process of copying a Web site's files to a server.
- Web sites that have been published to a server are called **server-based Web sites**.

Finding a Server

- Web designers can find servers for publishing in a number of locations:
  - Large companies often have their own internal network servers called intranets.
  - Many schools and universities also have network servers that can be used for publishing.
  - Some Internet service providers (ISPs) allow their subscribers to publish Web sites to the ISP server either as part of the service agreement or for an extra fee.
  - Web site hosting services provide server space and support for both personal and corporate Web sites.

Selecting a Server Protocol

- FrontPage 2003 authors can choose from three server protocols to publish to.
- The best option for a FrontPage Web site is a server that runs FrontPage or SharePoint extensions.
- **FrontPage extensions** are programs and scripts that allow a Web designer to author and edit a Web site in FrontPage and enable a server to display FrontPage components and features.
- A server that has FrontPage extensions supplies full functionality for FrontPage Web sites. This means that special components such as form handlers and hit counters will work correctly on pages published to this server, and also that FrontPage will maintain the Web site's files and links automatically.
- When a server has FrontPage extensions, Web sites can be published to that server using **HTTP (HyperText Transfer Protocol)**.
- An author may also choose to publish to servers that support FTP and WebDAV.
  - **FTP (File Transfer Protocol)** is a very common method of uploading files to a server. This protocol requires an author to specify a user name and password to gain access to the site.
  - **WebDAV (Web-based Distributed Authoring and Versioning)** is a protocol that allows for collaboration among authors to edit and manage a remote Web site.

    ✓ *WebDAV provides a set of extensions to the HTTP protocol. An author may need to supply not only the server name but also a user name and password to publish to a WebDAV server.*
- FrontPage will alert the designer to any components or features in the Web site that require FrontPage extensions and thus will not display correctly when published using the FTP or WebDAV option.
- Besides the consideration of how pages will display on the chosen server, a designer needs to be aware of some security issues when publishing to servers that do not run FrontPage extensions.

  ✓ *Exercise 38 covers the subject of publishing and Web site security.*

Using a Personal Web Server

- Authors working on Windows systems have an additional server option: the **personal Web server** included with these operating systems.
- The personal Web server may be referred to as the PWS (Personal Web Server) or IIS (Internet Information Services). Different versions of Windows support specific personal Web server versions.

  ✓ *For example, Windows NT 4 Workstation supports Personal Web Server; Windows 2000 Professional supports IIS 5.0; Windows XP Professional supports IIS 5.1. Windows XP Home cannot run a personal Web server.*

- Many Web developers publish Web sites to a personal Web server to test FrontPage features before publishing a Web site to a server connected to the Internet.
- A personal Web server can be configured with FrontPage extensions just like any other server.
  - ✓ *Personal Web servers do not support all of FrontPage 2003's components but are still useful for testing a Web site.*
- Web sites published to a personal Web server are stored on the hard drive in a specific location: the C:\Inetpub\wwwroot folder.

Insert Hit Counter

- A **hit counter** is a FrontPage component that counts the number of visitors to a Web site.
- A hit counter updates each time a visitor opens or refreshes the Web page that contains the counter.
- The hit counter component will not work correctly unless the Web page on which it is inserted is published.
- For this reason, a hit counter can be used to determine if a Web site has been successfully published to a server.
- Insert a hit counter from the Insert Web Component dialog box. Use the Insert>Web Component command on the menu bar and click the Hit Counter component.
- Authors have five hit counter styles to choose among (see illustration at the top of the next column), as well as the option to insert a custom picture for a counter.
- Authors can also choose a beginning number for the counter (to avoid starting from 0) and set the number of digits the counter will display.
- When inserted on a Web page, the hit counter component displays the counter style graphic as a placeholder. Only after the Web page is published does the counter display the designated number of digits and update correctly.

Hit Counter Properties dialog box

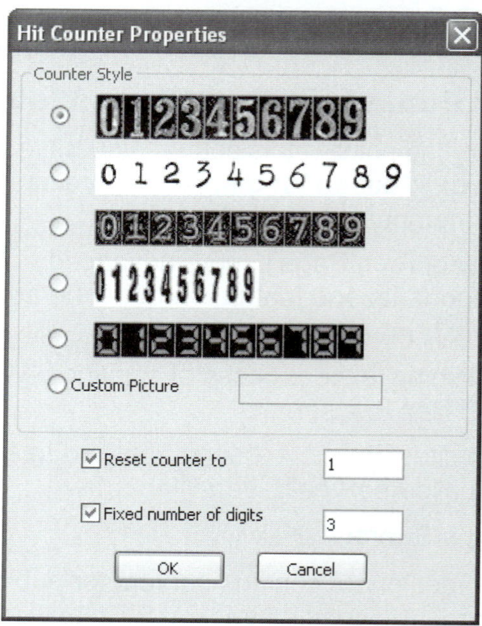

Publish Web Site

- The publishing process is the same whether a Web developer publishes to an Internet-connected server or to a personal Web server.
- Begin the process by displaying the Web Site pane and clicking the Remote Web site option at the bottom of the pane. Then click the Remote Web Site Properties button at the top of the pane to open the Remote Web Site Properties dialog box (see illustration at top of next page).
  - ✓ *An author can also display this dialog box using the File>Publish Site command on the menu bar.*
- In this dialog box, the author first specifies the remote server type. Note that along with the FrontPage/SharePoint, FTP, and DAV (WebDAV) server types, a designer can specify File System to publish the Web site to a disk or local location.
  - ✓ *You learn more about this option later in this exercise.*
- Next, the author specifies the remote Web site location. If a Web site has recently been published, the Remote Web site location box may already contain a path to a server.

Remote Web Site Properties dialog box

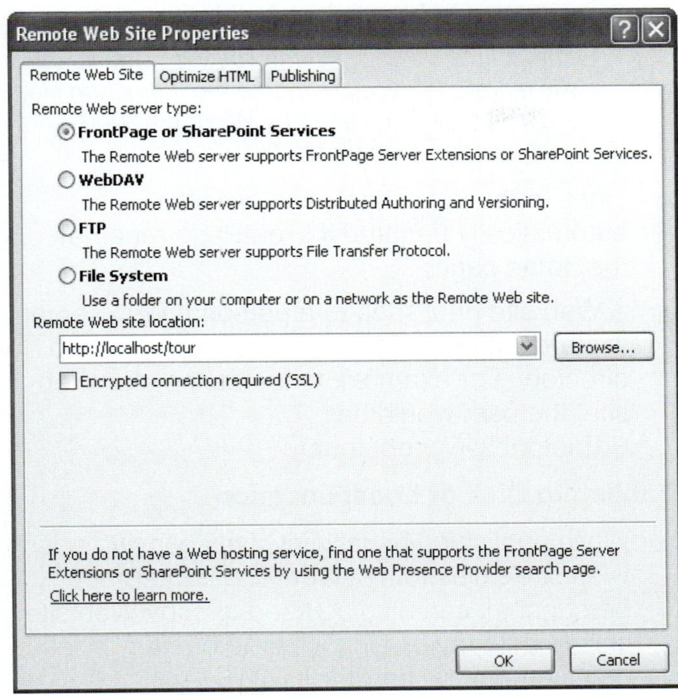

- Type the correct path or use the Browse button to specify the path to the server.
- The default destination for a personal Web server is http://localhost. *Localhost* is the name of the computer on which the personal Web server is running.
  - ✓ *This name may vary depending on individual computer setup.*
- The destination for an Internet-connected server will be http://[servername], where [servername] is the server's domain name.
- The publishing destination must also include the Web site's name (*tour* in the illustration at left).
- If the designer chooses to publish using FTP, the dialog box changes to display boxes that allow the designer to specify the FTP path and directory.
- If the Web site does not already exist on the server at the location specified in the Remote Web Site Properties dialog box, FrontPage asks the user if it should be created (see illustration below).

FrontPage asks if it should create a Web site

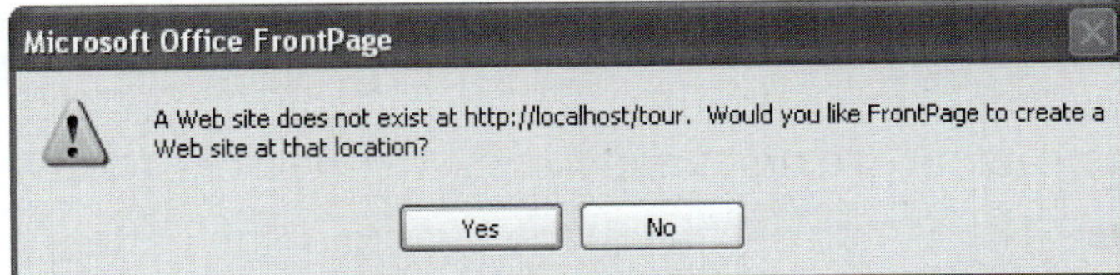

- When publishing to an Internet-connected server, the Web author must supply a proper user name and/or password to establish access to the server.
- Once the destination is correctly set, FrontPage displays both the local and remote site in the Web Site pane (see illustration below).

Web Site pane

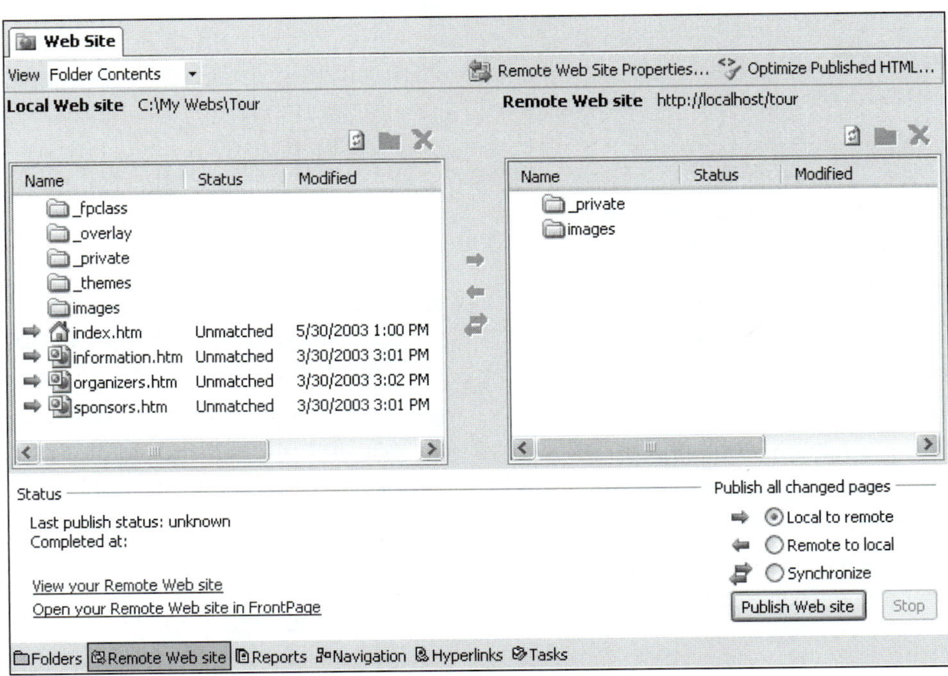

- At the left side of the pane, files and folders of the local site are listed, with left-pointing arrows indicating the pages that are ready to publish.
- The right side of the pane shows the remote site containing the two standard FrontPage folders, _private and images, ready to receive files from the local site.
- The View drop-down list at the top left of the pane indicates the current view. By default, FrontPage displays Folder Contents, which shows the site's folders and pages. A designer can change the view to show files that will be published, files that won't be published, or files that have a conflict to be resolved before they can be published.

  ✓ *You will learn more about changing publishing options in Exercise 38.*

- Both the local and remote site panes give information about status, modification date, author, file type, and file size for all files.
- The Status section at the bottom of the pane allows the author to specify a publishing option. The default option is to publish from local to remote, but an author can also choose to publish from the remote to the local site or simply synchronize the two sites so their content is identical.
- Clicking the Publish Web site button begins the actual copying of files from one location to another (for example, from a computer's hard disk to a server).
- FrontPage displays a box that shows the process of copying files.
- When the publishing operation is complete, the author can use the links at the bottom left of the Status area to perform several tasks:
  - Use the *View your publish log file* link to review the log of the publishing operation.

    You will view a publish log file in Exercise 38.

  - Use the *View your Remote Web site* link to jump right to the published Web site on the browser or view the publish log file.
  - Use the *Open your Remote Web site in FrontPage* link to launch another FrontPage window containing the remote Web site.

    ✓ *This can be very handy when you want to work further with the published version of the Web site.*

- FrontPage may rename the index.htm file as Default.htm during the publishing process.

  ✓ *The IIS 5.1 used by Windows XP Professional will not automatically rename the index.htm file, but IIS version 5.0 used by Windows 2000 usually does rename the file.*

- Links to the index.htm page are also automatically updated if FrontPage renames the home page.
- A Web site published to a personal Web server is stored in the wwwroot folder in the Inetpub directory. For example, to locate the tour Web site, the path would be C:\Inetpub\wwwroot\tour.

Publish to Disk or Local Location

- While publishing usually involves copying a Web site's files to a server (either Internet or personal), it can also be used to copy Web site files to a floppy or Zip disk or to another location on a computer's hard disk.
- Publishing is a good way to make a backup copy of a Web site for storage or to move Web sites from one location on a hard disk to another.
- Publishing a Web site from one location to another ensures that all necessary files stay together and links between pages are maintained.
- Publishing to a disk or another local location creates another disk-based Web site.
- To publish a Web site to a disk or other local location, use the File System option in the Remote Web Site Properties dialog box and then enter the path to the desired location, making sure to include the name of the Web site at the end of the path.

  ✓ *Use the Browse button to locate a specific disk or folder.*

- For example, to publish a Web site named Lacrosse to the Storage folder on the C: drive, type the path C:\Storage\Lacrosse.
- FrontPage displays a warning during publishing for any page which contains features that will work only when published.

Optimize Published HTML

- A new feature in FrontPage 2003 allows an author to clean up HTML code in a Web site's pages. Optimizing HTML removes unnecessary codes that can slow downloading.

- An author can optimize HTML at the authoring stage, to remove codes supplied by other applications such as Word, for example, or at the publishing stage.

  ✓ *You will use this feature on an imported Word page in Lesson 8, Exercise 44.*

- One benefit of optimizing at the publishing stage is that FrontPage will optimize the pages as they are being published.
- This means that unnecessary codes are stripped out of the remote site pages, while the local site pages remain the same. A designer can continue to see all code in the local pages for easy editing.
- To optimize HTML at the publishing stage, click the Optimize HTML tab in the Remote Web Site Properties dialog box, or click the Optimize Published HTML button at the top right of the Web Site pane with Remote Web site information displayed.
- When optimizing at the publishing stage, the author has three major areas of optimization, as shown on the Optimize HTML tab below: comments, whitespace, and generated HTML.

Optimize HTML dialog box

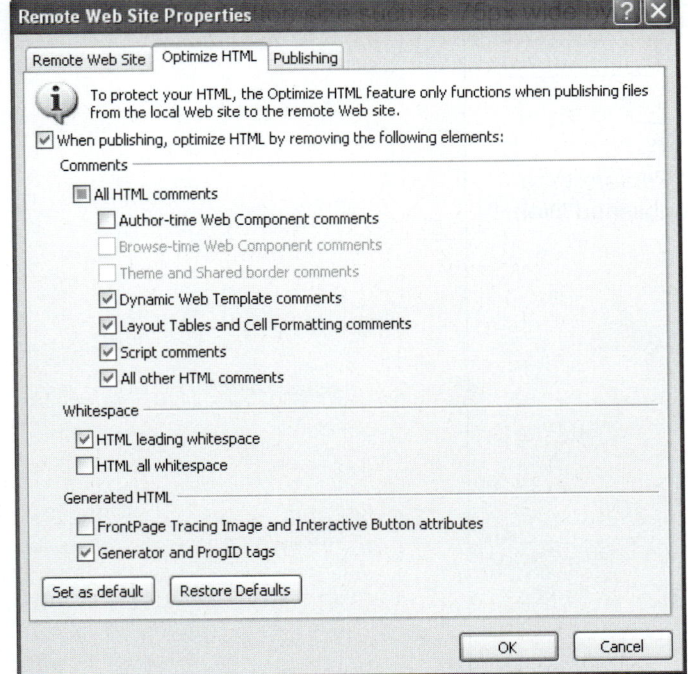

- *Comments* are remarks included in code to identify elements or settings or give further information about a component. Comments appear gray in code and are surrounded by wickets, an exclamation point, and two hyphens.
- The illustration below points out a comment inserted in code to identify a layout table.

Comments in HTML code

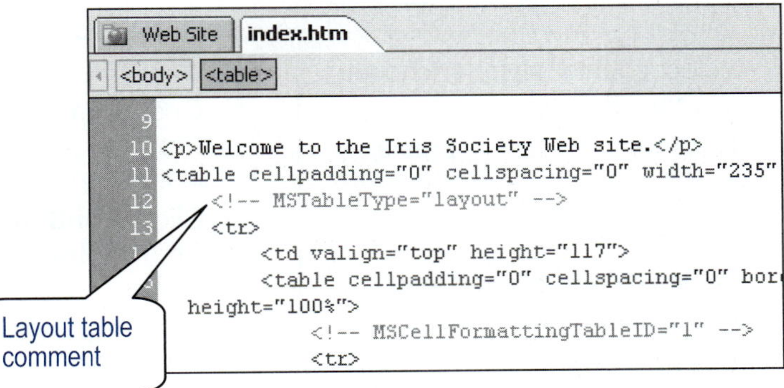

- Comments are not necessary for code to work correctly, so the author can choose to eliminate comments for a number of different features, such as cell formatting or dynamic Web templates.
- Whitespace options control the amount of white space in HTML code, such as between lines of code. Removing this white space causes code to run together rather than each new tag beginning a new line.
- Generated HTML includes HTML code created by features such as Trace Image and interactive buttons, as well as meta tags such as Generator and ProgID that may be added by other applications.

Procedures

Insert Hit Counter

1. Click **Insert** .... Alt+I
2. Click **Web Component**....... C
3. Select **Hit Counter**.
4. Click Finish **Finish** button .... Alt+F
5. Select counter style, or choose **Custom Picture**.
   - ✓ *If inserting a custom picture, the picture must be created in advance and named custom.gif.*
6. Select **Reset counter to** check box to set a starting number for counter.
7. Select **Fixed number of digits** and type number to set number of digits that will display in counter.

Publish Web Site to Internet-Connected Server

1. Click **Web Site** tab in FrontPage window.
2. Click **Remote Web site** option at bottom of pane.
3. Click **Remote Web Site Properties** at top of pane.

   OR

   a. Click **File**............... Alt+F

   b. Click **Publish Site** .... U

In Remote Web Site Properties dialog box

4. Select remote Web server type.
5. Type **http://[servername]/[Web site name]**
6. Click OK.
7. Supply user ID and/or password if necessary.
8. Click OK if FrontPage asks to create a Web site at the destination.
9. Click Publish Web site to begin publishing process.
10. Click *View your Remote Web site* link to see published Web site in browser.

Publish to Default Destination

- To publish to a default destination without changing publishing options, click (**Publish Web** button) on the Standard toolbar.

Publish Web Site to Personal Web Server

1. Open Remote Web Site Properties dialog box (see instructions at left).
2. Click **FrontPage or SharePoint Services** server option.
3. Type **http://localhost/[Web site name]**
   - ✓ *Some computers may have a name different from "localhost," depending on setup. If localhost does not work, consult a technical support person or your instructor.*
4. Click OK.
5. When FrontPage asks to create a Web site at the destination, click OK.
6. Click Publish Web site to begin publishing process.
7. Click *View your Remote Web site* link to see published Web site in browser.

Optimize Published HTML

Before publishing Web site to remote site

1. Open Remote Web Site Properties dialog box (see instructions in first column).
2. Click **Optimize HTML** tab.

   OR

   Click **Optimize Published HTML** at top right of Web Site pane in Remote Web site view.
3. Select **When publishing, optimize HTML by removing the following elements** check box to activate options.
4. Select options for optimizing.
5. Click OK and proceed with publishing.

Exercise Directions

✓ *This exercise assumes you are using a Windows 2000 Professional or Windows XP Professional personal Web server and that the personal Web server has been correctly set up for your computer. If you are able to publish to an Internet-connected server, make the appropriate change to the server name in the Remote Web Site Properties dialog box.*

1. Start FrontPage 2003.
2. Open **Tour**.
3. Open **index.htm**.
4. Scroll down the page and locate the shaded, shadowed box at the bottom right of the page. Insert a hit counter in the blank line between the two lines of text. Use the first counter style in the Hit Counter Properties dialog box.
5. Set the counter to begin at **1** and display three digits.
6. Save the page.
7. In Split or Code view, look for the comments related to the layout table and layout cell formatting. Return to Design view.
8. Begin the publishing process. Select the FrontPage or SharePoint Services server option and set the publishing destination as **http://localhost/tour**.

   ✓ *If your computer uses a different name for its personal Web server, use that name. If you are publishing to an Internet-connected server, supply the server name and any necessary user ID or password.*
9. Accept FrontPage's offer to create a Web site at the destination.
10. In the Web Site pane, choose to optimize published HTML. Select layout tables and cell formatting comments.
11. Publish the Web site.
12. When the publishing process is complete, click the *View your Remote Web site* link.
13. Scroll if necessary on the home page to see the hit counter. It should display 001.
14. Test the links and return to the home page. Use the browser's Refresh button to refresh the page several times.
15. The bottom of the home page should resemble Illustration A.
16. Close the browser.
17. Click the *Open your Remote Web site in FrontPage* to launch another FrontPage window.
18. Open **index.htm** or **Default.htm** and display code in Split or Code view. Note that the layout table and cell formatting comments have been removed from the code.
19. Close both versions of the Web site.
20. Exit FrontPage 2003.

Illustration A

Preservation is important to Clifton residents. Though some homes have deteriorated over time, many have been refurbished and renovated to their former glory. Residents who own outstanding properties like the Victorian pictured at the right have proved themselves willing to pay the sometimes high costs of restoration and maintenance to preserve the area's history.

Refurbishment doesn't stop at the front door. Many Clifton homeowners have restored interiors, as much as is practical, to their new state. This means rescuing beautiful moldings that were wrenched off and thrown behind the furnace decades ago, uncovering original fireplaces, hanging authentic wallpaper patterns, removing many layers of paint from woodwork, refinishing floors, and restoring windows. These are not easy jobs, but the results are rewarding.

Clifton is fortunate to have historic homes built by some of the pre-eminent architects of the past two centuries, including Samuel Hannaford and Frank Lloyd Wright. You might drive past these homes every day without knowing their rich and varied histories. Why not join us and learn more about the neighborhood and the homes that make it special.

On Your Own

1. Start FrontPage 2003.
2. Create a new Web site of at least two pages that gives a history of your neighborhood, town, or city and offers visitors a tour of the high points. Name the site **OYO37.**
   ✓ *Use the Tour Web site you worked with in this exercise as a guide for your Web site.*
3. Insert pictures if available or use clip art pictures or photos to illustrate the Web site.
4. Establish a navigation structure for the Web site and insert link bars to link pages.
5. Insert a hit counter on the Web site's **index.htm** page. Choose a hit counter style appropriate for your Web site.
6. Optimize the site's HTML.
7. Publish the Web site to your personal Web server or to any other available server that has FrontPage extensions.
8. View the published Web site and check that the hit counter is working correctly.
9. View the remaining page or pages of your Web site.
10. Close the browser.
11. Close the Web site.
12. Exit FrontPage 2003.
13. Summarize the development of each of the following Internet protocols: hypertext transfer protocols, gopher, file transfer protocol (FTP), telnet, and wide area information systems. Do research online if you need more information on any of these protocols.

Exercise 38

◆ **Set Publishing Options** ◆ **Exclude Pages During Publishing**
◆ **View Publish Log File** ◆ **Publish to Different Server Location**
◆ **About Web Site Security**

On the Job

After making changes to a Web site, a Web designer can publish changed pages only or replace all pages. Pages can be excluded during publishing so they do not appear in the published Web site. A designer can check the publishing process in the publish log file. An author can republish a published Web site to a different server or a different location on the same server. To maintain Web site security, the author can (in some cases) set permissions to limit access to a Web site.

In this exercise, you will continue to work with the Tour Web site. You will exclude a page, publish the Web site to a new server location, and view the publish log file. You will make changes throughout the Web site and republish all pages. Finally, you will make one additional change and publish only the changed page.

Terms

permissions
Authorizations that specify who can create, modify, administer, or visit a Web site.

publish log
A file that shows each action that takes place during the publishing process.

Notes

Set Publishing Options

- A Web author must often make changes to a Web site even after it has been published.
- The author can make changes to either the disk-based Web site from which a Web site was published or to the published Web site itself.

  ✓ *To make changes to the server-based Web site, it must be opened from the server where it is stored.*
- After changes have been made to a disk-based Web site, affected pages must be republished to take effect in the server-based Web site.
- Changes made to a server-based Web site do not have to be republished, only saved and then refreshed in the browser.
- Click the Publishing tab in the Remote Web Site Properties dialog box to set publishing options for the changed pages (see illustration at top of next page).
  - Choose *Changed pages only* to publish only pages that have been changed since the Web site was last published.
  - Choose *All pages, overwriting pages already on destination* to replace all pages in the published Web site with changed pages.

Set publishing options in Remote Web Site Properties dialog box

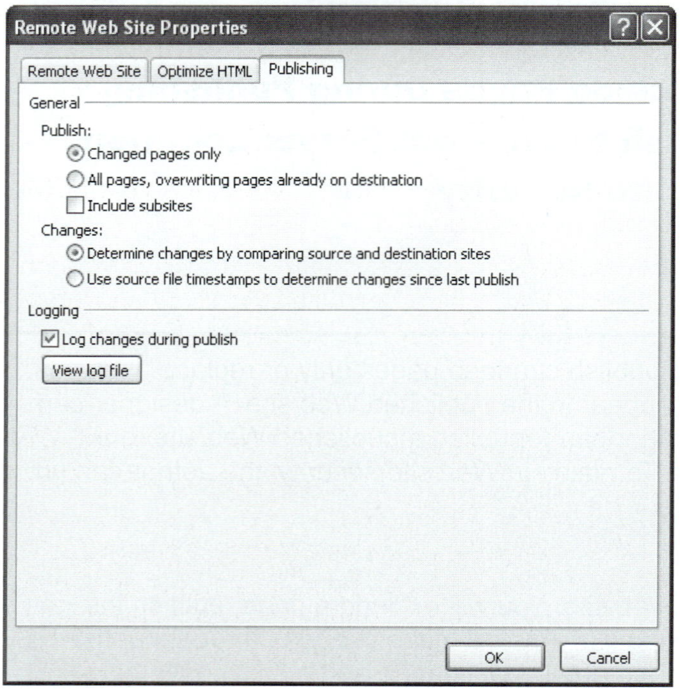

- Select *Include subsites* to include subsites in the publishing process.

  ✓ *Subsites are folders that can contain a Web site different from but related to the main Web site. You will learn more about subsites in Lesson 10, Exercise 52.*

- By default, FrontPage determines which pages to change by comparing pages in the source Web site (the one currently open) with the destination Web site (the published Web site).
- Pages that have been changed in the source Web site display a status of Changed to indicate that they don't match up with the destination Web pages (see illustration below).

Two pages have been changed

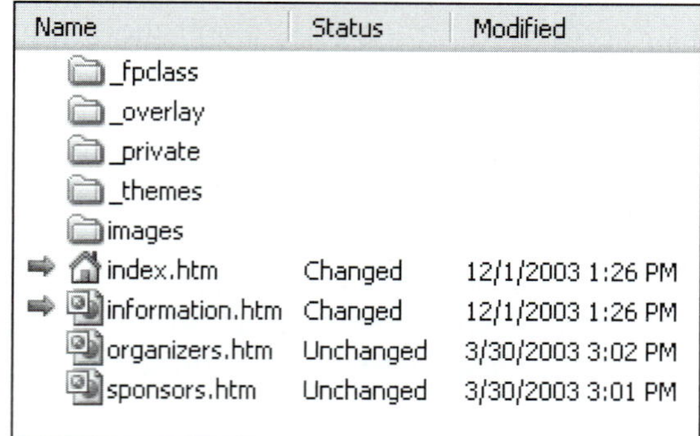

Name	Status	Modified
_fpclass		
_overlay		
_private		
_themes		
images		
index.htm	Changed	12/1/2003 1:26 PM
information.htm	Changed	12/1/2003 1:26 PM
organizers.htm	Unchanged	3/30/2003 3:02 PM
sponsors.htm	Unchanged	3/30/2003 3:01 PM

- If a file has a status of Conflict, the designer should confirm that he or she wants to publish the changed source file to the destination Web site.
- FrontPage requests that the author either skip the file in conflict or overwrite the file in both Web sites.
- Status of both local and remote pages may change depending on the option chosen in the Publishing tab of the Remote Web Site Properties dialog box.
- If *All pages* is selected, for example, the status will change to Publish for all local pages and Unmatched for remote pages.
- A designer may on occasion wish to synchronize local and remote files. Synchronizing downloads files from the remote site to the local site so that the author can work on all versions locally.
- Use the Synchronize option in the Publish all pages section of the Remote Web site pane to synchronize files.
- Similarly, the designer may wish to replace a page on the local site with a page from the remote site. Use the Remote to local option to publish from the remote site to the local site.

Exclude Pages During Publishing

- In some cases, the Web designer might not want to publish all pages of a Web site; for example, if a page is still under construction.
- Pages can be excluded from the publishing process in the Remote Web site pane.
- Right-click the page to exclude and choose Don't Publish from the shortcut menu. A small red circle with a white x in it displays next to the page (see illustration at the top of the next page).

  ✓ *Pages can also be excluded from the Folder List in Page view.*

- If pages are not to be included in the final published Web site, they should be excluded before the Web site is published. Once a Web site has been published, it is not possible to exclude a page by republishing the Web site. The only way to remove a page from a published Web site is to delete it from its published location.

Exclude a page from publishing

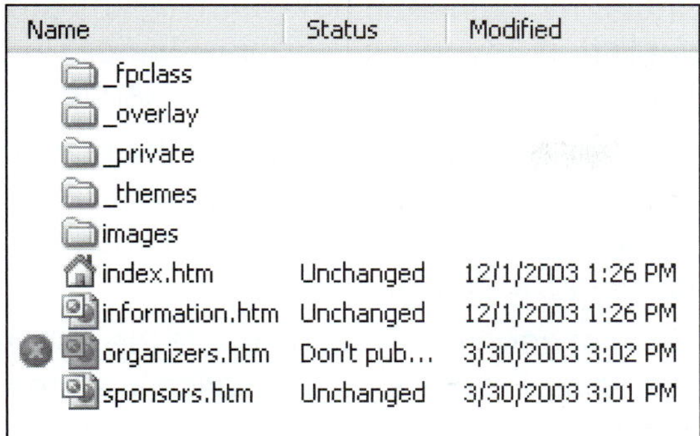

Name	Status	Modified
_fpclass		
_overlay		
_private		
_themes		
images		
index.htm	Unchanged	12/1/2003 1:26 PM
information.htm	Unchanged	12/1/2003 1:26 PM
organizers.htm	Don't pub...	3/30/2003 3:02 PM
sponsors.htm	Unchanged	3/30/2003 3:01 PM

- Delete a page from a published Web site by right-clicking the page in the destination side of the Remote Web site pane and click Delete on the shortcut menu.

  ✓ *If a deleted page is part of a navigation structure, FrontPage automatically removes links to the deleted page in link bars.*

- An excluded page can be published at any time by right-clicking it and deselecting Don't Publish.

View Publish Log File

- The **publish log** is a file the Web author can display after publishing to show the actions that took place during publishing.
- Click the *View your publish log file* link in the Status area of the Remote Web site pane to open the publish log in the browser.

  ✓ *The publish log can also be displayed by clicking the View log file button on the Publishing tab of the Remote Web Site Properties dialog box.*

- The publish log is set up in tabular form and shows the date and time for each action (see illustration below).
- Use the Show only drop-down list to select specific actions to view. The author can view eight different options: Publish Starts, Folder Creations, File Copies, File Renames, File Deletions, Confirmations, Warnings, and HTML Optimizations.
- For example, selecting the File Copies item on the Show only list modifies the list to show only the files that were copied into the Web site.

Publish to Different Server Location

- An author can easily republish a published Web site to a different location on the same server or on a different server.
- For example, Web designers commonly publish a Web site to a personal Web server first, work out any problems, and then publish the Web site to an Internet-connected server.
- To publish a published Web site to a different server, open the Remote Web Site Properties dialog box and specify a new server location.
- To publish to a different location on the same server, change only the Web site name in the Remote Web Site Properties dialog box.

Publish log file

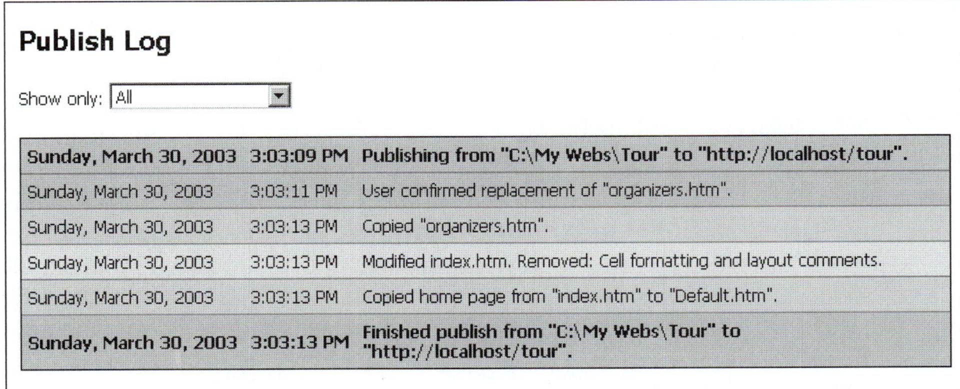

Publish Log

Show only: All

Sunday, March 30, 2003	**3:03:09 PM**	**Publishing from "C:\My Webs\Tour" to "http://localhost/tour".**
Sunday, March 30, 2003	3:03:11 PM	User confirmed replacement of "organizers.htm".
Sunday, March 30, 2003	3:03:13 PM	Copied "organizers.htm".
Sunday, March 30, 2003	3:03:13 PM	Modified index.htm. Removed: Cell formatting and layout comments.
Sunday, March 30, 2003	3:03:13 PM	Copied home page from "index.htm" to "Default.htm".
Sunday, March 30, 2003	**3:03:13 PM**	**Finished publish from "C:\My Webs\Tour" to "http://localhost/tour".**

About Web Site Security

- Security is an important consideration when publishing a Web site from a local server (or publishing a disk-based Web site) to an Internet-connected server.
- To maintain the security of a Web site published to an Internet-connected server, the author can limit access to the Web site by setting permissions.
- **Permissions** are a set of authorizations that specify who can create, modify, administer, or visit a Web site.
- Permissions are assigned to users depending on their roles as visitors, authors, or administrators:
  - Visitors have only *browsing* permission; they can view a published FrontPage Web site but can make no changes to it.
  - Authors have *authoring* permission; they can open and edit a published FrontPage Web site.
  - Administrators have *administering* permission; they can work with FrontPage extensions, set permissions for other users, and perform other administrative tasks.
- Permissions cannot be set in FrontPage for personal Web servers and Windows NT servers. As a general rule, permissions are set and maintained by a server's administrator.

  ✓ *You will learn more about setting permissions in Lesson 10, Exercise 52.*

- When selecting a server to host a Web site, an author should find out how permissions are established and test permissions before publishing a final Web site to that server.
- An author should also verify that the server has the latest updates and patches necessary to maintain server security, as well as good antivirus protection.
- Choice of server may also impact the security of a Web site. FrontPage automatically stores sensitive files such as form results and discussion postings in a file named _private, which is hidden on servers running FrontPage and SharePoint extensions.
- Other servers, such as FTP or WebDAV servers, may not hide this folder by default, which can allow site visitors access to these private files.
- For this reason, designers need to use care when publishing to these server types.
- Finally, an author should take care when synchronizing files in the Remote Web Site view. Synchronizing downloads files from the remote Web site to the local Web site. If the remote Web site has been hacked, it is possible to download corrupted files from the remote site, thereby also corrupting the local site. Making sure that the remote server has good security in place that limits access to the site can make a designer feel more secure about all publishing operations.

Procedures

Open Published Web site

- In Remote Web site view, click *Open your Remote Site in FrontPage* link.

OR

1. Click **File** .... Alt+F
2. Click **Open Site** I

   OR

   Click (**Open** button) down arrow and click **Open Site** I

In Open Web dialog box

3. Click folder that shows network places.
4. Click published Web site name (or navigate to Web sites within localhost).
5. Click Open ..... Alt+O

Set Publishing Options

1. Click **Web Site** tab in FrontPage window.
2. Click **Remote Web site** option at bottom of pane.
3. Click **Remote Web Site Properties** at top of pane.

   OR

   - Click **File** .... Alt+F
   - Click **Publish Site** .... U
4. Click **Publishing** tab.
5. Select **Changed pages only** to publish only pages that have changed since last publish.
6. Select **All pages, overwriting pages already on destination** to replace all pages in the published Web site with pages from the source (current) Web site.
7. Select **Include subsites** ..... 

Exclude Pages During Publishing

1. Click **Web Site** tab in FrontPage window.
2. Click **Remote Web site** option at bottom of pane.
3. Right-click file to exclude.
4. Click **Don't Publish** .... P

   ✓ *A small red stop sign with a white x in it displays to the left of the excluded file.*

5. To include an excluded file, right-click the file and deselect **Don't Publish** .... P

   OR

   Right-click file name in Folder List in Page view and select **Don't Publish** .... P

6. Delete a file from the published Web site:
   - Right-click the file to delete and click **Delete** .... D

View Publish Log File

- Click *View your publish log file* link in Status area of Remote Web site view.

OR

1. Click **File** .... Alt + F
2. Click **Publish Web** .... U
3. Click **Publishing** tab.
4. Click View log file.
5. Show only specific actions in the publish log by clicking **Show only** down arrow and selecting type of action to show.

Publish to Different Server Location

1. Click **Web Site** tab in FrontPage window.
2. Click **Remote Web site** option at bottom of pane.
3. Click **Remote Web Site Properties** at top of pane.
4. Type new server name in **Remote Web site location** text box to publish to different server.

   OR

   - Type new Web site name in Remote Web site location text box to publish to different location on same server.

Exercise Directions

1. Start FrontPage 2003.
2. Open **tour** from your personal Web server or server. (This is the published version of the Tour Web site you created in Exercise 37.)
3. Open the Remote Web Site Properties dialog box to begin the publishing process. Change the Web site name to **tour1** to publish the Web site to a new location on the personal Web server.

   ✓ *FrontPage will create a new Web site with the new name and then display the local and remote files and folders.*

4. The **organizers.htm** page in this Web site contains phone numbers that shouldn't be available to all viewers of the published Web site. In the Remote Web site view, exclude the **organizers.htm** page and then publish the Web site.
5. View the published Web site and click the Organizers link. The page cannot be found, because it was excluded from the Web site.
6. Return to FrontPage and click the *View your publish log file* link to review the publish log.
7. Use the Show only drop-down list to display only the folders FrontPage created during the publish.
8. Return to FrontPage. In Navigation view, exclude the Organizers page from all link bars.
9. Republish the Web site to the same location, choosing to replace all existing pages.
10. Refresh the home page in the browser. Notice that the published Web site now displays the revised link bar.
11. Return to FrontPage.
12. To make the home page stand out, remove its theme background.
13. Save the page and republish the Web site, choosing to publish only changed pages.

    ✓ *Don't forget to change the publishing option to Changed pages only on the Remote Web Site Properties dialog box's Publishing tab.*

14. Refresh the home page in the browser. Your Default.htm page should look similar to Illustration A.
15. Close the browser.
16. Close the Web site.
17. Exit FrontPage 2003.

Illustration A

Clifton Historic House Tour

Tour Information | Sponsors

Welcome to the annual Clifton Historic House Tour! If you have joined us before, you know the treat in store for you. Some of Clifton's many historic homes are open one Sunday a year so that visitors from all over the city and surrounding regions can appreciate their exceptional architecture and environments.

Founded over 150 years ago, Clifton was from its inception home to influential citizens, including wealthy industrialists and politicians. These early Clifton residents built their houses in a variety of styles, from stone mansions to quaint cottages surrounded by acres of garden. Drive down any street in the historic area and you'll find sturdy German-influenced brick homes rubbing shoulders with Queen Annes and Tudors, Italianate palaces overlooking Dutch colonials, and arts and crafts style homes peacefully coexisting with medieval revival mini-castles.

On Your Own

1. Start FrontPage 2003.
2. Open the Web site you created in the last On Your Own exercise.
3. Choose a page in the Web site to exclude. If you do not have a page that can easily be excluded, add an appropriate page and insert text indicating that the page is under construction.
4. If you inserted a Web page, add it to the navigation structure.
5. Publish the Web site to a new location on the server and exclude the Web page in the Remote Web site view.
6. View the published Web site and the publish log file.
7. Modify the navigation structure so the excluded Web page will not appear in link bars.
8. Apply a theme to all pages in the Web site, or modify an existing theme.
9. Republish the Web site so that all existing pages are replaced.
10. Center the hit counter on the home page, or change its style.

    ✓ *To center the hit counter, click it to select it and then click the Center alignment button on the Formatting toolbar.*

11. Republish the home page and specify that only changed pages be published.
12. View the published Web site in the browser and check all links and changes.
13. Close all browser pages.
14. Close the Web site.
15. Exit FrontPage 2003.

Exercise 39

◆ **About Searching** ◆ **Use Search Page Template**
◆ **Customize Search Page** ◆ **Use Search Form**

On the Job

To allow a site visitor to search a Web site for a specific word or phrase, FrontPage supplies a search feature. Use the Search Page template to create a page that contains a search form and instructions for using the form, or insert a search form on any Web page. The search page can be customized to match other pages in a Web site. A search form will work correctly only in a published Web site.

In this exercise, you will continue to work with the Clifton House Tour Web site. You will add a page that uses the Search Page template, customize the page to match other pages in the Web site, and test the search form after publishing the Web site to a new location.

Terms

search form
A form that allows a visitor to find specific words or phrases in a Web site.

Notes

About Searching

- Web sites often contain a considerable amount of text spread over many pages.
- Make such a site more accessible to visitors by adding a **search form** to the Web site.
- A FrontPage search form allows a visitor to type words or phrases to find. After the visitor clicks a button to start the search, FrontPage opens a search results page that displays the locations of the found text as links.
- The visitor can click a link to jump to a page where the word or phrase appears.
- When a Web site is published on a server that uses FrontPage extensions, FrontPage indexes the text on the Web site's pages. The search form compares text entered in the form with the text index and returns the list of matching results.
  - ✓ *FrontPage does not index common words such as "a," "an," "the," and so on.*
- FrontPage offers two easy ways to insert a search form:
  - Use the Insert Web Component dialog box to insert a search form on any Web page (see illustration below).

Insert a search form on any page

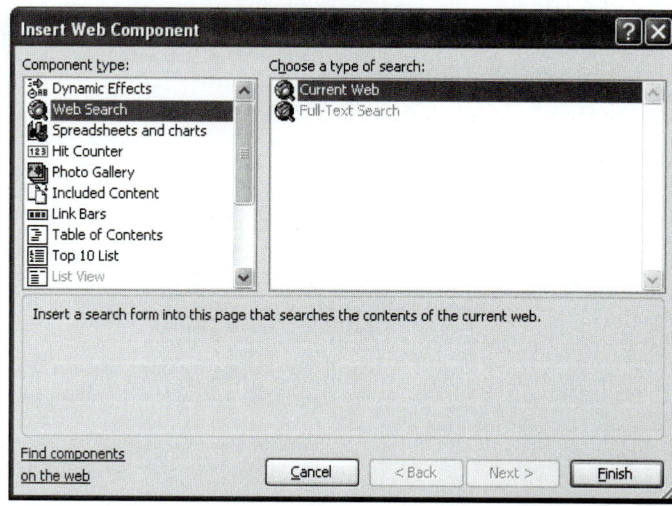

- Use the Search Page template to create a new page that contains a search form.

Use Search Page Template

- FrontPage's Page Templates dialog box contains a number of page templates to help Web authors create special Web pages, for example, pages that contain multiple columns or other complex layouts.
- The Search Page template creates a page containing a search form, a generic introduction, instructions on how to use the search form, and generic copyright information (see illustration below).
  - ✓ *The Search Page template also includes bookmarks and links to control navigation on the page, a comment that explains what the search page does, and several horizontal rules to divide sections of the page.*
- The actual search form appears in the middle of the page and consists of a form label (Search for), the form field (the blank box), and two push buttons (Start Search and Reset).
  - ✓ *You will learn more about forms in Lesson 8, Exercise 41 and Exercise 42.*

Customize Search Page

- Web authors can customize search pages in a number of ways:
  - Format a search page with a theme, fonts, backgrounds, or pictures to match or complement other pages in the Web site.
  - Modify the generic instructions above the search form to tailor the search page for a specific audience.
  - Modify the Query Language section if desired, or move it to a different page and link it to the search page.
  - Modify the properties of the search form itself.
- To modify the search form's properties, double-click the search form (or right-click and choose Search Form Properties) to open the Search Form Properties dialog box (see illustration at the top of the next page).
- In this dialog box, change:
  - The label for the search form field.
  - The width of the form field (the default width is 20 characters).
  - The labels for the buttons that start the search and reset the form for the next use.
- The Search Results tab in this Search Form Properties dialog box gives the Web developer additional control over the scope of the search and what information will display on the search results page.

New search page created from Search Page template

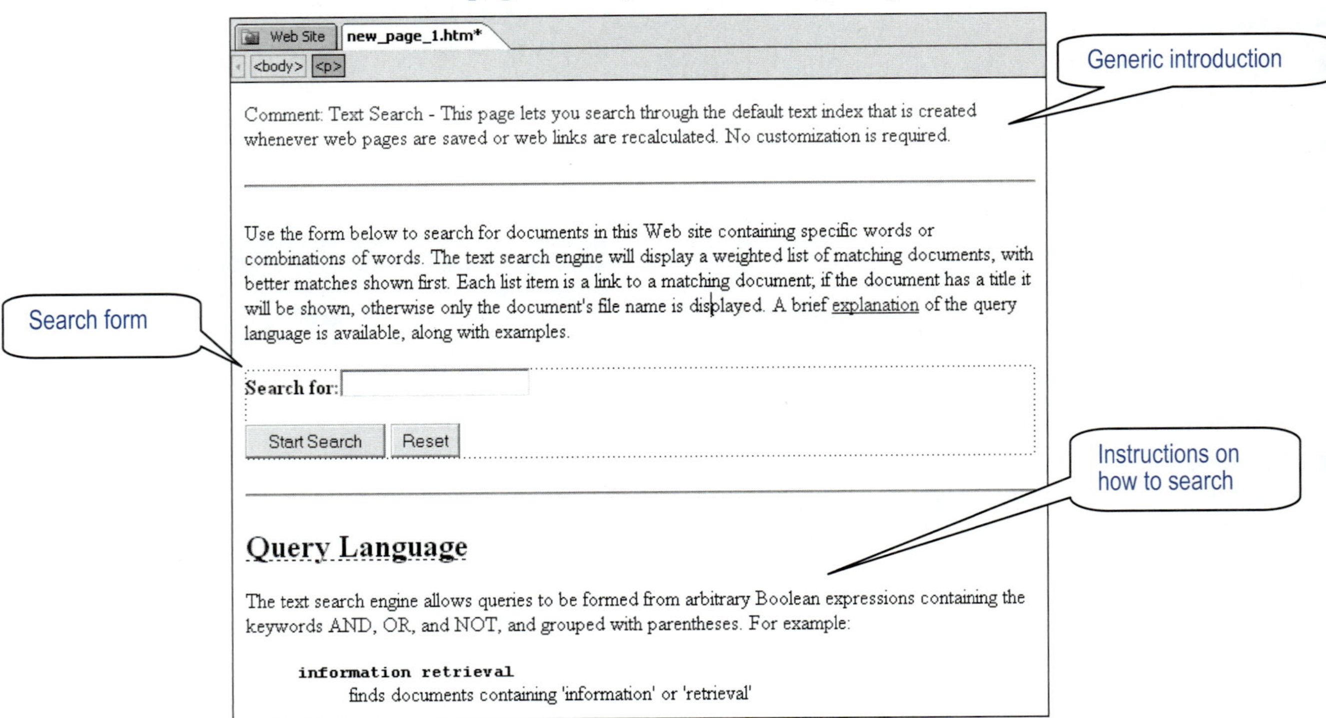

Search Form Properties dialog box

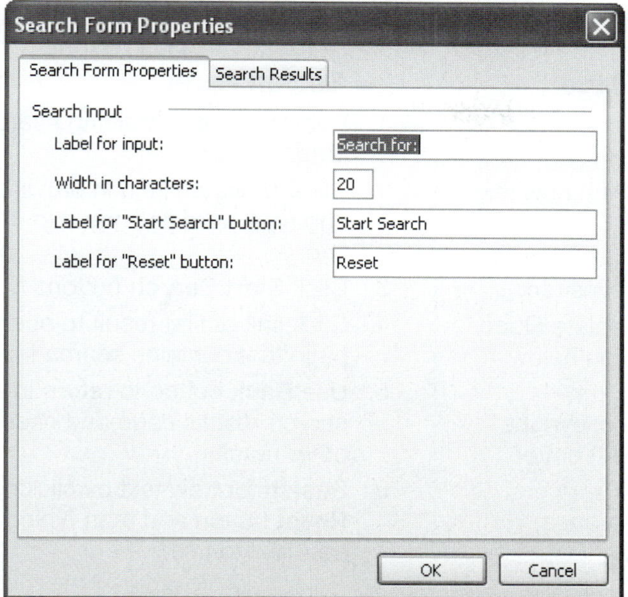

Use Search Form

- To work properly, a search form must be published to a server that uses FrontPage extensions.
  - ✓ *If an author attempts to use the search form in a disk-based Web site, FrontPage will display an error page.*
- Test a search form in the browser after the Web site has been published by typing some text in the search form field that definitely appears somewhere in the Web site.
  - ✓ *The browser may "remember" previous form entries. If form text matches a previous entry, a drop-down list displays the matching entry. Click a list item to insert it in the form field.*
- FrontPage displays the search results page that lists the location(s) of text that match the search text (see illustration below).
  - ✓ *If no matches are found for the search text, FrontPage displays the message "No documents found. Please try again."*
- The Search Results table contains several items of information: the name of the page where the search text appears, the date and time the page was modified, and the page size (see illustration below).
  - ✓ *Information displayed in this table can be modified on the Search Results tab of the Search Form Properties dialog box. Displayed items vary depending on whether a search page is added as a new page or added to an existing page.*

Search results page

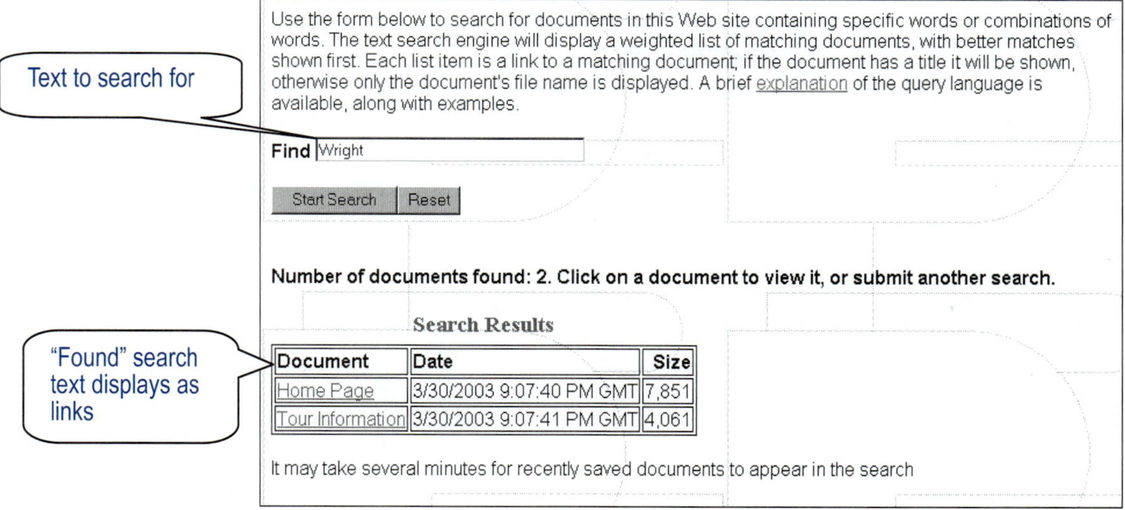

Procedures

Insert Search Form on Any Web Page

1. Position insertion point at location where search form should appear.
2. Click **Insert** .... Alt+I
3. Click **Web Component**....... C
4. Select **Web Search** and click [Finish] **Finish** button .... Alt+F.
5. Modify the search form's properties if desired.

Use Search Page Template

1. Click **File** .... Alt+F
2. Click **New** .... N
3. Click **More page templates** link in the New task pane.

   OR

   a. Click Create a new normal page down arrow.
   b. Click **Page** .... P
4. Click **Search Page** template.

Customize Search Page

1. Modify page text:
   a. Delete or replace comment at top of page with new text or heading.
   b. Edit introductory text above search form as desired.
   c. Edit, move, or delete Query Language section below search form.
   d. Edit or remove copyright information at bottom of page.
2. Modify page appearance:
   a. Apply a theme or background.
   b. Change text formatting.
3. Modify search form properties:
   a. Double-click search form to open Search Form Properties dialog box.

      OR

      Right-click search form and select **Search Form Properties**..................... O
   b. Change:

      Search for label.

      Search field width.

      Labels for Start Search and Reset buttons.
   c. Specify scope of search and information to display in Search Results table on Search Results tab.

Use Search Form

1. Publish page containing search form.
2. Click in search field in browser and type word or phrase to find.
3. Click **Start Search** button.
4. Click link of first result to open page that contains search text.
5. Use **Back** button to return to search results page and check other results.
6. Search for new text by clicking **Reset** button and then typing new text to find.

Exercise Directions

1. Start FrontPage 2003.
2. Open **tour1**.
   ✓ *Don't forget that you have to open this Web site from your personal Web server file location (use Web Folders or My Network Places in the Open Web dialog box to locate the Web site).*
3. Create a new page in the Web site using the Search Page template.
4. Save the new Web page as **search.htm** with the page title **Search**.
5. Add the **search.htm** Web page to the navigation structure to the right of the Sponsors page.
6. On the **search.htm** Web page, delete the comment at the top of the page and the horizontal rule below the comment.
7. Insert the Heading 1 heading **Search** at the top of the page and change its color to match that of the other Heading 1 headings in the Web site.
8. Insert a navigation bar on the Web page that matches those on other pages.
9. To help visitors understand how the search page works, modify the introductory text above the search form to read as follows:

   Use the form below to search for specific words or combinations of words. The text search engine will display a weighted list of matching pages, with better matches shown first. Each list item is a link to a matching page. A brief explanation of the query language is available, along with examples.

   ✓ *Do not change the explanation link to the Query Language bookmark.*
10. Scroll to the bottom of the Web page and remove the bottom horizontal rule and the copyright information below it.
11. Modify the search form properties as follows:
    - Change the Search for label to Find:.
    - Change the search field width to **35**.
    - On the Search Results tab, choose to display file size and score.
12. Save changes to the **search.htm** page.
13. Publish the Web site to your personal Web server or other server with the new name **toursearch**.
    ✓ *If you receive a message about the changed navigation structure during the publishing process, let FrontPage handle merging the changes.*
14. Display the Search page and test the search form by entering **Frank Lloyd Wright** in the Find box and clicking the Start Search button.
15. Your search results page should resemble Illustration A. (Your Score numbers may differ.)
16. Click each link in the Search Results table to find the search text.
    ✓ *Use the browser's Back button to return to the search results page. If you use the Search link in the link bar, you will open the page ready to start a new search.*
17. Close the browser.
18. Close the Web site.
19. Exit FrontPage 2003.

Illustration A

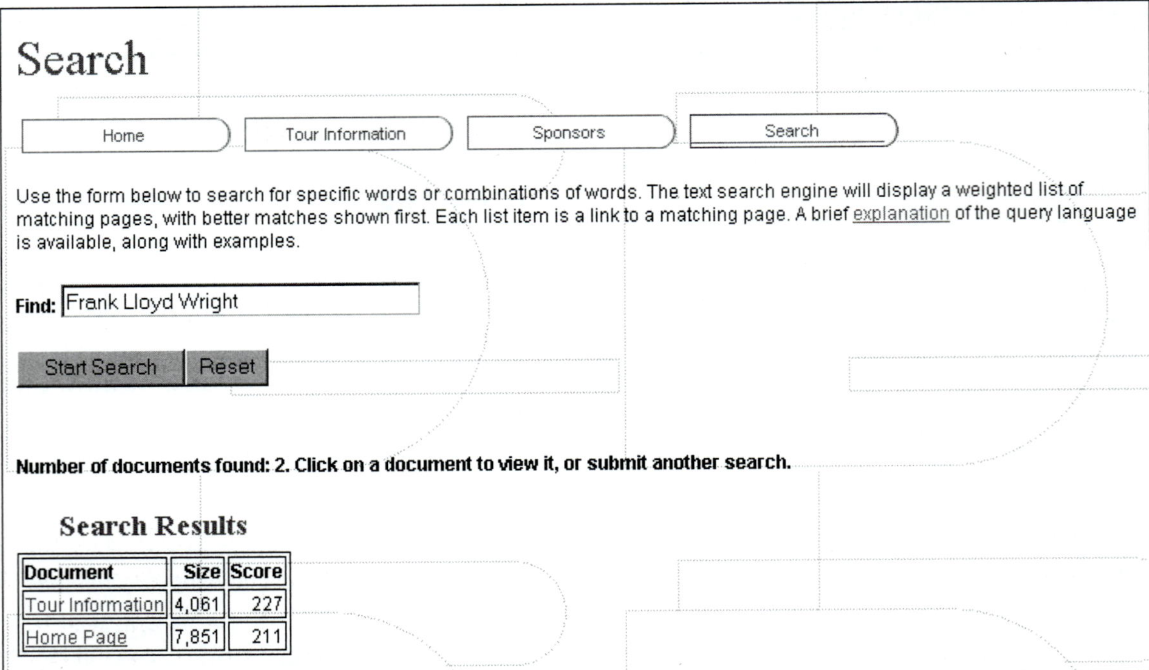

On Your Own

1. Start FrontPage 2003.
2. Open the Web site you published in the last exercise.
3. Create a new Web page using the Search Page template.
4. Save the page with an appropriate name and page title.
5. Customize the Web page as desired to match the other pages in your Web site.
6. Add the Web page to the navigation structure and insert a link bar on it.
7. Publish the current Web site to a server using a different Web site name.
8. Test the search page by typing a word or words that you know are somewhere in your Web site (such as the name of your neighborhood, town, or city).
9. Test each link on the search results page.
10. Close the browser.
11. Close the Web site.
12. Exit FrontPage 2003.

Exercise 40

◆ **Critical Thinking** ◆ **Challenge**

In this exercise, you will work on a Web site for Midwest University's Alumni Association. You will add a hit counter, publish the Web site, make changes to the Web site, and republish pages. You will add and customize a search page and publish the Web site to a new location.

Exercise Directions

1. Start FrontPage 2003.
2. Open **Alumni**.
3. Open **index.htm**
4. In the left-hand shaded layout cell, insert the text **You are visitor** and press Enter.
   - ✓ *Use your own judgment about the placement of this text in the layout cell.*
5. Insert a hit counter. Choose an appropriate style, start counting at 001, and specify 3 digits.
6. Exclude the **updates.htm** page (this page is still under construction) and publish the remaining files to your personal Web server (or other server, if you have access to one). Publish the Web site as **alumnifirst** and verify that the hit counter works correctly.
7. View the publish log file.
8. Return to FrontPage and change the color of *You are visitor* to another of the theme's colors and apply bold formatting. Center both the text and the hit counter in the layout cell.
9. Save the page, and then republish the changed page only.
10. Check each page in the Web site and notice that only the home page has page links.
11. Return to FrontPage and add link bars to the **homecoming.htm** and **classes.htm** pages.
12. Adjust page titles if desired to fit navigation buttons.
13. Republish the Web site, overwriting all pages. Check links in the published Web site.
14. Return to FrontPage and add a search page to the Web site. Give the page an appropriate file name and page title.
15. Customize the search page as desired.
16. Add the page to the navigation structure and insert a link bar.
17. Insert a link to the search page in the layout cell on the **index.htm** page.
18. Your review of the site has convinced you the theme backgrounds on all pages other than **index.htm** make the site seem dark. Remove the background picture on all pages where it appears. (Deselect Vivid Colors, if necessary, so you can apply a plain white background.)
19. You are now ready to publish the final version of the Web site. First choose to optimize the site during publishing to remove layout table and cell comments and HTML leading whitespace.
20. Publish the Web site to a new location, using **alumnifinal** as the Web site name.
21. Test the search form by finding where on the Web site the Homecoming Parade is discussed.
    - ✓ *If the search form does not find this information, make sure indexing is turned on, if necessary, or try searching for* Parade.
22. Your search results should look similar to Illustration A.
23. Close the browser.
24. Close the Web site.
25. Exit FrontPage 2003.

Illustration A

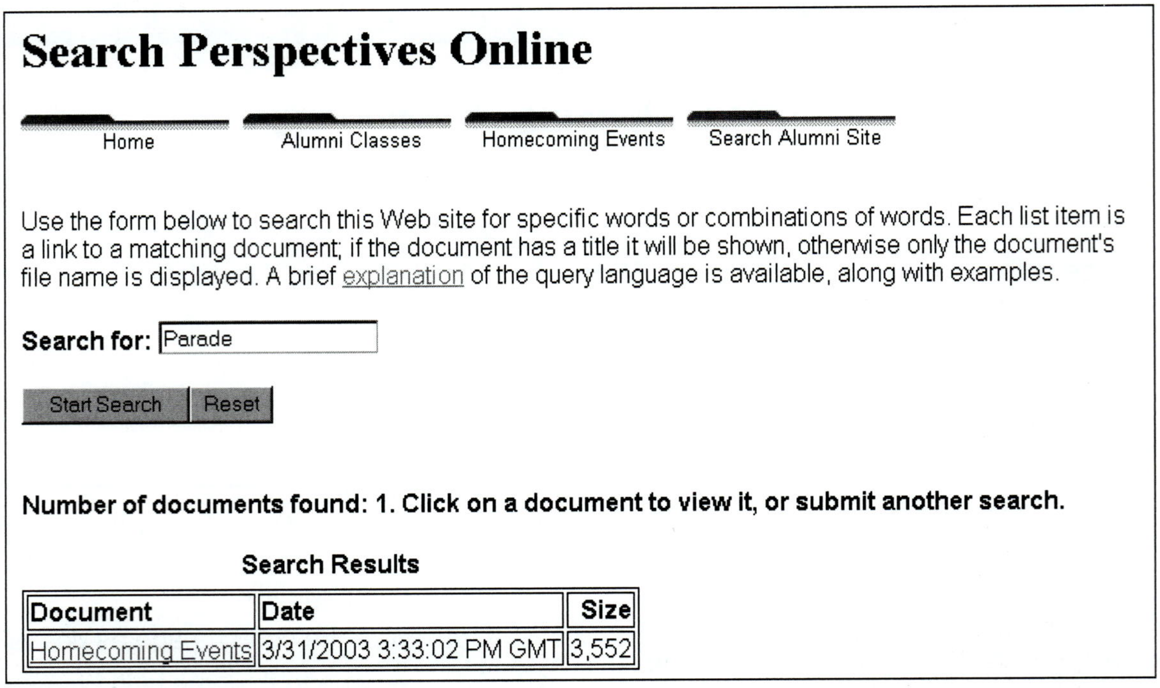

Search Perspectives Online

Home | Alumni Classes | Homecoming Events | Search Alumni Site

Use the form below to search this Web site for specific words or combinations of words. Each list item is a link to a matching document; if the document has a title it will be shown, otherwise only the document's file name is displayed. A brief explanation of the query language is available, along with examples.

Search for: Parade

Start Search | Reset

Number of documents found: 1. Click on a document to view it, or submit another search.

Search Results

Document	Date	Size
Homecoming Events	3/31/2003 3:33:02 PM GMT	3,552

Challenge Exercise

1. Using FrontPage's Help files and any other technical documentation you can find, write a short report that answers the following questions:
   - What security measures does FrontPage provide?
   - How would you set passwords that would allow only certain visitors to access your Web site?
   - What security methods do Web servers have available for protecting against hackers, viruses, etc? What security methods do you think would work best?
2. What factors should you examine when choosing a Web server? (For example, cost, availability of FrontPage server extensions, etc.)
3. What are the technical needs of a Web server, with regards to the following:
   - RAM
   - Hard disk capacity
   - CPU speed
   - Methods of connectivity
   - Appropriate software

LESSON 8

Interactive Web Site Features: Forms and Other FrontPage Components

Exercise 41

◆ **About Web Site Forms**
◆ **Insert Form Component** ◆ **Insert Form Fields**
◆ **Modify Form Field Properties**

On the Job

Web developers can create forms on Web pages to collect data from site visitors. FrontPage offers a number of different form fields to collect different types of data. Developers can modify form field properties to make it easier to identify and analyze collected information.

In this exercise, you will work on a Web site for the Save Our Schools school levy campaign. You will create a form that site visitors can fill out online to volunteer their services. You will insert a form component, add form fields to the form, and modify properties for each form field.

Terms

form
A collection of *form fields* used to gather information from visitors to a Web site.

form component
A FrontPage component that contains all the fields for a form.

form field
The form element that allows a visitor to supply a specific type of information.

label
Word or phrase that identifies what kind of information a form field requires.

Notes

About Web Site Forms

- A **form** is a collection of fields used to gather different types of information from the person who fills out the form.
- In the past, forms were always produced on paper and had to be filled in by hand with a pencil, pen, or typewriter. In the Internet age, forms are commonly created on Web pages.
- When a Web-site visitor types information in a Web site form, that information is stored in a file in the Web site so that the Web site's author can easily review and analyze the information.
- Web authors use forms to gather various types of information from Web site visitors; for example, contact information, feedback, or product orders.
- A Web site form must be published to work correctly.

Insert Form Component

- The first step in creating a Web site form is to decide what types of information to collect in the form.

  ✓ *It can be helpful to sketch the form layout on paper before beginning work on the form.*

- The second step is to insert a **form component**, the FrontPage component that will contain all the form information.

- Insert a form component using the Insert>Form>Form command on the menu bar.
- A new form component initially contains only two buttons (Submit and Reset) surrounded by a dotted-line box (see illustration below).

New form component in a Web page

The Save Our Schools levy campaign needs your help. If you can volunteer your time (or even just your yard or your bumper), fill out the form below and submit it. We will contact you as soon as possible.

Submit Reset

- The insertion point displays to the left of the Submit button. Press the Enter key to add a blank line and enlarge the form component.
- To work properly, all form elements must be enclosed within the dotted-line form component box.

Insert Form Fields

- Once the form component has been added to a page, the Web author can add **form fields** to the form to collect information.
- A form field provides a means for the visitor to supply a specific type of information. For example, a Textbox form field allows a visitor to type text in the field.
- The Insert>Form menu offers eight different form fields for use in forms as well as Advanced Button, Picture, and Label options.
- Use these form fields as follows:

Form Field	Use to . . .
Textbox	Let a visitor type a single line of text.
Text Area	Let a visitor type multiple lines of text.
File Upload	Allow a visitor to type the name of a file or use a Browse button to locate a file to upload.
Checkbox	Allow a visitor to select a choice if desired.

Form Field	Use to . . .
Option Button	Allow a visitor to select only one from a group of options.
Group Box	Separate a group of related fields or text from the main form.
Drop-Down Box	Let a visitor select from a drop-down menu of choices.
Push Button	Enable a visitor to perform a specific action.
Advanced Button	Customize text on a button.
Picture	Insert a picture within the form component.
Label	Enable a visitor to select an option by clicking either the form field or its label.

- To insert a form field, first type a **label** that identifies what type of information the form field requires (see illustration below).
- Insert the form field itself by clicking Insert>Form and selecting the desired field from the pop-out menu. The following illustration shows a Textbox form field and two push buttons.
- After inserting the first form field, press the Enter key to move down in the form component.
- To align labels and form fields neatly on a page, insert them in table cells within the form component.
- Delete a form field by clicking a field once to select it and then pressing Delete.

Modify Form Field Properties

- To make the results collected from a form easier to understand, the Web author can set or change properties for each type of form field.
- To change a form field's properties, double-click the form field, or right-click the field and select Form Field Properties from the shortcut menu.

Textbox form field and label in form component

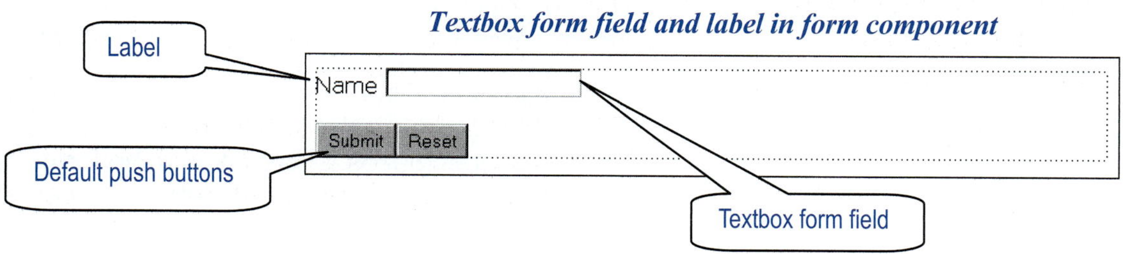

- The properties dialog box offers different properties for each type of form field. The illustration below shows the properties dialog box for a Textbox form field.

Text Box Properties dialog box

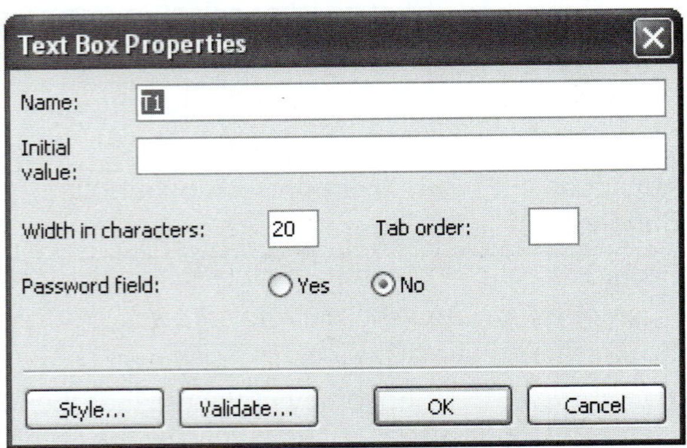

- In addition to setting other properties for a field, the author can set tab order for each field.
- Tab order controls which field the insertion point will jump to when a visitor uses the Tab key to move from field to field. The default tab order follows the position of the fields on the page.
  ✓ *If fields are positioned in a table, tab order moves from the first cell to the next column(s) to the right before moving down to the next row.*

Change the Name Property

- FrontPage gives each form field in a form component a default name based on its type.
- For example, the first Textbox form field in a form is named T1.
- The Web developer should rename each form field with a name that tells exactly what information will be entered in that field.
  ✓ *Field names become important when viewing confirmation pages and form results, as discussed in Exercise 42.*

  ✓ *When renaming a field, use a single word, run multiple words together, or connect multiple words with underscores. For example: Zip, ZipCode, or Zip_Code.*

Set Textbox and Text Area Properties

- Both Textbox and Text Area form fields can be resized in the Properties dialog box. Select a new width and, for Text Area, the number of lines of text the field can contain.
- The author can also enter a word or phrase that will initially appear in the field. The initial value can be used to tell the visitor what kind of information to supply.

Set Checkbox and Option Button Properties

- Checkbox and Option Button form fields allow the author to set a value that will display when the field is chosen.
- The default value for a Checkbox field is ON. This means that if a visitor clicks in the checkbox, the form results will display "ON" to indicate that the field was turned on.
- Changing the value from ON to Yes makes it easier to understand the form results (see illustration below).

Checkbox properties

Check Box Properties
Name: List
Value: Yes
Initial state: Checked Not checked
Tab order:
Style... OK Cancel

- Web site visitors can select more than one checkbox in a list or group.
- FrontPage assumes that option buttons will appear in a group. For this reason, the Option Button properties dialog box allows the Web developer to specify a group name (see illustration below).

Option Button Properties dialog box

Option Button Properties
Group name: Location
Value: House
Initial state: Selected Not selected
Tab order:
Style... Validate... OK Cancel

- Changing the value for an option button from its default (such as V1) to be the same as the button's label makes it very clear in the form results which button has been selected (see illustration above).

- Web site visitors are limited to selecting only one option button from a group of option buttons.
- For both checkboxes and option buttons, the author can choose to have the box or button selected (or checked) by default. This means the box or button will already be selected each time the form is opened.

  ✓ *Generally, checkboxes are not checked by default. For a group of option buttons, consider which your visitors are most likely to select and have that option selected by default.*

Set Properties for a Group Box

- Use a Group Box form field to separate text or form fields from other content on a Web page or within a form (see illustration below).

Group box separates related text and fields from remainder of form

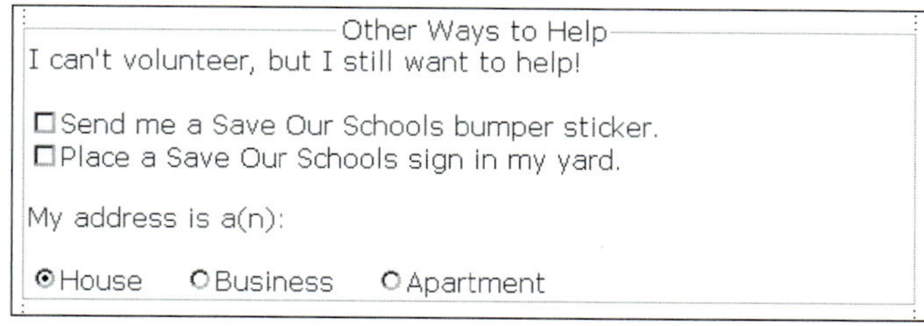

- Name the Group Box in the Group Box Properties dialog box. This name displays in the form as part of the group box's border.
- Specify default (left), center, or right alignment for the group box name.

  ✓ *Adjust the group box size by pointing to the bottom or right border and clicking to select the box. Drag the bottom-right corner handle to reduce width and height at the same time.*

Set Properties for a Drop-Down Box

- A Drop-Down Box gives visitors a number of choices (generally more than three) from which they can usually select only one.

  ✓ *To allow visitors to select more than one, change the Allow multiple selections property.*

- Enter the selection choices in the Drop-Down Box Properties dialog box by clicking the Add button and typing each choice (see illustration at the top of the next column).
- To record a value different from the choice, select the Specify Value checkbox in the Add Choice dialog box and then type the value.

Add choices for a drop-down box

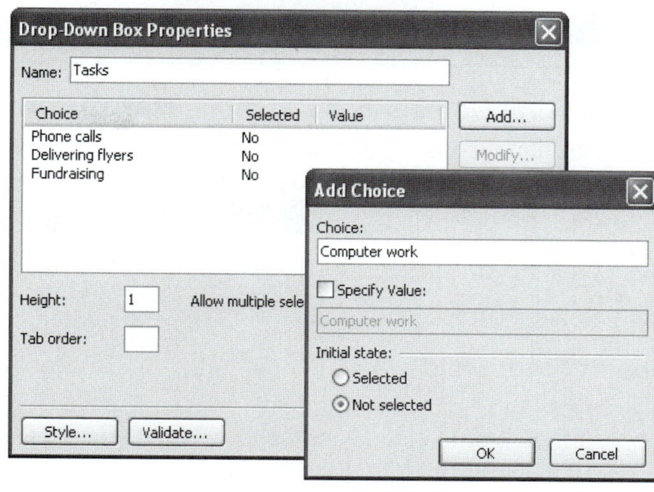

- The drop-down box expands automatically to fit the width of the longest choice.
- The Web developer can also change the number of choices to display on the form (the default is to display only one choice).
- Move choices on the choice list using the Move Up and Move Down buttons or delete a choice from the list using the Remove button.

  ✓ *To make a drop-down box easier to use, place the most popular choices at the top of the list or list choices in alphabetical order.*

Change Submit and Reset Properties

- Every new form component includes Submit and Reset buttons. Properties can be changed for these buttons just as for other form fields.
- Inserting new Value/label text changes the button's label on the form (see illustration below).

Change push button properties

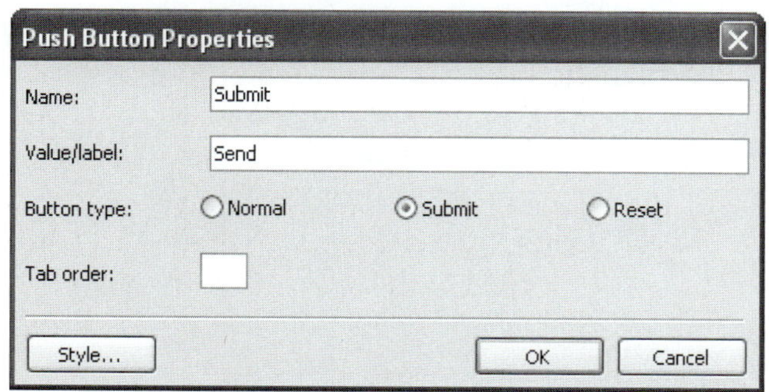

- The Submit and Reset push buttons have associated scripts that perform specific actions. Do not change the button type for either of these buttons.

Procedures

Insert Form Component

1. Position insertion point at location for form.
2. Click **Insert** .... Alt+I
3. Click **Form** .... R
4. Select **Form** .... F

Insert Form Field

1. Press the **Enter** key in a new form to create blank line above Submit and Reset buttons.
2. Move insertion point into blank line. Type label if necessary.
3. Click **Insert** .... Alt+I
4. Click **Form** .... R
5. Click desired form field:
   - **Textbox** .... T
   - **Text Area**....................... E
   - **File Upload** .... U
   - **Checkbox**...................... C
   - **Option Button**............... O
   - **Group Box** .... G
   - **Drop-Down Box**............ D
   - **Push Button** .... B
   - **Advanced Button** V
6. Insert picture in form component:
   a. Click **Picture**.................. P
   b. Locate picture using Picture dialog box.
   c. Modify picture field name and size in Picture Properties dialog box.
7. Allow visitors to select an option button or check box by clicking either the field or the label:
   a. Type label and insert form field.
   b. Select both field and label and click **Label** .... A

Modify Form Field Properties

1. Double-click form field.

   OR

   Right-click form field and click **Form Field Properties** .... M
2. Change properties for each type of field:
   a. Modify **Textbox**:
      - Change field name by typing new name.
      - Insert text to appear in textbox in Initial value box.
      - Change field width by typing new value.
   b. Modify **Text Area**:
      - Change field name by typing new name.
      - Insert text to appear in textbox in Initial value box.
      - Change field width by typing new value.
      - Change field height by increasing or decreasing number of lines.
   c. Modify **Checkbox**:
      - Change field name by typing new name.
      - Change Value from ON to another word such as Yes.
      - Specify Checked or Not checked for default appearance in form.
   d. Modify **Option Button**:
      - Change field name by typing new name.
      - Type value for option button.
      - Specify Selected or Not selected for default appearance in form.
   e. Modify **Group Box**:
      - Change field name by typing new name.
      - Change alignment of field name.
   f. Modify **Drop-Down Box**:
      - Change field name by typing new name.
      - Click Add... .
      - Type choice and specify value if desired.
      - Continue until all choices are added.
      - Change height of drop-down box to display more than one choice.
      - To allow visitors to select more than one choice, click **Yes** for **Allow multiple selections**.
   g. Modify **Push Button**:
      - Change field name by typing new name.
      - Change label that will appear on button in form.

Exercise Directions

1. Start FrontPage 2003.
2. Open **Levy**.
3. Open **volunteering.htm** and insert a form component below the text paragraph.
4. Insert a blank line in the form component and on the blank line, type **Name**.
5. Press **Spacebar** once and insert a Textbox form field.
6. Change the Textbox form field name to **Name** and set a width of **35** for the field.
7. Click in the form component to deselect the Textbox field and press the **Enter** key.
8. Type **Address**, press **Spacebar**, and insert another Textbox form field.
9. Change the form field name to **Address** and set a width of **35** for the field.
10. On a new blank line, insert the label **City**, a space, and a Textbox form field. Press **Spacebar** twice and insert the label **ZIP**, a space, and another Textbox form field.
11. Name the City field **City** and the ZIP field **ZIP**. Change the width of the ZIP field to **10**.
12. On a new blank line, insert the label **Phone**, a space, and a Textbox form field. Rename the form field **Phone**.
13. Press **Spacebar** three times and insert the label **E-mail**, press **Spacebar** once, and insert a Textbox form field. Name the form field **Email**.
14. On a new blank line, insert the following text:

    Do you have children attending Franklin Schools? If so, please indicate their ages and schools:
15. On a new blank line, insert a Text Area form field. Change the field name to **Schools**, set a width of **30**, and set number of lines to **3**.
16. On a new blank line, insert the following text: **I can help with:**
17. On a new blank line, insert a Drop-Down Box form field. Change the field name to **Help**.
18. Add the following choices: **Phone calls**, **Delivering flyers**, **Computer work**, **Fundraising**, and **I can't volunteer at this time**.

    ✓ *None of the choices should be selected or have other values.*
19. On a new blank line, insert a Group Box field and label the Group Box **Other Ways to Help**.
20. Center the Group Box name.
21. On the first line in the group box, insert the following text: **I can't volunteer, but I still want to help!**
22. On a new line insert a Checkbox form field and then type **Send me a Save Our Schools bumper sticker.**
23. Rename the Checkbox field **Sticker** and change its value to **Yes**.
24. Press **Shift+Enter** to insert a Break tag (<br>) and insert another Checkbox form field. Then type **Place a Save Our Schools sign in my yard**.
25. Rename the Checkbox field **Sign** and change its value to **Yes**.
26. On a new blank line, insert the following text: **My address is a(n):**
27. On a new blank line, insert an Option Button form field, type **House**, press **Spacebar** three times, insert a second Option Button field, type **Business**, press **Spacebar** three times, insert a third Option Button field, and type **Apartment**.
28. Name the first option button **Location** and change its value to **House**. Specify that the button is not selected.
29. Change the value of the second option button to **Business** and the value of the third option button to **Apartment**.

    ✓ *Both of these option buttons should have Location as the Group Name and neither should be selected.*
30. Change the Value/label of the Submit push button to **Send**.
31. Preview the Web site. Your form should look similar to the one shown in Illustration A.
32. Try selecting option buttons and selecting a choice from the drop-down list.
33. Close the Web site.
34. Exit FrontPage 2003.

Illustration A

Name [ ]

Address [ ]

City [ ] ZIP [ ]

Phone [ ] E-mail [ ]

Do you have children attending Franklin Schools? If so, please indicate their ages and schools:

[ ]

I can help with:

Phone calls ▾

Other Ways to Help

I can't volunteer, but I still want to help!

☐ Send me a Save Our Schools bumper sticker.
☐ Place a Save Our Schools sign in my yard.

My address is a(n):

○ House ○ Business ○ Apartment

Send | Reset

On Your Own

1. Start FrontPage 2003.
2. Create a new Web site of at least two pages for a club or organization to which you belong. Name the site **OYO41**.
   - ✓ *If you do not belong to a club or organization, make up information about a new club.*
3. Create a home page with general information and a membership page that will allow new members to join online.
4. Establish a navigation structure and add link bars.
5. Plan the type of information you need to collect for new members (such as name, address, phone, e-mail address, membership level).
6. Insert a new form on the membership page and add form fields to the form.
7. Use as many different types of form fields as you can to collect information.
   - ✓ *At a minimum, insert a Textbox, Text Area, Checkbox, Option Buttons, and Drop-Down Box form fields.*
8. Give each form field an appropriate name and change its properties as necessary.
9. Close the Web site.
10. Exit FrontPage 2003.

Exercise 42

◆ **Customize Push Buttons** ◆ **Validate Form Fields**
◆ **Specify Form Results File** ◆ **Test FrontPage Form**
◆ **View Form Results Files**

On the Job

FrontPage's Advanced Button form field allows a Web author to customize a push button with text and other formats. Use validation rules for some form fields to control how data is entered. Data entered into a form is captured by a form handler and stored in the designated form results file. The author can specify a format for the form results file and view the file from FrontPage.

In this exercise, you will continue to work with the Levy Web site. You will replace a standard push button with an Advanced Button, apply validation rules to some fields, and set up a file to store the form results. Finally, you will test the form by publishing it and entering data, and then you will view the form results file from FrontPage.

Terms

confirmation page
A page displayed in the browser when data has been successfully entered in a form.

form handler
A program on a server that delivers the form information to a results file.

form results file
File located within FrontPage that stores form data.

validation
Data entry rules that control how data is entered in a form field.

Notes

Customize Push Buttons

- Default push button form fields allow the Web developer little leeway for modification: the developer can change the name and value, but the value is also the button label.
- The Advanced Button form field allows the developer to type any text desired right on the button.
- An Advanced Button can be further customized in several ways (see illustration at right):
  - A developer can insert a Value different from the button's label.
  - The developer can specify exact width and height measurements for the button.

Customize an Advanced Button

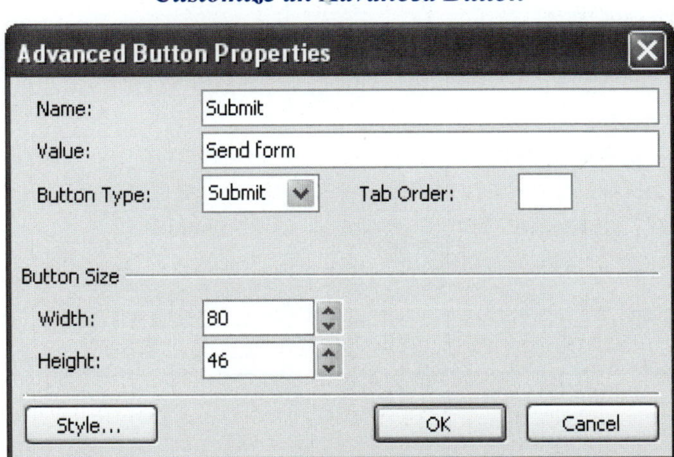

- The developer can further customize the Advanced Button (as well as most form fields) by clicking the Style button in a Properties dialog box and selecting font, paragraph, border, and other formatting options.

Validate Form Fields

- **Validation** can be set for Textbox, Text Area, Drop-Down Box, and Option Button form fields. Validation is a set of data entry rules that control how text is entered in a form field.
- To validate a form field, click the Validate button in the form field's Properties dialog box.
- After a Web author applies validation to a form field, a message will display if a visitor enters information that does not follow the validation rule.

  ✓ *For example, if the Name field is required to have an entry and the visitor has left that field blank, a message displays at the time the form is submitted to tell the visitor to please enter a value for the Name field.*

Textbox and Text Area Validation

- Textbox and Text Area form fields offer the most options for validation. Options become available in the Text Box Validation dialog box depending on the Data type chosen: Text, Integer, or Number (see illustration below).

Textbox validation options

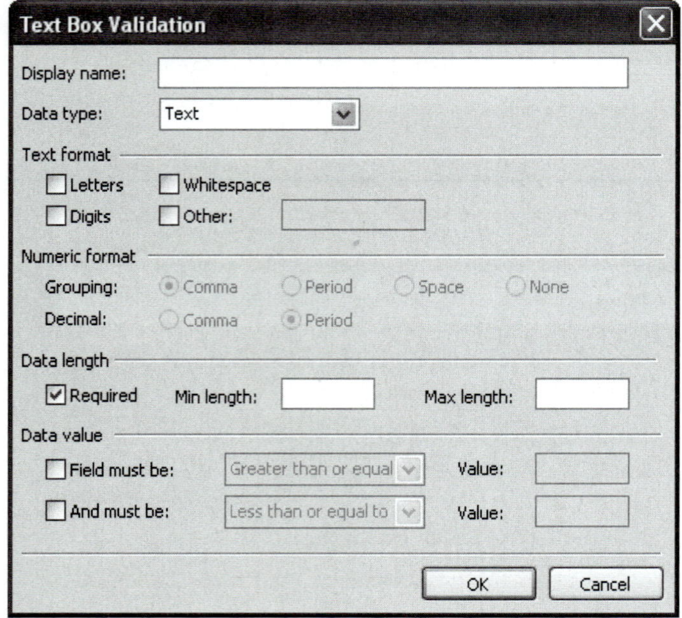

- For the Text data type the author can specify:
  - What kind of text the field should contain (such as only letters or only digits).
  - That the field is required to have an entry, and, if desired, a minimum or maximum length for the entry.
  - A particular range or value for an entry.
- For the Integer data type, the author can specify how numbers display a thousands separator: using commas, periods, or spaces.
- For the Number data type, the author can specify whether the decimal is indicated by a comma or period.

  ✓ *For the Number data type, the author can select both Grouping and Decimal options, but choosing options in both areas allows the visitor to enter any number format. To limit the decimal type effectively, choose None for Grouping.*

Drop-Down Box Validation

- Drop-Down Box form fields have only two validation options (see illustration below):
  - The Web designer can specify that a choice is required for the field.
  - If the designer has included an instruction at the beginning of the choice list (such as "Choose one option"), that option can be "locked" so visitors cannot choose it by accident.

Drop-Down Box validation options

Drop-Down Box Validation
Display name: Help
☑ Data required
☐ Disallow first choice
OK Cancel

- The Drop-Down Box Validation dialog box also asks for the name of the field being validated. This name will be used in the warning message that displays if the validation rule is broken.

Option Button Validation

- Option Button fields have only one validation option: Data required.
- Supply the group name to be used in the warning message.
- Applying the Data required validation to one option button automatically applies it to all buttons in the group.

> **Code Cues**
>
> You can easily change form field properties in Split or Code view. Form fields are identified by tags such as <input> with attributes such as type, name, and size for which you enter values just as in a properties dialog box. To specify validation, you must insert webbot coding. The following webbot coding specifies that digits are required in a field: <!--webbot bot="Validation" s-data-type="String" b-allow-digits="TRUE" -->

Specify Form Results File

- FrontPage uses a **form handler** to manage information submitted in a form.
  - ✓ *FrontPage's default form handler is included in the FrontPage extensions. For this reason, a FrontPage form must be published to a server that uses FrontPage extensions to work correctly.*
- The form handler collects the data entered and stores it in a **form results file** located within the FrontPage Web site that contains the form.
- The form results file is stored in the _private folder located in the FrontPage Web site.
- The user can specify the type of file that will store form results. The most common options are to store the results in a text file or as an HTML file, but the author can also specify XML format, a Microsoft Word document, or an Excel worksheet.
  - ✓ *It is also possible to send the form results in an e-mail message if the server is configured to do so.*
  - ✓ *Form data may also be sent directly to a Microsoft Access database. You will learn how to send form data to a database in Lesson 9, Exercise 48.*
- A form results file saved as a text file can be opened in any text editor (such as Notepad). An HTML file can be opened right in FrontPage. XML files can be used by a wide variety of applications to share data on the World Wide Web.
- To specify the form results file, open the Form Properties dialog box using the Insert>Form>Form Properties command on the menu bar.
  - ✓ *Or right-click anywhere in the form and click Form Properties on the shortcut menu.*
- The default form results file name is form_results.csv (see illustration below), which will open form results in Microsoft Excel.
  - ✓ *The .csv extension stands for "comma separated values." This format can be read in a number of applications, including Microsoft Excel.*

Form Properties dialog box

Form Properties

Where to store results
Send to
File name: _private/form_results.csv Browse...
E-mail address:
Send to database
Send to other Custom ISAPI, NSAPI, CGI, or ASP Script
Form properties
Form name:
Target frame:
Options... Advanced... OK Cancel

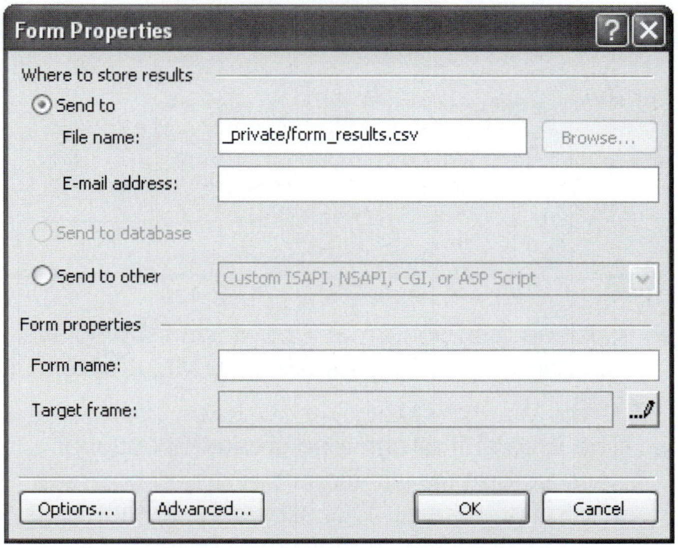

- Change the form results file name by deleting the existing name and typing a new one. FrontPage creates the new file and stores it in the _private folder.
  - ✓ *Do NOT delete the _private/ portion of the name, or the file will not be stored in the correct location.*
- The author can also use the Browse button in the Form Properties dialog box to locate an existing Web page or file within the Web site to store the form results.
- Including a file extension such as .txt (for a text file) or .htm (for an HTML file) when creating a new form results file tells FrontPage what kind of file to create.
- The Web author can also specify a format for the form results file by clicking the Options button in the Form Properties dialog box to open the Saving Results dialog box (see illustration on following page).

Set display options for form results

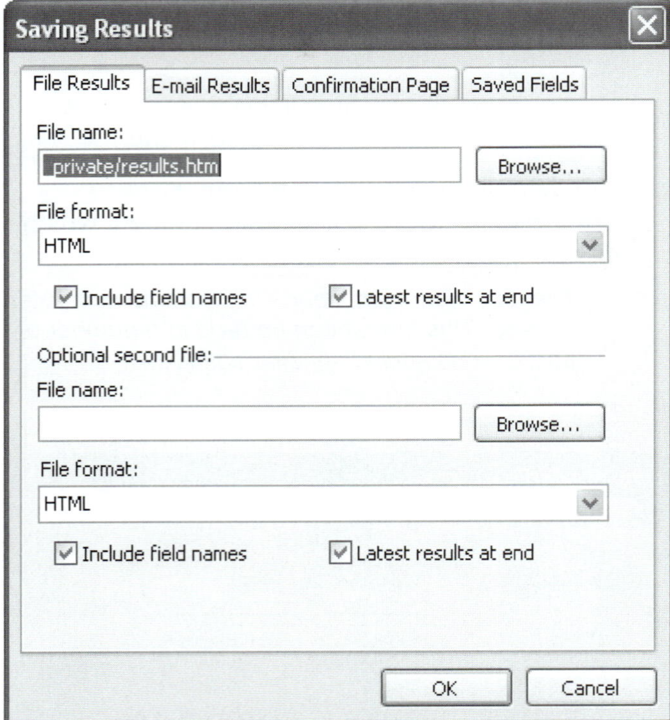

- Clicking the File format drop-down list displays a number of options for XML, HTML, and text files.
- The Web author can also create an optional second form results file in this dialog box (see illustration above). This allows the author to store form results in more than one format.

Test FrontPage Form

- A FrontPage form must be published to a server that uses FrontPage extensions to work correctly.
- After the page containing the form is published, the Web developer can enter data in the form as it is displayed in the browser to test the form.
- Clicking the Submit button in the browser immediately displays a **confirmation page** that shows the form user what information has been inserted in each field.
- FrontPage supplies a default confirmation page that lists each field name and the data entered into the field, along with a link to return to the form (see illustration below).

Default confirmation page

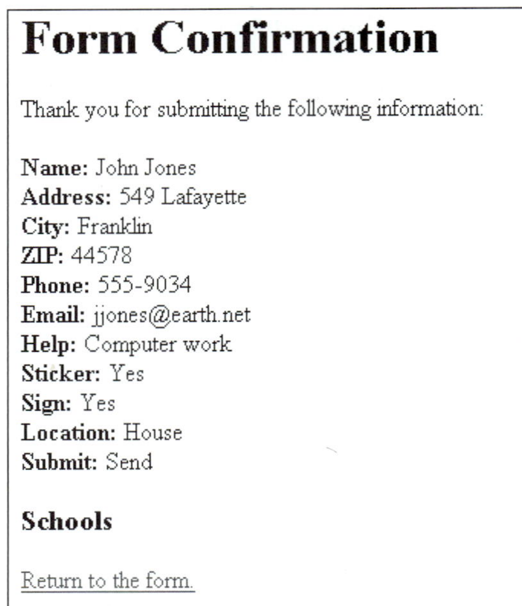

✓ *Web developers can also create their own confirmation pages or use the FrontPage Confirmation Page template. Specify a new confirmation page on the Confirmation Page tab in the Saving Results dialog box.*

- After a form has been published, the published Web site can be opened from the server in FrontPage and the form can then be tested using the Preview in Browser command.

View Form Results Files

- To view the form results file in FrontPage, the Web author *must* open the published Web site from the server.
- Locate the form results file in Page view by clicking the plus sign next to the _private folder in the Folder List to display the folder's files. Double-click the form results file to open it.

✓ *Or switch to Folders view and double-click the _private folder to open it and display its files. Double-click the form results file to open it.*

- An HTML form results file displays field labels by default. Horizontal rules separate the results from each submitted form. (See illustration below.)
- HTML form results can also be displayed as bulleted lists, definition lists, or formatted HTML text.

HTML form results file

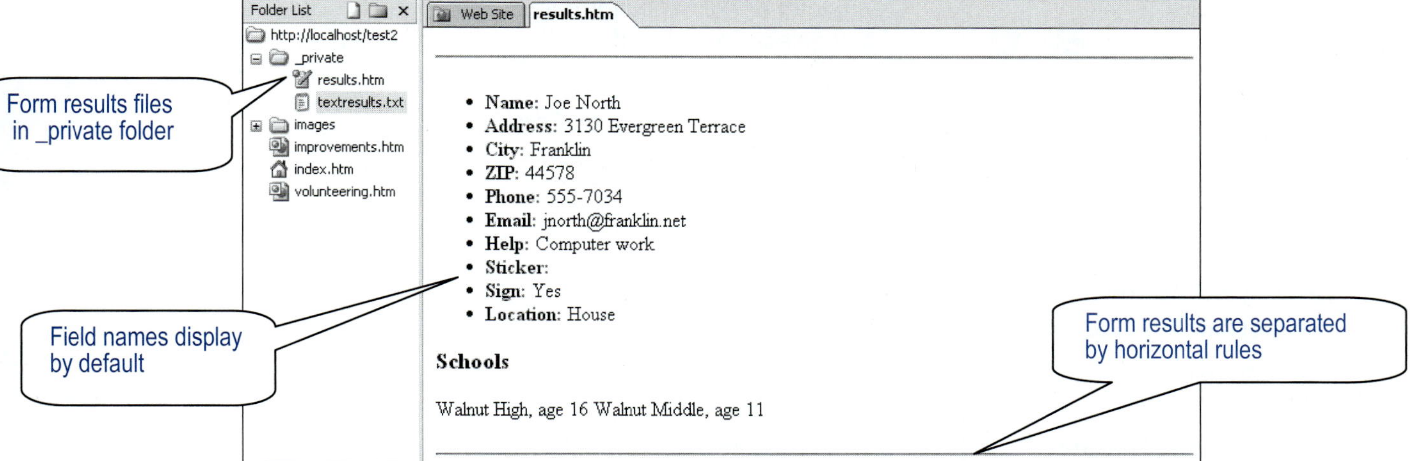

- A text form results file can be displayed in FrontPage or in a text editor such as Notepad, as shown in the illustration below.

Text form results file in Notepad

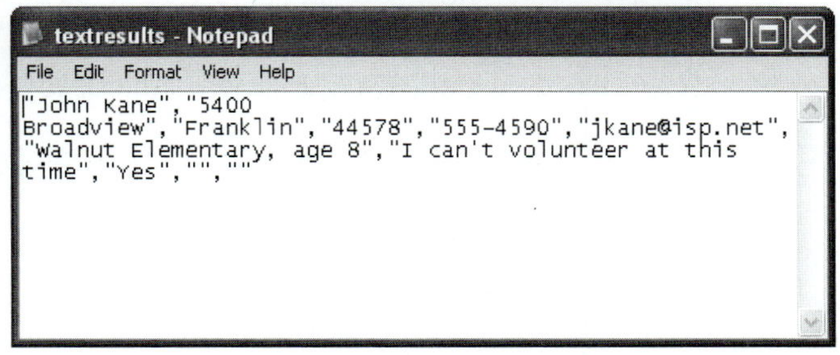

- By default, field data is surrounded by quotation marks and fields are separated by commas, tabs, or spaces (see illustration at left).
- A text form results file may also be formatted to display field names and data in columns, with lines of asterisks between each form.

Procedures

Customize Push Buttons

1. With insertion point in form component, click **Insert** .... Alt+I
2. Click **Form** .... R
3. Click **Advanced Button** V
4. Type label text on button.
5. Modify button properties:
   a. Right-click button and click **Advanced Button Properties** .... N
   b. Change name and value of button, if desired.
   c. Specify button size and width, if desired.

Specify Form Results File

With insertion point in form component

1. Click **Insert** .... Alt+I
2. Click **Form** .... R
3. Click **Form Properties** .... R

   OR

   Right-click in form component and click **Form Properties** . R

In Form Properties dialog box

4. Accept default form results file name (form_results.csv) or type new file name.
   ✓ *Do NOT delete _private/ portion of file name. New file name should read _private/[newname].*
5. Use .txt extension to create a text form result file that can be viewed in Notepad.
6. Use .htm extension to create an HTML form result file that can be viewed in FrontPage.
7. Modify format of form results file by clicking Options... and select option on File format list.

Validate Form Fields

1. Double-click form field to validate, or right-click form field and select **Form Field Properties** .... M
   ✓ *You can validate Textbox, Text Area, Drop-Down Box, and Option Button form fields.*
2. Click Validate... .
3. Validate Textbox or Text Area field:
   a. Choose data type (Text, Integer, or Number).
   b. Select Text options for Data type, Data length, and Data value.
   c. Select Integer Grouping options.
   d. Select Number Decimal options.
4. Validate Drop-Down Box field:
   a. Select Data required and/or Disallow first choice.
   b. Type field name in Display name text box for use in warning message.
5. Validate Option Button field:
   a. Select Data required.
   b. Type field name in Display name text box for use in warning message.
      ✓ *Setting validation for one option button in a group sets validation for all buttons in the group.*

Test FrontPage Form

1. Publish FrontPage Web site that contains form.
2. Click *View your Remote Web site* link and navigate to page that contains form, if necessary.
3. Enter data in form and click Submit button.
4. View confirmation page that shows data entered in each field.
5. Continue testing as form is developed by opening published Web site from server and previewing form in browser.

View Form Results File

1. Open published Web site from server.
2. Click plus sign next to _private folder in Folder List to expand folder.

   OR

   Switch to Folders view and double-click _private folder to open it.
3. Double-click form results file to open it.
   ✓ *When a text file is double-clicked, Notepad opens to display the form results.*

Exercise Directions

1. Start FrontPage 2003.
2. Open **Levy**.
3. Open **volunteering.htm**.
4. Delete the Send button from the form component.
   ✓ *Click the Send button once to select it and press the Delete key.*
5. Insert an Advanced Button form field at the same location and type **I Can Help!** on the button.
6. Modify the Advanced Button field's properties:
   - Change the name to **Submit** and the Value to **Send Form**.
   - In the Button Type list, select Submit.
   - Modify the style of the button to have a color background and bold white text.
     ✓ *Click the Style button in the Advanced Button Properties dialog box and then click Format. Choose Border and then click the Shading tab and apply a background color that goes well with the theme. You may also want to apply a border choice. Choose Font from the Format menu to change text color and style.*
   - Specify a button size such as 75px wide by 25px high.
7. Validate the Name text box so that visitors are required to enter at least one character in the field.
8. Validate the ZIP field to accept only digits (select Text from the data type list and then in the Text format section of the Text Box Validation dialog box, choose Digits).
9. Specify that the form handler send results to a file named **results.htm** in the _private folder.
10. Set up the file results to appear as an HTML bulleted list.
11. Publish the Web site to your personal Web server (or other server) with the new Web site name **levyform**.
12. Click the *View your Remote Web site* link and navigate to the Volunteer Form page.
13. Enter the following data in the form:

Address:	**3130 Evergreen Terrace**
City:	**Franklin**
ZIP:	**4457d**
Phone:	**555-7034**
E-mail:	**jnorth@franklin.net**
Schools text area:	**Walnut High, age 16** **Walnut Middle, age 11**
Help box:	**Computer work**
Sign checkbox:	**Click to check box**
Address option:	**House**

14. Click the **I Can Help!** button to submit the form.
15. FrontPage should display an error page that asks you to supply an entry of at least one character in the Name field and digits only in the ZIP field.
16. Use the browser's Back button to return to the form.
17. Insert the name **Joe North** and change the ZIP entry to **44578**.
18. Submit the form again.
19. Check entries in the confirmation page.
20. Close the disk-based **Levy** Web site and open the server-based **levyform** Web site from your server.
    ✓ *Or, click the Open your Remote Web site in FrontPage link in the Status area of the Remote Web Site view.*
21. Open the _private folder in the Folder List and double-click **results.htm** to view the form results file. Your file should look similar to the one shown in Illustration A.
    ✓ *If the form_results.csv form results file displays in the _private folder, you can delete the file.*
22. Preview the Web site in the browser and enter data for several more volunteers in the form. (Make up data for each field.)
23. Return to FrontPage, open the **results.htm** page if necessary, and click the **Refresh** button to display the new form information.
24. Close the browser.
25. Close the Web site.
26. Exit FrontPage 2003.

Illustration A

- **Name:** Joe North
- **Address:** 3130 Evergreen Terrace
- **City:** Franklin
- **ZIP:** 44578
- **Phone:** 555-7034
- **Email:** jnorth@franklin.net
- **Help:** Computer work
- **Sticker:**
- **Sign:** Yes
- **Location:** House

Schools

Walnut High, age 16 Walnut Middle, age 11

On Your Own

1. Start FrontPage 2003.
2. Open the Web site you created in the last exercise.
3. Replace one or both form component buttons with Advanced Button form fields.
4. Customize the advanced buttons with text, names, values, and, if desired, sizes and styles that complement your form.
5. Apply validation to some of the fields to make sure visitors supply all necessary information in the form.
6. Change the default form results file format to create a text results file.
   - ✓ *Your results file name should be similar to _private/results.txt.*
7. Specify that field names for the results file do NOT display and that the results are set up as a text database using a comma as a separator.
8. Publish the Web site with an appropriate name on a personal Web server or other server.
9. Test the form by entering data for one or two new club or organization members. Leave out information you validated to make sure your validation rules work correctly.
10. Close the disk-based Web site and open the server-based Web site from the server.
11. Open the form results file in Notepad to check the results. Close the file.
12. Preview the Web site in the browser and add several more records.
13. Refresh FrontPage and open the form results file to check that your new information has been added to the file.
14. Close the browser.
15. Close the Web site.
16. Exit FrontPage 2003.

Exercise 43

◆ **Create Custom Link Bar** ◆ **Insert Top 10 List**
◆ **Schedule Page** ◆ **Schedule Picture**
◆ **Add Information Components**

On the Job

FrontPage's custom link bar component allows a Web author to link pages without first creating a navigation structure. Another component displays a top 10 list of usage statistics for a Web site, such as pages browsed most often or browsers used to visit a site. Two other FrontPage components, Page Based On Schedule and Picture Based On Schedule, allow the author to schedule display of a Web page or a picture. Give a site a professional touch with a component that displays weather or news headlines.

In this exercise, you will work on a Web site for the Shelby Sharks Aquatic Club. You will create custom link bars for the site's pages and add a Top 10 List component to the Web site. You will also schedule insertion of a picture and a page of text on one page of the Web site. Finally, you will add a component that displays the current weather.

Terms

custom link bar
FrontPage component that allows a Web author to create links to pages in the current Web site as well as external Web sites without first establishing a navigation structure.

external link
A link to a Web page outside the current Web site.

Top 10 List
FrontPage component that lets a Web developer compile usage data for a Web site in the form of a list or table.

Notes

Create Custom Link Bar

- FrontPage link bars create and maintain links based on a navigation structure.
- A Web developer can also create a **custom link bar** that does not require a navigation structure.
- The Web developer can name a new custom link bar and then select the links that will display in the link bar.
- The custom link bar can have links not only to pages in the current Web site but also to pages outside the Web site.
- Begin creating a custom link bar by opening the Insert Web Component dialog box using either the Insert>Web Component or Insert>Navigation command on the menu bar.
- In the Link Bars component type options, choose Bar with custom links. After selecting link bar style and orientation, supply a name for the custom link bar.
- In the Link Bar Properties dialog box, use the Add link button to open the Add to Link Bar dialog box (see illustration on following page).

- The Add to Link Bar dialog box has options very similar to those in the Insert Hyperlink dialog box. Here, the Web author can select a Web page in the current site to add to the link bar.
- By default, FrontPage uses the actual Web page name for the link. Type new text for the link in the Text to display text box.

Add to Link Bar dialog box

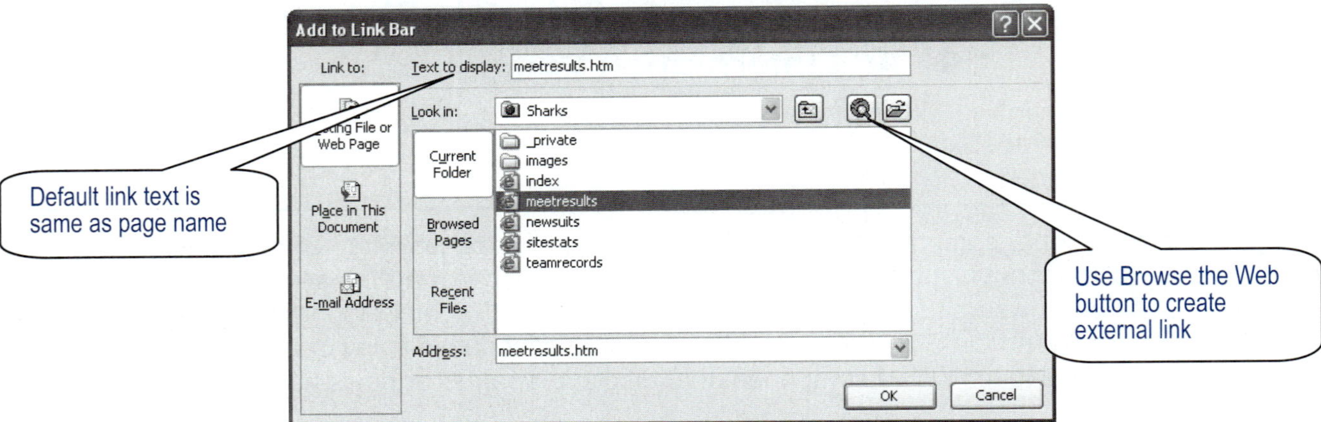

- As each link is established, it appears in the Links list of the Link Bar Properties dialog box (see illustration below). Links on this list can be deleted, modified, or moved on the list.

Links for the custom link bar shown in the Links list

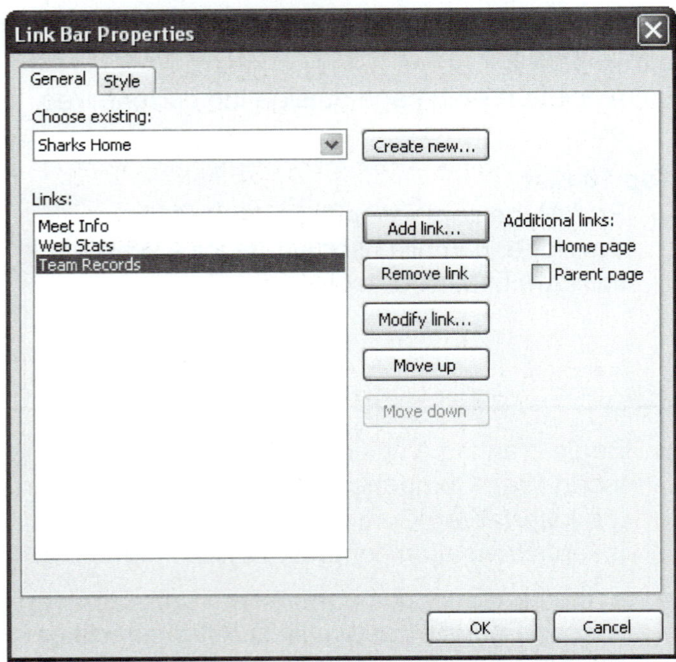

- The Link Bar Properties dialog box also allows the Web author to add a link for the home page or the parent page, just as when creating a FrontPage link bar.
- The author can, if desired, change the style of the link bar buttons by clicking the Style tab in the Link Bar Properties dialog box and selecting a new style.
- Custom link bars allow the Web author to create an **external link** (a link to a page outside the current Web site) in the link bar.
- Add an external link using one of these methods:
  - Type the address of the external page in the Address box of the Add to Link Bar dialog box.
  - Use the Look in list box to locate a page elsewhere on the system, or use the Browse the Web button to locate the page online.

    ✓ *After locating the page online, select the Web site's address in the browser's Address box and then return to the Add to Link Bar dialog box. The address of the Web page appears automatically in the Address box.*
- A custom link bar looks the same on the page as a FrontPage link bar, except that it displays a "+add link" link at the end of the link bar to signify that additional links may be added.

  ✓ *The* +add link *link will not appear in the browser.*
- A custom link bar sets up its own navigation structure to the right of the existing structure in Navigation view (see illustration on next page).

Navigation structure created by link bar

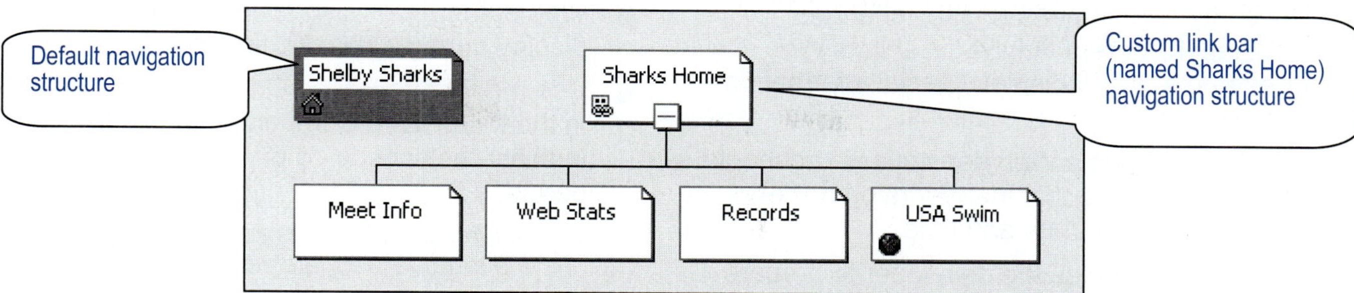

✓ *Pages of the link bar structure are white in contrast to the yellow pages of the default navigation structure.*

- After creating a custom link bar, a Web developer can apply the link bar to other pages in a Web site.
- To insert an existing link bar on a Web page, use the Bar with custom links option in the Insert Web Component dialog box. Choose not to create a new link bar, and select the existing link bar from the Choose existing list.
- A Web developer can create more than one custom link bar in a Web site. Link bars can thus be customized for specific pages in the Web site.

Insert Top 10 List

- The **Top 10 List** component allows the Web designer to gather information about visitors to a Web site.
- For example, a Top 10 List component can track how often each page in a Web site is visited, search strings used to locate the Web site, and visitors' operating systems and browsers.
- Insert a Top 10 List component from the Insert Web Component dialog box. The designer can choose what item to track and then the format of the list itself (see illustration at the top of the next column).
- Change the title of the component, if desired, and specify whether the date of the latest update will display in the component.

Choose format for Top 10 List component

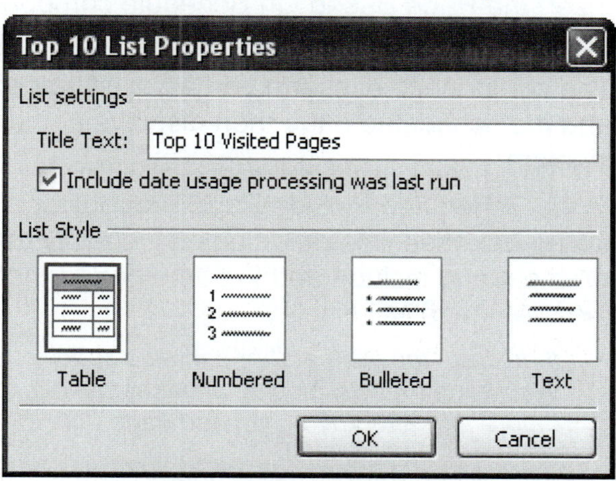

- By default, usage data is processed on a weekly basis. After the designated update day, the Top 10 List component displays the requested statistics (see illustration below).

✓ *The author must open the Web site from the server and view the page in the browser to see the usage data.*

Top 10 list of visited pages

Schedule Page

- The content of some Web sites changes occasionally or regularly. A gift shop's Web site, for example, might display special information during sales or holiday seasons.
- FrontPage allows a Web developer to schedule insertion of text so that it appears on a Web page at a specific date and time.
- This feature enables the developer to prepare changing text well in advance and automatically display it on schedule.
- Use the Insert Web Component dialog box to insert the Page Based On Schedule component from the Included Content component list.
- The component is inserted on an existing page, and the scheduled page then displays at that location.
- In the Scheduled Include Page Properties dialog box (see illustration below), specify the Web page to include and the time period that the Web page will display.
  - ✓ *If desired, the Web author can also specify a Web page that will display at the same location before and after the scheduled page.*

Specify page to include and time period

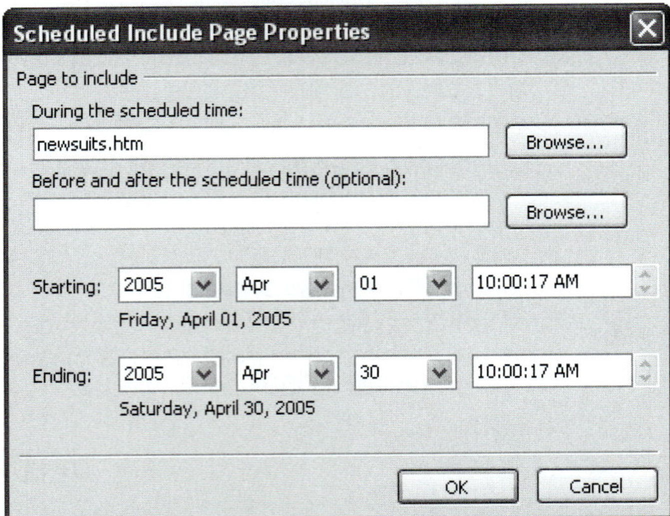

- The component displays the message *[Scheduled Include Page]* on the Web page until the date and time for display.
  - ✓ *This message does not appear when the Web page is viewed in the browser.*
- A scheduled page change can be viewed in Page view. Simply refresh the page after the scheduled time begins to see the inserted page.

Schedule Picture

- Web authors can also schedule pictures to display during a specific time period.
- Use the Picture Based On Schedule component in the Insert Web Component dialog box to indicate the scheduled picture and its display period.
  - ✓ *Pictures should be saved in the images folder and sized appropriately before being scheduled.*
- As for text, a scheduled picture can be alternated with another picture before and after the display period.
- The component will display *[Scheduled Picture]* on the Web page until the date and time for display.

Add Information Components

- The Insert Web Component dialog box includes additional components that can add a professional touch to a Web site.
- Use the Expedia components to add a map or a link to a map to help users locate a place.
- Use the MSN components to add a Web site search component or stock information to a page.
- The MSNBC components allow an author to add news, business, travel, sports, and technology headlines, as well as the latest weather forecast for a specific location.
- To add one of these information components, select the component and supply any necessary information, such as the location for the map or the ZIP code for the weather forecast.
- The information component displays on the page just as it will in the browser. The MSNBC Weather Forecast component displays a sample (see illustration below) but will display the correct city location in Preview view or in the browser.

Sample weather forecast

Procedures

Create Custom Link Bar

1. Click at location where custom link bar will display.
2. Click **Insert** .... Alt+I
3. Click **Navigation** V

OR

a. Click Web Component C

b. Click **Link Bars**.

4. Click **Bar with custom links**.
5. Select style and orientation for link bar and click

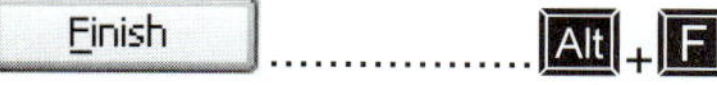
.... Alt+F

6. Type name of new link bar in Create New Link Bar dialog box.

✓ *If creating a new custom link bar in a Web site that already has one, click Create New to open the Create New Link Bar dialog box.*

7. Click Add link... in Link Bar Properties dialog box.
8. Choose page to link to in Add to Link Bar dialog box, and type link text in **Text to display** box.
9. Continue adding links as desired.
10. Add external link:
    - Type address of Web page to link to in **Address** box in Add to Link Bar dialog box.

OR

a. Click (**Browse the Web** button) in Add to Link Bar dialog box and navigate in browser to Web page to link to.

b. Click in browser's Address bar to select address of current Web page.

c. Return to Add to Link Bar dialog box and make sure Web address appears in Address text box.

✓ *To edit an existing custom link bar, select its name from the link bar list.*

Insert Top 10 List

1. Click at location where Top 10 List component will display.
2. Click **Insert** .... Alt+I
3. Click **Web Component** C
4. Click **Top 10 List**.
5. Choose an item to track from usage list.
6. Click Finish .... Alt+F
7. Customize Top 10 List by:
    - Changing title text.
    - Specifying display of the date usage was updated.
    - Choosing a list style.
8. Publish page containing Top 10 List and visit it a number of times.
9. After a week (or other specified time period), open Web site from server to see updated Top 10 List.

Schedule Page

1. Click at location where scheduled page will display.
2. Click **Insert** .... Alt+I
3. Click **Web Component** C
4. Click **Included Content**.
5. Click **Page Based On Schedule**.
6. Click Finish .... Alt+F
7. Click Browse... and locate page to schedule.
8. Locate page that will display before and after scheduled page, if desired.
9. Click down arrows to select Starting year, month, and date.
10. Click hour, minute, second, and AM or PM and use up or down spin arrows to set time.
11. Use same procedure to set Ending year, month, date, and time.

Schedule Picture

1. Click at location where scheduled picture will display.
2. Click **Insert** .... Alt+I
3. Click **Web Component**....... C
4. Click **Included Content**.
5. Click **Picture Based On Schedule**.
6. Click Finish .... Alt+F
7. Click Browse... and locate picture to schedule.
8. Locate picture that will display before and after scheduled picture, if desired.
9. Click down arrows to select Starting and Ending year, month, and date.
10. Use spin arrows to set hours, minutes, seconds, and AM or PM.

Add Information Components

1. Click at location where information component will display.
2. Click **Insert** .... Alt+I
3. Click **Web Component**....... C
4. Click desired component group: Expedia Components, MSN Components, or MSNBC Components.
5. Choose desired component.
6. Supply necessary information for component, such as map location or ZIP for weather forecast.
7. Click Finish .... Alt+F

Exercise Directions

1. Start FrontPage 2003.
2. Open **Sharks**.
3. Open **index.htm**.
4. Below the page banner, insert a custom link bar named **Sharks Home** that contains links to the **meetresults.htm**, **sitestats.htm**, and **teamrecords.htm** pages. The link text for these pages should be **Meet Info**, **Web Stats**, and **Records**.
5. Add an external link to the USA Swimming site at http://www.usswim.org. Use the link text **USA Swim**.
6. Open **meetresults.htm**.
7. Create another custom link bar named **Sharks Web** that has links to the home page and **meetresults.htm**, **sitestats.htm**, and **teamrecords.htm** pages. Use the same link text as for the links in the Sharks Home link bar.
   - ✓ *In the Link Bar Properties dialog box, click the Create new button to create a new link bar.*
8. Apply the Shark Web link bar to the **sitestats.htm** and **teamrecords.htm** pages.
   - ✓ *To save time, copy the Sharks Web link bar from meetresults.htm and paste it on the other pages.*
9. Activate the **index.htm** Web page.
10. Insert a new line above the *Summer Swimming* heading. In the new line, schedule the insertion of the **newsuits.htm** Web page.
11. Specify that the Web page begin displaying in 10 or 15 minutes from the current time. Schedule the ending date for a year from the current date.
12. Below the schedule page component, schedule the insertion of the **newsuit.jpg** picture from the images folder. (It should appear in a new line above the *Summer Swimming* heading.)
13. Set the same starting and ending information for the picture as for the page.
14. At the bottom of the page, below the last paragraph, insert the Weather Forecast MSNBC component. Use the ZIP code for your city or town.
15. Save the page.
16. Open or activate the **sitestats.htm** page.
17. At the bottom of the page, insert a Top 10 List component that will track visited pages.
18. Change the Title Text to **Pages Visited Most Often**.
19. Select the Bulleted list style.
20. Publish the Web site as **sharkweb** and view the Web site in the browser.
21. Test all links on all pages. Your **sitestats.htm** page should look similar to Illustration A.
    - ✓ *No usage data display for the Top 10 List component because no visitors have yet visited and the component has not been updated.*
22. Navigate back to the home page and scroll down to view the weather report. Refresh the page to see your scheduled page and picture in place.
    - ✓ *You might need to refresh several times to see the page and picture.*
23. Close the browser.
24. Close the Web site.
25. To track usage on your Web site, visit the site a number of times and open some (but not all) of its pages on your browser each time. If you have published the Web site to a server with the proper extensions, you should see usage data at the end of a week.
26. Exit FrontPage 2003.

Illustration A

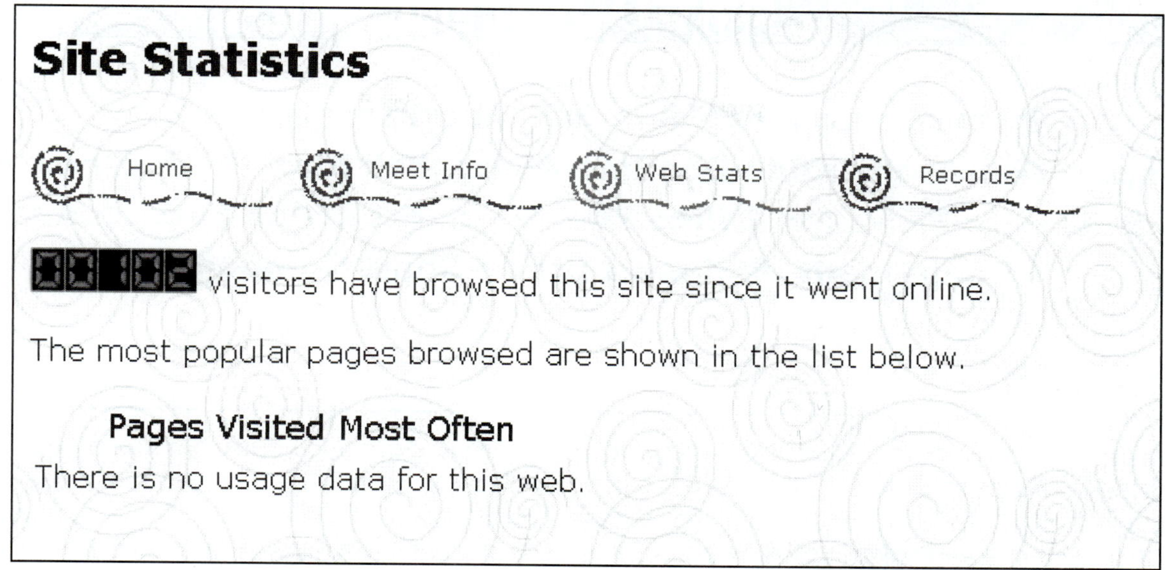

On Your Own

1. Start FrontPage 2003.
2. Open **Striders**.
3. Open **index.htm**.
4. In the empty top left layout cell, insert the MSNBC Sports Headlines component.
5. Create a new custom link bar below the *Southside Striders* head for the home page named **Home Links**.
6. Add links to the **events.htm**, **mileage.htm**, **visitors.htm**, and **walking.htm** pages. Use appropriate text for the link names and add a link for the home page.
7. Insert the Home Links link bar on the **mileage.htm**, **visitors.htm**, and **walking.htm** pages.
8. On the **events.htm** page, create a new link bar with the same links that are on the home page, **events.htm**, **mileage.htm**, **visitors.htm**, and **walking.htm** pages.
9. Add an external link to the North American Racewalking Foundation at http://members.aol.com/RWNARF. Supply appropriate link text.
10. On the **index.htm** page, schedule insertion of the **snow.jpg** picture where indicated by the placeholder in the left table cell. Schedule the picture to display from November 1 of the current year to February 1 of the next year.
11. Schedule the **winter.htm** page to display in the right table cell for the same period.
12. Schedule the **shoes1.jpg** picture and **features.htm** page to display in the table cells before and after the scheduled picture and page.
13. On the **visitors.htm** page, insert a Top 10 List component at the bottom of the page to track visited pages (or other usage statistics of your choice). Format the Top 10 List as desired.
14. Publish the Web site as **striderweb** and view all pages in the browser.
15. Close the browser and the Web site.
16. Exit FrontPage 2003.

Exercise 44

◆ **Integrate FrontPage with Microsoft Office 2003** ◆ **Import Microsoft Office Document into Web Site** ◆ **Optimize HTML** ◆ **Link to Microsoft Office File** ◆ **Insert Office Spreadsheet Component** ◆ **Insert Office Chart Component**

On the Job

All applications in the Microsoft Office 2003 integrated suite are designed to share information easily. Web pages created in Microsoft Office applications can be imported into FrontPage. Data can be copied from a Web page to a Microsoft Office document or spreadsheet, and vice versa. Microsoft Office documents can be stored in a Web site and linked to Web pages. When importing a Web page created in another application, use the optimize HTML feature to clean up that application's code. FrontPage's Office Spreadsheet and Office Chart components allow the Web author to create Excel workbooks and charts right on a Web page.

In this exercise, you will continue to work with the Sharks Web site. You will import a Word document and optimize it. You will also create a Word document from information in the Web site and then link it to a Web page so visitors can download it. Finally, you will insert a Microsoft Office Spreadsheet component and a Microsoft Office Chart component to display the meet results data.

Terms

data range
A group of contiguous cells in a spreadsheet.

data series
The data points plotted in a chart. Each data series has its own color or pattern.

integration
Sharing information among applications in a suite such as Microsoft Office 2003.

Notes

Integrate FrontPage with Microsoft Office 2003

- Microsoft Office 2003 is a collection of applications designed to perform specific tasks, such as word processing (Word), analysis and manipulation of numerical data (Excel), and data organization and storage (Access).
- Applications included in Microsoft Office depend on the Microsoft Office version.
- Microsoft Office applications are designed to make it easy for users to share data among applications. For example, table data in Word can be copied into Excel to create a worksheet.
- Sharing information among applications is called **integration**.
- As a Microsoft Office application, FrontPage can easily share information with other Microsoft Office applications. Integrate FrontPage and other Microsoft Office applications in several ways:

- Create Web pages in Word or Excel and import them into a FrontPage Web site.
- Copy information from FrontPage and paste it in a Word document or Excel worksheet.
- Copy information from Word or Excel and paste it in a FrontPage Web site.
- Link from a FrontPage Web page to a Microsoft Office file to allow a visitor to view information in the Office application used to create the information.
- Send form data to an Access database or display Access data in a Web page.

  ✓ *You will learn how to work with Access databases in Lesson 9, Exercises 48–50.*

- Insert a spreadsheet or chart component directly on a FrontPage Web page.

  ✓ *You will insert both spreadsheet and chart components in this exercise.*

Import Microsoft Office Document into Web Site

- Office applications such as Word, Excel, and Access have options for creating Web pages right in their respective applications.
- Documents created in any of these applications can be imported into a FrontPage Web site using the File>Import command on the menu bar.
- By default, a Web page created in another application will open in that application even when stored in a FrontPage Web site.
- To ensure that an imported page opens in FrontPage, right-click it in the Folder List, select Open With, and then click FrontPage (Open as HTML).

Optimize HTML

- Web pages created in Microsoft Office applications require coding not only for correct display in a browser, but also for proper appearance when viewed and printed from the native application.
- For this reason, a Microsoft Office document may contain a great deal of coding that FrontPage doesn't need.
- The illustration at the top of the next column shows a portion of the unnecessary information included in the HTML code for a Word Web page opened in FrontPage.

Split view shows Word document information in code

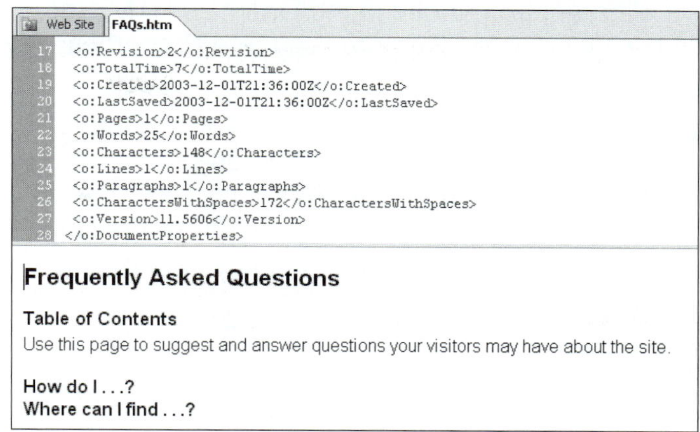

- An author can "clean up" HTML coding in Microsoft Office applications using the Optimize HTML feature.

  ✓ *You have already used this feature to optimize code before publishing.*

- Click Tools>Optimize HTML to open the Optimize HTML dialog box shown below.

Optimize HTML dialog box

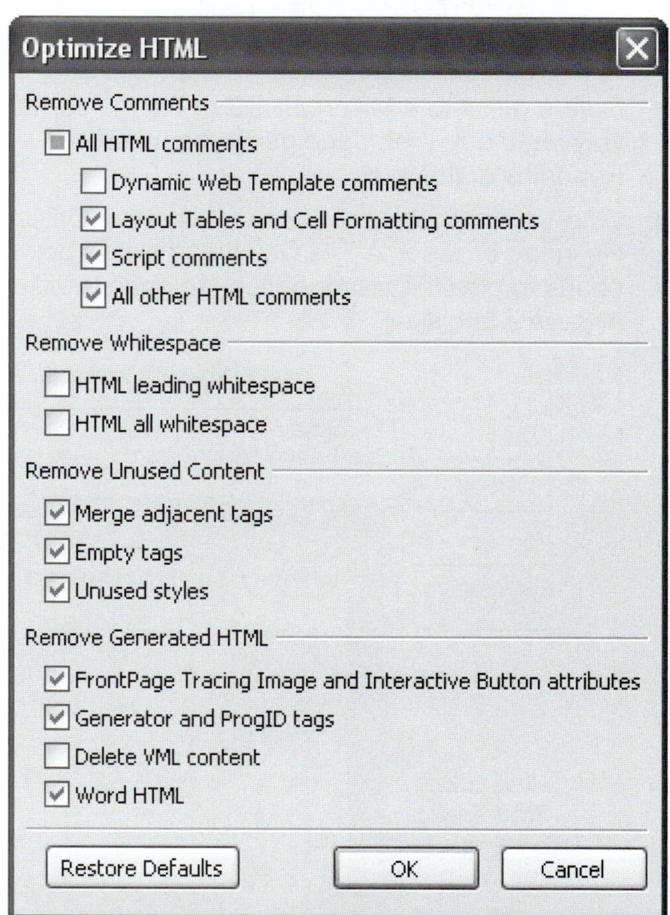

- Note that this dialog box has some options different from those in the Optimize HTML tab included in the Remote Web Site Properties dialog box.
- Besides the option to remove Word HTML code, for example, an author can remove unused styles and delete VML content (generated when the Microsoft Office drawing tools are used to created objects on a page).

Link to Microsoft Office File

- Besides importing Web pages from other applications, an author can import Microsoft Office files such as Word documents and Excel spreadsheets in their native file formats.
- Such documents can be stored in a FrontPage Web site and linked to a page in the Web site without having to convert them to HTML format.
- Linking a Microsoft Office file to a FrontPage Web site is a good way to make information available to site visitors in a form that is easier to view or print.
- For example, a Word version of Web page information can be formatted in columns to make the information easier to read and print.
- Create a link to a Microsoft Office file the same way as to any Web page using the Insert Hyperlink dialog box.
- When a visitor clicks a link to a Microsoft Office file in the browser, a File Download dialog box opens to give the visitor options to open the file or save it to disk.

Insert Office Spreadsheet Component

- A Web author can insert spreadsheet data on a Web page by simply copying it from the worksheet and pasting it on the Web page.
- Data inserted this way takes the form of a table that can be formatted the same way as any other FrontPage table.
- FrontPage also allows an author to insert a spreadsheet right in a Web page using the Office Spreadsheet component.
- The Office Spreadsheet component allows an author to enter and manipulate spreadsheet data even if Excel is not installed on the computer used to create the Web site.
- A spreadsheet inserted this way looks very similar to an Excel worksheet. Data can be entered and analyzed in a number of ways just as in an Excel worksheet.
- For example, in the illustration below, tools in the spreadsheet component can be used to sum the total points and format text and numbers. The data can even be entered in the browser and totaled using a formula already inserted in the spreadsheet.
- Insert an Office Spreadsheet component from the Insert Web Component dialog box. Click the Spreadsheets and charts component type and select Office Spreadsheet.

Spreadsheet data in Spreadsheet component

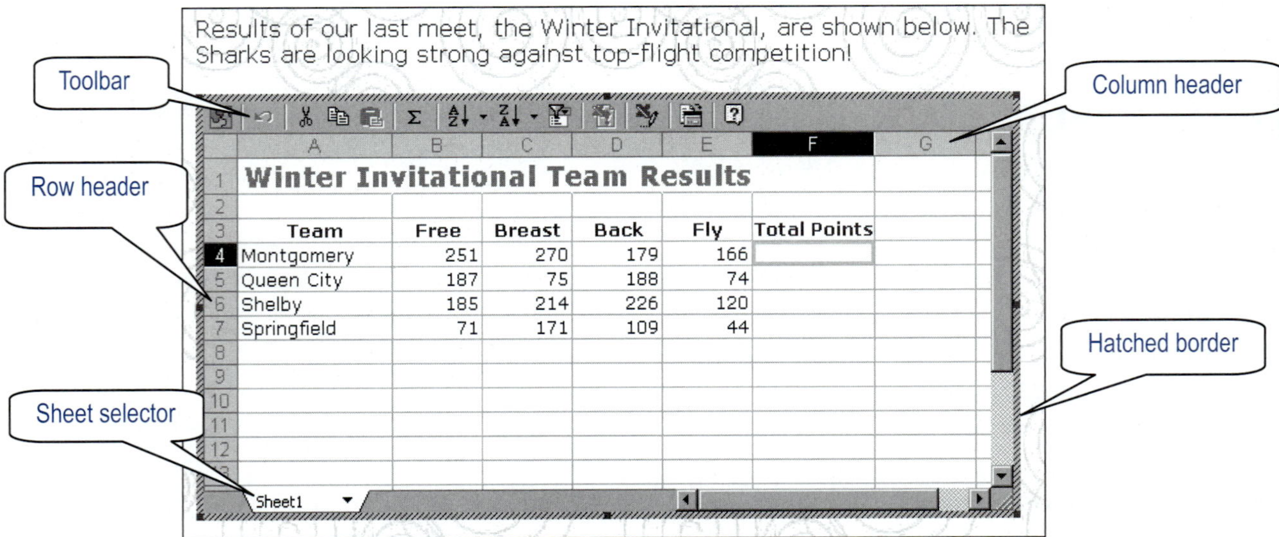

- The new Office Spreadsheet component appears at the insertion point. Click in the component to make it active.
  - ✓ *The active spreadsheet component displays a colored, hatched border and sizing handles.*
- By default, the spreadsheet component contains cells for data entry and a toolbar containing standard tools for manipulating text and numbers.
- The component also displays scrollbars, a sheet selector that names the current worksheet, and row and column headers.

Insert Data in Spreadsheet Component

- Enter data in the Office Spreadsheet component just as in Excel or any other spreadsheet program by typing data in each cell.
- A Web author can also import existing spreadsheet data into the component if it has already been created in a spreadsheet application.
- Data to be imported must be in XML, HTML, or CSV format.
  - ✓ *XML and CSV formats are used to store data as text files that can read by many applications.*
- To import data, click the Commands and Options button on the spreadsheet component's toolbar to open the Commands and Options dialog box and use the Import tab to locate and import the file.

Format Data in Spreadsheet Component

- The Commands and Options dialog box (see illustration at top of next column) contains a number of tabs that can be used to format and otherwise work with the spreadsheet data.
- On the Format tab (see illustration at top of next column), change text formats such as font, font style, alignment, and color; number format; and cell borders, fills, and protection.
  - Use the Formula tab to create formulas and name cell ranges in the component.
  - The Sheet tab supplies a Find feature and allows the author to display/hide row and column headers and gridlines.
  - The Workbook tab lets the author specify automatic or manual calculation; display/hide the scrollbars, toolbar, and sheet selector; and name the worksheet.

Commands and Options dialog box

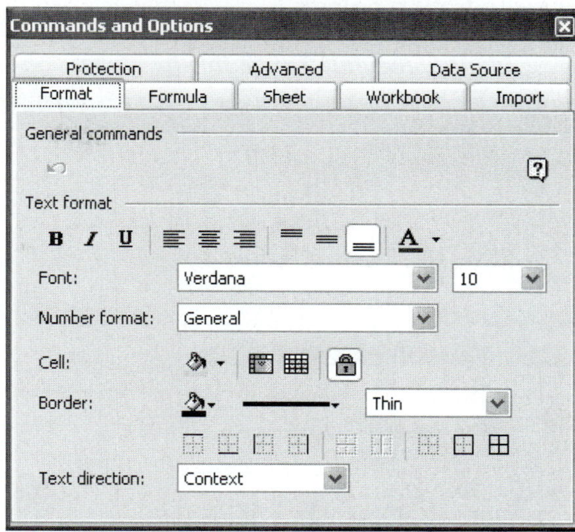

- The Protection, Advanced, and Data Source tabs contain additional options for protecting the spreadsheet data, linking the data to a source, and adjusting text display.

Resize Spreadsheet Component

- If data added to the spreadsheet component does not fill all cells, or fills more than the default number of cells, the component can be resized to eliminate blank cells or display all data.
- Drag a corner or side handle in the desired direction to display data attractively.
  - ✓ *For best control of the resizing operation, drag very slowly when resizing.*

Insert Office Chart Component

- A Web author can insert an Office Chart component to display spreadsheet data in a graphic format.
- Selecting the Office Chart component from the Insert Web Component dialog box starts a wizard in the Commands and Options dialog box to help the author create the chart.

Create Chart

- After indicating the source of the data to be charted, the author can set the **data range** for the chart.
  - ✓ *The data range contains the cells that will provide data for the chart.*
- As soon as the author identifies a data range, FrontPage displays a sample chart in the Office Chart component.

- Data can be charted by rows or by columns (see illustration below).

Identify the data range for the chart

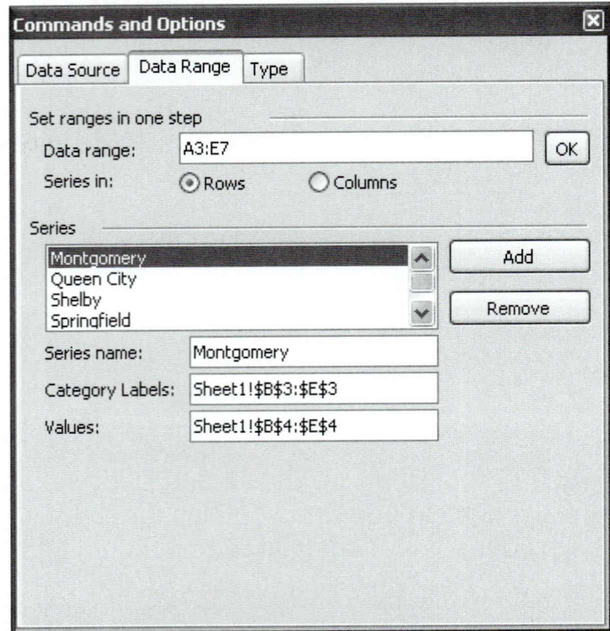

  - When charting by rows, the row data is used as the **data series** and the column headings are used as labels.
  - When charting by columns, the column data is used as the data series and the row headings are used as labels.

  ✓ *The author can change the series option from Columns to Rows (and vice versa) and click OK to see the sample chart display each option.*

- By default, the Office Chart component creates a Column chart. The author can use the Type tab to select from 11 other chart types, including Bar, Line, Pie, and Area charts.

Format and Resize Chart

- After creating a chart, a Web designer can modify its format in the Commands and Options dialog box.
- Before modifying the chart, the designer must select it by clicking it once to display a colored hatched border and handles.
- Double-clicking on a particular chart area opens the Commands and Options dialog box with tabs containing options for that chart area.
- Or, right-click any part of the white space within the chart's hatched border and choose Commands and Options from the shortcut menu.
- The Commands and Options dialog box that displays (see illustration below) displays tabs that allow the Web developer to change any chart element.

Change chart formats in the Commands and Options dialog box

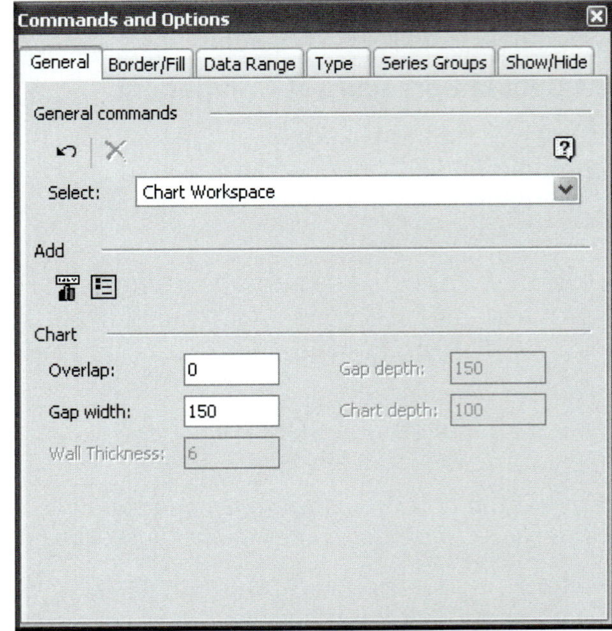

  - Use options on the General tab to select a part of the chart to format, add a title or legend, or set the gap between data series.
  - The Border/Fill tab lets the author change the border and fill color for a specific chart element.
  - Change the data range or data series on the Data Range tab.
  - Choose a different chart type on the Type tab.
  - Add a new series group or axis on the Series Groups tab.
  - Choose chart elements to display or hide on the Show/Hide tab.

- Resize a chart in the same way as a spreadsheet component. Drag handles slowly for best control of the chart component.

Procedures

Integrate FrontPage with Microsoft Office 2003

Copy text from FrontPage to another Microsoft Office 2003 document

1. Select text.
2. Click (**Copy** .... Alt+C button) on Standard toolbar.
3. Open Microsoft Office 2003 document.
4. Click (**Paste**.......... Alt+V button) on Standard toolbar.

Copy text from Word or Excel to FrontPage

5. Select text in Word or cell data in Excel.
6. Click (**Copy** .... Alt+C button) on Standard toolbar.
7. Open FrontPage Web page in Page view.
8. Click (**Paste**.......... Alt+V button) on Standard toolbar.

Import Office Document into Web Site

1. Click **File**.................... Alt+F
2. Click **Import**.................... M
3. Click Add File... .... Alt+A
4. Select drive and folder of file to be imported.
5. Click file to import.
6. Click Open ..... Alt+O
7. Click OK .... Enter
8. Specify to open page with FrontPage:
   a. Right-click imported page in Folder List.
   b. Click **Open With**............ W
   c. Click **FrontPage (Open as HTML)**.

Optimize HTML

1. Open the page to optimize in FrontPage.
2. Click **Tools** .... Alt+T
3. Click **Optimize HTML**.. Alt+H
4. Select options in the Optimize HTML dialog box.
5. Click OK.

Link to Microsoft Office File

1. Select text to become link, if desired.
2. Click **Insert**................. Alt+I
3. Click **Hyperlink** I

   OR

   Click (**Hyperlink** ... Alt+K button) on Standard toolbar.
4. Set up link as for any Web page.

Insert Office Spreadsheet Component

1. Click **Insert**................. Alt+I
2. Click **Web Component** C
3. Click **Spreadsheets and charts**.
4. Click **Office Spreadsheet**.
5. Click Finish......... Alt+F
6. Import spreadsheet data:
   a. Click inside component to activate it.
   b. Click (**Commands and Options** button).
   c. Click **Import** tab.
   d. Change data type, if necessary.
   e. Click (**Browse** button) and locate file to import.
   f. Click Import Now.
7. Format spreadsheet data:
   a. Click (**Commands and Options** button).
   b. Click **Format** tab.
      - Change font, font style, font size, or font color.
      - Change number format.
      - Change cell border or fill.
8. Show/hide spreadsheet elements:
   - Click **Sheet** tab in Commands and Options dialog box to show/hide row headers, column headers, and gridlines.
   - Click **Workbook** tab in Commands and Options dialog box to show/hide scrollbars, toolbar, and sheet selector.
9. Resize spreadsheet component by dragging handle slowly in direction to size.

Insert Office Chart Component

1. Click **Insert** .... Alt+I
2. Click **Web Component**...... C
3. Click **Spreadsheets and charts**.
4. Click **Office Chart**.
5. Click Finish .... Alt+F
6. Choose location of data source.
7. Click Ranges... .
8. Type data range to be plotted.
9. Click OK.
10. Select **Rows** or **Columns** and click OK to see display change.
11. Select chart type on **Type** tab.
12. To add legend after chart has been created:
    a. Right-click in white area around chart.
    b. Click **Commands and Options** .... O
    c. Click **General** tab.
    d. Click (**Add Legend** button).
13. Resize chart component by dragging handle slowly in direction to size.

Exercise Directions

1. Start FrontPage 2003.
2. Open **sharkweb**.
   ✓ *Open the Web site from the server where you published it.*
3. Open **teamrecords.htm**.
4. Select and copy the table on this page.
5. Open Microsoft Word and paste the copied table in a new, blank document.
6. Save the document as **records.doc** in the Data folder.
7. Import the **records.doc** Word file and **sharkfaqs.htm** Word Web page into the **sharkweb** Web site.
   ✓ *In the Add File to Import List dialog box, click the first file, hold down Ctrl, click the second file, and then click Open.*
8. Link the *Download Word table* text on **teamrecords.htm** to the **records.doc** file.
9. Specify that the **sharkfaqs.htm** page will open with FrontPage, and open it.
10. Use Split or Code view to view the code Word adds to this page.
11. Optimize the HTML for this page, choosing to remove script comments, all other HTML comments, and unused styles, as well as the other default selections.
12. View the code again to see how FrontPage optimized the code.
13. Link *Back to Home Page* to **index.htm** or **Default.htm**.
14. On **index.htm** or **Default.htm**, insert the following sentence at the end of the second paragraph:

    Click here for answers to frequently asked questions.
15. Link the word *here* in this sentence to **sharkfaqs.htm**.
16. Open **meetresults.htm**.
17. Delete the text *[Results under construction!]*.
18. Insert an Office Spreadsheet component at the insertion point and activate the component.
19. If necessary, display the Commands and Options dialog box and import the **results.htm** file from the Data folder.
   ✓ *Don't forget to change the Data type from XML to HTML on the Import tab.*
   ✓ *Click OK if FrontPage alerts you that the page accesses data on another domain.*
20. Click in cell F4 and use the AutoSum button to sum the total points for the Montgomery team.
21. Sum the total points for the remaining teams.
22. Center all point values in their cells.
   ✓ *Use the Format tab of the Commands and Options dialog box.*
23. Change the color of the spreadsheet title (*Winter Invitational Meet Results*) to Midnight Blue.
   ✓ *Use the Format tab of the Commands and Options dialog box.*
24. Hide the row headers, column headers, sheet selector, scrollbars, and toolbar.
   ✓ *Use the Sheet and Workbook tabs of the Commands and Options dialog box.*
25. Resize the spreadsheet component to hide blank cells to the right and below the data.
26. Click below the spreadsheet and insert an Office Chart component:
   - Choose the *Data from the following Web page item* option. (FrontPage automatically suggests the spreadsheet already inserted on the Web page.)
   - Click the Ranges button to move to the Data Range tab.
   - Type **A3:E7** as the data range and select the **Rows** option. Click OK.
27. Close the Commands and Options dialog box and review the chart.
28. With the chart still selected, right-click in the white area inside the hatched outline and choose Commands and Options from the shortcut menu.
   ✓ *If you see only an ActiveX Control Properties command, or if you do not see six tabs in the Commands and Options dialog box, the chart component is not selected or you have not right-clicked in a white area.*
29. Click the Add Legend symbol on the General tab to add a legend to the chart.
30. Resize the chart using a corner handle to be about as wide as the spreadsheet component.

31. Save changes and publish the Web site as **sharkresults**.
32. View the Web site. Test the link on the home page to display the FAQs page. Try the links on the FAQs page to see how this Word Web page works.
33. Display the **meetresults.htm** Web page. Your Web page should look similar to Illustration A.
34. Close the browser.
35. Close the Web site.
36. Exit FrontPage 2003.

Illustration A

Results of our last meet, the Winter Invitational, are shown below. The Sharks are looking strong against top-flight competition!

Winter Invitational Team Results

Team	Free	Breast	Back	Fly	Total Points
Montgomery	251	270	179	166	866
Queen City	187	75	188	74	524
Shelby	185	214	226	120	745
Springfield	71	171	109	44	395

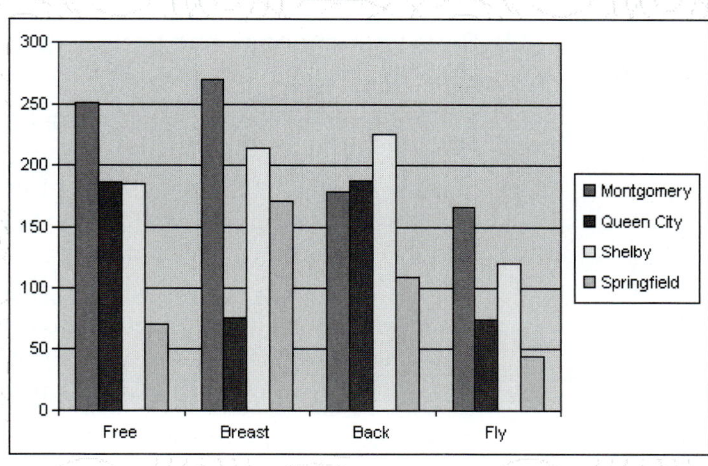

On Your Own

1. Start FrontPage 2003.
2. Open **strideweb**.
   ✓ *Open the Web site from the server where you published it.*
3. Import the Excel worksheet named **dailylogs.xls** from the Data folder.
4. Open **mileage.htm**.
5. Delete the text *[Coming soon: October mileage]*.
6. Type the following text: **Download daily logs**.
7. Link this text to the **dailylogs.xls** worksheet.
8. Below the link, insert an Office Spreadsheet component.
9. Import spreadsheet data in the **mileage.htm** file.
10. Change the *October Mileage* heading in the spreadsheet to dark brown and bold.
11. Change the column headings to dark brown and bold and add a dark brown border below the column headings.
12. Center the column headings.
13. Total the weekly mileage for each name using the AutoSum button.
14. Format the weekly totals so they stand out.
15. Hide the column headers, row headers, gridlines, scrollbars, and sheet selector.
16. Resize the spreadsheet component to hide blank cells.
17. Below the spreadsheet component, insert an Office Chart component that uses the spreadsheet data on this page as its data source.
18. Type the data range **A3:E8** and choose to plot the data by columns.
19. Select the first Bar chart type (or any other chart type that represents the data clearly).
20. Add a legend to the chart.
21. Resize the chart to be about an inch wider than the spreadsheet component.
22. Save your changes and preview the Web page in the browser.
23. In the browser, change one of the names in the October Mileage spreadsheet to your name and insert new mileage numbers to see how the worksheet automatically adjusts the total and the chart data.
    ✓ *Changes made in the browser will not appear in the spreadsheet in FrontPage. To make a permanent change to the data, you must do so in FrontPage.*
24. Publish the Web site as **stridermileage**.
25. Close the browser.
26. Close the Web site.
27. Exit FrontPage 2003.

Exercise 45

◆ Critical Thinking ◆ Challenge

In this exercise, you will work on a Web site for a public radio station on your university campus. You will add a form that visitors can use to become members or renew membership, create custom link bars, add several FrontPage components to track visitors and pledge information, schedule a page and picture, import and optimize a Word Web page, and create a link to a Microsoft Office 2003 document. Finally, you will publish the Web site, test the form, and view the form results.

Exercise Directions

1. Start FrontPage 2003.
2. Open **Pledge**.
3. Open **index.htm**.
4. Create a custom link bar with links to **form.htm**, **support.htm**, and the National Public Radio (NPR) Web site at www.npr.org and position it in the shadowed layout cell.
   - ✓ *If you are publishing to a server that does not support custom link bars, create a navigation structure and insert a FrontPage navigation bar.*
5. Create custom link bars on **form.htm** and **support.htm** with links to these pages and the home page.
6. Import **playlist.htm** into the Web site from the Data folder and optimize the Web page's HTML.
7. On **index.htm**, use the words *sample playlist* in the first bullet item to link to **playlist.htm**.
8. Delete the *[Schedule page]* placeholder in the table on **index.htm** and schedule the **pledge.htm** page to appear in this table cell starting tomorrow and ending one week from tomorrow.
9. Delete the *[Schedule picture]* placeholder in the table on **index.htm** and schedule the **pledge.jpg** picture to appear in this table cell starting tomorrow and ending one week from tomorrow.
10. At the bottom of the **index.htm** page, insert a Top 10 Component to track the pages visited on this site. Change the heading as desired and choose a style for the list.
11. Center the Top 10 List component.
    - ✓ *Select the component and click the Center button on the Formatting toolbar.*
12. Import **mailform.doc** into the Web site from the Data folder.
13. Open **form.htm**. Link the words *printable form* in the first paragraph to **mailform.doc**.
14. Create the form shown in Illustration A, using a table if desired to align form elements. Modify the properties as follows:
    - Give all text boxes and text areas appropriate names and widths.
    - Name the *Membership type* drop-down box **Membership** and add **New member**, **Rejoining**, and **Renewing membership** as the choices.
    - Name the *Pledge amount* drop-down box **Amount** and add **$25**, **$40**, **$50**, and **$100** as the choices.
    - Name the *Payment options* drop-down box **Payment** and add **Discover**, **MasterCard**, and **Visa** as the choices.
    - Give the option buttons within the group box the values **Student**, **Alumnus**, and **Community**. All option buttons should have the group name **Member** and should not be selected.
    - Name the first check box **Thanks** and the second **AirComments**. Set a value of **Yes** for both checkboxes.
15. Remove the Submit button and replace it with an advanced button that reads **Send Pledge**. Change properties and formats for the button as desired.

16. Validate form fields so that all fields with an asterisk require an entry. The ZIP and Card number fields should have digit entries (use the Digits text format).
17. Specify that form results be stored in an HTML file named **results.htm**.
18. Open **support.htm**.
19. Insert an Office Spreadsheet component below the second paragraph and import into the component **summerpledge.htm** from the Data folder.
20. Copy the formula in cell B7 and paste it into cells C7, D7, and E7.
21. Boldface the totals and change their color to one used by the current theme.
22. Make any other changes desired to improve the spreadsheet component's appearance.
23. Insert an Office Chart component below the last paragraph on the page. Use the data from the spreadsheet on the page and specify the data range **A3:E6**. Plot the data by rows.
24. Add a legend to the chart and make any other changes desired to improve the chart component's appearance. A sample page appears in Illustration B.
25. Publish the Web site as **pledgeweb**. Fill in the form for at least two new or renewing members.
26. Open the Web site from the server and view the form results file.
27. Close the browser.
28. Close the Web site.
29. Exit FrontPage 2003.

Illustration A

Name*

Address*

City* State* ZIP*

E-mail*

Home phone* Work phone

Membership type* New member

Pledge amount $25 Other $

Payment options Discover

Card number* Expiration*

Comments

Member Information

I am currently a(n)

MU student MU alumnus Community supporter

May we thank you on the air?

Yes, you can use my name on the air.

You can use my comments on the air.

Send Pledge Reset

Illustration B

Community Support

Home | Pledge Form | Community Support

WMUX is proud of its wide support from students and area listeners. Our last pledge drive resulted in over 500 new members from various groups in our community.

Pledges by amount and group are shown in the following spreadsheet:

Summer Pledge Drive

	$25	$40	$50	$100+
Students	35	21	16	10
Alumni	38	45	35	42
Community	46	52	87	95
Totals	119	118	138	147

The chart below shows this information more clearly:

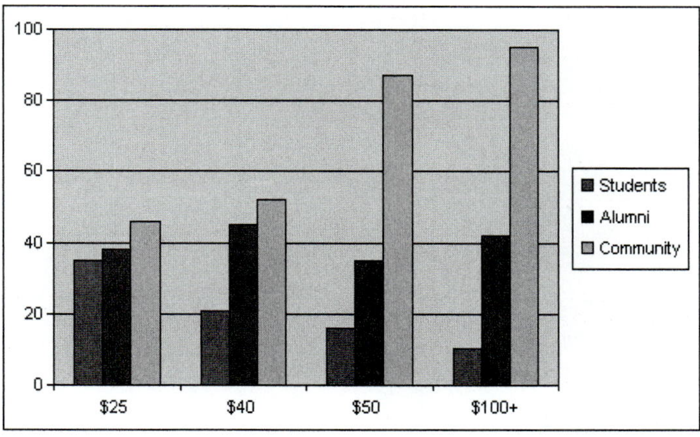

Challenge Exercise

1. People commonly use online forms in order to purchase items, and in doing so enter their credit card numbers and other sensitive information. Investigate ways that both you as consumer and you as Webmaster can make transactions secure. Write a short report on your findings, citing your sources.
2. With permission from your instructor and guardian, access a secure site in order to conduct a secure transaction, for example the purchase of a product, such as a book or music CD.

LESSON 9

Advanced Interactive Web Site Features: Discussion Groups and Databases

Exercise 46

◆ About Discussion Groups ◆ Set Up Discussion Group (Wizard)
◆ Change Discussion Group Page Formats
◆ Post Article ◆ Reply to Article

On the Job

FrontPage's Discussion Web Site Wizard makes it easy for a Web developer to create a discussion group Web site or add a discussion group to an existing Web site. After the developer selects discussion and display options, the Wizard creates all pages for the discussion group. The developer can then change discussion group page formats if desired and test the discussion group by posting articles and replies.

In this exercise, you will create a discussion group for the Ariel Books Web site. You will add the discussion group to the Web site, change its page formats to match other Web pages, and then test the discussion group by posting messages and replying to messages.

Terms

article
Message posted to a discussion group.

discussion group
An interactive Web site that lets Web site visitors discuss topics with each other by *posting* and replying to messages.

footer
Text or graphic that appears at the bottom of each page of a discussion group or Web site.

header
Text or graphic that appears at the top of each page of a discussion group or Web site.

post
Add a new *article* to a discussion group.

threaded discussion
Series of messages or *articles* in which replies are nested directly below the article they refer to.

Notes

About Discussion Groups

- A **discussion group** is an interactive Web site that encourages site visitors to discuss topics with each other.
- Visitors take part in discussions by **posting articles** to the discussion group and replying to articles that other visitors have posted.
- A FrontPage discussion group usually includes a search form to allow visitors to find topics of interest posted to the group.

Set Up Discussion Group (Wizard)

- FrontPage's Discussion Web Site Wizard automates the process of creating a discussion group.
- A Web designer can use the Discussion Web Site Wizard to create a new discussion group Web site or add a discussion group to an existing Web site.

- A discussion group can be created in either a disk-based or server-based Web site, but some options are unavailable when the discussion group is created in a disk-based Web site. For best results, use a server-based Web site.
- Begin creating a discussion group by opening the Web Site Templates dialog box:
  - Click the File>New command on the menu bar and click the *More Web site templates* link in the New task pane.
  - Click the Create a new normal page down arrow on the Standard toolbar and click Web Site.
- Choose the Discussion Web Site Wizard and specify a name for a new Web site or click the *Add to current Web site* checkbox to insert the discussion Web site in the current Web site.

Supply Information for Wizard

- The Wizard requests information from the designer that will be used to set up the discussion group:
  - The Wizard first asks the designer what features to include in the discussion group. By default, the Wizard creates a submission form, threaded replies, and a confirmation page. An author can also choose to create a table of contents and a search form.

    ✓ *An author can eliminate any of these features except the Submission form, which is required.*
  - The Wizard requests a title for the group and a name for the folder where articles will be stored (see illustration below).

Name discussion group and folder for articles

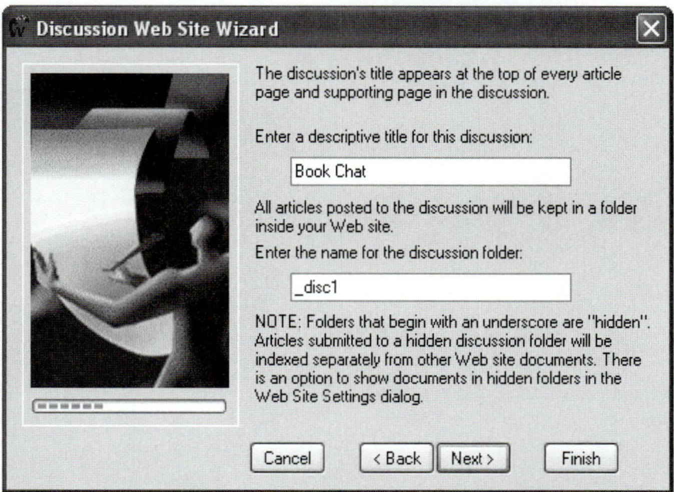

✓ *The discussion folder is hidden by default. You will learn how to display hidden folders in the next exercise.*

- The Wizard then asks the designer what fields should appear on the submission form. These are the fields that visitors use to post their messages. Subject and Comments fields are standard. The designer can also request a Product field or a Category field.
- Next, the Wizard asks the designer to specify who can post articles to the discussion group. If the discussion group is part of an existing Web site, the designer can restrict access to visitors who have permission to use that Web site.
- The Wizard asks how the table of contents should sort articles. The default option is to display articles from oldest to newest.
- The Wizard asks if the discussion table of contents page should become the Web site's home page. If the discussion group is being created within an existing Web site, the default option is no.

  ✓ *Answering Yes overwrites any existing index.htm page.*
- The designer can next specify what information displays with search results, including Subject, Size, Date, and Score.
- If the discussion group is being created as a standalone Web site (not added to an existing Web site), the Wizard allows the designer to choose a theme for the group pages.

  ✓ *If the discussion group is being added to an existing Web site that has a theme applied to all pages, the group pages will automatically format with that theme.*
- Next the Wizard proposes layout options for the discussion group pages (see illustration at the top of the next page). The Wizard suggests a dual interface that uses frames if a browser supports frames and normal Web pages if a browser cannot display frames.
- In the last dialog box, the Wizard gives the designer information about displaying hidden folders and the main pages in the discussion group.

Choose a layout for contents page

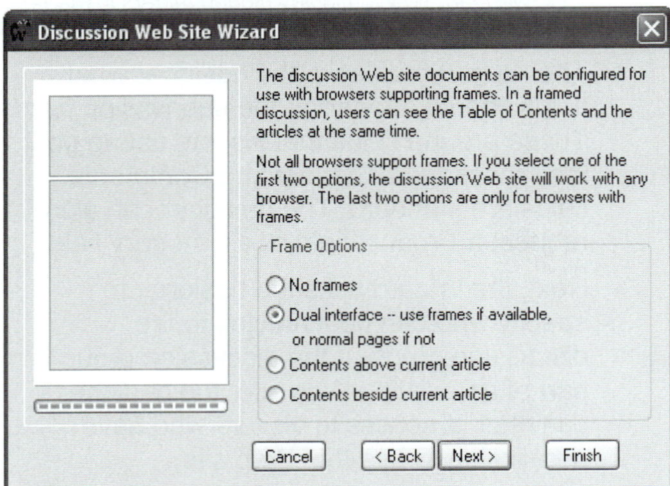

- After the designer clicks the Finish button in the last dialog box, FrontPage creates the discussion group pages in the Web site.

Discussion Group Pages

- The number and type of Web pages the Wizard creates depends on the layout option the Web author selected.
- If the author chose the default Dual interface option, the Wizard creates a frames page in which to display discussion group Web pages.
- Choosing the No frames option results in fewer discussion group pages because no frames page is created.
- The Wizard creates the following pages for the dual interface layout:
  - The discx_cfrm.htm page is the Confirmation page that displays after a visitor posts an article to the discussion group.

    ✓ *The x in the above page name stands for a number that will differ depending on the discussion group folder name.*
  - The discx_frm.htm page is a frames page that displays the discussion group's contents in the top frame and other pages (the Welcome page, the Confirmation page, and the Post Article page) in the main frame (see illustration below).
  - The discx_post.htm Web page is the Post Article page visitors use to add new articles to the discussion group.

    ✓ *In the dual interface layout, this page displays in the main frame of the discx_frm.htm page.*
  - The discx_srch.htm page contains a search form visitors can use to search for articles.
  - The discx_tocf.htm page is the Contents page that displays in the top frame of the discx_frm.htm page.

    ✓ *In the No frames layout, this page is named discx_toc.htm.*
  - The discx_welc.htm page is the Welcome page that displays in the main frame of the discx_frm.htm page.

    ✓ *The Wizard does not create this page if the designer selects the No frames option.*

Default dual interface frames page

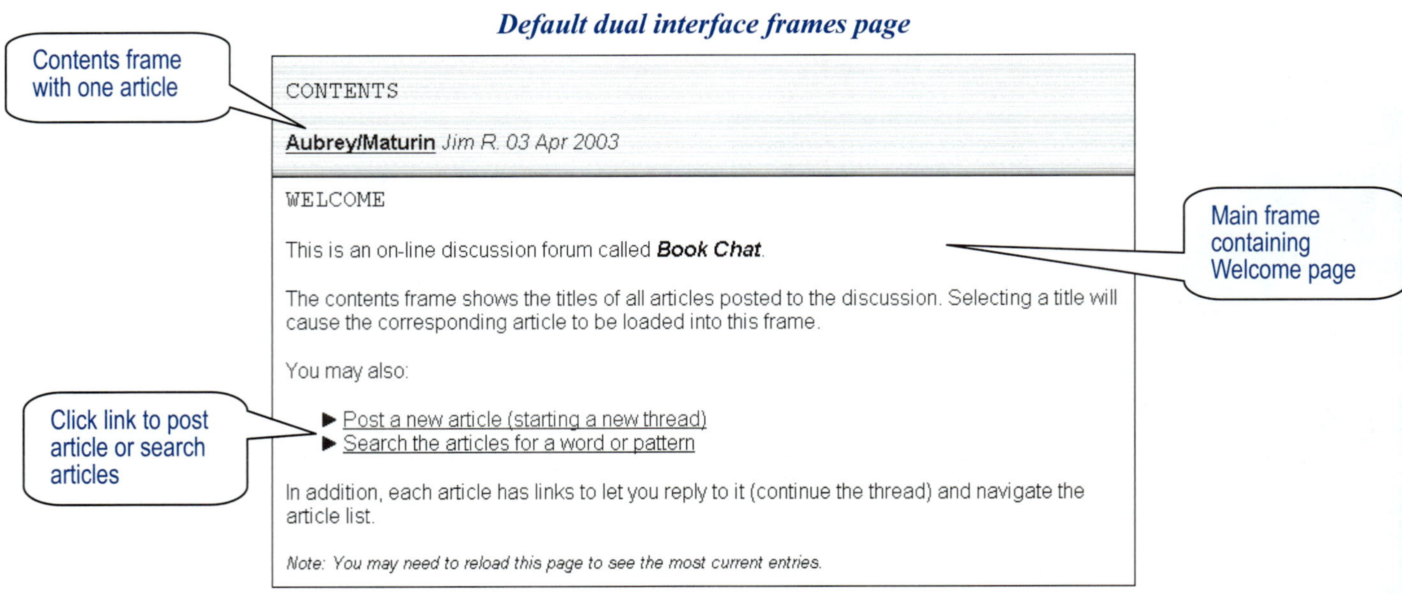

Change Discussion Group Page Formats

- After creating a discussion group, the Web author can change discussion group page formats as desired.
- Change fonts, colors, theme elements, alignments, and the default text supplied on the Welcome and Confirmation pages.
- By default, most discussion group pages display a **header** that contains a page title, links to other discussion group pages, and a horizontal rule (see illustration below).
- Discussion group pages also display a **footer** that contains the current date and a horizontal rule (see illustration below).

  ✓ *Headers and footers are actually inserted on discussion group pages using the Include Page component.*

Header and footer on discussion group page

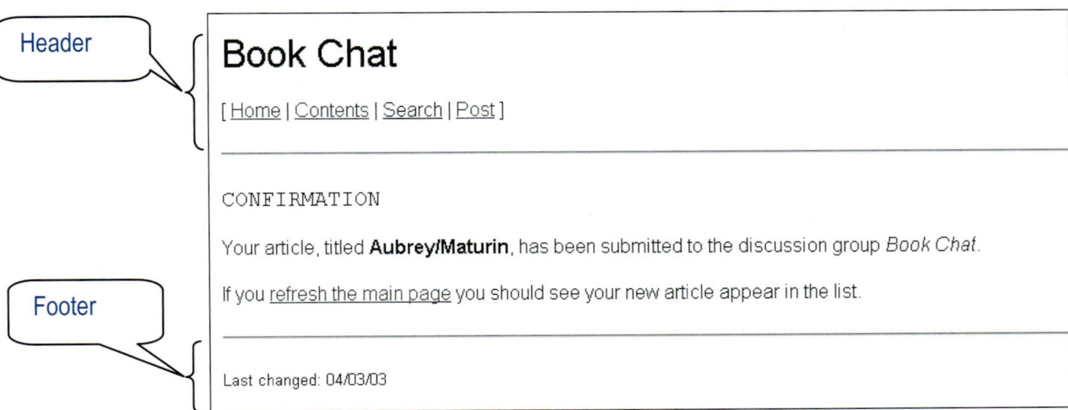

- The pages that contain the header and footer material are stored in a hidden folder. The Web author must instruct FrontPage to display hidden folders and their contents to access these pages.

  ✓ *You will display hidden folders and change header properties in the next exercise.*

Post Article

- Visitors post articles to a discussion group from the browser.
- If the discussion group uses frames, the visitor can click the *Post a new article (starting a new thread)* link to open the Post Article page in the frame (see illustration on previous page).
- If the discussion group does not use frames, the visitor can click the Post link in any page of the group to open the Post Article page.
- To post a new article, use the form fields supplied on the Post Article page to insert a subject, name, and comments (see illustration at right).
- After the visitor clicks the Post Article button, FrontPage displays a Confirmation page such as the one shown above.

Post a new article

CONTENTS

Book Chat

[Home | Contents | Search | Post]

POST ARTICLE

Subject:

Aubrey/Maturin

From:

Jim R.

Comments:

What is the first book in the Aubrey/Maturin series? This series was recommended to me, but I don't know where to start. Thanks!

Post Article | Reset Form

- The posted article does not immediately appear in the Contents frame (or on the Contents page). The visitor can click the *refresh the main page* link on the Confirmation page to update the Contents page.
- A posted article displays as a hyperlink in the Contents frame or page. (See illustrations at right and below.)

Reply to Article

- FrontPage's discussion group feature allows visitors to create **threaded discussions**.
- In a threaded discussion, replies to an article are indented (or nested) directly under the original article, as shown in the illustration at right. All replies to an article are indented the same distance.
- Visitors can also reply to a reply. A reply to a reply is indented below the reply (see illustration at right).

Replies nested below an article

CONTENTS

Aubrey/Maturin *Jim R. 03 Apr 2003*

    Re: Aubrey/Maturin *Leslie M. 03 Apr 2003*

    Re: Aubrey/Maturin *Elliot Q. 03 Apr 2003*

        Re: Aubrey/Maturin *Lucy C. 03 Apr 2003*

- To reply to an article, click the article link in the Contents frame or page to open an article page that supplies information about the posted article (see illustration below).

Click article link to display information about article

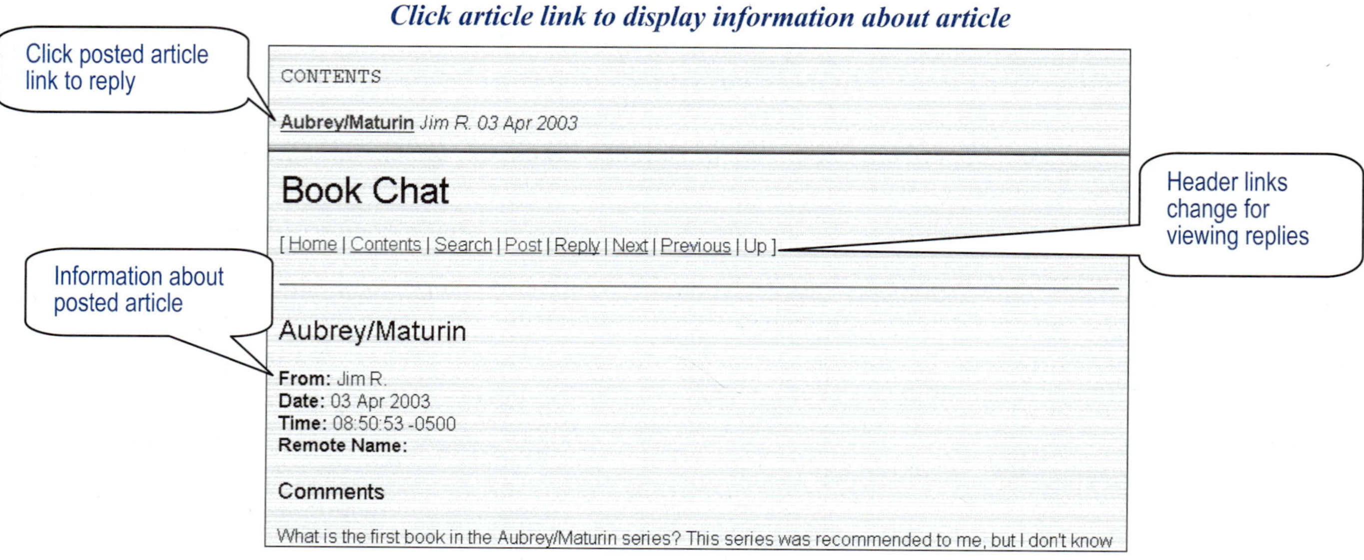

- The information displayed about the article's author, date and time of the posting, and the name of the computer from which the article was posted is returned from FrontPage's Discussion Form Handler.
  - ✓ *The Remote Name is concealed in the illustration above for security.*
  - ✓ *The information displayed on this page can be adjusted by changing options for the Discussion Form Handler. You will modify this information in Exercise 47.*
- A visitor can reply to the article by clicking the Reply link on this page. A page similar to the Post Article page opens to allow the visitor to supply his or her name and comments.
  - ✓ *The subject field is already filled in with Re: and the name of the article to which the visitor is replying.*
- After a discussion group has a number of articles, visitors can browse the articles easily by clicking an article link and then using the Next and Previous links (see illustration above) to move backward and forward among articles and their replies.
- To find specific text in discussion group articles, visitors can use the discussion group's search form.
  - ✓ *You will learn how to use the search form in Exercise 47.*

Procedures

Set Up Discussion Group (Wizard)

For best results, publish Web site before adding discussion group.

1. Click **File** .... Alt+F
2. Click **New** .... N
3. Click **More Web site Templates** link in New task pane.

   OR

   a. Click (**Create a new normal page** button) down arrow.
   b. Click **Web Site** .... W

In Web Site Templates dialog box

4. Click **Discussion Web Site Wizard**.
5. Type name for new Web site in *Specify the location of the new Web site* box.

   OR

   Click to select **Add to current Web site** checkbox.

Supply Information for Wizard

1. Click Next > in first Wizard dialog box to begin Wizard.
2. Choose features for the discussion group and click Next >.
3. Supply a title for the discussion group, designate the folder name where articles will be stored, and click Next >.
4. Choose an option for input fields and click Next >.
5. Choose who can post articles to the discussion group and click Next >.
6. Choose an option for sorting posted articles (oldest to newest or newest to oldest) and click Next >.
7. Specify whether the Table of Contents page of the discussion group will become the home page of the Web site and click Next >.
8. Choose what information will be displayed in the search results and click Next >.
9. Choose a theme for the discussion group, if it is not being added to an existing Web site, and click Next >.
10. Choose a layout option for displaying discussion group pages and click Next >.
11. Click Finish to complete the Wizard.

Change Discussion Group Page Formats

1. Open a discussion group page from the Folder List by double-clicking page name.
2. Use Formatting toolbar buttons or Format menu commands to apply new formats or change existing formats.

Post Article

In browser

1. Click **Post** or **Post a new article (starting a new thread)** link to open Post Article page.
2. Click in **Subject** field and type subject of article.
3. Click in **From** field and type your name.
4. Click in **Comments** field and type the body of the article.
5. Click Post Article.
6. Click the **refresh the main page** link in Confirmation page to see the article in the Contents frame or page.

Reply to Article

In browser

1. Click link of article to reply to.
2. Click **Reply** link in article page.
3. Click in **From** field and type your name.
4. Click in **Comments** field and type the body of the article.
5. Click Post Article.
6. Click the **refresh the main page** link in Confirmation page to see the reply nested below the original article in the Contents frame or page.

Exercise Directions

1. Start FrontPage 2003.
2. Open **Books**.
3. Publish the Web site as **booksweb**.
4. Close the disk-based **Books** Web site and open the server-based **booksweb**.
5. Click the Discussion Web Site Wizard in the Web Site Templates dialog box and choose to add the discussion group to the current Web site.
6. Click **Next** in the first Wizard dialog box to begin the Wizard.
7. Supply information for the Wizard as follows, clicking **Next** to move to the next dialog box:
   - Select all checkboxes to create a table of contents, search form, threaded replies, and confirmation page.
   - Type the title **Book Chat** as the name of the discussion group and change the name of the folder, if necessary, to **_disc1**.
   - Accept the default input fields (*Subject, Comments*).
   - Accept the default option for who can post to the discussion group (*No, anyone can post articles*).
   - Accept the default option for sorting the posted articles (*Oldest to newest*).
   - Click the **No** option if necessary to make sure the current home page is not overwritten by the discussion group's Table of Contents page.
   - Choose the **Subject** option if necessary for information the Search Form will display.
   - Choose the **Dual interface** option if necessary for the layout of the discussion pages.
   - Click **Finish** to complete the Wizard.
8. Format the discussion group pages as follows to make them match other pages in the site:
   - Apply the Straight Edge theme with background picture and without vivid colors to each discussion group page.
   - On the **disc1_cfrm.htm** page, change the *Confirmation* heading to Arial with an initial capital *C* and the remaining letters lowercase. Change the heading color to the theme's dark red color.
   - On the **disc1_post.htm** page, modify the *Post Article* heading using the same formats as for the *Confirmation* heading.

     ✓ *To save time, use the Format Painter to copy the formats from the disc1_cfrm.htm page and then lowercase all letters except the P and the A in Post Article.*
   - On the **disc1_srch.htm** page, format the *Search for Article* heading as on other pages (Arial, dark red color, and capital letters only on the *S* of *Search* and the *A* of *Article*).
   - On the **disc1_frm.htm** page, apply the Heading 2 style to the *Contents* and *Welcome* headings. Change their font to Arial and lowercase all but the first letter of each heading.
   - Open the **disc1_tocf.htm** and **disc1_srch.htm** pages again and make sure they don't have a blank line above the first heading.
9. Open the **index.htm** or **Default.htm** Web page and create a link from the Book Chat interactive button to the **disc1_frm.htm** page.
10. Also create a link to the **disc1_frm.htm** page from the first instance of *Book Chat* in the last paragraph on the **index.htm** or **Default.htm** page.
11. Save all changes, then open the **index.htm** or **Default.htm** page and preview it in the browser.
12. Click the **Book Chat** link to open the discussion group frames page and click the **Post a new article (starting a new thread)** link.
13. Create the following article:

Subject:	Adventure query
From:	[type your first name and last initial]
Comments:	Does anyone know when the next volume of the Wheel of Time series is due out?

14. Click the **Post Article** button to post the article.
15. Click the **refresh the main page** link on the Confirmation page to see the article in the Contents frame.
16. Click the **Adventure query** link in the Contents frame to open the article page.
17. Click the **Reply** link in the article page.

18. Create the following reply:

    From: [use a classmate's first name and last initial]

    Comments: The hardback version is on sale now. The paperback version is due out in November.

19. Post the article and then refresh the main page to view the reply nested below the original article.

20. Post at least one other article (either a new article or a reply) to the discussion group on a book-related topic.

21. Your frames page should look similar to the one shown in Illustration A. (Your dates will differ.)

22. Close the browser.

23. Close the Web site.

24. Exit FrontPage 2003.

Illustration A

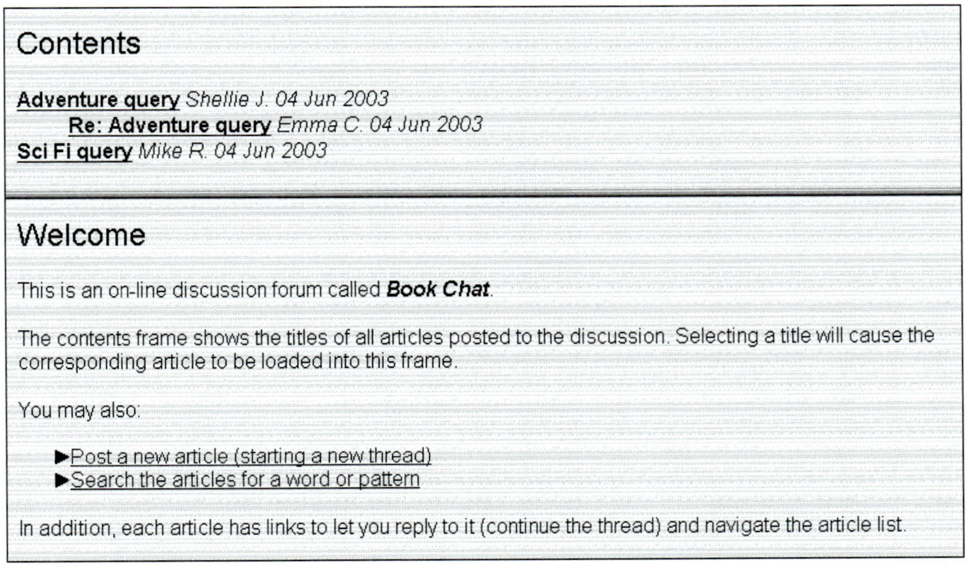

Contents

Adventure query *Shellie J. 04 Jun 2003*
  Re: Adventure query *Emma C. 04 Jun 2003*
Sci Fi query *Mike R. 04 Jun 2003*

Welcome

This is an on-line discussion forum called ***Book Chat***.

The contents frame shows the titles of all articles posted to the discussion. Selecting a title will cause the corresponding article to be loaded into this frame.

You may also:

▶Post a new article (starting a new thread)
▶Search the articles for a word or pattern

In addition, each article has links to let you reply to it (continue the thread) and navigate the article list.

On Your Own

1. Start FrontPage 2003.
2. Create a new discussion group for a topic that interests you. You can devote the entire Web site to the discussion group or add the discussion group to a Web site.
   ✓ *If desired, use a Web site you have already created for this course. Publish the Web site first to have access to all discussion group options.*
3. Run the Discussion Web Site Wizard and choose options for your discussion group. Name the folder that will store the articles **_disc1**.
4. After the Wizard has created the discussion group pages, format the pages as desired.
5. If you added the discussion group to an existing Web site, set up links to the discussion group's frames page (or table of contents page if you chose the No frames option).
6. Publish the Web site if necessary and then view the Web site in the browser.
7. Post several articles and replies to the discussion group.
8. Close the browser.
9. Close the Web site.
10. Exit FrontPage 2003.

Exercise 47

◆ **Search Discussion Group** ◆ **Display Hidden Folders**
◆ **Modify Discussion Page Properties**
◆ **Manage Discussion Group Articles**

On the Job

FrontPage developers can include a search form in a discussion group to allow visitors to find words or phrases among posted articles. To edit some discussion group properties and manage articles, a developer must display the hidden folders in which discussion group articles and pages are stored.

In this exercise, you will continue to work with the Ariel Books discussion group. You will test the search form and display hidden folders. You will modify article properties and formatting in discussion page headers. Finally, you will edit article content and delete an article.

Terms

hidden folder
A folder in a Web site that does not display by default. Folders are usually hidden for security reasons.

Notes

Search Discussion Group

- To make a discussion group more useful for visitors, a Web author can include a search form within the discussion group.
- If included in the discussion group, the search form appears on the discx_srch.htm page.
- In a discussion group that uses the dual interface layout, the Welcome page includes a link that opens the Search for Article page in the main frame.
- Visitors can also open the Search for Article page by clicking the Search link in any page header.
- The discussion group search form works the same way as the standard FrontPage search form: Visitors type a word or phrase to find and the search form displays any resulting matches below the form (see illustration at right).

Results of search in discussion group

Search for Article

Find articles posted to this discussion containing matching words or patterns.

Search for: Wheel

Start Search | Reset

Number of documents found: 1. Click on a document to view it, or submit another search.

Search Results

Document
Adventure query

- The Search Results table lists links to articles that contain the search text. Click the link to go directly to that article.

Display Hidden Folders

- FrontPage stores some Web site information in **hidden folders**. To change discussion group headers or footers or manage articles in a discussion group, a Web author must display FrontPage's hidden folders.
- Display hidden folders using the Tools>Site Settings command on the menu bar.
- In the Site Settings dialog box, click the Advanced tab and select the *Show hidden files and folders* checkbox (see illustration below).

Show hidden folders

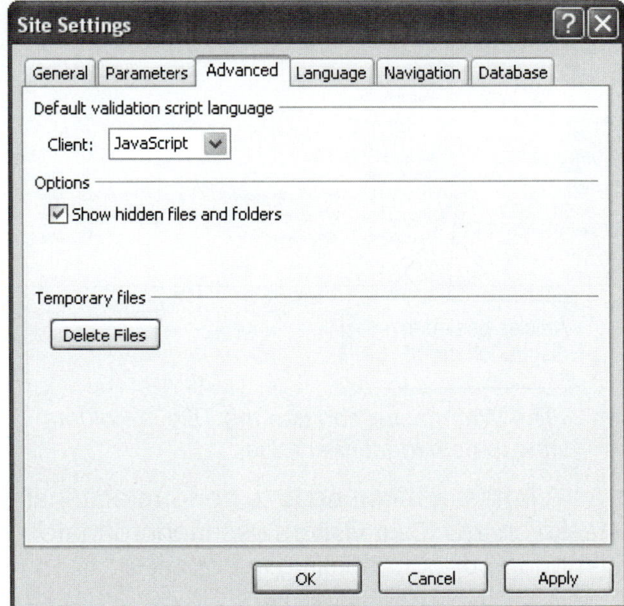

- FrontPage requires the author to refresh the Web site and then displays hidden folders in the Folder List.
- The number and type of hidden folders displayed depend on the Web site's contents.
- A Web site formatted with a theme has a _themes hidden folder. A discussion group Web site has a _borders folder that contains header pages and the _discx folder that stores articles.
- When an author has finished work on hidden folder files, he or she should hide the folders again.
- To hide folders again, deselect the *Show hidden files and folders* checkbox on the Advanced tab in the Site Settings dialog box.

Modify Discussion Page Properties

- Web designers can modify discussion page properties to make the pages more useful or attractive.
- Recall the information displayed when a visitor clicks an article to reply to it (see illustration below). The Web designer might wish to modify or delete some of this information.

Information displayed on article page

Aubrey/Maturin

From: Jim R.
Date: 03 Apr 2003
Time: 08:50:53 -0500
Remote Name:

Comments

- Modify article information by displaying form properties for the discx_post.htm page. In the Form Properties dialog box, click the Options button and then the Article tab (see illustration below).

Change items displayed on article page

Options for Discussion Form Handler
Discussion | Article | Confirmation Page
URL of header to include: _borders/disc1_ahdr.htm [Browse...]
URL of footer to include: _borders/disc1_aftr.htm [Browse...]
Date and time:
Date format: 02 Dec 2003
Time format: 10:57:42 TZ
Additional information to
☑ Remote computer name ☐ User name
[OK] [Cancel]

- The designer can change date and time formats and choose to display the remote computer name or the user name of the visitor who posted the article.

- The designer can modify information in discussion page headers and footers by opening the _borders folder to display the pages used to create the headers and footers.
- A discussion group has two sets of headers and footers (see illustration below).
  - Discx_head.htm and discx_foot.htm display on all pages except the article pages.
  - Discx_ahdr.htm and discx_aftr.htm display only on article pages (the pages that give information on posted articles).

Header and footer pages in _borders folder

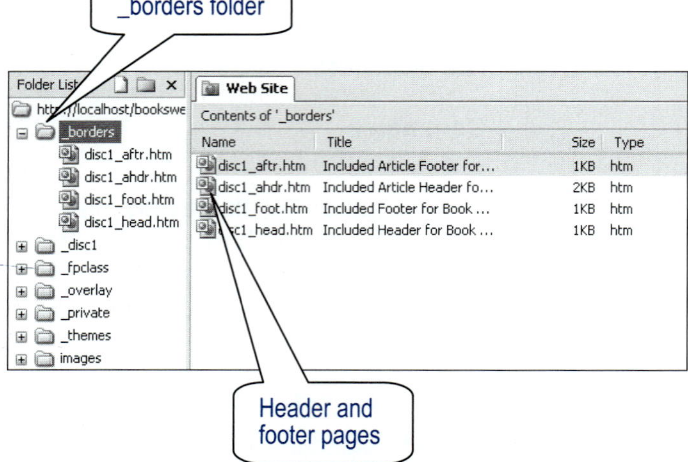

- Note in the illustration above that the header and footer page titles indicate the headers and footers are "Included." Header and footer pages display on discussion group pages by means of the Included Content Web component.
- To modify a header or footer, display the contents of the _borders folder in Folders view and double-click a header or footer page to open it.

  ✓ *Edit the content of a header or footer page just as for any other Web page.*

Manage Discussion Group Articles

- A Webmaster in charge of a discussion group occasionally needs to manage discussion group content.
- The Webmaster can manage discussion group articles by opening them from the _disc*x* folder and editing or deleting them.
- Each article posted to a discussion group receives a numeric file name (see illustration below). Articles are thus ordered by number, not by subject or content.

Articles stored in _discx folder

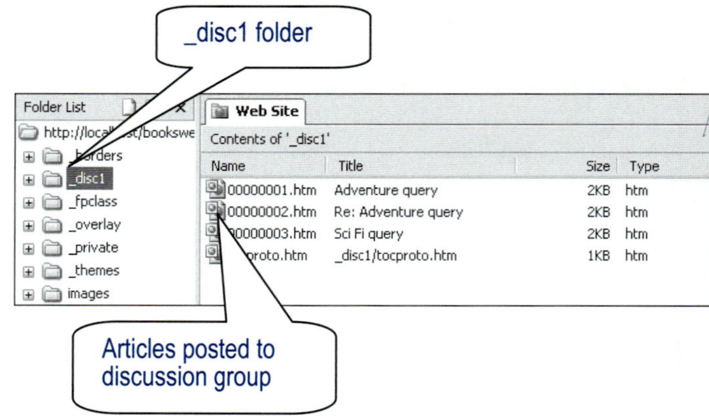

✓ *The Webmaster can use the Title in Folders view to help identify articles.*

- A Webmaster might need to perform editorial tasks on articles if visitors use inappropriate language or poor spelling in an article.
- To edit an article, display the contents of the _disc*x* folder in Folders view and double-click an article to open it.
- The Webmaster can edit text on the article page just as for any Web page.
- Revisions display the next time the article page is opened or refreshed in the browser.
- If an article is out of date or inappropriate for the discussion group, the Webmaster can delete the article using the Edit>Delete command on the menu bar.

  ✓ *Or right-click the article in Folders view and click the Delete command on the shortcut menu.*

Procedures

Search Discussion Group

In browser displaying discussion group Web site

1. Click **Search the articles for a word or pattern** link on Welcome page or click **Search** link on any discussion group page.
2. Click in **Search for** box and type word or phrase to search for.
3. Click [Start Search].
4. Review list of matches and click link to go to that article.
   - ✓ *If no matches are found, the Search for Article page displays "No documents found."*

Display Hidden Folders

1. Click **Tools** .... Alt+T
2. Click **Site Settings** I
3. Click **Advanced** tab.
4. Select **Show hidden files and folders** checkbox.
5. Click [Apply].
6. Click [Yes] when asked to refresh the Web site.
7. Hide folders again using same process and deselecting checkbox.
8. Click [Yes] when asked to refresh the Web site.

Modify Discussion Page Properties

Modify information displayed on article pages

1. Open discx_post.htm page from Folder List.
2. Click in form.
3. Click **Insert** .... Alt+I
4. Click **Form** .... R
5. Click **Form Properties** .... R

   OR

   Right-click in form and click **Form Properties** .... R
6. Click [Options...] .... Alt+O
7. Click **Article** tab.
8. Choose options to display on article page:
   - Modify date or time format.
   - Choose to display remote computer name or user name.

Modify header or footer information

1. Switch to Folders view.
2. Click **_borders** folder in Folder List.
3. Double-click header or footer page to modify.
4. Modify as for any Web page.

Edit Discussion Group Articles

1. Switch to Folders view.
2. Click **_disc*x*** folder in Folder List.
3. Double-click article to modify.
4. Modify as for any Web page.

Delete Discussion Group Articles

1. Switch to Folders view.
2. Click **_disc*x*** folder in Folder List.
3. Select article.
4. Click **Edit** .... Alt+E
5. Click **Delete** .... D

   OR

   Right-click article and click **Delete** .... D

Exercise Directions

1. Start FrontPage 2003.
2. Open **booksweb**.
   ✓ *Open the Web site from the server where it was published.*
3. Open **index.htm** or **Default.htm** and preview this page in the browser.
4. Click the **Book Chat** link to open the first discussion group frames page.
5. In the Welcome page, click the **Search the articles for a word or pattern** link to open the search page.
6. Search for the word *Wheel*.
7. FrontPage should locate an instance of this word in the *Adventure query* article.
8. Click the **Adventure query** link to read the article that contains the search word.
9. Return to FrontPage and open **disc1_post.htm**.
10. Open the Form Properties dialog box and click the **Options** button and the **Article** tab.
11. Change the date format to the Mon-01 pattern (e.g., Feb-01) pattern and the time format to the HH:MM PM pattern (e.g., 12:58 PM).
12. Deselect the **Remote computer name** checkbox.
13. Display hidden folders.
14. Change the *Book Chat* heading to Heading 2 style in both header pages (disc1_ahdr.htm and disc1_head.htm) in the _borders folder.
15. Save all pages and refresh the Web site in the browser.
16. Post a new article to test your changes to the form properties:

Subject	Wheels
From	K.D.
Comments	People who read those Wheel books are complete geeks. Get a life!

17. Refresh the main page to see the new article and click it to see its information in the article page. Your page should look similar to Illustration A.
18. Return to FrontPage and display the articles in the _disc1 folder.
19. Open **00000002.htm** and change the word *version* to *edition* in two places in the Comments. Save your changes to this file.
20. The Wheels article does not conform to Book Chat's policy of free nonjudgmental discussion of books. Delete this article. (This article has the highest number in the list of articles in the disc1 folder.)
   ✓ *You might need to refresh Folders view to see the latest article.*
21. Refresh the browser and notice that the Wheels article disappears. View the first Adventure query reply to see the editorial change you made.
22. Close the browser.
23. Hide hidden folders again.
24. Close the Web site
25. Exit FrontPage 2003.

Illustration A

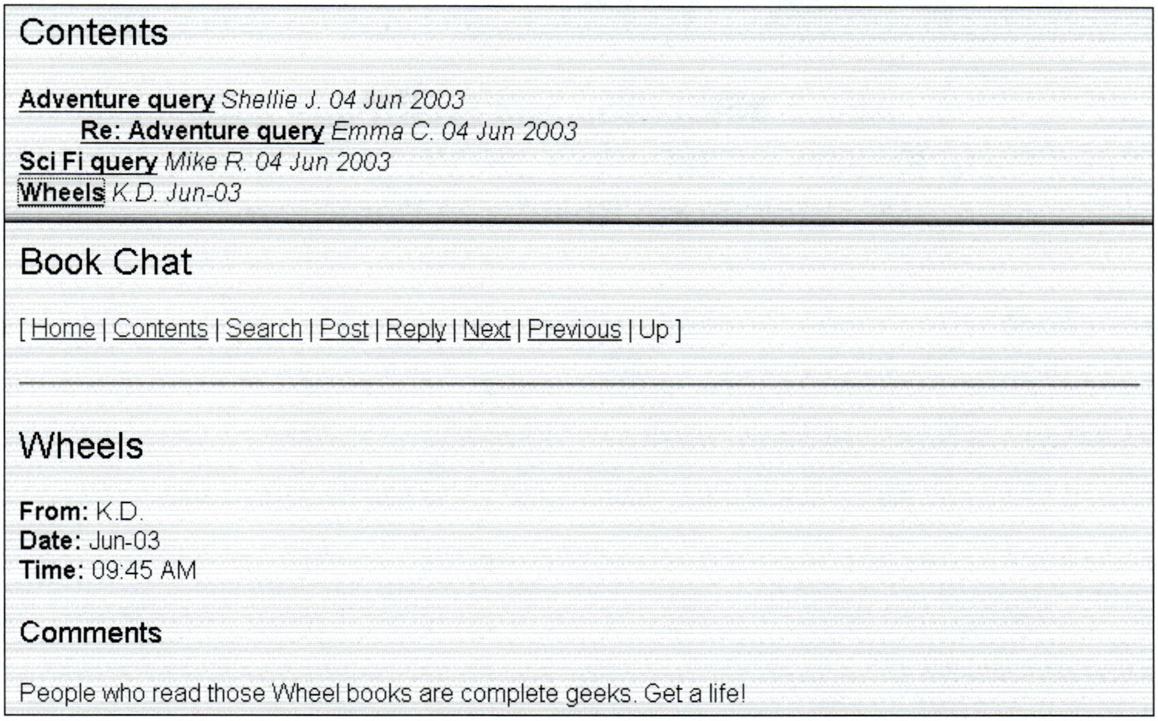

Contents

Adventure query *Shellie J. 04 Jun 2003*
Re: Adventure query *Emma C. 04 Jun 2003*
Sci Fi query *Mike R. 04 Jun 2003*
Wheels *K.D. Jun-03*

Book Chat

[Home | Contents | Search | Post | Reply | Next | Previous | Up]

Wheels

From: K.D.
Date: Jun-03
Time: 09:45 AM

Comments

People who read those Wheel books are complete geeks. Get a life!

On Your Own

1. Start FrontPage 2003.
2. Open the Web site you worked on in the last On Your Own exercise. (Open the published Web site from the server.)
3. Test the discussion group's search form by searching for a word or phrase you know appears in one of the posted articles.
4. Change the properties of the form on the **disc1_post.htm** page so that the article page does not display the remote computer name or the time an article is posted.
5. Display hidden folders.
6. Change text for both footers to read **Updated:** and the date format to the pattern that gives the Day of Week, Month, Day, and Year (e.g., Monday February 27, 2005).
7. Make any other changes to the headers and footers desired to improve the appearance of the discussion pages.
8. Post a new article to see your changes to article formats.
9. Edit an existing article to correct spelling or improve comprehension.
10. Delete one of the articles and then rehide hidden folders.
11. Check your changes to the discussion group in the browser.
12. Close the browser and the Web site.
13. Exit FrontPage 2003.

Exercise 48

◆ **About Databases and FrontPage 2003**
◆ **Send Form Results to Database** ◆ **Verify Database Connection**
◆ **View Form Results in Database**

On the Job

FrontPage is designed to integrate with a database program such as Microsoft Office Access in a number of ways. FrontPage can send form results directly to a database table. The developer can create a database from within FrontPage to handle form results. After verifying the database connection, the developer can test the form and then open the database from within FrontPage to see the form results.

The Ariel Books Web site you have been working with includes a contact form. In this exercise, you will create a database from within FrontPage to store results from the contact form. After you configure the new database, you will use the form to create several records. Finally, you will open the database within FrontPage to view the form results.

Terms

Active Server Page (ASP)
An HTML page that contains *server-side* scripts, which are processed by a server before being sent to a visitor's browser. Active server pages use the .asp file extension.

database
A file that contains related information organized so that the information can be searched or retrieved easily.

database table
In Microsoft Office Access, a collection of data on one specific topic. An Access database can contain more than one table.

field
A specific item of information about an object, such as a first name or part number.

record
The complete set of fields for an object.

server-side
Taking place on a Web server rather than in the Web developer's computer.

Notes

About Databases and FrontPage 2003

- Interactive Web sites can generate a considerable amount of data. One of the best ways to store data is in a database.
- A **database** organizes related information in such a way that a user can easily search for or retrieve data.
- A database stores data in **fields**. A field is one piece of information about the database's subject.
  - ✓ *An employee database, for example, will have first name, last name, address, phone, and social security number fields, among others.*
- A complete set of fields for one item is called a **record**.

Portion of Access database table

Members : Table

MemberID	First	Last	Club	Phone
1	Janey	Fox	Mysteries	555-3409
2	Mike	Mowbry	History	555-9387
3	Nancy	Meadows	Mysteries	555-2910
4	Harris	Kelly	Romances	555-3019
5	Shelley	MacArthur	History	555-6474
6	Indri	Chaudhuri	Science Fiction	555-1080
7	Tim	Norgaard	Mysteries	555-0330
8	Ellen	Bernstein	Science Fiction	555-7843
9	Taylor	Bradford	Romances	555-5789
10	Paul	Haverford	History	555-8684
11	Terry	Newsome	Romances	555-4289

Record: 1 of 30

Field name

Field entries

Record for one member

- A database's fields and records create a grid of columns and rows that makes it easy to find a single piece of information in a database (see illustration above).
- A Web developer can use databases in several ways:
  - Use a database to store FrontPage form results.
  - Insert a Database Results region to display database information on a Web page.

    ✓ *You will insert a Database Results region in Exercise 49.*
  - Maintain a database from within FrontPage using the Database Interface Wizard.

    ✓ *You will use the Database Interface Wizard in Exercise 50.*
- Because FrontPage is one of the Microsoft Office 2003 applications, FrontPage integrates easily with Microsoft Office's database application, Microsoft Office Access.
- Access stores database information in **database tables**. The Access database itself is a "container" that can store a number of tables and other database objects such as forms and reports.

  ✓ *In Access, tables are the primary storage object. Forms, queries, reports, and data access pages are all based on the information stored in tables.*

Send Form Results to Database

- Storing form data in a database allows the Web developer to manipulate data using the database's tools.
- For example, the developer can easily sort data stored in a database by one or more fields, use a query to display only data that meet certain conditions, or create a report that summarizes the data.
- FrontPage has a standard option in the Form Properties dialog box to send form results to a database.
- Selecting this option and then clicking the Options button opens the Options for Saving Results to Database dialog box (see illustration below).

Select or create database connection

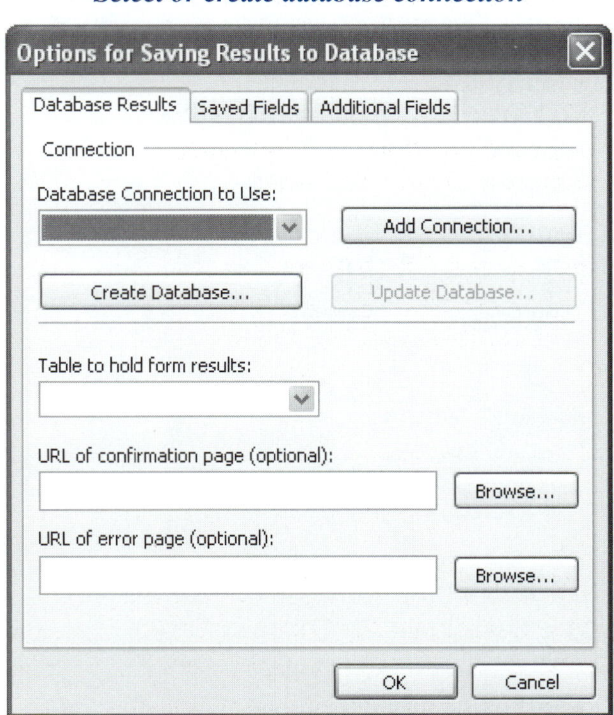

- The Web author can specify an existing database (one that has already been imported into the Web site), create a new database connection, or create a new database to store the form results.
  - ✓ *You will learn how to import a database in Exercise 49.*

Create Database from FrontPage

- A Web author does not have to leave FrontPage to create a database for form results.
- Clicking the Create Database button in the Options for Saving Results to Database dialog box prompts FrontPage to create the new database.
- FrontPage places the new database in a folder named fpdb. By default, the database name is the same as the page on which the form appears and the database table that stores the data is named Results.
- FrontPage uses the form field names in the FrontPage form as field names in the new database.
- Clicking the Saved Fields tab in the Options for Saving Results to Database dialog box shows the author how the form fields match up with the database table fields (see illustration below).

Check that saved fields match form fields

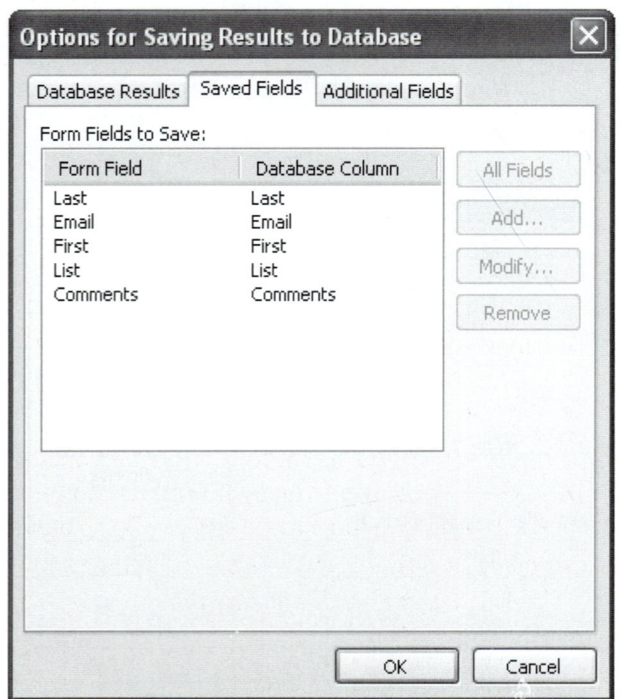

- When FrontPage creates the database, these field names will match exactly.
- If the author is using an existing database whose fields do not have precisely the same names as the form field names, the author can click on a form field name and choose the database field that should receive the form field's data.
- FrontPage also creates four additional fields in the new database to store information about the visitor sending the form data (see illustration below).

Specify additional data if desired

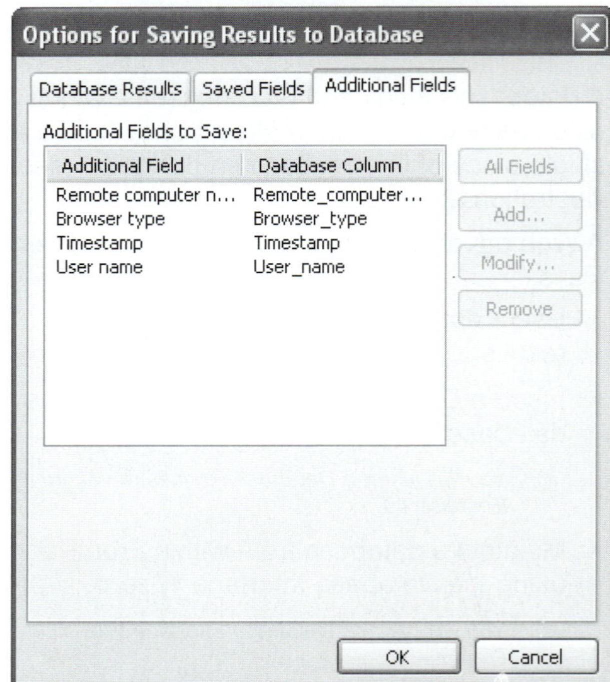

- If the author does not want to capture this information, he or she can click each Additional Field item and then click the Remove button.
- As soon as FrontPage makes a connection to a database, it adds the global.asp file to the Folder List. This file stores information about the connection between FrontPage and the database.

About Active Server Pages

- After the Web developer specifies a database to receive form results, FrontPage prompts the developer to change the page's file type to one with an .asp extension.

- The .asp extension identifies an **Active Server Page (ASP)**. Using an ASP page allows the author to combine HTML content with scripts that run on the server (**server-side** scripts) to display interactive Web site elements.
- To change an HTML page to an ASP page, rename the page in Folders view. Change only the extension and leave the remainder of the file name the same.
  ✓ *FrontPage will warn the author about changing the extension and offer to update any links to the changed page.*
- The author must verify that the server on which a Web site is published is able to run Active Server pages.
  ✓ *ASP technology is built into some Microsoft Web servers and personal Web servers, but the author should check to be sure.*
- Check to make sure Active Server Pages will run correctly by clicking the Tools>Page Options command on the menu bar.
- In the Page Options dialog box, click the Authoring tab (see illustration below) and make sure the *Active server pages* checkbox is selected.
  ✓ *For servers other than personal Web servers, the systems administrator is in charge of authoring settings.*

Check ASP status in Page Options dialog box

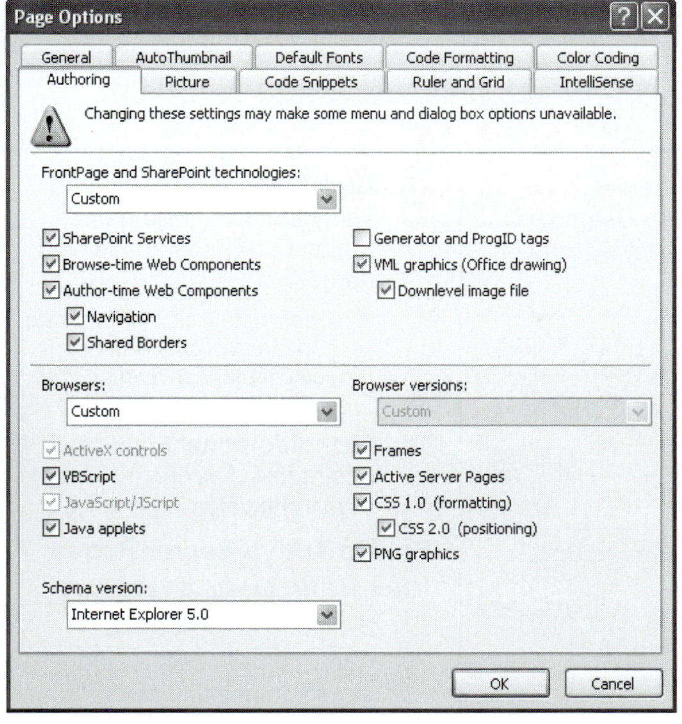

Verify Database Connection

- After adding a database to a Web site, the author must verify the database connection. By verifying the connection, the author ensures that the Web site and the database are correctly linked.
- To verify a database connection, use the Tools>Site Settings command on the menu bar and then click the Database tab in the Web Settings dialog box.
- Immediately after a database has been added to a Web site, the database connection shown on the Database tab has a question mark to the left of the database name (see illustration below).
- After the author clicks Verify and FrontPage checks the connection, a green checkmark displays to the left of the database name to indicate the connection is active.

Verify database connection

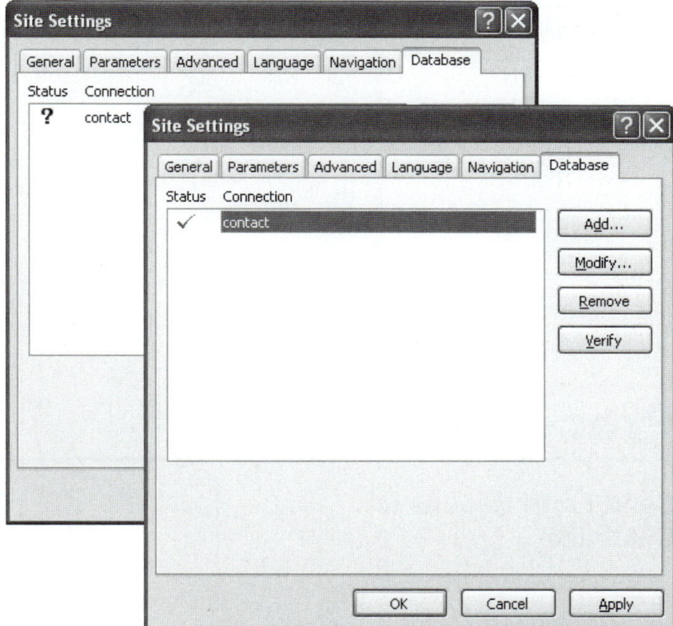

View Form Results in Database

- When a FrontPage form sends form results to a database, the author can open the database from within FrontPage to check the form results.
  ✓ *The author may need to click the Refresh button in FrontPage before opening the database to see recent data.*
- Open the database by clicking the plus sign to the left of the fpdb folder in the Folder List and then double-clicking the database name.

- The database opens to give the author access to the form results data.
- When Microsoft Office Access opens, it displays the Database window for the current database (see illustration below).
- The Web developer must click the Tables object in the Database window to display the tables stored in the database.
- The developer can then double-click the name of the form results table to see the data stored in the table
- The author can use the database's standard tools to manipulate form data:
  - Sort the data according to the entries in any field using a Sort command or tool.
  - Apply a filter to display records that match specific criteria.
  - Create a query that will display specific fields and data that match criteria.
  - Create a report that shows data from chosen fields in a format suitable for printing.

Open a table in Access

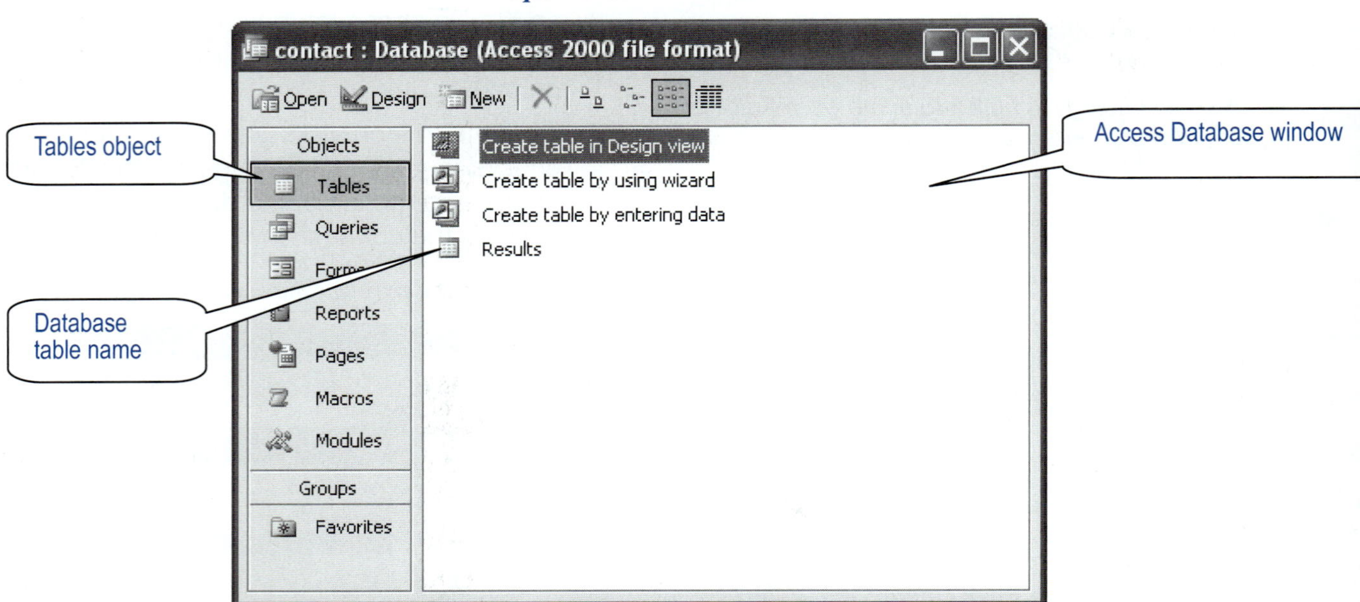

Procedures

Send Form Results to Database

1. Click in FrontPage form.
2. Click **Insert** .... Alt+I
3. Click **Form** .... R
4. Click **Form Properties** .... R

   OR

   Right-click in form and click **Form Properties** .... R
5. Select **Send to database** option.
6. Click Options... .
7. Choose database connection:
   - Click **Database Connection to Use** down arrow and select existing database.

   OR

   - Click Add Connection... to add a new database connection to Web site .... Alt+A

   OR

   - Click Create Database... to create new database................. Alt+C
8. Choose database table if necessary.
9. Click **Saved Fields** tab and verify that form field names match up with database field names.

   ✓ *If necessary, click a form field name and click* ***Modify*** *to select database field to store data from that field.*
10. Click **Additional Fields** tab, if desired, and verify or remove additional fields.

Set Up Active Server Pages

Rename HTML page to ASP page

1. Switch to Folders view.
2. Click name of page twice, slowly, to position insertion point in name.

3. Delete .htm extension and type .asp extension.
4. Click **Yes** if FrontPage asks if you really want to make this change.
5. Click **Yes** if FrontPage offers to update hyperlinks.

Verify ASP status

1. Click **Tools** .... Alt+T
2. Click **Page Options** .... A
3. Click **Authoring** tab.
4. Verify that there is a checkmark in the **Active Server Pages** checkbox.

Verify Database Connection

1. Click **Tools** .... Alt+T
2. Click **Site Settings** I
3. Click **Database** tab.
4. Click name of database to verify.
5. Click Verify .... Alt+V

View Form Results in Database

1. Click (**Refresh** button) on Standard toolbar to update Web site in FrontPage.
2. Click plus sign to expand **fpdb** folder in Folder List.
3. Double-click database name to open database program.

In Microsoft Access, click Tables object in Database window to list database's tables.

4. Double-click name of database table, if necessary, to open table that stores form results.

Exercise Directions

1. Start FrontPage 2003.
2. Open **booksweb**.
3. Publish the Web site as **booksdata**.
4. Close **booksweb** and open **booksdata** from the server.
5. Open **contact.htm**.
6. Open the Form Properties dialog box and choose to send form results to a database.
7. Create a new database to store the form results.
8. Check the Saved Fields tab to make sure the form field names match up with database field names.
9. On the Additional Fields tab, remove all additional fields.
10. After closing the Form Properties dialog box, save the **contact.htm** page and then rename it as **contact.asp** in Folders view.
    - ✓ *Answer Yes to update hyperlinks to this page.*
11. Check in the Page Options dialog box to make sure the Web site is set to run Active Server Pages.
12. Verify the connection to the **contact** database.
    - ✓ *On the Tools menu, click Site Settings and then click the Database tab to verify the database connection.*
13. Preview the **contact.asp** page in the browser and fill out the form with made-up data to create at least four records.
14. Open the **contact** database from within FrontPage.
15. Click the Tables object in the Database window, if necessary, and open the **Results** table.
16. Your form results should look similar to Illustration A. (Your data will differ.)
17. Close the browser.
18. Close the Web site.
19. Exit FrontPage 2003.

Illustration A

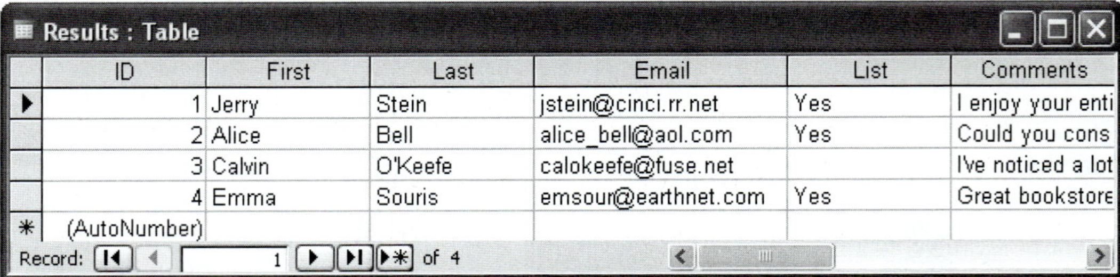

Results : Table

	ID	First	Last	Email	List	Comments
▶	1	Jerry	Stein	jstein@cinci.rr.net	Yes	I enjoy your enti
	2	Alice	Bell	alice_bell@aol.com	Yes	Could you cons
	3	Calvin	O'Keefe	calokeefe@fuse.net		I've noticed a lot
	4	Emma	Souris	emsour@earthnet.com	Yes	Great bookstore
*	(AutoNumber)					

Record: 1 of 4

On Your Own

1. Start FrontPage 2003.
2. Open the Web site you worked on in the last On Your Own exercise and publish it with a different name.
3. Open the new version of the Web site.
4. If necessary, add a form to the Web site containing three or four fields that relate to the Web site's subject.
5. Name and validate the form fields as desired.
6. Create a new database to store the form results.
7. Verify that form fields and database fields have the same names.
8. Remove additional fields as desired.
9. Rename the page that contains the form to make it an Active Server Page.
10. Verify the database connection.
11. Test the form in the browser by filling out the form several times.
12. Open the database from within FrontPage to see the form results.
13. Close the browser.
14. Close the Web site.
15. Exit FrontPage 2003.

Exercise 49

◆ **Import Database** ◆ **Insert Database Results Region**
◆ **Query Database from FrontPage**

On the Job

Web developers can import an existing database into FrontPage and then use a Database Results region to display records from the database on a Web page. The Database Results region can include a search form that allows visitors to query the database from the Web page.

In this exercise, you will work with the Ariel Books intranet Web site, which stores information about Ariel Books' operations. You will import a database that stores data in three different tables and add Database Results regions and search capability.

Terms

Database Results region
FrontPage component that inserts data from a database on a Web page.

Notes

Import Database

- If database information a Web author wants to use is already stored in a database file, the author can import the database into FrontPage.
- Import a database the same way as any other file using the File>Import command on the menu bar.
- After the author has added the database file to the Import dialog box and clicked the OK button, FrontPage asks the author to create a database connection (see illustration at right).
- FrontPage suggests that the imported database be stored in the fpdb folder.
- The author must verify the database connection for an imported database as discussed in Exercise 48 using the Tools>Site Settings command on the menu bar.

Create the database connection

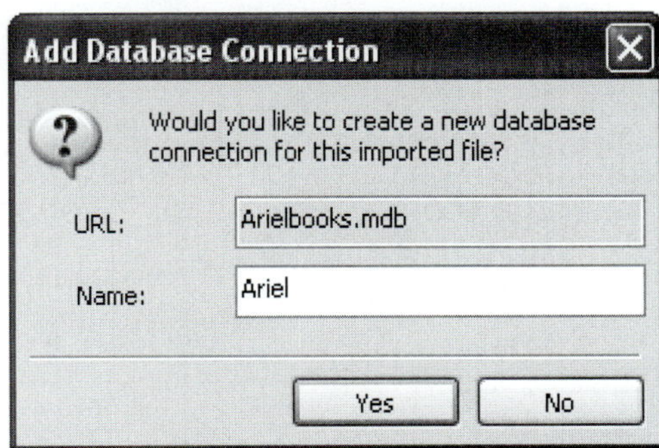

Insert Database Results Region

- After a database has been added to a FrontPage Web site, the Web developer can insert a **Database Results region** on any page in the Web site to display data from the database.
- Begin the process of adding a Database Results region by clicking the Insert>Database>Results command on the menu bar. The Database Results Wizard starts.

- FrontPage's Database Results Wizard automates the process of inserting and formatting the Database Results region.
  - The Wizard first asks the author to specify the database to be used. The author can use a sample database, select an existing database connection, or create a new database connection.
    - ✓ *The wizard will also suggest either ASP or ASP.NET format for the database results region. You must use ASP unless you are publishing to an ASP.NET server.*
  - The Wizard then asks the author what record source to use. For an Access database, the author selects a table from the database.
  - By default, the Wizard adds all database fields to the Results region. The author can remove or rearrange fields in Step 3 of the Wizard by clicking the Edit List button to open the Displayed Fields dialog box (see illustration at top of next column).
  - In Step 4 of the Wizard, the author can choose how to display records in the Results region: as a table, as a list, or as choices in a drop-down list.
    - ✓ *Formatting options differ depending on which of these three formats the author chooses.*
  - In the last step of the Wizard, the author can choose to display records together or in groups of five records.
    - ✓ *If the author chose the Drop-Down List option, records cannot be displayed in groups.*
  - If the page on which the Database Results region appears is not an Active Server Page, FrontPage prompts the author to rename the page with the .asp extension.

Specify database fields for results region

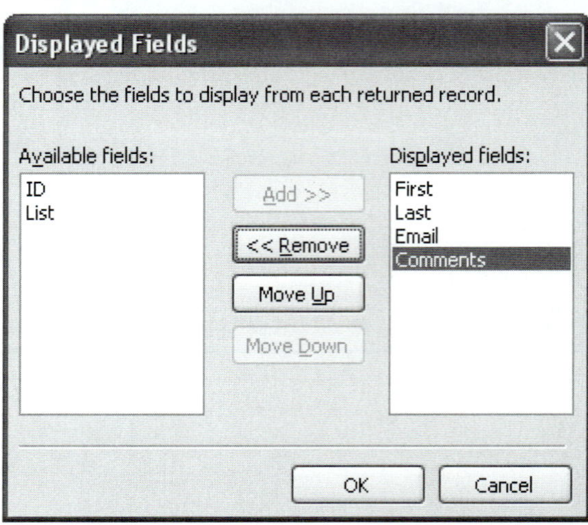

- The Database Results region displays on the Web page and may include additional instructions to the author about publishing the page (see illustration below).
- In a Database Results region set up as a table, FrontPage includes navigation buttons at the bottom of the table (see illustration below) and numbers in brackets to indicate the number of groups of records and the current group.
- Both the field names and the data in a Database Results region can be formatted the same way table text is formatted.
- A Database Results region cannot be used to enter data into a database or edit existing data. The Results region merely displays data from the designated database table.
- To keep a database up to date, the Web author can open the database from within FrontPage and add or edit records in the database table.

Database Results region in disk-based Web site

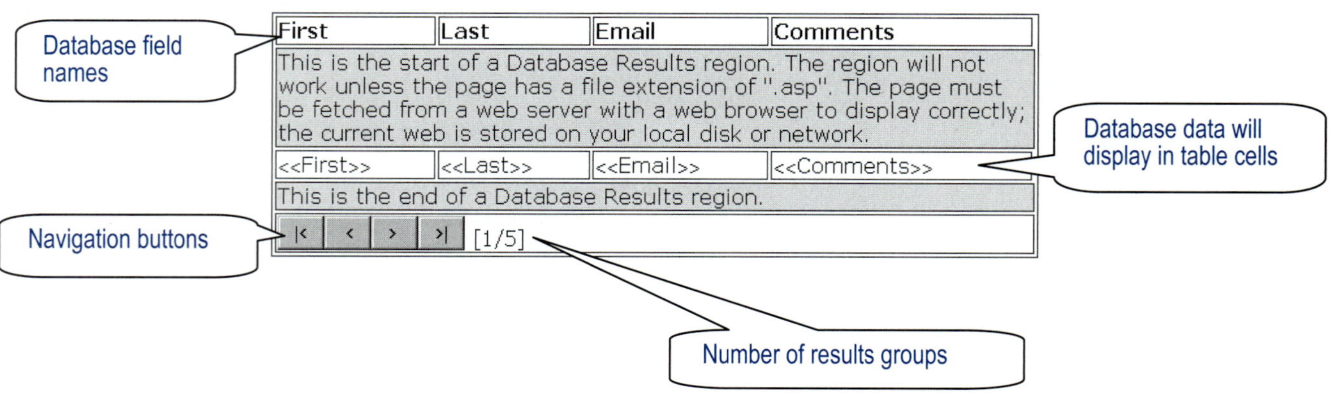

Query Database from FrontPage

- To make a Database Results region more useful for visitors, the Web designer can add a search form to the page to query the database.
- The designer adds the search form during the process of inserting a Database Results region.
- The designer selects a field (or fields) from the database to use for the search form. When a visitor types in the search form a value that appears in that field, the results region displays only the records that match the value in the search form.
- To insert a searchable Database Results region, start the Database Results Wizard and specify the database connection and the desired table.
- In Step 3 of the Database Results region, click the More Options button. In the More Options dialog box click the Criteria button.
- The Criteria dialog box shows fields that will be used for the search. To set up criteria for a search, click the Add button to open the Add Criteria dialog box (see illustration below).

Specify criteria for the search

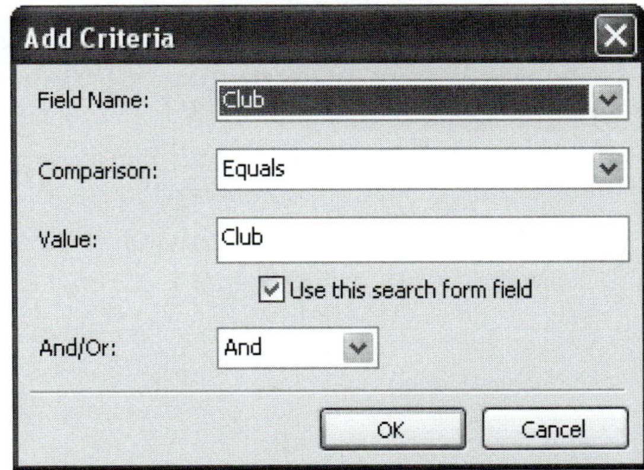

- Choose the field for the search. FrontPage automatically suggests the Equals comparison and a value the same as the field name.
  - ✓ *Accepting these defaults means that the search text a visitor enters for a field must match an entry in that field exactly for FrontPage to display the record.*
- Available comparisons depend on the type of field chosen for the search. Choosing a comparison other than Equals filters records in specific ways.
  - ✓ *For example, choosing the Greater Than comparison for a Last Name field allows the user to type a letter such as H to see all records in which the last name begins with H or a letter after H in the alphabet.*
- The author can select more than one field to search by continuing to add criteria to the Criteria dialog box. When using more than one field, the author must specify the And or Or operator (see illustration below).

Specify more than one field to search

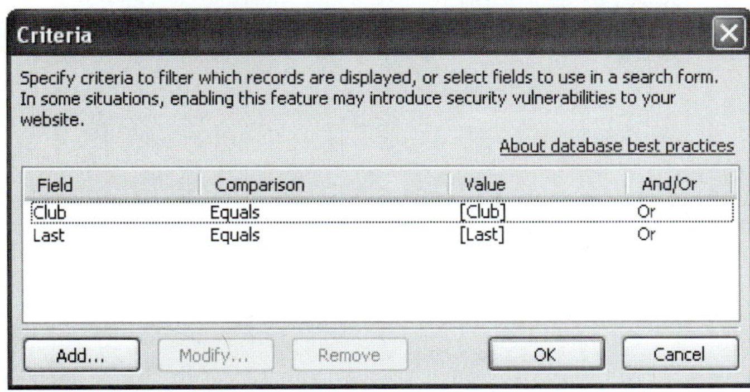

  - ✓ *Use And to display only records where both criteria are met; use Or to display records meeting either criterion.*
- After setting up criteria, the author can also choose to sort the search results by a particular field.
- Click the Ordering button in the More Options dialog box to display the Ordering dialog box (see illustration below). Choose a field and click the Add>> button to sort by that field.

Sort search results

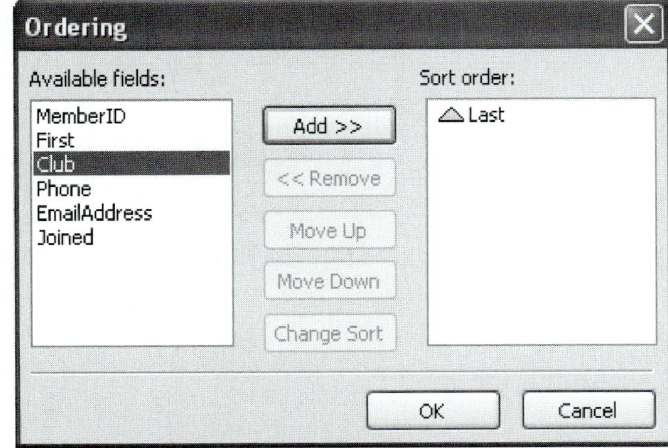

- After choosing criteria for the search and setting ordering options, the designer completes the Database Results Wizard just as for any Results region.

Procedures

Import Database

1. Click **File** .... Alt+F
2. Click **Import** .... M
3. Click [Add File...] .... Alt+A
4. Use **Look in** box to locate folder of file to import.
5. Click file to import.
6. Click [Open] .... Alt+O
7. Click [OK] in Import dialog box.
8. Create database connection by accepting default name (Database1) or supplying new name.
9. Choose to store database in fpdb folder.
10. Verify database after import:
    a. Click **Tools** .... Alt+T
    b. Click **Site Settings** I
    c. Click **Database** tab.
    d. Click name of database to verify.
    e. Click [Verify] ... Alt+V

Insert Database Results Region

1. Click **Insert** .... Alt+I
2. Click **Database** .... D
3. Click **Results** .... R

In Database Results Wizard

4. Specify database connection for results region in Step 1 of the Wizard and click [Next >].
   ✓ *Or create new connection if desired.*
5. Choose table from database in Step 2 and click [Next >].
6. Click [Edit List...] in Step 3 to choose fields to display in results region.
   - Remove a field by selecting it and clicking [<< Remove].
   - Return a removed field to the list by selecting it and clicking [Add >>].
7. Click [Next >].
8. Choose to display records as a table, list, or drop-down list and click [Next >].
9. Choose to display records together or in groups and click [Finish].
10. If necessary, save page containing the Results region as an ASP page.

Query Database from FrontPage

1. Start the Database Results Wizard.
2. Specify database connection for results region in Step 1 of the Wizard.
3. Choose table from database in Step 2.
4. Click [More Options...] in Step 3.
5. Click [Criteria...].
6. Click [Add...].
7. Select field name from **Field Name** drop-down list.
8. Choose **Comparison** option if desired.
9. Click [OK] twice to return to More Options dialog box.
10. Click [Ordering...] if desired.
11. Click field to sort results by and click [Add >>].
12. Continue with Database Results Wizard.
13. If necessary, save page as ASP page.

Exercise Directions

1. Start FrontPage 2003.
2. Open **Ariel**.
3. Import the **Arielbooks.mdb** database file from the Data folder. Name the database connection **Ariel** and store the database in the fpdb folder.
4. Verify the database connection.
5. Open **contactinfo.htm**.
6. Insert a Database Results region below the text on this page as follows:
   - Use the Ariel database connection.
   - Choose the Contact table in the database.
   - In Step 3 of the Wizard, edit the field list to remove the ID and List fields.
   - Choose to display the Results region as a table.
   - Choose to display the records in groups of 5.
7. Rename the **contactinfo.htm** page as **contactinfo.asp**.
8. Change the table properties for the database results region to apply a white background.
9. Publish the Web site as **arielinside**. Close the Ariel Web site and open **arielinside** from the server.
10. Preview the Web site and view the database results on the Web site Contacts page. Display the second page of results using the [>] navigation button.
11. In FrontPage, rename **bookclubs.htm** as **bookclubs.asp**.
12. With the insertion point below the last paragraph of text on **bookclubs.asp**, start the Database Results Wizard. Insert a searchable Results region as follows:
    - Use the Ariel database connection.
    - Choose the Members table in the database.
    - In Step 3 of the Wizard, edit the field list to remove the MemberID and Joined fields to limit the results to the most important fields from the database table.
    - Still in Step 3, click **More Options**, then click Criteria, then click Add to begin the process of setting up the query.
    - Select the Club field from the Field Name drop-down list because you want users to be able to search for members who belong to specific clubs, such as Science Fiction.
    - Click **OK** twice to return to the More Options dialog box and click **Ordering**. Click the **Last** field and click the **Add>>** button. This will display records that match the search criterion in alphabetical order by last name.
    - Click **OK** twice and continue with the Database Results Wizard, accepting the defaults in the last two dialog boxes.
13. Apply a white background to the database results table.
14. Save the **bookclubs.asp** page and preview it in the browser.
15. Test the search form by displaying all book club members in the Science Fiction book club.

    ✓ *Type Science Fiction in the Club form field and click Submit Query. Your results region should display seven club members on two different pages.*
16. Your page should look like Illustration A.
17. Close the browser.
18. Close the Web site.
19. Exit FrontPage 2003.

Illustration A

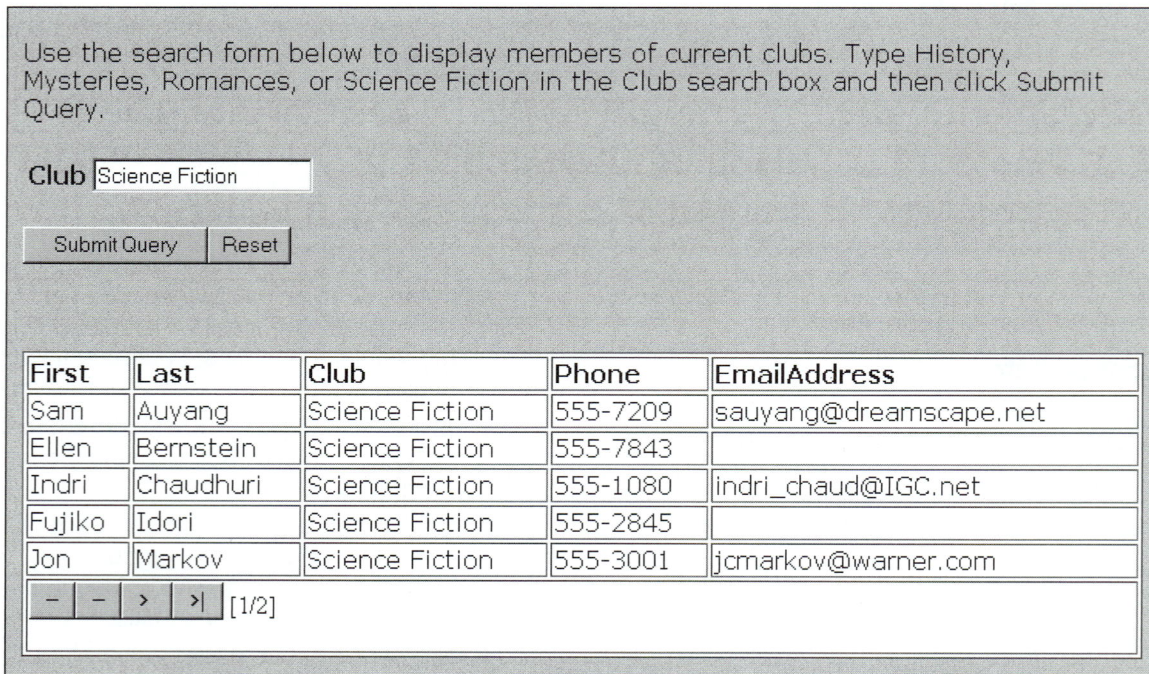

First	Last	Club	Phone	EmailAddress
Sam	Auyang	Science Fiction	555-7209	sauyang@dreamscape.net
Ellen	Bernstein	Science Fiction	555-7843	
Indri	Chaudhuri	Science Fiction	555-1080	indri_chaud@IGC.net
Fujiko	Idori	Science Fiction	555-2845	
Jon	Markov	Science Fiction	555-3001	jcmarkov@warner.com

On Your Own

1. Start FrontPage 2003.
2. Open **Wedding**.
3. Import the **wedding.mdb** database file from the Data folder. Name the database connection **Wedding** and store the database in the fpdb folder.
4. Verify the database connection.
5. Rename **lodgings.htm** as **lodgings.asp**.
6. Open **lodgings.asp** and insert a searchable Database Results region below the text as follows:
   - Use the Wedding database.
   - Use the Lodgings table.
   - Use all fields from the database table.
   - Use the Accommodations field as the criteria for the search.
   - Order the results by the Name field.
   - Use a table for the results region.
   - Display all records together rather than in groups.
7. Publish the Web site as **weddingweb** and preview the Lodgings page.
8. Test the search form by finding lodgings in the Moderate category.
9. The text in some of the fields wraps to several lines. In the server-based **weddingweb**, change the font of the headings and results text to 10 point.

   ✓ *Place the pointer just to the left of a row until the pointer becomes a small, black, left-pointing arrow and then click to select all cells in the row.*
10. Save the page and refresh it in the browser to check the modified font size.
11. Close the browser.
12. Close the Web site
13. Exit FrontPage 2003.

Exercise 50

◆ **About Database Interface Wizard**
◆ **Add Database Interface to Web Site**
◆ **Modify Database Interface Pages**
◆ **Work with Database Editor**

On the Job

The Database Interface Wizard creates Web pages that can be used to manage a database even if the database program is not available. The Wizard can create a login page for security and pages that allow the user to add, edit, and delete records in a database from the browser.

In this exercise, you will use the Database Interface Wizard to set up an interface to manage employee records for Ariel Books. You will add interface pages, modify form fields, and format the interface pages. Finally, you will add, edit, and delete records in the browser.

Terms

Database Editor
A Database Interface element that allows users to view, insert, edit, and delete records from a database.

Database Interface Wizard
Feature in FrontPage that creates Web pages used to manage database records.

Notes

About Database Interface Wizard

- The **Database Interface Wizard** is a FrontPage feature that creates Web pages which allow a Web user to manage a database from the browser.
- The advantage of using the Database Interface Wizard is that the Web author does not require access to a database program to set up and manage database records.
- As for a discussion group, the Database Interface Wizard can create interface pages in a new, empty Web site or can add the interface pages to an existing Web site.
- The Database Interface Wizard can set up three interface objects:
  - A Results Page similar to a Database Results region that shows records from the database on a Web page.
  - A Submission Form like any other FrontPage form that contains fields used to enter data in the database.
  - A **Database Editor** frames page that shows all database records in a table and allows the user to add, edit, and delete records in a secondary frame.

Add Database Interface to Web Site

- Start the Database Interface Wizard from the Web Site Templates dialog box.

  ✓ *Open the Web Site Templates dialog box from the New task pane or click the Create a new normal page down arrow and click Web Site.*

- The Wizard gives the Web developer the option of creating a new database, using an existing database connection, or using a sample database connection.
  - If the developer chooses to create a new database, the Wizard asks for a name and then allows the developer to define field names and form field types.
  - If the developer uses an existing database connection, he or she can select the connection and the table within the database.
- When the Wizard lists the field names and form field types (see illustration below), the developer can change the form field type by clicking the Modify button.

Change form field types

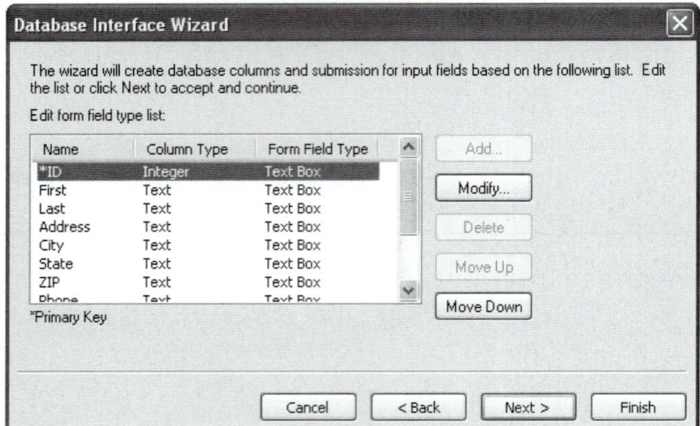

- A Text Box form field type can be changed to a Drop-Down Box or Option Buttons, and the developer can choose how many options to create.
- Next the Wizard asks what interface pages to create (see illustration at the top of the next column): a Results Page, a Submission Form, or a Database Editor.

  ✓ *The developer can choose to create any or all of these pages. The Database Editor, however, allows the user to submit and display data so the other two pages are not essential.*

Choose interface pages to create

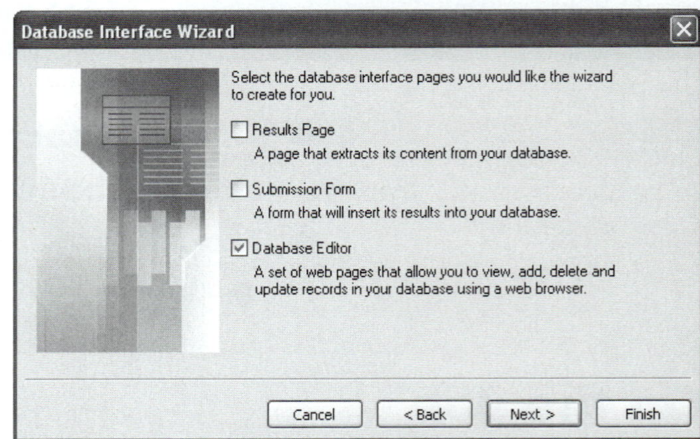

- The Wizard allows the Web developer to set up a user name and password that will be required to access the records (see illustration below) if the developer has chosen to create a Database Editor.

  ✓ *To allow anybody to access the records, select the Don't protect my Database Editor with a username and password checkbox.*

Specify user name and password

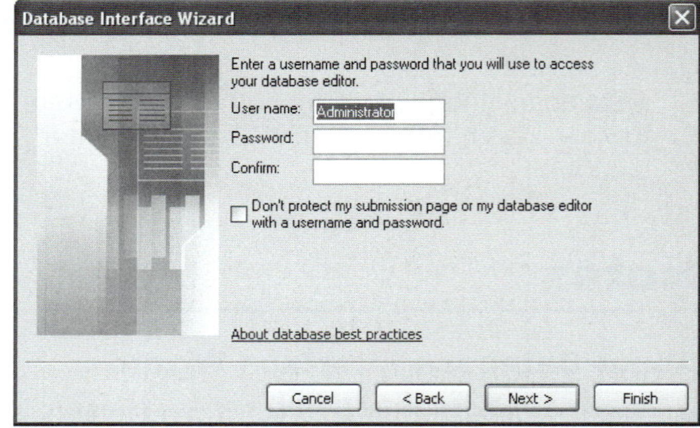

- The Wizard then creates all interface pages and stores them within a folder (such as Ariel_interface). This folder displays in the Folder List along with the rest of the Web site's pages.

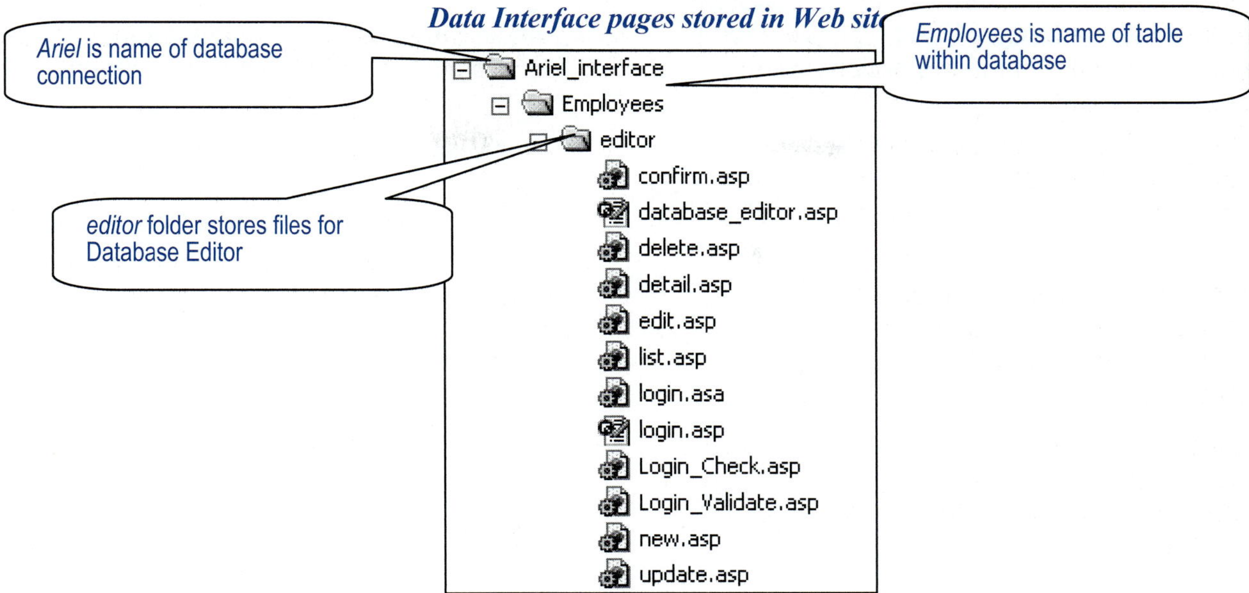

Data Interface pages stored in Web sit

- The files created depend on what interface pages the designer asked the Database Interface Wizard to create (see illustration above).
  - ✓ *Note that most interface pages are Active Server Pages.*
- The illustration above shows the files created when an author chooses to create only the Database Editor:
  - The database_editor.asp page is the frames page that displays the list.asp page in the top frame and various other pages (confirm.asp, edit.asp, delete.asp, detail.asp, and so on) in the bottom frame.
  - The list.asp page contains a Database Results region that displays records currently stored in the database.
  - The login.asp page is created if the author chose to protect the Database Editor with a user name and password.
  - The new.asp page is the Submission Form page used to enter data into the database.
  - Other pages, such as confirm.asp and delete.asp, display in the bottom frame of the frames page to pass messages or allow the author to edit records.

Modify Database Interface Pages

- Database Interface pages are formatted by default using table structures and distinctive headings.
- These pages can be modified like other Web pages by adding a theme or applying text or paragraph formatting.
- If the Database Interface has been added to an existing Web site, the author should also create links to an interface page (such as the login.asp or database_editor.asp page).
  - ✓ *If the author creates more than one interface object (such as a Submission Form and a Results Page), the interface pages include links to each other.*
- The author might also need to adjust some form fields on the new.asp and edit.asp pages.
- Modify form fields just as in any FrontPage form.
- The illustration below shows a portion of the new.asp page. Option buttons have been inserted for a field that originally had Yes or No entries. Note that the default labels for the option buttons are Option 1 and Option 2.

Modify form fields as in any form

Hired

<%=Date%>

Salary

○ Option 1

○ Option 2

- To make this form more meaningful, the author should change the Option 1 and Option 2 labels to Yes and No and change the option button values to match the labels.
  - ✓ *Note also that the Hired field contains an initial value that might be confusing to users. This value can deleted in the Text Box Properties dialog box.*

Work with Database Editor

- The Submission Form and Results Page interface pages work very similarly to other FrontPage forms and Database Results regions.
- The Database Editor, however, provides a neat and efficient system for managing database records within a single frames page.
- The illustration below shows the Database Editor displaying the Submission Form in the bottom frame.
- The user can perform a number of tasks in this frames page:
  - Drag the horizontal frame border down to show the Database Results region containing records from the database.
  - Click the Add New Record button to open the Submission Form in the bottom frame.
    - ✓ *After the user has filled out the form and clicked the submit button, a confirmation page displays.*
  - Click in the checkbox to the left of a record to select the record.
  - Click the Delete Selected Records button to remove all records with checkmarks.
    - ✓ *The Database Editor asks the user to confirm the delete and then removes records from the database.*
  - Click a record's link to display the record's details page in the bottom frame. The author can click the Edit button in this page to modify a record or the Delete button to delete it.

Database Editor frames page

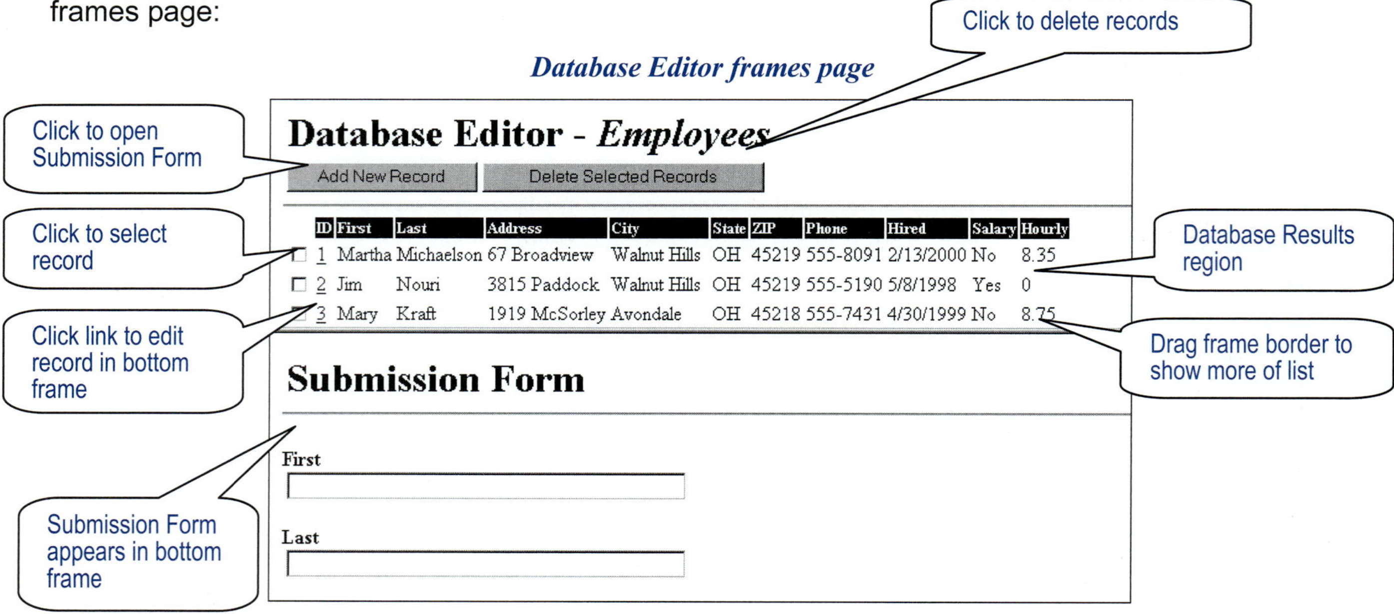

Procedures

Add Database Interface to Web Site

1. Click **File** .... Alt+F
2. Click **New** .... N
3. Click **More Web site templates** link in New task pane.

OR

a. Click (**Create a new normal page** button) down arrow.

b. Click **Web Site** .... W

4. Click **Database Interface Wizard**.
5. Type name for new Web site in *Specify the location of the new Web site* box.

   OR

   Click to select **Add to current Web site** checkbox.
6. Click **OK** .... **Enter**

In Database Interface Wizard

1. Choose to create new database or select existing database connection and click [Next >].
2. Supply name for new database or choose table for existing database and click [Next >].
3. Add and modify fields as necessary:
   - For a new database, supply field names and form field types.
   - For an existing database, modify form field types if desired by clicking [Modify...] and choosing new field type from *Form field input type* drop-down list.
4. Click [Next >].
5. Choose pages to create (Results Page, Submission Form, and/or Database Editor) and click [Next >].
6. Type a User name and Password, and then confirm password if using the Database editor.

   OR

   Select Don't protect my Database Editor with a username and password checkbox.
7. Click [Finish].

Modify Database Interface Pages

To modify interface page appearance

- Apply theme, if desired.
- Change fonts, font sizes, font styles, or font colors of any text on any interface page.
- Add interface page to navigation structure to include page in FrontPage link bars.
- Modify appearance of Database Results region.

To modify interface page properties

- Add link(s) to interface page(s) to link to other pages in Web site, if desired.
- Modify form fields by changing properties of individual fields.

Work with Database Editor

With Web site open in browser

1. Log in to Database Editor, if necessary.
2. Drag horizontal frame border to view more records in top frame.
3. Add new record:
   a. Click [Add New Record] button to open Submission Form in bottom pane.
   b. Fill in form fields in Submission Form and click [OK].
4. Edit record:
   a. Click a record's link to see details of record in bottom frame.
   b. Edit record in bottom frame by clicking [Edit] and then making changes in form fields.
   c. Click [OK] when finished.
5. Select records by clicking in checkboxes to left of record.
6. Delete records:
   a. Click [Delete Selected Records]
   b. Confirm deletion by clicking [OK].

Exercise Directions

1. Start FrontPage 2003.
2. Open **arielinside**.
3. Publish the Web site as **arielemployees**. Close **arielinside** and open **arielemployees** from the server.
4. Start the Database Interface Wizard and add the Database Interface to the current Web site:

   ✓ *Make sure to select the Add to current Web site check box in the Web Site Templates dialog box after you select the Database Interface Wizard.*

   - Choose the existing Ariel database connection.
   - Choose the Employees table.
   - Change form field type for the Salary field to Option Button with 2 choices.
   - Select only the Database Editor checkbox (deselect Results Page and Submission Form).
   - Enter the Username **Ariel** and the password **books**. Confirm the password by typing it again in the Confirm text box.
   - Click **Finish**.
5. Display interface pages by expanding the Ariel_interface folder, the Employees folder, and the editor folder in the Folder List.
6. Add the **login.asp** page to the Web site's navigation structure and change its page title to **Employees Login**.
7. Open the **login.asp** page and make the following changes:
   - Change the heading font to Verdana.
   - Enlarge the cell that contains the heading so the heading will appear on one line.

8. Open the **list.asp** page and make the same changes to the heading as on the **login.asp** page.
9. On the **list.asp** page, click just to the right of the *Delete Selected Records* button and press **Spacebar** once or twice (you may need to enlarge the cell first). Insert a hyperlink using text that says **Ariel Home** and links to **index.htm** or **Default.htm**. Format the text as desired.

   ✓ *This link will appear in a frames page, so make sure to set the target frame correctly to display Default.htm as a whole page.*

10. Open **new.asp** and change the heading to darkest blue Verdana 18 point and, if necessary, expand the table cell so the heading fits on one line.
11. Make the following changes in the submission form on **new.asp**:
    - Remove the entire initial value in the Hired form field. (Double-click the form field to open the field's properties so you can delete the initial value.)
    - Change the Option 1 label to **Yes** and the Option 2 label to **No**. Remove the paragraph break so these two options appear on the same line and insert several spaces between them.
    - Change the Yes option button value to **Yes** and the No option button value to **No**.
    - Remove the empty paragraph below the option buttons.
12. Also change the option button properties on the **edit.asp** page (and make sure neither option button is selected).
13. Save and close all pages.
14. Open **index.htm** or **Default.htm** and preview the page in the browser.
15. Click the **Employees Login** link to open the Database Editor Login page and type the username (**Ariel**) and the password **(books**).
16. Drag the frame border down to see all records in the Database Results region in the top frame.
17. Click the Add New Record button.
18. Insert the following information for a new employee:

First	Sarah
Last	Schuster
Address	135 Anniston
City	Avondale
State	OH
ZIP	45218
Phone	555-7703
Hired	[Use last Monday's date]
Salary	No
Hourly	8.35

19. Click **OK** and check the results region to see the new record (go to the second page of results to see the record).
20. Leni Patterson and Mike Foster have both left Ariel Books. Click in the checkboxes to the left of their names and then click Delete Selected Records.
21. The bottom frame shows the two records and asks if you are sure you want to delete the records (see Illustration A).
22. Click **OK** to delete the records.
23. Close the browser.
24. Close the Web site.
25. Exit FrontPage 2003.

Illustration A

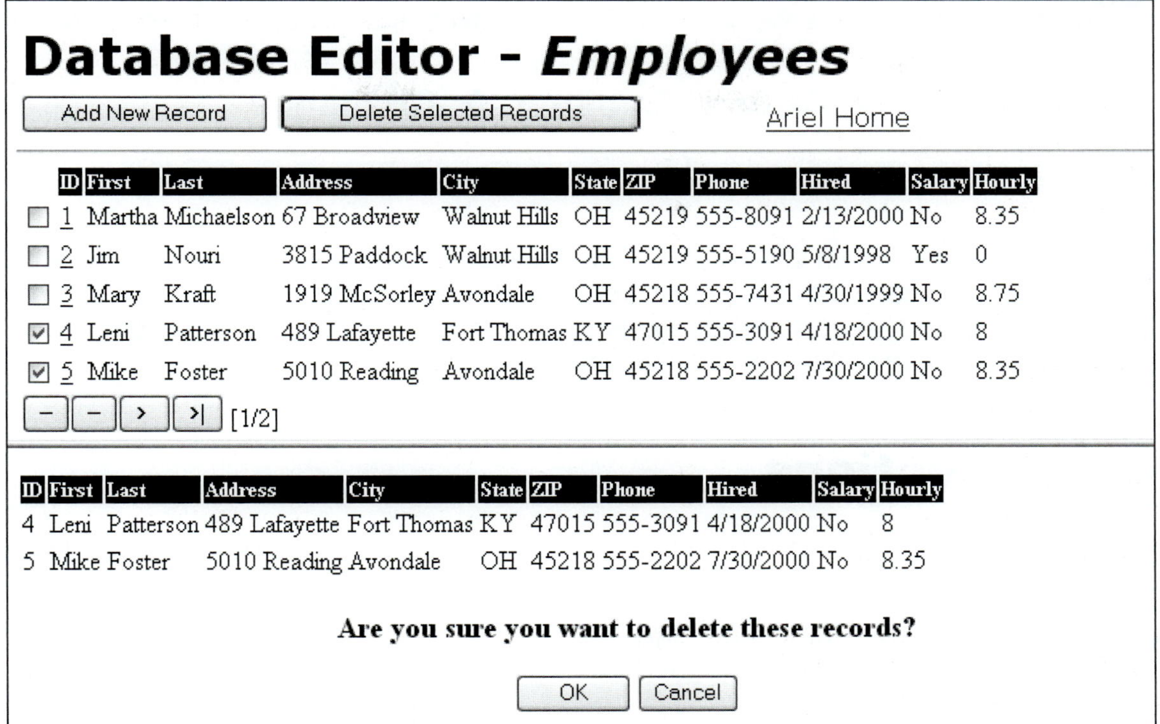

On Your Own

1. Start FrontPage 2003.
2. Open **weddingweb** and publish it as **weddingguests**. Close **weddingweb** and open **weddingguests** from the server.
3. Start the Database Interface Wizard and add the Database Interface to the current Web site:
   - Choose the existing Wedding database connection.
   - Choose the Guests table.
   - Change form field type for the Attending field to Option Button with 2 choices.
   - Select only the Database Editor checkbox (deselect Results Page and Submission Form).
   - Do not set a username or password for the database.
   - Click **Finish**.
4. Add the **database_editor.asp** page to the Web site's navigation structure and change its page title to **Guests**.
5. Modify the interface pages as desired to make them look similar to the other pages in the Web site and present data attractively.
6. Insert a link on the **list.asp** page to **index.htm** or **Default.htm**.

   ✓ *This link will appear in a frames page, so make sure to set the target frame correctly for Default.htm.*
7. Modify the **new.asp** and **edit.asp** page option buttons to have more meaningful labels and values.
8. Save and close all pages.
9. Open **index.htm** or **Default.htm** and preview the page in the browser.
10. Click the Guests link to open the Guests page.
11. Drag the frame border down if necessary to see all records in the Database Results region in the top frame.
12. Click the Add New Record button and add your name and address information. You will be attending the wedding.
13. Mr. and Mrs. Burroughs have discovered they cannot attend after all. Select and delete their record.
14. Close the browser.
15. Close the Web site.
16. Exit FrontPage 2003.

Exercise 51

◆ **Critical Thinking** ◆ **Challenge**

In this exercise, you will work on a Web site for CyberExchange, an online "marketplace" where visitors can trade information and computer equipment. You will add and customize a discussion group for the Web site, import a database, send survey form results to the database, display database data on a Web page, and create a database interface to manage mailing list data.

Exercise Directions

1. Start FrontPage 2003.
2. Open **Exchange**.
3. Publish the Web site as **exchangeweb**. Close **Exchange** and open **exchangeweb** from the server.
4. Start the Discussion Web Wizard to add a discussion group to the Web site. Use these settings:
   - Accept the default features for the discussion group.
   - Give the discussion group the title **CyberForum** and change the name of the discussion folder to **_disc1** if necessary.
   - Accept the *Subject, Comments* option for input fields.
   - Allow anyone to post articles.
   - Display articles from oldest to newest.
   - Choose **No** to avoid overwriting the home page.
   - Display only the Subject in the search form.
   - Choose the **No frames** option.
5. Display hidden folders and change the heading *CyberForum* to Heading 2 style on both header pages.
6. Add **disc1_toc.htm** to the navigation structure to the left of the Exchange page and change the title to **CyberForum**.
7. Open **index.htm** or **Default.htm** and create a link from the word *CyberForum* in the first bullet item to **disc1_toc.htm**.
8. From the browser, post the following articles to the CyberForum discussion group:

   Subject: Voice recognition

   From: Jenny C.

   Comments: Has anyone worked with voice recognition in Office? Is it worth pursuing?

   Subject: Networking

   From: Jim J.

   Comments: I'm interested in networking my home computers. Can anyone tell me the difference between a switch and a hub?
9. Reply to the Voice recognition article as follows:

   From: Terry G.

   Comments: Lots of people use it religously. You have to check your text pretty carefully, though, because you may end up with real words that aren't the right words.
10. Search the discussion group for the word *switch* and then display the article that contains that word.
11. Reply to the article as follows:

    From: Buzzer

    Comments: These are the same thing, I think.
12. Reply to Buzzer's article as follows:

    From: J.D.L.

    Comments: Any fool knows they're not the same!
13. Edit the discussion group articles as follows:
    - Locate the reply to the Voice recognition article. The author of this article typed *religously* instead of *religiously*. Correct the spelling.

- The last article posted (the reply to the Networking reply) is unnecessarily rude. Delete it.

14. Hide the hidden folders.
15. Import the **cyber.mdb** database from the Data folder and name the database connection **Cyber**.
16. Verify the database connection.
17. Open **whatsnew.htm**.
18. Open the Form Properties dialog box and specify form results as follows:
    - Send the form results to the Survey table in the Cyber database.
    - Click the **Saved Fields** tab and double-click each form field to associate it with a database field.
    - Click the **Additional Fields** tab and remove all additional fields.
19. Rename the **whatsnew.htm** page as **whatsnew.asp** and save it.
20. Preview **whatsnew.asp** in the browser and fill out the form using several different names and responses.
21. Open the Survey table from within FrontPage to see the form results added to the table.

    ✓ *Open the Survey table by first clicking the plus sign to the left of the fpdb folder and then double-clicking the Cyber.mdb database file. Then display the Tables objects and double-click Survey.*
22. Rename **exchange.htm** as **exchange.asp**.
23. Open **exchange.asp**. Insert a searchable Database Results region below the text as follows:
    - Use the Cyber database connection.
    - Use the Exchange table.
    - Remove the ID field from the Database Region.
    - Allow visitors to search using the Component field.
    - Order results by the Maker field.
    - Display the Results region as a list using the bullet list option and display all records together.
24. Preview the **exchange.asp** page and test the search field by searching for all Peripheral components. Your page should look like Illustration A.
25. Start the Database Interface Wizard and add interface pages to the current Web site as follows:
    - Use the Cyber database connection.
    - Use the List table.
    - Modify the Tips field to use Option Buttons with 2 choices.
    - Create only the Database Editor.
    - Set a username of **Cyber** and a password of **exchange**.
26. Add the **login.asp** page to the navigation structure and name it **List Login**.
27. On the **list.asp** page, add a link in the empty table cell to the right of the page's main heading to the **index.htm** or **Default.htm** page. Use your own judgment for the actual text of the link and its formatting.
28. Change the Option 1 and Option 2 option buttons on the **new.asp** and **edit.asp** pages to Yes and No labels and values.

    ✓ *Assign the name Tips and the value Yes for the first button and the name Tips and the value No for the second button. Make sure neither button is selected. Change the labels next to the option buttons to Yes for the first button and No for the second button.*
29. Format the interface pages as desired.
30. Preview **index.htm** or **Default.htm** in the browser and click the List Login link.
31. Add a new record to the e-mail list:

First:	Jake
Last:	Pantoliano
Email:	jakepanto@IGC.net
Tips:	No
32. Check the Results region in the top frame to locate the new record.

    ✓ You may need to display a new page to find the record.
33. John Schaefer has changed Internet service providers. Edit his record to change his e-mail address to johnschaefer@msn.com.
34. Fran Valentine and Isaac Weber have requested that their names be removed from the e-mail list. Select and delete these records.

    ✓ *Because these names are on different Results pages, you will have to select and delete them one at a time.*
35. Your Database Editor should look similar to Illustration B.
36. Close the browser.
37. Close the Web site.
38. Exit FrontPage 2003.

Illustration A

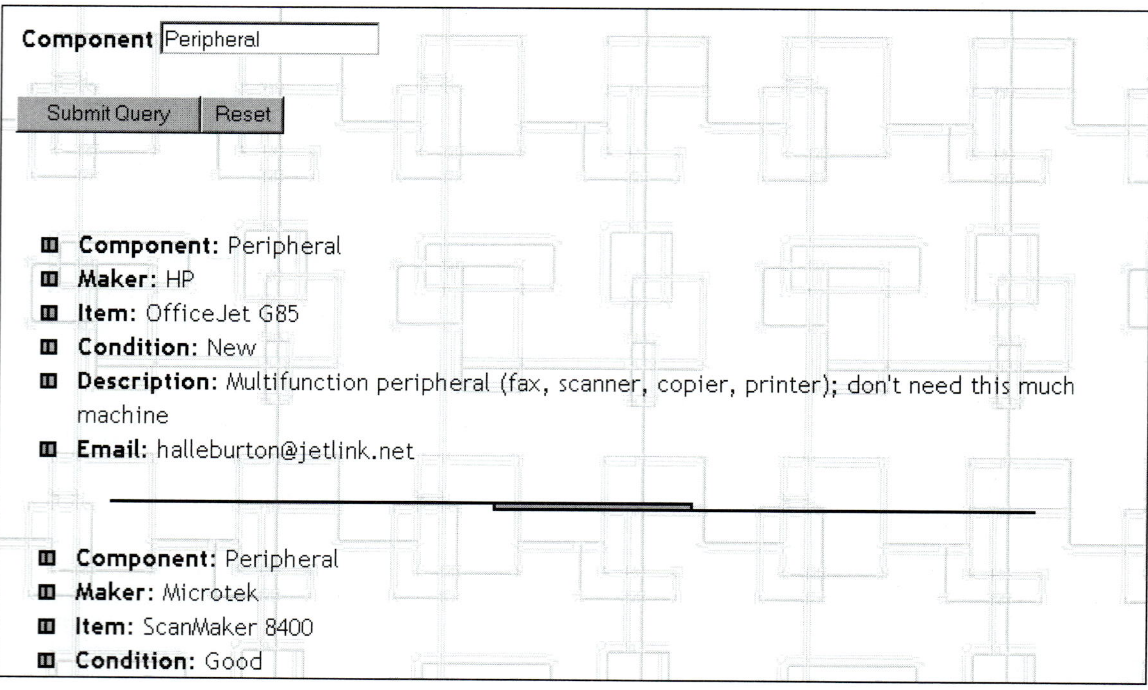

Illustration B

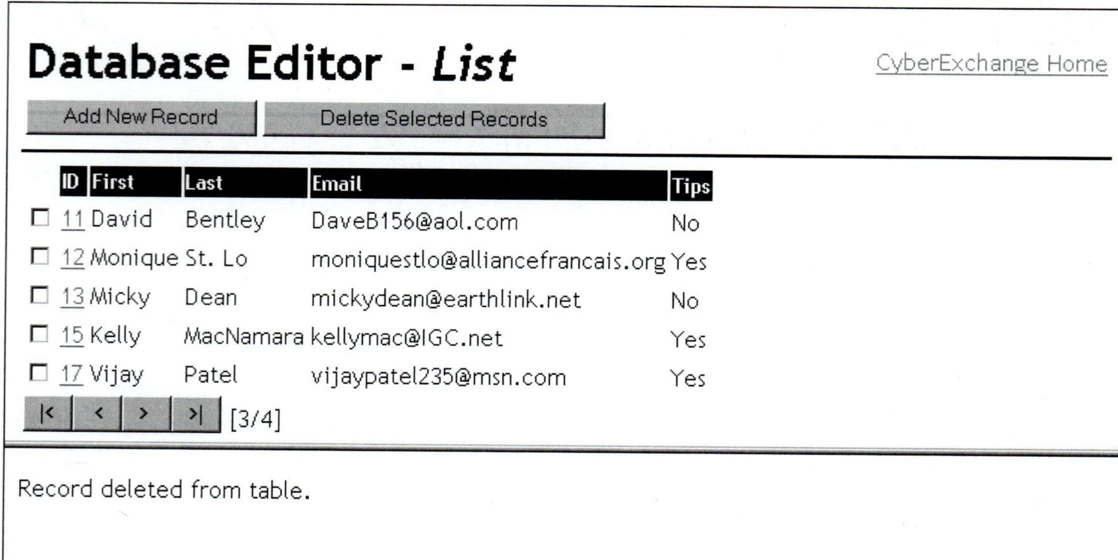

Challenge Exercise

1. Break into groups of three or four based on a common elective course (fine arts, foreign language, physical education, health, etc.).
2. Set up a discussion group to discuss a topic or multiple topics that have been covered in that course.
3. Each person in the group should start at least one thread; others should participate in each started thread.
4. Invite other students in your class to join the discussion groups.
5. Keep the discussion group running through the remainder of the course.

LESSON 10

Web-Site Management

Exercise 52

◆ Create Folder to Manage Files
◆ Create Subsite from Folder ◆ Set Permissions for Subsite
◆ Check Pages In and Out (Source Control)

On the Job

FrontPage includes a number of features that can be used to organize a Web site and manage Web-site tasks. An author can create a folder to hold related pages. Folders within Web sites can become subsites with their own formats and permissions. To manage Web-site editing, a Web-site administrator can turn on source control to require authors of a multi-author Web site to check pages in and out.

In this exercise, you will work with a Web site for Madison Wildlife Center. You will create a folder for related pages, convert the folder to a subsite, and learn how to set permissions for the subsite. You will turn on source control to prevent more than one person from editing pages at the same time.

Terms

permissions
Authorizations that specify who can create, modify, administer, or visit a Web site.

root Web site
The top-level Web site that contains a subsite.

source control
Security system that requires editors of a multi-author Web site to check pages out before working on them and check them back in after finishing edits.

subsite
A Web site nested within another Web site.

Notes

Create Folder to Manage Files

- By default, FrontPage Web sites contain several folders used to store related files or pages.
- The images folder, for example, is supplied with every new Web site to store pictures.
- As a developer builds a Web site, he or she may create a number of related pages. To avoid cluttering the Folder List, the Web developer can create a folder in which to store related pages.
- Create a new folder in Folders view by clicking the Create a new normal page down arrow and selecting Folder.

  ✓ *Or right-click in a blank area of the Folder List or Contents pane in Folders view and select New>Folder on the shortcut menu.*

- The new folder displays already selected so the developer can rename it as desired (see illustration at top of following page).
- After creating a new folder, the author can move pages into the folder by selecting them and dragging them on top of the folder.

New folder in Folders view

✓ *To select more than one page in Folders view or the Folder List, click the first, hold down Ctrl or Shift, and click additional pages. Release the Ctrl or Shift key before dragging the selected pages into the folder.*

Create Subsite from Folder

- A Web author can further organize pages in a Web site by creating a **subsite**. A subsite is a Web site nested within an existing Web site. The Web site in which a subsite is stored is called the **root Web site**.
- One of the easiest ways to create a subsite is to first create a folder for related pages and then convert the folder to a subsite.
- Convert a folder by right-clicking it in the Folder List and selecting Convert to Web on the shortcut menu.
- FrontPage displays a warning about the possible consequences of converting the folder (see illustration below).

Convert a folder to a subsite

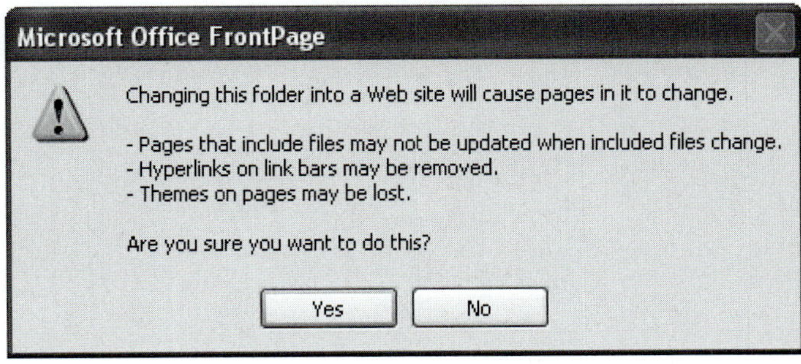

- After the conversion process, FrontPage displays the folder with the "world" symbol that indicates it stores a Web site (see illustration at the top of the next column).
- After creating a subsite, the author can establish a navigation structure in it separate from that of the root Web site.

Folder converted to subsite

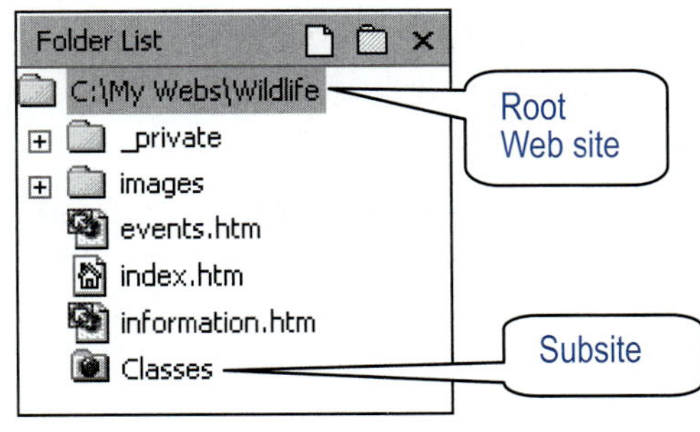

- Subsite pages can also be formatted with a theme or shared borders that will not apply to the root Web site.
- To open a subsite from the root Web site, double-click the subsite folder in the Folder List. A new version of FrontPage launches to display the subsite.
- A subsite can exist on its own on a server, with no link to its root Web site. Or, if the author wants a visitor to be able to navigate to and from a subsite, the subsite can be linked to the root Web site.
- To link *to* a subsite page, double-click the subsite folder in the Insert Hyperlink dialog box's list of pages and folders to display the contents of the subsite.

- To link *from* a subsite, use the Up One Folder button in the Insert Hyperlink dialog box to display the contents of the root Web site.
- When publishing a Web site after creating a subsite, the author must make sure to select the *Include subsites* checkbox in the Remote Web Site Properties dialog box (on the Publish tab) to include the subsite with other published pages.

Set Permissions for Subsite

- One of the chief reasons to create a subsite is for security, because subsites can have **permissions** different from those of the root Web site.
- Recall that three basic levels of permissions can be assigned to Web site users:
  - *Browsing* permission allows a visitor to view a published FrontPage Web site but make no changes to it.
  - *Authoring* permission allows a user to open and edit a published FrontPage Web site.
  - *Administering* permission allows a user to work with FrontPage extensions, set permissions for other users, and perform other administrative tasks.

✓ *Some servers, such as those using SharePoint extensions, may offer additional permission levels, such as Advanced Author or Contributor.*

- Moving sensitive Web pages into a subsite allows an author to set a more restrictive permission for those pages.
- An author's ability to set permissions for subsites depends on access to the server on which the root Web site and subsite are published.
- Different servers also have different systems for managing permissions.
- The illustration below shows how an author can specify unique permissions for a subsite on a SharePoint server site.

✓ *The Web site must be opened from the server for an author to view and/or set permissions.*

To set unique permissions for a subsite, click the subsite folder to select it and then use the Tools>Server>Permissions command on the menu bar.

Specify unique permissions for subsite

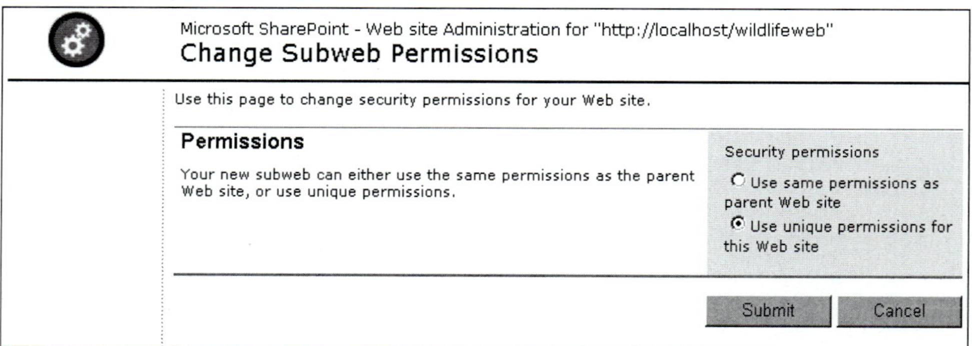

- After specifying that unique permissions are to be set for the subsite, the author can then set permissions for specific users by adding users or editing their current permissions, as shown in the illustration below.

  ✓ *A user with administering permission is usually in charge of managing users for a Web site.*

Add new user or change user permissions

Use this page to add a user or group to your site.

User

Choose whether you want to add a new user account or use an existing account or group.

◉ Add a new user with the following information:

User name: Ellen

Password: ********

Confirm password: ********

○ Add user or group name (For example, DOMAIN\name):

User Role

Choose a role or roles for this user.

Select a role for this user

☐ Administrator - View, add, and change all server content; manage server settings and accounts.

☐ Advanced author - View, add, and change pages, documents, themes, and borders; recalculate hyperlinks.

☑ Author - View, add, and change pages and documents.

☐ Contributor - View pages and documents, view and contribute to discussions.

☐ Browser - View pages and documents.

Check Pages In and Out (Source Control)

- Web sites are often managed by teams of authors who collaborate to keep the site up to date.
- In a collaborative setting where authors have the same permissions, it is possible for more than one author to open and work on a specific Web page at the same time, which can result in conflicting page versions.
- To control access to a Web site's pages so that only one author at a time can work on a specific page, the team can turn on **source control**.
- When source control is on, a Web developer must check a page out before working on it and check it back in after completing the work.
- A page that is checked out to one user cannot be opened by another.
- To turn on source control, use the Tools>Site Settings command on the menu bar. Select the *Use document check-in and check-out* checkbox on the General tab and select the location from which pages must be checked out.
- FrontPage warns the author that he or she has changed source control for the Web site and requires the author to confirm the change, as shown below.

Confirm source control

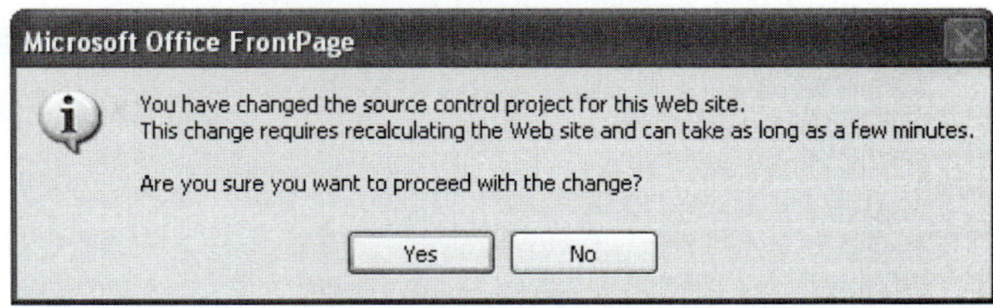

- Before an author can open a page, he or she must check it out.
- Check out a page by selecting it and using the Edit>Check Out command on the menu bar.

  ✓ *Or right-click the page and select Check Out from the shortcut menu, or double-click the page and then answer Yes when asked to check out the page.*

- A page that has been checked out shows a green checkmark to the left of the page name in the Folder List and in Folders view, as shown in the illustration below.

Checkmark indicates page checked out

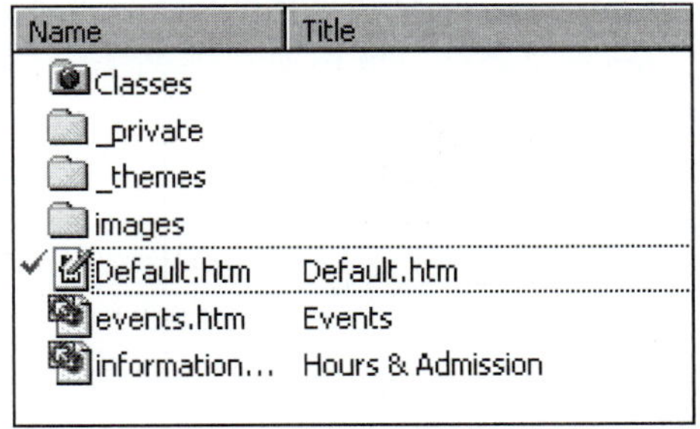

- After completing work on a page that has been checked out, the author must check the page in before another user can open it.
- Check a page in using the Edit>Check In command on the menu bar, or right-click the page and select Check In.
- When source control is turned on for a Web site that contains a subsite, only the root Web site pages are affected. The author must turn on source control within the subsite to affect the subsite's pages.

Procedures

Create Folder to Manage Files

In Page view or Folders view

1. Click (**Create a new normal page** button) down arrow.
2. Click **Folder** .... F

   OR

   - Right-click in blank area of Folders view or Folder List.
   - Click **New** .... N
   - Click **Folder** .... F
3. Type new name for folder.

Create Subsite from Folder

1. Right-click folder in Folder List.
2. Click **Convert to Web**......... W
3. Click Yes .... Alt+Y when asked to confirm the conversion.
4. Open a subsite by double-clicking subsite folder in Folder List.
5. Link from root Web site to a subsite page:
   a. Select text or picture to become link.
   b. Open Insert Hyperlink dialog box.
   c. Double-click subsite folder to display pages in subsite.
   d. Click subsite page to select it as the target.
6. Link from subsite to root Web page:
   a. Select text or picture to become link.
   b. Open Insert Hyperlink dialog box.
   c. Click (**Up One Folder** button) to open root folder.
   d. Click root Web page to select it as the target.

Set Permissions for Subsite

In published Web site

1. Click **Tools** .... Alt+T
2. Click **Server**......................... V
3. Click **Permissions** .... P

   ✓ *Dialog box or Web page that displays will vary by server.*
4. Click an option that allows you to set unique permissions for the subsite.
5. Add users or modify user permissions as permitted.

Check Pages In and Out (Source Control)

1. Click **Tools**................. Alt+T
2. Click **Site Settings**............. I
3. Click **General** tab, if necessary.
4. Select **Use document check-in and check-out** checkbox.
5. Click option of location from which pages can be checked out.
6. Check out page:
   a. Select page in Folder List or Folders view.
   b. Click **Edit** .... Alt+E
   c. Click **Check Out** .... O

   OR

   - Right-click page and click **Check Out** .... O

   OR

   - Double-click page to check out and click Yes when asked if you want to check it out.
7. Check in page:
   a. Save and close page after editing.
   b. Select page, if necessary.
   c. Click **Edit** .... Alt+E
   d. Click **Check In** I

   OR

   - Right-click page and click **Check In** I

Exercise Directions

1. Start FrontPage 2003.
2. Open **Wildlife**.
3. Create a new folder in the Web site and name it **Classes**.
   ✓ *For best results, create the folder in the Folders view, rather than in the Folder List.*
4. Drag the **classes.htm**, **classes3-7.htm**, **classes8-13.htm**, and **classesadults.htm** pages into the new folder.
5. Turn on source control for the local Web site.
6. Expand the Classes folder in the Folder List and check out the **classesadults.htm** page. Open the page.
   ✓ *Click Yes if you are asked if you want to open a newer version of the page.*
7. Locate the heading that reads *Our Environment—* and type **Wildlife Habitats** after the em dash in the heading.
8. Insert the following paragraph below the heading:

   You might think wildlife habitats exist only in faraway lands, but your own backyard is a habitat for many kinds of wildlife. Join us for coffee and conversation about preserving urban and rural habitats.
9. Insert the date for this program, **April 8**.
10. Save your changes and check the page in so someone else can open it.
11. Turn off source control.
12. Create a subsite from the **Classes** folder.
13. Publish the Web site as **wildlifeweb**, being sure to include the subsite.
    ✓ *Select the Include subsites check box on the Publishing tab in the Remote Web Site Properties dialog box before clicking the Publish Web site button.*
14. Close **Wildlife** and open **wildlifeweb** from the server.
15. Click the **Classes** subsite folder and, if permitted, set an authoring permission for yourself for this Web site.
16. Double-click the **Classes** subsite to open the subsite's pages. You may need to click the Refresh button to see the subsite files.
17. Open **classes.htm**. Notice that no theme is currently applied to the page.
18. Apply the Edge theme to all pages in the subsite.
19. Create a navigation structure in the subsite by dragging the **classes.htm** page into the Navigation pane and then adding the other three pages as child pages of this page.
20. On **classes.htm**, position the insertion point below the main heading and type **Back to Madison Wildlife Center**.
21. Link this text to the **index.htm** or **Default.htm** page in the root Web site.
    ✓ *Use the Up One Folder button in the Insert Hyperlink dialog box to display the pages in the root Web site, or type the complete path to the root Web site.*
22. Add link bars to the three child pages in the subsite. Set up the link bars to link to child level pages and the parent page.
23. Close the subsite and return to the version of FrontPage that shows the root Web site.
24. Open **index.htm** or **Default.htm** and preview this page in the browser. Click the Classes link to open the first page of the subsite. Your page should look similar to Illustration A.
25. Return to the first page of the root Web site.
26. Close the browser.
27. Close the Web site.
28. Exit FrontPage 2003.

Illustration A

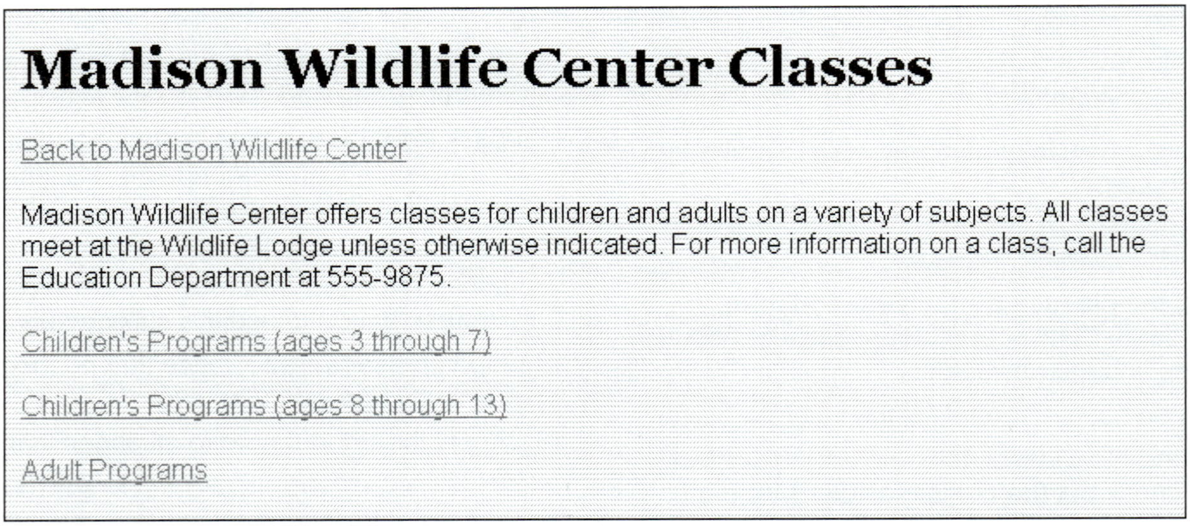

Madison Wildlife Center Classes

Back to Madison Wildlife Center

Madison Wildlife Center offers classes for children and adults on a variety of subjects. All classes meet at the Wildlife Lodge unless otherwise indicated. For more information on a class, call the Education Department at 555-9875.

Children's Programs (ages 3 through 7)

Children's Programs (ages 8 through 13)

Adult Programs

On Your Own

1. Start FrontPage 2003.
2. Open **Reinhardt**.
3. Create two folders to hold the pages for the Dayton and Springfield branches of the Reinhardt family.
4. Turn on source control.
5. Check out and open the **springfieldnews.htm** page. Add a paragraph of news information about the Springfield Reinhardts and some news about recent trips the Reinhardts have taken.
   - ✓ *Add a picture if desired using any picture in the Data folder or clip art. Save the picture in the Springfield folder.*
6. Check out and open the **springfieldgatherings.htm** page and add information about when and where the party can be found.
7. Check in all pages and turn off source control.
8. Create subsites from the Dayton and Springfield folders.
9. Publish the Web site as **reinhardtweb** with subsites.
10. Open **reinhardtweb**. If permitted, set an authoring permission for yourself for both subsites.
11. Open each subsite and format as desired. Provide links from page to page in the subsites and from each subsite to the **index.htm** or **Default.htm** page in the root Web site.
12. Test the Web site in the browser. (Don't worry about the missing picture on **daytonnews.htm**; you'll fix that problem in a future exercise.)
13. Close the browser.
14. Close the Web site.
15. Exit FrontPage 2003.

Exercise 53

◆ **Review Hyperlinks View** ◆ **Change Hyperlinks Display**
◆ **Recalculate Hyperlinks**

On the Job

FrontPage's Hyperlinks view displays links between pages in a Web site. Viewing links for each page allows an author to identify pages that are not correctly linked. An author can change the way items are displayed in Hyperlinks view using shortcut menu options and recalculate hyperlinks to correct linking problems.

In this exercise, you will continue working with the Wildlife Center Web site. You will check hyperlinks in the Web site to identify any linking problems. After recalculating hyperlinks, you will correct any remaining link problems.

Terms

broken link
A hyperlink whose target is not available in the current Web site.

recalculate hyperlinks
Check hyperlinks automatically using the FrontPage Recalculate Hyperlinks command.

Notes

Review Hyperlinks View

- Recall that FrontPage's Hyperlinks view gives the Web site developer a graphic representation of the way pages are linked in a Web site.
- A selected Web page appears in the middle of the Hyperlinks pane with links *from* other pages to the left and links *to* other pages to the right (see illustration below).

Hyperlinks view showing broken links

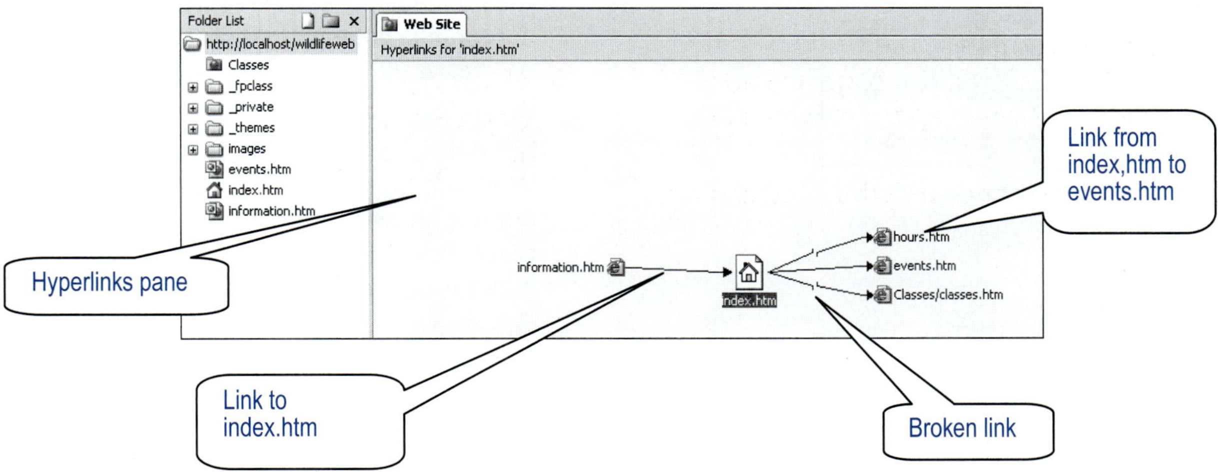

- A developer can identify some link problems easily in Hyperlinks view, such as the **broken links** shown in the illustration on the previous page.
- By viewing links to and from each page in the Web site, the developer can ensure that all pages are correctly linked with each other.

Change Hyperlinks Display

- After opening Hyperlinks view, the Web author must select a page from the Folder List to display at the center of the Hyperlinks pane.
- View links to a different page by selecting that page from the Folder List.
- If a page icon in Hyperlinks view includes a small plus sign, it has links to other pages. The Web author can click a plus sign to expand the page's links (see illustration below) and follow the links from page to page.

Expand a page's links by clicking plus sign

✓ *After it is clicked, the plus sign becomes a minus sign. Click the minus sign to collapse the links.*

- The Web author can also use commands on a shortcut menu (see illustration below) to modify the Hyperlinks view display.

Hyperlinks view shortcut menu

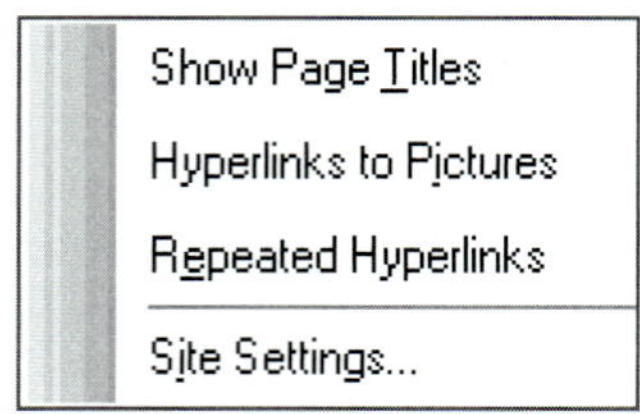

- These commands can be used to modify Hyperlinks view as follows:
  - Show Page Titles displays the page title, rather than the name, of each page in the Hyperlinks pane (see illustration below).
  - Hyperlinks to Pictures shows links to pictures embedded on the selected page (see illustration below).

  Lines to pictures are gray and end in a bullet rather than an arrow.

Page titles and links to pictures

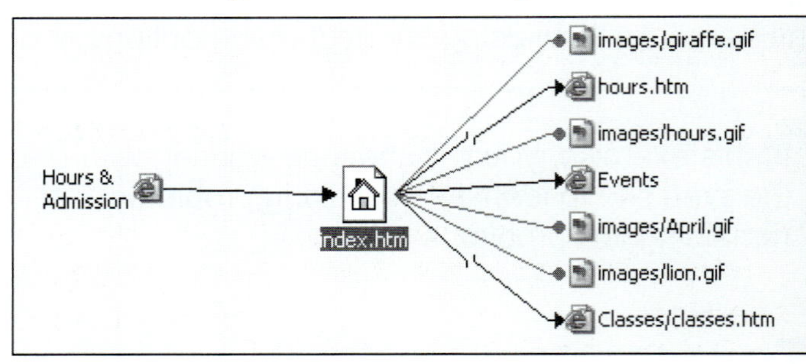

  - Repeated Hyperlinks shows all links to all pages, even if some links are duplicates (if, for example, both a picture and text link to a target page).

    ✓ *The Site Settings command on the shortcut menu opens the Site Settings dialog box, where authors can make global changes to Web site settings if desired.*

Recalculate Hyperlinks

- If a Web author has created links between pages manually, he or she can check and update links using the Recalculate Hyperlinks command.

  ✓ *If the author is using only FrontPage link bars, there is no need to recalculate links because FrontPage maintains the links automatically.*

- When FrontPage **recalculates hyperlinks**, it not only checks and repairs links throughout a Web site but performs other "housekeeping" chores as well, such as deleting unused themes, updating components, and synchronizing database information.

- For this reason, a Web author can recalculate hyperlinks regularly while creating and managing a Web site.
- To recalculate hyperlinks, in Hyperlinks view use the Tools>Recalculate Hyperlinks command on the menu bar.
- FrontPage displays the warning box shown at the right.
- Some other FrontPage operations, such as turning on source control, recalculate hyperlinks as part of their operations.

Recalculating hyperlinks

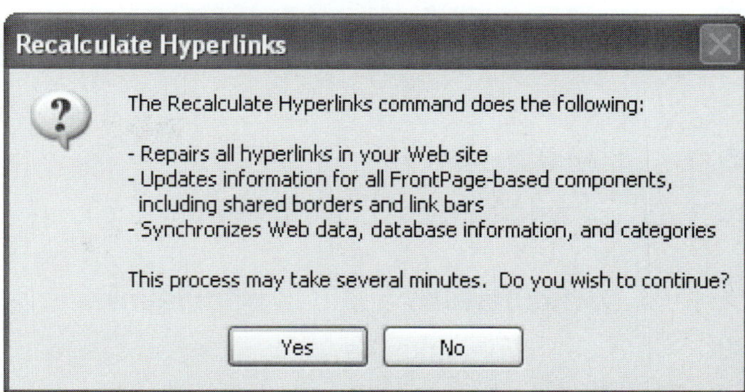

Procedures

Change Hyperlinks Display

1. Switch to Hyperlinks view.
2. Select page from Folder List to display links to and from that page.
3. Click plus sign in linked page to see links from that page.
4. Click minus sign to collapse links from a page.
5. Modify display by right-clicking in Hyperlinks pane to display shortcut menu:
   - Click **Show Page Titles** .... T to display page titles rather than page names.
   - Click **Hyperlinks to Pictures** .... I to show links to pictures embedded on selected page.
   - Click **Repeated Hyperlinks** .... E to show all duplicate links to all pages.

Recalculate Hyperlinks

1. Switch to Hyperlinks view.
2. Click **Tools** .... Alt+T
3. Click **Recalculate Hyperlinks** .... R
4. Click Yes .... Alt+Y

Exercise Directions

1. Start FrontPage 2003.
2. Open **wildlifeweb**.
3. Publish **wildlifeweb** as **wildlifelinks**, including the subsite.
4. Close **wildlifeweb** and open **wildlifelinks**
5. Switch to Hyperlinks view.
6. Click **index.htm** or **Default.htm** in the Folder List if necessary to display links to and from the home page. Notice the broken links to **hours.htm** and the Classes folder.
   ✓ *Recall that the Classes folder was converted to the Classes subsite.*
7. Recalculate hyperlinks to see if this command will fix the broken links. After recalculating, FrontPage fixes the broken link to the Classes subsite, but the link to **hours.htm** is still broken.
8. Show page titles in the Hyperlinks pane and note that there is a link from the Hours & Admission page to the home page but no link from the home page to Hours & Admission. Also note that the **hours.htm** page does not have a page title. In the Folder List, the **hours.htm** page has been renamed as **information.htm** without updating all links in the Web site.
9. Open **index.htm** or **Default.htm** in Page view and modify the links from the hourglass picture and *Hours & Admission* to open **information.htm** rather than **hours.htm**.
10. Save the page and return to Hyperlinks view. Notice that the broken link has been fixed.
11. Notice that there is a link from the home page to Events, but no link from Events to the home page.
12. Check the links to Events by selecting **events.htm** in the Folder List. Pages are linked to this page but not from this page.
    ✓ *You will see linked pages on the left of the events.htm page, but not to the right of the page, indicating that there are no links from events.htm to other pages.*
13. Open **events.htm** in Page view and create links in the navigation bar to **index.htm** or **Default.htm** and to **information.htm**.
14. Save the page and return to Hyperlinks view. Events now has links to and from the page.
15. Select **index.htm** or **Default.htm** in the Folder List and display links to pictures embedded on the page.
16. Display repeated hyperlinks. Notice that there are two links to the Hours & Admission and Events pages (from a picture and a text link) but only one link to the **classes.htm** page in the Classes subsite. There should be two links.
17. Open **index.htm** or **Default.htm** in Page view and check to see if there is a link to the **classes.htm** page in the Classes subsite from the lion picture. Create this link.
    ✓ *You may need to open the Classes subsite and refresh to display pages so you can create the link.*
18. Save the page and return to Hyperlinks view. There should now be two links to each page linked from the home page, as shown in Illustration A.
19. Open the Classes subsite and display hyperlinks to and from the **classes.htm** page. Click the plus sign in any page and follow links from page to page by expanding links.
20. Collapse all links.
21. Close both Web sites.
22. Exit FrontPage 2003.

Illustration A

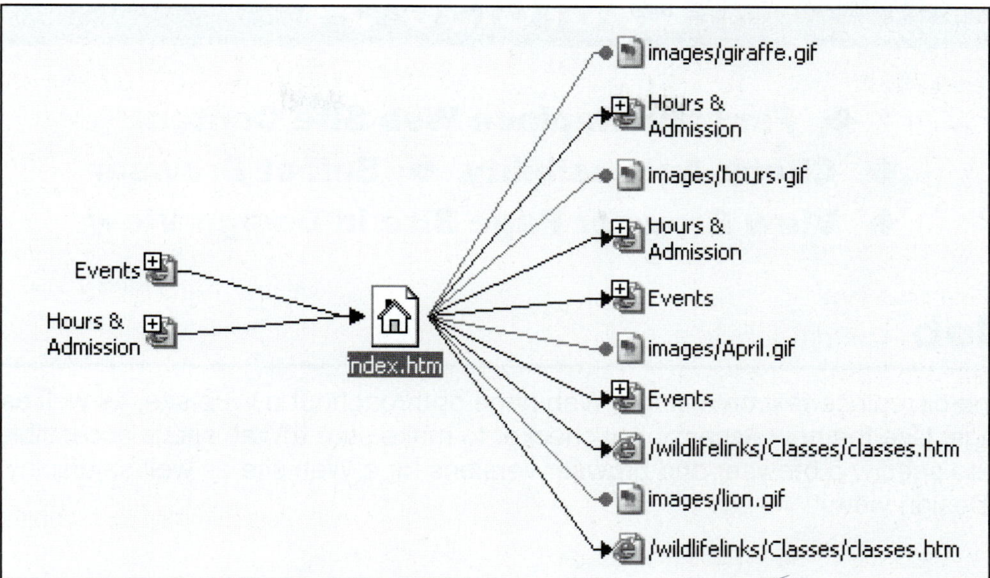

On Your Own

1. Start FrontPage 2003.
2. Open **reinhardtweb**.
3. Publish **reinhardtweb** as **reinhardtlinks**, including the subsites.
4. Close **reinhardtweb** and open **reinhardtlinks**.
5. Switch to Hyperlinks view and display links to the **index.htm** or **Default.htm** page.
6. Recalculate hyperlinks to repair the links to the subsite folders.
7. Open each subsite and display links to all pages and pictures.
8. Fix any broken links you find.
9. Close all open Web sites.
10. Exit FrontPage 2003.

Exercise 54

◆ **Find and Replace Web Site Content**
◆ **Check Accessibility** ◆ **Select Browser**
◆ **View Browser Page Size in Design View**

On the Job

An author can find or replace text on a single Web page or throughout a Web site, as well as find and replace HTML tags. Use the new Accessibility checker to make sure a Web site is accessible to all users. An author can also specify a browser and browser versions for a Web site as well as display browser size settings right in Design view.

In this exercise, you will work with a new Web site for Clifton Village. You find and replace text and HTML codes. Then you will check the site for accessibility problems. Finally, you will learn how to specify a browser for a Web site and se a browser size in Design view.

Terms

accessibility
Making sure a Web site or document can be used effectively by all users, including those with various vision or motor impairments.

World Wide Web Consortium (W3C)
A consortium of educational and business institutions that conducts research and suggests standards for the World Wide Web.

Notes

Find and Replace Web Site Content

- As a Web author builds a Web site, he or she might need to find or replace content on one or more Web pages.
- In FrontPage 2003, Web designers can use a robust find and replace feature that allows them to find or replace not only text, but also HTML tags.
- The Edit>Find or Edit>Replace command on the menu bar allows the author to locate or locate and replace text or tags on a single Web page or on all pages of a Web site.

  ✓ *Selecting either command opens the Find and Replace dialog box with the appropriate tab (Find or Replace) selected.*

Find and Replace Text

- Finding and replacing text in a Web site is a process very similar to finding and replacing in a word processing application.
- Type the word or phrase to find in the Find what box and choose to find the text in all Web pages, open pages, or the current page.
- To replace text, type the word or phrase to find in the Find what box and then type the replacement text in the Replace with box.
- The author can refine the Find or Replace operation by selecting the Match case or Find whole word only checkbox.
- The author may also choose to ignore whitespace differences or use regular expressions (similar to wildcards) to find patterns of text.

✓ *For example, use the regular expression race* to find race, races, raced, or racers throughout a Web site.*

- An author can also locate text that appears in source code by selecting the Find in source code checkbox.
- Specify whether to search the current page, open pages, or all pages of the site.
- Clicking the Find in Site button generates a list of pages that contain the word or phrase in the Find what box with red circles in the Status column, as shown in the illustration below.

List of pages where text in Find what box appears

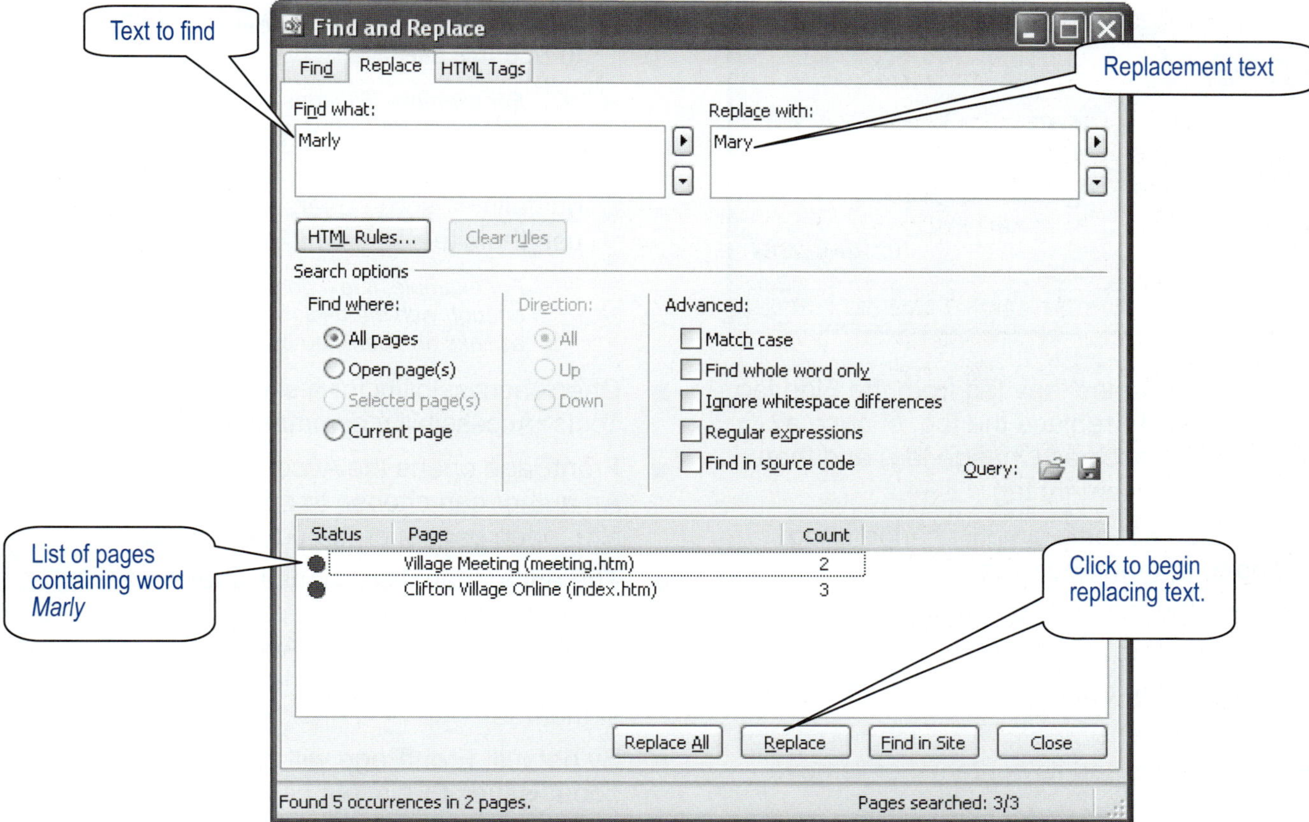

- Begin the process of finding text by double-clicking an item in the list. To begin a replace operation, click Replace or double-click the first item in the list.
- FrontPage opens the first page that contains the found text, highlights the found text, and allows the author to decide whether to replace the text.

  ✓ *If replacing, the author can also click the Replace All button, but using this button can be risky. To avoid unexpected replacements, use this button only when very sure of Web site content.*

- After the author replaces text on a page, FrontPage displays the Continue with next page? dialog box so the author can go on to the next page on the list or return to the list.

  ✓ *FrontPage allows the author to save and close each page after making a replacement.*

- After the author has replaced all occurrences of the text, the Find and Replace list shows yellow circles and the message *Edited* in the Status column.
- If the replacement operation is one that the author anticipates using again, he or she can save it as a query using the Save query icon in the Find and Replace dialog box.
- A saved query can then be opened in any Web site using the Open query icon.

Find and Replace Code

- FrontPage 2003 allows Web authors to find and replace HTML code throughout a Web site.

- Click the HTML Tags tab in the Find and Replace dialog box to display the dialog box shown at the top of the next page.

HTML Tags tab of Find and Replace dialog box

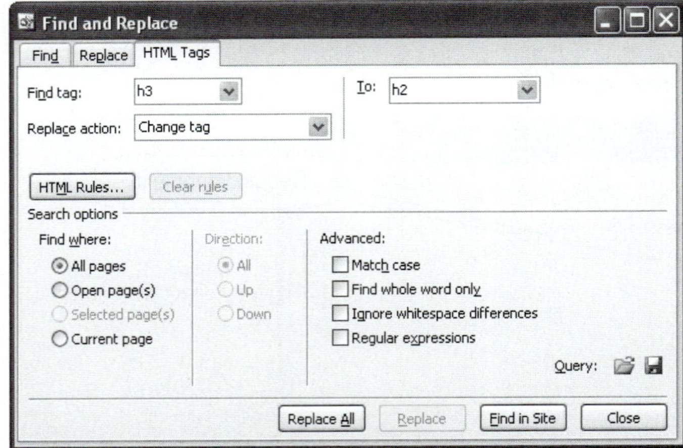

- The author can select any tag from the Find tag drop-down list. To replace the tag, choose a replace action (such as Change tag) and then specify the replacement tag.
- An author can not only simply change a tag from one to another, but also:
  - Replace the tag and its contents or contents only.
  - Add a new tag before or after a start tag or an end tag.
  - Remove a tag and its contents, or remove the tag only.
  - Change or remove a tag's attribute.
- For more complex replacement operations, an author can create rules by clicking the HTML Rules button and then configuring the rules in the HTML Rules dialog box.
- Clicking the Find in Web Site button starts the find or replace operation, just as when locating or replacing text. Use the Replace button to replace each instance of code just as for text.

Check Accessibility

- A new feature in FrontPage 2003 allows a designer to check pages throughout a site for **accessibility** problems.
- Accessibility checking can identify issues that may make the site difficult to use for visitors with vision or motor impairments.
- The **World Wide Web Consortium (W3C)** has prepared a list of accessibility guidelines called Web Content Accessibility Guidelines (WCAG) that can help an author ensure a site is accessible to a wide range of users.
- These guidelines are divided into two sets of priorities: Priority 1 and Priority 2.
  - If a site doesn't comply with Priority 1 guidelines, some users will find it impossible to use the site.
    - ✓ *For example, if images are used extensively without alternate text descriptions.*
  - If a site doesn't comply with Priority 2 guidelines, some users will find it difficult to use the site.
    - ✓ *For example, if text doesn't contrast strongly enough with the background or information such as links are identified by color alone.*
- Check accessibility for a site using the Tools>Accessibility command on the menu bar.
- FrontPage opens the Accessibility dialog box. An author can choose to check all pages in the site, open pages, or the current page.
- The author can also choose what accessibility standards to check against: WCAG Priority 1, WCAG Priority 2, and/or Access Board Section 508 (the Federal government's accessibility standards).
- By default, FrontPage will display warnings about issues that might be corrected and errors—problems that must be corrected to meet accessibility standards.
- Click the Check button to check the desired page or pages and generate a list of warning and errors such as those shown in the illustration at the top of the next page.
- The results show the name of the page that has a problem, the line number in the code where the problem occurs, the guideline the warning or error applies to, and a description of the warning or error.
  - ✓ *Click on a warning or error to see a full description below the list in the Problem details section of the dialog box.*
- To make it easy to check and resolve problems, an author can click the Generate HTML Report button to add a report page to the Web site containing a checklist of the problems identified.

- The author can easily refer to this page, or print it using the Print button on the Standard toolbar for even easier reference.
- After the user closes the dialog box, he or she will find that FrontPage has automatically switched to Split view to make editing simpler.

Results of accessibility check

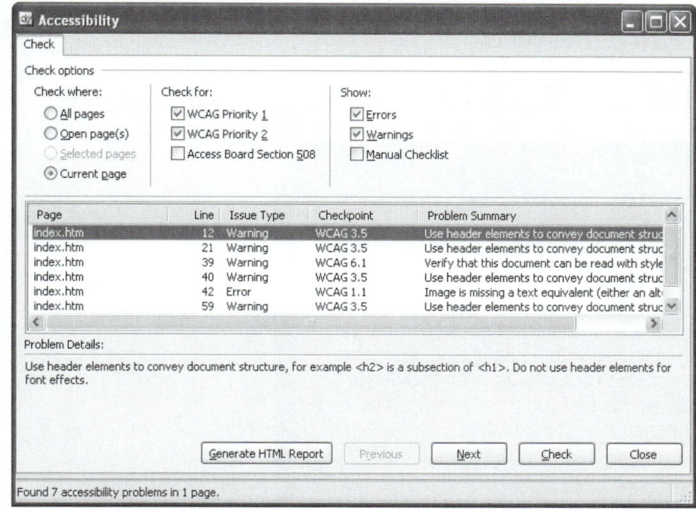

- Not all accessibility problems can be identified with the Accessibility command. For example, this feature cannot check whether link bars are in the same location on each page (WCAG 13.4).
- Clicking the Manual Checklist checkbox in the Accessibility dialog box generates a checklist of accessibility issues an author should check on each page of a Web site as a supplement to the other warnings and errors listed in the dialog box.

Select Browser

- By and large, a Web author will want his or her Web site to display properly in as many different types of browsers as possible to encourage many visitors.
- If a Web site contains components that require a specific browser or browser version to display properly, however, the author can select the browser and version.
- Select a browser and version using the Tools>Page Options command on the menu bar.
- Click the Authoring tab (see illustration at right) and select the desired browser and/or browser version from the Browsers and Browser versions drop-down lists.

Select browser and browser version

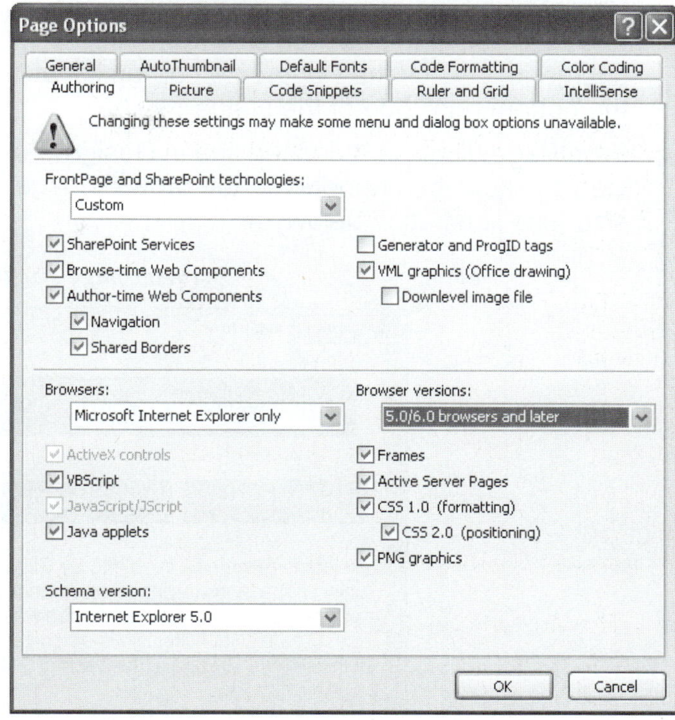

- When a Web developer selects a specific browser and/or browser version, FrontPage determines which of its features the browser will be able to display.
- Any features that are not supported by a browser or browser version will be unavailable for use (menu commands will be dimmed).
- If a specific browser/version is required for a Web site, the author should select the browser/version at the beginning of the project. In that way, he or she will know as pages are created if their features will display properly in the chosen browser.

View Browser Page Size in Design View

- You may remember from earlier in this course that FrontPage 2003 allows an author to specify the screen size of the browser in which a Web site will be previewed.
- Another new feature lets the author set a desired browser page size so that he or she can see in Design view, without previewing, how the page's content will lay out in the browser.

- To specify a page size in Design view, use the View>Page Size command on the menu bar and then select the desired size from the submenu, or click the Page Size pop-up list at the bottom right side of the status bar.
- FrontPage displays a dashed line in Design view to show the boundary of the browser page size (see illustration below).
- If a designer wants to optimize Web pages for a specific browser size, he or she should set page size at the outset of a project.
- This allows the designer to construct pages so their content will display efficiently and pleasingly in the browser.

Browser page size indicated in Design view

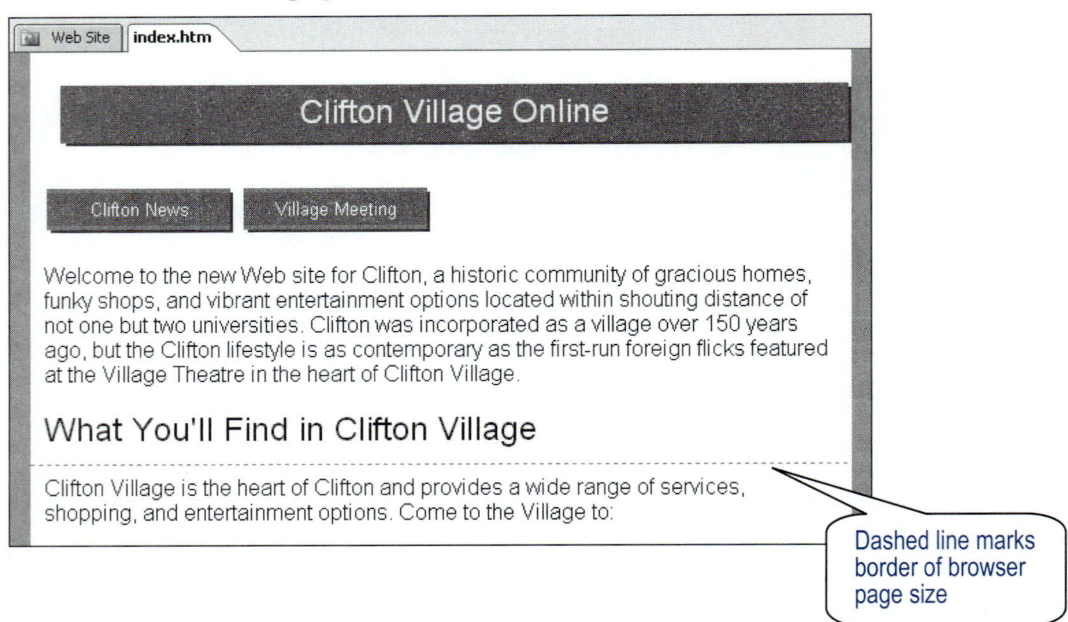

Procedures

Find and Replace Web Site Content (*Ctrl + F, Ctrl + H*)

1. Click **Edit** .... Alt+E
2. Click **Find**........................... F

   OR

   Click **Replace** .... E

Find or replace text

3. Type text to find in **Find what** box and, if desired, replacement text in **Replace with** box.

Find or replace code

4. Click **HTML Tags** tab.
5. Click **Find tag** down arrow and select tag.
6. Click **Replace action** down arrow and select action if replacing.
7. Select HTML code or attribute if necessary to replace.

For both text and code

8. Select **All pages**, **Open page(s)**, **Selected page(s),** or **Current page** option.
9. Click Find Next to find on current page.
10. Click Find in Site to find on all pages.
11. Double-click first occurrence on list or click Replace if desired to go to first occurrence.

    ✓ *Or click* Replace All *to replace all occurrences without reviewing each one.*

12. Click Next Page to go to next occurrence on list or click Back To List to return to list.

Check Accessibility (*F8*)

1. Click **Tools**................. Alt+T
2. Click **Accessibility** .... Y
3. Select **All pages**, **Open page(s)**, **Selected pages,** or **Current page** option.
4. Select guidelines to check accessibility for.
5. Click **Manual Checklist** checkbox if desired.
6. Click Check to begin check.
7. Review warnings and errors and then click Close.

   OR

   - Click Generate HTML Report to add a report page to Web site.
   - To print the report, click (**Print** button) on the Standard toolbar.

Select Browser

1. Click **Tools** .... Alt+T
2. Click **Page Options** .... A
3. Click **Authoring** tab.
4. Click **Browsers** drop-down list and select browser type.
5. Click **Browser versions** drop-down list and select browser version.

View Browser Page Size in Design View

1. Click **View** .... Alt+V
2. Click **Page Size** .... Z
3. Select desired browser page size.

Exercise Directions

1. Start FrontPage 2003.
2. Open **Clifton**.
3. Open **index.htm**.
4. Open the Page Options dialog box, click the Authoring tab, and select the **Microsoft Internet Explorer only** choice from the Browsers list.
5. Click the Browser version list and select **5.0/6.0 browsers and later** and notice that the PNG graphics checkbox becomes selected to indicate that these browsers can work with this graphic format.
6. Click **Cancel** to close the dialog box without making changes.
7. The name of the Clifton Town Meeting Web site coordinator has been misspelled throughout the Web site. Find the name **Marly** and replace it with **Mary** on all pages.
8. Check accessibility on **index.htm** using default options (make sure both Errors and Warnings are selected to check). FrontPage should find seven accessibility problems. Resolve them as follows:
   - First generate an HTML report so you have a checklist of problems to refer to. Then close the Accessibility dialog box.
   - The image on this page requires alternate text. Open its Picture Properties dialog box and type this alternate text in the Long Description box on the General tab: **Grayson's ice cream uses only the freshest and best-tasting ingredients**
   - If something should happen to the style sheet's background color for this Web site, the light yellow text would be hard to read. Solve this problem by applying a new theme to all pages. Use the Sandstone theme with no background and no vivid colors.
   - The accessibility report notes that headings should be properly subordinated. This page uses <h3> headings rather than <h2> headings that would be expected. Use the Replace feature to change <h3> headings to <h2> headings throughout the site.
9. Close the Accessibility Report without saving changes and check accessibility again on the current page. You can disregard the two warnings about style sheets.
10. Open **news.htm**. Supply the following long description for the picture on this page:

    Clifton Library will be closed for renovation until the fall of this year
11. Check accessibility on this page. You should receive no errors or warnings.
12. Open **meeting.htm**. Check accessibility on this page. FrontPage finds six problems, mostly relating to table structure.
13. Generate an HTML report and then resolve issues as follows:
    - The first issue suggests using the <th> table header tag to format the table's column headers. Modify the HTML code for the table as shown in Illustration A below. (Use Split view and locate the correct line as shown.)

Illustration A

```
<tr>
  <th>Membership Levels</th><th>Per Year</th><th>Two Years</th>
</tr>
<tr>
```

Membership dues confer the right to vote on Clifton issues.

Membership Levels	Per Year	Two Years

✓ *You may need to reapply table border formatting to show borders around the heading cells. Use black for both light and dark borders in the Cell Properties dialog box.*

- Because this is not a layout table and doesn't contain a lot of data, you can ignore the remaining warnings that relate to tables.
- You can ignore the one warning about document structure, which refers to the fact that the table has only a single <h1> heading.

14. Close the Accessibility Report page without saving. Check accessibility again, and this time also select **Manual Checklist**.
15. Generate an HTML report and take some time to look at the issues. You can ignore the table and heading warnings you have already looked at on this page.
16. The manual checklist gives some suggestions you can use on this Web site. Make the following final adjustments:
    - The link bar on **index.htm** is near the bottom of the page. Move it just below the page banner so it will be in the same position as on other pages (WCAG 13.4).
    - Change this link bar to use the theme's style, as on other pages.
    - **Index.htm** also has two links on it that rely on color only, which could be a problem for someone who can't distinguish colors easily (WCAG 2.1). Add underline formatting to these links.
    - The table on **meeting.htm** uses an absolute value for width (450 pixels). To comply with WCAG 3.4, change the width to 50%.
17. Close the accessibility report without saving.
18. Activate **index.htm** and change the page size to 600 by 300 (640 by 480, Maximized).
19. Click the Preview tab in Page view to see how your page would look in a browser at this size. Your page should look similar to Illustration B in Page Preview view.
20. Restore the default page size. Close the Web site.
21. Exit FrontPage 2003.

Illustration B

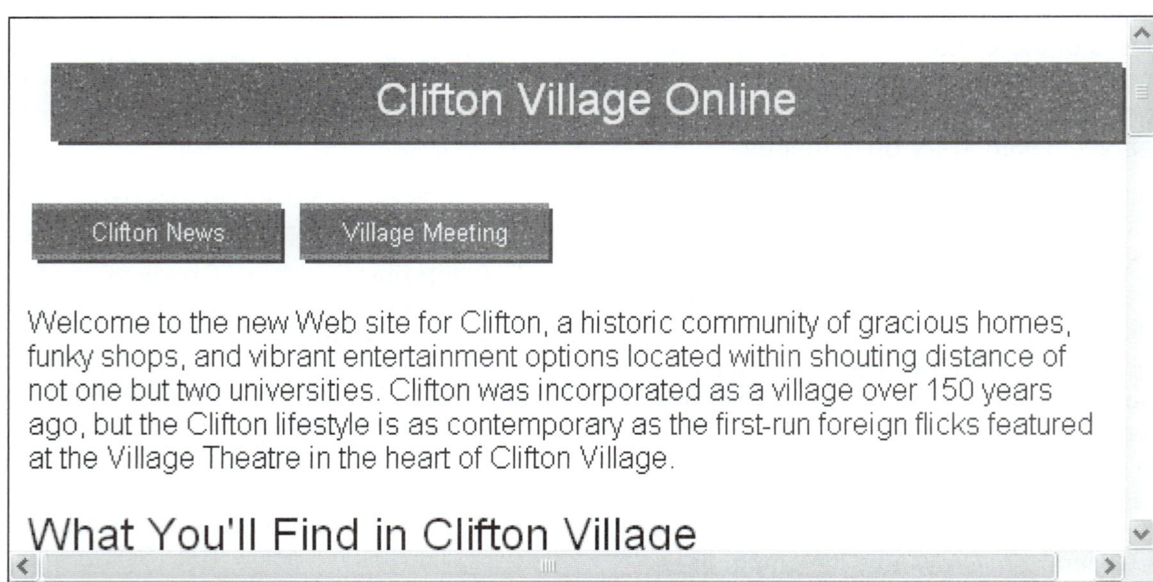

On Your Own

1. Start FrontPage 2003.
2. Open any Web site you have created in this course.
3. Check accessibility for all pages in the site.
4. Make changes you think necessary to ensure the site is accessible to all users.
5. If necessary, use the Find and Replace feature to change HTML tags throughout the site.
   ✓ *For example, change heading levels or add attributes to change text face or style.*
6. Create a manual accessibility report and print it for easy reference. Use suggestions on the report to fine-tune the site.
7. Specify a different browser for the site and then look at FrontPage menus to see options that aren't available for that browser.
8. Publish the Web site with a new name and preview it in the browser.
9. Close the browser.
10. Close the Web site.
11. Exit FrontPage 2003.

Exercise 55

◆ Review Reports View ◆ View Reports ◆ Site Summary Report ◆ Files Reports ◆ Shared Content Reports ◆ Problems Reports ◆ Workflow Reports ◆ Usage Reports ◆ Print Report

On the Job

FrontPage's Reports view lets a Web author run many types of reports on a Web site to identify problems and analyze Web site statistics. Five categories of reports deliver information on Web site files, shared content, problems, workflow status, and site usage.

In this exercise, you will work with a new Web site for PlantScapes, an online landscape materials company. You will run reports in all five report categories, plus a Site Summary report, to track progress on the Web site and identify problems that should be fixed before publishing.

Terms

Files reports
Reports that give the developer information on the files that make up a Web site.

Problems reports
Reports that display problems in the Web site such as broken links or slow pages.

Shared content reports
Reports that display information about features used by groups of pages in a Web site, such as themes and shared borders.

Site Summary report
A report that displays an overview of the Web site's statistics.

Usage reports
Reports that display information about visits to a Web site and visitors' browsers and systems.

Workflow reports
Reports that show the status of files and assignments for Web pages.

workgroup
A team of developers who work together to create a Web site (or other document).

Notes

Review Reports View

- FrontPage's Reports view allows a Web developer to display many different types of information about a Web site that can be used to eliminate problems and analyze data.
- Reports can (and should) be run at any time during the process of creating a Web site to help a Web developer identify problems before the Web site is published.
- After a Web site has been published, reports can be used to track important information such as number of site visits by month or week, most popular pages or browsers, and so on.

View Reports

- Reports view consists of column headers and items similar to Tasks view. The column headers and the report items change depending on what report is active.

- Select a report to view using the View>Reports command on the menu bar. On the pop-out Reports submenu, choose a category and then a report from the category's submenu.

Use Report Tools

- An author can also click the Report drop-down list just below the Web Site tab in Reports view to select a report category (see illustration below).
- Click a right-pointing arrow to display a submenu of reports for that category.
- At the right side of this space are several tools that can be used in Reports view.
- The Report Setting menu allows the user to refine a report with a specific setting, such as a date or time interval for the chosen report.

Report tools in Reports view pane

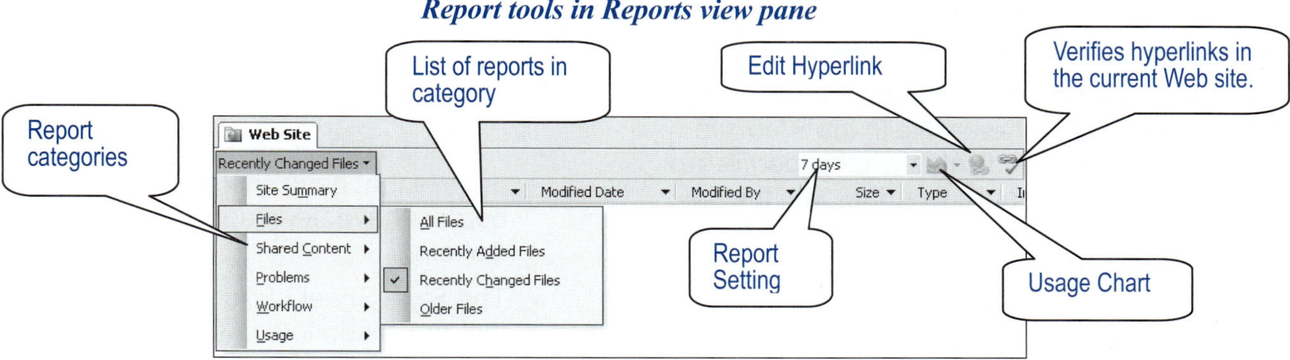

- The Reporting toolbar also includes three buttons:
  - Use the Usage Chart button to prepare a chart from usage data.
  - Use the Edit Hyperlink button to fix an incorrect hyperlink.
  - Use the *Verifies hyperlinks in the current web* button to verify hyperlinks in the Web site.

You will learn more about verifying links later in this exercise.

Site Summary Report

- By default, Reports view displays a **Site Summary report** for the current Web site when first opened (see illustration below). A Site Summary report provides an overview of the Web site's statistics.

  ✓ *By default, Reports view doesn't display a grid. You can turn on the grid using the Tools>Options command, selecting the Reports View tab, and selecting* Display gridlines when viewing reports.

Site Summary report

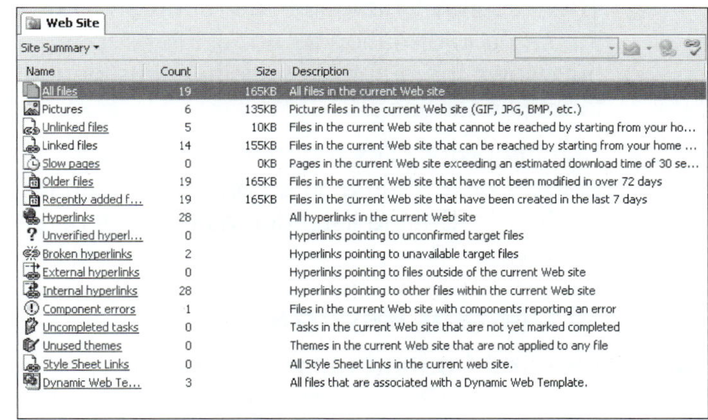

Web Site

Site Summary

Name	Count	Size	Description
All files	19	165KB	All files in the current Web site
Pictures	6	135KB	Picture files in the current Web site (GIF, JPG, BMP, etc.)
Unlinked files	5	10KB	Files in the current Web site that cannot be reached by starting from your ho...
Linked files	14	155KB	Files in the current Web site that can be reached by starting from your home ...
Slow pages	0	0KB	Pages in the current Web site exceeding an estimated download time of 30 se...
Older files	19	165KB	Files in the current Web site that have not been modified in over 72 days
Recently added f...	19	165KB	Files in the current Web site that have been created in the last 7 days
Hyperlinks	28		All hyperlinks in the current Web site
Unverified hyperl...	0		Hyperlinks pointing to unconfirmed target files
Broken hyperlinks	2		Hyperlinks pointing to unavailable target files
External hyperlinks	0		Hyperlinks pointing to files outside of the current Web site
Internal hyperlinks	28		Hyperlinks pointing to other files within the current Web site
Component errors	1		Files in the current Web site with components reporting an error
Uncompleted tasks	0		Tasks in the current Web site that are not yet marked completed
Unused themes	0		Themes in the current Web site that are not applied to any file
Style Sheet Links	0		All Style Sheet Links in the current web site.
Dynamic Web Te...	3		All files that are associated with a Dynamic Web Template.

- The Name column lists items such as Pictures and Linked files and counts how many of these items the Web site includes.
- The Name column also contains links to other reports, such as *All files* or *Slow pages*. Clicking one of these links changes the display to show the results of that report.

  ✓ *These reports are also available on the View>Reports submenus or the Report drop-down list's submenus.*

- The Count column shows how many items or problems have been counted in the current Web site.

- The Size column indicates file sizes for pages or items counted, and the Description column tells the author exactly what the item or report link in the Name column is tracking.
- As in the Tasks view, the author can change the order of items listed by clicking a column heading to sort items by that heading.

Files Reports

- The **Files reports** give the Web author an overview of the files that make up a Web site.
- FrontPage offers four Files reports:
  - The All Files report lists the name, page title, size, and type for each file in the Web site. This report also indicates what folder files are stored in, if applicable, the date the file was last modified, and who modified it.
  - The Recently Added Files report includes the same information as an All Files report but shows the date each file was created rather than its modified date. The author can use the Report Setting list on the Reporting toolbar to specify a date range.
  - The Recently Changed Files report shows the same information as an All Files report, but allows the author to specify a time period to track changes.
  - Use the Older Files report to identify files that are older than a time period specified by the Report Setting list, such as 60 days or 90 days.

Shared Content Reports

- The **Shared Content reports**, new in this version of FrontPage, show information about features that are used by groups of pages, including themes, dynamic Web templates, and shared borders.
- FrontPage has four Shared Content reports:
  - The Dynamic Web Templates report shows all pages in the Web site and which are attached to dynamic Web templates (see illustration below).

Dynamic Web Templates report

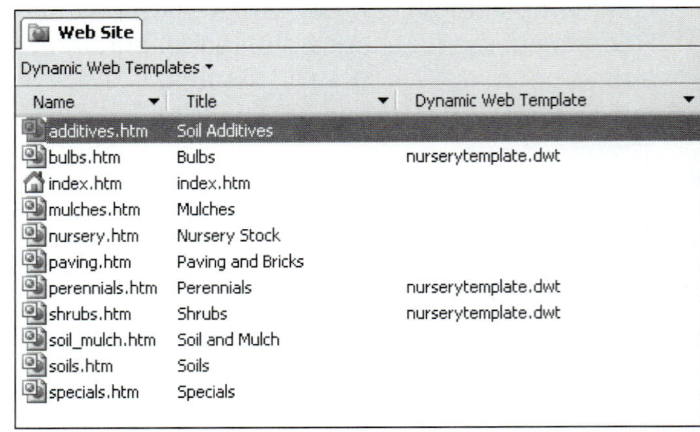

Web Site

Dynamic Web Templates

Name	Title	Dynamic Web Template
additives.htm	Soil Additives	
bulbs.htm	Bulbs	nurserytemplate.dwt
index.htm	index.htm	
mulches.htm	Mulches	
nursery.htm	Nursery Stock	
paving.htm	Paving and Bricks	
perennials.htm	Perennials	nurserytemplate.dwt
shrubs.htm	Shrubs	nurserytemplate.dwt
soil_mulch.htm	Soil and Mulch	
soils.htm	Soils	
specials.htm	Specials	

  - The Shared Borders report shows pages in the site that have shared borders and which borders have been applied, such as Top or Bottom.
  - The Style Sheet Links report displays pages that are linked to a cascading style sheet and the name of the style sheet.
  - The Themes report lists pages that are formatted by a theme and the name of the theme. The report will also indicate if a theme is the default site theme.

Problems Reports

- The **Problems reports** display problems in the Web site that can affect performance, such as broken links and component errors. Running the reports in this category before publishing can eliminate problems visitors might otherwise encounter.
- FrontPage has four Problems reports:
  - The Unlinked Files report lists the name and page title of files in the Web site that are not linked to other pages, as well as each file's folder, type, modified date, and modifier.
  - The Slow Pages report lists the name, page title, size, and type of pages that take longer than the default 30 seconds to download. The author can modify the download time using a Report Setting option.

- The Hyperlinks report identifies pages that have broken hyperlinks (links to nonexistent pages or pictures). (See illustration below.)

Hyperlinks report

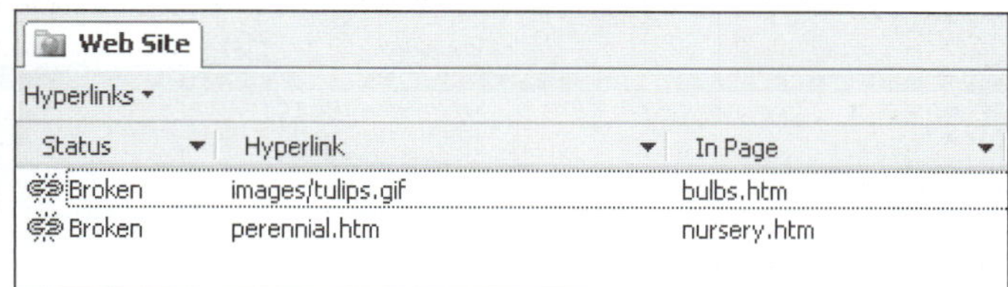

- The Component Errors report identifies errors that have been made in configuring FrontPage components.

■ As reports identify problems, the Web author can correct problems directly on pages by double-clicking the page name in the Name column to open the page in Page view.

■ When fixing hyperlink problems from Reports view, the author can double-click a page name to display the Edit Hyperlink dialog box (see illustration at the top of the next column). Open the page to edit or replace the incorrect hyperlink in this dialog box.

■ The Web author can also identify hyperlink problems without running the Broken Hyperlinks report by clicking the *Verifies hyperlinks in the current web* button on the Reporting toolbar.

Edit Hyperlink dialog box

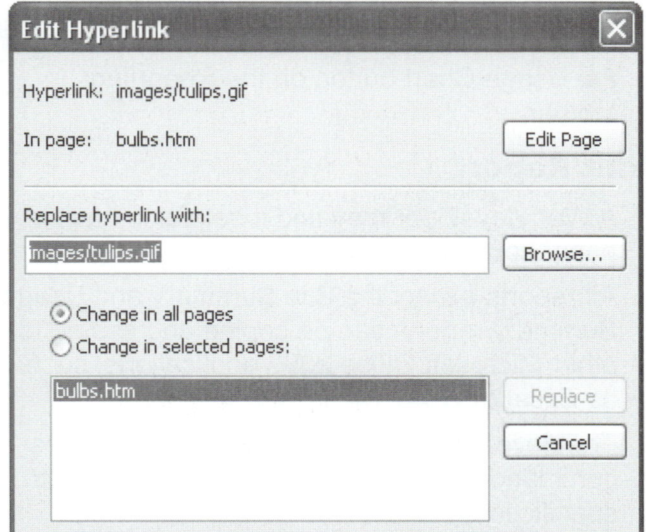

Workflow Reports

■ The **Workflow reports** show the status of files and assignments for files in the Web site. These reports are most useful when a Web site is being managed by a **workgroup**.

■ To simplify workgroup collaboration, the Web developer can assign a Web page to a category and assign a workgroup member to work on the page (see illustration below). The developer can also set the current review status.

Workgroup tab in Properties dialog box

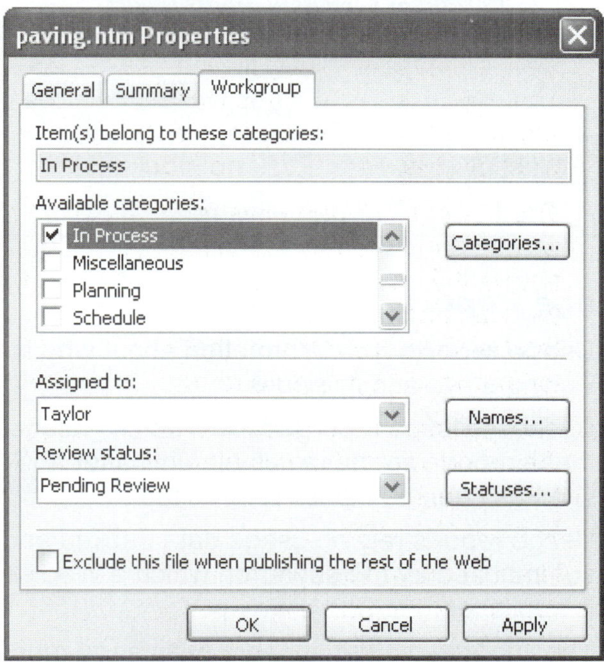

✓ *You will learn more about categories in the next exercise.*

■ FrontPage offers five Workflow reports:

- The Review Status report shows the review status for each page or file that has been assigned to a workgroup member. This report also shows the name, page title, type, review date, and reviewer.
- The Assigned To report shows the name, page title, and assigned workgroup member for each Web page. The report also shows the date the page was assigned and who made the assignment.
- The Categories report shows the name, page title, type, and the categories to which each page has been assigned.

- The Publish Status report indicates whether pages are ready to be published. This report also shows review status as well as modified date and file type and size.
- When source control is turned on, the Checkout Status report shows which pages have been checked out for editing. This report also shows who checked out the page, its version, and the date and time the page was locked for editing (see illustration below).

Portion of Checkout Status report

Web Site

Checkout Status

Name	Title	Checked Ou...	V...	Locked Date
✓ index.htm	index.htm	MAX\Cat	V1	12/3/2003 9:57 AM
✓ mulches.htm	Mulches	MAX\Cat	V1	12/3/2003 9:57 AM
✓ paving.htm	Paving and Bricks	MAX\Cat	V1	12/3/2003 9:57 AM
form_resul...	_private/form_results.csv			
specials.htm	Specials		V1	

Usage Reports

- **Usage reports** give information about who is visiting a site and its pages.
- Because Usage reports track Web site usage, these reports are not available until after a Web site has been published and visited.
- Usage reports rely on usage data tracked and summarized by the server on which a Web site is published.
- The information that appears in a usage report, therefore, may vary depending on the server's usage settings.
- Servers that track usage data specify an update interval. Usage data may be updated daily, weekly, or monthly. A Web author might have to wait days or weeks to see usage data for the Web site.
- The Usage Summary report, shown below, provides an overview of usage information, including total visits, total page hits, top Web browser used to access the Web site, and top operating system.

  ✓ *A "visit" is when a user opens a Web site's Default.htm page. A "page hit" is when a user opens a page in a Web site.*

- Click any of the links in the Name column to see a more detailed report:
  - Summary usage data can be displayed by day, week, or month.
  - Page hits can also be displayed by day, week, or month.

Usage Summary report for new Web site

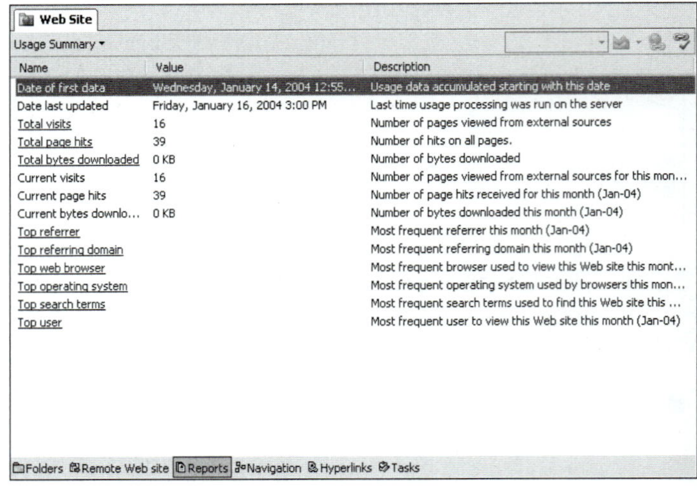

Web Site

Usage Summary

Name	Value	Description
Date of first data	Wednesday, January 14, 2004 12:55...	Usage data accumulated starting with this date
Date last updated	Friday, January 16, 2004 3:00 PM	Last time usage processing was run on the server
Total visits	16	Number of pages viewed from external sources
Total page hits	39	Number of hits on all pages.
Total bytes downloaded	0 KB	Number of bytes downloaded
Current visits	16	Number of pages viewed from external sources for this mon...
Current page hits	39	Number of page hits received for this month (Jan-04)
Current bytes downlo...	0 KB	Number of bytes downloaded this month (Jan-04)
Top referrer		Most frequent referrer this month (Jan-04)
Top referring domain		Most frequent referring domain this month (Jan-04)
Top web browser		Most frequent browser used to view this Web site this mont...
Top operating system		Most frequent operating system used by browsers this mon...
Top search terms		Most frequent search terms used to find this Web site this ...
Top user		Most frequent user to view this Web site this month (Jan-04)

Folders Remote Web site Reports Navigation Hyperlinks Tasks

  - The Referring URLs and Referring Domains reports show what other Web sites and domains are referring visitors to the site using hyperlinks.
  - Use the Browsers and Operating Systems reports to show the browsers and operating systems used most frequently by visitors.
  - Use the Visiting Users report to track user names of frequent visitors.
  - Use the Search Strings report to identify search strings used to reach the site.
- The developer can chart the numerical data displayed in these detailed reports by clicking the Usage Chart button on the Reporting toolbar.

Print Report

- A Web developer may find it helpful to have a paper copy of a report.
- All reports *except* the Site Summary and Usage Summary reports can be copied and pasted to other Microsoft Office 2003 applications, such as Excel or Word.
- The developer can also use the File>Save As command on the menu bar to save a report to a specific location.
- Once the report has been copied or saved in a new location or application, it can be printed using that application's print settings.

Procedures

View Reports

1. Click **View** .... Alt + V
2. Click **Reports** .... R

   OR

   Click report down arrow on Site Summary drop-down list.
3. Click report category:
   - **Site Summary** .... M
   - **Files** .... F
   - **Shared Content** C
   - **Problems** .... P
   - **Workflow** .... W
   - **Usage** .... U
4. Click desired report on submenu.

Site Summary Report

1. Display list of reports as described in *View Reports*.
2. Click **Site Summary** .... M
3. Click report link in **Name** column to run report.

Files Reports

1. Display list of reports as described in *View Reports*.
2. Click **Files** from the Site Summary drop-down list...... F
3. Click desired report on submenu:
   - **All Files** .... A
   - **Recently Added Files** .... D
   - **Recently Changed Files** .... H
   - **Older Files** .... O
4. Use Report Setting options to refine dates for Recently Added Files, Recently Changed Files, and Older Files reports.

Shared Content Reports

1. Display list of reports as described in *View Reports*.
2. Click **Shared Content** C
3. Click desired report on submenu:
   - **Dynamic Web Templates** .... D
   - **Shared Borders** .... S
   - **Style Sheet Links** L
   - **Themes** .... T

Problems Reports

1. Display list of reports as described in *View Reports*.
2. Click **Problems** .... P
3. Click desired report on submenu:
   - **Unlinked Files** .... U
   - **Slow Pages** .... S
   - **Hyperlinks** .... H
   - **Component Errors** .... E
4. Use Report Settings options at the top right of the pane to refine speed for Slow Pages report.
5. Click (**Verifies hyperlinks in the current web**) button on Reporting toolbar to verify hyperlinks.
6. Double-click page name to fix broken hyperlinks:

   a. Click Edit Page to open page.

   b. Click Browse... to locate correct target page, or type correct link in **Replace hyperlink with** box.

   c. Click Replace to replace incorrect hyperlink with correct target.

Workflow Reports

1. Display list of reports as described in *View Reports*.
2. Click **Workflow** .... W
3. Click desired report on submenu:
   - **Review Status** .... R
   - **Assigned To** .... T
   - **Categories** C
   - **Publish Status** .... P
   - **Checkout Status** .... K
4. Use Report Setting option to indicate category for Categories report

Usage Reports

1. Display list of reports as described in *View Reports*.
2. Click **Usage** .... U
3. Click desired report on submenu:
   - **Usage Summary** .... U
     - Choose daily, weekly, or monthly summary.
     - Choose daily, weekly, or monthly page hits.
   - **Visiting Users** V
   - **Operating Systems** ...... O
   - **Browsers** .... B
   - **Referring Domains** .... R
   - **Referring URLs** L
   - **Search Strings** .... S

Print Report

1. Click **File** .... Alt + F
2. Click **Save As** .... A
3. Save report with new name or location and print from that location.

OR

1. Right-click in report and select **Copy Report** .... R
2. Paste report in new application and print from that application.

Exercise Directions

1. Start FrontPage 2003.
2. Open **Plantscapes**.
3. Switch to Reports view.
4. Run a Site Summary report, if this report does not display when you open Reports view.
5. Review the items and reports tracked in this report. Note that there is also 1 Component error listed. This error appears because of the form on the specials.htm page.
   ✓ *This error will disappear after the Web site is published.*
6. Adjust Slow Pages settings to make sure all pictures download quickly:
   - Click the **Slow pages** link in the Name column to run the Slow pages report.
   - Click the Report Setting down arrow and select **10 seconds** if necessary.
   - There are two pages that exceed this download time.
   - Open **nursery.htm** and resample the picture on this page. Save the page.
   - Resample the picture on **paving.htm** and save the page.
7. Return to Reports view. The problems have been resolved.
8. Use the Report toolbar to run all of the Files reports, noting the information each displays about the Web site's files.
9. Use the reports toolbar to verify hyperlinks in the Web site. Two broken hyperlinks are identified, one on the **bulbs.htm** page and one on the **nursery.htm** page. Fix these links as follows:
   - Open **bulbs.htm** and note that the **tulips.gif** image is missing. Use FrontPage clip art to locate and insert a clip art picture of a tulip in the empty picture area. Resize the picture to fit the layout cell.
   - Make the background transparent if necessary and save the picture as a GIF file in the images folder.
   - In Reports view, double-click the perennial.htm hyperlink to open the Edit Hyperlink dialog box. Use the **Browse** button to select the intended target, **perennials.htm**. Click the **Replace** button.
10. Run the Unlinked Files report. The form results page appears at the top of the list (because the Web site has not yet been published), but two other pages also display, **mulches.htm** and **specials.htm**. Fix these errors as follows:
    - Double-click **mulches.htm** in the Name column and use *Up* below the heading to link to **soil_mulch.htm**.
    - Open **soil_mulch.htm** and link the word *Mulches* in the list to **mulches.htm**.
    - Save all pages and return to Reports view.
    - Double-click **specials.htm** in the Name column to open the page.
    - Insert a new paragraph below the heading and type **[Home]**. Link the word *Home* to the **index.htm** page.
    - Open **index.htm** and locate the reference to the Specials page at the bottom of the page. Link *Specials* to **specials.htm**. Save all open pages.
    - Return to Reports view and note that all unlinked files have been fixed.
11. Run the Dynamic Web Templates report to see which pages in the Web site are attached to a template.
12. Run the Themes report to see the default theme for the site.
13. Turn on source control and check out the **index.htm** page. Then run the Workflow reports to see the information each displays.
14. Save the Assigned To report as **assignments.htm** in your solutions folder.
15. Turn off source control and run a final Site Summary report. Your report should look similar to Illustration A.
16. Publish the Web site as **plantscapeweb**. If you are publishing to a server that tracks usage data, visit your site several times during the tracking interval specified by your server.
17. After the update day and time, open **plantscapeweb** from the server and run several usage reports to see data collected for your visits.
18. Close the Web site.
19. Exit FrontPage 2003.

20. Start Excel 2003 and open the **assignments.htm** file from your solutions folder. Print the worksheet.
    - ✓ *If you open this file from FrontPage or from Windows Explorer, it will open in your browser.*
21. Close the worksheet.
22. Exit Excel 2003.

Illustration A

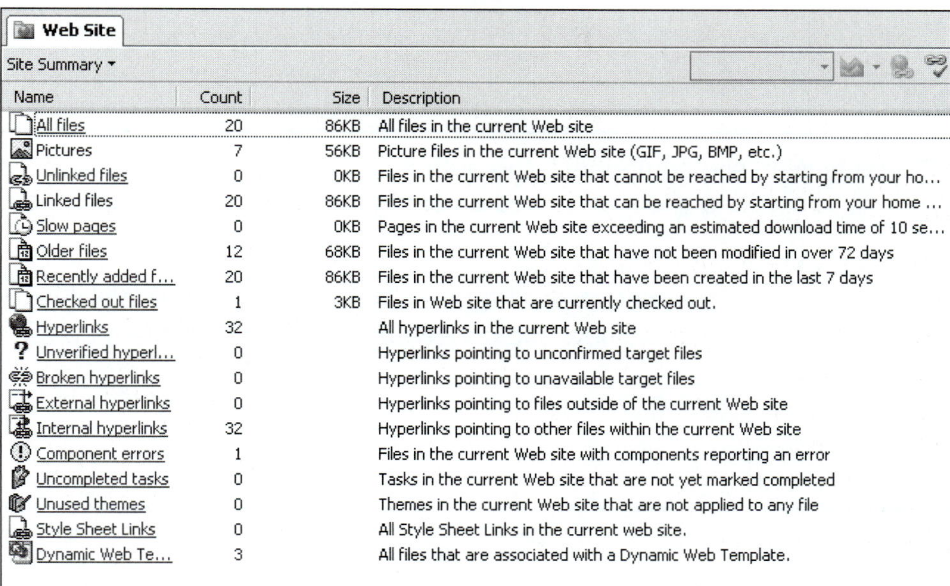

Web Site

Site Summary ▾

Name	Count	Size	Description
All files	20	86KB	All files in the current Web site
Pictures	7	56KB	Picture files in the current Web site (GIF, JPG, BMP, etc.)
Unlinked files	0	0KB	Files in the current Web site that cannot be reached by starting from your ho...
Linked files	20	86KB	Files in the current Web site that can be reached by starting from your home ...
Slow pages	0	0KB	Pages in the current Web site exceeding an estimated download time of 10 se...
Older files	12	68KB	Files in the current Web site that have not been modified in over 72 days
Recently added f...	20	86KB	Files in the current Web site that have been created in the last 7 days
Checked out files	1	3KB	Files in Web site that are currently checked out.
Hyperlinks	32		All hyperlinks in the current Web site
Unverified hyperl...	0		Hyperlinks pointing to unconfirmed target files
Broken hyperlinks	0		Hyperlinks pointing to unavailable target files
External hyperlinks	0		Hyperlinks pointing to files outside of the current Web site
Internal hyperlinks	32		Hyperlinks pointing to other files within the current Web site
Component errors	1		Files in the current Web site with components reporting an error
Uncompleted tasks	0		Tasks in the current Web site that are not yet marked completed
Unused themes	0		Themes in the current Web site that are not applied to any file
Style Sheet Links	0		All Style Sheet Links in the current web site.
Dynamic Web Te...	3		All files that are associated with a Dynamic Web Template.

On Your Own

1. Start FrontPage 2003.
2. Open **reinhardtlinks** from the server.
3. Publish the Web site as **reinhardtreports**. Include the subsites. Close **reinhardtlinks** and open **reinhardtreports**.
4. Run a Site Summary report on the root Web site.
5. Verify all hyperlinks in the Web site.
6. Run an Unlinked Files report to identify any unlinked files.
    - ✓ *Don't worry if you see a message about the paris.jpg file. This file is used in the Springfield subsite.*
7. The **branches.htm** page is not linked to any other page in the Web site. Create links from the **Default.htm** page to **branches.htm** and from **branches.htm** to **Default.htm**.
8. Run a Site Summary report in the Dayton subsite.
9. Verify hyperlinks in the Dayton subsite and notice that the **deer3.jpg** picture is missing on the **daytonnews.htm** page. Insert this picture from the Data folder and position it as shown by the empty placeholder on this page.
10. Verify all links in the Springfield subsite.
11. Visit this site several times during your server's usage reporting interval, then open the Web site from the server and run the Usage Summary report to see information on your visits.
12. Close the Web site.
13. Exit FrontPage 2003.

Exercise 56

◆ **About Site Maps** ◆ **Create Table of Contents**
◆ **Create Site Map Using Categories**

On the Job

Using the Table of Contents Web site component, the author can create a simple table of contents for a Web site using page titles or create a site map based on categories assigned to each page.

In this exercise, you will continue to work with the PlantScapes Web site. To help visitors find all the pages in the site, you will assign pages to new categories and then create a site map based on the categories.

Terms

category
A keyword or phrase used to organize pages or other items.

site map
An ordered list of hyperlinks that open pages in a Web site. A site map may be a list of page titles or pages assigned to specific categories.

Notes

About Site Maps

- A **site map** displays links to pages in a Web site so that site visitors can easily find their way to specific pages.
- FrontPage 2003 offers two site map options: a simple table of contents based on a Web site's page titles and a site map based on page **categories**.
- Both options use the Table of Contents Web site component found in the Insert Web Component dialog box.

Create Table of Contents

- Create a table of contents on a page with other Web site content or on a new page.
- Use the Insert>Web Component command on the menu bar to open the Insert Web Component dialog box and select the Table of Contents component type.
- After an author selects the For This Web Site option, FrontPage displays a dialog box that allows the author to set up the table of contents (see illustration below).

Table of Contents Properties dialog box

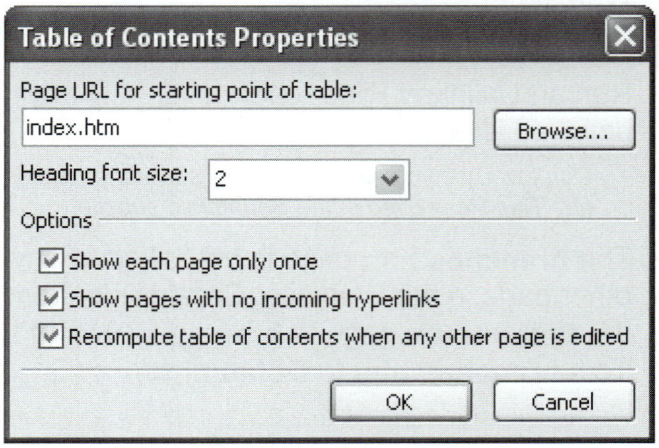

- Supply the name of the page that will start the table of contents (usually the home page) and specify a heading level for the first table of contents heading.
- The author can choose three options to configure the table of contents:
  - Choose *Show each page only once* to create a single link to a page (even if there are multiple links to a page in the Web site).
  - Choose *Show pages with no incoming hyperlinks* to include unlinked pages in the table of contents.
  - Choose *Recompute table of contents when any other page is edited* to have FrontPage automatically update the table of contents as pages are added or renamed.
- FrontPage inserts the table of contents component in the Web page. It must be viewed in the browser to display the links (see illustration below).

Table of contents in browser

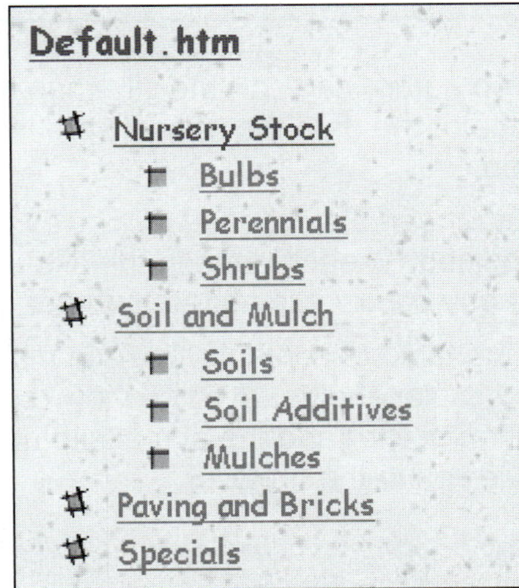

✓ *To display subordinate links as shown above, pages must be organized in a navigation structure.*

Create Site Map Using Categories

- A Web developer can create a more sophisticated site map by assigning pages to categories and then using the Based on Page Category Web component to create links to all pages in a specific category.
- In the partial site map shown at the top of the next column, for example, the links are to pages that have been assigned to the Nursery category.

Partial site map showing Nursery category pages

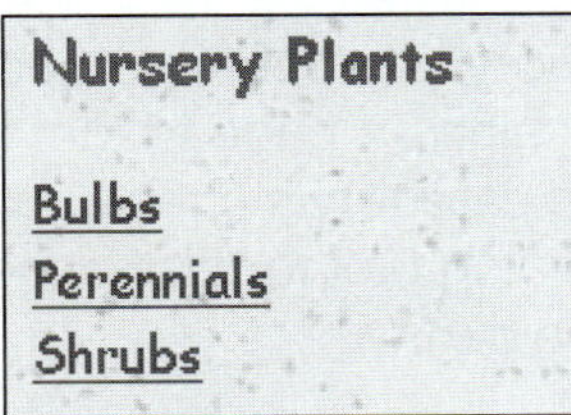

Create New Category

- FrontPage 2003 (and other Microsoft Office 2003 applications) has a standard set of categories that may be assigned to Web pages.
- A Web developer can also create categories specifically for a Web site.

  ✓ *Categories created within a Web site are not available for other Web sites.*
- Begin the process of creating a category by right-clicking a page (in the Folder List or in Folders view) to be assigned to a new category, then click the Workgroup tab in the Properties dialog box.
- The Workgroup tab shows FrontPage's default categories. Click the Categories button to open the Master Category List dialog box (see illustration below).

Add category to the Master Category List

Master Category List
New category:
Nursery
Add
Business
Competition
Expense Report
Goals/Objectives
Ideas
In Process
Miscellaneous
Planning
Schedule
Travel
VIP
Waiting
Remove
Reset
OK
Cancel

- Create a new category by typing the category name in the New category box and clicking the Add button.

  ✓ *After clicking the Add button, the new category name is highlighted in the New category text box. To add other categories, simply begin typing to replace the previous category name.*

Assign Page to Category

- After a category has been created, the Web developer assigns a page to that category by selecting the category's checkbox in the Properties dialog box for that page (see illustration below).

Assign a page to a category

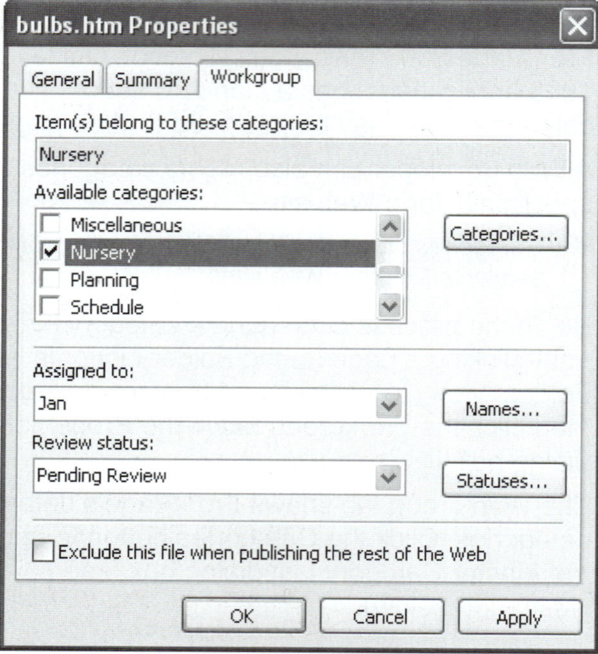

- The developer can also use this dialog box to assign a page to a workgroup member and to establish a review status for the page.
- Web pages may be assigned to more than one category, one of the benefits of creating this type of site map rather than a simple table of contents.

Add Categories to Site Map

- After all relevant pages have been assigned to categories, the Web developer can create headings for each category on a Web page (either a new page or one that already contains other content).
  - ✓ *The heading does not have to be exactly the same as the category name.*
- Below the heading, the developer then inserts the Based on Page Category Web site component. FrontPage requests the developer to choose the category for the component (see illustration below).

Choose category for site map component

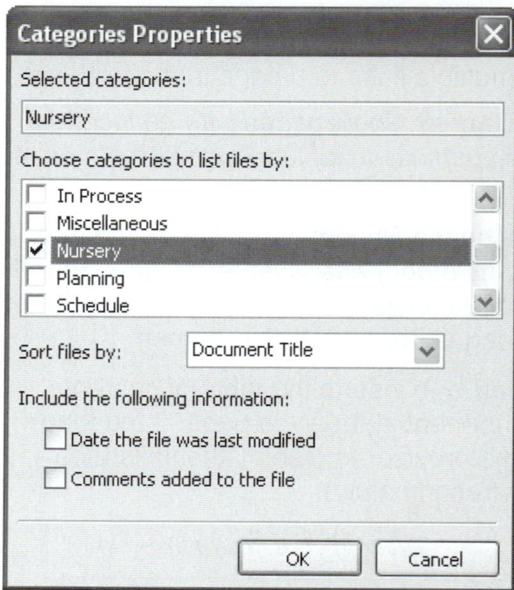

- The Web author can sort the site map links by page title or the date the pages were last modified.
- The author can also choose to display the date last modified for each page in the site map as well as any comments added to the page file.
- As for the table of contents, the site map displays a placeholder in Page view (see illustration below) and the actual site map links when viewed in the browser.

Site map heading and component in Page view

- Site map components can be modified at any time by double-clicking the component in Page view to open the Categories Properties dialog box.

Procedures

Create Table of Contents

On new page or page containing other Web site text

1. Position insertion point where table of contents should appear.
2. Click **Insert** .... Alt+I
3. Click **Web Component**........ C
4. Click **Table of Contents** component type.
5. Click **For This Web Site**.
6. Click Finish.
7. Use Browse... to locate page that should appear at top of table of contents (usually Default.htm or index.htm).
8. Select:
   - **Show each page only once** to limit links to a single link for each page.
   - **Show pages with no incoming hyperlinks** to display pages with no links to the top-level page.
   - **Recompute table of contents when any other page is edited** to automatically update table of contents when pages are added or renamed.

Create New Category

1. Right-click page to assign to new category in Folder List or Folders view.
2. Click **Properties** .... R
3. Click **Workgroup** tab.
4. Click Categories... .... Alt+C
5. Type name of new category in **New category** box.
6. Click Add .... Alt+A

   ✓ *To add additional categories, keep typing them in New category text box.*

Assign Page to Category

1. Right-click page to assign to category in Folder List or Folders view.
2. Click **Properties** .... R
3. Click **Workgroup** tab.
4. Locate category in **Available categories** list and select category checkbox.

   ✓ *A page can be assigned to a new category in the Properties dialog box immediately after creating the new category.*

   ✓ *A page can be assigned to more than one category.*

Create Site Map

1. Insert headings for each category on a new page or page containing other Web site text.
2. Click **Insert** .... Alt+I
3. Click **Web Component**....... C
4. Click **Table of Contents** component type.
5. Click **Based on Page Category**.
6. Click Finish .... Alt+F
7. Choose category for pages to list in Categories Properties dialog box.
8. Choose to sort files by page title or date last modified.
9. Select:
   - **Date the file was last modified** to display last modified date in site map.
   - **Comments added to the file** to display any comments attached to the page file.

Exercise Directions

1. Start FrontPage 2003.
2. Open **plantscapeweb**.
3. Publish the Web site as **plantscapesite**.
4. Close **plantscapeweb** and open **plantscapesite**.
5. Your client would like more comprehensive links on the home page. You will create a site map instead. As a first step, open **index.htm** or **Default.htm** and delete the *Nursery stock*, *Soil and mulch*, and *Pavers and bricks* links on the page.
6. Create new categories as follows:
   - In Folders view, right-click **additives.htm** and open this page's Properties box.
   - Create a new category named **Soil**.
   - Create additional new categories named **Nursery**, **Information**, and **Paving**.
   - Assign the current page to the Soil category.
7. Assign pages to categories as follows:

Soil	mulches.htm soil_mulch.htm soils.htm
Nursery	bulbs.htm nursery.htm perennials.htm shrubs.htm
Information	nursery.htm paving.htm soil_mulch.htm
Paving	paving.htm

8. On **index.htm** or **Default.htm**, insert the following Heading 3 headings below the first paragraph, with a blank paragraph after each:

   PlantScape Departments

   Nursery Stock

   Paving Solutions

   Soils and Mulches
9. On the blank line below the *PlantScape Departments* heading, insert a Table of Contents component and select the Based on Page Category type.
10. Select the Information category and make no other changes in the Categories Properties dialog box.
11. Insert components below each of the other headings, using the Nursery category for *Nursery Stock*, Paving for *Paving Solutions*, and Soil for *Soils and Mulches*.
12. Save the page and view it in the browser. The top of your site map should look similar to Illustration A.
13. Close the browser.
14. Close the Web site.
15. Exit FrontPage 2003.

Illustration A

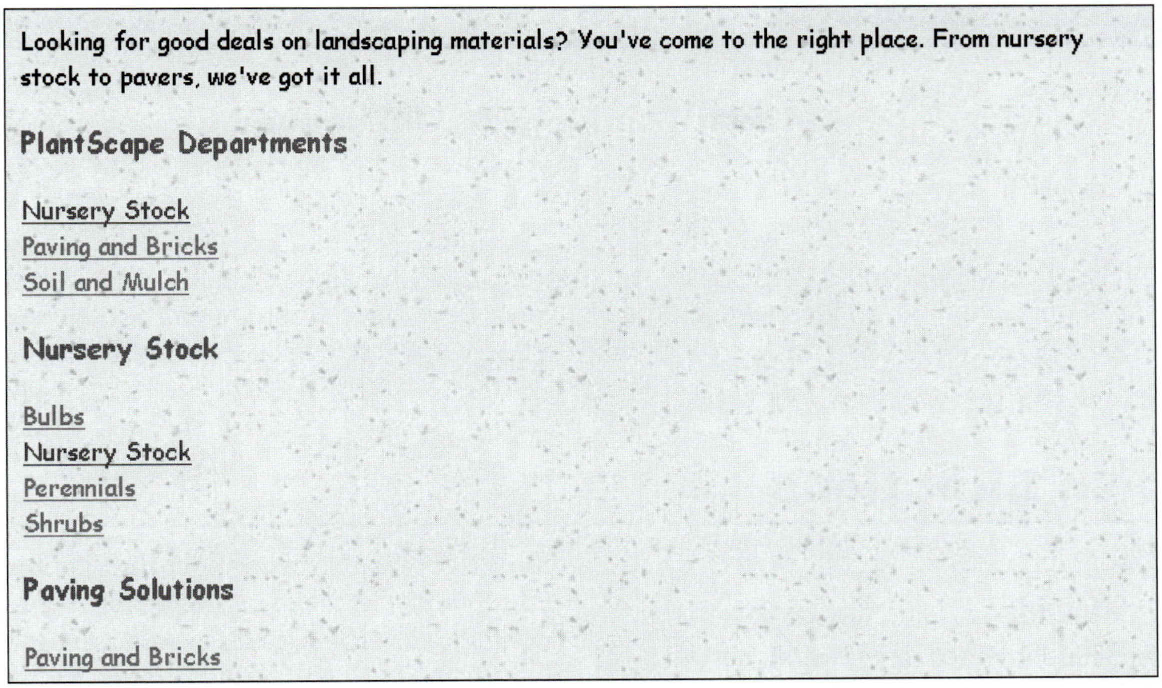

Looking for good deals on landscaping materials? You've come to the right place. From nursery stock to pavers, we've got it all.

PlantScape Departments

Nursery Stock
Paving and Bricks
Soil and Mulch

Nursery Stock

Bulbs
Nursery Stock
Perennials
Shrubs

Paving Solutions

Paving and Bricks

On Your Own

1. Start FrontPage 2003.
2. Review the Web sites you have created for this course in Exercises and On Your Own Exercises.
3. Choose a Web site that has a number of pages (such as one of the frames pages Web sites from Lesson 4).
4. Create a table of contents for the Web site on a new page or an existing page.
   ✓ *If you create the table of contents on a new page, be sure to link it to other pages in the Web site.*
5. Create a site map on the Web site's home page or on a new page. If necessary, add new categories and then assign pages to the categories.
6. Supply appropriate headings for the category pages and insert the components for each category.
7. Publish the Web site, if necessary, with an appropriate name and then preview the site map and the table of contents in the browser.
8. Close the browser.
9. Close the Web site.
10. Exit FrontPage 2003.

Exercise 57

◆ **Critical Thinking** ◆ **Challenge**

In this exercise, you will work on a Web site for Safe Harbor, a local children's shelter. The Web site is in the process of being created, so you need to organize files, check links, and run reports to identify potential problems. As part of your organization tasks, you will create a subsite and a site map for the Web site.

Exercise Directions

1. Start FrontPage 2003.
2. Open **Harbor**.
3. Several different people have worked on this Web site, and one developer has used Safe Shelter rather than Safe Harbor on his pages. Use Replace to replace all occurrences of Safe Shelter with **Safe Harbor**.
4. Turn on source control and check out the **products.htm** page. Add this sentence to the last paragraph:

   We ship via UPS or first-class mail.
5. Check the page in and turn off source control.
6. Switch to Hyperlinks view and view links to and from **index.htm**.
7. Notice the broken link to **tellme.htm**. This link should be to **information.htm**. Fix the link on the **index.htm** page.
8. Return to Hyperlinks view and display page titles.
9. Note that there is no link from the Tell Me More page to the **index.htm** page.
10. Open **information.htm** and create a link to **index.htm** using the *Safe Harbor* text at the top of the page below the picture.
11. Return to Hyperlinks view and display links to pictures and repeated links for **information.htm**.
12. You should have a repeated hyperlink from Tell Me More to **index.htm**, but only one appears. Return to **information.htm** and create a hotspot in the lighthouse picture at the top of the page that links to **index.htm**.
13. Check hyperlinks for the **products.htm** page and expand links for the pages at the left side of the Products page.
14. Switch to Reports view and check the Site Summary report.
15. One slow page is listed. Open the page, select the picture, and resample the picture to reduce its size.
16. Save the page and its picture and return to Reports view.
17. Verify hyperlinks and note that two broken links are identified to the **brittle.htm** page.
18. Double-click the first link to fix and browse to select the correct page, **brittles.htm**. Fix the link on both pages.
19. Shared borders were applied to all pages of the Web site by mistake and then removed, but some borders may remain. Run the Shared Borders report and then turn off shared borders on all pages *except* **index.htm**.
20. Run the Review Status report to check on the status of pages being reviewed.
21. Save this report as **status.htm** in the folder where you're saving Web sites.
22. Start Excel 2003 and open the report. Print the report.
23. Close the report and Excel 2003.
24. Check accessibility on the following pages: **index.htm**, **products.htm**, **information.htm**, and **brittles.htm**. Make the following corrections to the pages:

- On **index.htm**: Type the following long description for the lighthouse image:

  Safe Harbor is a shelter for children and teens
- On **products.htm**:
  - Supply the same long description for the lighthouse picture.
  - Double-click the hotspot in the lighthouse picture and add a ScreenTip that reads **Home Page**.
  - Supply an appropriate long description for the other picture on this page.
- On **information.htm**:
  - Supply the same long description for the lighthouse picture.
  - Double-click the hotspot in the lighthouse picture and add a ScreenTip that reads **Home Page**.
- You can ignore any warnings about headings on any page or about the form on information.htm.

25. You noticed when you checked the **brittles.htm** page that the products are listed numerically, but they would look better as bulleted lists. Use the Replace feature to change the <ol> tag to <ul> on all pages.
26. Create a folder named **Products** to contain the food products portion of this Web site.
27. Add all files to the folder *except* **index.htm** and **information.htm**.
28. Create a subsite from the **Products** folder.
29. Publish the Web site (including the subsite) as **harborweb**.
30. Close **Harbor** and open **harborweb**.
31. Recalculate hyperlinks to fix links to the subsite.
32. If permitted, assign an authoring permission to yourself for the subsite.
33. Open the subsite and apply a theme of your choice to all pages in the subsite.
34. Create four new categories for the subsite: **Items**, **Confections**, **Jams**, and **Nuts**.
35. Assign subsite pages to the categories as follows:

Items	confections.htm jams.htm nuts.htm
Confections	brittles.htm fudge.htm
Jams	fruitbutters.htm fruitjellies.htm
Nuts	brittles.htm roastednuts.htm

36. Open **products.htm** in the subsite and create a link back to the **index.htm** or **Default.htm** page in the root Web site using the *Safe Harbor* text at the top of the page below the picture.
37. Below the first paragraph of text, insert the following headings in Heading 3 style for a site map: **Gift Items**, **Confections**, **Jams and Spreads**, and **Nuts**.
38. Insert table of contents components that use page categories below each heading.
39. Save the page and preview it in the browser. Your site map should look similar to the one shown in Illustration A.
40. Return to the root Web site and open **index.htm** or **Default.htm**. Preview the page in the browser and test the Web site.
41. Close the browser.
42. Close the Web site and subsite.
43. Exit FrontPage 2003.

Illustration A

Gift Items

Confections
Jams and Spreads
Nuts Savory and Sweet

Confections

Brittles
World Famous Fudge

Jams and Spreads

Fruit Butters
Fruit Jams and Jellies

Nuts

Brittles
Roasted Nuts

Challenge Exercise

✓ *Congratulations! You are almost done with this course.*

As a student, you probably did not make the decision of which software to use in this class. In this last exercise, now that you have an idea of what you as a Webmaster need from a Web-design program, do research and write a short report that compares and contrasts various Web-design programs.

Some factors to consider:

1. Cost
2. What other programs integrate with the program?
3. How easy is the program to learn and use?
4. How effective and efficient is the program?
5. What kind of online help and documentation are available for the program?

Appendix A
Computer and Networking Basics

Introduction to Operating Systems

- An **operating system** is a software program that enables your computer hardware and all other software programs to run. Also referred to as an OS, an operating system, such as Windows, Linux, or the Macintosh OS, is the brain that controls the processes, resources, and memory in your computer.
- Operating systems can consist of a number of types of files. For example, Windows contains short software programs, such as games and WordPad, as well as system files that help your hardware to run, and resources, such as fonts and Windows desktop icons.
- An operating system controls how you manage files, modify your desktop display, allocate disk space, and even set your computer clock and date.
- New versions of operating systems are released every few years as enhancements in technology become available. That is why you may have heard of or worked with Windows 95, Windows 98, Windows NT, Windows 2000, Windows ME, and Windows XP. They are all versions of the Windows operating system.
- Software that runs on your computer, such as word processors and spreadsheet programs, is also released in new versions every few years; these versions are designed to work on the then-current version of an operating system.
- Most operating systems are **backwardly compatible**, meaning that software that worked on an earlier version will probably run adequately on a newer version (though some operating systems will require new versions of software or device drivers) . However, if you have an older version of an operating system, you are not likely to be able to use software written for a later version.

Overview of Software

- Software is essentially made up of a set of features you can use to get work done, such as designing company brochures or creating a department budget. Software contains sets of features that you can use through tools such as menus and toolbar buttons.
- Software can fall into several categories. For example, you could use:
  - Financial software that works with numbers and calculations, such as Quicken® or spreadsheet programs such as Excel.
  - Word processing software, such as Microsoft Office Word or Corel™ WordPerfect®, which is used for writing documents such as letters and reports.
  - Desktop publishing and Web design software, such as Adobe PageMaker, Microsoft Office Publisher, Macromedia® Dreamweaver®, or Microsoft Office FrontPage®, which provides tools for designing documents such as newsletters and brochures or Web pages.
  - **Utilities** that help to maintain your system or manage files; for example, antivirus programs to prevent and clean up computer infections and zip programs to compress large files into smaller files.
  - **Drivers**, which are software applications that run your hardware, such as print drivers for a printer and a display driver to enable your operating system to interact with your computer monitor.
- To use software, you first **install** it on your computer. You can then open the software program by using your operating system; for example, you can start installed software programs on a Windows computer by selecting the program name from the Windows Start menu. You can also start a software program by opening any file originally created in that program.

- When you save a document you have created in a software program, it will be saved in that software format with a name you give it. The file name will include an indication of the file format.
- For example, a Microsoft Word document might be called "Rent Letter.doc," where Rent Letter is the name you give the file to identify its contents and the .doc extension indicates that this is a Word document.
- Some common file extensions are .txt for Text file, .rtf for Rich Text Format files, and .xls for Excel spreadsheets.

Computer Communications

- All computers communicate. The central processing unit (CPU) talks to the hard drive controller; the video card communicates with the monitor and the CPU. The printer and the CPU talk to each other. Each element uses a communications protocol—a set of send and receive signals following rules that have been agreed upon by computer manufacturers or established by governmental or professional organizations.
- For example, when you print a document, the program in the computer that handles printing sends a signal to the printer that asks whether it is ready to receive data. The printer normally signals that it is ready. When its print buffer (a place where the document "lines up" waiting for the printer to be available) is full, the printer signals the computer that it cannot receive more data. The computer waits, periodically asking if the printer is ready for more, until the printer signals its readiness.
- When people talk of computer communications, however, they usually mean the ability of one computer to talk with other computers. When personal computers became common in businesses, users began to look for ways to make it possible for personal computers to share data and programs with one another.
- The first solution was **sneaker net**. Users copied files from one computer and carried them to another on a storage media such as a floppy disk.
- That method, however useful, had limits. If the receiving computer was across town, it took a while for the communication to be completed. In addition, businesses have large amounts of data residing under the control of their mainframe computers (a mainframe computer is a powerful computer that serves an entire organization), but the personal computers on desktops at first couldn't make use of that data. Communication was a problem that needed to be solved.

PC-to-Mainframe Communications

- To use a company's mainframe computing capacity, workers require a **terminal**. Terminals are pieces of hardware that have no software of their own. They are connected to the mainframe computer via cables and their communication is managed by a **controller**, another piece of hardware that provides the link between terminals (one controller can handle many terminals) and the mainframe.
- Terminals are single-use devices; they cannot function apart from the mainframe. If they get disconnected from the computer or the mainframe stops working, their users are no longer able to compute.
- In the first days of the personal computer, users thought it would be good to use computers just like terminals. But terminals operate differently from PCs. PCs do not require controllers and ordinarily do not speak the same language as controllers. Often workers who needed both a personal computer and access to the company's mainframe had both a PC and a terminal on their desks. Soon after the introduction of IBM's PC in the early 1980s, however, both hardware and software solutions were created.
- **Terminal emulation software**, programs that mimicked mainframe terminals, was created as early as 1981 for computers built by Digital Equipment Corporation. DEC mainframes used ASCII (American Standard Code for Information Interchange) for encoding characters. Since PCs also used ASCII, it was possible to create software that let a PC work with a DEC mainframe.

- IBM mainframes, however, were a different matter. Rather than use ASCII codes, they use a coding system called EBCDIC (sometimes pronounced EB-sid-ick, short for Extended Binary Coded Decimal Interchange Code).
- Differences between the ASCII and EBCDIC coding systems made it necessary to create **terminal emulation hardware** so the PC and the IBM mainframe could communicate.
- In most installations where PCs and mainframes communicate today, a combination of hardware and software does the job. In many companies, users are connected to a local area **network** and log on (or sign on) to the organization's mainframe without disconnecting from the network. The personal computer then operates not only as an independent machine but also as a network workstation and as a mainframe terminal. PC users can communicate with colleagues in remote locations through networks, electronic mail, and the Internet and World Wide Web.
- If you use a personal computer in a reasonably large organization—school, university, or company—you probably work on a Local Area Network or LAN. Your computer can work locally, using the programs and drives that are installed on it. Your computer, however, is also a workstation; that is, a machine that can use the drives, folders, files, and programs on the computer network.

Compatibility Issues

- In the early days of computing, operating systems and applications that ran on them created files that could not be used by other operating systems and applications. These compatibility problems are known as **cross-platform** issues because they involve different operating systems.
- As discussed above, IBM mainframe systems used the EBCDIC coding system for alphabetic and numeric, and when they became available, personal computers used the ASCII coding system for. Special translation hardware or software is required to allow IBM mainframes to communicate with personal computers.
- In the world of personal computers, you may encounter problems in transporting text from a MAC OS machine to a Windows machine. Applications attempt to account for the differences in the two operating systems so that you can create an Excel document on your iMac that can be read by Excel on a Windows PC. Such a file can be e-mailed, made available on a network, or written to a CD. Usually, you cannot take a removable medium, such as a ZIP disk from a MAC to a Windows machine, but you can almost always take a Windows ZIP disk and read it with a MAC. Apple has tried to make its operating system flexible enough to handle Windows removable media.
- Within an operating system, compatibility issues can also arise. Especially in the early days, applications created files that could not be read by other, similar applications. For example, in DOS, the WordStar word processor used special coding to mark the ends of words. When a user opened a WordStar document in a different word processor, the words looked odd and the text was not understandable. Many software manufacturers, therefore, included conversion utility programs that cleared up most incompatibilities. On personal computers now, you can open a Corel QuattroPro spreadsheet in Excel (and vice-versa) without using a separate conversion program; the manufacturers include the conversion capabilities within the application.

Network Systems

- LANs generally operate in one of two configurations:
  - **File server**, in which a central computer or group of computers controls access to the network's facilities.
  - **Peer-to-peer**, in which users share the resources of their local machines with one another.

File Server Local Area Networks (LANs)

- On **file server** networks, one or more computers act as the central filing system for the **clients** on the network. Data and programs that are to be shared reside on the disk drives controlled by the network programs.

- File server LANs usually connect users in the same building or group of neighboring buildings that can be connected directly by cables.

File Server Network Components

- File server networks include the following elements:
  - The **server** provides files or services to other computers. The server has hard drives and programs that let it communicate with other computers and provide services to them.
  - **Client workstations** are computers that request files or services from servers. Most modern networks can mix computers of different types and capabilities, including Apple machines running Mac OS, PCs running Windows or DOS, and computers running the Unix or Linux operating systems. In a peer-to-peer network, each computer operates as a client when it requests services from other computers and as a server when it provides services to other computers.
  - **Printers** may be shared across the network. Each shared printer is identified by a name. When users want to print, they choose a printer through the application they are using. Other peripherals, such as scanners or plotters, are managed in the same way as printers. (For more information on peripherals, see Appendix B.)
  - **Network cards** convert data from the computer into signals that can be transmitted over cables to and from other computers. Computers use the binary system of 1s and 0s to encode data. Each workstation requires a network card. Network cards are specific to the type of network to which the workstation is connected.
  - **Cables** connect computers to one another and to the server.
  - When network wiring stretches over long distances, a series of **hubs** may be used to strengthen signals transmitted along the cables. The distance from one hub to another depends on the cable type; fiber optic cables allow the longest runs without a hub to boost the signal.

Wireless LANs

- In smaller business or home computing settings, a wireless network solution makes most of the cabling of other networks unnecessary. Using radio frequencies or infrared optical signaling and protocols such as Bluetooth, computers can communicate and share peripheral devices such as printers by use of a network card and wireless access point.
- One problem with wireless networks today is that communication can be interfered with by walls, pillars, or other equipment that can disrupt a radio signal. However, in smaller offices and homes where computers can be set up to avoid these obstacles, wireless networks are a handy networking solution.

Network Use

- When you turn on a computer attached to a network, the computer boots up, but before you can start using it, you are requested for a **login name** or **username** and **password**.
- The login name (also called **user ID**) identifies you to the network and the password ensures that only an authorized person can use the name. If you do not have a valid login name or you don't remember your password, you are not allowed to use the network.
- If you cancel the login process, you can use the machine as a stand-alone computer, but some drives, programs, data files, and printers may be unavailable.

  ✓ *All the illustrations in this section are drawn from a Novell file server network. The objects on your network will have different names.*

Windows Login Screen for Novell Network

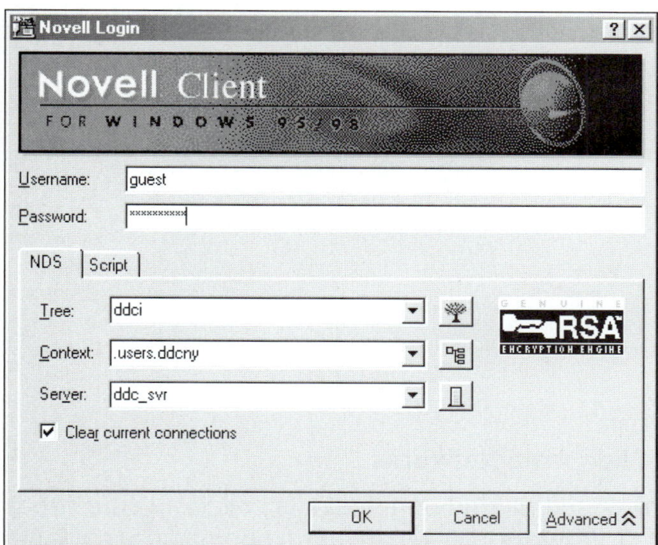

MacOS Login Screen for Novell Network

- The **login name** is a string of characters assigned by network administration that identifies you as a network user. The rights to use network folders and files are associated with the login name.
- On LANs, your access is usually restricted to certain drives, folders, and files. On a file server network, maintaining access rights is the job of the **network administrator**. The network administrator assigns login IDs, defines and maintains access rights, ensures that backups are performed regularly, and works to keep the network operating smoothly.

Structure of a File Server Network

- A Novell file server network has a hierarchical structure:

Sample Tree in Windows

Tree
Ddci
DDCNY
Organization
USERS
Organization unit
DDC_EDITORS
DDC_SVR_EDITORS2
DDC_SVR_SYS
DDC_SVR_VOL2
DDC_SYS

  - **Tree.** A network may have several trees. In the preceding illustration, Ddci is the tree.
  - **Organization.** A tree may have several organizations. In the sample tree illustration, DDCNY is the organization.
  - **Organization unit.** An organization may have several organization units. In the sample tree illustration, USERS is the organization unit.
  - **Server.** An organization unit may have several servers. Server names usually represent disk drives under the server's control.
  - **Volume.** A volume is a name given to a disk drive or a portion of a disk drive. In Windows, drive identifiers (letters) are **mapped** (assigned) to a volume or portion of a volume. These drive letters appear in Windows Explorer just like local drives. On the Macintosh, a volume to which you have access appears on the desktop.
  - **Folder.** A container for files on a volume.

Introduction to Peer-to-Peer Networks

- On **peer-to-peer** networks, each workstation has disk areas that are accessible to other users. In such a network, no machine acts solely as a server. If you want a file from another workstation, you act as a client and the other machine is the server; if someone retrieves files from your machine, your workstation is the server and the other is the client.

- Peer-to-peer networks usually work best when only a few users are involved. Because they require direct cable connection from workstation to workstation, they are usually restricted to a single geographic location.
- Combinations of file server and peer-to-peer networks often exist within a single company. Several users who are working on the same project may work on a peer-to-peer network. They may need, for example, to retain close working-group control of specific files. But when members of the group need to communicate with or use files that belong to the organization as a whole, they may access the file server network that everyone in the company uses.

Explore a Peer-to-Peer Network on Windows

- You can explore a peer-to-peer network on Windows through Windows Explorer. The illustration that follows shows a five-workstation, peer-to-peer network displayed in Windows Explorer.

Five-Workstation, Peer-to-Peer Network on Windows

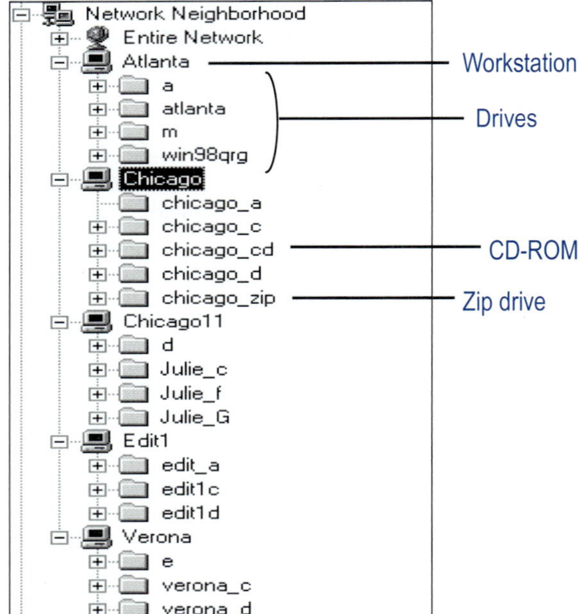

- Any drive on a machine can be shared. Note, for example, the Chicago workstation can give other users access to its CD-ROM and a Zip drive that provides additional storage on 100 MB, removable disks.
- When you right-click on one of the workstations or drives, a shortcut menu appears, as shown in the illustration that follows.

Windows Peer-to-Peer Workstation Shortcut Menu

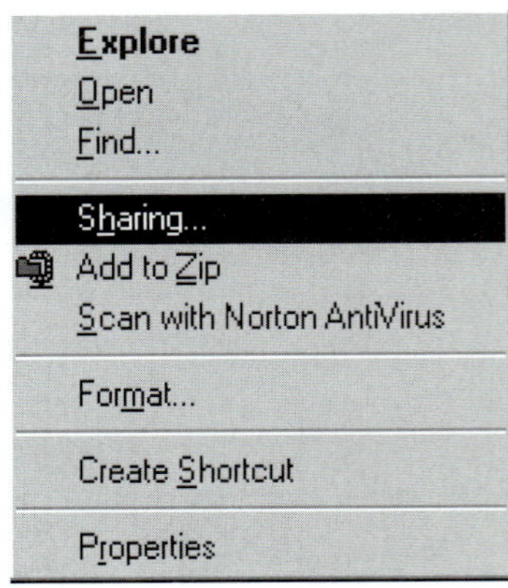

Wide Area Networks

- Another kind of network is called a **Wide Area Network** (**WAN**). In some companies, a WAN is used to connect workers in different geographic locations.
- In the central location, the network operates like a LAN. Workers outside the central location communicate with the network via modem, satellite, or leased telephone lines through hardware and software facilities called **gateways**. The gateways give distant users access to the services of the central location.
- Some people reserve the term WAN for networks that serve only members of the same company or organization. Others consider AOL, Prodigy, CompuServe, World Wide Web, and even the Internet as WANs.

Intranets

- Many users within an organization may have access to the Internet, using their Internet browsers to find information, send e-mail, and exchange files with co-workers. But when they leave the Internet, many of them have to use other applications to review information and exchange files.
- Increasingly, therefore, companies are creating internal Webs to allow employees to access company information using the same application they use to access the Internet. These internal Webs are known as **intranets**.

- Intranets are created and managed within an organization. Users outside the organization generally cannot gain access to them. This means that information that is inappropriate for an Internet site, such as personnel policies or intra-company news, can be provided on an intranet. Using their Internet browsers, workers can use the intranet in the same way they use the Internet.
- Some companies also provide access to their intranets to authorized outside users. For example, a company may wish a supplier to be able to review specifications for a purchase that is about to be made. The supplier then uses an Internet browser, contacts the intranet (often through the Internet), and gains access to the intranet by using an ID and password. The companies that provide such access call this an **extranet**.
- An intranet may have connections to the Internet, but these connections are constructed to prevent unauthorized access. The term **firewall** is used to describe software or hardware that protects a network or computer from unauthorized access.

Telecommuting and Networks

- More and more workers are working away from the office. Some of them simply use their PCs as local machines and communicate with the office only when they have files they want to send or receive. Such users may use the Internet or e-mail service as their way to communicate with the office and never actually log in to the office's computers.
- Other workers, however, connect via telephone lines and work directly on the office network. Telecommuting of this type requires hardware and software on both the workstation and the server. Usually the telecommuter starts the communications software on the workstation, dials up the office computer, and logs in as a network user. The full facilities of the company's network are then available to the workstation.

On Your Own

- After having read about operating systems, demonstrate the appropriate use of the operating system used in your classroom. Visit a computer store and try another operating system.
- Create a PowerPoint presentation demonstrating your knowledge of communication and networking components.
- If you have access to both a Windows and MAC OS machine, create an Excel workbook on a Windows machine and send it to a MAC OS machine. Can the MAC OS version of Excel open the Excel workbook?
- If you have access, create a Word document on a MAC OS machine and send it to a Windows PC. Can the Windows version of Word read the MAC OS word document?
- If you have both Word and Corel WordPerfect on your computer, create a Word document on a Windows PC and try to open it with Corel WordPerfect. Can you tell if any features didn't convert properly? If you know how to use Reveal Codes in WordPerfect, look at the codes for the converted Word document. What do you notice?
- Delineate compatibility issues including cross-platform connectivity. Can RTF files be exchanged across platforms? Try exchanging an RTF file across platforms. Make any necessary adjustments to the file regarding compatibility issues including cross-platform connectivity.
- Investigate the hardware/software solutions necessary to allow a company that uses Windows PCs to read and write data using the company's IBM mainframe applications.
- Prepare a report on the major differences between LANS and WANS. Talk to the network administrator at your school; find out how the school network is setup and what security procedures are in place to protect the integrity of the network.
- Research and discuss the difficulty involved in sharing information for someone who is using an iMac computer with someone who is using a Windows computer. What files are easily transferred between platforms and what files pose problems? How can these issues be addressed so that the files can be shared? For example, are JPEG files easily shared? Can RFT files be exchanged across platforms?

Appendix B
Peripherals and Storage Devices

Introduction to Computer Peripherals

- The hard drive that holds the operating system to run your computer and installed software is located in a central processing unit (CPU). But it's nearly impossible to actually take advantage of all that information and computing power without the use of computer peripherals.
- A **peripheral** is a device such as a printer, keyboard, or monitor that is attached to the CPU and managed by the computer's microprocessor. That attachment may be connected through any of a variety of cable types such as parallel or USB (universal serial bus), or through a wireless infrared connection.
- Peripherals require software called **drivers** to enable them to communicate with the computer and function. A peripheral driver is very specific to the device it works with. By using drivers to control peripherals, the computer operating system is freed from the task of incorporating those controls within its own program and allows the operating system to coordinate with a wide variety of hardware products.
- **Plug and play** refers to the ability of a computer to make automatic settings to configure a peripheral you add through a cable or wireless connection. Plug and Play is also the name of the set of specifications developed by Intel and Microsoft that enables this automatic configuration to occur. The preferred connection for plug and play devices is the USB interface. A USB-equipped computer is capable of supporting up to 127 USB devices—simultaneously!

Input Devices

- The process of computing is, at its most basic, the process of putting information into a computer, having the computer manipulate that information, and generating output, such as a business letter or budget.
- The process of putting information into your computer, whether in the form of commands or content, is called **input**. Various devices can be used to input data into a computer, including a mouse, keyboard, speech commands, and something called pen technology which allows you to write on a computer screen with a special form of pen.
- One of the concerns about most input devices is the area of **ergonomics**. (Ergonomics studies the design of equipment and furnishings with the intention of maximizing productivity and minimizing worker fatigue and discomfort.) Because input devices are used repetitively and for long periods of time, they can cause damage to the user.
- For example, using a keyboard for years on end can lead to a condition affecting the nerves in the wrists called Carpal Tunnel Syndrome. For this reason, you will see some models of input devices touted as being ergonomically designed.

Mouse

- The mouse is a pointing and selection device. Although the mouse itself isn't the primary way to enter content into your computer, it is considered an input device because it enables you to interact with computer data. A mouse can also be used to select commands through tool buttons or menus to perform various actions such as formatting text or saving a file.
- A mouse can be used to place your computer's insertion point in a document so that you can begin to enter content with a keyboard or other method. A mouse can also be used to select objects by clicking on them, and to select text and move it around a document through a method known as drag and drop. The mouse is also the primary device used by most people to draw objects.
- Early mouse models sported a trackball on their underside that the user rolled around a mat on the desktop. The movement of the mouse around the desktop was mirrored in the movement of the cursor on the computer screen.

- Later mouse models moved the trackball to the top of the device, where, instead of moving the mouse itself around the desktop, the user could roll the trackball with the thumb or finger and that movement was mirrored on screen.
- Today, there are optical mouse models. An optical mouse uses light sensors that detect movement, rather than any moveable part such as a trackball. Many new mouse models are also cordless, helping to get rid of some of the clutter of wires surrounding a computer setup.
- The mouse of today typically offers three parts: a left button, a right button, and a center button called a scroll wheel. The left button is used to select things; the right button displays context-sensitive shortcut menus, and the scroll wheel makes moving through a document—especially lengthy Web pages—easier.
- You can control how your mouse functions to a large extent by using your operating system controls.

The Windows Mouse dialog box, accessed through the Control Panel

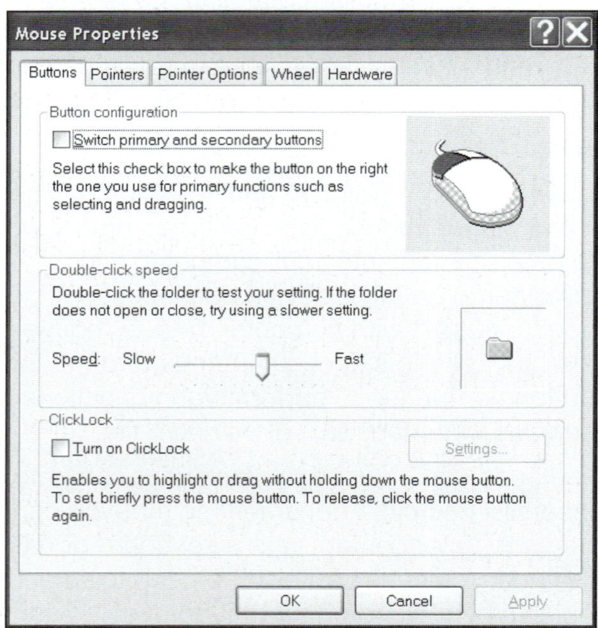

Keyboard

- The keyboard used with your computer has as its ancestor a typewriter keyboard. The arrangement of letters on the keys themselves, called QWERTY after the six letters in the top left corner, has remained largely intact from the old-fashioned manual typewriter to the modern-day keyboard.
- In addition to the letters, numbers and functional keys such as the Enter or Spacebar that a typewriter included, a computer keyboard may contain several other types of keys:
  - A function key is a key numbered from F1 to F12 that may be displayed across the top of the keyboard, or, with certain portable keyboards, embedded within the standard keys. A function key invokes a function such as displaying a help screen or activating a menu bar. Function keys are sometimes used in conjunction with other keys such as the Alt or Ctrl key to perform secondary functions.
  - Internet-ready keys give you one touch access to online elements such as your e-mail or home page.

  ✓ *Internet-ready keyboards have up to seven programmable Internet-ready keys. You can set these up to access areas of the Internet you visit frequently with a single keystroke.*

  - Directional keys allow you to move your insertion point around a document. In addition, keys such as Home, End, Page Up, and Page Down allow you to move quickly to another area of a document or screen.
- There are a variety of keyboard designs available, with most designed to ease repetitive stress to the user's hands and wrists. Ergonomic keyboards may have a curvy appearance, or even be split into two sections. Many keyboards provide a wrist rest area at the bottom of the keyboard, or you can buy a wrist rest at any office supply store to work with any keyboard.
- Wireless keyboards provide some freedom for the user. Wireless keyboards can either use infrared technology (just like a television remote control) or radio frequencies to establish a wireless connection. With infrared technology, the computer and keyboard have to have their infrared ports facing each other. With radio frequency, the connection can be made with the equipment in any position, and often up to 30 feet apart.

Speech

- Speech recognition (also called voice recognition) is a technology that is still evolving. Voice recognition software can be trained to your own speech patterns by having you read sample text into a microphone attached to your computer. The software then matches your patterns to stored speech patterns and turns your spoken words into text in a document. Speech can also be used to dictate voice commands, such as “Save,” or “Open.”
  - ✓ *Speech recognition is useful for those with visual impairments and provides one viable way for these people to interact with a computer.*
- Because there is such a wide variety of accents and inflections among human beings, speech recognition software is not 100 percent accurate. Content entered using speech sometimes needs to be corrected using a mouse and keyboard. For that reason, few computers make do with only speech recognition as a method to enter content.

Pen

- Pen technology has been around for the last ten years or so. Pen technology uses a combination of handwriting recognition software and a specialized pen device that you can use to write either on an input panel or directly on certain computer screens.
- Pen technology is traditionally used by people who work with graphics, because it provides a much more natural method to enter drawings into a computer document. However, to date, this technology has been slow to be accepted.
- With the release of a new computer format called Tablet PC in the fall of 2002, pen computing is undergoing something of a renaissance. The handwriting recognition software that underlies pen technology in Windows XP for Tablet PC has advanced to the point where approximately 97 percent of what you write can be converted to text automatically with no error.
  - ✓ *One big advantage to pen input is that even those who don’t know how to type can input content into a computer using it.*

Scanners

- Scanners are another method of getting input into your computer, though they are usually not considered an input device. These peripherals allow you to scan a hard copy document into an electronic format, creating a computer graphics file. Scanners come with their own software to perform the scan and also to manipulate, edit, and save the scanned image in a computer file.

A scanned image displayed in the HP 2210 flatbed scanner software

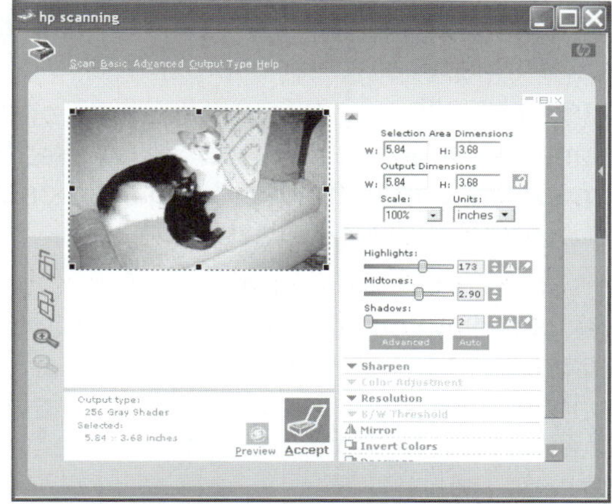

- One important feature of a scanner is the degree of image resolution it can produce. The higher the resolution, the better the image quality.
- Images are made up of tiny dots called pixels. The higher the resolution of an image, the more pixels per inch. An optical resolution of 1,200 dots per inch (also called dpi), for example, would be very high quality (and more than most consumers need for their purposes). For most people’s needs, 300 dpi is adequate.
- The speed with which you can transfer data from a scanner to a computer is a consideration. A USB connection allows transfers of 12 megabits per second, compared to only 2 megabits per second through a parallel port.
- Scanners are available in flatbed models, which allow you to place documents, or media such as a book, flat on a panel for scanning. They also come in sheetfed models where you must feed a printed document through the device. This makes scanning bulkier document formats such as books and magazines impossible.
- Some multipurpose machines may include printing, faxing, copying and scanning capabilities in a single unit.

Output Devices

- Getting content into a computer is only half of the process. Peripheral devices are also used to generate output. Output may come in the form of a printed document or a faxed document.
  - ✓ *By networking computers, you can share peripheral devices such as printers or fax machines among several computers.*

Printers

- Printers today provide a lot of technology for a very reasonable cost. Purchasing a color printer with very satisfactory print quality is within the means of most computer users. Printers come in two main types:
  - Laser printers use a laser beam to create an image on a drum that holds an electrostatic charge. The charge attracts toner (ink), then uses heat to apply the toner to a page.
  - Inkjet technology sprays a liquid ink onto paper to form letters or graphic images. Inkjet printers can produce output quality similar to that of laser printers, though they are typically slower.
- You can find both black and white and color printers, though the color feature has become so affordable that most newer printers are color printers.
- Printers print with various resolutions, a measure of the quality of the output. A good-quality resolution would be 1,200 × 1,200 dots per inch, though both higher and lower quality exists.
- The speed with which a printer can print a document has always been a consideration. Newer printers take advantage of a USB connection to provide faster transfer of data from the computer to the printer. Printers will output a certain number of pages per minute, a gauge of actual printing speed.

Faxes

- Faxing sends a copy (or a facsimile) of a document in digitized form over a phone line. Originally faxing technology was available only through machines connected to a phone line through which you would feed a document. The recipient of the fax also had to have a machine that printed the digitized version of the document (typically a bitmap image) on paper.
- Today many people find it convenient to skip the fax machine altogether and fax digital files directly from one computer to another, or one computer to a fax machine, via a fax modem that uses faxing software. The recipient who receives the fax on his or her computer then prints it out on a standard printer.
  - ✓ *If a document isn't available in a digital file format, you can use a scanner to scan it and save it as a computer file, then fax that file from your computer.*
- To fax from a computer, you essentially print a document to a fax rather than to a printer. Faxing software walks you through entering recipient information, and even building fax cover sheets.

The Windows fax wizard

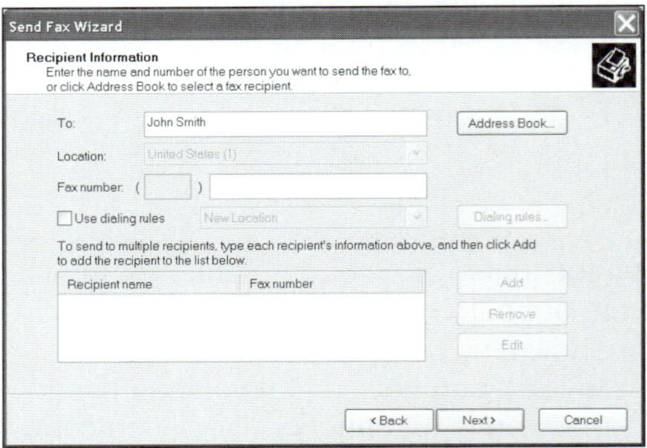

Storage Devices

- Computer files are saved on storage devices using drives. The storage medium itself, called a disk, is placed in the drive and your computer writes data to the disk.
- Your computer's hard drive is one kind of storage device built into your computer. Hard drive capacities today are measured in gigabytes. Other kinds of storage media include:
  - Floppy disks; though no longer floppy (they are encased in hard plastic), these contain a film that is coated with particles that can hold a magnetic field. A computer writes data to the disk in binary code using 1s and 0s.
  - Zip or Jaz disks are similar in appearance to a floppy disk, but they can hold up to 100 megabytes of data.

- CD-ROMs (compact disc read-only memory) are compact discs that contain data, such as software program or even music. CD-ROMs are read only, meaning the user cannot save data to them.
- CD-RWs are rewriteable CDs, meaning that you can both read information off of them and save information to them.
- CD-ROMS and CD-RWs can hold around 650 megabytes of data, much more than floppy disks or even zip disks.

✓ *Note that a floppy or zip medium is called a disk, but a CD is named a disc.*

Computer Displays (Monitors)

- Not much can be accomplished with your computer without a monitor to show you what you're doing.
- Most monitors today use a CRT display. A CRT is similar to a television screen, but the images on them are even more precise.
- In the CRT model, electron guns send beams of electrons to the end of a tube covered with phosphors. The glowing of these phosphors results in images on your monitor. CRTs are analog devices and though their image quality can be high, their analog nature means they can produce inaccuracies when rendering video images.
- Flat panel monitors are the wave of the future. These display devices use a liquid crystal display technology (LCD) that has been popular in notebook computers for years.
- LCD displays put liquid crystals between two layers of glass. Voltage is actually applied to the crystals to rearrange them in a way that allows light to come through, forming an image. The introduction of thin film transistor (referred to as TFT or active-matrix) technology to the scene provides better quality by giving each pixel in the image its own controlling transistor.
- Improvements that are occurring in flat panel technology will bring their refresh rates (how frequently all the information on the screen has to be redrawn) and color quality in line with the traditional CRT standards. As that happens, flat panels will be preferred for their thin size and more accurate digital image technology.
- You can set your monitor resolution and other display controls using your computer's operating system controls.

The Windows Display Properties dialog box

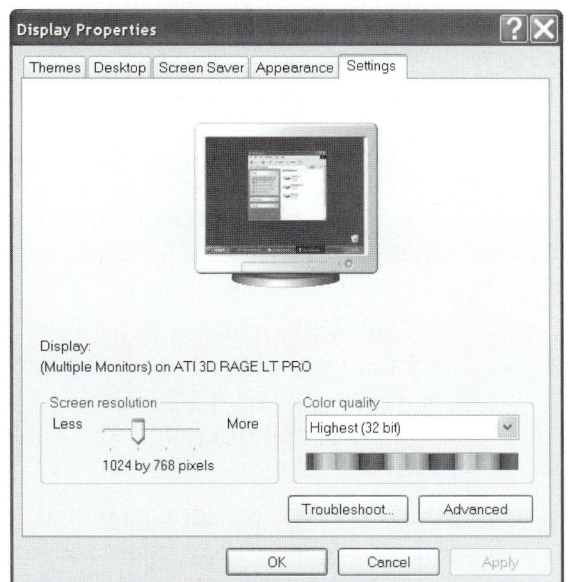

On Your Own

- Create a document and outline differences among a variety of electronic input devices. Compare and contrast the following input devices: keyboard, speech recognition, and pen technology.
- Use PowerPoint to illustrate the advantages/disadvantages of various input devices. Illustrate the devices that would be appropriate for a variety of functions (e.g., music files, video files, etc.).
- Work with a partner to describe different types of output devices. Compare and contrast at least three types of devices that you discuss. Present your information to the class.
- Create a PowerPoint presentation that compares and contrasts the various primary/secondary storage devices.

Appendix C
Using the Internet and Intranets

The Internet and Intranets

- The **Internet** is a worldwide network of computers that makes it possible to view and access information of all kinds. The Internet consists of all the computers, telephone lines, satellites, and connection devices and organizations that enable this exchange of information.
- The **World Wide Web** is a component of the Internet created to allow you to use an easy, **graphical interface** to view information organized as pages. Web pages support graphics as well as audio and video files. The coding used to create Web pages also supports **hyperlinks**, used to move quickly from one Web document to another.
- An **intranet** is similar to the Internet, in that it is a network of computers that allows people to view and access information. However, rather than being a publicly available network, an intranet is usually internal to a company or other organization and accessed mainly by the employees or members of that organization.
- Company networks such as LANs and WANs also store information and can be searched for information and used to share resources.
- **Gopher** is a menu system that allows you to search various sources available on the Internet through a browsing system of directories. Gopher predates the World Wide Web.
- **Telnet** is a program that allows one computer to log onto another host computer. Telnet allows you to access servers remotely.
- **WAIS (Wide Area Information Server)** is a system that allows for searches based on contents of files, not just file titles; this system is somewhat outdated.

The Structure of the Internet

- The computers linked on the Internet are linked together using a variety of connections—such as cables, telephone lines, and satellites. They pass information back and forth using the communications protocol called **TCP/IP** (Transmission Control Protocol/Internet Protocol). TCP/IP is actually a suite of protocols that work together to make the Internet work.
- TCP/IP performs the following communications functions:
  - Permits login from remote computers.
  - Routes data between Internet servers.
  - Makes sure that data packets are error-free and assembled in the right sequence.
  - Converts text-based domain names into numerical IP (Internet Protocol) addresses.
- The computers that form the Internet or intranets can be divided into the following groups:
  - **Clients** are computers that connect to the Internet to do research and send e-mail. Most personal computers that access the Internet fall into this category. Client computers access the Internet in one of three ways:
    - Online service, such as America Online (AOL) or Prodigy.
    - Internet Service Provider.
    - Direct access through a dedicated communications line (telephone or cable, for example) that is continuously connected to the Internet.
  - **Online services** provide a variety of shopping, research, and e-mail services and also provide access to the Internet. America Online (AOL), Prodigy, and MSN are popular online services. Such services are not actually part of the Internet, but most users do not distinguish between AOL and the Internet.

- **Internet Service Providers (ISPs)** are computer servers that provide other computers with access to the Internet. Networks such as Earthlink, NetCom, and AT&T Worldnet are ISPs.
- **Internet servers** (sometimes called hosts) are computers that provide access to information. When an Internet user contacts an Internet site, the computer that contains the site is a server. Internet servers may also act as clients when they request a link to another site. Some servers offer specialized services, such as e-mail and file transfer.
- **Search engines or sites** are Internet computers dedicated to providing information about other Internet sites. Yahoo!, Excite, and Lycos started life as search engines but now have expanded to offer a wide range of services in addition to search capabilities.
- **E-mail servers** are computers that provide electronic mail boxes and e-mail services.
- **File transfer protocol (FTP) servers** are computers dedicated to allowing the transfer of files from one computer to another.

Internet Addresses—URLs (Uniform Resource Locators)

- Because the Internet is not a single network but a collection of networks, a naming system called the **domain name system** is used to identify the exact location of Internet servers and their primary Internet activity. It is something like the telephone numbering system that includes country codes, area codes, and individual phone numbers.
- An Internet address (IP address) is made up of a four-part series of numbers. The domain name system translates the numbers into a user-friendly system of text-based names. So instead of typing in 128.337.392.449 to order a pizza over the Internet, you can type in "www.pizzahut.com." Text is simply easier to remember.
- To locate an Internet site, you enter an address called a **URL (uniform resource locator)**. Usually this address is a group of characters that looks like the following: http://www.amazon.com
- In this address, note the following items:
  - **http** stands for HyperText Transfer Protocol, the communications protocol used by sites on the World Wide Web. (An FTP site's address would be preceded by ftp instead of http.)
  - **www** stands for World Wide Web, the largest part of the Internet.
  - **amazon** is the name used to identify the organization responsible for the content of the site. It is usually some form of the name of the company or organization; for example, amazon is the identifier for Amazon.com, an online store.
  - **com** is the **domain** identifier. Different types of organizations have different domain names.
- Common Internet domains include the following:

Domain:	Used By:
.com	commercial/business
.gov	government
.edu	educational
.org	various organizations, usually non-profit
.mil	military
.net	network resources

- In addition, many domain names include an abbreviation of the country where the site is located; for example, *uk* in a URL indicates a site in the United Kingdom (Great Britain and Northern Ireland).
- Companies or personal users can obtain a domain name by purchasing an existing domain name or by registering a new one. To register a domain name, you can go to any number of authorized registry sites (see http://www.icann.org/registrars/accredited-list.html) to confirm that your choice is unregistered and pay for your domain name.

Using a Browser

- To use the Internet or an intranet, you need an **Internet browser**, such as Microsoft Internet Explorer or Netscape Navigator. A browser is an application that:
  - Lets you connect to the Internet/intranet either directly or through a modem and a telephone line using an ISP or online service.
  - Lets you enter URLs.
  - Displays information provided by an Internet/intranet site.
  - Lets you save or print displayed information so it can be reviewed later.
  - Recognizes and lets you activate connections (called **hyperlinks)** to other addresses.
  - Lets you save addresses that you'd like to visit again using **favorites** (Internet Explorer) or **bookmarks** (Netscape Navigator).

Web Page Basics

- Though Web pages differ widely in design and format, many Web pages share some common features.
- On many Web pages, information is organized using **frames**. Often, a frame at the left side of the Web page holds links that act as a table of contents for the Web site.
- The browser window that displays the Web page has additional features that will be familiar to you from other applications:
  - The title bar displays the name of the current Web page.
  - A menu bar offers menus of commands for displaying and controlling Web pages.
  - A toolbar contains buttons for executing frequently used commands and functions.
  - If the page has more content than can be displayed in the current window size, scroll bars become active.
  - The address bar displays the Internet address of the current Web page.
  - The standard Windows sizing controls also appear in the Internet Explorer window.
  - The status bar displays the progress of a Web page as it **loads** on your computer screen. It also displays the current Web page address and changes to show the addresses of links as you point to them.

Sample Web Page

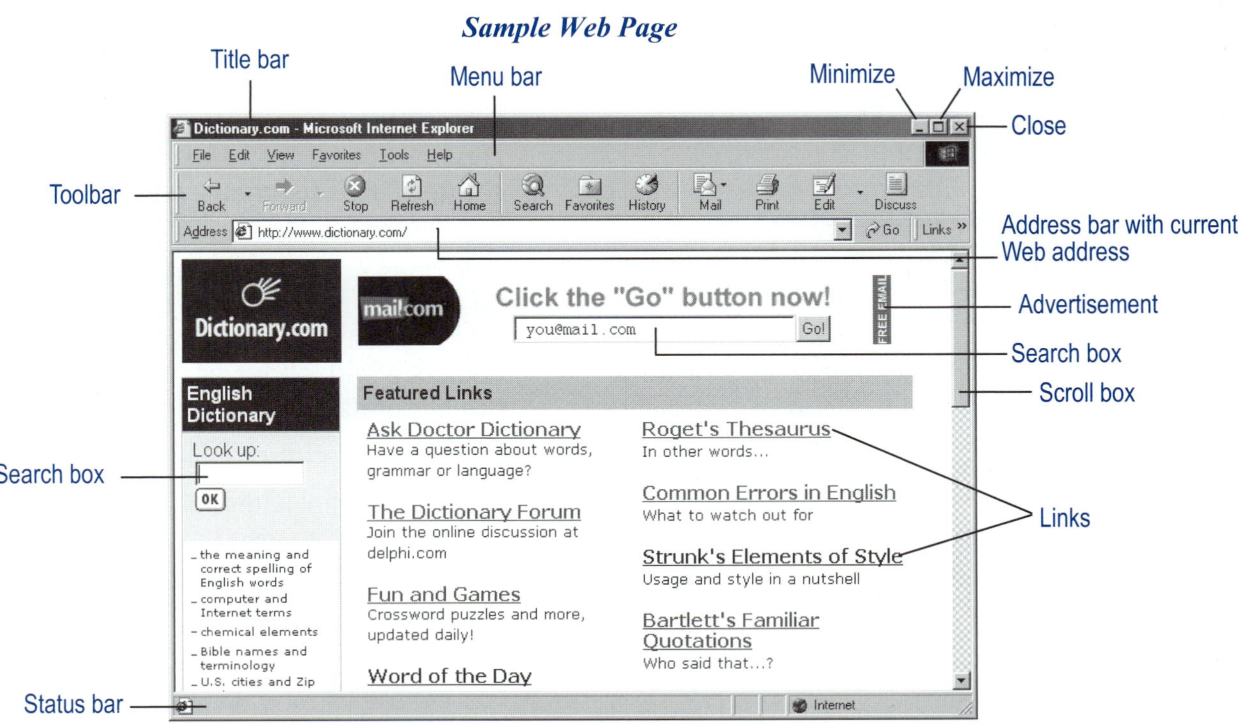

Standards of Online Behavior

- The Internet is a great resource for everything from understanding the do's and don'ts of buying a new car, to paying bills, to researching school term papers.
- Over the Internet you can purchase concert tickets, order steaks for the weekend cookout, and print maps for your next road trip. The ability to communicate with people and visit places all over the world from the comfort of your home, classroom, or office is amazing.
- It is important, however, to use this great communication tool responsibly. Respectful communication with others and a cooperative attitude are indispensable when taking advantage of the many resources available.

Netiquette

- Generally speaking, there are very few actual "Net Laws" at this writing (excluding Federal laws for prosecuting Internet hackers, virus terrorists, and other "cybercriminals"). Those that exist are generally devised by the Internet community itself.
- For example, when you sign up with an Internet service provider (ISP), you will probably be asked to agree to adhere to strict usage rules that, if you disobey them, can result in a loss of service—and possible prosecution.
- Netiquette (net + etiquette) has developed over time as a set of behaviors that should be adhered to while working online.

FTP Etiquette

- FTP, or File Transfer Protocol, allows you to transfer data files and software programs from FTP sites to your computer over the Internet. If you are using a browser program to access an FTP site, you will use anonymous FTP. This means that you won't need a login name or password to gain access to the FTP site server.
- We are allowed access to these vast storehouses of information through the generosity of the individual FTP host institutions (universities, organizations, etc.); therefore; it is important that we play by their rules.

Some FTP Netiquette Hints and Tips

- Respect any posted hours at an anonymous FTP host. As a general rule, most sites ask that you not access their databases between the hours of 8 am and 5 pm, as these are the hours when they are busiest. Remember to verify time zones: for example, when it is 5 pm on the East Coast it is only 2 pm on the West Coast.
- If you log on to an anonymous FTP site (without using a browser application) as an anonymous user, it is recommended that you use your full Internet e-mail address as your password.
- Use available site help files before asking for help. Many sites provide README and INDEX files that provide answers to commonly-asked questions.
- Many FTP hosts post rules particular to their site. Be aware of these postings and follow the rules strictly.
- Download only files you know you will need. Don't tie up the network downloading information you don't need.

E-Mail Etiquette

- The written word is a powerful tool for communication, so you should exercise caution in how you use words on the Internet. Remember: an e-mail message will almost always be taken at face value. The reader is not afforded the luxury of perceiving nuance.
- Since your message will not be accompanied by facial expression or vocal inflection, it is imperative that you write with clarity and courtesy. Keep sarcasm to a minimum, or avoid it altogether.
- This does not mean that mail to friends cannot be funny or mildly satiric, but be aware that your message can be misinterpreted. Know your audience and, above all, minimize the risks or misinterpretation.

Some E-Mail Netiquette Hints and Tips

- Using all capital letters gives a word very strong emphasis. It can also have the effect of SHOUTING! In general, it is better to use upper- and lowercase letters as you would when writing a letter.

- Enclosing a word with *asterisks* has a different effect. Asterisks indicate a mild emphasis and serve the same purpose as italics.
- Signature "smileys" can help to indicate mood or tone of voice:

:-)	I'm happy. (Made with a colon, hyphen, and right parenthesis. Tilt head to the left for full effect.)
;-)	Just joking. (Made with semicolon, hyphen, and right parenthesis.)
:-(	I'm unhappy. (Made with colon, hyphen, and left parenthesis.)

- Be careful when replying to a message. If your reply is to be automatically sent back to the originating address, verify that the address is not connected to a list or group. A personal response intended for a specific person may end up in the hands of many.
- Electronic mail is not protected and not private. Your message can be forwarded or copied to anyone, anywhere. Think of it as an electronic postcard—fully exposed and able to be read by anyone who comes in contact with it.
- Computer and network hackers can easily access anything sent across the Internet. Assume that anyone with a computer has the potential to read your message.
- Never send chain letters over the Internet. Not only are they annoying, but they are forbidden by many Internet service providers, and if you participate in sending them, your privileges may be revoked.
- Sending angry or heated messages is called "flaming." Everyone seems to agree that "flames" are childish and never necessary. If you are feeling emotional, take the time to calm down before sending responses.
- Use the subject or RE: line to clearly state the topic of your message. This is the first thing the recipients will see in their e-mail directory.
- Keep messages concise. When replying to a message, be sure to include enough information from the original message so that your reply is understood. Delete anything from the original message that is irrelevant.
- Messages should have lines that are no more than 65–70 characters in length and generally no more than 12 lines. Do not assume that the person has the same size screen or that the wrap feature will automatically make the message "fit."
- If you send a long message, it is a good idea to tell the recipients at the beginning of the message so that they have the option of downloading the message to read later.
- There are many other rules and procedures that you will learn as you become an experienced Net user. Typically, the ISP service contract to which you have agreed will contain specific rules about sending e-mail through its server. School labs and office environments will have their own procedures that are strictly enforced. Check with your teacher or network administrator for more information.

Internet Ethics

- Ethics is the study of standards of conduct and moral judgment. Ethical behavior is as important when you use the Internet as it is in any other part of your life.
- Internet ethics is a hot topic on the Internet, as users attempt to define standards of behavior that all can adhere to. Remember that, generally speaking, the Internet is regulated only by those who use it.
- Use the following points as a guideline for ethical behavior when you use the Internet:
    - **Plagiarism:** The Internet is a vast resource of information. If you use material from a source on the Internet, cite the source properly.
    - **Privacy:** Networked systems make it all too easy for determined snoopers to read other people's e-mail or review documents on their computers. Respect the privacy of others, as you expect them to respect yours.
    - **Piracy:** Piracy of copyrighted materials, such as software or music, has always been a serious problem. Do your part to respect copyrights.
    - **Hacking and Viruses:** Hacking and the spreading of destructive viruses are legal issues. No matter how much fun you might find it to access a server illegally or pull a prank with a virus, you can face serious charges if you do so.
    - Avoid "spamming"—sending the same e-mail message to many recipients.

- Respect the privacy of other Internet users.
- Adhere to any guidelines set up for you in the setting in which you will use the Internet, such as your business or school.

- Remember that whenever you use the Internet, you are part of an entire community of users who rely on you to behave sensibly and ethically. Keep both ethics and Netiquette in mind as you use the Internet.

Searching Online

- Searching is the systematic approach to finding information on the Web. This differs from surfing, which is simply jumping from link to link.
- With the help of online Internet search tools and a basic knowledge of how to search, you can greatly increase your chances of finding specific information.
- When you use a search tool, you are not searching the Internet live. You are searching a database or **index** maintained by the search site. Because methods for compiling databases differ among search sites, you can expect search results to differ as well from site to site.
- There are two major types of search tools available on the Web: **search engines** and **directories**.

  ✓ *Some Internet guides refer to all search tools as search engines.*

- Both directories and search engines maintain Web sites that you can access just like any other Web site: click a link or type the site's address in your browser's address bar.
- Some search sites provide special features that direct you to certain kinds of results. Google, for example, is a search site that allows you to search for certain types of files (such as PDF or non-HTML), retrieve news stories related to your search term, to restrict your search to their directory (which contains over 3 million sites), or to a specific Web site.

Evaluating and Validating Online Information

- There are millions of pages of information to be mined on the World Wide Web and on the Internet. Not all of that information can be trusted.
- A healthy skepticism about all information found on the Internet is a good thing. Anyone with a computer, very little technical expertise, and an opinion can post information on the Internet.
- Following are a few suggestions to keep in mind as you explore the Internet:
  - Check to see when the site was last updated. Most sites include this information somewhere on the home page.
  - Be wary of sites that contain many typographical or grammatical errors.
  - Go to sites run by established organizations.
  - Long Internet addresses with many backslashes (/) and tildes (~) often indicate personal Web pages.
  - Check several sources before deciding whether information is accurate.
  - Look at the end of the Internet address to see what type of organization is running the site. For example a .gov at the end of an address indicates a government site, and an .edu indicates an educational organization such as a university.

Searching Basics

- You perform a search in a search engine by entering a keyword or phrase in the search text box, then clicking a button typically labeled "Search" or "Go." The search engine then displays matching sites.

  ✓ *Most search engines display results with a ranking of how relevant each item might be to the keyword you entered.*

- Web sites get listed in search databases with associated keywords that they feel relate to the interests of those searching and to the topic of their site. When you perform a search, the search engine looks for matches between your keyword and the keywords organizations and individuals have associated with their sites.
- You can use as many keywords as you like, dividing them with commas that act like the word "and" to add words to the search string. However, too many words can result in a less accurate list of results. Where the keywords **Dogs, Retriever** might get the results you want, **Dogs, Retriever, Golden, Puppies, Canine** will probably provide an odd mix of results.
- Google works a bit differently from some other sites. Google searches only sites that contain all the words you enter. So if you enter **golden retriever,** you won't get sites with the words **golden** but not **retriever** and sites with the word **retriever** but not **golden**, as you may with other

search engines. This feature helps narrow down your search quickly.

- If you want a specific phrase to be found, put those words in quotes. For example, if you want to find the World Health Organization, enter the keyword as "**World Health Organization**". Only specific matches to the phrase will be searched for, rather than sites that match either World or Health or Organization.

Use the NOT (-) Operator

- You can *exclude* information from your search results using the **NOT operator**. The NOT operator helps you to eliminate certain search results that you know you will not want.
- Some search engines require you to use andnot rather than not, as shown in the illustration below.
- Suppose you want to explore the Web for pages relating to grandfathers, and you want to eliminate references to grandfather clocks. You would create a search string like this:
  - grandfather NOT clock
- Running the search with this search string displays Web pages relating to many other kinds of grandfathers, but not to grandfather clocks.

  ✓ *You might still receive hits for "grandfather clocks" from the previous search string, because the search engine understands that* clock *is different from* clocks.

- Generally, you can use the – sign (use the hyphen key or the minus sign on your keyboard's number pad) in place of the NOT operator, in the same way you use the + sign:
  - Grandfather –clock

  ✓ *Google ignores words such as **how** and **where** in its searches, as well as single characters such as numbers or letters. You can use the + sign ahead of such a common word to have it included in your search.*

Alltheweb Search Using the andnot Operator

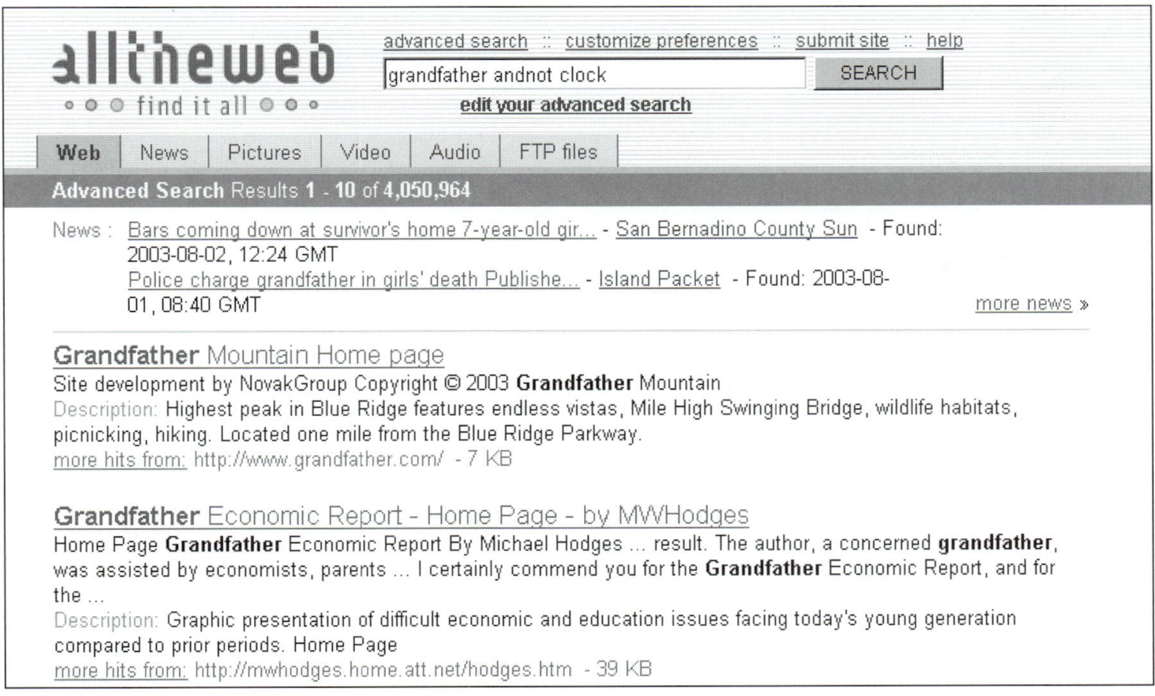

Use the OR Operator

- The **OR operator** is used to broaden a search. An OR search string looks like this:
  - El Nino OR La Nina
- This search string will find any pages that contain El Nino or any pages that contain La Nina.
- The OR operator can be very useful when you are not sure how a particular subject might be indexed in a search engine's database.
- For example, if you want to find Web pages relating to pottery, you could create the following search string to make sure you find as many sites as possible:
  - pottery OR ceramics

Use Truncation (Wildcards)

- Some search engines, such as Northern Light, automatically search for plurals of singular words, as well as singulars of plural words.
- Other search engines consider all words created from a common stem to be different in terms of search results, so that the following search strings may yield very different search results:
  - Run
  - Runs
  - Runners
  - Running
- **Truncation** allows you to create a search string using a word stem such as *run* along with the *** wildcard**.
- The * symbol stands for any number of letters at the end of the keyword, so you can find information about a particular subject without having to enter multiple keywords. The search string *run** would find all the variations listed above.
- Wildcards can also help you find information when you're not sure of the spelling.

  ✓ *You can insert a wildcard anywhere in a keyword, not just at the end of the word.*
- Suppose you want to find sites that contain the phrase *compu*, such as CompuTek, computing, computers, and so on. You could set up the following search string:
  - compu*
- Running this search in Google gives information about any site containing a word that begins with *compu*.
- Not all search engines support the use of truncation and wildcards. You can find out if a search engine does by checking its Help page.

Google Wildcard Search

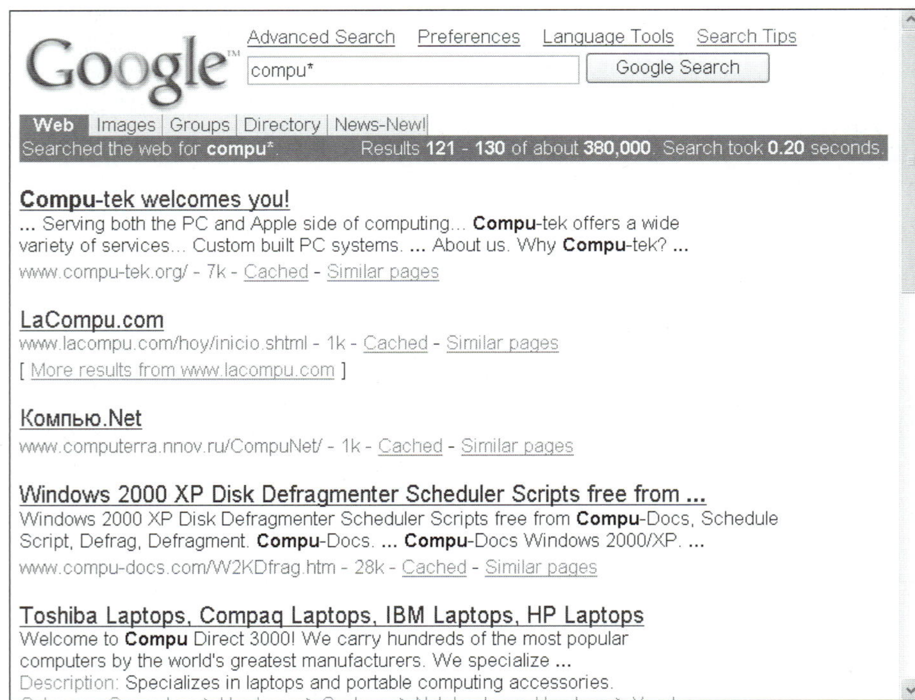

Use Multiple Operators

- You can use more than one operator in a search string along with keywords to further limit your search results.
- Suppose you're looking for information on flyfishing in the Great Smoky Mountains. To get the most responses, you should consider using both *fishing* and *flyfishing* as keywords. You could create the following search string:
  - fishing OR flyfishing AND Smoky Mountains

✓ *You can use operators and signs interchangeably in a search string. For example, you can compose a search string using both the (+) and the AND operators.*

Use Parentheses

- You can further control search results when using multiple operators by enclosing some keywords and operators in parentheses.
- As in a mathematical expression, parentheses tell a search engine how to relate the keywords in the search string.
- Suppose you want to find a resort for your vacation. You might want to golf or go sailing at this resort (but not necessarily both). You could create the following search string:
  - resort AND (golf OR sailing)
- The parentheses tell the search engine that it should find Web pages that contain both resort and golf OR resort and sailing.

Using Multiple Operators in HotBot

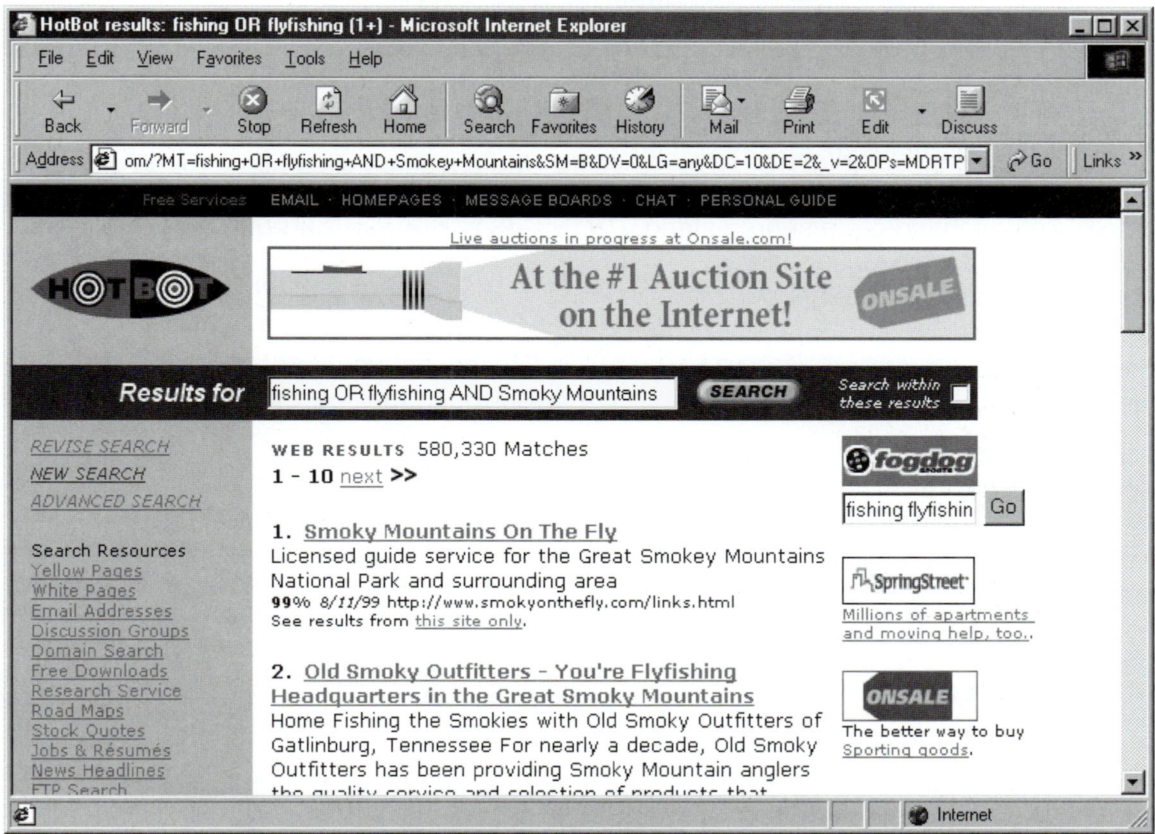

Alltheweb Search Using Parentheses

- To further refine a search, it is possible to nest parentheses within parentheses, just as you do in a mathematical equation.
- For example, you might create a search string to find out information on Baroque music, specifically violin compositions by Bach or Handel.
  - Baroque AND (“violin” AND (Bach OR Handel))

    ✓ *Just as in mathematics, you have to have a closing parenthesis for each opening one. Make sure you have all your parentheses in the right places.*
- The more comfortable you become working with a search engine, the easier you will find it to create complex searches that give you just the informaton you need.

About Natural Language Queries

- Many search sites allow you to create search strings in the form of a question. These questions are called **natural language queries**.
- A typical natural language query might be:
  What is the capital of Assyria?
- Notice that you do not need to use quotes to surround the search string. Nor do you need to use operators. The search engine extracts keywords from your question and bases the search on them.
- Most search engines allow this type of searching. In addition, the Ask Jeeves(sm) Web site is designed specifically to handle natural language searches.

  ✓ *To find out if a search engine supports natural language searching, check the search engine's Help pages.*

Perform a Natural Language Search

- Natural language searches are among the easiest searches you can perform. All you need to do is think up a fairly specific question.
- Suppose you want to know who is the richest person in the world. You could create a search string like this:

  Who is the richest person on earth?

  ✓ *To help the search engine locate proper information, be sure to capitalize terms and proper names as you would see them in a reference book.*

- Running this query in Ask Jeeves results in sites that exactly match your query.
- As with other kinds of keyword searching, it pays to be as specific as possible when creating a natural language search. For example, these queries will yield different results:
  - *What are the seven wonders of the world?*
  - *What are the seven natural wonders of the world?*
  - *What are the seven wonders of the ancient world?*

Ask Jeeves Natural Language Search

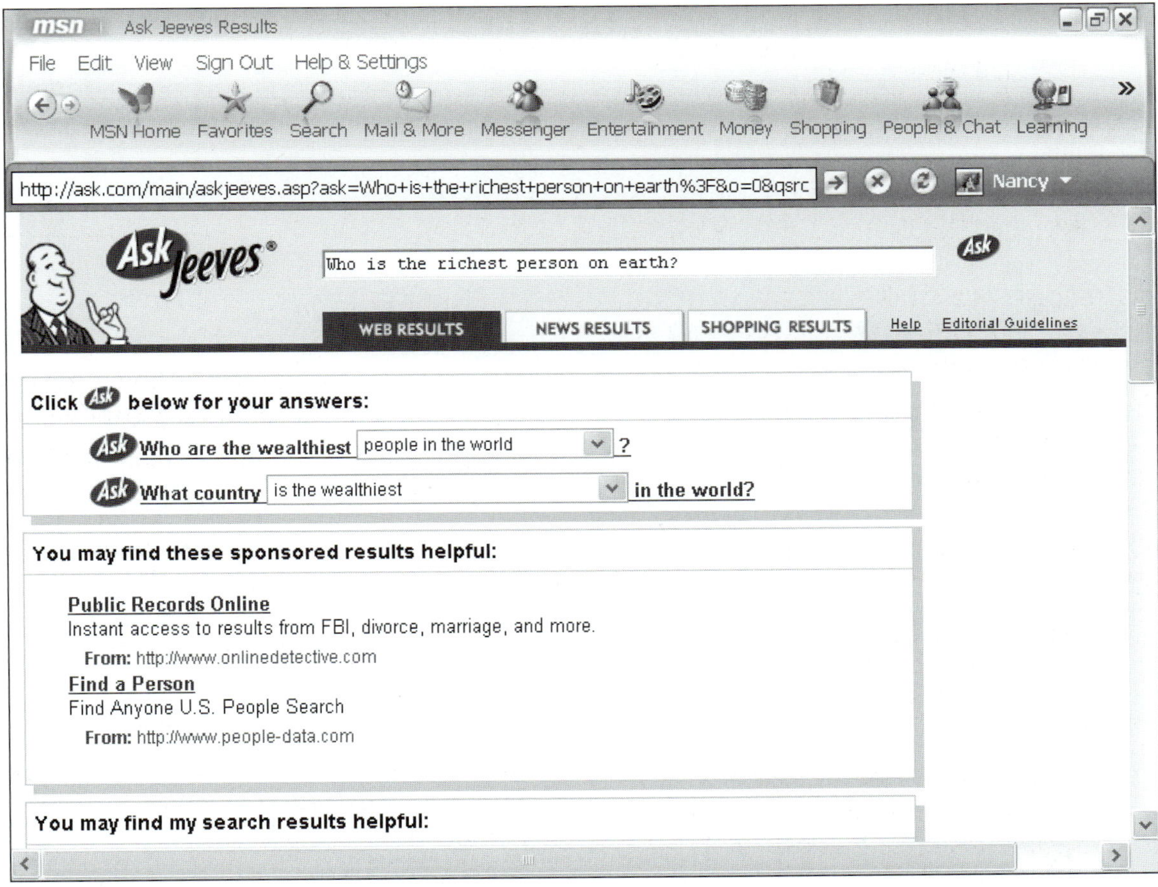

Use a Metasearch Engine

- Powerful search sites called **metasearch engines** have become popular. These sites do not have databases of their own. Instead, they use the databases of other search engines to find results for your search string.
- Major metasearch engine sites include:
  - ProFusion® (www.profusion.com)
  - MetaCrawler (www.metacrawler.com)
  - InfoSpace (www.metafind.com)
  - Search.com (www.search.com)
  - Dogpile (www.dogpile.com)
- Because they submit your search string to a number of different search engines and directories at one time, you get the benefit of seeing results from a variety of different databases.
- Metasearch engines also do you the favor of weeding out duplicate pages so that you see a page's URL only once. Search results are usually summarized under headings and identified by the search engine that found the page.

Profusion Search

Results of search on metasearch site.

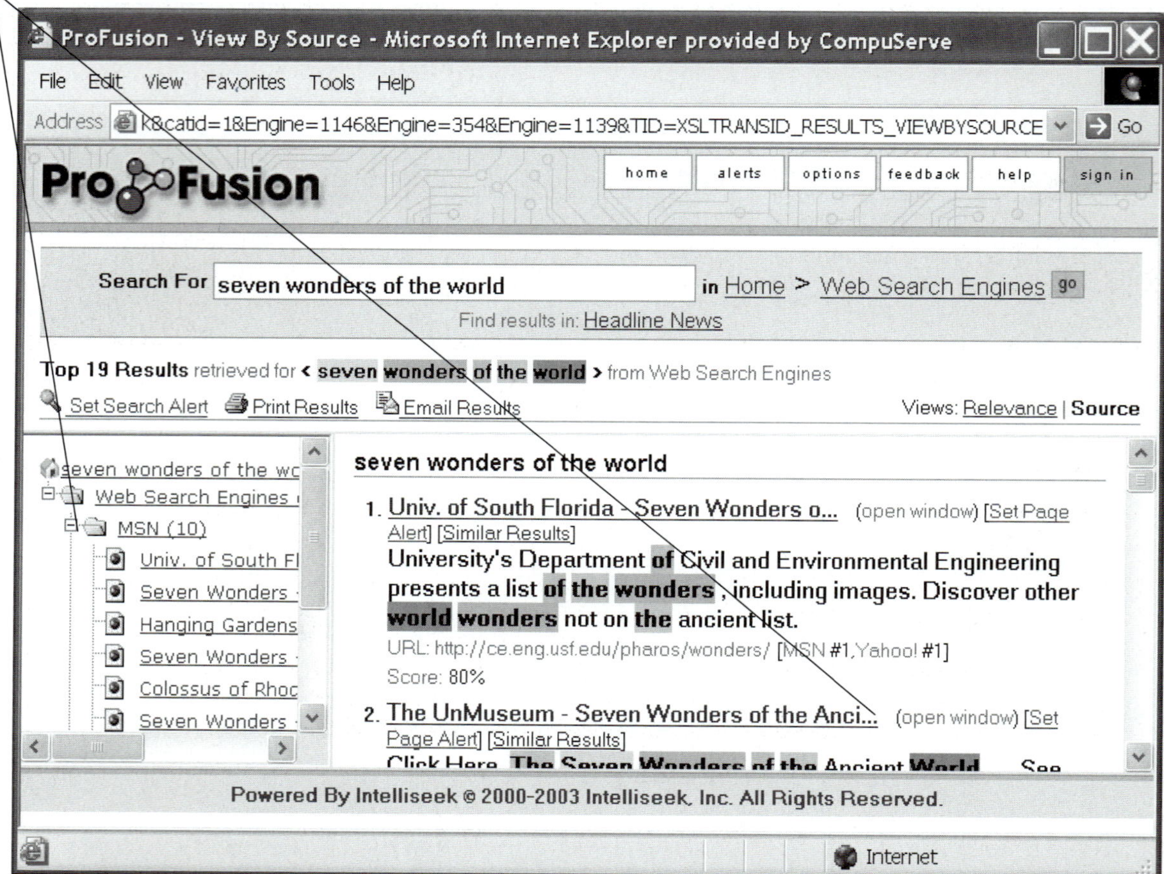

- Most metasearch engines allow you to customize your search options to choose the search engines and directories you want to use for a search.
- You usually also have a number of options you can choose from to control the way the metasearch engine passes your search string to other engines.
- One downside to using a metasearch engine is that one or more of the search engines queried may be "busy" at the time the metasearch engine sends the search string, so you don't get results from as many sources as you expect. The metasearch engine usually tells you which search engines responded to the search string so you know from which search engines you have received results.
  - ✓ *If you do not receive results from as many search engines as you want, run the search additional times until all the search engines respond.*
- Metasearch engines support the same search conventions as other search engines. You can use multiple keywords and operators, quotes, and parentheses to create your search strings.
  - ✓ *If a particular search engine does not support the operator you use in your search string, the metasearch engine takes care of rephrasing your string so that search engine gets the proper information.*
- The Ask Jeeves Web site deserves additional mention at this point. Designed as a natural language search site, Ask Jeeves is also a metasearch engine of sorts.
- In addition to answering questions from its own database, Ask Jeeves supplies possible answers from other search engines. You can click the link to the other search engines to see their answers to the search string.
- Using metasearch sites such as Ask Jeeves can save you considerable time in creating search strings and sorting through the search results.

Ask Jeeves' Answer to a Question

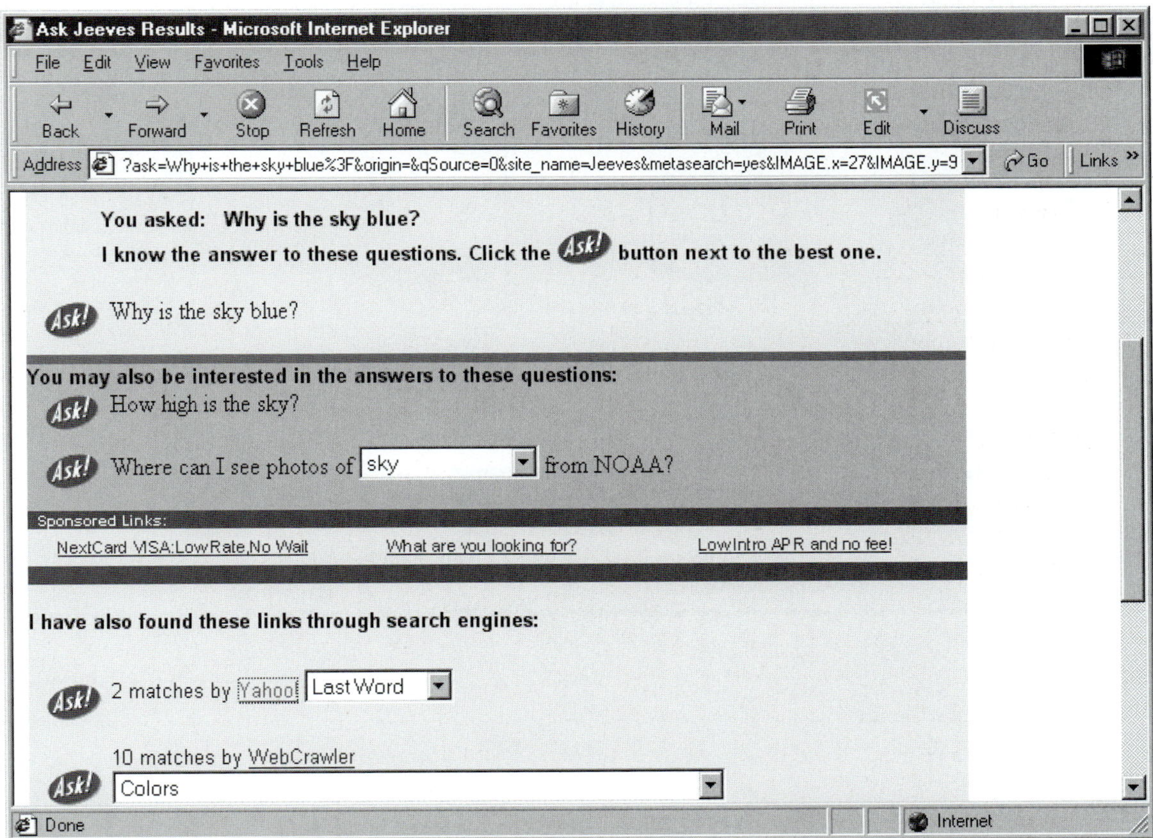

Search for Items other than Web Pages

- Up until now, your searches have concentrated on finding Web sites and Web pages as well as listings in directories.
- You can also, however, search for very specific items on the Internet, such as pictures, sounds, companies, publications, and so on. You can also restrict your searches to parts of Web pages, such as URLs or titles.
- When you open a search engine's Web site, take a moment to look at the options available for searching. Some search engines, such as Google and Lycos give you options right on the home page to find pictures, sounds, video, or specific types of results such as news stories.
- After you select one of these options, keywords you enter will give you search results specific to the option you selected.
- Suppose you want an interesting bird picture to use as wallpaper on your desktop. In Google, you can click the Images option and then type the keyword *birds* to display search results containing only pictures of birds.

Google Image Search

Images option selected

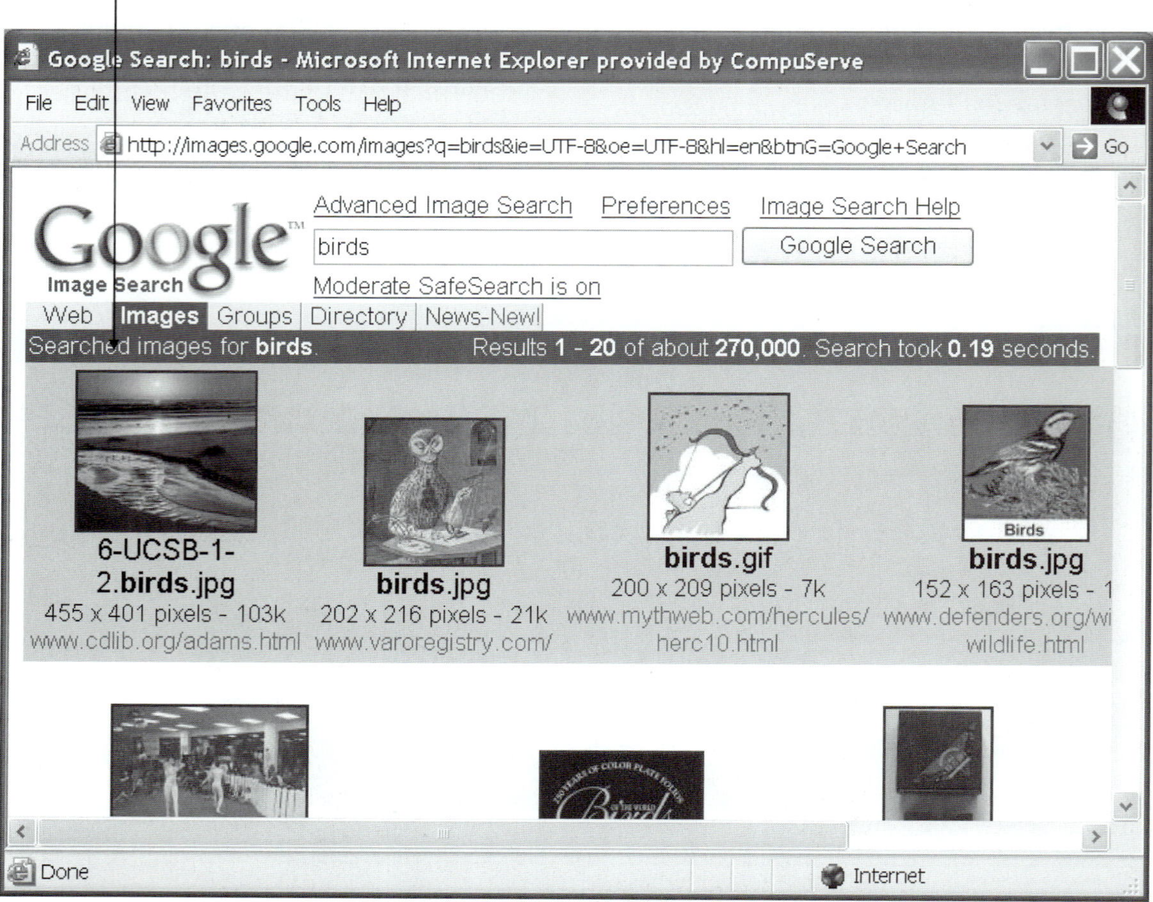

- If the search engine doesn't offer a specific option such as Images, you can often find pictures, sounds, and video links simply by typing a search string containing the keyword of the medium you want to find.
- For example, the search string *bird pictures* will provide you with many hits containing images of birds.
- If you want to locate information based on only a part of the indexed Web page, you can do so by selecting an option or typing a specific keyword in the search box. For example:
  - Type URL: and a keyword to find URLs with the keyword in them.
  - Type TITLE: and a keyword to find that keyword in Web page titles.

Use Advanced Search Options

- A number of search engines offer you additional help with advanced searches. Clicking a link such as Advanced Search, More Search, or Advanced Text Search opens a page containing a series of fields you fill in to define your search string.
- Advanced search assistants often give you a number of choices for refining a search that you cannot specify any other way, including:
  - Language of search results
  - Category to which the search topic belongs
  - Specific type of item, such as a book, dictionary, home page, or even recipe
  - Date of Web page creation
  - Area of the Web page that should be searched
  - Keywords that must be excluded
  - Media type for search results
  - Number of results to display
- After you have filled in the advanced search form, you can run the search just as you usually do in the search engine.

  ✓ *Google advanced search even allows you to search all government sites, all university sites, or all mail order catalogs.*

HotBot's Advanced Search Assistant

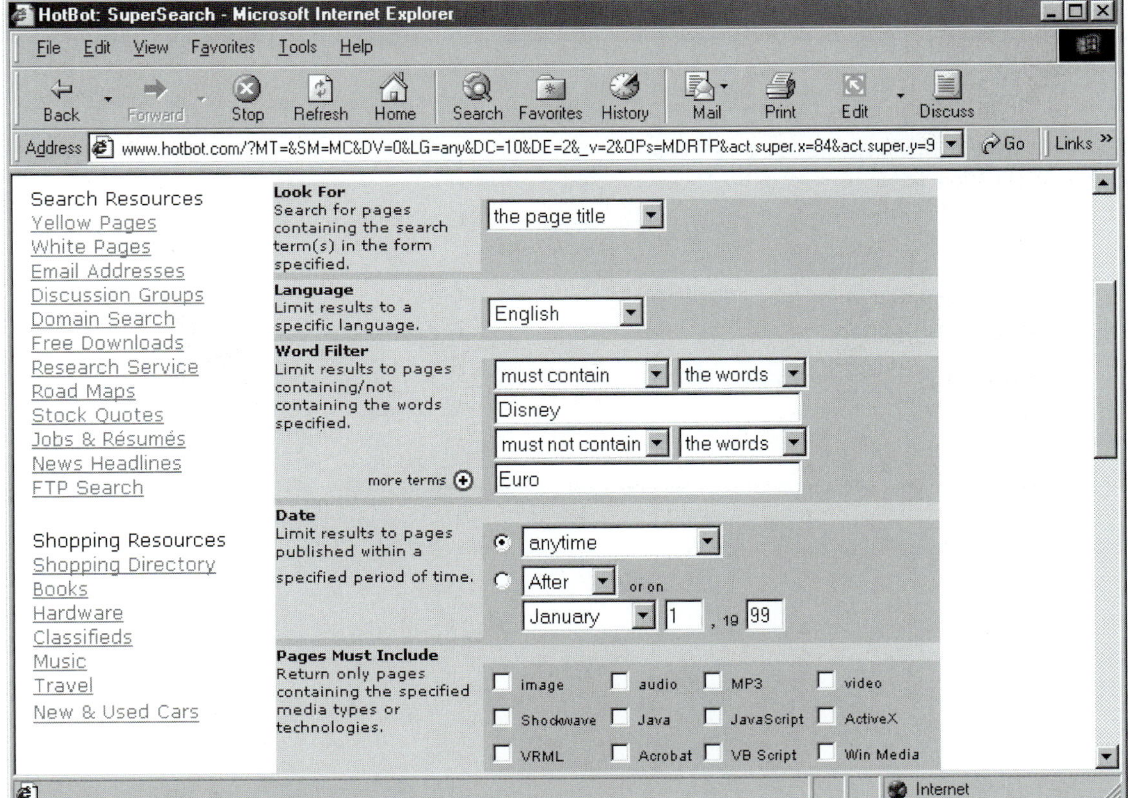

Copyrights and Source Citation

- When you find information that is useful to you on the Internet, you cannot use it as your own because of copyright laws that protect peoples' and organizations' intellectual property. Just because information or other content has been posted online, it is not available for the taking.
- If you use text or images or sound files, you must provide appropriate credit and in some cases obtain written permission. Obtaining written permission is necessary if you are using material in a publication you will sell rather than for personal use, if you take large amounts of information that you do not put in your own words, or you use media such as a photograph or piece of music.
- References to electronic information are similar in format to those for offline articles, in that you must provide the author and title of the content. However, you also need to let your reader know how to find the content, which means you must list the online provider of the content and any medium on which the content is available, if relevant.
- If data exists both online and in print, it's useful to provide information about how to locate both sources. You might also list the length of the publication on a Web page using paragraphs rather than number of pages.
- Here are some examples of citations for online sources:
  - **Internet site**: Schwartz, Delmore, "Survey of Our National Phenomena." The *New York Times Magazine*, April 21, 1996; 17 paragraphs. Available http://www.nytimes.com/specials/magazine/titles.html.
  - **E-mail messages**: Smith, John (john@microsoft.com). "New Product Overview." E-mail to Nancy Jones (jones@home.com). August 22, 2002.
  - Discussion board: "The Next Threat to Homeland Security." Online newsgroup posting. Discussion of Homeland Security. Available e-mail: listserve@national.edu.Homeland/asp. November, 2001.

On Your Own

- Research Internet sites (e.g., http://www.ciolek.com/WWWVLPages/QltyPages/QltyEtiq.html) that discuss issues related to copyright and fair-use issues for material that you find on the Internet.
- Discuss with your class the complex issues related to the issues of usage of material that you acquire from the Internet.
- How can you avoid illegal use of material you acquire from the Internet?

Index

D

E

F

G

H

I

Notes

Notes

SINGLE PC LICENSE AGREEMENT AND LIMITED WARRANTY

READ THIS LICENSE CAREFULLY BEFORE OPENING THIS PACKAGE. BY OPENING THIS PACKAGE, YOU ARE AGREEING TO THE TERMS AND CONDITIONS OF THIS LICENSE. IF YOU DO NOT AGREE, DO NOT OPEN THE PACKAGE. PROMPTLY RETURN THE UNOPENED PACKAGE AND ALL ACCOMPANYING ITEMS TO THE PLACE YOU OBTAINED THEM. THESE TERMS APPLY TO ALL LICENSED SOFTWARE ON THE DISK EXCEPT THAT THE TERMS FOR USE OF ANY SHAREWARE OR FREEWARE ON THE DISKETTES ARE AS SET FORTH IN THE ELECTRONIC LICENSE LOCATED ON THE DISK:

1. GRANT OF LICENSE and OWNERSHIP: The enclosed computer programs and data ("Software") are licensed, not sold, to you by Pearson Education, Inc. ("We" or the "Company") and in consideration of your purchase or adoption of the accompanying Company textbooks and/or other materials, and your agreement to these terms. We reserve any rights not granted to you. You own only the disk(s) but we and/or our licensors own the Software itself. This license allows you to use and display your copy of the Software on a single computer (i.e., with a single CPU) at a single location for academic use only, so long as you comply with the terms of this Agreement.

2. RESTRICTIONS: You may not transfer or distribute the Software or documentation to anyone else. Except for backup, you may not copy the documentation or the Software. You may not network the Software or otherwise use it on more than one computer or computer terminal at the same time. You may not reverse engineer, disassemble, decompile, modify, adapt, translate, or create derivative works based on the Software or the Documentation. You may be held legally responsible for any copying or copyright infringement which is caused by your failure to abide by the terms of these restrictions.

3. TERMINATION: This license is effective until terminated. This license will terminate automatically without notice from the Company if you fail to comply with any provisions or limitations of this license. Upon termination, you shall destroy the Documentation and all copies of the Software. All provisions of this Agreement as to limitation and disclaimer of warranties, limitation of liability, remedies or damages, and our ownership rights shall survive termination.

4. LIMITED WARRANTY AND DISCLAIMER OF WARRANTY: Company warrants that for a period of 60 days from the date you purchase this SOFTWARE (or purchase or adopt the accompanying textbook), the Software, when properly installed and used in accordance with the Documentation, will operate in substantial conformity with the description of the Software set forth in the Documentation, and that for a period of 30 days the disk(s) on which the Software is delivered shall be free from defects in materials and workmanship under normal use. The Company does not warrant that the Software will meet your requirements or that the operation of the Software will be uninterrupted or error-free. Your only remedy and the Company's only obligation under these limited warranties is, at the Company's option, return of the disk for a refund of any amounts paid for it by you or replacement of the disk. THIS LIMITED WARRANTY IS THE ONLY WARRANTY PROVIDED BY THE COMPANY AND ITS LICENSORS, AND THE COMPANY AND ITS LICENSORS DISCLAIM ALL OTHER WARRANTIES, EXPRESS OR IMPLIED, INCLUDING WITHOUT LIMITATION, THE IMPLIED WARRANTIES OF MERCHANTABILITY AND FITNESS FOR A PARTICULAR PURPOSE. THE COMPANY DOES NOT WARRANT, GUARANTEE OR MAKE ANY REPRESENTATION REGARDING THE ACCURACY, RELIABILITY, CURRENTNESS, USE, OR RESULTS OF USE, OF THE SOFTWARE.

5. LIMITATION OF REMEDIES AND DAMAGES: IN NO EVENT, SHALL THE COMPANY OR ITS EMPLOYEES, AGENTS, LICENSORS, OR CONTRACTORS BE LIABLE FOR ANY INCIDENTAL, INDIRECT, SPECIAL, OR CONSEQUENTIAL DAMAGES ARISING OUT OF OR IN CONNECTION WITH THIS LICENSE OR THE SOFTWARE, INCLUDING FOR LOSS OF USE, LOSS OF DATA, LOSS OF INCOME OR PROFIT, OR OTHER LOSSES, SUSTAINED AS A RESULT OF INJURY TO ANY PERSON, OR LOSS OF OR DAMAGE TO PROPERTY, OR CLAIMS OF THIRD PARTIES, EVEN IF THE COMPANY OR AN AUTHORIZED REPRESENTATIVE OF THE COMPANY HAS BEEN ADVISED OF THE POSSIBILITY OF SUCH DAMAGES. IN NO EVENT SHALL THE LIABILITY OF THE COMPANY FOR DAMAGES WITH RESPECT TO THE SOFTWARE EXCEED THE AMOUNTS ACTUALLY PAID BY YOU, IF ANY, FOR THE SOFTWARE OR THE ACCOMPANYING TEXTBOOK. BECAUSE SOME JURISDICTIONS DO NOT ALLOW THE LIMITATION OF LIABILITY IN CERTAIN CIRCUMSTANCES, THE ABOVE LIMITATIONS MAY NOT ALWAYS APPLY TO YOU.

6. GENERAL: THIS AGREEMENT SHALL BE CONSTRUED IN ACCORDANCE WITH THE LAWS OF THE UNITED STATES OF AMERICA AND THE STATE OF NEW YORK, APPLICABLE TO CONTRACTS MADE IN NEW YORK, AND SHALL BENEFIT THE COMPANY, ITS AFFILIATES AND ASSIGNEES. HIS AGREEMENT IS THE COMPLETE AND EXCLUSIVE STATEMENT OF THE AGREEMENT BETWEEN YOU AND THE COMPANY AND SUPERSEDES ALL PROPOSALS OR PRIOR AGREEMENTS, ORAL, OR WRITTEN, AND ANY OTHER COMMUNICATIONS BETWEEN YOU AND THE COMPANY OR ANY REPRESENTATIVE OF THE COMPANY RELATING TO THE SUBJECT MATTER OF THIS AGREEMENT. If you are a U.S. Government user, this Software is licensed with "restricted rights" as set forth in subparagraphs (a)-(d) of the Commercial Computer-Restricted Rights clause at FAR 52.227-19 or in subparagraphs (c)(1)(ii) of the Rights in Technical Data and Computer Software clause at DFARS 252.227-7013, and similar clauses, as applicable.